SCIENCE AND ART DEPART
OF THE COMMITTEE OF COUNCIL ON EDUCATION,
SOUTH KENSINGTON MUSEUM.

A LIST

OF

BUILDINGS IN GREAT BRITAIN AND IRELAND HAVING MURAL AND OTHER PAINTED DECORATIONS,

OF

DATES PRIOR TO THE LATTER PART OF THE SIXTEENTH CENTURY,

WITH

HISTORICAL INTRODUCTION AND ALPHABETICAL INDEX OF SUBJECTS,

BY

C. E. KEYSER, M.A., F.S.A.

[COMPILED FOR THE USE OF SCHOOLS OF ART IN THE UNITED KINGDOM.]

THIRD EDITION, ENLARGED.

LONDON:
PRINTED BY EYRE AND SPOTTISWOODE,
PRINTERS TO THE QUEEN'S MOST EXCELLENT MAJESTY.
FOR HER MAJESTY'S STATIONERY OFFICE.
AND SOLD AT THE SOUTH KENSINGTON MUSEUM.

1883.

Price Two Shillings and Threepence.

CONTENTS.

THE first edition of the present work was a thin pamphlet of 24 pages, which was issued in 1871. A second edition of 58 pages appeared in 1872, to which was prefixed the following Note :—

1. The present brief notices are the commencement of an attempt suggested by the Director of the South Kensington Museum to collect existing evidences of painting in England from the earliest times to the Reformation.

2. For the present the list is necessarily imperfect, and notices of omissions will be gratefully received. Valuable aid has been received from many correspondents, to whom the compiler's best thanks are due, towards completing this second and much enlarged issue of the list.

3. Where printed notices of Mural Paintings have been found, references of such notices have been given. The brief descriptions have been taken, where special sources of information were not available, from the authorities quoted. A few names are left of places where paintings formerly existed, and of which records or copies are preserved, as the paintings of St. Stephen's Chapel, Westminster, coloured copies of which were published by the Society of Antiquaries in the *Vetusta Monumenta*, Vol. VI.

4. As almost all early Churches in England had some mural painting, and the progress of "restoration" has brought much of this to light, there are, no doubt, other examples that I have not yet heard of or found described, and many, it is to be feared, have perished without any record being preserved.

5. Paintings on screens or other wood-work have been included in the present list.

R. H. SODEN SMITH.

So much interest was taken in these comparatively brief lists, that it was determined to collect materials for a fuller and more comprehensive account of the ancient mural paintings still existing in this country. This work has been carried out, as a voluntary task, in friendly compliance with my request for aid, by Mr. Charles E. Keyser, without whose generous assistance, involving prolonged literary labour and journeys to all parts of England, the Editor could not have looked for success. In fact, all that is of most value in this edition is practically Mr. Keyser's work, and the result is to produce, as the Editor believes, a fairly complete, though necessarily brief, notice of every ancient mural painting as yet recorded to have been discovered in Great Britain.

R. H SODEN SMITH.

South Kensington Museum,
    June 1883.

Information of additional examples will be most thankfully received, addressed to the Secretary, Science and Art Department, South Kensington Museum.

PREFACE TO THE THIRD EDITION.

THE present list, though still doubtless imperfect, will, it is hoped, furnish the most complete record of the art of mural painting, and the decoration of our churches and other buildings in the Middle Ages, which has yet been published. Almost all the recorded examples are included in this new edition, nearly every work on British topography brought out during the present century having been carefully consulted. With a few exceptions, the references to the sources whence the information has been obtained are given, and it may be here stated, that where the account in the list differs from that in the authority cited, the former may be taken as correct, the variation of the account being obtained in consequence of personal inspection or thoroughly reliable information. As far as possible, all the more important examples have been visited by the Compiler of the present edition, and all doubts as to identification of saints, subjects, &c. in the majority of instances cleared up by personal examination, or an application to those most likely to be well informed an the subject.

To the present edition has been appended an alphabetical index of the saints, subjects, &c. portrayed, as well as of screens, roofs, monuments, &c. still or till recently retaining traces of their original colouring; and this will, it is hoped, prove an assistance to the student in any particular branch of this subject, and will serve to illustrate the varying popularity of the several subjects and saints during the period comprehended by the list.

In conclusion, the Compiler begs to express his thanks to the many gentlemen who have assisted him by furnishing him in various instances with most valuable information, and he feels that he should especially state his obligation to Mr. E. L. Blackburne, F.S.A., who allowed him to inspect his considerable collection of notes on this subject, and to extract therefrom all the necessary details for the present list.

C. E. KEYSER.

June 1883.

TOPOGRAPHICAL CLASSIFICATION ALPHABETICALLY UNDER NAMES OF COUNTIES.

. *See* Lists of Later examples, p. 297, and of additional ditto, p. 300, in case any name here quoted is not found in the Principal List.

(I.) ENGLAND.

BEDFORDSHIRE.

Ampthill.
Arlesey.
Barford, Great.
Barford, Little.
Bedford.
Biddenham.
Biggleswade.
Bletsoe.
Blunham.
Caddington.
Campton.
Cardington.
Chalgrave.
Clapham.
Clifton.
Cople.
Dean.
Eaton Bray.
Eaton Socon.
Edworth.
Eggington.
Elstow.
Felmersham.
Gravenhurst, Lower.
Gravenhurst, Over.
Harlington.
Houghton Conquest.
Houghton Regis.

Husborne Crawley.
Kempston.
Keysoe.
Leighton Buzzard.
Luton.
Marston Moretaine.
Oakley.
Odell.
Pertenhall.
Roxton.
Sandy.
Sharnbrook.
Shelton.
Shillington.
Stagsden.
Stanbridge.
Stevington.
Stotfold.
Tempsford.
Tilbrook.
Tilsworth.
Toddington.
Turvey.
Warden Abbey.
Warden, Old.
Willington.
Wilshampstead.
Wymington.

BERKSHIRE.

Abingdon.
Avington.
Bisham.

Blewbury.
Bradfield.
Bray.

BERKSHIRE—*cont.*

Brimpton.
Chilton.
Drayton.
Enborne.
Englefield.
Fyfield.
Goosey.
Hagbourne.
Hampstead Norris.
Hanney.
Poughley Priory.
Reading (3).

Ruscombe.
Stanford Dingley.
Sutton Courtenay.
Theale.
Tidmarsh.
Upton.
Wallingford.
Wantage.
Warfield.
Windsor.
Windsor, Old.
Wittenham, Long.

BUCKINGHAMSHIRE.

Amersham.
Ashendon.
Ashridge.
Astwood.
Aylesbury.
Beachampton.
Bradwell.
Brickhill, Great.
Broughton.
Chalfont St. Giles.
Cheddington.
Chenies.
Chesham.
Chesham Bois.
Chetwode.
Cholesbury.
Clifton Reynes.
Crawley, North.
Denham.
Dorney.
Drayton Beauchamp.
Eddlesborough.
Ellesborough.
Eton.
Grendon Underwood.
Hanslope.
Hillesden.

Horton.
Kimble, Great.
Kimble, Little.
Lathbury.
Lavendon.
Leckhampstead.
Marston, North.
Marsworth.
Mentmore.
Moreton, Maid's.
Nettleden.
Newton Longueville.
Olney.
Padbury.
Preston Bissett.
Quainton.
Ravenston.
Risborough, Monks.
Shenley Mansell.
Stewkley.
Stoke Hammond.
Swanbourne.
Upton.
Whaddon.
Wing.
Wingrave.
Wycombe, High.

CAMBRIDGESHIRE.

Abington, Great.
Barrington.
Bartlow.

Borough Green.
Bottisham.
Bourn.

CAMBRIDGESHIRE—*cont.*

Caldecote.
Cambridge (12).
Cherry Hinton.
Chesterton.
Chevely.
Chippenham.
Comberton.
Coton.
Cottenham.
Ditton, Fen.
Ditton, Wood.
Duxford.
Ely (2).
Eversden.
Foxton.
Fulbourn (2).
Grantchester.
Guilden Morden.
Haddenham.
Hardwick.
Hauxton.
Hildersham.
Histon.
Horningsey.
Ickleton.
Impington.

Isleham.
Kennet.
Landbeach.
Melbourne.
Meldreth.
Milton.
Newton.
Oakington.
Orwell.
Quy.
Rampton.
Shelford, Little.
Shepreth.
Soham.
Sutton.
Swaffham Bulbeck.
Swaffham Prior.
Teversham.
Toft.
Trumpington.
Waterbeach.
Whittlesea.
Whittlesford.
Wilburton.
Willingham.

CHESHIRE.

Astbury.
Barthomley.
Bramall Hall.
Bunbury.
Chester (6).
Daresbury.
Gawsworth.

Harthill.
Malpas.
Moreton Hall.
Northenden.
Siddington.
Waverton.
Wilmslow.

CORNWALL.

Advent.
Blisland.
Callington.
Cardynham.
Cury.
Davidstow.
Grade.
Gunwalloè.

Helland.
Lanivet.
Lanreath.
Launcells.
Launceston.
Lostwithiel.
Ludgvan.
Mabe.

CORNWALL—*cont.*

Madron.
Mawnan.
Minster.
Mylor.
Pengersick.
Poundstock.
St. Anthony in Roseland.
St. Budoc.
St. Buryan.
St. Clements.
St. Columb.
St. Endellion.
St. Enodoc.
St. Feock.
St. German's.
St. Gulval.

St. Just in Penwith.
St. Levans.
St. Michael's Mount.
St. Minver (2).
St. Teath.
St. Thomas by Launceston.
St. Winnow.
Saltash.
Sancreed.
Sennen.
Sheviocke.
Talland.
Tamerton.
Tintagel.
Trevalga.
Tywardreth.

CUMBERLAND.

Carlisle (2).
Crosthwaite.
Greystoke.
Holm-Cultram.
Lanercost.
Millom.

Naworth.
St. Bees.
Stapleton.
Thursby.
Yanwath.

DERBYSHIRE.

Allestree.
Ashbourn.
Ashover.
Bakewell.
Barlow.
Beauchief Abbey.
Bolsover.
Breadsall.
Chaddesden.
Chelmorton.
Chesterfield.
Dale Abbey.
Derby.
Derwent Chapel.
Dovebridge.
Eyam.
Haddon Hall.
Hartington.
Hucknall, Ault.

Langley, Kirk.
Longstone, Great.
Marston Montgomery.
Melbourne.
Morley.
Newton Solney.
Norbury.
Norton.
Osmaston.
Pentrich.
Repton.
Sawley.
Scropton.
Staveley.
Steetly.
Winfield, North.
Wirksworth.
Youlgrave.

DEVONSHIRE.

Allington, East.
Alphington.
Alvington, West.
Ashburton.
Ashford.
Ashton.
Atherington.
Axminster.
Bampton.
Barnstaple.
Beer Ferrers.
Berry-Pomeroy.
Bideford.
Bigbury.
Bovey Tracey.
Bradfield.
Bradninch.
Bratton Clovelly.
Brent, South.
Bridestow.
Bridford.
Broadclist.
Buckland-in-the-Moor.
Buckland Monachorum.
Burlescombe.
Chagford.
Chawleigh.
Chivelston.
Chudleigh.
Chulmleigh.
Churston Ferrars.
Clayhanger.
Clyst St. George.
Clyst St. Lawrence.
Cockington.
Coleridge.
Combe Martin.
Crediton.
Cullompton.
Dartington.
Dartmouth (2).
Dittisham.
Downe, West.
Exeter (7).
Feniton.
Gidleigh.
Haccombe.
Harberton.
Hartland (2).

Hatherleigh.
Heavitree.
Hempston, Little.
Hennock.
Holcombe Burnell.
Holcombe Rogus.
Holne.
Honiton.
Horwood.
Ilfracombe.
Ilsington.
Ipplepen.
Kenn.
Kentisbeare.
Kenton.
Kerswell, Abbot's.
Landkey.
Lapford.
Lustleigh.
Lympstone.
Mamhead.
Manaton.
Martinhoe.
Meavy.
Molton, North.
Newton Tracey.
Nympton, St. George.
Ogwell, West.
Ottery St. Mary.
Paignton.
Payhembury.
Pinhoe.
Plymstock.
Plymtree.
Pool, South.
Portlemouth.
Rewe.
Ringmore.
Seaton.
Shaugh Prior.
Shebbear.
Staverton.
Stoke Fleming.
Stoke Gabriel.
Stoke-in-Teignhead.
Swimbridge.
Talaton.
Tavistock (2).
Tavy, Peter.

Tawstock.
Tawton, Bishop's.
Teignton, King's.
Throwley.
Tiverton.
Tor Bryan.
Tor Mohun.
Totnes (2).
Trentishoe.
Trusham.

Uffculme.
Ugborough.
Wear Gifford.
Whimple.
Widecombe-in-the-Moor.
Widworthy.
Woodland.
Woodleigh.
Woolborough.

DORSETSHIRE.

Abbotsbury.
Beaminster.
Bere Regis.
Bradford Abbas.
Cerne Abbas.
Chickerell, West.
Compton, East.
Cranborne.
Durweston.
Fordington.
Frampton.
Hawkchurch.
Hazelbury Bryan.
Hilton.
Mappowder.
Margaret Marsh.
Marnhull.
Melcombe Horsey.

Milton Abbas.
Netherbury.
Piddletown.
Portisham.
Pulham.
Shaftesbury.
Sherborne (2).
Stockland.
Stourton Candel.
Studland.
Sturminster Marshall.
Sturminster Newton.
Thornford.
Whitchurch Canonicorum.
Wimborne Minster.
Winfrith Newburgh.
Worth Matravers.
Yetminster.

DURHAM.

Brancepeth.
Durham (4).
Finchale.
Hartlepool.

Lanchester.
Pittington.
Staindrop.

ESSEX.

Ardleigh.
Aveley.
Barking (2).
Barling.
Beleigh Abbey.

Bentley, Great.
Blackmore.
Braintree.
Braxted, Little.
Brentwood.

ESSEX—*cont.*

Brightlingsea.
Bures, Mount.
Bycknacre.
Canewdon.
Canfield, Great.
Chelmsford.
Childerditch.
Chishill, Great.
Clacton, Great.
Coggeshall, Great.
Coggeshall, Little (2).
Colchester.
Copford.
Corringham.
Danbury.
Easton, Little.
Feering.
Frating.
Hadleigh.
Ham, East.
Ham, West.
Hedingham, Castle.
Horkesley, Little.
Hornchurch.
Horndon-on-the-Hill.
Ilford, Little.
Ingatestone.
Inworth.
Kelvedon (2).
Latchingdon.

Latton.
Layer Marney.
Littlebury.
Margaretting.
Newport.
Ongar, Chipping.
Ongar, High.
Orsett.
Prittlewell.
Rainham.
Romford.
Saffron Walden.
Shenfield.
Stanford-le-Hope.
Stifford.
Tey, Marks.
Thorington.
Totham, Great.
Upminster.
Wakering, Great.
Wakering, Little.
Waltham Abbey.
Waltham, Great.
Weathersfield.
Wicken Bonant.
Wickham.
Woodford.
Writtle.
Yeldham, Great.

GLOUCESTERSHIRE.

Ampney Crucis.
Ashchurch.
Ashton Keynes.
Awre.
Barnwood.
Baunton.
Berkeley (2).
Beverstone.
Bibury.
Bisley.
Bledington.
Bristol (10).
Buckland.
Cerney, North.
Cheltenham (2).

Cirencester.
Cleeve, Bishop's.
Cowley.
Deerhurst.
Duntisbourne Rouse.
Fairford.
Gloucester (3).
Icomb.
Kempley.
Lassington.
Leckhampton.
Mitcheldean.
Notgrove.
Quinton.
Rissington, Great.

GLOUCESTERSHIRE—*cont.*

Shenington.
Shurdington.
Slymbridge.
Stanley St. Leonard.
Tewkesbury.

Westbury-on-Trym.
Winstone.
Wolston.
Wotton.

HAMPSHIRE.

Alton.
Amport.
Basing, Old.
Basingstoke.
Bramdean.
Bramley.
Breamore.
Christchurch.
Clatford, Goodworth.
Colmer.
Compton.
Easton.
Exton.
Farnborough.
Hartley Wintney.
Havant.
Heckfield.
Hound.
Ibsley.
Idsworth, Chalton.
Kingsclere.

Meon, East.
Micheldever.
Netley Abbey.
Romsey.
Rowner.
Selborne.
Sherborne, Monks.
Silchester.
Soberton.
Southampton.
Sparsholt.
Stoke Charity.
Tichborne.
Upton Gray.
Warblington.
Wellow.
Winchester (9).
Winchfield.
Worthy, Headbourn.
Yately.

ISLE OF WIGHT.

Arreton.
Bonchurch.
Chale.
Godshill.

Newport.
Northwood.
Shorwell.
Whitwell.

HEREFORDSHIRE.

Abbey Dore.
Aconbury.
Almeley.
Aston.
Brinsop (2).
Dilwyn.
Dormington.
Eardisley.

Eaton Bishop.
Hereford (6).
Hereford, Little.
Hope Mansel.
Kenderchurch.
Kington.
Leominster.
Madley.

HEREFORDSHIRE—*cont.*

Marcle, Much.
Michaelchurch Eskley.
Moccas.
Mordiford.
Orleton.
Pembridge.

Ross.
Rowlstone.
Stretton Grandison.
Upton Bishop.
Weobley.
Weston Baggard.

HERTFORDSHIRE.

Albury.
Aldbury.
Aldenham.
Anstey.
Ardeley.
Ashwell.
Aspenden.
Aston.
Barkway.
Barnet, East.
Bengeo.
Bennington.
Berkhampstead, Great (2).
Bovingdon.
Braughing.
Broxbourne.
Buckland.
Eastwick.
Flamstead.
Flaunden.
Furneaux Pelham.
Gaddesden, Great.
Gaddesden, Little.
Hadham, Much.
Hinxworth.
Hitchin.
Hunsdon.
Ickleford.
Kelshall.
Kensworth.

Kimpton.
Knebworth.
Langley, Kings.
Marston, Long.
Mimms, North.
Munden, Great.
Munden, Little.
Northchurch.
Pirton.
Puttenham.
Rickmansworth (2).
Ridge.
Royston.
Rushden.
St. Albans (3).
St. Stephens.
Sandridge.
Sarratt.
Standon.
Stevenage.
Stortford, Bishop's.
Therfield.
Walden, King's.
Walkern.
Ware.
Watford.
Watton.
Wheathampstead.
Widford.

HUNTINGDONSHIRE.

Bluntisham.
Broughton.
Bury.
Covington.
Easton.
Glatton.
Hemingford Abbas.
Huntingdon.
Kimbolton.

Morborne.
Newton, Water.
Overton Longueville.
St. Neots.
Spaldwick.
Stow Longa.
Swineshead.
Upwood.
Yaxley.

KENT.

Adisham.
Alkham.
Ash.
Barfreston.
Baston.
Biddenden.
Birchington.
Brabourne.
Bredhurst.
Bridge.
Brook.
Canterbury (4).
Capel Le Ferne.
Chatham.
Chevening.
Chiselhurst.
Cliffe.
Cobham (2).
Cooling.
Cudham.
Darent.
Dartford.
Ditton.
Doddington.
Dover (2).
Eastry.
Elham.
Faversham.
Gillingham.
Harbledown.
Harty.
Hastingleigh.
Horn Hill.

Horton, Monks.
Ightham.
Kemsing.
Leeds.
Lenham.
Lydd.
Maidstone.
Malling, East.
Minster.
Newington - by - Sitting-
    bourne.
Postling.
Preston.
Rainham.
Reculver.
Rochester (4).
Ruckinge.
St. Lawrence.
Sandwich (3).
Sheldwich.
Sittingbourne.
Smarden.
Southfleet.
Staplehurst.
Stone.
Stone-by-Faversham.
Swanscombe.
Ulcomb.
Upchurch.
Wickham, East.
Wickham, West.
Wye (2).

LANCASHIRE.

Altham.
Cartmel.
Cartmel Fell.
Claughton.
Furness.
Leyland.

Manchester.
Ormskirk.
Sefton.
Stydd.
Warton.

LEICESTERSHIRE.

Allexton.
Ashby Folville.
Barrow-on-Soar

Bottesford.
Burrow-on-the-Hill.
Cranoe.

LEICESTERSHIRE—*cont.*

Edmondthorpe.
Gaddesby.
Harborough, Market.
Kilworth, North.
Kilworth, South.
Laund Abbey.
Leicester (4).
Loughborough.
Lutterworth.

Medbourn (2).
Melton Mowbray.
Overton, Cold.
Sproxton.
Thurnby.
Tilton-on-the-Hill.
Twyford.
Wartnaby.
Wyfordby.

LINCOLNSHIRE.

Addlethorpe.
Alford.
Anwick.
Asgarby.
Barkston.
Billinghay.
Blyborough.
Boston (2).
Bratoft.
Broughton, Brant.
Burton-upon-Stather.
Bytham, Castle.
Caythorpe.
Cockerington, South.
Corringham.
Croft.
Croyland.
Deeping, Market.
Donington.
Dowsby.
Epworth.
Folkingham.
Frieston.
Friskney.
Fulbeck.
Gainsborough.
Grimsby, Great.
Hainton.
Horbling.
Kirton-in-Lindsey.
Leasingham.

Lincoln (2).
Louth (2).
Ludborough.
Navenby.
Pinchbeck.
Rauceby.
Ropsley.
Saltfleetby, All Saints.
Saltfleetby, St. Peters.
Sedgbrook.
Sleaford.
Somerby.
Somercotes, South.
Sotby.
Spalding.
Spilsby.
Stamford (5).
Stow.
Stroxton.
Sutton, St. Mary's.
Swaton.
Swinderby.
Tealby.
Uffington.
Waddington.
Wainfleet.
Welbourne.
Whaplode.
Winterton.
Winthorpe.
Worlaby.

MIDDLESEX.

Bedfont.
Drayton, West.

Enfield.
Finchley.

O 8954.

MIDDLESEX—*cont.*

Hadley, Monken.
Hampton Court.
Harefield.
Harlington.
Harmondsworth.
Harrow.
Hayes.

Heston.
Ickenham.
London (15).
Northolt.
Ruislip.
Stoke Newington.
Westminster (5).

MONMOUTHSHIRE.

Abergavenny.
Caerleon.
Chepstow.
Llanarth.

Llangwm Isaf.
Llangwm Ucha.
Magor.
Monmouth.

NORFOLK.

Acle.
Acre, Castle, (2).
Acre, South.
Alburgh.
Aldburgh.
Arminghall.
Ashmanhaugh.
Ashwellthorpe.
Aslacton.
Attleborough.
Aylmerton.
Aylsham.
Babingley.
Banham.
Barnham Broom.
Barningham Winter.
Barton Bendish (2).
Barton Turf.
Beachamwell.
Beeston, St. Mary's.
Beeston Regis.
Beighton.
Belaugh.
Billingford.
Binham Abbey.
Bircham.
Blofield.
Bradfield.
Breckles.
Bridgham.

Brisley.
Brockdish.
Brooke.
Broome.
Brunstead.
Buckenham, New.
Buckenham Ferry.
Burgh, St. Peter.
Burlingham, St. Andrew.
Burlingham, St. Edmund.
Burnham Norton.
Burnham Overy.
Buxton.
Carbrooke.
Carlton Rode.
Caston.
Catfield.
Catton.
Cawston.
Cley.
Colkirk.
Coltishall.
Creake, North.
Creake, South.
Cressingham, Great.
Cringleford.
Cromer.
Crostwick.
Crostwight.
Dalling, Field.

NORFOLK—*cont.*

Dalling, Wood.
Denton.
Denver.
Deopham.
Dereham, East.
Dereham, West, (2).
Dersingham.
Dickleburgh.
Diss.
Ditchingham.
Downham Market.
Drayton.
Dunham, Little.
Easton.
Eaton.
Eccles.
Edgfield.
Edingthorpe.
Elmham, North.
Elsing (2).
Emneth.
Erpingham.
Fakenham.
Fersfield.
Filby.
Fincham.
Foulden.
Foulsham.
Foxley.
Freethorpe.
Fring.
Fritton.
Fundenhall.
Garboldisham.
Garvestone.
Gately.
Gillingham.
Gooderstone.
Gresham.
Gressenhall.
Grimstone.
Guist.
Haddiscoe.
Happisburgh.
Hardwick.
Harling, East.
Harpley.
Heigham, Potter.
Hemblington.
Hemesby.

Hempstead.
Hethersett.
Hickling.
Hilgay.
Hingham.
Hockering.
Honing.
Horningtoft.
Horsham, St. Faith's.
Horstead.
Houghton-le-Dale.
Hunstanton.
Ickburgh.
Ingham.
Irstead.
Kenninghall.
Ketteringham.
Knapton.
Lessingham.
Letheringsett.
Limpenhoe.
Litcham.
Loddon.
Longham.
Ludham.
Lynn, King's.
Lynn, South.
Marsham.
Martham.
Massingham, Great.
Mattishall.
Mautby.
Merton.
Middleton.
Morley.
Morston.
Moulton.
Mulbarton.
Narburgh.
Neatishead.
Necton.
Northwold.
Norwich (28).
Ormesby, St. Margaret.
Outwell.
Oxburgh.
Paston.
Plumstead, Great.
Poringland.
Postwick.

NORFOLK—*cont.*

Pulham St. Mary Magda-
lene.
Pulham St. Mary the Virgin.
Rackheath.
Rainham, South.
Randworth.
Redenhall.
Reepham.
Repps.
Repps, North.
Ringland.
Rising, Castle.
Rudham.
Rushall.
Ruston, East.
Salhouse.
Sall.
Salthouse.
Sandringham.
Saxthorpe.
Scarning.
Sco-Ruston.
Sculthorpe.
Sedgford.
Seething.
Shelfhanger.
Sheringham.
Shimpling.
Shingham.
Shouldham Thorp.
Sloley.
Smallburgh.
Snetterton.
Snettisham.
Somerton, West.
Sparham.
Sporle.
Stalham.
Stanfield.
Starston.
Stokesby.
Stow Bardolph.
Strumpshaw.
Suffield.
Swaffham.
Swafield.
Swainsthorpe.
Swanton Morley.
Taverham.
Terrington St. Clements.

Thetford (4).
Thornham.
Thorpe Abbots.'
Thrigby.
Tibenham.
Tilney All Saints.
Toft Monks.
Tofts, West.
Tottington.
Trimmingham.
Trunch.
Tuddenham, North.
Tunstead.
Upton.
Upwell.
Wacton Magna.
Walcot.
Walpole St. Peter's.
Walsham, North.
Walsham, South.
Walsingham, New.
Walsoken.
Walton, West.
Weeting.
Wellingham.
Wells.
Wendling.
Wesenham.
Westfield.
Weston Longueville.
Westwick.
Whissonsett.
Wickhampton.
Wickmere.
Wiggenhall   St.   Mary
Magdalene.
Wiggenhall St. Mary the
Virgin.
Wighton.
Wilton.
Wimbotsham.
Witchingham, Great.
Witton.
Wiveton.
Worstead.
Worthing.
Wrotham, Great.
Wymondham (2).
Yarmouth, Great, (2).
Yelverton.

NORTHAMPTONSHIRE.

Addington, Great.
Aldwincle St. Peter's.
Ashby St. Leger's.
Ashby, Castle.
Ashby, Mears.
Aston-le-Walls.
Badby.
Bainton.
Barnack.
Barton Segrave.
Barton, Earl's.
Bowden, Little.
Bozeat.
Brigstock.
Brington, Great.
Brixworth.
Broughton.
Bugbrooke.
Burton Latimer.
Castor.
Charwelton.
Courteenhall.
Cransley.
Crick.
Dene.
Denford.
Doddington.
Dodford.
Duston.
Edgcott.
Etton.
Evenley.
Fawsley.
Floore.
Glinton.
Grafton Regis.
Grendon.
Haddon, West.
Hannington.
Hardwick.
Hargrave.
Harringworth.
Heyford, Nether.

Higham Ferrers (2).
Higham, Cold.
Holdenby.
Irthlingborough.
Kettering.
Lichborough.
Marholme.
Marston St. Lawrence.
Middleton Cheney.
Newnham.
Newton Bromswold.
Northampton (2).
Oakley, Little.
Orlingbury.
Oundle.
Peakirk.
Peterborough.
Pytchley.
Raunds.
Ravensthorpe.
Ringstead.
Rothersthorpe.
Rothwell.
Rushden.
Rushton.
Slapton.
Spratton.
Stanford.
Stanion.
Sutton, King's.
Tansor.
Towcester.
Walgrave.
Warkworth.
Warmington.
Weekley.
Wellingborough.
Winwick.
Woodford.
Woodford Halse.
Wootton.
Yardley Hastings.

NORTHUMBERLAND.

Alnwick.
Chillingham.
Chipchase.

Hexham.
Newminster Abbey,

xxii

NOTTINGHAMSHIRE.

Blyth.
Carlton-in-Lindrick.
Clayworth.
Collingham, North.
Flawford.
Gonalston.
Kelham.
Langford.
Leake, West.
Lenton.
Newark.
Nottingham (2).
Southwell.
Strelley.
Sutton Bonnington.
Thurgarton.
Worksop.
Wysall.

OXFORDSHIRE.

Adderbury.
Alkerton.
Alvescott.
Aston, Steeple.
Balscot.
Bampton.
Barford, Little.
Beckley.
Bloxham.
Broughton.
Burford.
Cassington.
Chalgrove.
Charlton-on-Otmoor.
Checkendon.
Cowley.
Cropredy.
Cuddesdon.
Deddington.
Dorchester.
Drayton.
Ewelme.
Eynsham.
Hampton Poyle.
Handborough.
Hanwell.
Haseley, Great.
Headington.
Heyford, Lower.
Horley.
Hornton.
Iffley.
Islip.
Kidlington.
Leigh, North.
Leigh, South.
Mapledurham.
Merton.
Milcomb.
Milton, Great.
Minster Lovel.
Newington, South.
Norton, Chipping.
Oxford (6).
Rollwright, Great.
Rotherfield Peppard.
Rycote.
St. Bartholomew's.
Sandford.
Shutford.
Stanton Harcourt (2).
Stanton St. John's.
Swalcliffe.
Swincombe.
Tadmarton.
Tew, Great.
Thame.
Westcott Barton.
Westwell.
Wiggington.
Witney.

RUTLANDSHIRE.

Ashwell.
Brooke.
Egleton.
Empingham.

RUTLANDSHIRE—*cont.*

Exton.
Ketton.
Langham.
Luffenham, North.
Lyddington (2).
Preston.
Ridlington.

Seaton.
Stoke Dry.
Uppingham.
Wardley.
Weston, Edith.
Whissendine.
Wing.

SHROPSHIRE.

Albrighton.
Alveley.
Ashford Carbonell.
Barrow.
Burford.
Claverley.
Edstaston.
Halesowen.
Leighton.
Ludlow.
Moreton Corbet.
Neen Savage.
Quat.

St. Kenelm's.
Shawbury.
Shiffnal.
Shrewsbury (2).
Staunton, Long.
Tong.
Wellington.
Whittington.
Willey.
Wistanstow.
Worfield.
Wroxeter.

SOMERSETSHIRE.

Ashton, Long.
Axbridge.
Backwell.
Banwell.
Bath.
Bathampton.
Blackford.
Bleadon.
Bruton.
Brympton d'Evercy.
Cadbury, North.
Cadbury, South.
Camel, West.
Chard.
Charlton Horethorne.
Cheddar.
Chew Magna.
Chilton Cantelo.
Clapton-in-Gordano.
Cleeve, Old.
Compton Martin.
Corston.

Cothelstone.
Creech St. Michael's.
Curry-Rivell.
Curry, North.
Ditcheat.
Doulting.
Dunster.
Englishcombe.
Evercreech.
Farleigh-Hungerford.
Frome.
Glastonbury (2).
Harptree, East.
Henstridge.
Huish Episcopi.
Kelston.
Kewstoke.
Keynsham.
Kingston.
Langport.
Limington.
Locking.

SOMERSETSHIRE—*cont.*

Loxton.
Lydeard, Bishop's.
Lytes Cary.
Martock.
Mells.
Minehead.
Muchelney (2).
Norton Fitzwarren.
Pilton.
Podymore Milton.
Porlock.
Portbury.
Poyntington.
Puckington.
Ruishton.
St. Catherine.

Stoke-sub-Hamdon.
Sutton Bingham.
Sutton, Long.
Taunton (2).
Trent.
Uphill.
Wedmore.
Wellington.
Wellow.
Wells (4).
Weston-in-Gordano.
Winsham.
Wraxall.
Yatton.
Yeovil.

STAFFORDSHIRE.

Alrewas.
Areley, Upper.
Brewood.
Checkley.
Colton.
Elford.
Hanbury.

Leek.
Lichfield.
Norbury.
Tamworth.
Tettenhall.
Weston.
Wolverhampton.

SUFFOLK.

Ashby.
Athelington.
Bacton.
Badley.
Bansfield.
Bardwell.
Barking.
Barningham.
Barrow.
Barton.
Beccles.
Bedfield.
Belton.
Bildestone.
Billingford.
Blakenham, Little.
Blundeston.
Blythburgh.

Boxford.
Boxted.
Bradfield-Combust.
Bramfield.
Bramford.
Brandon.
Bricett, Great.
Brockley.
Bures.
Burgate.
Burgh.
Burgh Castle.
Bury St. Edmund's (2).
Chellesworth.
Cotton.
Cove, North.
Cove, South.
Covehithe.

SUFFOLK—*cont.*

Cowling.
Cratfield.
Creeting.
Culford.
Dalham.
Darsham.
Dennington.
Easton.
Elmham, South.
Eriswell.
Erwarton.
Eye.
Flempton.
Framlingham.
Freckenham.
Fritton.
Gisleham.
Gorleston (2).
Grundisburgh.
Hadleigh.
Halesworth.
Haverhill.
Hawkedon.
Hengrave.
Herringfleet.
Hessett.
Hevoningham.
Hitcham.
Honnington.
Hopton.
Horham.
Hoxne.
Huntingfield.
Ilketshall, St. Margaret.
Ipswich (3).
Ixworth.
Kersey.
Laxfield.
Lowestoft.
Melford, Long, (2).
Mellis.
Mendham.
Mendlesham.
Mickfield.
Mildenhall.
Newbourne.
Oulton.
Pakefield.
Palgrave.
Parham.

Preston.
Ringsfield.
Ringshall.
Risby.
Rougham.
Rushmere.
Saxham, Little.
Sibton.
Somerleyton.
Sotterley.
Southwold (2).
Sproughton.
Stanningfield.
Stanton.
Stoke Ash.
Stoke-by-Clare.
Stoke-by-Nayland.
Stonham Aspall.
Stonham, Earl.
Stow, West.
Stowlangtoft.
Stradbroke.
Sudbury (4).
Thurlow.
Timworth.
Troston.
Ufford.
Uggeshall.
Walberswick.
Walsham.
Walsham-le-Willow.
Walton.
Wangford.
Wattisfield.
Wenham, Great.
Wenham, Little.
Westhall.
Westley.
Wickham Market.
Wilby.
Wingfield.
Wissett.
Wiston.
Withersfield.
Woodbridge.
Woolpit.
Worlingworth.
Yaxley.
Yoxford.

SURREY.

Alfold (2).
Beddington.
Byfleet.
Capel.
Caterham.
Chaldon.
Charlwood.
Chipstead.
Cranley.
Croydon.
Fetcham.
Godalming.
Guildford (2).
Horley.
Kingston-on-Thames.

Lambeth.
Limpsfield.
Lingfield.
Merstham.
Merton.
Newdigate.
Oakwood.
Ockham.
Pirford.
Putney.
Reigate.
Southwark.
Stoke d'Abernon.
Warlingham.
Woking.

SUSSEX.

Alfriston.
Amberley (2).
Arlington.
Arundel.
Barlavington.
Battle (2).
Bepton.
Bersted, South.
Binstead.
Bosham.
Boxgrove.
Brighton.
Broadwater.
Chichester (4).
Chiddingly.
Chiltington, West.
Clapham.
Climping.
Cuckfield.
Fernhurst.
Findon.
Hardham.
Harting.
Hastings.
Henfield.
Hooe.
Horsham.
Horsted Keynes.
Hurstmonceux.
Hurstpierpoint.

Icklesham.
Ifield.
Iford.
Isfield.
Keymer.
Kirdford.
Lavant, Mid.
Lewes (2).
Lindfield.
Lurgashall.
Maresfield.
Mayfield.
Patcham.
Pevensey.
Plumpton.
Poling.
Portslade.
Preston.
Robertsbridge.
Rogate.
Rotherfield.
Rottingdean.
Rye.
Shipley.
Shulbrede, Fernhurst
Slaugham.
Slindon.
Stedham.
Steyning.
Treyford.

SUSSEX—*cont.*

Westfield.
Westmeston.
Wilmington.
Winchelsea.
Wisborough-Green.

Wiston.
Withyam.
Wittering, West.
Wivelsfield.

WARWICKSHIRE.

Astley.
Aston.
Beaudesert.
Birmingham.
Brailes.
Claverdon.
Compton Wynyate.
Coventry (2).
Eatington, Lower.
Guy's Cliff.
Henley-in-Arden.
Hillmorton.
Kenilworth.
Knowle.
Lapworth.

Merevale.
Newnham Regis.
Nuneaton.
Polesworth.
Shotteswell.
Southam.
Stoneleigh.
Stratford-upon-Avon (2).
Tanworth.
Ullenhall.
Warwick.
Withybrook.
Wolston.
Wootton Wawen.

WESTMORELAND.

Bowness.
Kirkby Lonsdale.

Levens Hall.

WILTSHIRE.

Amesbury.
Avebury.
Bedwin, Great.
Berwick Bassett.
Berwick St. James.
Berwick St. Johns.
Boyton.
Bradenstoke.
Bradford-on-Avon.
Bremhill.
Britford.
Bromham.
Broughton Gifford.
Cannings, Bishop's.
Chalfield, Great, (2).
Chippenham.

Clyffe Pypard.
Codford St. Mary's.
Colerne.
Collingbourn Kingston.
Combe.
Combe, Castle.
Compton Bassett.
Corsham.
Devizes (2).
Ditteridge.
Durrington.
Eaton, Castle.
Edington.
Enford.
Harnham, West.
Heytesbury.

WILTSHIRE—*cont.*

Highworth.
Homington.
Hullavington.
Idmiston.
Keevil.
Kingston Deverill.
Langford, Steeple.
Laycock (2).
Ludgershall.
Lyncham.
Malmesbury.
Manningford Bruce.
Milston.
Monkton Farleigh.
Orcheston St. Mary.
Pitton.
Potterne.

Salisbury (6).
Sarum, Old.
Shorncote.
Somerford Keynes.
Stanton, St. Quintin's.
Stapleford.
Stockton.
Tidworth, North.
Upavon.
Warminster.
Westwood.
Wilsford and Lake.
Winterbourne Dauntsey.
Winterbourne Earls.
Wootton Bassett.
Yatesbury.

WORCESTERSHIRE.

Astley.
Besford.
Bordesley.
Bredon.
Broadwas.
Broadway.
Bromsgrove.
Bushley.
Chaddesley Corbet.
Droitwich.
Elmley Castle.
Evesham.
Flyford Grafton.
Hampton Lovett.
Holt.

Icomb.
Leigh.
Malvern, Great.
Overbury.
Pensax.
Pershore.
Pinvin.
Ribbesford.
Salwarpe.
Sedgberrow.
Strensham.
Tredington.
Wickham, Child's.
Worcester (2).

YORKSHIRE.

Almondbury.
Aysgarth.
Bainton.
Barforth.
Bedale.
Bempton.
Beverley (2).
Bolton Abbey.

Bolton-on-Swale.
Broughton-in-Airedale.
Burnsall.
Burton Agnes.
Campsall.
Conisborough.
Coverham.
Doncaster (2).

YORKSHIRE—*cont.*

Easby (2).
Edlington.
Fangfoss.
Fishlake.
Flamborough.
Fountains Abbey.
Frodingham, North.
Guisborough.
Halifax.
Hampsthwaite.
Harewood.
Hemingborough.
Hooton Roberts.
Hornby.
Hovingham.
Hubberholme.
Hull.
Hunmanby.
Jervaulx Abbey.
Kirby Hill.
Lastingham.
Leake.
Leeds.
Methley.
Northallerton.

Pateley Bridge.
Pickering.
Pickhill.
Preston-in-Holderness.
Richmond.
Ripon.
Roche Abbey.
Rotherham.
Roystone.
Salton.
Selby (2).
Skipton.
Slingsby.
Snaith.
Sprotborough.
Stillingfleet.
Thirsk.
Treeton.
Wakefield (2).
Wath (2).
Watton.
Wilton, Bishop's.
Woodchurch.
York (3).

(II.) WALES.

ANGLESEY.

Beaumaris.
Llaneilian.

Llanidan.
Penmynydd.

BRECKNOCKSHIRE.

Brecon (2).
Merthyr Cynog.

Partricio.

CARDIGANSHIRE.

Llanbadarn Fawr.

Strata Florida.

CARMARTHENSHIRE.

Eglwyscummin.
Laugharne.

Llandawke.

CARNARVONSHIRE.

Gloddaeth.
Gyffin.

Llandudno.
Rhos.

DENBIGHSHIRE.

Cerrigydruidion.
Clocaenog.
Efenechtyd.
Gyffiliog.
Llanarmon in Yale.
Llanelian.

Llanrhaiadr in Kinmerch.
Ruabon.
Ruthin.
Valle Crucis Abbey.
Wrexham.

FLINTSHIRE.

Bangor-is-y-Coed.
Holywell.

Mold.
St. Asaph.

GLAMORGANSHIRE.

Coychurch.
Llandaff.
Llantwit Major.

St. Donats.
Swansea.

MERIONETHSHIRE.

Llanaber.

Llandanwg.

MONTGOMERYSHIRE.

Buttington.
Guilsfield.
Llanfihangel-yng-nghwnfa.
Llangurig.
Llanidloes.

Llanwyddyn.
Meifod.
Newtown.
Pennant Melangell.
Welshpool.

PEMBROKESHIRE.

Caldey Island.
Gumfreston.
Newport.
Penally.

St. David's.
St. Twinnel's.
Stackpole Elidur.

RADNORSHIRE.

Michaelchurch-on-Arrow.

(III.) SCOTLAND.

ABERDEENSHIRE.

Aberdeen. | Turriff.

EDINBURGHSHIRE.

Borthwick. | Edinburgh.
Craigmillar.

FIFESHIRE.

Dunfermline.

LANARKSHIRE.

Douglas.

MORAYSHIRE.

Elgin. | Pluscardine.

PERTHSHIRE.

Fowlis Easter.

RENFREWSHIRE.

Houston.

(IV.) IRELAND.

CLARE.

Killaloe.

CORK.

Ballyvourney. | Youghal.

GALWAY.

Knockmoy.

KERRY.
Kilmelchedor.

KILKENNY.
Kells.

TIPPERARY.
Cashel.

(V.) CHANNEL ISLANDS.

Guernsey (2). | Jersey (6).

INTRODUCTION.

It has been thought that a short introduction giving an outline of the history and progress of mural and decorative painting will be of service to those who take an interest in these subjects. The following slight sketch has, therefore, been prefixed to the "List," the intention being simply to point out, as briefly as possible, the most noticeable facts connected with this branch of decorative art.

Numerous articles have already been written dealing with the subject generally, and many more, treating of its various branches, reference to all of which will be found fully set out in the "List," to enable those interested in the whole or any individual subject to glean the most complete information which can be obtained. Perhaps the most interesting series of illustrations of wall paintings, screens, roofs, &c., is contained in the collection of coloured drawings made by the late Mr. Dawson Turner, with a view to the publication of a new edition of Blomefield's History of Norfolk, and now in the manuscript department of the British Museum. The history of decorative painting is also comprehensively treated by Mr. E. L. Blackburne, in his work published in 1847, and the principles of colour, in a volume recently issued by Messrs. W. and G. Audsley, entitled "Polychromatic Decoration as applied to buildings in the mediæval styles." Valuable information may be obtained from a paper on the "Polychromy of the Middle Ages," by J. Whichcord, junr., published in Weale's Quarterly Papers, Vol. iv., and in Vol. x. of the British Archæological Association Journal, from three articles in the Builder for 1864, and two in the Civil Engineer and Architects Journal for 1850-51, also from one on Chalgrove Church in Archæologia, Vol. xxxviii., and on Charlwood Church in Vol. xxi. of the Archæological Journal, from a short essay on Mural Painting by A. Billing, 1872, &c. &c. The respective Archæological Societies' publications, as will be noticed from the numerous references to them in the "List," teem with illustrations and detailed accounts of the various mural and other painted decorations recently discovered or existing in the churches &c. of Great Britain. These records are in too many instances the only surviving memorials of the paintings, as it may be safely asserted that in the majority of cases wall paintings especially have only been discovered to be destroyed, or to be concealed by a fresh coating of whitewash, and thereby irretrievably injured. Although this destruction may often be excused on the ground of the imperfect or indistinct condition of the paintings, or the perishable and crumbling character of the material on which they are delineated, still it is lamentable to think of the number of examples which have perished through the wilful negligence or prejudice of those who might have preserved them.* It may be stated here, without fear of contradiction, that there is not a single pre-reformation church in England which was not adorned with painted decorations, and there are very few where, with ordinary care, some remains of these paintings could not have been, 'or may not be, brought to light, in spite of the layers of ▸whitewash or paint with which they have been from time to time overladen. It is hoped that one important result of the present list will be to stimulate the interest in this subject, and to be the means of collecting together from every available source all the information which can be acquired, so that a future edition may contain a complete history of the decorative arts as applied to the Churches, &c., of Great Britain during the Middle Ages.†

* Numerous instances might be mentioned of the prejudice and caprice to which Mural paintings have been subjected. For instance, at Catfield, the very remarkable series of paintings were, at the cost of great labour, most carefully uncovered by the son of one rector, only to be whitewashed over by his successor. At Pickering and St. Thomas', Salisbury, numerous interesting pictorial subjects were found beneath the whitewash some few years back, and again plastered over. Many of these are being again brought to light under the auspices of the present incumbents. In a church in the Midland Counties a wall painting of our Crucified Saviour was discovered, and a neighbouring clergyman came over with the intention of sketching it, but not having time to complete the drawing, left the work to be finished on the following day. The extremely evangelical rector, however, disapproving the subject, managed in the interim to have both the sketch and the original painting destroyed. Of the remarkable series at St. John's, Winchester, St. Olave's, Chichester, Westmeston, Whaddon, Bardwell, and Stow Bardolph, not a vestige remains, and as a rule the searcher after these relics will meet with disappointment in prosecuting his researches. The same vandalism has been equally busy with the screens and other remains of painted woodwork. The damage done in this direction, even during the present century, is incalculable. Even during the most recent restorations, many surviving screens have been most ruthlessly swept away, as interfering with the modern ideas of ritual, or the uninterrupted view of the whole church. As an instance of the utter want of feeling for these works of art, may be specified the case of Babingley Church, where a series of beautifully painted panels of a former screen, after lying neglected for many years, were finally utilised for firewood. Fortunately Mr. Dawson Turner has preserved for our benefit a set of coloured drawings of this unique series.

On the other hand, great care has often been taken to preserve the paintings. At Canterbury Cathedral, the necessary measures have been carried out for fixing the plaster and bringing out the colours of the subjects in St. Gabriel's Chapel, and of the legend of St. Eustace in the north choir aisle, and at Eastbridge Hospital in the same city the chief subjects have been similarly treated. At Great Canfield, a very interesting representation of the Virgin and Child has been carefully secured from further injury. More complete restoration at Patcham, South Leigh, &c., has hardly been attended with such satisfactory results. At Castor a blind is kept drawn over the subjects, and at Overton Longueville folding doors enclose the interesting painting of St. Christopher, found about 40 years ago. At Turvey, the recess, within which is a representation of the Crucifixion, has been glazed over.

† The practice of scraping the interior walls of churches so as to expose and leave bare the rough and wide-jointed masonry, seems on every ground a most reprehensible and unreasonable form of treatment. It is quite impossible that the walls, whose external surfaces have been so carefully smoothed over and jointed, could have been intended to present the rude internal effect we now so often see. In the earlier

It is hardly necessary to reiterate the assertion which is now confidently made, that from the earliest times colour was universally adopted as an embellishment to the most excellent and delicate workmanship. Amongst the Egyptians, Greeks, and Romans, colour was freely applied as a necessary adjunct to the most highly finished sculpture.* In Great Britain many examples of decorative colouring on the walls and elsewhere in buildings of the Roman era have been discovered, but these are not included within the scope of the present list, which only professes to commence with the period when Christianity was generally established in our Islands. It seems tolerably clear that for many years after the destruction of the Roman Empire in Britain the art of painting was lost, as we read, and this is the earliest record on the subject, on the authority of the Venerable Bede, that in the year 678 Benedict Biscop brought back from France, for his monastery at Weremouth, portraits of the Virgin and Twelve Apostles, some of the histories of the Evangelists, and subjects from the Apocalypse. And again in 685 he further embellished his monastery with the following subjects : Isaac carrying the wood for a burnt offering ; Christ bearing the Cross ; the Serpent exalted by Moses ; and the Crucifixion. The art of decoration thus introduced seems to have been generally adopted, and paintings and tapestry hangings became the regular adornments of the early Churches. Even before these dates, namely, in the year 674, Wilfrid, Bishop of York, had the walls, the capitals of the columns, and the sacrarium arch of his church decorated "historiis et imagi- "nibus et variis celaturam figuris ex lapide prominentibus et " picturarum et colorum grata varietate."† At the beginning of the 9th century the practice of decorating churches must have been common. At the second Council of Calcuth in Northumberland, held in the year 816, a canon was issued requiring every bishop before consecrating a Church to see painted on the walls or over the altar thereof a portraiture of the Patron Saint.‡ Mention of an early painting on panel at Peterborough Cathedral occurs in the following passage, "There was within these few years a " door in the Church having the picture of Abbot Hedda, and the

---

buildings both the outer and inner faces were plastered over, and in the later, though the outer surface was most carefully finished off, the inner was still left in the rough as being better suited for the adhesion of the layer of plaster on which the painting was to be executed. In such instances as Rushden, Finedon, and Walgrave (Northants), Preston, Morcott, and South Luffenham (Rutland), Bosham (Sussex), &c., the contrast between the carefully finished details and the rough interior wall surfaces is sufficiently startling.

* "Every ancient edifice, whether of Egyptian, Greek, Roman, or Mediæval times, was carefully faced internally with wrought stone or with plaster, and decorated throughout in colour, or it might be encrusted with marbles and mosaic. The notion of leaving the interior of a building as rough and rugged as an exterior generally must be has been from a very early date abandoned by civilized men."—*G. G. Scott, An Essay on the History of English Church Architecture, p. 100.*

† *Ricardi Prioris Hagustaldensis*, lib. I, cap. iii.

‡ "Seu etiam præcipimus unicuique episcopo, ut habeat depictum in pariete oratorii aut in tabula, vel etiam in altaribus, quibus sanctis sint utraque dedicata."—*Wilkins' Concilia*, i. 169.

" King or Captain of the Danes, as it were expostulating the
" business, and underneath were these four Verses written in ancient
" Saxon Letters, as if they had been spoken by the Abbot."*

It is doubtful whether any remains of pre-Norman decoration
have come down to our time. At Deerhurst mention is made of a
painting of the Saxon period. Again on the wall of the apse of
Swincombe Church, a painting of Our Lord in Glory was found
partially destroyed by the insertion of a Norman window. At
St. Mary's, Guildford, on the north and south sides of the tower,
which is alleged to be Saxon, are long narrow windows on the splays
of which have been depicted figures of Saints. The lower part of
the windows and the paintings have been cut through by the present
arches opening into the transepts, which are of early Norman
character. On the south of the Chancel of the very early Church
of St. Martin's, Canterbury, a doorway has recently been found,
which had been walled up for many generations. It is of the
rudest possible workmanship, and is reputed to be a portion of the
original Church in which St. Augustine preached. On the soffit
or under side of the arch are remains of a decorative pattern in red,
apparently of early character. At the Church of Britford are two
walled-up doorways of very early date, the jambs of which are
ornamented with scroll work picked out with colour. Again at
Headbourn Worthy is a very ancient stone Rood still retaining faint
traces of colouring. On some of the sculptures on the west front
of Lincoln Cathedral, which by some are thought to have belonged
to a building prior to the edifice erected by Remigius soon after the
Norman conquest, are distinct remains of chromatic decoration, and
lastly some very rude sculptured figures found in the walls of
St. Nicholas Church, Ipswich, were likewise observed to retain
considerable traces of their original colouring. These instances
will, however, hardly justify a positive assertion that we can claim
to possess any remains of decorative art as undoubtedly practised
before the period of the Norman occupation.

During the Saxon period the practice of painting the Dedication
or Consecration Crosses on the walls seems to have become general,
and a few special remarks about them may here be fitly introduced.
A full account of the Ceremony of consecrating a Church is given
in Archæologia, Vol. xxv. p. 325. It seems to have been the
invariable custom to decorate the interior walls with 12 crosses,
three on each cardinal face, on the exact spots anointed by the
bishop with the holy oil during the ceremony of dedication. In
many cases, also, though it is doubtful if this was always done,
12 crosses were likewise carved or painted on the exterior walls.
It may of course be assumed, unless there is positive evidence to
the contrary, that the crosses are coëval with the walls on which
they are delineated. The painted crosses, as a rule, were of simple
character, with four equal arms expanding towards their extremities,

* Gunton, Hist. of the Church of Peterburgh, p. 9.

and enclosed within a plain circle, being of the pattern commonly denominated the cross patée, formée, or Maltese. Where the crosses are painted, the colour used was almost invariably the dark indian red. Though more elaborate forms are often found, this simplest type continued to be the most prevalent, and appears equally in buildings of Norman date, as at Kempley, Barfreston, Ditteridge, &c., and in those of the latest perpendicular, as at Henry VII.'s Chapel at Westminster Abbey, &c., &c. On the apsidal chancels at Swincombe and Manningford Bruce have been found the original crosses, which may perhaps be of pre-Norman date, in the former instance the colouring being blue instead of red. Many examples exist and have been found of more elaborate character. At Climping is a large and elegant specimen, probably of late 12th century date. At Salisbury Cathedral were 12 beautiful silver inlaid crosses, both on the inner and outer walls. The crosses themselves have all been abstracted long ago, but their outlines are deeply impressed on the walls where they were let in, and traces still remain of colouring having been applied to heighten their effect. During the 15th and early part of the 16th century, the crosses were commonly of more varied design and colouring, green being constantly introduced in conjunction with the red. Occasionally also they were adorned with texts, initials, and inscriptions, as have been noted on specimens found at Arminghall and St. Saviour's, Norwich. Most of the exterior crosses have long since ceased to display the colouring, with which, if ever, they were once adorned, but in recent times traces have been distinguishable on examples at Shurdington, North Repps, and Blythburgh.

During the prevalence of the Norman style,* the art of painting seems to have made considerable progress. To this period may be ascribed some of the most interesting Mural paintings which still survive to our time. As far as one can judge, a greater depth of colour was used then than in later times, or perhaps this result may be due to the restoration which must doubtless from time to time have been applied, but certain it is, that many of the paintings of this era exceed in brightness of colouring and excellence of condition those of much later date. We have numerous proofs of the extent to which decoration was carried. The fine chancel arches at Bishops Wilton and Kempley and the Galilee arches at Durham Cathedral, had their zigzag mouldings picked out with varied colouring. Numerous richly coloured mouldings have been found in the walls of Westminster Hall, and of the churches of Paignton and Wellington (Somerset). At Rochester Cathedral the tympana within the triforium arches are sculptured with a diaper pattern, and have been further decorated with polychrome. The richly sculptured shaft and capital in the crypt at Canterbury Cathedral, at the entrance to

---

* In the Archæological Journal, xxxiv., 275-279, a list of Churches containing paintings of this period is given. This might now be very largely supplemented, many discoveries having been made and much fresh information having been acquired within the last five years.

St. Gabriel's Chapel were found to have been delicately coloured, the preservation of these colours being due to the fact of the pillar having at some distant period been walled up. The plain surfaces of the sculptured portions of buildings were likewise ornamented with colour, as on the soffit of the chancel arches of Copford and Kempley, where were delineated the signs of the zodiac. On the chancel arch of Walsoken, on a plain intermediate moulding, is a scroll pattern, while on that of Castle Rising has been a text in large capital letters. Even the tympana of the doorways seem to have been coloured, as traces have been noted on those at Fordington, Malmesbury, and Wiston (Suffolk), and still exist on those at Leckhampstead, Bridge and Ditteridge. Where the arches are without sculptured moulding, they are often found with the ordinary ornamentation represented in colour. In the north transept of Winchester Cathedral, the very early Norman arches are decorated with medallions containing foliage, &c. At Canterbury Cathedral, the arch opening from the north choir aisle to St. Andrew's chapel, which is a portion of Prior Conrad's glorious work, is richly ornamented with decorative colouring, the several orders of the arch being embellished with varied designs. St. Andrew's Chapel also retains numerous very early wall patterns, which are probably the most ancient remains of colouring in the Cathedral. At Worcester Cathedral a plain roll moulding on an arch in the south transept is painted in imitation of the cable pattern. Round the arches of Norwich and Ely Cathedrals are considerable remains, as also on an arcade in the east wall of Brabourne Church. But undoubtedly the most interesting examples have been found at St. Albans Cathedral and Elstow Church. In the former building the arches, some in three and some in two orders, have been ornamented with oblong patterns in three colours, while bands of foliage have been carried round as a kind of hoodmould above them. The soffits of the arches have been likewise embellished with varying patterns of chevrons, no two being exactly similar. On the jambs of some of the arches and windows in the transepts imitation shafts and capitals have been painted. So, too, round the arches at Elstow, the most interesting decorative patterns, such as interlacing semicircular arches, &c., &c., were recently visible through the whitewash, but these, as is much to be regretted, have been entirely destroyed. The variety of decorative patterns made use of is very considerable. At Copford are some unusual designs which may have been suggested by Roman remains existing at the neighbouring town of Colchester, the patterns bearing a strong resemblance to many of those forming the borderings of the Roman mosaic pavements. At Kempley is a kind of "tau" pattern of a character said to be distinctly Byzantine. At Leominster a variety of ornaments are depicted, the zigzag and scallop being the most common. Good designs were found and are still partially visible at Ifiley, the lozenge ornament at Pytchley and Avington, the zigzag or chevron at Stewkley and Tintagel, and the indented at Patcham and Winchfield. At St. Cross, Winchester, and St. John's, Devizes, ornamental patterns have been discovered and restored in a manner which would hardly commend itself to the original artists. Scroll and foliage patterns are not uncommon, the designs being very stiff and conventional, and inferior to those introduced in the succeeding century. They seem generally to belong to a late period in this architectural era. At Stoke sub Hamdon are two windows with a pattern of stars and roses on the splays. One of these affords a good example of genuine Norman decoration, as it has only been recently opened, having doubtless been closed up since the early part of the thirteenth century, a lancet window, which cuts partly through it, having been inserted in its stead. Varieties of decoration have been recently found within the window splays at Willey and Neen Savage, the groundwork being yellow; and many other instances will be found in the list, with the authorities cited, whence fuller information may be acquired. Bands of red and yellow round the window splays and arches are not uncommon, and may be seen at Canterbury Cathedral, Barfreston, Kempley, and elsewhere. Imitation hangings are sometimes depicted on the walls, and occur at the Cathedrals of Durham and Canterbury, also at Romsey, Barfreston and Cashel. On the nave piers at Leckhampstead are sentences in red letters. We have but few remaining paintings of scenes, figures, &c., which can with certainty be ascribed to the Norman period. In the crypt at Worcester Cathedral is an early example of an angel swinging a thurible, and an angel with a censer is also to be seen at St. Albans Cathedral. At Chichester Cathedral, Castle Hedingham, and Hadleigh (Essex), are figures of bishops, at the last named the portrait of St. Thomas of Canterbury being, of course late in the 12th century. At Wisborough Green is a curious representation of the Crucifixion, and above St. James introducing pilgrims to our Saviour in Heaven. At Westmeston a very interesting series were discovered. Those of Norman date included the "Agnus Dei," The Adoration of the Magi, Betrayal, Scourging, Descent from the Cross, and Christ seated in Glory, and delivering the keys to St. Peter and the book to St. Paul. At West Chiltington are figures of the Apostles, and some lettering on scrolls and a portion of a vesica, indicates that a figure of our Lord in Glory was also here represented. At the little church of Hardham, one of the most interesting series of early paintings has been discovered, though it is difficult to identify some of the subjects. In the chancel seems to have been depicted Christ in Majesty, though only the seated figures of the Apostles remain. In the nave has, perhaps, been a Doom and various scenes in the life of Christ upon earth. There is also a representation of St. George on horseback, by far the earliest example of this subject in painting which has yet been discovered in Great Britain. At Romsey are several subjects within medallions, perhaps the history of a bishop. At Brook (Kent), the whole of the chancel walls seem to have been decorated with a series of subjects, within medallions, commemorating Christ's life on earth and His Majesty in Heaven. The medallions have not been completely cleansed of their numerous coatings, and very few of the subjects can be identified with certainty. On the nave walls are also some earlier subjects within larger medallions, but too much obscured to make it safe to hazard a conjecture as to their interpretation. At Barfreston the chancel was found to be covered with paintings probably coeval with the church itself. Figures of our Lord, saints, and seraphim, within medallions, archbishops and bishops, and early New Testament subjects, were discovered about 40 years ago, but only a representation of the Annunciation has been preserved. Fortunately an elaborate series of coloured drawings of these paintings exists in the library of the Society of Antiquaries. On the east wall of the Galilee at Durham Cathedral was a large painting of the Crucifixion, with portraits, as is supposed, of Richard I. and Bishop Pudsey. At St. Albans Cathedral on the Norman piers are several representations of the Crucifixion, of which one or perhaps two may be assigned to the late Norman period. At Chaldon is a very large representation of the Ladder of Salvation of the Human Soul and the Road to Heaven. The Tortures of the Wicked, St. Michael weighing Souls, &c., are also included in the subject. This dates from quite the end of the 12th century. Over the chancel arch at Patcham is a curious representation of the Doom, which seems to have been partly retouched, though evidently originally executed in the 12th century. At Pirford are some very early paintings supposed to illustrate scenes in the life of St. Nicholas. At St. Mary's, Guildford, on the ceiling of the chapel of St. John the Baptist, are the well-known series of paintings portraying our Lord in Glory and (as asserted by the various authorities, though the correctness of the interpretation is doubtful), the tortures of the wicked after death. But undoubtedly the most interesting examples of this early period, are those in the chapel of St. Gabriel in the crypt of Canterbury Cathedral, and at the small and unimportant churches of Copford and Kempley. As may be gathered from a reference to the list all have been fully illustrated and described. At Canterbury on the vault of the nave or outer chapel are various subjects within medallions which are certainly late in the 12th century, and probably of a subsequent date to those in the chancel or inner chapel. Here on the vault we have a representation of Christ in Majesty, and on the north and south walls are portrayed the events connected with the nativity of our Saviour and St. John the Baptist. On an arch in the east wall is St. John writing the Apocalypse, and the angels of the seven churches, and the seven stars within medallions, and on buttress strips on the north and south sides are cherubim with wings full of eyes. The whole is in fair condition and has recently been preserved from further injury. In the chancel at Copford is likewise a picture of Christ in Majesty occupying the vault, while on the north and south walls are figures of the Apostles, angels and ornamental patterns filling up the subsidiary spaces. These paintings have been declared on good authority to date from the 12th, but to have received a considerable amount of renovation in the 14th century.

The series at Kempley are still more interesting. As in the other two examples, on the vault of the chancel is depicted a representation of Christ in Glory, in this instance, surrounded by angels, several figures, and the stars, golden candlesticks, &c., in conformity with the description given in the book of Revelation. On the north and south sides are the Apostles, while the other wall spaces are occupied by figures of angels within medallions, the Virgin, St. James Major, two bishops and ornamental patterns. There can be no doubt that here, at Copford, and probably also at Hardham the design of the painter was to make the chancel of the church figuratively to portray the glories of Heaven, Christ's everlasting Kingdom. On the nave walls and window splays (at Kempley), are some early paintings, viz., over the chancel arch a Doom, also the figure of a saint, St. Michael weighing Souls, St. Anthony, and several varieties of decoration. Only red, yellow, and black is used, all the figures being left in outline on a red ground, but, as at Canterbury and Copford pale green and blue tints are introduced, it seems probable that these also originally existed at Kempley.

There is no doubt that decorative patterns, &c., of Norman architectural character were still used at least for the first 20 years of the 13th century, and it is probable that some of the above-mentioned examples may belong to this period. It is by some supposed that the elaborate painted decorations at St. Albans Cathedral were of this date, as it is recorded that one Walter de Colchester was employed to decorate various portions of the Abbey Church, by Abbot Trumpington, who rebuilt the western portion of the nave early in the 13th century.

The examples of painted woodwork of the Norman period are extremely uncommon, and it is doubtful whether any instances have come down to us, with the exception of the roof of the nave and transepts of Peterborough Cathedral. These roofs are flat and highly coloured, that over the south transept being plainer and somewhat earlier than that over the nave. On the latter are numerous figures within lozenge-shaped medallions of the Agnus Dei, various saints, and grotesque and allegorical figures.[*]

During the long and troubled reign of Henry III., the art of painting seems to have received considerable encouragement. Many entries appear in the Court rolls, &c., which mention the names of the painters employed, the various subjects delineated by them, and the amount of remuneration received by them for their work.[†] It is clear that at this time many foreigners were attracted to England, but the purely English character of most of the paintings of this

[*] This roof has been fully illustrated in a work by Strickland, entitled "The Ancient Painted Ceiling in the Nave of Peterborough Cathedral."

[†] As one example out of many, may be cited on the authority of Sir R. C. Hoare, in his history of Wiltshire, the numerous contracts entered into with various painters for embellishing the Royal Palace at Clarendon. Another instance, worthy of special mention, is the order for a painting of St. Christopher, to be executed in the Chapel of St. Peter within the Tower, being perhaps the earliest record of the introduction into England of this legendary subject, which afterwards became so universally popular.

date shows that this immigration served only to arouse a healthy competition on the part of the English painters and to cause a marked improvement in the execution of the various works. It is generally supposed that many of the finest pictures were painted by travelling monks or other ecclesiastics, but even if this were the case, there is ample evidence to prove that, both at this period and still more in later times, abundant patronage was extended to professional artists, whose services were in constant request both in the religious and secular edifices.

It seems almost incredible, but is certainly a fact, that the finest workmanship and materials were still further overlaid with colour. As an instance of this it may be mentioned that the black marble shafts in the choir of Rochester Cathedral, showed distinct traces of early red colouring. The beautiful monument of Archbishop Walter Gray at York Minster, composed of the finest marble, shows that there also colour had been freely applied, and many other examples might be adduced to prove the universality of this practice. The decorations of this period consist chiefly of masonry patterns, scroll, and foliage, still very conventional in character, and a few more elaborate designs. The masonry patterns are the simplest form of decoration, lines intersecting each other at right angles, dividing the wall surface into oblong divisions. This is especially common within the splays of lancet windows. Good examples may be seen in the south choir aisle and transept of St. Albans Cathedral, at Royston, Little Coggeshall, &c. Sometimes in this as in the succeeding century, roses were painted within the divisions as st Potterne, Moor Hall, Harefield, and elsewhere. At Notgrove and North Luffenham are masonry patterns and scroll decorations on the nave arches. At Ketton is a running scroll round the eastern tower arch, and similar ornamentation is visible on the soffits of the beautiful early English arches at Elstow. At Charlton on Otmoor, the nave arches are all ornamented with a running scroll, while on the soffits is a diaper of stars, crescents, and roses. The west respond on the north side is decorated with large chevrons similar to those which are visible on the columns of the nave at Hunstanton. Within the splay of a lancet window at Cheveley, a kind of fleur de lis ornament is introduced. The chancel walls of Bramdean Church are decorated with an early diaper pattern. The dogtooth moulding, so distinguishing an ornament in 13th century work, is not often represented in painting, owing to the difficulty of depicting it in the then deficient knowledge of perspective. On the south wall of the presbytery of St. Albans Cathedral, and in the churches of Godalming, St. Olave's, Chichester, and Killaloe, attempts have been made to delineate it. On a corbel in the south porch at Barnack the indented ornament occurs. The walls of Berkeley Church were found to have been entirely covered with various ornamental decorations. Some of these have been repainted and still exist. A series of interlacing semicircular arches run along the west wall, which are clearly of early 13th century date. Between the clerestory windows at West Walton are some very interesting decorations with varied diapers representing tapestry hangings. The practice of painting the external portions of buildings was, as in the preceding century, constantly in vogue. The west front of Wells Cathedral shows traces of colouring, as does the exterior of the Lady Chapel of Hereford Cathedral. At East Harptree the head of a churchyard cross was found in an old chimney stack, the drapery of the several figures sculptured on it still retaining their former decorative painting.

Some remains of 13th century screen work also retain traces of their original colouring, as at Hullavington and Swanscombe. It will, however, be more convenient to make some special remarks on the subject of screens and other painted woodwork, and of monuments, sculpture, &c., later on, and, as far as possible, to confine this portion of the essay to the subject of the wall paintings.

There are still, or have been till recently, existing numerous pictorial representations of saints, subjects, &c., which can with certainty be ascribed to this century. The practice of depicting a series of events in the history of the life of Christ upon earth, of the Virgin, SS. Catherine, Thomas of Canterbury, and others, seems to have become very common, the former subject generally appearing on the walls of the chancel, the others being most commonly found on those of the nave. Very interesting series of the life of Christ have been found on the walls of the nave at Winterbourne Dauntsey and West Chiltington, of the chancel at Easby, Chalgrove, Timworth, East Wickham, and Preston (Sussex), also at Wiston (Suffolk), and Headington, in the chapel of the Holy Sepulchre at Winchester Cathedral, and on a pillar at Faversham. At St. Albans Cathedral, on the north nave piers, most of the series of paintings of the Crucifixion with the Annunciation below belong to this period. On the east wall of the refectory of St. Martin's Priory at Dover, is a 13th century painting of the Last Supper. At Easby, the subject of the creation and fall of man is delineated, and at Shenley Mansell on the wall of the south transept, three small pictures forming the first of a series of old testament subjects still remain. At St. Thomas', Newport, Isle of Wight, amongst other paintings, were discovered a portrait of King David, and a female figure blindfolded with crown falling off and sword near her. It is probable that this figure may be emblematical of the fall of the Mosaic dispensation or may be intended for St. Osyth, some lettering at the side appearing to be "S." "OSA." At Wiston (Suffolk) and Godalming, St. John the Baptist is portrayed, and within the window splays at Chalgrove, some of the Apostles and other Saints occur. Representations of the Doom of this period occur at Wiston (Suffolk), Headington, and St. John's, Winchester. At the last-named church a very interesting series was found, which has fortunately been illustrated in the Winchester volume of the British Archæological Association, as no traces of the original work now remain. Here were found, amongst other subjects, the martyrdom of St. Andrew, the Crucifixion, unusually treated, the figures on either side of the Cross being Isaiah and St. Francis, instead of SS. John and Mary the Virgin, as almost invariably introduced. In the north aisle was painted the murder of St. Thomas of Canterbury, who undoubtedly became one of the most popular of English Saints, and whose portrait and martyrdom were amongst the commonest subjects delineated by the artist. At Hauxton, Bramley, and Preston (Sussex), are remaining good examples of 13th century date. Another was discovered at Mentmore and destroyed. At St. Cross, Winchester, a number of incidents in his life are depicted. Another painting at St. John's, Winchester, was the representation of the Seven Acts of Mercy (the first six) as detailed in St. Matthew, xxv. 35. This is certainly an early instance of what seems to have become a common subject, though not many examples have survived to the present time. At Chesterton, within the splay of a window in the north aisle, is perhaps a contemporary illustration of this same subject, though its interpretation is very doubtful. At Rochester Cathedral is another early example of what may be termed the "Morality" subjects, viz. a wheel of fortune, which has been fully described in the Gloucester volume of the British Archæological Association, page 179. At Kempley and Leominster are similar wheels and executed about the same period. At Winchester Cathedral, in the chapel of the Holy Sepulchre, which is now almost blocked up by the new apparatus attached to the organ, is the earliest existing example in England, being of the beginning of the 13th century, of what afterwards became one of the most popular subjects in Mural painting, viz., the history of St. Catherine of Alexandria. Her conversion to Christianity, defiance of the emperor Maximian, miraculous escape from being torn to pieces by the breaking of the wheels to which she was attached, the martyrdom of those whom she converted, and finally her own death by decapitation and apotheosis, are constantly represented. At Preston (Sussex), is a figure of St. Catherine forming part of a very interesting series of subjects which have been most fully illustrated and described. We find (at Preston) besides events in the life of Christ and the martyrdom of St. Thomas of Canterbury, a painting of St. Margaret, who also became one of the most popular of English Saints, and the curious and very early traditional subject of St. Michael weighing souls. Figures of St. Margaret of this date are to be found on the ceiling of the sacrist's room at Norwich Cathedral, where she is represented within a medallion in the company of St. Mary the Virgin and St. Catherine, while in an adjoining medallion occur SS. Paul, Andrew, and Peter, the latter, habited as an archbishop, being a unique representation. In the next medallion is a figure of St. Richard de la Wych, bishop of Chichester, a saint who rarely appears, though, as he is portrayed without an emblem, many of the unidentified figures of bishops may be intended for him. The legend of St. Margaret was also discovered at Charlwood, where was also depicted the history of St. Nicholas, who was undoubtedly one of the most popular of English Saints, as evidenced by the large number of churches bearing his name and containing special chapels or altars dedicated to him, and it is therefore a somewhat remarkable circumstance that comparatively few representations of this Saint, either in sculpture, painting, or stained glass, have survived to our time.* Another very popular Saint, especially in the eastern counties, was St. Edmund, king and martyr, and we find representations of his martyrdom as being discovered at Ely Cathedral and at Stow Bardolph, beneath a later painting of St. Christopher. Another instance occurs at Stoke Dry, where are also representations of the Virgin and Child, the torture of a female saint, &c., and a portion of a St. Christopher, which has been painted subsequently to and over this series. It is sometimes difficult to discriminate between the pictures of St. Edmund and St. Sebastian, a Saint who does not seem to have been venerated in England till a later period, though, as a general rule, it may be laid down that the former is always crowned and more completely clad than the latter. Both are usually delineated as fixed to a tree or stake and being shot to death, St. Edmund† being usually pierced by more arrows than St. Sebastian. A series of events commemorating the martyrdom of St. Edmund was discovered at Cliffe at Hoo. There, as also at East Wickham and West Chiltington, the several scenes are represented beneath and separated from each other, by a continuous arcade of trefoil-headed arches, early English in its character, though the paintings are reputed to be of the latter part of the 13th century. Another series of events, probably the history of some sainted bishop, occur under triangular-headed arches on the wall of the south aisle at Upchurch. No conjecture as to the legend represented has as yet been hazarded. The practice of painting figures, &c., within medallions seems to have been common both in the latter part of the 12th and throughout the 13th century. Over the chancel arch at Eastry are a series of circles enclosing animals, foliage, &c. On the ceiling of the chapter house at Christ Church, Oxford, are large figures of SS. Peter, Paul, &c., and in the chapel of the Guardian Angels at Winchester Cathedral are demi-figures of angels, in each case within medallions. On the ceiling of the angel choir and transepts of Lincoln Cathedral have been numerous subjects, many of which have been destroyed. At Salisbury Cathedral the vault of the choir has been repainted, the original scheme, which comprised the following subjects, viz., Christ in Majesty, the Apostles, Evangelists, Prophets, Seasons, &c., having been carefully copied.

---

* The same remarks which have been made about St. Richard of Chichester will apply still more forcibly to St. Nicholas. He was generally portrayed without any distinctive emblem, and, in the opinion of the late Dr. Husenbeth, *British Archæol. Assoc. Journ.*, xiv. 176, it may be assumed that where a bishop is represented without name or emblem, St. Nicholas is intended. In later times the remark will seem to refer more appropriately to St. Martin. An archbishop without name or emblem may be generally considered to portray St. Thomas of Canterbury.

† On the panels of screens, St. Edmund is generally represented as in regal attire and holding an arrow.

The paintings of the 14th century do not show any marked advance over those of the preceding era, though a greater diversity of subjects was then introduced and the pictures seem on the whole to have been more skilfully executed. The same careful attention to the due preparation of the wall surface appears often to have been neglected, and many interesting series of paintings have been discovered in too perishable a condition to be capable of preservation, owing to the decay of the plaster on which they have been delineated. The decorative patterns of this date are in many cases more elaborate than those made use of in the previous century. As in sculpture, so in painting, the designs for the foliage, flowers, &c., are taken from real instead of conventional examples. Beautiful arabesque patterns with foliage, flowers, &c., on a red ground seem to have been not uncommon. Bold interlacing scrolls were often introduced as borderings and to fill up vacant spaces, as at Dodford and Newington by Sittingbourne. A powdering of roses may often be found of this as of the preceding century, and may still be seen at the Saints Chapel, St. Albans Cathedral, and elsewhere. A fleur de lis pattern was also not uncommon and is still visible at Northolt, and in conjunction with heraldic lions in the north transept of St. Albans Cathedral. A masonry pattern of double lines seems to be a special design of the early part of this century, and may be observed on the splay of a window at Much Hadham. A curious example of decoration exists at Chalfont St. Giles, where above the chancel arch are painted battlements, &c., causing the arch to present the appearance of a fortified gateway. Heraldic designs began to prevail, as evidenced by the rich colour and gilding on the stone screens enclosing the choirs of the Cathedrals of Rochester and Canterbury. So again in the vestibule between the cathedral and chapter house at York are remains of decorative painting on the vaulting ribs, with shields, roses, &c., on the walls. The practice of enriching with colour and gilding the ornamental sculpture seems to have been universally prevalent. As an example, may be cited the beautifully diapered stone work on the south of the high altar of Canterbury Cathedral, and at the back of the monuments in the south aisle at Winchelsea Church. The diaper work in the triforium storey at Westminster Abbey, of rather earlier date, also bears traces of having been once richly coloured. The Lady Chapel at Ely Cathedral must have formerly presented a gorgeous appearance, traces of rich gilding and colour being still everywhere visible through the whitewash. The groined roof with sculptured representations of events in the life of the Virgin, the numerous niches, and beautiful arcading were all profusely decorated, and it is hoped that by a careful removal of the whitewash, ere long its former magnificence may be in some measure recovered. Even the exterior arcade exhibited remains of coloured decoration.

In pictorial subjects the same general method of arrangement, as in vogue in the previous century, seems to have been followed, the chancel walls being generally decorated with scenes from the New

Testament, while legends of saints, the "Moralities," &c. adorned
the other portions of the edifice, the subject of the Doom usually
occupying the space over the chancel arch. On the chancel walls at
North Cove are scenes from the life of Christ on earth, of about the
same date. On the north wall of the nave of Battle Church are faint
traces of pictures of our Lord's passion. At Warblington in the
nave were a series of Christ's miracles, and various events in His
earthly life also occur on the nave or aisle walls at West Somerton,
Crostwight, Islip, Bedfont, Plumpton, &c. At St. Stephen's
Chapel, Westminster, a beautiful series were executed for King
Edward III., and copies of some of these, which include portraits of the
King and his family, are preserved in the rooms of the Society of Antiquaries. The subject of the great Doom, with Christ seated in Judgment, was not an uncommon one during this period, and examples
may be noted at Bedfont, Newington by Sittingbourne, Plumpton,
Houghton Conquest, West Somerton, &c. Amongst the most
beautiful remnants of 14th century work are the paintings on the
east wall of the chapter house at Westminster Abbey, where are
portrayed the three persons of the Blessed Trinity with the seraphim
and cherubim. The name of the painter, John of Northampton, is
recorded in the annals of the monastery. The series of subjects
illustrating the Apocalypse are of much later date. Of other
scriptural subjects, have been recorded the last scenes from the life
of the Virgin at Wimborne Minster, the Virgin and Child, of unusual
merit, at Great Canfield, the history of St. John the Baptist at Cold
Overton, Elsing, and Chalfont St. Giles, admirably executed figures
of the apostles at Newington by Sittingbourne, the temptation of our
first parents and their expulsion from Paradise at Colton. Of saintly
portraits and legends, have been until recently, or still are, in
existence, representations of St. Michael weighing souls, with the
Virgin interceding on the souls' behalf,* at Toddington, Islip, and
Lenham, the history of St. Catherine at Castor, Bardwell, and
Chalfont St. Giles, the martyrdom of St. Thomas of Canterbury at
Whaddon, and of St. Erasmus at Cirencester. At Birmingham was
depicted the history of St. Martin, at Norwich Cathedral, SS. Wulstan
and Edward the Confessor, and at Westminster Abbey, St. Faith. At
Little Kimble are an interesting series of paintings, including a portrait
of St. George on foot, and in the armour of the period, his name being
recorded below. At Bardwell and Charlwood were representations of
St. Edmund, or possibly in the latter case of St. Sebastian, who, in
conjunction with St. Anthony, appears at Irthlingborough, while
St. Nicholas was portrayed at Colton and Tamworth. At Rauceby is
an unusual subject described by some of the authorities as St.
Matthew and Satan, by others as St. Anthony and the panther. The
correctness of either of these definitions seems doubtful. Some
interesting paintings have recently been discovered at Farnborough,
where, side by side, are depicted SS. Eugenia, Agnes, and Mary

* For a full explanation of the origin of this legend, see Archæological Journal,
xxxiv. 238.

Magdalene, the names of the first two being inscribed above, and of the third across, the figures in characters which show them to belong to the reign of Edward II. St. Eugenia is not recorded to have been portrayed elsewhere in England, and the presence of these three saints, none of whom seem to have been specially honoured in this country, points to the fact of some foreigner having at that time settled in the parish. On the nave piers of St. Albans Cathedral are four large paintings executed during the rule of Abbot Delamere, circ. 1360. They represent large figures of St. Christopher, St. Thomas of Canterbury, St. Citha, and King Edward the Confessor and the Pilgrim.* The legend of St. Christopher, which became so favourite a subject during the 15th century, had hardly yet become universally popular, but examples ascribed to the reign of Edward III. have been found at Croydon, Shorwell, &c. This latter example is the most interesting illustration of the legend which has yet been brought to light, and, besides the general representation of the Saint carrying the Infant Saviour across the stream, depicts his conversion to the Christian faith, and his martyrdom. But undoubtedly the most interesting series of this century was found in the nave of Catfield Church, the paintings having been most carefully divested of their covering of whitewash by the son of one incumbent, only to receive a fresh dose and be again concealed by his successor. Fortunately they have been copied, and coloured drawings remain in the "Dawson-Turner" collection. The subjects all run into each other, and the whole of the wall surface was covered with the pictures, which illustrate scenes in Christ's life upon earth, the history of St. John the Baptist, an event in the life of St. John the Evangelist, the martyrdom of SS. Lawrence and Catherine, and representations of the Wheel of Fortune, similar to those at Kempley, &c., of the tree of the Seven Deadly Sins, and the Seven Virtues or Acts of Mercy, and seven Sacraments of the Church of Rome. Of the last class of subjects an example of one of the Vices of this date was found at Melbourne (Derbyshire). At Starston a representation of an entombment, date 1300, gave rise to a long and somewhat controversial correspondence in *Notes and Queries*; in this case, as in many others, the attempt being made to attach a significance to the subject which could not reasonably be maintained.

To the 15th and early portion of the 16th century, perhaps the largest number of Mural paintings which exist or have been discovered belong, and this is the less surprising, from the numerous proofs which remain of the want of respect for the workmanship, both architectural and pictorial, of their predecessors, displayed by the architects and artists of mediæval times. Such instances may be cited as those at St. Lawrence, Reading, Pinvin, Hovingham, Tintagel, &c , where one series has been found to have been painted over another, the subjects of the later pictures being often, and in fact generally, quite distinct from those of the earlier period. These

---

* The identification of the two last subjects is somewhat doubtful.

cases strikingly exemplify the changes of religious sentiment, and the rising or waning popularity of the various saints and subjects. As in most of the examples hitherto noted, the older paintings are in better preservation than those by which they have been overlaid, it could not therefore have been owing to the fact of their being faded or decayed that a renewal of the wall decoration was deemed necessary. The numerous beautiful screens and painted wooden roofs, of which a more detailed account will be given hereafter, were mainly executed in the latter part of the 15th or early portion of the 16th century.

It will be impossible in the space within which it is advisable to confine this essay, to do more than refer briefly and in general terms to the multiplicity of subjects of which we have recorded examples, and the additional saints and representations introduced at this period, owing to the more extended commerce of our British merchants, and consequently a more intimate connexion with the peoples and religious observances of other countries. The many foreigners who were induced and encouraged to settle in England, as for instance, the Flemings in the eastern counties, soon began to exercise a considerable influence in religious matters, and to their industry and consequent wealth and generosity we owe many of the magnificent ecclesiastical structures which have been erected in the districts where they were located. The presence of mural paintings portraying unusual subjects and saints not commonly worshipped in England, generally affords evidence that the early settlers in the parish, or benefactors to a particular church, were thus influenced by foreign religious sentiment, and where the earlier history of the several parishes has been explored, this indirect evidence of the paintings has been almost invariably confirmed.

The decorative patterns of this period chiefly consist of natural foliage, and diapers of various initials, shields, &c. Chevrons of different colours, and spiral ornamentation on shafts, groining ribs, &c., similar to that exhibited on barbers' poles, are also very common. Of the chevron ornament the piers and arches of Stanion Church afforded a very rich example, which was unfortunately not preserved. A chapel on the north side of Laycock Church, and the Dean's Chapel at Canterbury Cathedral, are also good instances of the style of decoration of this period. At St. Peter's, St. Alban's, the vaulting-shafts in the south aisle are ornamented with a pattern of single oak leaves. The nave of Lathbury Church, including the whole of the walls, arches, and clerestory window splays, is ornamented with a bold foliage pattern which encircles various subjects, such as the Seven Sacraments, St. Michael weighing souls, &c. Within the window splays of the Lady Chapel at St. Alban's Cathedral is a beautiful arabesque pattern of vine leaves on a pale red ground, and a somewhat similar design exists on the piers of the chancel arch at Meldreth. At South Leigh, besides the interesting series of pictorial subjects, are running scrolls with foliage, birds, &c., and numerous ornamental designs. The pomegranate pattern became a favourite

subject, especially on the panels of screens, and it has been found as
a wall decoration at Ridge, Newton Bromswold, and elsewhere. The
sacred monograms "ihc," "χρς," are also constantly depicted, as are
also diapers of crowned "M"s for St. Mary the Virgin. A few
instances occur of the initials of other saints, as "T" for St. Thomas
of Canterbury, "N" for St. Nicholas. At St. Mary's, Bury St.
Edmunds, is a rather uncommon representation of the sacred
monogram within a collar of "SS." On the north nave clerestory
wall at Charlton on Otmoor are numerous crowned "I"s. The
eastern portion of the crypt at Canterbury Cathedral has a diaper of
crowned "M"s on the roof, and one large crowned "M" appears on
each of the nave pillars of Old Warden Church. Heraldic designs
are not uncommon in mural painting, though more usually found on
screens, roofs, and monuments. As instances may be mentioned
examples on the east wall of the choir of Peterborough Cathedral,
on the walls of the chapel of St. Mary in the crypt of Canterbury
Cathedral (these being probably of the end of the 14th century), and
in the Scadbury Chantry, Chiselhurst. On the walls of the Swayne
Chantry at St. Thomas, Salisbury, are numerous St. George's shields
within a garter, and of pots of lilies, on a red ground.

Of the pictorial subjects, the most common representations were
scenes from Christ's life upon earth, the Doom, or Great Day of
Judgment, the Life and Miracles of St. Mary the Virgin, the history
of St. Catherine, the murder of St. Thomas of Canterbury, and the
Legendary Moralities, amongst which may be included SS. Christopher and George, saints of mythical origin, who became the objects
of the most intense and superstitious reverence amongst all classes of
society in England. Representations of St. George have been noted
even in mural painting as early as the 12th century, and several
sculptured tympana of Norman doorways still remain, exhibiting in
somewhat rude carving his combat with the dragon. In the later
wall paintings he is generally portrayed on horseback trampling the
dragon beneath the feet of his charger, while behind him kneels the
princess whom he has rescued from the monster, and whose parents
survey the contest from a distant tower. St. George was the special
patron of English soldiers, and his aid was always invoked in the
various campaigns. Most of the examples of this subject have been
executed in the 15th century, but besides those at Hardham and
Little Kimble already referred to, another instance, namely, that
found at Croydon Church, may be attributed to an earlier period.
Very interesting examples have been discovered at Witton, Drayton,
and Fritton, Norfolk, and may still be seen at St. Gregory's,
Norwich, Broughton (Bucks), Dartford, &c. At Astbury an unusual
representation of the subject, which probably formed a portion only
of a series, formerly existed, in which St. George is depicted as having
dismounted from his horse, while the princess expresses her
gratitude to him for his timely rescue, and a second picture
exhibits the Virgin holding the Infant Saviour, and conferring upon
him the honour of knighthood as a reward for his prowess.

St. Christopher, who seems to have become even more popular than St. George,[*] does not appear to have been generally recognised in England before the 15th century, during which period it is conjectured that every English church possessed a figure, either in painting or sculpture, of this Saint. There are a few representations which may be ascribed to the latter half of the 14th century, as for instance, those at St. Alban's, Croydon, and Shorwell, already referred to, and perhaps also an example at Witton. Among the 13th century paintings in the nave at West Chiltington is a figure of Saint Christopher, of the same date apparently as the remainder of the series. If so, this is certainly the earliest existing example in England. St. Christopher owed his peculiar popularity to the superstitious notion that any one who looked on his portrait would be secure from a violent death during that day, and two verses commemorating this belief are often found on scrolls above and below the picture. It is for this reason that the paintings of St. Christopher usually occupy the situation most easily seen by any one entering the church, and are generally found on the wall, or sometimes, as at Watford, South Bersted, &c., on a pillar facing the principal doorway, so that they may be even visible to any one passing by the church.[†] Thus it is constantly found painted over subjects which had previously filled the coveted position, as at Stow Bardolph already referred to, where also a second and later example occupied a similar position over the other doorway. The instances are very rare, where this subject is represented elsewhere than on the wall facing the principal entrance, or one of the doorways. At Ufford, without any apparently special reason, it occurs quite on the eastern portion of the north wall. At St. James, South Elmham, St. Christopher occurs on one splay, while the attendant hermit appears on the opposite side of a window. At Burnham Overy is a painting of this subject on the Chancel wall, another one having been found in the nave. At Salisbury Cathedral, Tewkesbury, Cirencester, and Latton, examples have been noted in Chantry Chapels, and a portion of one in a similar situation at Stoke Dry, and facing the entrance to the chapel, still remains. In the chapel at the east end of Canterbury Cathedral, known as "Becket's Crown," a large painting of this saint was visible a century ago. This is supposed to have formed

* The instances where SS. George and Christopher are portrayed in the same church are comparatively numerous, and a list is here appended. They are sometimes depicted on opposite walls, but more generally close together, and very often side by side; those which are thus represented being distinguished by an asterisk. Pickering,* Gawsworth, Raunds, Slapton, Hargrave, Houghton Conquest, Eversden, Witton,* Drayton (Norfolk),* Fritton (Norfolk),* Preston (Suffolk), Troston, Sproughton,* Bradfield Combust,* Chellesworth, Croydon, Stedham, Devizes, St. Mary's,* Wilsford and Lake,* and Whimple.* At Bradninch they both appear on the rood screen, while at Horsham, St. Faith's, St. George is painted on the screen and St. Christopher on the pulpit. At Randworth and Winchester Cathedral are wall paintings of St. Christopher and paintings on panel of St. George.

† At Stockerston Church, Leicestershire, where the arrangement of the nave is somewhat remarkable, a large window fills up the space opposite the main entrance. This window contains an interesting representation in ancient stained glass of the legend of St. Christopher.

one of the series of subjects executed at the expense of Cardinal Pole, the last Roman Catholic prelate interred in the Cathedral. As in other cases, so in this, the artists all followed the same principle of treatment. St. Christopher is represented as a man of gigantic proportions, grasping a staff, and with the Infant seated behind his head, or on his shoulder, holding an orb and in the act of benediction. The saint is usually bare legged, with a garment down to his knees, and is in the act of wading across the water, which, though only reaching somewhat above his ankles, is meant to be of considerable depth, as quaint fishes and occasionally a mermaid are depicted in the stream, and sometimes ships sailing down it. On either side is a high bank, and not uncommonly an angler is introduced. On one side is always a hermitage, and the hermit is represented holding a lantern to light the Saint across the ford. St. Christopher always appears to be bowed down by the weight of his burden, and scrolls are often introduced with the well known verses recording the conversation between the Infant Saviour and the Saint. One or two examples show a rather more elaborate treatment of the subject. That at Shorwell has already been recorded, and a somewhat similar representation seems to have been discovered and destroyed at Portisham. At Sedgford the Infant is portrayed with three heads, in illustration of the doctrine of the Blessed Trinity. Many of the finest examples have been found in Norfolk, though but few have been preserved. At Raunds, Overton Longueville, and Hayes, interesting pictures of this subject still remain.

Another very popular legendary morality was "Les Trois Rois Morts et les Trois Rois Vifs," which was intended to illustrate the vanity of human greatness. Three kings sometimes on foot, and sometimes on horseback, with hawks and other hunting appliances, and clad in royal apparel, are represented as being suddenly confronted by three skeletons, who admonish them that as they too were once kings, so ere long will the kings be such as they. At Raunds is a very large example of this subject. Closely akin to it is "The Dance of Death," illustrating the absolute sway of death, and the vanity of all earthly ambition and aspirations. In an example at Newark a young civilian is represented as receiving the dread summons from a skeleton, emblematical of Death, and in the Hungerford Chapel, now destroyed, at Salisbury Cathedral, and on the screen of Sparham Church were similar representations. Another of the Moralities, which seems to have been a popular subject for the brush of the artist during this period, was the "Purging of the Seven Deadly Sins." These were "Superbia," Pride; "Ira," Anger; "Socordia," Sloth; "Gula," Gluttony; "Luxuria," Lust; "Avaritia," Covetousness; and "Invidia," Envy. The picture sometimes represented a tree placed over the flames of hell, as at Crostwight and St. John's, Bristol, sometimes a figure within a wheel, the various sins being represented within medallions, as at Ingatestone and Arundel, or, as at Raunds, a large figure of Pride, she being considered the chief and origin of all the other sins, by illustrations of which she is surrounded. The "Seven Acts of Mercy" seems also to have been a favourite subject at this period, and an example in compartments remains at Arundel. The "Seven Sacraments" of the Romish Church have also been found in mural painting, though they are more commonly met with, as sculptured on the Norfolk and Suffolk fonts of the 15th century. A most interesting example was found at Kirton in Lindsey, where in the centre is our Saviour on the cross with the Virgin and St. John on either side. Streams of blood from His wounds are directed towards the representations of the Seven Sacraments, which are depicted on each side. The doctrine of the "Literal Transubstantiation of the Wafer," commonly denominated St. Gregory's Mass, has been found at Slapton and Beverstone, and a highly coloured sculpture of this same subject is preserved in Stoke Charity Church. In each case is represented the conversion of the consecrated wafer into the actual body of Christ by St. Gregory in consequence of the disbelief of a certain woman in the doctrine of Transubstantiation.*

A large picture of the Doom or Great Day of Judgment seems to have been painted in the 15th century in a very large number of churches, where one had not been previously in existence. The usual place for this subject was over the Chancel arch, or on the east wall of the nave, though from various causes it is often found elsewhere in the church. Where there is sufficient space, the following general scheme seems to have been almost invariably followed. In the centre is a figure of Christ seated on the rainbow, with hands upraised and feet and side bare so as to display the wounds received on the Cross. On either side are Angels bearing the Cross and other implements of the Passion, while on His right kneels the Virgin Mother in the act of supplicating on behalf of mankind. Below Him is St. Michael weighing souls. The saved are represented on His right, sometimes in procession towards the gate of heaven, which is guarded by St. Peter, while on His left are the condemned being dragged off by demons to the regions of eternal torments, where some are already portrayed as suffering the most fearful punishments. In most cases the mouth of hell is represented by the jaws of an immense fish, a gigantic demon armed with a trident standing within them, and pushing the miserable wretches deeper down into the hideous depths below. In the lower part of the picture are Angels blowing trumpets, and figures rising from their graves, their rank being denoted by crowns, mitres, tonsures, &c. A very large and late example of this subject has been recently again uncovered at St. Thomas', Salisbury. Here all the above mentioned details may be seen, except that the legend of St. Michael weighing souls is omitted. On the upper part of the north side of the picture are the heavenly mansions, with numerous figures looking out of the windows, and beneath the figure of Christ are the twelve apostles seated. At Trinity Church, Coventry, South Leigh, Chesterton, and West

---

* For fuller details, see Archæological Journal, xxxiv. 234.

Ham are other well known representations of this subject. At St. Michael's, St. Alban's, owing to the want of space over the Chancel arch, part of the painting was executed on a large panel, which was inserted within the upper part of the arch, and is still preserved. Another large painting, entirely on panel and of very late date, also still exists at Gloucester Cathedral. A rather unusual painting of Our Lord in Judgment with a sword in His mouth may be seen at Widford. The representations of the Blessed Trinity seem to have been not uncommon during the 15th and early 16th centuries, though owing to a special order emanating from the leaders of the Commonwealth to destroy all the then existing examples, but few have survived to our time. At Winterbourne Earls one was found, the date of which is considered to be as early as 1200. At St. Albans Cathedral, on a pier onthe north side of the Choir, is an example of probably 14th century date. Edward the Black Prince held in special veneration the doctrine of the Blessed Trinity, and most of the pictorial representations remaining are subsequent to his time. Instances have been noted at Gorleston, Latton, Aldenham, Tewkesbury, and Pinvin, and a very fine example still remains at Cowley (Oxon). The ordinary mode of illustrating this subject was by delineating the Almighty seated, with our Saviour on the Cross between His knees, and the Holy Spirit introduced in the form of a Dove or Star. The examples in sculpture are much more numerous than those recorded in wall or panel paintings. This subject was also very commonly represented on the brasses of the late 15th and early 16th century.

Of scenes in the life of Christ, one of the most interesting series has been recently uncovered at Friskney, where are large pictures representing the Nativity, with the Adoration of the Magi, and the Shepherds, The Last Supper, and the Resurrection ; at Little Easton and Wrexham are the events connected with the Passion of Christ ; at Maids Moreton, the Last Supper and Crucifixion ; at Attleborough the Crucifixion ; at Abbotsbury was the Resurrection ; and at St. Alban's Cathedral may still be seen the Incredulity of St. Thomas. At Friskney, in juxtaposition to the large painting of the Last Supper, is depicted the Children of Israel gathering the Manna in the Wilderness, the only example of this subject in mural painting in England. At Attleborough, above the west tower arch, was found a very large painting of the Adoration of the Cross, viz., a large cross in the centre with Seraphin, Prophets, &c., reverently beholding it, the subject being evidently intended to stimulate the worship due to Christ for His great sacrifice on behalf of mankind. The history, legends, and miracles of St. Mary the Virgin seem also to have been popular during this era. In St. Thomas', Salisbury are the Annunciation, Salutation, and Adoration of the Magi ; at Hastingleigh is a large representation of the Annunciation, a cock and hen being introduced in the background. At St. Cross, Winchester, is a large subject of the Virgin with the dead body of her Divine Son on her lap, commonly known as a "Pieta" or "Mater Dolorosa."

An uncommon instance of this occurs at Broughton (Bucks), where all the bones of our Saviour are represented as being disjointed, though none are broken. The Five Joys of the Virgin have been found at Broughton (Oxon) and her Assumption, or being borne to Heaven by Angels, occurs at Friskney, Ruislip, &c. Her Coronation, or receiving the Crown of Joy in Heaven at the hands of the glorified Christ, has been depicted at Pickering and elsewhere. The Miracles of the Virgin have been represented by a numerous series of pictures in compartments at the Lady Chapel at Winchester Cathedral, and at Eton College, and though the two do not exactly correspond, it has been surmised that they were executed by the same artist. One of the chief subjects at Eton is the story of the Roman Empress unjustly accused of infidelity by her husband, but miraculously preserved and her purity most fully demonstrated through the direct intervention of the Virgin. Some of this series still remain behind the stalls. At Winchester the paintings still exist, though the manner in which they have been scratched and scored over, proves the trouble which has at some time been taken as far as possible to obliterate them. At Eton College, between each compartment has been introduced a female figure standing on a pedestal. The series comprises most of the Saints who were popular at that date, and one or two, such as St. Sidwell, a Devonshire Saint not commonly met with. Two Saints have emblems not easy to identify. One may be St. Theodosia, the other St. Ulph or Sira; none of whom are recorded as occurring elsewhere. A somewhat similar disposition of subjects and Saints, and of about the same date, seems to have been adopted at Buckland, in Gloucestershire. The legend of St. Michael weighing souls continued to be commonly represented, and examples have been noted at Slapton, Stotfold, Lathbury, Beckley, Ruislip, Lingfield, Lindfield, Netherbury, Cullompton, &c. At Worsted and St. Clements, Jersey, were representations of his contest with Satan, a subject more commonly found on the panels of screens. Portraits of the Apostles, though very numerous on the screens, are not often found in mural painting at this period. St. Peter occurs at St. John's, Bristol, SS. Andrew and Bartholomew at Brisley, St. James Major at St. Thomas', Salisbury. At Wellow (Somerset) are numerous large figures of Saints, amongst which the Virgin, SS. Bartholomew, Thomas, Stephen, and Margaret can be identified. St. John the Baptist occurs in the series at Friskney and Witton, and three scenes in his life are depicted in the Oxenbridge Chapel, at St. George's, Windsor, having been painted in or about the year 1522. In the Hasting's Chapel, also at St. George's, Windsor, are four incidents in the history of St. Stephen, of the end of the 15th century. St. Mary Magdalene appears on many of the screens, but not often in wall painting of this date. Representations of her have been noted at St. Clement's, Jersey, and of Christ appearing to her after his Resurrection, at Bray. Besides St. Christopher and St. George, St. Catherine continued to be universally popular, and many mural paintings illustrating her life and martyrdom, especially in the eastern and midland counties, have been found. At Raunds, a series of pictures still remain, which were originally painted early in the 15th century, and partly renewed about 100 years later. At Tempsford, the representation of the Saint bound to the wheels may be seen in a good state of preservation, at St. Mary's, Beverley, her history was delineated on the ceiling of the south aisle in 14 compartments, while at Sporle no less than 24 scenes in the legend are depicted within small square divisions. They all date from quite the beginning of the 15th century, though it is thought that the later events in the series were inferior in execution, and painted by a different hand to the earlier ones. A figure of the Saint, probably dating from the 15th century, was discovered at St. Martin's, Leicester. It has been destroyed, but drawings have been preserved, and if these are correctly delineated, the original may certainly be considered one of the most beautiful specimens of this branch of art which have yet been found in England. The other female Saints, though very common on the screens, do not appear often in wall paintings. St. Margaret has been noticed at Lingfield and Lindfield, and a very elegant portrait of her still remains at Cassington. St. Agatha was formerly visible at Winchester Cathedral, SS. Ursula and Lucia at Stoke by Nayland, and SS. Ursula and Modwenna at the chapel of the Guild of the Holy Cross, Stratford-on-Avon, SS. Clare and Bridget at Cullompton, St. Barbara at St. Clement's, Jersey, probably St. Winifred at Mells, and St. Helen in conjunction with St. Dunstan at Broughton (Bucks). Of the male Saints, St. Thomas of Canterbury still maintained his popularity, and his martyrdom continued to be a favourite subject, and doubtless more pictures would have survived to us had not all representations of this Saint been specially condemned at the time of the Reformation. SS. Edmund and Edward the Confessor were also specially reverenced as heretofore. SS. Anthony, Sebastian, and Roche, seem also to have been highly esteemed, a portrait of the last still remaining at Kettering, and another having been recently discovered at Grendon. St. Erasmus seems also at this period to have been very popular, and mural paintings have been found at Ampney Crucis and Whitwell depicting his horrible martyrdom by disembowelling. Of other Saints, St. Martin perhaps occurs at Ruislip, North Tidworth, and Grendon; St. Lawrence at Ruislip, North Tidworth, and Great Chishill; St. Clement at South Leigh and Lingfield; St. Blaise at Kingston-upon-Thames; St. Dunstan at Latton and Broughton (Bucks); and King Henry VI. at Witton and Alton. All these Saints are more commonly met with, as will hereafter be mentioned, on the panels of the screens. At Hardwick (Cambs) is the legend of St. Cyriac, a subject not recorded elsewhere in England. At the chapel of the Guild of the Holy Cross at Stratford-on-Avon are a series of paintings representing the legend of the finding of the Cross on which Christ suffered, of which no other example in mural painting has come to light. During the 15th century the practice of inscribing texts on the walls seems to have prevailed, though it became far more general after the period of the Reformation. The following list will denote the churches in which the most interesting series of paintings of the perpendicular period have been found, and full particulars of most of them can be obtained from the authorities referred to in the list : Pickering, Gawsworth, Friskney, Raunds, Slapton, Lutterworth, Stratford-on-Avon, South Leigh, Broughton (Bucks), Brooke (Norfolk), Eaton, Earl Stonham, Chellesworth, Hessett; Latton, Salisbury, St. Thomas', and St. Clement's, and St. Brelade's, Jersey.

Very interesting series of paintings, the dates of which have not been specified here, have been found at Pinvin, Notgrove, Limpenhoe, Drayton (Norfolk), Gorleston, Milton Abbas, Lanivet, Llanwyddyn, and Pluscardine Abbey. At St. Kenelm's Chapel was a representation of the history of St. Kenelm, found also at the neighbouring church of Halesowen. At Pinvin some of the paintings still remain in good preservation, and seem to be as early as the 13th century. At Notgrove the whole of the east wall has been profusely decorated with New Testament subjects, and in many of the other above-mentioned examples the whole or some special portion of the walls have been covered with varied pictorial representations from Scripture history or the saintly calendar. Within an arch in the north choir aisle of Canterbury Cathedral is a very interesting painting, representing the Conversion, Trials, and Martyrdom of St. Eustace, the only instance in England where this Saint is portrayed in mural painting. At Cowley (Oxon) numerous subjects have been discovered, including a very fine representation of the Blessed Trinity over the east window, which has been preserved. Some of this series are of early 14th century date.

At St. Lawrence's Church, Reading, no less than five distinct series of paintings were discovered, painted one over another, and similarly at Hovingham, Yorkshire, several courses of decoration were found and destroyed.

At Wimborne Minster, on the walls of the crypt or chapel beneath the Choir, was a painting, now destroyed, stated to have been a genuine fresco. If so, it is the only painting in fresco recorded in England. It is very doubtful, however, as to whether the assertion can be maintained.*

Besides the ordinary wall spaces, decorative colouring and historical subjects were often introduced elsewhere in the churches, in the window splays, within recesses, at the back of sedilia and monuments, &c., &c. The splays of the windows of the Norman and early English period seem almost always to have been embellished

---

* It will doubtless have been noticed that both in this Essay and in the List, the use of the common expression for mural paintings, viz., "fresco," has been most carefully avoided. The difference between the process of painting in distemper or tempera, and painting in fresco, as to a certain extent adopted in Italy, will be pointed out at length at the conclusion of this Essay. The following quotation will give the opinion of an authority on this subject. "The term fresco is so constantly used, and is so exceedingly " improper, that it ought at once to be given up. All mediæval paintings in our " Churches are in tempera, and of a common kind."—*Surrey Archæol.*, vi. 304, note.

with painting, and good examples of pictorial subjects of Norman date are recorded at Kempley, Little Wakering, and Barfreston. Of later date we find the series (?) of the Acts of Mercy at Chesterton, full length figures of saints at Eaton, Chalgrove, Cassington, Newington, and St. Cross, Winchester, and of subjects of doubtful import at Little Kimble, Lanivet, &c. At South Elmham is an unusual representation of St. Christopher in this situation. At Easby are depicted the four seasons. At Kimpton on either side of the east window are deep recesses, with figures painted on them. On the splays of some few of the low side windows, coloured decoration has also been discovered, as at Hannington, where are ornamental designs of the 13th century, and at Buckland (Herts) where are paintings of the Virgin and Child. The examples of figures and floral and other decorations on the various arched recesses are very common. In some Churches these arched recesses, generally of early date, occur on one or both sides of the Chancel arch, and seem to denote the former existence of an altar beneath them. Instances may be mentioned at Castle Rising and Doddington (Northants), where the Crucifixion is thus depicted, at Brixworth, where was a "Gloria," at Hauxton, St. Thomas of Canterbury, at West Harnham, and elsewhere. In the north transept of Stow Church, St. Thomas of Canterbury is portrayed on the back of a recess over an altar, and in a similar position in the south transept at St. Cross, Winchester, are a series of scenes in his life and the Crucifixion. Within an arch in the east wall of the first storey of the tower of Brook Church, Kent, is depicted Our Lord in Glory, and in a similar situation at Warminster was a painting of St. Denis. These tower chambers are conjectured to have been oratories or residences for the priests. So again there are instances where painting has been discovered in the parvise or chamber above the porch, as at Harrow and Breamore, and on the inner wall of the porch itself, as at Wardley and Broughton Gifford.

The niches for the images of Saints, &c., many of them ornamented with delicately-sculptured canopies, which are found in the walls of most churches, have been usually enriched with colour and gilding. In many instances plain colouring has been applied to form a background to the image, as at St. Mary's, Oxford, and on the screens at St. Albans Cathedral. At Lichfield Cathedral and Ottery St. Mary are a series of canopied niches similarly decorated. At the Lady Chapel, St. Albans Cathedral, are some beautiful canopies with gilded foliage on the upper portion. At Melbourne (Cambs), the canopies of two niches, retain their gilding, while at Witney a rich diaper still remains on the background. At Market Deeping, on the lower part of two niches are painted shields, charged with crosses. At the back of one at Staepole Elidur is painted a large cross and an angel holding a shield of St. George. At Llantwit Major is a very elaborate example, the niche being surrounded by a band of sculptured scroll work enclosing a stem of Jesse, the whole retaining traces of its original illuminations. Even on the exterior of the churches remains of colouring have been in like manner discovered, as at Bolton Abbey, over the original western entrance, our Lord and two Angels, and simple decorative colouring at Bottisham, Axbridge, Bleadon, &c.

The wall surface at the back of the sedilia was often adorned with painting, and sometimes with figure subjects. Three very rich examples have been noted at Tewkesbury, Dorchester, and Chatham, upon which rich diaper patterns, picked out with gilding, have been found, and, in the latter instance, destroyed. At Winchelsea the elegant sculptured diaper is further enriched with colour. At Great Yarmouth and Hornchurch were traces of figures, and other examples are noted, viz., at Little Coggeshall, the head of Christ ; at Puckington, Elias and other figures ; and at Easby Church, arch- bishops seated. On the sedilia at Westminster Abbey, both on the side towards the presbytery and on the back facing the south presbytery aisle, were full-length figures of St. Peter, St. Edward the Confessor, King Sebert, Henry III., and an ecclesiastic. A representation of the Last Supper may also still be seen at Maid's Moreton. The canopies and other sculptured portions were likewise often overlaid with gilding and colouring, as evidenced by portions of very early sedilia found at Paignton, also of later date, recently dug up at St. Alban's Cathedral. Traces can still be made out on the beautiful example at Furness Abbey.

In like manner, several instances exist or have been recorded where the piscina has been ornamented with colour, the fenestella or canopy being thus decorated, and sometimes subjects being intro- duced within the piscina itself. A good instance of this was found at Frome, where a somewhat rare specimen of a roodloft piscina was found retaining its original illumination. On an example at Anstey are two shields, and on another at Cheltenham a consecration cross. At the back of a piscina at St. Mary's, Bury St. Edmunds, is the sacred monogram within a collar of SS., and in a similar situation at Lichfield Cathedral is painted the Crucifixion; at Sproughton, St. Mary the Virgin ; at Widford, traces of figures ; and in the Lady Chapel at Winchester Cathedral a portrait of Prior Silkstede.

Many instances are noted where the reredos remains, or has been found in a more or less mutilated condition, but still bearing evidence of its former splendour and gorgeous colouring. Most of the examples are of the 14th and 15th centuries. The more elaborate specimens are composed of alabaster, but, as in the case of the monuments and effigies shortly to be mentioned, even this beautiful material was always lavishly overlaid with colour and gilding. In place of the elaborate sculptured altar pieces about to be described are often simple recesses over the altar space, with figures of the saints to whom the altar was dedicated, &c. depicted on the wall surface. Thus at Wivelsfield is a pattern of diaper and lozenge work of 13th century date; over the altar in the chapel of St. Faith, Westminster Abbey, is a picture of St. Faith; at Stow and St. Cross, Winchester, scenes in the life and martyrdom of St. Thomas of Canterbury ; at Great Canfield, the Virgin and Child, &c., &c. At

Whissendine was found, during the restoration of the church, a plain slab of stone on which was painted the Crucifixion, with the Virgin and St. John, SS. Andrew, Margaret, and the emblems of the Evangelists. Beneath these subjects, which are probably of 15th century date, were clear traces of an earlier and more elaborate design. In Norwich Cathedral is preserved a beautiful reredos, conjectured to date from 1370 and to be the work of the Siennese school, on which are sculptured representations of the Scourging, Christ bearing his Cross, the Crucifixion, Resurrection, and Ascension. A reredos of somewhat similar character, though of earlier date, is preserved in the south presbytery aisle of Westminster Abbey, with figures of Christ and St. Peter, and the Adoration of the Magi, and the Raising of Lazarus. Examples with richly coloured and gilt canopies and niches have been found at Ludlow, Reigate, Micheldever, &c., and fragments with figures, &c. at Preston in Holderness, Great Yarmouth, Tofts, Sandy, Drayton (Berks), Wimborne, and Cobham. At Blunham were found portions with sculptured representations of the Virgin and Child, Christ bearing His Cross, and the Descent from the Cross, on the panels. At Whittlesford are numerous fragments of an altar piece similarly sculptured. Figures of the Virgin, St. Anne instructing the Virgin, our Saviour on the Cross, and St. Sitha can alone be identified. The figure of the Virgin, which is larger than the others, and probably a portion of the central panel of the reredos, is a most elegant specimen of sculpture and colouring. At Smarden a reredos has been recently noticed with representations of a "pieta," the entombment, and various figures. At Cury was discovered what was probably a portion of the principal altar piece, with the upper part of the figures of our Saviour blessing the Cup and the Apostles. At Somerton is preserved a very beautiful 14th century reredos with representation of the Last Supper, but none of the original colouring in this instance remains. A small portable altar-piece called an "iconula" seems to have been a not uncommon possession of the wealthier classes. One is recorded to have been found at Fountain's Abbey, and another is noticed, and an illustration of it given in Schnebbelie's Antiquaries' Museum. A third is still preserved in Amport Church, having in the centre the head of St. John the Baptist on a charger, above angels holding his soul in a napkin, and below the Resurrection, and figures of saints on either side. The date is probably about 1500. The whole is of alabaster richly illuminated with colour and gilding. Of the more elaborate altar screens only a few survive. At St. Cuthbert's, Wells, in the east wall of each transept are very beautiful examples, that in the south transept having a sculptured representation of the stem of Jesse. At Wellington (Somerset), another very rich specimen was discovered, with illustrations of the Crucifixion, SS. Christopher, Catherine, Michael, &c. It is now preserved in the Taunton Museum. At Beauchief Abbey was an altar-piece on which was carved the martyrdom of St. Thomas of Canterbury. This is now in private possession. At All Souls College, Oxford, the high altar of the chapel has been recently discovered and restored, and new figures inserted in the niches. In its pristine condition it must have been an unusually elaborate specimen. Of the detached altar screens only four retaining their colouring can be recorded as having survived to the present day, viz., the high altar screens at Westminster Abbey (restored) and at the Cathedrals at St. Alban's and Winchester, both probably designed by the same architect,* and the screen of the once richly endowed chapel of our Lady, in the crypt of Canterbury Cathedral. All these examples were probably erected during the latter part of the 15th century. In Gunton's History of the Church of Peterburgh, an illustration is given of the beautiful altar screen formerly existing in the Cathedral there, which was destroyed by the fanaticism of the soldiers of the Commonwealth. It was of earlier date than those at Winchester, &c., and was, as we read in page 97, "exquisitely carved and beautified with guilding and painting." The screen now dividing the nave and choir of St. Alban's Cathedral, and erected about the year 1360, formerly served the double purpose of an altar screen to the parochial church and a division between that and the portion of the church to the eastward of it, which was reserved solely for the services of the abbey. It is a very elegant example, with numerous canopied niches, and retains some traces of colouring.

There are not many examples of stone rood or choir screens which have survived to our day, and only a few of these retain remnants of their former profusion of illumination. The magnificent choir screen at Salisbury Cathedral of 13th century date was removed by Wyatt to the north-east transept, where it still remains, a brilliant example of gilded splendour. During some excavations at Finchale Abbey, the lower part of the screen was found in situ, still exhibiting its former rich colouring. At Totnes, the rood screen has been decorated with heraldic shields, and outlines of saints appear on the panels, and on the mutilated screen at Ingham traces of decoration still remain. On the interior of the beautiful choir screen at St. David's Cathedral, erected by Bishop Gower, are depicted the Crucifixion, emblems of the Evangelists, and scroll and other ornamental patterns. On the present organ screen at Exeter Cathedral are a series of panel paintings illustrating scenes from the Old and New Testament. Between the choir and north choir aisle of the Chapel of St. Cross, Winchester, is a stone screen with outlines of figures on the panels. The choirs of the Cathedrals of Canterbury and Rochester are enclosed by stone screen work, in each case bearing traces of elaborate early 14th century heraldic decoration. At Weston in Gordano colouring was found on the verge of the altar stone. No other instance of this has been recorded.

* Screens of similar character still remain at St. Saviours, Southwark, and Christchurch, Hampshire, but no mention has been made of any of their original decoration being still, or till recently, in existence.

On the few shrines which have entirely or partially survived to our day, gilding and colour seem to have been most lavishly made use of. The shrine of St. Edward the Confessor, at Westminster Abbey, retains sufficient of its gilding, enamel, and colouring to demonstrate clearly its pristine splendour, and similarly those of St. Hugh at Lincoln, and of St. Alban and St. Amphibalus at St. Albans, bear traces of their early decorations. On the shrine of St. Alban, which is entirely composed of a dark marble, a series of panels have been coloured red and blue, and enriched with gilding on the tracery. The shrine of St. Werburgh at Chester Cathedral is fully described in the new edition of Ormerod's History of Cheshire, vol, i., pp. 298, 299. It is of the time of Edward III., and is richly painted and gilt. Upon it, within niches, are 30 statues of kings and saints of the Royal line of Mercia, and relations by blood to St. Werburgha. At Christchurch Cathedral, Oxford, portions of the shrine of St. Frideswide have been found, the mouldings of 13th century date having been decorated with a plain band of gilding. Fragments of highly enriched shrines have been recently dug up at Corne Abbas and Guisborough.

A few examples of reliquaries have also survived to our time. A very early one of Norman character was dug up on the site of the cathedral of Old Sarum, and is now preserved in the Salisbury Museum. One of the 13th century, found in the wall of Kewstoke church, and supposed to have been brought from the neighbouring priory of Woodspring, and to have contained a relic of St. Thomas of Canterbury, may be seen in the museum at Taunton. A beautiful and richly gilt example in Limoges enamel belongs to Shipley church, and is kept at the neighbouring mansion of Knepp Castle.* A handsome specimen in alabaster, of the latter part of the 15th century, was accidentally discovered on Caldey Island, and is now in private possession. At Haslingden, Lancashire, two bones, retaining traces of gilding, and supposed to have been relics of St. James, were dug up. This instance has not been included in the list, as it is thought to be hardly within its present scope.

Only three examples can be adduced where traces of colour and gilding have been recently noticed on the bishops' thrones in our cathedrals, viz., at Durham, Wells, and Exeter; and it is doubtful whether in any of these cases a particle of the original decoration survives at the present time. Of the stone pulpits, which are chiefly found in Devonshire and Somersetshire, only a few have been noted as retaining traces of their original colouring. Very gorgeous and elaborately sculptured examples of late date remain at Paignton, Harberton, and Dartmouth, and, with the colouring restored, at Cheddar and St. Catherines. At Totnes traces of nimbi prove that figures of saints had been depicted on the panels; and at Bovey Tracey the saints, &c. still remain. These have been executed in plaster,

* Two similar reliquaries, the property of Lord Zouche, are now in the loan collection, South Kensington Museum. Another belongs to and is preserved in the library of the Society of Antiquaries, London.

and coloured, and have recently been repainted. The Devonshire antiquary, Dr. Oliver, seems to have had some doubts as to the genuine antiquity of these figures. Only one example of a stone lectern retaining its colouring has been recorded, viz., at Ottery St. Mary, though other early examples have been found at Much Wenlock Abbey, Crowle (Worcestershire), &c., but no remains of decoration have been recorded as being noticed upon them.

There is no doubt that in very many instances the fonts were decorated with varied illumination; but as these have been unfortunately, during the past two centuries, either cruelly neglected and thrust on one side, or, what was worse, the special objects of the attention of successive churchwardens, but few have survived with any considerable remains of their original colour and gilding. Sky blue and other brilliant hues were deemed appropriate colours by the aforesaid custodians; and to make a stone font simulate the appearance of marble was considered to be a triumph of art. Thus it is that so meagre a list has been compiled; and even of these most of the examples exhibit merely the faintest traces of their undoubted original decoration. The font in the old parish church of Lenton, a fine Norman specimen, ornamented with rude though elaborate sculptures of the Crucifixion, &c., has experienced numerous vicissitudes, but is still thought to retain some slight remnants of its original colouring. On the Norman font at Great Kimble, some decoration in red still remains on the bowl, which may be coeval with the font itself. So again on the transitional Norman example at Hornton some early colouring still exists. Of later date are noticed painted fonts at Wolston (Warwickshire), circ. 1320, and at Wickham Market of about the same period. There are numerous instances, especially in the 15th century, where the armorial bearings of the benefactors to the church, or donors of the font, were properly blazoned on shields, generally sculptured, but sometimes simply painted, on the panels or elsewhere, but, with rare exceptions, the tinctures have been completely effaced. Traces of these have been noticed within the past few years on an early 14th century font at North Cove; on one of about the year 1400, at Hagbourne; and of a third at Aslacton. Another not uncommon subject on the 15th century fonts, especially in the Eastern Counties, was a representation of the Evangelistic emblems; but of the numerous instances which could be cited, only that at Ludham can be mentioned as still clearly retaining traces of its original polychrome. The Seven Sacraments of the Romish Church were deemed appropriate subjects for the panels of the bowls of the more ornate examples of the third pointed period, and a long list might be appended, but, as in the other instances, only a few can be cited as clearly displaying evidences of their former decoration, viz., at Brooke, East Dereham, Gresham, Loddon, New Walsingham, and Great Witchingham, Norfolk, and at Gorleston, Westhall, and Woodbridge, Suffolk. All these examples are octagonal, and exhibit remains of rich gilding and varied colouring on the sculptures. At Brooke, East Dereham, New

Walsingham, and Woodbridge, the eighth panel has a representation of the Crucifixion; at Gorleston of the Resurrection; at Loddon of the Virgin and Child; and at Great Witchingham of the Assumption of the Virgin.

Of the Easter Sepulchres, which probably, either as permanent structures or movable erections, had a place in almost every church during the 15th century, but few remain, and of these only a very limited number retain any traces of decoration. None is recorded as being now visible on the well known examples at Patrington (Yorkshire), Hawton (Notts), Lincoln Cathedral, and Heckington (Lincoln), Northwold (Norfolk), or Woodleigh (Devon), though it may without hesitation be asserted on the general principle already affirmed, that their mouldings and sculptures were formerly further enriched with decorative colouring. Traces have been found on specimens at Withybrook, St. Mary de Crypt, Gloucester, and Smarden, also on that at Stanton Harcourt, which, as was not unfrequently the case, served the double purpose of a tomb and Easter Sepulchre. At the back of the one at Huntingfield is a painting of Christ seated in Judgment; while on that at South Pool is the more natural representation, in sculpture, of the Resurrection. In the course of the restoration of the church of Preston in Holderness, in 1881, numerous fragments in alabaster of an Easter Sepulchre, &c., of the middle of the 14th century, were found beneath the floor, two of which represented the Resurrection.

The monumental effigies and canopied tombs have been most fully treated of and described by various distinguished antiquaries and others most competent to deal with the subject, and their evidence clearly proves that there can be little doubt that colour and gilding were here also most lavishly applied in all cases where the designs were fully carried out. Cruel neglect and wilful mutilation have done much irretrievably to ruin these most interesting memorials, and to injure beyond repair the works on which the skill of the sculptor and painter was so successfully employed. It is a common occurrence, even in the present day, to hear of the monuments being destroyed, and to find the effigies of former benefactors buried or thrust out of the churches. One can hardly sufficiently condemn the ignorant or parsimonious spirit which can thus consent to the degradation of the memorials of those with whom the earlier history of the district or parish has been inseparably connected. It is doubtful whether any effigies retaining traces of their original colour remain of an earlier date than the 13th century. Of military effigies, that of King John at Worcester Cathedral is probably one of the earliest. Traces of gilding were noticed some few years ago on some of the cross-legged and other early effigies in the Temple Church, London. The first William Longespée, Earl of Salisbury, who died in 1227, is commemorated by a beautiful sculptured figure, now placed in the nave of Salisbury Cathedral, and exhibiting considerable remains of its former decoration. So do the two 13th century examples to Thomas and the second Maurice, Lords

Berkeley, in Bristol Cathedral, another one, date circ. 1250, to
Sir Stephen de Haccombe, at Haccombe church. The effigies of
Edmund Crouchback, Earl of Lancaster, and Aymer de Valence,
Earl of Pembroke, at Westminster Abbey, still exhibit traces of their
original coloured decorations, as do those of Gervase and Stephen
Alard at Winchelsea. Three mutilated examples, but all retaining
their early colouring, have been, within the past few years, dug up
respectively on the sites of the monasteries at Robertsbridge, Lewes,
and Monkton Farleigh. In most of the instances the representation
of the armour was carved and then coloured, but in some few
examples it was merely painted on a flat surface, as may still be
noticed on an effigy at Hampton Poyle. The effigy of Sir Stephen
de Haccombe " is formed of a block of red sandstone, on which a
" coat of plaster has been laid, moulded to represent chain mail, and
" once richly gilt."—*Murray's Handbook for Devon.* The armour is
similarly represented on the effigy at Ash. Many of the early cross-
legged figures are of wood, and these will be referred to hereafter.
Two small cross-legged effigies with remains of colour may be seen
at Mappowder and Horsted Keynes.* The examples of the later
military effigies are very numerous. The more important examples
are placed on elegant altar tombs, with richly panelled sides and
delicately carved canopies. It is difficult to pick out any specially
ornamented monuments, as in too many cases the most beautiful
specimens have been the most cruelly mutilated, and often all traces
of the colouring have been intentionally obliterated. Monuments
and effigies still retaining rich decoration may be mentioned as
existing at Chillingham, Staindrop, Harewood, Methley, Bunbury,
Elford, Warwick, Arundel, Battle, Porlock, North Cadbury, Henstridge, and Callington. Of effigies of civilians, the coloured
examples are not very numerous. At Elford, on the north of the
chancel, is one of date about 1500. At Yatton is another to Lord

---

* The following list of cross-legged or early military effigies in stone or marble, on which colour has been noted, may be appended as interesting:—
Buckinghamshire.—Ashendon.
Cambridgeshire.—Rampton.
Devonshire.—Exeter Cath., Haccombe, Landkey.
Dorsetshire.—Mappowder.
Durham.—Hurworth.
Gloucestershire.—Bristol Cath. (2), Bristol, St. Mark's Chapel, Bishop's Cleeve, Leckhampton.
Kent.—Ash, Minster.
Leicestershire.—Tilton-on-the-Hill.
Middlesex.—Westminster Abbey (2), London, Temple Ch. (10).
Monmouthshire.—Monmouth.
Nottinghamshire.—Gonalston (2).
Oxfordshire.—Hampton Poyle.
Shropshire.—Leighton.
Suffolk.—Erwarton.
Sussex.—Horsted Keynes, Ifield, Lewes, Robertsbridge, Winchelsea.
Warwickshire.—Birmingham, Lower Eatington, Guy's Cliff.
Wiltshire.—Salisbury Cath., Monkton Farleigh, Great Bedwin.
Worcestershire.—Worcester Cath.
Yorkshire.—Bedale.

Q 3254.

Chief Justice Newton, late 15th century; and at Long Ashton one
to another judge, Sir Richard Choke, also of the end of the 15th
century. At Ashburton portions of a figure habited in a scarlet
robe with a powdering of golden flours de lis, were found in the wall,
and, again, built up into it. At St. Nicholas, Guildford, is the effigy
of Arnald Brocas, coloured red, of the end of the 14th century. At
Berkeley church are three small figures, supposed to commemorate
children of Thomas, eighth Lord Berkeley, of about the same date.
The effigy of William of Hatfield, who died in 1344, in York Minster,
represents him in the costume of a gentleman of the period. Similar
figures also exist at Haccombe and Westminster Abbey. Of the
effigies of ecclesiastics, the list of coloured examples is also somewhat
meagre. At Axminster is a very early example. At Bathampton is
a figure of a priest of the 13th century. At Christ Church Cathedral,
Oxford, is a fine effigy of a prior, circ. 1330; and at Edington, of an
ecclesiastic of somewhat later date. But the finest example is
undoubtedly that of Bishop John de Sheppey, at Rochester Cathedral, of date 1360. This had been concealed in the wall for many
years, and, owing to this fact, the colouring and gilding have preserved their brightness, and present us with an admirable exemplifi-
cation of the rich ecclesiastical vestments worn in the 14th century.
At Wells Cathedral the effigy of Bishop Beckington, which has been
removed from the chantry chapel, wherein it previously lay, is still
richly coloured, dating from about the year 1460. At Exeter Cathedral the recumbent effigy of Bishop Bronescombe still retains its
colouring, of the end of the 13th century, though the canopy above
it is of much later date. Priestly effigies are noted at Fersfield and
South Pool, of late 15th century, and at Poughley Priory, recently
found in the ruins. At St. John's Church, Glastonbury, is a richly-
coloured monument and effigy to a bursar to the abbot of the neighbouring wealthy abbey, said to have been brought from the abbey
at the time of the dissolution of the monasteries. Of the female
figures, in many instances bright colouring on the dresses and
gilding on the girdles, head-dresses, &c., still remains. At Axminster
is a very early effigy. At Stoke Fleming is an example of late 13th
century; and a portion of another of the same period remains at
Stevenage. At Bradford on Avon is preserved an example of the
14th, and at Much Marcle and Horwood of the 15th century. A
richly coloured effigy has been recently found in the wall at Abbots
Kerswell. At Polesworth is a highly decorated specimen of the figure
of an abbess; and other female effigies of uncertain date may be noted
at Bedale, Holt, Landkey, Shebbear, and Llandawke. The table
tombs, as has already been mentioned, upon which the effigies were
often coloured, generally displayed the armourial bearings of the
deceased, blazoned in proper colours within the panels. A rather
curious and late example of this exists at Willington, where are two
16th century table tombs, with the armorial bearings painted on the
lower portion, which is otherwise unornamented. The canopies of
the tombs are often lavishly decorated with colour and gilding, as

may still be seen on the monuments of Archbishop Peckham at Canterbury Cathedral, of the Countess of Lancaster and Aymer de Valence at Westminster Abbey, and at Bainton, Borough Green, and Winchelsea, all of these dating between the years 1290–1350. The canopies above the effigies of Bishops Bronescombe and Stafford, at Exeter Cathedral, are rich examples of early 15th century date; while those of Bishop Beckington and Joanna, Viscountess Lisle, at Wells Cathedral, may be cited as highly decorated specimens of somewhat later date. At Porlock is another fine monument with considerable traces of its former rich colour and gilding still remaining. The noble monument of Elizabeth, Lady Montacute, at Christchurch Cathedral, Oxford, still retains the colouring with which it was everywhere embellished. The ceiling of the aisle and the arches above the tomb have been decorated with painting at the same period. In some cases colouring only remains on the lower panels, as at Reepham, where the "weepers" on the tomb of Sir Roger de Kerdiston are noted as having been painted. At Hereford Cathedral the sides of the chantry chapel of Bishop Audley are filled in with panels containing portraits of 33 saints. At Newark, on the monument of Robert Markham, only one panel, with a scene from the Dance of Death, remains. On two panels of a 16th century altar tomb at Stoke Charity are depicted the Virgin and Child and St. Thomas of Canterbury. On the south side of the monument of Lord Bourchier, in Westminster Abbey, are traces of elaborate colouring. Considerable traces of red colouring are still visible on the noble canopied tomb of Archbishop Walter Gray, in York Minster. Of much later date, the chantry chapels of Lord de la Warr at Boxgrove, and of Lord La Warre at Broadwater, have been highly enriched examples of decorative art. The beautiful monumental chapels of Bishops Alcock and West, at the east end of Ely Cathedral, still exhibit traces of their former elaborate decoration. In the Hungerford Chapel (now destroyed) at Salisbury Cathedral, in the chantry chapel of Peter Arderne at Latton, and in some of those at Tewkesbury Abbey, numerous subjects were depicted on the walls and monument itself. On that of John Clopton, at Long Melford, are painted the Resurrection, &c., with portraits of the deceased and his family at the head and foot of the tomb. On the eastern wall of the chantry of Prince Arthur at Worcester Cathedral is a richly gilt sculpture of the Descent from the Cross. On the ceiling of the lower portion of the elegant monument of the Duchess of Suffolk, at Ewelme, is painted the Annunciation and other subjects. Perhaps the earliest monument with remains of its ancient colouring is the one still existing at Whitchurch Canonicorum, stated to be of late 12th century workmanship. In many instances, where the monuments are placed within recesses in the walls, and in some few other cases, various subjects, inscriptions, &c., are depicted on the wall surface at the back. Thus at Narburgh was an inscription in gilt letters of the end of the 13th century; at St. Peter's, Sandwich, inscriptions and the Crucifixion; at Rochester Cathedral, on the back of the monument of St. William, is a good example of 13th century scroll work. At Turvey and Knockmoy Abbey we find the Crucifixion; and at St. Edmund's, Salisbury, traces of an indistinct subject—apparently Christ and the Apostles. On Bishop Bronescombe's tomb, at Exeter Cathedral, are SS. John, James, and Jude; at Weston Baggard, St. Mary the Virgin between two censing angels; and at Gorleston the Blessed Trinity, with other figures and shields charged with the implements of the Passion. At Ingham was an alleged representation of St. Hubert hunting, now quite gone. In some cases a sculptured bas-relief is inserted above, or at the back of, the monument, as at Horbling, where we find the Resurrection, and at Long Ashton, two angels supporting a "gloria." The portraits of the deceased were often introduced, as at the back of the monument of Simon de Apulia, at Exeter Cathedral, where is the bishop seated; at Silchester, the portrait of the lady whose effigy lies below; at Bedale, on the dado of the tomb of Brian Fitzalan, the knight, St. Peter and the conveyance of the soul to Heaven; at Dodford, the departed soul being borne to Heaven by angels; at Hereford Cathedral, on the back of a monument of a dean, the dean kneeling to St. Anne instructing the Virgin; at Maidstone, the Annunciation, with St. Catherine and (probably) St. Margaret, and kneeling figure of Dr. Wootton, the master of the college, and an archbishop and bishop within panels at the head and foot of the tomb respectively; and, as a last and very late instance, may be mentioned the kneeling figure of Precentor Bennet, with scrolls, at Salisbury Cathedral, dating from about the year 1558.

A rare example of red colouring occurs on the cross of a stone coffin lid of 13th century date at Hildersham. At Barrow Gournay is an incised slab of early 14th century date, where the lines have been coloured blue. Some few instances of painted shields, &c., occur on the incised alabaster slabs, which are principally found in the Midland counties, and usually of date between the years 1480–1580. In an example dug up at Dale Abbey were traces of red colouring in the grooves, and blazoned armorial shields are noted on specimens at Watton (Herts), Claverley, and St. Chad's, Shrewsbury.

The beautiful brass effigies at Westminster Abbey of Edward III., Richard II., and Henry VII., and their Queens, have been overlaid with gilding. In some instances the inlaid brass figures were embellished with colouring, the heraldic bearings being thus represented on the ladies' dresses, &c., but the process here employed was generally that of enamelling. Gilding was also introduced on the fine brasses at Marholme, Ketteringham, and Aspenden, where the other heraldic colours are represented in enamel. In a few instances the armorial shields are emblazoned in dry earth colours, as at Cople, Wing (Bucks), &c., all these dating in the 16th century.

Numerous coloured statuettes, and richly sculptured subjects in bas relief or alto relievo, which cannot be identified as belonging

either to monuments or altar pieces, have been at various times
discovered in the churches. Of the statuettes several of St. Mary
the Virgin have been found, viz., at Broughton in Airedale, Worksop,
Anwick, Shimpling, Barling, Arundel, Great Bedwin, and Stewkley,
also of the Assumption at Sandford. Several effigies of St. John the
Baptist have been found, viz., at Easton (Hants), Hereford Cathedral,
and, dug up with several other figures, at St. Mary's Abbey, York,
At Bideford, a small effigy, formerly in the church, when cleaned
was found to be a figure of this saint, and to have been executed
either by Donatello himself or one of his pupils. It is supposed to
have been presented to the church by one of the Devonshire worthies,
the heroic admirals in the time of Queen Elizabeth. It is now in
private possession. Figures of St. Peter have been discovered at
Flawford and Beachamwell; of St. Margaret, at St. Margaret's,
Westminster; of St. Leonard, at Milton; of St. Ethelbert, at
Hereford Cathedral; of St. Erasmus, at Trinity Church, Cambridge,
and a portion of another at St. Albans Cathedral; of St. Eligius, at
Freckenham; of St. Dominic, at Barling; of St. Gobnet, at Ballyvourney; and of Henry VI. at Alnwick. Richly coloured representations of the Blessed Trinity have been found at Carlton in
Lindrick, Brant Broughton, and Upton (Bucks). Three very early
sculptured figures were found embedded in the wall of St. Nicholas
Church, Ipswich, one perhaps being intended for St. James Minor.
Amongst the earliest coloured sculptures are those on the west front
of Lincoln Cathedral, chiefly representing Old Testament subjects,
the colour being especially visible on some of those which are concealed behind the later Norman work. The figures composing the
very early Rood at Headbourn Worthy bear traces of colour, and a
sculpture of Christ in Majesty, surrounded by the Evangelistic
Emblems, found face downwards in St. Giles' Church, Durham,
was also richly embellished with decoration. Of more elaborate
composition, we find notices of coloured sculptures of the Nativity at
Bolsover, the Adoration of the Magi at Long Melford, the flagellation of Christ at Thursby, the Descent from the Cross at
Beachamwell, and a "Pieta" at Breadsall. The flaying of St. Bartholomew is noticed at Lostwithiel, the martyrdom of St. Erasmus
at Buckenham Ferry, and a Pope inaugurating a bishop at St. Mary's,
Nottingham. At Stoke Charity is a sculptured representation of the
literal transubstantiation of the wafer, or St. Gregory's mass, which
has been entirely overlaid with bright vermilion colouring. At the
church of St. Peter Mancroft, Norwich, was an alabaster tablet with
several figures of female saints. At Warwick are a series of niches
containing figures of the Heavenly Hierarchy and several female
saints. At Madron are several figures, also alleged to be the
Heavenly Hierarchy. At Hillesden, round the upper walls of the
chancel are numerous sculptured figures of angels holding musical
instruments, all highly coloured and gilded. On the walls of an
oratory in Norwich Castle are certain rude sculptures of St. Chris-

topher, &c., bearing evidence of chromatic decoration.* Sometimes, but not often, subjects were moulded in plaster and then coloured. A curious and late example was found in the wall behind the papering of a room at Rushton Hall, a former seat of the Treshams. This is a large representation of the Crucifixion, with the two thieves and a variety of other figures. The saints on the pulpit of Bovey Tracey are of plaster, coloured.

The stone bosses placed at the intersection of the groining ribs of the roofs were often most carefully sculptured, and further enriched with colour and gilding. Thus, at Exeter Cathedral, the colouring on those in the nave and Lady Chapel has been restored from traces of the original decoration, and those in the Lady Chapel of Chester Cathedral, and in the nave and aisles of St. George's Chapel, Windsor, have been similarly treated. In the south choir aisle of Lichfield Cathedral, and in the choir of Christchurch Priory Church, considerable remains of gilding are still visible. The roof of the Lady Chapel of Ely Cathedral everywhere shows signs of its former elaborate decoration, especially on the beautifully carved bosses whereon are represented the Nativity, Crucifixion, and history of the Virgin. At St. Helen's, Norwich, are numerous beautifully sculptured and painted bosses, and on them are displayed, the Annunciation, Nativity, Resurrection, and Ascension, figures of Apostles and Saints, and the Coronation of the Virgin, which forms the central and principal subject. But by far the most interesting series are those at Norwich Cathedral, which have been fully illustrated and described by Dr. Goulburn, and on which are exhibited the principal events of Old Testament history, from the Creation to the Judgment of Solomon, and of the New Testament from the birth of Christ to the final Judgment.

Before drawing attention to the fine painted screens, roofs, and other remains of ecclesiastical furniture and decorated wood-work, which exist, or have from time to time been discovered, a few remarks may here be fitly inserted on the subject of mural decoration as applied to domestic buildings. Numerous instances still remain, or have at various times been found, which demonstrate the prevalence, if not the universality, of the practice of adorning with painting the walls of the chief apartments of castles and other mansions, and of the principal chambers of the ecclesiastical establishments. Some valuable information on this subject is given in an account of a painting of the Annunciation, discovered in an old house at Salisbury.† Very early specimens of decoration have been found in an upper arcade in Westminster Hall, where bright

* A similar figure of St. Christopher exists at Guildford Castle, but it is uncertain whether it was ever coloured, as no traces now remain. In Blomefield's History of Norfolk, mention is often made of images of St. Christopher being in the churches. Many of these seem to have been statuettes, but none now remain. In the South Kensington Museum are some interesting sculptured representations of this Saint chiefly brought from the Tyrol, and all still retaining rich colour and gilding.

† British Archæol. Assoc. Journ., iv. 91.

colouring had been laid on the shafts and imposts of, and masonry patterns on the wall within, the arches, the date being about the year 1100. On the walls of Bishop Gundulph's foundation at Rochester, and at the Bishop's Palace at Hereford, some very ancient painting has also been discovered. The encouragement given to this art by and during the reign of Henry III. has already been referred to, and numerous records exist of paintings executed during this period at the castle of Guildford, the palaces of Clarendon and Winchester, &c., &c. One of the most important series which have been noticed are those in the Painted Chamber, Westminster Hall, where are depicted numerous events in the Old Testament history, two scenes connected with King Edward the Confessor, and certain allegorical subjects. At Chipchase Castle various wall decorations remain in a fragmentary condition, and considerable remains of later date have been found at Rochford Tower, Boston, at Gainsborough, Medbourne, Bradfield (Devon), Gloddaeth, &c. At Cowdray House, which has been entirely burnt out, and whose tottering walls still stand to attest its former grandeur, were a series of sacred and mythological subjects painted on the walls of the great hall, and another of historical incidents on those of the dining parlour, all probably executed during the reign of Edward VI. On the walls of the Carpenters' Hall, London, a series of paintings were found some few years back, and are still preserved.

As might be expected, the chapels of the more important military and domestic buildings were adorned on the same principle as the churches. In the chapel of the Bishop's Palace at Chichester are some 13th century paintings, while of the two succeeding periods considerable remains have been noticed in the chapels of Prior Crauden at Ely, of Haddon Hall, Elsing Hall, Magdalen Hospital, Winchester, Harbledown Hospital, &c. In an old house at Bristol an oratory was discovered adorned with scriptural paintings. At East Bridge Hospital, Canterbury, are three very interesting wall paintings only recently discovered, and apparently of the 13th century. The finest represents Christ in Majesty, within a vesica and surrounded by the emblems of the Evangelists. Below this is a representation of the Last Supper, and at the side, the martyrdom of St. Thomas of Canterbury. A masonry pattern is mixed up with and seems to be of later date than the other paintings. At Berkeley Castle chapel numerous texts from the book of "Revelation" were found, which are reputed to have been painted about the year 1400, an early example of this kind of decoration. In the several apartments of the monastic and other religious establishments coloured decorations were also freely applied. The Chapter Houses were often most handsomely decorated, as, for instance, we may still see at York, Canterbury, Salisbury, Oxford, Westminster, Jervaulx, Beleigh, Laycock, &c., and read of at Hereford. In the Frater House at Durham was a wall painting of the Crucifixion, with the Virgin and St. John. In the refectory at Cleeve Abbey is a similar painting, and in that at St. Martin's Priory, Dover, is a representation of the Last Supper. At the Guesten Hall, Worcester, was depicted the Adoration of the Magi. On the wall of a room adjoining the abbey church at Selby were portrait figures within compartments, and an inscription of early 16th century date. Various decorative patterns, &c , have been found on divers portions of the domestic buildings belonging to Norwich Cathedral, and at the abbeys of Fountains, Mendham, Battle, Cleeve, and elsewhere, some as early as the 12th century. Even the walls of the cloisters were often decorated with subjects and ornamental designs. In the Dean's Cloister, at Windsor, a crowned head has been conjectured to be a portrait of King Henry III. At the college of Ashridge were a series of forty stone panels, on which were depicted as many scenes from the life and passion of Christ, most of which were destroyed at the beginning of this century, when the present stately mansion was erected. In the cloisters of Old St. Paul's, London, it is recorded that a painting of the Dance of Death was executed, and it is asserted that traces of decoration are still visible over the entrance to the ancient refectory of Westminster Abbey.

Next to the wall paintings, and other remains of decoration in distemper, attention may now fairly be directed to the various panel paintings, timber mouldings enriched with colour and gilding, &c., with which our churches were formerly so bountifully adorned. Except in the very early examples, the process adopted in colouring the woodwork was different from that employed in the wall paintings, and will hereafter be briefly described. And first ought to be noticed the rood and chancel screens, which, it is believed, formed a necessary portion of the furniture of, and consequently formerly existed in, every church in Great Britain, though, chiefly owing to the vandalism of the Puritans, or the restorers of recent date, comparatively few examples were permitted to remain in anything approaching a perfect condition. Above or on the top of the rood screens always hung or was placed the Holy Rood, consisting of representations, almost invariably in wood, of Christ on the Cross, with the Virgin and St. John on either side. At the time of the Reformation these ornaments were swept away, and, as a rule, utterly destroyed. A specimen was found not long ago at Ludham, concealed perhaps purposely in the staircase leading to the roodloft, and panel paintings at Cartmel Fell and West Somerton are likewise conjectured to have formed part of the rood. Several instances might be recorded where the rood beam has survived to our time, but only on examples at Martham, Ufford, Postling, and Brabourne has the ancient colouring been observed.

It may be assumed that all screens prior to the time of the Reformation were originally decorated with colour and gilding, but in the majority of instances paint and varnish have totally and beyond recovery destroyed their former splendour. The greater number of the screens were of wood, but some few examples in stone remain with traces of their former illumination, and have already been noticed. Most of the wooden screens surviving to our time belong to the latter part of the 15th or early 16th century, and especially to the reigns of Henry VII. and Henry VIII. The finest still existing are to be found in Norfolk, Suffolk, and Devonshire, as may be seen at once by a reference to the list. It is doubtful as to whether any remains of coloured screen work of earlier date than the 13th century have survived to our time. During the 13th and 14th centuries, as far as can be ascertained from the few specimens remaining, the mouldings of the screens were enriched with colour, and the panels decorated with plain green and red tints, and sometimes powdered with flowers, stars, &c., but during the 15th and early part of the 16th century, figures of saints, sacred subjects, and rich diapers were depicted on the lower panels, in some instances as many as 40 different personages being thus portrayed.

One of the earliest examples of this branch of our subject may still be seen at Rochester Cathedral, where, forming a kind of base to the present stalls, are on each side of the choir, a row of tri-foliated arches of early 13th century date still retaining their original colouring. At Hullavington is the lower part of a screen of early English character, the colouring on which may be also of this period. At Swanscombe and Willingham are screens of pure decorated character, the latter in a sadly mutilated condition, both of them retaining traces of simple colouring. At Lower Gravenhurst is a screen reputed to be of the same age as the church, which was re-built about the year 1350. The mouldings of the upper part have been varnished over, but exhibit traces of red colouring; the lower portion has been boarded, but not panelled, and is ornamented with a decorative pattern in chocolate on a pale yellow ground. At Edingthorpe, the screen belongs to the decorated period, and the painted and gilt mouldings are probably of 14th century date, but the figures still existing on the lower panels are not earlier than the succeeding century. At Newtown, the screen has been conjectured to be of decorated character, and to have been executed in the early part of the 14th century, but comparing it with similarly carved ornamental woodwork, the date of which is undoubted, it may with far more probability be deemed a work of the latter part of the 15th century.

In a treatise which professes to deal only with the subject of decorative colouring, it may perhaps be deemed beyond its scope to attempt any general remarks upon the screens, as in so many of the finest examples, no traces of colouring now exist, nor can it be actually proved that they ever were decorated. It may, however, be again confidently asserted that every church in the 15th century possessed its roodscreen, and that the screen was invariably enriched with colour and gilding. The roodscreens seem generally to have occupied the space beneath the chancel arch, so as to form a division between the nave and chancel. In the more important examples, the screen supported a gallery, called the roodloft, where the choir were located and some portions of the service administered. "The

" roodloft generally projected in front of both sides of the screen, so
" as to form a kind of groined cove, the ribs of which sprang or
" diverged from the principal uprights of the screen beneath, and
" this cove supported the flooring of the loft."[*] In many instances
the colour and gilding on this upper portion still remains. As it
cannot be disputed that these screens to a certain extent interfere
with the due performance of the reformed service, continuing as they
do, according to the ancient intention, to constitute a barrier between
the nave and chancel, and looking at the inconvenience thereby
caused to the minister and congregation, it is perhaps surprising that
so many have survived to our day. Several fine examples still
remain in an almost perfect state in Wales, though the ancient
colouring has been in most cases destroyed. At Newark is a very
fine chancel screen with projecting canopy, but here again varnish
has successfully obliterated the colouring, and only a little gilding
on the mouldings has been preserved and renewed. At Tilbrook, the
projecting canopy remains with its original colouring, the mouldings
being beautifully carved and gilt, and the groundwork of the spaces
between being painted a delicate pale blue. At Charlton on Otmoor
is another richly decorated screen, with canopy of very late date and
partly Italian in its character, the carving of the shafts being
decidedly of the classic order. Here the original colour and gilding
is in very good condition. At Oakley is an earlier screen, which
seems to have had a canopy extending across the chancel and aisles,
but only that in the north aisle remains. On this has been some
more than usually elaborate colouring, viz., a representation of
Christ seated in Judgment, and showing the wounds, with an angel
holding the instruments of the Passion, the general groundwork
being painted red with a diaper of stars. At Maidstone, on the
north side of the chancel, is a similarly constructed screen, but very
little of the colouring has survived, though enough remains to show
how richly decorated it once was. Both of these last-mentioned
screens are probably of the end of the 14th century. A very fine
example of later date is preserved at Long Sutton, and another with
the original colour on the canopy only at Stoke Dry.[†] At Great
Rollwright and Avebury, the roodlofts are now placed above the
chancel arch. On the cornices are generally beautifully carved
patterns of running foliage, the vine leaf being the most common ;
and often shields charged with the arms of the benefactors, and
sometimes also black letter inscriptions recording the names, and
soliciting prayers for the souls of the donors, as at Aylsham, Fritton
(Norfolk), &c. Very fine screens with richly gilt mouldings restored
may be seen at Long Ashton and Banwell, and also have been noted
at Flamborough, Hexham, Litcham, Llangwm Ucha, St. Buryan,
&c., &c. At Brancepeth are numerous carved panels on which are

---

[*] Bloxam, Principles of Gothic Architecture, 11th ed., ii. 38.

[†] This screen is a late and curious example. On its west side at each extremity is a projecting framework, apparently intended as a canopy over the pulpit and reading desk.

sculptured various geometrical designs, retaining traces of colour and gilding, and conjectured to have belonged to a screen. A very late example of a roodscreen with its original colouring exists at Hubberholme, the date of its erection being 1558.

The panels of the screens were often the most elaborate portions with rich traceried canopies, the ground decoration being generally red and green, though very often a richly gilded diaper occurs, especially in the Norfolk examples, very ornate specimens still remaining at Randworth, North Elmham, Gooderstone, and elsewhere. As has been already stated, a powdering of leaves, flowers, stars, &c., seems to have been the earlier method of decorating the panels, and interesting examples may be seen at Ashby Folville, Luton, Trumpington, Dickleburgh, and Burlingham St. Edmunds. At Stevington, on the panels are depicted numerous white harts, heraldic badges, probably denoting the erection of the screen during the reign of Henry VI. It is uncertain when the practice of portraying figures of saints, &c. on the panels was first introduced, and also whether this custom was generally adopted throughout the country, as the existing examples are rare, except in Norfolk, Suffolk, Devonshire, and Cornwall. It seems, however, tolerably clear that no example has survived to our time of an earlier date than the 15th century, and that with a very few exceptions, most of the extant specimens date from the latter part of the 15th or early in the 16th century. A glance at the "List" will demonstrate the wonderful variety of saints depicted on these screens, and as in the case of the mural paintings, so equally, and perhaps even more directly, from the figures on these screens, may deductions be drawn as to the professions, &c., of the principal residents at the time of their erection. In almost all the examples, each main panel or division of the screen is sub-divided into two portions, on each of which is depicted a distinct figure or subject. An exception to this rule may be seen at Kelshall, where the four saints severally occupy the whole surface of the undivided panels. The most common arrangement seems to have been to portray the Apostles or Evangelists and the Doctors and Fathers of the Western Church, the latter usually occupying the panels of the doors of the central portion. Thus at Morston we find the Doctors of the Church and the Evangelists; at Gooderstone, the Apostles and Doctors of the Church; at Elsing, Irstead, Gisleham, &c., the Apostles alone. St. Paul is generally included in the series, in the place of St. Matthew, as at Hunstanton, Trunch, Tunstead, Westwick, &c. He is also introduced in lieu of St. Thomas at Lessingham, and of St. Matthias at Randworth. At Belaugh and Aylsham, SS. Paul and John the Baptist occupy the places of SS. Philip and Matthias, in the former case Moses being also introduced in the place of St. John the Evangelist. The Apostles were sometimes represented as holding scrolls, on which were inscribed sentences from the Creed, as at Mattishall, Weston Longville, Ringland, and St. Peter's, Thetford. At Clifton (Bedfordshire), are portions of a former screen; on the panels are pairs of

figures, one being an Apostle and the other a duplicate figure
holding a scroll, supposed to be the corresponding prophet.* At
Bovey Tracey, Kenton, and Chudleigh the Apostles and Prophets
alternately are similarly represented. At St Peter Mancroft, Norwich,
are a series of panels with paintings of the Apostles and Prophets of
very late, probably post Reformation, date. There does not appear
to have been any regular order of arrangement in these series of the
Apostles, except that St. Peter almost always occupies the panel
immediately to the north, and St. Paul to the south of the doors of
the central screen. A series of the Prophets are not uncommonly
found, though as a rule these are of very late execution, as at Monks
Risborough. Screens of very elaborate character with these panel
portraits of the Prophets still are, or till recently have been, in
existence at Thornham, Harpley, Marston Moretaine, &c. In most
of the examples each Prophet holds a scroll on which is inscribed a
sentence from his book referring to the Messiah, as at Poringland,
North Crawley, &c. It is uncertain whether in each instance the
same text is given to each particular Prophet, but in the cases where
the scrolls can be decyphered, there are many divergencies from the
series of inscriptions now given to the Prophets depicted on the
vault of the choir of Salisbury Cathedral.† In the series of the
Prophets, king David is often introduced as at Thornham, Poringland, North Crawley, and elsewhere, and Baruch occurs at Bedfield
and Southwold. Another series of subjects which are found together
are the "Holy Families," as still to be seen at Houghton Le Dale
and Randworth, where are represented, the Virgin and Child,
and SS. Mary Cleopas and Salome, each with their respective
families. At the former church are also depicted St. Anne and the
Virgin, SS. Elizabeth and John the Baptist, and SS. Monica and
Augustine.‡ St. Mary the Virgin being taught to read by her
mother St. Anne, the Annunciation and Salutation were subjects
not uncommonly delineated on the screens, while the Coronation of
the Virgin appears chiefly upon the central doors, as at Holne and
Portlemouth. Scenes from the life of Christ are not uncommon, as
at Loddon. At Plymtree and Buckland in the Moor may be seen
the Adoration of the Magi; at Westhall and Ashton, the Transfiguration; at Broadclist, Christ with the Woman of Samaria; at
Upwell, St. Michael at Plea, and SS Simon and Jude, Norwich, are
scenes from the Passion; at Fowlis Easter, Hexham, and Kenn, is
the Crucifixion; and at Ashton, Romsey, and Upwell, the Resurrection. The screen at Fowlis Easter, is almost, if not actually, the

* An early example of this arrangement may be seen on the brass of Abbot Delamere, at St. Albans Cathedral.

† The north aisle ceiling of St. Helen's, Abingdon, has a series of full length figures of royal personages and prophets, conjectured to have been intended to illustrate the genealogy of Christ, and to have originally formed part of a screen. The prophets holding scrolls are also represented in ancient stained glass at Oxburgh and in the ante-chapel of New College, Oxford.

‡ With the exception of SS. Monica and Augustine, these all occur in glass of contemporary date in the ante-chapel of All Souls College, Oxford.

only one which has escaped the fury of the Scotch reformers, and strange to say, it remains in admirable condition. On the lower portion is a most complete representation of the Crucifixion with the thieves on either side and a multitude of beholders all around. Figures of St. John the Baptist and St. Mary Magdalene often occur especially in Norfolk and Devonshire. A representation of Lazarus stepping forth from his tomb exists on the screens at Thornham and Roxton. St. Joacim, the father of St. Mary the Virgin, is represented with St. Anne and the Virgin on the south door of the screen at Harpley. St. Stephen, habited as a deacon, is also not uncommon. The only recorded picture of St. Barnabas is to be found at Woodbridge, where several other rare saints are also depicted. At Barton Turf, the main portion of the screen is beautifully illuminated, and illustrations of the Heavenly Hierarchy are delineated on the panels. This subject occurs also at Southwold, and is said to have decorated the screen at Tavistock, though not now remaining. We find similar representations in mural painting at Irstead, and in sculpture at Warwick and Madron. In glass the subject seems to have been not uncommon. Portraits of St. Michael are often found, representing him both in the act of contending with Satan, and of weighing souls. At Gooderstone, above all the figures are introduced busts of arch-angels, and a similar arrangement occurs above some of the principal panels at Randworth.

It will be impossible to do more than to refer to the various saints depicted on the panels of the screens. A large number of portraits still remain either altogether unidentified or unsatisfactorily appropriated, owing either to the absence of any distinguishing emblem, or to the uncertainty as to whom any particular emblem is intended to apply. In Norfolk and Suffolk the various saints can in most cases be identified by the emblems as given in "Husenbeth's Emblems of Saints," of which a third edition has just been published, but in other counties, and especially in Devonshire and Cornwall, the emblems represented do not seem to denote the same personages, and it is unfortunate that the scope of Dr. Husenbeth's work was not enlarged prior to the publication of the last edition, in which, as in the previous ones, almost all the illustrations from England are taken from examples in Norfolk and Suffolk. For instance, in the fine screens at Plymtree, Holne, Manaton, Woolborough, &c., many interesting figures occur, whose identity is still undetermined, or can only be hazarded from a possible resemblance to some certified example, and there can be no doubt that many erroneous appropriations have thus been inserted in the present work.

Numerous examples occur of St. George represented on foot and trampling upon the dragon, also of SS. Anthony, Benedict, Clement, Blaise, Martin, Lawrence, Sebastian, and Roche, the two latter being constantly found together, as at Stalham, North Tuddenham, Holne, Plymtree, &c. Although there are not a great many instances where it can clearly be proved that St. Martin is portrayed, yet as he was

generally depicted, as being simply habited as a bishop, and without
any distinguishing emblem, it is probable that many of the episcopal
portraits, which it has not been possible to identify, may be applied
to him. Representations of SS. Leonard, Giles, Nicholas, Eligius,
Erasmus, Francis, Denis, and Louis, seem to have been not uncommon, though only a few examples have survived. At Litcham is a
painting of St. Hubert, the only portrait which can with certainty be
identified with the saint. At Suffield we find St. Julian Hospitator,
an unique example, or possibly the figure may be St. Jeron or
Geron, who is also stated to occur at North Tuddenham. At
Houghton-le-Dale is a figure of St. Sylvester ; at Oxburgh, St. Willebrod ; at Woodbridge, St. Quintin ;* at Somerleyton, St. Zeno ;
at Guilden Morden, St. Erkenwold ; in each case this being the only
recorded picture of the saint in England remaining in this situation.
The popular St. Christopher does not seem to have been often
depicted on the screens, doubtless because his picture occupied a
more prominent position. There are examples still remaining on the
panels of the screens at Binham Abbey, Roxton, and Bradninch.†
On some of the Devonshire screens are numerous saints, which have
not yet been satisfactorily identified ; for instance, at Plymtree may
be found figures, perhaps intended for SS. Cyr, Romuald, and Odilo,
none of whom occur elsewhere ; at Portlemouth is St. Cornelius and
possibly SS. Machutus and Bruno, also unique examples in panel
painting, though the former occurs in glass in the church of North
Walsham, and at Cossey Hall Chapel, Norfolk. At Woolborough,
where the figures in some cases have been repainted, are numerous
saints whose identity is uncertain ; amongst them seem to be
SS. Irenæus and Pancras, the latter also occurring at Holne, but the
former has not been noticed elsewhere, except in one or two cases
where he has been mistaken for St. Hieronymus (Jerome).

Of the English saints the most commonly represented were
SS. Edmund, Edward the Confessor, Edward king and martyr, and
Walstan, of the royal personages, these being all most usually met
with in the Eastern Counties. SS. Oswald and Olave also occur,
and St. Kenelm was formerly visible at Woodbridge. St. Ethelbert
may still be seen at Burnham Norton, and St. Wandragesilas at
Horsham, St. Faiths. Of the ecclesiastical saints, St. Thomas of
Canterbury occurs by far the most often, and it may safely be
asserted that where an archbishop appears without name or emblem,
St. Thomas of Canterbury is generally intended to be portrayed.
SS. Dunstan and Cuthbert are occasionally met with. St. William
of York is noticed at Garboldisham, and St. Robert at Erpingham.
At Hempstead, amongst several other figures occur SS. Theobald
and John of Burlington (or this may be St. John of Beverley, who

* At St. Hilaire, Poitiers, are considerable remains of wall paintings, amongst them a
figure of a bishop, with the name "Quintian Eps."

† There is also a similar representation on one of the panels of the pulpit of Horsham
St. Faith's church.

also appears on a screen at Hexham, and the roof of St. Mary's, Beverley), neither of whom are found in painting elsewhere. At Randworth is a bishop, conjectured to be St. Felix. On one of the screens at Hexham, now used as a vestry screen, are a series of early English saints not recorded as occurring elsewhere. Another English saint, of whom a few representations remain, is St. William of Norwich, who was crucified by the Jews, and afterwards canonized on account of the numerous miracles performed at his tomb. King Henry VI. and Sir John Shorne, neither of whom were ever actually canonised, are often found in the Eastern Counties included among the series of saints. The legend connected with Sir John Shorne is curious, tradition crediting him with the feat of imprisoning the Devil in a boot, and in all the representations he is depicted holding a boot whence a demon is emerging. It is somewhat singular that there is not a single representation remaining either in panel or mural painting which can be identified as portraying such popular and well-known English saints as St. Augustine the Apostle of England, St. Chad, St. Botolph, St. Alban, and others, whom we should rather have expected to find, than those foreign saints who are so constantly introduced.

The representation of the female saints was also very common. In many cases both male and female saints appear on the same screen, and are sometimes placed alternately on the panels, as at Blyth, North Tuddenham, &c., and in three instances, viz., at Babingley, Ufford, and Tilbrook, the latter alone are depicted. At Babingley no less than 18 panels remained till within the last 50 years, and though the originals have been destroyed, excellent coloured drawings exist, being included in the collections of the late Mr. Dawson Turner, and now preserved in the British Museum. Many of the saints there depicted bear emblems which are not found elsewhere, and their identification has been to a certain extent conjectural. At Ufford no emblems are given to the several figures, which are of very late character, but the names still remain below them.

The most favourite saints as shown by these panel paintings were SS. Catherine of Alexandria, Margaret, Etheldreda, Agatha, Agnes, Appollonia, Barbara, Helen, Dorothy, and Ursula. Several portraits remain of SS. Bridget of Sweden, Sitha, Faith, Clara, Juliana, Sidwell, Petronilla, Withburgha, Christina, and Genevieve. Of the more uncommon representations we find St. Gertrude at Babingley, Hennock, and Woolborough; St. Blida, mother of St. Walstan, at St. James', Norwich, and perhaps at Babingley; St. Scholastica at Romsey and Kenn; St. Gudule at Berry Pomeroy and Walpole St. Peter; St. Elizabeth of Hungary at Gately and Fulbourne; St. Joan of Valois at Barnham Broom, Upton (Norfolk), and St. James', Norwich; St. Catherine of Siena at Horsham St. Faith's and Portlemouth; St. Wilgefortis at Worstead and perhaps at North Walsham; while single examples occur of St. Euphemia at Blyth; St. Florence at Ufford; St. Mary of Egypt at North Walsham; St. Puella Ridibowne at Gately; St. Winifred at Bab-ingley; and St. Anastasia at Hennock.* On the former screen of Pennant Melangell were a series of events in the life of St. Melangell. The mythical St. Veronica, usually represented emblematically by a napkin on which is delineated the head of Christ, also occurs both in Norfolk and Devonshire. On the screen at Bradninch are a full series of the Sybils bearing their respective emblems. It is possible that the same figures are portrayed at Ugborough. On the screen at Sparham are two scenes from the Dance of Death, a subject similarly represented on the screens at Hexham and Yoxford. In one or two instances portraits are supposed to have been painted on the screens. The most interesting example is that at Plymtree, where the Magi are said to be portraits of King Henry VII., Prince Arthur, and Cardinal Morton, Bishop Fox being also introduced. At Bloxham is a figure supposed to be a likeness of Cardinal Wolsey. The practice of representing on the screens the donors and their families has been already alluded to. Thus at Aylsham we find Thomas Wymer; at Fritton (Norfolk), Sir John Bacon and Family; and of unknown benefactors at Houghton le Dale, Burnham Norton, Ipswich, St. Matthew's, and Romsey. On the panels of the pulpit at Burnham Norton are portraits of John and Katherine Goldale, and on the panel of a cupboard at King's Lynn is the kneeling figure of a priest. None of these examples are earlier than the end of the 15th century.

In some few instances a second tier of panels is introduced within the open tracery of portions of the screen, as at Attleborough and Randworth. At Morley, St. Botolph's Church, Norfolk, above the screen is a panel with portrait of the rector between the two churches over which he presided. At Strensham the panels of the screen are incorporated in a western gallery, and many examples might be mentioned of the removal of the screens, or portions of them, to different situations in the church. At North Elmham the very fine screen has been subjected to many changes, and even within the past few years so many screens have been cut down, and even entirely removed, that it is unsafe to make any positive assertions as to the present condition or situation of any particular example. Many cases might also be mentioned where all the paint, varnish, &c., have been so thoroughly removed that not a vestige of the original colouring has survived the process of scraping or washing to which the surface of the screen has been subjected. In some few instances small sculptured figures grouped round the doors, &c., are also introduced. At Beeston St. Mary's are carved and coloured repre-sentations of SS. George, Michael, &c. At Manaton are SS. Stephen, Paul, and the majority of the Apostles. A similar arrangement

---

* St. Anastasia also occurs in ancient stained glass in the ante chapel at All Souls College, Oxford.

occurs at North Bovey, also in Devonshire, but no traces of colouring are there recorded.[*]

On the back of the choir stalls at Carlisle Cathedral are some very interesting panel paintings, illustrating the histories of SS. Augustine, Anthony, and Cuthbert. At Chichester Cathedral are two large and elaborate pictures in a similar situation, executed at the charge of Bishop Sherborne and commemorating two important events in the history of the See.

At the churches of Sall and Aylsham are galleries for the bell ringers ; the screen work across the tower arches retains traces of the former decoration.[†] At Weston in Gordano is a singular wooden platform within the porch and over the inner entrance, the use of which has not been satisfactorily ascertained. Considerable remains of painting are still apparent.

Of wooden pulpits of pre-Reformation date, retaining their ancient colouring, only a few specimens remain, and these, as in the case of the screens, are chiefly to be found in Norfolk. At Burlingham St. Edmunds the pulpit has richly painted and gilded mouldings and cresting, and a diaper of various ornaments on the panels. At Long Sutton is another very rich example of about the year 1530. At St. Michael's, Coventry, was an early and very interesting specimen of date about 1400, with some gilding on the tracery and mouldings. We sometimes find figures of saints depicted on the panels, as at Warmington, our Saviour, and various saints ; at Castle Acre, the four Doctors of the Church, who also appear at Burnham Norton, together with the portraits of the donors. At Horsham, St. Faith's, are numerous saints, including a representation of St. Christopher, one of the few instances known of his portraiture on panel in England.

Of wooden lecterns, a handsomely carved and coloured example has been noticed at Littlebury, and another one, with the eagle, of St. John, the motto "In Principium," and musical inscription depicted on it, at Randworth. Colouring formerly existed on specimens still preserved at Peakirk and Leighton Buzzard. At Hexham, a litany desk with panel paintings is still preserved.

Of wooden fonts, which are of exceeding rarity, the only recorded example, with remains of its original polychromatic decoration, is to be found at Mark's Tey. Several instances of the font covers remain, with rich colouring and illumination on the mouldings and intermediate surfaces. Many of them are shaped like a spire, with numerous tiers of delicately carved canopies, gradually diminishing towards the summit, and reaching almost to the beam in the roof,

---

* The following screens may be enumerated as being specially interesting, owing to the number of figures depicted on the panels. In many instances the screens are continued across the aisles, and sometimes also enclose small chantry chapels, &c. Fowlis Easter ; Hexham ; Worstead, North Walsham, Aylsham, Barton Turf, Repps, Cawston, Houghton-le-Dale, Hunstanton, Babingley, Gooderstone, Randworth, North Elmham Loddon, Walpole, St. Peter ; Woodbridge, Somerleyton, Westhall, Southwold, Eye ; Roxton, Clifton ; North Crawley ; Strensham ; Kenn, Kenton, Ashton, Woolborough, Tor Bryan, Manaton, Holne, Portlemouth, Ugborough, Bradninch, Plymtree ; and St. Budoc.

†

whence they are suspended. One of the earliest recorded is that at Elsing, which is of the decorated style of architecture, and dates from the 14th century. Another very beautiful example remained at Randworth until the early part of the present century, when it was swept away as useless lumber during the carrying out of certain repairs to the church. Magnificent specimens still exist at South Acre, St. Gregory's Sudbury, Ufford, and Worlingworth. At Plymstock is a late, but also elaborate, specimen, and one of about the same age has recently been restored to its original position in Shaugh Prior Church. At Foulsham, the interior of the font cover was adorned with paintings of the Evangelists. A very late example at Terrington, St. Clement's, is similarly ornamented with scriptural subjects. At Trunch and St. Peter, Mancroft, Norwich, are baptisteries, composed of wood and retaining traces of their original gilding and coloured decorations. Both these examples have rich canopies of late character supported on shafts, and enclosing the space within which the font is placed. At Luton, a similar but much earlier baptistery in stone has been denuded of the decoration with which it was once probably enriched. The painted beam whence the font cover was suspended still remains at Sall, Sheringham, and Trunch.

Of other painted church furniture may be mentioned a curious hexagonal stand at Burlingham St. Andrew's, the bench ends with coloured decorations at Hemingborough and Great Brington, and the carrel or stall at Bishop's Cannings. Several examples of ancient church chests still remain with their original decorations in fair preservation. The most interesting of these, as well as the earliest, may still be seen at Newport, in Essex, where on the inner side of the lid are paintings of the Crucifixion, the Virgin, and SS. John, Peter, and Paul. These date from the latter part of the thirteenth century, and are conjectured to be almost the earliest instances known of paintings in oil. At Durham Cathedral and Burgate are ornamental chests of the time of Richard II. On the lid of the former are heraldic bearings, and on the latter two knights tilting. At Rainham (Kent) is a beautifully carved specimen with traces of colouring. At Great Yarmouth the hutch or corporation chest, supposed to have belonged originally to some church, is decorated with various colours and some diaper patterns.

Some few examples of painted panels, which appear not to have belonged either to screens, pulpits, or roofs, still remain. At Mitcheldean a series of panels illustrate the earthly life of Christ and the Day of Judgment. The latter subject still exists at St. Michael's, St. Alban's, and of late date at Gloucester Cathedral, and another example, now destroyed, was within the past few years preserved at Enfield. The former was in existence at Burford (Salop) and St. Germains. Figures of Our Saviour occur at Axbridge, His Crucifixion at Winsham and Bradninch, and His Entombment at Southwold. At Warton are portrayed St. Mary the Virgin and various ecclesiastics, and a panel with the Coronation of the Virgin depicted upon it is preserved in the Bishop's Palace, Llandaff. At the back of the altar at Wilton Church, Norfolk, are SS. John the Baptist and John the Evangelist, with two priests kneeling at an alter. At Herringfleet and Romsey are also figures of ecclesiastics, and on the door of a cupboard in the vestry of St. Nicholas, King's Lynn, a priest kneeling with supplicatory scroll to St. Peter. At North Creake are three of the Cardinal Virtues and the emblematical representation of St. Veronica. At Ingham were formerly three panels, which are now in private possession, on which are delineated scenes in the life of St. Nicholas. A curious painting has been preserved at a farmhouse close to the abbey of Strata Florida, illustrating Temptation. At Loddon are portraits of Sir John Hobart and lady, and at St. Michael's, St. Alban's, and Wesenham, of Henry VI. At the head of the monument of king Henry IV., in Canterbury Cathedral, is a panel painting, now much worn, representing the murder of St. Thomas of Canterbury, whilst at the foot of the monument is an angel holding an armorial shield. At Milton Abbas are three panels incorporated with the present stalls, on which are depicted portraits of king Athelstan and his queen, and the Annunciation. At Cartmel Fell, on the Comer Hall pew, are various panel paintings of saints. In Gunton's History of the Church of Peterburgh, p. 95, mention is made of a series of very interesting painted panels, as formerly existing in the choir of that Cathedral. Upon these were delineated the Apostles, Prophets, the Salutation, Aaron's Rod budding, Boaz, David, Gedeon, and Moses, all with sentences in Latin verse.

Some few monuments have flat wooden canopies above them, adorned with gilding and colour. At Canterbury Cathedral, above the tomb of Edward the Black Prince, is one of these canopies, richly ornamented with his motto, and with a majestic representation of the Blessed Trinity, and evangelistic emblems on the under side. The monument of Henry IV. has a similar canopy, with the motto of the king and his queen on an ermine ground many times repeated on the verge and under side. At Westminster Abbey traces of colour are visible on the canopy above the monument of Queen Philippa. Above that of Richard II., on a richly gilded ground, are depicted the Coronation of the Virgin, Christ in Majesty, and two angels holding shields, charged respectively with the armorial bearings of the king and his royal consort. Above the Harington monument at Cartmel are some painted boards, with the emblems of the Evangelists depicted upon them. These, however, do not appear to occupy their original position.

There can be no doubt that the wooden effigies were invariably overlaid with colour and gilding, or, in a few instances, as in the case of the effigy of Henry V. at Westminster Abbey, with plates of metal enriched with enamel. The cross-legged effigy of William de Valence, also at Westminster Abbey, is still ornamented with a thin layer of enamel and gilding, which originally covered the whole figure. At Salisbury Cathedral the table on which the effigy of William Longespé, the first Earl of Salisbury, rests, is of wood, and

similarly enriched with enamel and gilding. Colour and gilding has
been noted on the following cross-legged effigies, viz., at Ashwell
(Rutland) ; Woodford (Northants) ; Weston (Stafford) ; Banham ;
Fersfield ; Bures ; Hildersham ; St. Saviour's, Southwark ; Abergavenny ; and Chew Magna. At West Downe the early effigy of a
judge, and at Tawstock of a lady, still retain their original colouring.
At Staindrop the monument and effigies of Henry, fifth Earl of
Westmoreland, and his two wives, are entirely composed of wood,
and have been profusely adorned with colour and gilding.

Of the timber roofs, numerous examples are still, or have been
till recently, in existence, where traces of the original colour remains,
but, with few exceptions, these are all of the fifteenth or early six-
teenth centuries. The flat roof at Peterborough Cathedral has
already been noticed as being probably the most ancient specimen
remaining, and perhaps the only coloured example in wood of the
Norman period, which has survived to our time. The roof which
spanned Conrad's glorious choir at Canterbury Cathedral was probably of similar character, as must have been that over the nave of
St. Alban's Abbey, though no remnants seem to have been retained
in the several ceilings which have succeeded it. It is uncertain
whether any examples of thirteenth century date can be adduced.
Of the succeeding century examples have been noted of bold floral
decoration on the groining of the passage leading from the cloisters
to the Chapter House at Salisbury Cathedral. The Chapel of the
Sanctuary between the retrochoir and Lady Chapel at St. Alban's
Cathedral has had a flat panelled ceiling, and traces of colour are
visible on the beams and bosses. At Shillington the roofs of the
aisles and chancel aisles have a chevron pattern running along the
central beam, and the east bay of the nave roof exhibits very
elaborate decoration, which has been renewed within the past few
years. At Edington the roofs still retain their fourteenth century
colouring.

But by far the greater number of examples belong to the perpendicular or third pointed period. In some few instances the whole
of the roofs are painted, but, as a rule, only the eastern bay of the
nave above the roodloft, or the east end of the aisles, or other special
portions of the churches, retain traces of their former decorations.
Perhaps the most interesting examples are to be found at St. Alban's
Cathedral. The roof over the choir to the west of the tower is flat,
and divided into a series of panels, on which are painted angels
holding the shields of the principal benefactors to the Abbey, round
and across which are scrolls with sentences from the "Te Deum."
On the central panels are the Coronation of the Virgin, and shields
charged with the instruments of the Passion, and the Trinity banner.
These panels seems to have been originally painted about the year
1390, and to have been restored and partially repainted between 1440
and 1460. The roof over the Presbytery and retrochoir is also of
wood, of high pitch, and embellished with a series of representations
within medallions, of the eagle of St. John the Evangelist, and the

lamb of St. John the Baptist, the patron saints of Abbot John de Whetehamstede, during whose rule in the fifteenth century the painting was executed. Some very well designed foliage patterns are also introduced, and the whole presents us with an admirable specimen of the decorative art of that period. At Ufford the roofs all retain traces of colour and gilding, the main beams and wall plate being most elaborately painted. At Blythburgh the fine though sadly decayed roofs exhibit traces of rich decoration, with the sacred monogram and floral patterns on the beams, and angels holding shields at the intersections. The roofs at Randworth, which were destroyed early in the present century, are recorded to have been very rich both in carving and gilding. At St. Mary's Church, Beverley, all the roofs appear to have been coloured; that over the nave previously to 1829, representing a serene sky with stars of gold; that over the choir has been repainted, and much of its interest has been thereby destroyed. On a numerous series of panels are depicted portraits of the kings of England from the mythical Brutus down to Henry VI., in whose reign the work was carried out. At Brant Broughton the nave roof has been very richly painted, as also at Kelshall, where the colouring has been renewed. At Southwold all the roofs seem to have been coloured; the eastern bay of the nave over the roodloft has been most highly decorated with angels with scrolls, and the implements of the Passion. At Ludlow, the roof over the nave and aisles had been magnificently coloured. At Necton, supporting the nave roof, are sculptured figures of Our Lord and six Apostles on one side, and of St. Mary the Virgin and the remaining Apostles on the other, all highly illuminated. At Ilsington, within image tabernacles supporting the nave roof, are several figures in oak, still bearing traces of chromatic decoration. At Aldenham the beams of the nave roof have been repainted; the design exhibited some unusual decoration; also angels holding shields, &c., on the principal timbers. At Meldreth are remains of delicate colouring on the east beam and along the wall plate of the nave roof. At Edingthorpe the two eastern bays of the nave roof have been richly painted, while at the neighbouring church of Knapton, the nave roof has been enriched with figures under canopies, angels, &c. At Biggleswade and Furneaux Pelham are still remaining good examples of painted roofs, and at St. Mary's and St. Martin's, Leicester, rich specimens were also formerly to be seen. In the chancel at Mapledurham, and the nave at Knowle, the ceilings have been painted and further embellished with a powdering of gilded metal stars, a not uncommon form of decoration, as, fo · instance, at Swimbridge and Payhembury. At St. Mary's, Bury St. Edmunds, the east bay of the magnificent nave roof has been re- painted. At the east end of the south aisle, above the monument of John Barrett, the roof is elaborately painted with various mottoes and monograms. At St. John's Maddermarket, Norwich, the ceilings over the east end of the aisles are divided into numerous painted panels, those in the north aisle portraying angels holding labels with sentences from the "Te Deum," and the name "Jesus" within a crown of thorns; those in the south aisle, angels bearing the legend "Ave Maria," and the name "Maria" crowned. At East Dereham, in the north aisle are depicted the two-headed eagle, and the initial "T" with martyr's crown, and in the south aisle the "Agnus Dei." These eagles seem to have been the insignia of certain guilds, and occur in a similar situation at Horstead, Redenhall, and the ancient chapel of the Hospital of St. Giles, Norwich. The eastern portion of the nave ceiling of Rainham Church, Kent, is divided into very large panels, each decorated with a large "rose en soleil," the badge of Edward IV. The roofs of Chantry Chapels at St. Mary's, Stamford, and Wellingborough are panelled, and exhibit a variety of painted decorations. In some late examples the panelled ceilings represent the heavens, with clouds, the sun, moon, and stars, as at Maids Moreton and elsewhere. At Empingham cherubs are also introduced.

In buildings other than churches, not a great many examples of coloured woodwork have survived to our time. At Monk's Horton Priory the ceiling of an upper room was flat and panelled, and on each panel was painted the sacred monogram within a crown of thorns. These panels, which were of the time of Edward III., were removed about the year 1840. At Castle Acre Priory, in a room belonging to the Prior's lodgings, is some panelling on which are painted red and white roses, indicating the date of their execution. At Icomb Place, and at an old inn at Kelvedon is some linen panelling with its original colouring. At Alfold House some of the ancient decoration remains on the beams and elsewhere in the hall. At the Old Blue Boar Inn, Leicester, on the roof of a room on the second story, painted scroll work appears on the principal beams, while at the Court House, Brinsop "there is some of the finest "timber work with polychrome in a very perfect state." At Queen's College, Cambridge, the roof of the chapel retains its 15th century colouring. At Baston Manor House a series of panels were found in one of the rooms on which were depicted numerous royal personages, only king Athelstan and Richard III. could be identified. At Amberley Castle, once the palace and stronghold of the bishops of Chichester, a similar series of panels formerly existed with representations of Sinope, Cassandra, &c. These have now been removed and are in private possession. They are supposed to have been painted by Theodore Bernardi, who is known for the works which he carried out under bishop Sherborne at Chichester Cathedral and Boxgrove. In an upper room in the tower of Pengersick Castle, "on the wainscot round the upper part of the "room are pictures in miniature, proverbs divided, and betwixt the "divisions, verses, all serving to illustrate each other, and to "enforce some moral instruction." These are of the time of Henry VIII. At Chalfield Manor House the hall screen still retains its coloring, and at an old house at Keavil the gallery in the hall has armorial shields depicted upon it.

A few remarks may here fitly be introduced on the subject of the destruction of the ancient paintings, and the adoption of a new order of church decoration in post Reformation times. It seems doubtful as to what changes took place at once with regard to the arrangement of church furniture, and the obliteration of the former venerated paintings, and it is probable that little was done except the public destruction of such images, &c., as had become notorious for the superstitious reverence with which they had been regarded, and for the miracles supposed to have been worked by them upon those who came to worship at their shrines. In many cases no doubt texts were painted over the existing pictures, but as has been mentioned, it was already a common custom to paint one series of subjects over those previously occupying the coveted position, the indifference to the works which had been executed at the cost of, and venerated by, their ancestors, being a remarkable feature of all ages. During the reign of Queen Mary an attempt was made to re-establish the former order of things, and we might expect to meet both with mural and panel paintings of this period. Perhaps the only certain examples were those on the walls of Becket's crown at Canterbury Cathedral, above the tomb of Cardinal Pole, which included a large and very poor representation of St. Christopher, now destroyed. In the beginning of the reign of Queen Elizabeth a stronger feeling seems to have been aroused against all relics of the popish religion, doubtless animated by the bitter intolerance displayed by the Papists during the brief period of the renewal of their supremacy during the preceding reign. Thus we have records of orders being sent out to destroy all images and to replace the paintings on the walls by texts from scripture. As an example, may be mentioned the following case, viz., of Thomas Lockwood, dean of Christchurch, Oxford, who received orders in 1559 to remove all popish relics and images, and to put sentences of scripture on the walls instead of "pictures and other like fancies," which was done. Thus we constantly meet with texts of the latter part of the 16th century, often within very elaborate borders. In the crypt at Canterbury Cathedral are a series of this date, and on the piers of the choir at St. Albans Cathedral are lengthy New Testament sentences in blue letter. Of more elaborate subjects the most common were the pictures of time and death, which seem to be all of post reformation date, and only a few of them as early as the 16th century. One of the earliest instances of this subject was found at Nuneaton, but is not now to be seen. The representations of Moses, Aaron, and king David, seem to have been common both in mural painting, and on panel and canvas throughout the 16th and 17th centuries. The series of paintings of the patriarchs at Hargrave and Burton Latimer are certainly as late as the reign of Queen Elizabeth, if not later. At Martock the apostles are similarly portrayed.

Of early 17th century paintings, a few instances of which have been included in an Appendix to the present work, some curious and interesting examples have come to light. In the nave of Exeter

Cathedral various heraldic bearings of this period have been recently discovered. At Bratoft, over the chancel arch, is depicted the destruction of the Spanish Armada. At Hadleigh (Suffolk) was a wall painting representing the interior of a church destroyed in 1834. Over the south door of Stevington church was a scene portraying a judge and two other figures, a text, and the date 1633. At Great St. Helen's Church, London, a series of paintings of the apostles and saints of about the year 1630 has been destroyed, and at St. Andrew Undershaft, also in London, were scenes from the life of Christ, and whole length figures of apostles and other saints of about the same date. In the chapel of Lytes Cary Manor House are numerous armorial shields, and in that of the Castle of Farleigh Hungerford, are considerable remains of wall decoration, viz., figures of apostles, coats of arms, &c., and a very interesting representation of St. George on foot and clad in the armour in vogue during the middle of the 17th century. Of paintings on panel, only three instances have been deemed worthy of being recorded. At St. Andrew Undershaft, London, on the roof of the sacrarium was the angelic choir in adoration. Another example is from Woolborough Church, where are four panel paintings of the Evangelists, probably dating from the reign of James I. The third is at Terrington St. Clements, where the interior of the font cover, which bears the date 1635, has paintings on the inner panels, representing the baptism of our Lord, two scenes from the Temptation and other subjects. It was about the middle of the 17th century, during the supremacy of the Commonwealth, that most of the wall paintings, &c., were obliterated, and such records as the journal of William Dowsing, relating his achievements in the eastern counties, prove to us the fanaticism of the Puritans, and their zeal not only in destroying all superstitious pictures and images, but also in recklessly mutilating ancient monuments and all the objects commemorating the piety and religious enthusiasm of their forefathers. This wholesale destruction of so many gems of early ecclesiastical art, though possibly at the time deemed a work of necessity, in order to crush finally the hopes and aspirations of the Roman Catholic party, cannot be too deeply deplored at the present day, as we can now only imagine or picture to ourselves the ancient splendour of our churches during the middle ages. Much has also been done through the neglect of those entrusted with the maintenance of the fabrics, or by the want of taste of successive generations of churchwardens during the past and early years of the present century, still further to reduce the store of objects of art, and to increase the number of those, the existence of which has been recorded, but of which no traces remain at the present day. Even during the present more enlightened times, incalculable injury has been done in the destruction of wall paintings, the sweeping away of screens, and the obliteration of all features of interest or antiquity in a church under the comprehensive title of restoration. It is certainly a sad, though undeniable fact, that there are but few cases where, during the necessary repairs of a church, many objects of archæological value have not disappeared owing to the want of supervision of those who should have made it their business to preserve them. It is perhaps hardly advisable to enlarge further upon these points here, but should the publication of this list produce a greater interest in the objects with which it deals, much will have been gained.*

It only now remains to allude to the post reformation paintings found in buildings which are not ecclesiastical. At Mendham Priory considerable remains of decorative painting of about the year 1550 existed on the walls of the buildings which had been erected on the site of the ancient Priory. So, too, on the walls of the banqueting hall at Lanercost Priory, various cinque cento designs, an armed figure, &c., have been noticed. In the Priors chamber at Shulbrede Priory, Sussex, some quaint paintings of the Nativity, &c., have been assigned to as late a date as the time of James I. At Paynes Place, Bushley, are couplets of verse on a white ground, circ. 1550. At Leven's Hall are shields of arms in plaster with their tinctures properly blazoned. At the Bury, Rickmansworth, on a wall apparently prepared for panelling, and partly in the timber work, are a series of representations of a decorative pattern in red, black, and white, probably of the time of Queen Elizabeth. At an old house at Great Berkhampstead were found beneath the panelling, some wall paintings of serving men, &c., and similar objects of somewhat later date have been noticed at Eastbury House, Barking, Essex. At the Manor House, Medbourn, have been found some interesting paintings representing an esquire, ladies, &c., which are late 16th or early 17th century work. On the wall of a room at the old Crown Inn, Rochester, was some late 16th century decoration, now destroyed. At West Stow Hall, in an upper chamber of the gate-house, are depicted the Ages of Man, and in an old house at Woodford, Essex, are 12 subjects exhibiting as many scenes from rural life, and dated 1617. At the ancient college of Wye, Kent, on the walls of a Jacobean staircase, are painted large representations of truth, justice, charity, &c., and on the staircase itself are coloured sculptured figures of warriors and other personages. A date, 1622, occurs on the wall. In the upper room of a house at Monken Hadley is depicted a stag hunt of the time of James I., and as a last instance may be mentioned a painting on the panel of the door of an upper chamber at the Manor House, Little Gaddesden, apparently of about the year

---

* It is a common thing to read in accounts of the restoration of churches such phrases as "The walls have been scraped and repointed," "The several coats of whitewash have "been removed, and the walls replastered," and other similar expressions. In both these cases, as a rule, the following simple process is employed. By the aid of a chisel and hammer the whole of the layers of whitewash, including those early courses on which the paintings have been executed, are rudely hacked away, no attempt being made to preserve or ascertain the subjects of these mementoes of mediæval times. It is no matter of surprise, then, that where this harsh treatment is adopted, one so often receives the answer to one's queries, that no discoveries have been made worthy of being recorded during the course of the restoration of the church. The unfortunate and somewhat prevalent practice of leaving the rough interior surface of the walls bare has already been commented upon and unhesitatingly condemned.

1554, representing an event which happened in that year, namely, the Princess, afterwards Queen, Elizabeth being summoned by Lord Howard to repair to London.

Such is a brief epitome of the history of this interesting subject, and a description of and reference to the most striking examples of the mural paintings and other painted decorations still or till recently existing, and it is sincerely hoped that it may prove of service to those anxious to cultivate a more intimate knowledge of this branch of art. It now only remains to explain the method employed and the ingredients and composition of the colours made use of by the artists, and then in conclusion to describe the most safe and effective mode of removing the washes or varnish by which the several subjects have been overlaid, and of preserving and bringing out the colours of the pictures when again exposed to view. In order to obtain the most valuable information on these points, the assistance of two of the greatest authorities in these matters has been solicited, and their consent has been most kindly and freely accorded. Their contributions which doubtless form the most important portion of this essay are herein-after fully set out, and are specially commended to the notice of all who are anxious to preserve these memorials of the piety of our ancestors during the middle ages, or who may take a general interest in the subject, and may wish to become more fully cognisant of an art, which is still imperfectly understood and appreciated.

C. E. KEYSER, M.A., F.S.A.

· The methods employed by our mediæval artists were of simplest character, particularly in the wall paintings of our churches. The latter were executed in "tempera," an Italian term represented by the English "distemper." It means no more than that which mixes or tempers the colours, and might be applied to any vehicle whatever. · But as generally understood, in former times as now, it is applied to that vehicle made of parchment size, or the superior egg-medium, i.e. eggs beat up with the juice of shoots of the fig-tree, but vinegar can also be used with the same effect. We have proof that both species of tempera were known and practised in England; but the former must always have been that used on walls, and it is this that we see in our mediæval churches. Both are of the greatest antiquity, known to Greeks and Romans, and also to the ancient Egyptians. Under reasonable conditions it is very durable, as indeed is shown by works executed in this manner enduring for many centuries the humidity of our climate and all kinds of neglect.

As regards the superior egg-medium it was chiefly employed in painting upon wood or panel, and when in our records we see the term "tabula" it either refers to a movable picture, as above an altar, or to those executed in panels on a screen. The practice in Italy did not differ in this respect. The use of the term "tempera" as restricted to the above processes, was gradual, as even Vasari occasionly applies it even to oil as "tempering" colours. But when the term "fresco" was in familiar use for painting on the *fresh* or wet plaster, and oil vehicles became general, it naturally was convenient to keep the word "tempera" to the process when it was first applied.

Our archæologists, though often corrected, still frequently call our mediæval wall paintings "frescoes." It is obviously most improper, as even the "fresco buono" of the Italians was not completely developed until the 14th century, though the system was known to the Greeks and Romans.

The colours generally used were of the commonest kind. Mostly earths, as in fresco, or of some mineral origin. The chief were colcotha or Indian red, for they are nearly the same, red ochre, yellow ochre, terra verte, verditer and native cinnabar. Neither of the two last are used in fresco painting, and verditer, both blue and green, are colours which fade and change very easily. To these may be added "lamp black" and white, made from lime. Cinnabar, which stands in the place of vermilion, grows black in contact with lime, and this accounts for some reds turning quite black, probably assisted by damp. All our earliest paintings are monochromes, or very nearly so.

As regards the decoration of oaken screens of which the Eastern counties show many fine examples, both "tempera" and oil were used. Indeed the latter was very much employed in this country, in early times, as our records prove. But it is very doubtful if this was for any delicate work. Many of the screens in Norfolk and Suffolk prove the influence of the Flemish artist, and we know many migrations from Flanders took place, bringing them superior manufactures, and doubtless a superior art practice. If we presume the use of oil in the painting of these screens, it seems always to have been applied on a ground of gesso, just as in preparation of panels by painters of both Flemish and Italian schools. But we cannot be sure that many which now seem to us as painted in oil were not first executed in tempera and afterwards varnished. It is, however, of little importance. But there are specimens of tempera simply, as well as in oil, or tempera varnished.

On the screens we get a superior range of colours; a finer blue, brighter green, a preparation probably of vermilion. The gilding is excellent, and in one or two instances, late in the 15th century, stamped processes are used for such parts as the shafts of the canopy, executed with much beauty and subtlety. Yaxley, Suffolk, offers an example.

As regards the best mode of removing whitewash from the underlying painting on walls, much depends upon the state of the latter. If these be sound and firm, an ordinary knife, if flexible, and thin from wear the better, can be used, or even a chisel, the rest depending on the care of the manipulator. But there will always be some portions still adherent, due to inequality of the surface and to other reasons. This may be removed by carefully damping with a squeezed out sponge, and again applying the knife, which then easily removes what remains. Even yet portions of white upon the colours will tend to render them fainter, but by a careful manipulation with diluted vinegar, cast on in a spray, this will disappear as the acid takes up and decomposes the lime. A spray of fresh water may afterwards follow to remove redundant acid. This process seems elaborate in description, but is less so in practice, but it depends, as all others, on the judgment and skill of the manipulator.

But should it happen, as it often does, that one series of paintings covers another, the removal of the whitewash from the upper series, and that alone, is not so easy. The second series will be on a ground laid over the other, with which the superincumbent whitewash will have a tendency to combine, and the chances are all will come away together. This, however, may often disclose the more interesting earlier series; possibly on the same subject; as was the case at Raunds, in Northamptonshire. Here the life of St. Katharine which has been uncovered, preserves some of two periods, viz., 14th century and late in 15th.

In discussing the mode of preserving these paintings by a varnish, it must be well considered. On stone, or upon a sound wall, no doubt some such manipulation may be very effective, if properly done. But the decay of wall-painting when exposed to the air, damp, &c., arises from the loss of the material by which the colours were originally tempered. The medium is not so durable as the colours, and damp succeeded by dryness, and the variations of our climate, tend to its disintegration; it comes off in dust or powder. This even takes place in "fresco buono," as may be seen in many churches in Italy, giving rise to the report of the colours fading. The colours do not fade, they simply disintegrate and fall off in dust.

To restore to the decaying tempera painting, the medium it has partially lost, could be done by means of a spray, casting upon the surface a dilution of size in alcohol and water to make it sufficiently thin for the process. This could be done to any wall, however soft, with success; but a hard varnish upon a soft wall would certainly hasten the decay.

J. G. WALLER.

The first step in the preservation of mural paintings in distemper is the complete removal of the whitewash, with which, in most cases, they have been coated. For this purpose I prefer ivory, bone or horn spatulas, thin at the end, but not pointed. These generally prove sufficiently powerful, but occasionally steel implements are necessary. Whatever the material, the working end of the instrument should be ground in such a way as to present a very slightly curved edge, not the usual semi-circular form. It may sometimes be necessary to assist the action of the spatula by means of slips of linen, wetted with hot strong glue, ironed on to the whitewash, and allowed to dry there before being torn off. Bellows and badger hair *softeners* are useful to clear away dust and reveal the work. They must always be used (or, if needed, stencil brushes) before applying the reviving, fixing and waterproofing liquid, which is made by the following recipe :—

Melt 2 ounces by weight of pure white beeswax, and pour the melted wax into 6 ounces by measure of oil of spike lavender or oil of orange peel. Warm the mixture until it is clear, and then add—

10 ounces by measure of picture copal varnish and 26 ounces of freshly distilled spirits of turpentine.

The above mixture is to be applied warm by means of a broad flat soft brush to the wall picture. Sometimes it is necessary, if the colour be at all easily detached to apply the fixing liquid to the wall by means of a *spray producer.* A scent distributor worked by an india-rubber ball, by bellows, or by Fletcher's foot-blower will answer.

Shelsley, Ennerdale Road, Kew,   A. H. CHURCH,
    26th January 1883.   *Professor of Chemistry in the
        Royal Academy of Arts.*

A LIST

OF

Buildings in Great Britain and Ireland having Mural and other Painted Decorations of Dates prior to the latter part of the 16th Century.

ABBEY DORE CHURCH, HEREFORDSHIRE.

Paintings and floral decorations of the 15th cent. *Murray's Handbook of Herefordshire. Archæologia Cambrensis*, 3rd series, xiii. 403.

On W. wall of choir; figures of King David and "Time." *J. H. James, Some Account of the Churches of Abbey Dore, &c.*, p. 4. *N. Stephenson, Hist. of Llanthony Abbey, &c.*, p. 27.

ABBOTSBURY CHURCH, DORSETSHIRE.

E. end of S. aisle; The Resurrection. ? Early 16th cent. Defaced in 1750. *Hutchins' History of Dorset*, 3rd ed., ii. 730.

ABERDEEN, ABERDEENSHIRE, ST. MACHAR'S CATHEDRAL.

Remains of colour and gilding on nave ceiling, and 48 armorial shields. *Billing's Antiquities of Scotland*, vol. i. *Antiquarian Cabinet*, vol. ix.

ABERGAVENNY CHURCH, MONMOUTHSHIRE.

Colour on the wooden effigy of George de Cantilupe, circ. 1275 ; on the canopies above the heads of Sir William Ap Thomas and his lady, and on the figures on slabs forming the lower part of the monument, circ. 1450. These probably were originally parts of a reredos.

Painted shields on, and colouring on sculpture at head of, monument of Richard Herbert of Ewias Harold, circ. 1510. *O. Morgan, The Abergavenny Monuments*, pp. 22, 42, 43, 64, 65. *Murray's Handbook of South Wales.*

ABINGDON, BERKSHIRE, ST. HELEN'S CHURCH.

Ceiling of N. aisle ; painted with full-length figures of royal personages of the family of Jesse and Prophets, a genealogy of Our Lord, time of Henry VI. ? Originally part of a screen. *Blackburne, Decorative Painting*, p. 45.

ABINGTON, GREAT, CHURCH, CAMBRIDGESHIRE.
N. wall of nave; part of a text. S. of chancel, on head of containing arch, band of colour.

ACLE CHURCH, NORFOLK.
Original colouring on font, circ. 1410. *East Anglian Notes and Queries*, ii. 28.

ACONBURY CHURCH, HEREFORDSHIRE.
Paintings, restored. *Havergal, Fasti Herefordenses*, p. 157.
On either side of W. window mural paintings; *destroyed.*
In S.W. corner, within a small chamber; ? an oratory, the Salutation, restored.

ACRE, CASTLE, CHURCH, NORFOLK.
Rood screen, pulpit, and font. *Civil Engineer and Architect's Journ.*, 1860, p. 5. *East Anglian Notes and Queries*, iii. 291.
On the panels of the screen; Our Lord and the Apostles.
On panels of pulpit; the four doctors of the Church.
Ceiling, E. end of N. aisle; a diaper of crowned " M"s and lilies.
Ceiling, E. end of S. aisle; a diaper of crowned " N"s with mitre above.
Chapels, E. end of aisles; coloured panelling.
Painted and gilt font cover repainted. *Blomefield, (Parkin,) Hist. of Norfolk*, ed. 1808, viii. 362. *Bloom Notices of Castle Acre, Hist. and Antiq.*, pp. 281–293.

ACRE, CASTLE, PRIORY, NORFOLK.
The Prior's lodgings; the panelling at the E. end of a room is painted with red and white roses. *Britton's Architectural Antiquities*, iii. 16. *Blackburne, Decorative Painting*, p. 46.
Similar paintings on the ceilings of all the rooms; time of Henry VII.
Carving on hearths, coloured scarlet.
Prior's Chapel; emblazoned shields of England and De Warenne, time of Henry VI.
On E. wall; "traces of an elaborate painting representing pinnacled canopies and shrine work, surmounted by what appears to be an inscription." *Bloom, Notices of Castle Acre, Hist. and Antiq.*, pp. 241–245. *Chambers, Hist. of Norfolk*, i. 381.

ACRE, SOUTH, CHURCH, NORFOLK.
Screen across N. aisle. *Chambers, Hist. of Norfolk,* ii. 662.
Traces of colour on the rood screen now under the tower. Date about 1350.
Remains of gilding and colour on the font cover. About 1500.

ADDERBURY CHURCH, OXFORDSHIRE.
Canopied niches of the reredos. *Gent. Mag.,* 1834, i. new series, 163.
Interesting paintings destroyed.
A head of a bishop, late 14th cent. ; in private possession.

ADDINGTON, GREAT, NORTHAMPTONSHIRE, ALL SAINTS' CHURCH.
Paintings, whitewashed over. Old wood panelling retaining the original painting worked up into pews. *Churches of the Archdeaconry of Northampton,* p. 98.

ADDLETHORPE CHURCH, LINCOLNSHIRE.
Painted roofs.
Roof of porch ; remains of colour.
Chancel screen ; enriched with colour and gilding.
Associated Architect. Societies' Repts., viii. 80.
Oldfield, Topog. and Hist. Account of Wainfleet, pp. 105, 106.

ADVENT CHURCH, CORNWALL.
Remains of colour and gilding on the nave roof. Date 15th cent. *Murray's Handbook of Cornwall. Exeter Diocesan Architect. Soc.,* v. 110. *Maclean, Hist. of the Deanery of Trigg Minor,* ii. 319.

ALBURGH CHURCH, NORFOLK.
Over N. door; St. Christopher. *Blomefield, Hist. of Norfolk,* ed. 1806, v. 354. *Chambers, Hist. of Norfolk,* i. 134.

ALBURY CHURCH, HERTFORDSHIRE.
N.E. corner of N. aisle; colouring on the effigies of Walter de la Lee and Lady, circ. 1396. *Cussans, Hist. of Hertfordshire,* vol. i., pt. ii., p. 166.

ALDBURGH CHURCH, NORFOLK.
Over N. door; St. Christopher. *Blackburne, Decorative Painting,* p. 16.

ALDBURY CHURCH, HERTFORDSHIRE.
N. side of chancel within the splay of a window; floral pattern.

ALDENHAM CHURCH, HERTFORDSHIRE.
Ceiling. *Civil Engineer and Architect's Journal,* 1851, p. 196.
E. wall of N. aisle; diaper pattern, &c. 15th cent. Partly whitewashed over.
Also "The Trinity" and the emblems of the Evangelists. An Elizabethan text has been painted over it. Whitewashed over.
Blackburne, Decorative Painting, p. 14.
Nave roof; scroll ornament, &c. Middle of 15th cent.
Blackburne, Decorative Painting, pp. 79, 80.
Screen of chapel, E. end of S. aisle; tracery, scroll ornament, banding, &c. Late 15th cent. Lithographed in *Blackburne, Decorative Painting,* p. 81.

ALDWINCLE ST. PETER'S CHURCH, NORTHAMPTONSHIRE.
Chancel; on either side of chancel arch two paintings, ? Consecration Crosses. *Associated Architect. Societies' Repts.,* vii. 243.

ALFOLD CHURCH, SURREY.
Over E. window; the Crucifixion.
On N. side of nave; flowerpots with lilies and roses. Recovered with whitewash.
Surrey Archæol., vi. 16.

ALFOLD HOUSE, SURREY.
Colouring on the beams and elsewhere in the hall, and on a doorway in the upper story. Date about 1500.
Surrey Archæol., vi. 18.

ALFORD CHURCH, LINCOLNSHIRE.
Lower part of screen; remains of gold and colour.
Associated Architect. Societies' Repts., x., xii.
On soffit of chancel arch; remains of figures enclosed within vesica-shaped medallions. 14th cent.

ALFRISTON CHURCH, SUSSEX.
Painting of the Doom, whitewashed over. *Neale and Webb's Durandus,* note p. 57.
N. wall of N. transept; St. Catherine. *J. M. Neale, Hierologus,* p. 295.

ALKERTON CHURCH, OXFORDSHIRE.
Walls and arches; extensive remains of early paintings.
Beesley, Hist. of Banbury, pp. 109, 143.

ALLESTREE CHURCH, DERBYSHIRE.

W. end of nave ; scroll patterns.

On either side of E. window ; Black-letter (Elizabethan) texts.

J. C. Cox, Churches of Derbyshire, iv. 296.

ALLEXTON CHURCH, LEICESTERSHIRE.

N. side of nave; colouring on two Norman arches. Not now visible. *Leicester Architect. and Archæol. Soc. Trans.,* ii. 172.

ALMELEY CHURCH, SHROPSHIRE.

E. part of nave roof; painted panels. Tudor period. *Archæologia Cambrensis,* 3rd series, ix. 373.

ALMONDBURY CHURCH, YORKSHIRE.

Inscription round the church below the roof. Date 1522. *Murray's Handbook of Yorkshire.*

ALNWICK CHURCH, NORTHUMBERLAND.

Coloured and gilt effigy of a king, ? Henry VI., with purse, rosary, globe, and sceptre, dug up in 1816. *A Descriptive and Hist. Account of Alnwick,* 2nd ed. 1822, p. 199. *Tate, Hist. of Alnwick,* ii. 111. *Mackenzie, View of the County of Northumberland,* i. 438.

ALPHINGTON CHURCH, DEVONSHIRE.

Rood screen.

ALREWAS CHURCH, STAFFORDSHIRE.

On the N. wall of the chancel ; a bishop accompanied by an acolyte, in the attitude of benediction. Date 15th cent.

ALTHAM CHURCH, LANCASHIRE.

Pillars, arches, and S. wall, decorated with a geo-metrical pattern, discovered in 1859 and destroyed.

W. A. Waddington, Architectural Sketches on the Calder and Ribble, article iii.

Murray's Handbook of Lancashire.

ALTON CHURCH, HAMPSHIRE.

Scenes in life of Christ, and portraits of King Henry VI. and several bishops. 15th cent. *Murray's Handbook of Hampshire. Black's Guide to Hampshire. Moody, Sketches of Hampshire,* p. 107.

ALVELEY CHURCH, SHROPSHIRE.
E. end of S. aisle; wall paintings. *Church Times*, 1879, p. 766.
S. wall of chapel; decorative colour. Representations of Time and Death.

ALVESCOTT CHURCH, OXFORDSHIRE.
Perpendicular chapel on S. side of chancel; painted and gilt ceiling. *Parker, Eccles. and Architect. Topog. of England, Oxford*, No. 176.
S. transept roof; painted panels with gilded stars and bosses. Three Consecration Crosses. *Antiquary*, 1872, ii. 105.

ALVINGTON, WEST, CHURCH, DEVONSHIRE.
Screen; repainted.

AMBERLEY CASTLE, SUSSEX.
The Queen's Room; Sinope, Cassandra, &c., said to have been painted by a Fleming, Theodore Bernardi. Early 16th cent. (On panels, removed.) *Archæol. Journ.*, xxii. 65. *Society of Antiquaries' Proceedings*, 2nd series, iii. 28. *Sussex Archæol.*, xvii. 205. *British Archæol. Assoc. Journ.*, xx. 315.
Removed to Parham.

AMBERLEY CHURCH, SUSSEX.
N.E. corner of S. aisle; The Virgin and Child, a priest, &c.
S. wall of S. aisle; the Salutation and other fragments. *Sussex Archæol.*, xvii. 231.
S. side of chancel arch and E. wall of S. aisle; Scripture texts with earlier painting below.
N. wall of nave; a consecration Cross. Early 12th cent.
Black's Guide to Sussex. Archæologia, xlvii. 165.

AMERSHAM CHURCH, BUCKINGHAMSHIRE.
N. aisle; mural paintings discovered and *destroyed*.

AMPNEY CRUCIS CHURCH, GLOUCESTERSHIRE.
Texts from the Bible, the Commandments, and the Lord's Prayer painted on the walls; Martyrdom of St. Erasmus.
N. wall; St. Christopher, with inscription. Signed "Thomas ye payntre of Malmesburie," in Black letters. (Much dilapidated.)

AMPNEY CRUCIS CHURCH, GLOUCESTERSHIRE—*cont.*

Les Trois Morts et Les Trois Vifs (?). 15th cent. (All plastered over again, 1871.)

Over chancel arch; the General Resurrection, part of a Doom. (Of later date than the former paintings.)
Ampney Crucis Parish Mag., May and June 1871 *Extract in the Art Library, South Kensington Museum.*

Remains of colour on the roofs. *British Archæol. Assoc. Journ.,* xxv. 193.

Remains of colour on wall pieces and trusses. *Bristol and Gloucestershire Archæol. Soc. Transactions,* 1877–8, pt. i. p. 23.

AMPORT CHURCH, HAMPSHIRE.

Let in to S. wall of S. transept; an iconuela, or small alabaster tablet, on which is sculptured the head of St. John the Baptist on a charger; above, two angels holding a napkin enclosing a soul; below, Our Saviour rising from the tomb; on either side, St. Peter, a royal abbess, ? St. Etheldreda, an archbishop, or abbot, and St. Catherine, all richly painted and gilt. Date circ. 1500. Found while pulling down an old house in the parish.

AMPTHILL CHURCH, BEDFORDSHIRE.

Over the porch; a painting formerly existed. *Ecclesiologist,* viii. 245.

ANWICK CHURCH, LINCOLNSHIRE.

Painted sculpture of the Virgin and Child; found in the rood loft staircase in 1859. *Trollope: Sleaford, Flaxwell, Aswardhurn,* p. 192. *Associated Architect. Societies' Repts.,* v.. xxi.

ARDELEY, OR YARDLEY, CHURCH, HERTFORDSHIRE.

S. wall of nave; St. Christopher.

S. aisle; red colouring.

Over chancel arch; angel blowing a trumpet, probably part of a Doom.

On either side of E. window; painted and gilt niche.
A Guide to Hertfordshire, 1881, p. 129.

ARDLEIGH CHURCH, ESSEX.

N. wall of nave; mural paintings destroyed in 1840. *Church Builder,* 1880, p. 26.

ARDSLEY, WEST. *See* WOODCHURCH.

ARELEY, UPPER, CHURCH, STAFFORDSHIRE.
Nave roof; traces of colour. *Garner, Natural History of the County of Stafford*, supplement, p. 33.

ARLESEY CHURCH, BEDFORDSHIRE.
E. beam of nave roof; pattern of chevrons. 15th cent.

ARLINGTON CHURCH, SUSSEX.
N. chancel chapel; on jamb of E. window, floral ornament.

ARMINGHALL CHURCH, NORFOLK.
St. Christopher; a diaper of the letter "A," with a consecration Cross below, and a text. 16th cent. *Destroyed. Norfolk Archæol.*, viii. 334.

ARRETON CHURCH, ISLE OF WIGHT.
On a window in the chancel; traces of a scroll pattern.
Scroll patterns discovered in the chancel, and *destroyed*.

ARUNDEL CHURCH, SUSSEX.
N. wall of N. aisle:—Over N. door; The Seven Deadly Sins. The Seven Acts of Mercy. *Restored. Archæologia*, xxxviii. 432. *Also British Archæol. Assoc. Journ.*, vi. 440. *Ecclesiologist*, xviii. 341. *Black's Guide to Sussex. Nibbs' Churches of Sussex*, No. 55.
An Angel holding the cloak of a Saint, part of a large painting.
S. wall of S. aisle; large and indistinct subject.
Several consecration Crosses remain. Date about 1390.
Fitz Alan or College Chapel; traces of colour visible through the whitewash.
Remains of gilding on the monument of Thomas Fitz Alan, Earl of Arundel. Date about 1415. *Blore's Monumental Remains of Noble and Eminent Persons.*
Remains of colour on the effigies of John Fitz Alan, Earl of Arundel, circ. 1434; and of William Fitz Alan, Earl of Arundel, and Lady, circ. 1487. *Stothard's Monumental Effigies*, pls. 119 and 137.
Effigy of the Virgin, richly painted and gilt: dug up in 1847. *Sussex Archæol.*, iii. 87.

ASGARBY CHURCH, LINCOLNSHIRE.
N. wall, E. end of N. aisle; painting of an Angel with scrolls. End of 15th cent. *Trollope: Sleaford, Flaxwell, Aswardhurn*, p. 331.

ASH, KENT, ST. NICHOLAS CHURCH.
Walls of N. transept; fragments of figures and scroll
and masonry patterns. *British Archæol. Assoc. Journ.*,
xx. 88. *J. R. Planché, A corner of Kent, Ash-next-
Sandwich*, p. 181 note.
N. side of chancel; painting and gilding on a cross-
legged effigy. *Glynne, Churches of Kent*, p. 128.
Archæol. Journ., viii. 302.

ASHBOURN CHURCH, DERBYSHIRE.
Monument of John and Edmund Cokayne, painted
panels. Circ. 1404.
S. transept; painted shields on monument of Sir
Humphrey Bradborne. Circ. 1580.
J. C. Cox, Churches of Derbyshire, ii. 382, 389.

ASHBURTON CHURCH, DEVONSHIRE.
S. aisle roof; painted panels. *Destroyed. Gent.
Mag.*, 1849, xxxi. new series, 194.
Screen, removed, formerly had figures of the Apostles
on the panels, sculptured in relief and painted.
Portions of a painted effigy found in the chancel.
C. Worthy, Ashburton and its Neighbourhood, pp. 11,
17, 18.

ASHBY CHURCH, SUFFOLK.
Last Judgment, St. Catherine, St. William of Norwich,
and history of St. Wulstan. All covered with a fresh
coat of whitewash.

ASHBY FOLVILLE CHURCH, LEICESTERSHIRE.
Panels and lower part of screen painted; traces of
colour on the roof; renewed in a different style.

ASHBY ST. LEGER'S CHURCH, NORTHAMPTONSHIRE.
Traces of colour on the rood screen.
Deacon, Hist. of Willoughby, p. 96.

ASHBY, CASTLE, CHURCH, NORTHAMPTONSHIRE.
Paintings within the splay of a chancel window. 15th
cent. *Gent. Mag.*, 1849, xxxii. new series, 185.

ASHBY, MEARS, CHURCH, NORTHAMPTONSHIRE.
Over chancel arch; the Day of Judgment. -
On wall of N. aisle; diaper pattern. *Destroyed.
Ecclesiologist*, xxi. (xviii. new series) 263, and xxv.
(xxii. new series) 305.

ASHCHURCH CHURCH, GLOUCESTERSHIRE.
Painted rood screen and loft. *Associated Architect. Societies' Repts.,* vi. 240.

ASHFORD, DEVONSHIRE, ST. PETER'S CHURCH.
W. end of N. wall; various figures. *Ecclesiologist,* vi. 40.

ASHFORD CARBONELL CHURCH, SHROPSHIRE.
Indications of painting on the walls.

ASHMANHAUGH CHURCH, NORFOLK.
Remains of screen.

ASHOVER CHURCH, DERBYSHIRE.
Rood screen; original colour and gilding scraped off in 1843. *J. C. Cox, Churches of Derbyshire,* i. 21.

ASHRIDGE HOUSE, BUCKINGHAMSHIRE.
Cloisters [or refectory or college hall]; on the walls, painted on 40 panels or compartments, passages from the life, death, and passion of Our Saviour, viz. : Our Saviour among the Doctors, His Baptism and Temptation, Miracles, Triumphal entry into Jerusalem, Last Supper, Betrayal, Trial before Pilate, Bearing the Cross, Crucifixion, Descent from the Cross, Burial, Descent into Hell, and the Ascension ; also the Trinity.
Almost all defaced in 1800. *Todd, Hist. of the College of Ashridge,* p. 58. *Sheahan, Hist. and Topog. of the County of Buckingham,* p. 732.

ASHTON CHURCH, DEVONSHIRE.
Rood screen and parclose. 15th cent.
On panels of screen ; SS. Appollonia, Barbara, Anthony, Sidwella, George, Blaize, the Virgin and Child, Mater Dolorosa; SS. John the Baptist, Stephen, Dorothy, Michael, the Four Evangelists, and Four Doctors of the Church.
In the interior of the screen; designs relating to the Resurrection, Annunciation and Visitation of the Virgin, and the Transfiguration, with scrolls.
Oliver's Ecclesiastical Antiquities of Devon, i. 195. *Exeter Diocesan Architect. Soc.,* 2nd series, ii. 90. *Ecclesiologist,* xx. 286. *Murray's Handbook of Devon.*

ASHTON KEYNES CHURCH, GLOUCESTERSHIRE.
On N. wall over the vestry door; ? the Trinity. Destroyed. *Builder,* 1877, p. 795. .

ASHTON, LONG, CHURCH, SOMERSETSHIRE.

Chancel and aisle screens ; richly painted and restored. 15th cent.

N. chapel, back of monument of Sir Richard Choke ; two Angels supporting a Glory, formerly enclosing the Crucified Saviour.

Bowman's Ecclesiastical Architecture, pp. 14, 15, plates 3–10.

Monument and effigies repainted and regilt.

ASHWELL CHURCH, RUTLANDSHIRE.

N. aisle ; wooden effigy. 14th cent.

N. chapel ; effigy of a priest, about 1500. Both shewing traces of colour and gilding.

Associated Architect. Societies' Repts., viii., lxiv. *Leicester Architect. and Archæol. Soc. Trans.*, iii. 88.

ASHWELLTHORPE CHURCH, NORFOLK.

Coloured effigies of Sir Edmund de Thorpe and Lady.

Stothard's Monumental Effigies, pl. 113.

ASLACTON CHURCH, NORFOLK.

On the font ; a painted shield.

ASTBURY CHURCH, CHESHIRE.

N. wall of nave ; a nearly obliterated painting, "the only one left of several which formerly adorned the walls," representing St. George receiving the thanks of the Princess, and the honour of knighthood from the Virgin, who holds the Infant Saviour. 15th cent. *Murray's Handbook of Cheshire.*

ASTLEY CHURCH, WARWICKSHIRE.

Coloured effigy of a lady. *W. H. H. Rogers, The Ancient Sepulchral Effigies, &c., in Devon*, p. 390.

Saints on panels over choir stalls ; removed and repainted in 1642.

Chancel ceiling ; 14th cent. decoration.

ASTLEY CHURCH, WORCESTERSHIRE.

N. chancel aisle ; coloured monument of the Blounts. Date 1561.

ASTON CHURCH, HEREFORDSHIRE.

Wall pattern. Norman period. *Kelly's Post Office Directory of Herefordshire.*

ASTON CHURCH, WARWICKSHIRE.
Coloured effigies of Sir Walter Arden and a Lady of the Arden family. *Hollis, Monumental Effigies*, pt. iv., pls. 7 and 8.

ASTON LE WALLS CHURCH, NORTHAMPTONSHIRE.
N. wall of N. aisle; St. Christopher. *Destroyed.*

ASTON, STEEPLE, CHURCH, OXFORDSHIRE.
The original painted roof has given place to a modern flat one. *W. Wing, Annals of Steeple Aston*, p. 4.

ASTWOOD CHURCH, BUCKINGHAMSHIRE.
Chancel screen. *Lipscomb, Hist. and Antiq. of Bucks,* iv. 6.

ATHELINGTON CHURCH, SUFFOLK.
Remains of rood screen, with painted mouldings and powdered panels.

ATHERINGTON CHURCH, DEVONSHIRE.
Rood screen.

ATTLEBOROUGH CHURCH, NORFOLK.
At the E. end on the inner wall; the Crucifixion.
Over the W. tower arch; the Legend of the Cross.
Painted screen with three upper panels on each side of the central doors. On the N. side are St. John the Evangelist, the Virgin and Child, and St. John the Baptist. On the S., an Archbishop, probably St. Thomas of Canterbury, the Trinity, and St. Bartholomew.
All are figured in *Barrett's Memorials of Attleborough Church*, pp. 108, 109, and 141. *British Archæol. Assoc. Journ.*, v. 99.

AVEBURY CHURCH, WILTSHIRE.
S. aisle; on splay of window; decorative pattern. 14th cent.
S. wall, E. end of nave; 14th cent. decoration.
N. wall, E. end of nave; 15th cent. decoration.
S. side of nave, on hoodmould of arches; painted zigzag pattern.
Built into chancel wall; coloured fragments of a Norman, ? the chancel, arch.
The Antiquary, 1881, iii. 45.
Above the chancel arch; upper part of rood screen painted and gilt. Early 15th cent.

AVELEY CHURCH, ESSEX.

Traces of colour on the nave columns. *Rev. W. Palin, Stifford and its Neighbourhood*, p. 167.

AVINGTON CHURCH, BERKSHIRE.

S. pier of chancel arch; a pattern of lozenges.
On the soffit of chancel arch; row of stars. Probably early 12th cent.
Archæol. Journ., xxxiv. 277. *British Archæol. Assoc. Journ.*, xvi. 60.

AWRE CHURCH, GLOUCESTERSHIRE.

"The colouring of the quatrefoils and ribs in the roof is a copy of the old work." *Builder*, 1875, p. 718.

AXBRIDGE CHURCH, SOMERSETSHIRE.

In the panel of a pew under the pulpit; painting of Our Saviour. Time of Edward III. *Kelly's Post Office Directory of Somersetshire. British Archæol. Assoc. Journ.*, xxxi. 465.
Panel paintings of St. Paul and Zacharias. 15th cent.; found nailed to the roof. *Long Ago*, 1873, vol. i., p. 93.
Aisle roofs, painted. Late 15th cent.
Above the arch opening from S. aisle to S. transept; part of a Doom. *Archæol. Journ.*, xxxviii. 87.
Above the arch opening from N. aisle to N. transept; part of a painting, the subject uncertain.
Eastern piers and arches of nave richly coloured. 15th cent.
At E. end of S. chancel aisle; reredos partly concealed by a 17th cent. monument, and a niche on each side, with remains of rich colour and gilding. 15th cent.
A niche over the W. doorway has traces of colour. 15th cent.

AXMINSTER, DEVONSHIRE, ST. MARY'S CHURCH.

Two painted effigies. 13th cent. *Murray's Handbook of Devonshire.*
Traces of painting beneath the whitewash against the wall of the tower. *J. Davidson, Hist. of Axminster Church*, p. 58.

AYLESBURY, BUCKINGHAMSHIRE, ST. MARY'S CHURCH.

Two or three panels of the rood screen forming the end of a pew, painted with figures of saints. *Ecclesiologist*, ii. 59.

AYLESBURY, BUCKINGHAMSHIRE, ST. MARY'S CHURCH—*cont.*
N. transept; effigy of a knight. 14th cent. With
remains of colour and gilding. *Lipscomb, Hist. and
Antiq. of Bucks,* ii. 55.
S. wall of S. transept; richly coloured niche. *Parker,
Eccles. and Architect. Topog. of England, Bucks,*
No. 175.

AYLMERTON CHURCH, NORFOLK.
Nave roof.

AYLSHAM CHURCH, NORFOLK.
Rood screen; the Apostles, omitting SS. John, Matthew,
and Philip, Moses, SS. Paul and John the Baptist, and
Thomas Wymer, the donor of the screen. Dated 1507.
Remains of painting on the ringers' gallery.
Roof of S. transept. Crowned M's.
Blomefield, Hist. of Norfolk, ed. 1807, vi. 278.

AYSGARTH CHURCH, YORKSHIRE.
Rood screen. 15th cent. Traditionally said to have
been removed from Jervaulx Abbey. *Associated Architect. Societies' Repts.,* i. 262.
Repainted. *R. S. Chattock, Wensleydale,* p. 25.
On the arches; "rude fresco paintings in small patterns." *Hardcastle, Wanderings in Wensleydale,* p. 34.

BABINGLEY CHURCH, NORFOLK.
Over door; St. Christopher. *Destroyed.*
Painted screen. *Destroyed.*
On the panels, *also destroyed*; SS. Catherine, Anne
instructing the Virgin, Mary the Virgin, Cecily, Mary
Magdalene, Helen, Agnes, Dorothy, and Margaret.

BACKWELL CHURCH, SOMERSETSHIRE.
N. chancel chapel; remains of colour on three shields
of a late 15th cent. monument.

BACTON CHURCH, SUFFOLK.
Over chancel arch; St. Peter receiving Souls at the
gate of Heaven; part of a Last Judgment. Late 15th
cent. *Archæol. Journ.,* xxx. 193.
Eastern bay of nave roof still richly coloured. *Brandon's Parish Churches,* ii. 68.

BACTON CHURCH, SUFFOLK—*cont.*

E. jamb of N.E. window of nave clerestory, and on E. pier adjoining chancel wall; ? the scourging of Our Lord.

Figures, &c. on W. wall of nave, on N. wall of N. aisle, and S. wall of S. aisle.

BADLEY CHURCH, SUFFOLK.

Painted rood screen.

BAINTON CHURCH, NORTHAMPTONSHIRE.

N. wall of N. aisle; indistinct subject with canopies showing through the whitewash. Late 14th cent.

BAINTON CHURCH, YORKSHIRE.

S. aisle; remains of colour on the canopy of the monument of a De Mauley. Early 14th cent.

BAKEWELL CHURCH, DERBYSHIRE.

Vernon chapel; effigies of Sir George Vernon and his two wives have been richly painted, the colouring partly renewed. Date about 1560. *J. C. Cox, Churches of Derbyshire,* ii. 21.

BALLYVOURNEY, ROMAN CATHOLIC CHAPEL, COUNTY CORK, IRELAND.

Coloured effigy of St. Gobnet. 14th cent. *Archæol. Journ.,* xii. 85.

BALSCOT CHURCH, OXFORDSHIRE.

On walls and arches; extensive remains of early paintings. *Beesley, Hist. of Banbury,* pp. 109, 123.

BAMPTON CHURCH, DEVONSHIRE.

In central compartments of screen; subjects emblematical of the Passion. *Oliver's Ecclesiastical Antiquities of Devon,* i. 169.

BAMPTON CHURCH, OXFORDSHIRE.

Stone reredos, painted. Early 15th cent. *Hall's Book of the Thames,* p. 52. *Giles, Hist. of Bampton,* p. 28.

BANGOR IS Y COED CHURCH, FLINTSHIRE.

Curious painting on S. wall; ? portrait of Dinoth, last Abbot of Bangor. Probably 16th cent. *Destroyed. Archæologia Cambrensis,* 4th series, vii. 154. *Thomas, Hist. of the Diocese of St. Asaph,* p. 800.

BANHAM CHURCH, NORFOLK. ·

E. end of N. aisle; painted screen. *Blomefield, Hist. of Norfolk*, ed. 1805, i. 354. *Chambers, Hist. of Norfolk*, ii. 702.

Wooden effigy of Sir Hugh Bardolph, died 1203; originally painted all over. *O. Morgan, The Abergavenny Monuments*, p. 24.

BANSFIELD HALL, SUFFOLK.

From the chapel at; painting on panel of two figures. *Bury and West Suffolk Archæol. Inst.*, ii. 209.

BANWELL CHURCH, SOMERSETSHIRE.

Rood screen. 15th cent. *Restored.* Said to have been brought from Bruton Abbey. *Rutter's Delineations of N.W. Somerset*, p. 138.

BARDWELL CHURCH, SUFFOLK.

Over the chancel arch; the Day of Judgment. About 1500.

Over N. door; St. Christopher. About 1500.

On N. wall of nave; the Legend of St. Catherine. Late 14th cent. And " Les Trois Morts." Early 16th cent.

On S. wall of nave; Tree of the Seven Deadly Sins, with group of minstrels, and the Martyrdom of St. Edmund. Late 14th cent.

Painted roof, with the date 1421 on an open book held by an angel.

Parker, Eccles. and Architect. Topog. of England. Suffolk, No. 360. *Suffolk Archæol.*, ii. 41. *British Archæol. Assoc. Journ.*, xxviii. 124.

All the paintings are whitewashed over.

BARFORD, GREAT, CHURCH, BEDFORDSHIRE.

N. of chancel; on the effigies and shields on the monument of the Anscells, gilding and colour, circ. 1591.

BARFORD, LITTLE, CHURCH, BEDFORDSHIRE.

Perpendicular rood screen; diapers. *Parker, Eccles. and Architect. Topog. of England, Bedford*, No. 105.

BARFORD, LITTLE, CHURCH, OXFORDSHIRE.

Chancel arch; scroll pattern. ·

BARFORTH, OR OLD RICHMOND, YORKSHIRE, RUINED CHAPEL OF ST. LAWRENCE.

Colour still remaining on the sheltered parts of the walls. *W. Hylton Longstaffe, Richmondshire, Its Ancient Lords and Edifices*, p. 144.

BARFRESTON CHURCH, KENT.

On the E. wall of chancel; nine medallions containing figures of saints, the central one, perhaps Our Lord, defaced, supported by two seraphims. Between each of these medallions are smaller ones, containing crosses, and with foliage on each side. Over the central medallion, part of a consecration cross. Below, and forming the background to the original altar, painting representing the folds of a curtain.

Within the splay of the central E. window; a nimbed head in the centre, and an angel on either side. Band of red and yellow round this and the other Norman chancel windows.

Within the S.E. window; the Annunciation.

Within the N.E. window; the Adoration of the Magi.

In the N.E. corner; two archbishops, one pointing down towards a consecration Cross. *Archæologia*, xlvii. 164, 165.

Above each of the E. windows; a seraph with an archbishop and bishop between them.

Above, on left side of the wheel window; an angel and two male figures.

On N. wall of chancel; within the splay of the eastern window, a male and female, perhaps the founders. Within the splay of the western window two figures one holding a scroll.

Between the windows, a figure seated, with four others looking towards him, and a nimbed archbishop behind him.

The paintings are probably co-eval with the church, viz., about 1180.

A complete set of coloured drawings in the Society of Antiquaries' Library. Only the painting of the Adoration of the Magi, and some traces of colouring in the N.E. corner, remain; the rest have been whitewashed over.

BARKING ABBEY, ESSEX.

Remains of bright colouring on the walls of a small side chapel or vestry of the Abbey Church. Discovered in 1875. *Builder*, 1875, p. 829. *British Archæol. Assoc. Journ.*, xxxii. 114.

BARKING CHURCH, SUFFOLK.

Rood screen; prophets. *Destroyed.*
Mural paintings, covered with whitewash.
Q

BARKSTON CHURCH, LINCOLNSHIRE.
Over N. door; St. Christopher. 15th cent. *Destroyed.*
Associated Architect. Societies' Repts., v. xxii., ix. 23.

BARKWAY CHURCH, HERTFORDSHIRE.
Found built up in E. wall; two groups of figures in
Italian alabaster, (i) the Holy Family, (ii) the decollation
of St. John the Baptist; the principal figures being em-
bellished with ornaments and aureoles of solid gold.
Cussans, Hist. of Hertfordshire, vol. i., pt. ii., p. 33.

BARLAVINGTON CHURCH, SUSSEX.
"Slight remains of wall painting." *M. A. Lower,
History of Sussex,* i. 27.

BARLING CHURCH, ESSEX.
Alabaster statuettes of the Virgin and St. Dominic,
richly coloured; found walled up in the N. aisle. *Essex
Archæol.,* iv. 120.

BARLOW CHURCH, DERBYSHIRE.
Scroll patterns. *Destroyed. J. C. Cox, Churches of
Derbyshire,* i. 64.

BARNACK CHURCH, NORTHAMPTONSHIRE.
On a corbel in the S. porch; painted imitation of the
indented moulding. 13th cent.

BARNET, EAST, CHURCH, HERTFORDSHIRE.
Pattern of lines, &c. Probably 13th cent. *Destroyed.
Associated Architect. Societies' Repts.,* iii. 359.
Painted roof; Angels, &c. 15th cent. *Ecclesiologist,*
xiii. 65.

BARNHAM BROOM CHURCH, NORFOLK.
Rood screen; St. Walstan, St. Joanna, St. Ursula,
St. Withburga, St. Mary Magdalene, &c. *The Ecclesiologist's Guide to the Deaneries of Brisley, &c.,* pp. 50,
54.

BARNINGHAM CHURCH, SUFFOLK.
Rood screen; perpendicular period. *Murray's Handbook of Suffolk. Parker, Eccles. and Architect. Topog.
of England, Suffolk,* No. 365.

BARNINGHAM WINTER CHURCH, NORFOLK.
A consecration Cross was discovered on the S. wall
of the chancel, and after being copied was re-covered with
whitewash.

BARNSTAPLE CHURCH, DEVONSHIRE.
S. wall of nave over tower arch ; part of large subject,
probably "Les trois Rois morts et les trois Rois vifs," and
kneeling figure of the donor below. 14th cent.

BARNWELL. *See* CAMBRIDGE, ST. ANDREW-THE-LESS.

BARNWOOD CHURCH, GLOUCESTERSHIRE.
N. side of nave ; scroll painting on piers and arches.
15th cent.

BARRINGTON CHURCH, CAMBRIDGESHIRE.
E. beam of nave roof ; traces of colour.

BARROW CHURCH, SHROPSHIRE.
A knight on horseback, and other mural paintings.
Discovered in 1851. *Murray's Handbook of Shropshire.*
Kelly's Post Office Directory of Shropshire.

BARROW CHURCH, SUFFOLK.
Remains of painted rood screen.

BARROW - ON - SOAR, LEICESTERSHIRE, HOLY TRINITY
CHURCH.
Remains of painting on tie beam at the E. end of the
roof of the nave. *Ecclesiologist,* vi. 184.

BARTHOMLEY CHURCH, CHESHIRE.
E. end of N. aisle ; effigy of (?) Robert Fulleshurst.
End of 15th cent.
Original colouring on the vestments, carefully washed
off. *E. Hinchliffe, Barthomley,* p. 33.

BARTLOW CHURCH, CAMBRIDGESHIRE.
S. wall of nave ; St. Christopher.

BARTON CHURCH, SUFFOLK.
Panel from a parclose screen formerly at, now in the
possession of Sir Henry Bunbury, Bart. ; a friar kneeling
to the Virgin, with scrolls. *Suffolk Archæol.,* i. 231.

BARTON BENDISH, NORFOLK, ST. ANDREW'S CHURCH.
On chancel arch, small circles. 13th cent. Colouring
and gilding on a niche in the N. wall of the nave. 15th
cent. Faint traces of painting on the S. wall of the nave.

BARTON BENDISH, NORFOLK, ST. MARY'S CHURCH.
On S. wall of nave ; an indistinct painting, perhaps
St. Catharine. Below a recumbent figure.
On the splay of the S. doorway, a crowned head. 15th
cent.

BARTON SEGRAVE CHURCH, NORTHAMPTONSHIRE.
Over the E. tower arch ; the Day of Judgment.
On N. wall of tower ; the Last Supper.
Discovered in 1878 during the restoration of the church.

BARTON TURF CHURCH, NORFOLK, is described· as having been, previous to 1793, covered with mural decorations. All were *destroyed* in that year in the course of restorations. The rood-screen was saved, and is richly painted with the Heavenly Hierarchy, and SS. Appollonia, Citha, and Barbara. Late 14th cent. *See* published account by Rev. J. Gunn.
S. aisle screen; Henry VI. (painted subsequently), St. Edward the Confessor, St. Edmund, and St. Olave. 15th cent.
Proceedings of the Royal Archæol. Institute, Norwich Vol. p. xxxix. *East Anglian Notes and Queries,* iii. 290. *Illustrations of Norfolk Topography,* p. 7. *Norfolk Archæol.,* iii. 19. *The Ecclesiologist's Guide to the Deaneries of Brisley, &c.,* p. 122. *Sacristy,* iii. 154.

BARTON, EARL'S, CHURCH, NORTHAMPTONSHIRE.
Painted chancel screen, partly repainted. Date about 1400.

BARTON, WESTCOTT. *See* WESTCOTT BARTON.

BASINGSTOKE CHURCH, HAMPSHIRE.
Decorative painting and mottoes. Elizabethan period. Drawing of them in the tower doorway. *Black's Guide to Hampshire.*

BASTON MANOR HOUSE, KENT.
Portraits of Kings Athelstan, Richard III., and other royal personages ; discovered painted on the panels of one of the rooms. Date, time of Henry VII. *Gent. Mag.,* c. pt. ii., p. 497. *Blackburne, Decorative Painting,* p. 19.

BATH ABBEY CHURCH, SOMERSETSHIRE.
Old colouring on the fan tracery vaulting renewed. *Builder,* 1875, p. 92.

BATHAMPTON CHURCH, SOMERSETSHIRE.
Recess in eastern exterior wall of chancel ; remains of colour on the back of the recess, and on an effigy of an ecclesiastic. 13th cent. *British Archæol. Assoc. Journ.,* xxiii. 292.

BATTLE ABBEY, SUSSEX.

On walls of refectory ; traces of masonry pattern.

On walls of chamber beneath the refectory ; vermilion stencilling. *C. L. W. C., A guide to Battle Abbey,* pp. 48, 53.

Remains of colour on the vault of the calefactory. *E. C. Mackenzie Walcott's Battle Abbey,* pp. 64, 65.

BATTLE CHURCH, SUSSEX.

Over the chancel arch ; Les Trois Morts, &c. *Archæol. Journ.,* v. 69.

N. side of nave ; The Passion, &c. Early 14th cent. *British Archæol. Assoc. Journ.,* ii. 141 ; and *Builder,* 1864, p. 733.

Colour and gilding on the monument and effigies of Sir Anthony Browne and Lady. Circ. 1540. *M. A. Lower, History of Sussex,* i. 36. *Antiquarian Repertory,* new ed., iii. 182.

Masonry patterns and other ornamental decoration discovered during the restoration, and *destroyed.* Late 12th cent. *Archæol. Journ.,* xxxiv. 278. *E. C. Mackenzie Walcott's Battle Abbey,* pp. 77, 86.

BAUNTON CHURCH, GLOUCESTERSHIRE.

N. wall of nave ; St. Christopher, with defaced inscription above. Over the chancel arch ; scenes from the Passion. *Builder,* 1876, p. 522 ; 1877, p. 46. *Church Builder,* 1876, No. LIX. p. 182.

On either side of chancel arch ; large turreted canopy work, alternately red and green.

BEACHAMPTON CHURCH, BUCKINGHAMSHIRE.

Coloured pattern much injured on the E. wall of the chancel, at the E. end of the S. aisle, and the adjacent bay of the arcade.

BEACHAMWELL CHURCH, NORFOLK.

Sculptures of the Descent from the Cross, and St. Peter ; curiously gilt and painted. *Blomefield, (Parkin,) Hist. of Norfolk,* ed. 1807, vii. 297. *Norfolk Archæol.,* i. 250. *Chambers, Hist. of Norfolk,* i. 42.

BEAMINSTER CHURCH, DORSETSHIRE.

Over chancel arch ; Last Judgment (*nearly destroyed*).

BEAUCHIEF ABBEY, DERBYSHIRE.

Altar piece formerly at, now in the possession of the Foljambe family, with sculptured representation of the Martyrdom of Thomas à Becket ; once rich in painting

BEAUCHIEF ABBEY, DERBYSHIRE—*cont.*
and gilding. *Figured in Smith's Sheffield and its Neigh-bourhood, in Addy's Hist. Memorials of Beauchief Abbey,* p. 11, *and in the Reliquary,* vii. 205.

BEAUDESERT CHURCH, WARWICKSHIRE.
Pattern on a Norman window.

BECCLES CHURCH, SUFFOLK.
Enrichments of the south porch, originally painted and gilt. *Suckling's History of Suffolk,* i. 15.

BECKLEY CHURCH, OXFORDSHIRE.
Belfry ; 2 series of floral ornaments. 13th and 15th cents.
End of S. aisle ; Virgin and Child under a cinquefoil canopy with diapered background. 14th cent.
Over this has been painted, St. Michael weighing Souls. 15th cent.
Over the W. tower arch ; the Last Judgment, and below, on either side, St. Peter and St. Paul. 14th cent. *Archæol. Journ.,* iv. 256; *Builder,* 1864, p. 725 ; and *Exeter Diocesan Architect. Soc.,* iv. 48.

BEDALE CHURCH, YORKSHIRE.
Remains of colour on the effigy of a Lady of the Fitz-Alan family. *Hollis, Monumental Effigies,* part iii. pl. 3. *Murray's Handbook of Yorkshire.*
Coloured effigy of Brian, Lord Fitz-Alan. Circ. 1302. *Blore's Monumental Remains of Noble and Eminent Persons. Hollis, Monumental Effigies,* pt. iv. pl. 4.
Dado of the tomb of Brian, Lord Fitzalan, built into exterior wall of vestry ; figures of the knight, St. Peter, and the conveyance of the soul to heaven. The colours are fast fading away.
A third knightly effigy has the flowers of his shield painted on his jupon. *W. Hylton Longstaffe, Richmond-shire, its Ancient Lords and Edifices,* p. 55.

BEDDINGTON CHURCH, SURREY.
Over chancel arch ; Scenes from the Passion. *Destroyed. Tracings in the Library of the Royal Archæological Institute. Archæol. Journ.,* vii. 298. *Surrey Archæol.,* I. report, p. ix.

BEDFIELD CHURCH, SUFFOLK.
Lower part of rood screen ; painted mouldings, and figures of Joel, Baruch, &c., depicted on the panels.

BEDFONT CHURCH, MIDDLESEX.

Within two arched recesses on N. of chancel arch.

(i.) In E. wall of nave; the Crucifixion with the Virgin and St. John. Late 13th or early 14th cent.

(ii.) In N. wall of nave; the Day of Judgment. Early 14th cent. *Copy in Art Library, South Kensington Museum.*

Portion of another painting. *Destroyed. Archæol. Journ.,* xxiii. 63, xxxviii. 84 (note), 89. *Ecclesiologist,* xxvi. (xxiii. new series), p. 318.

BEDFORD, BEDFORDSHIRE, ST. PAUL'S CHURCH.

Roof S. side of tower; signs of former painting and gilding. *Gent. Mag.,* 1849, xxxi. new series, 599. *Blyth. Hist. of Bedford,* p. 173.

Pulpit, ornamented with gilt tracery on a blue ground. *Lysons, Magna Britannia, Bedfordshire,* p. 52. *Builder,* 1881, vol. xli., p. 170.

BEDWIN, GREAT, CHURCH, WILTSHIRE.

N. transept; diaper work, with figures of St. John the Baptist, St. George, &c.

S. transept; Crucifixion, and what appears to be the history of a saint. Early 14th cent. *Gent. Mag.,* 1842, xviii. new series, 413.

On E. wall, above the space for an altar; paintings of ten or twelve saints; whitewashed over.

Within a recess in the S. wall of S. transept; Effigy of Sir Adam de Stokke, with remains of colour. Early 14th cent.

Northern respond, E. end of nave; Effigy of the Virgin, richly coloured and gilt.

Wilts Archæol. and Nat. Hist. Soc. Mag., vi. 278–280.

BEER FERRERS CHURCH, DEVONSHIRE.

Painted screens with figures of saints formerly depicted on the panels. Decorated period. *Archæol. Journ.,* i. 399.

BEESTON, NORFOLK, ST. MARY'S CHURCH.

Rood screen; St. Clement, and traces of painting on the panels and small sculptured figures of St. George and the Dragon, St. Michael, a ploughshare and tun, after the letter B, and an eagle. 15th cent. *Antiquary,* 1871, i. 152. *Carthew's Hundred of Launditch,* ii. 381.

Texts and inscriptions on the walls. *The Ecclesiologist's Guide to the Deaneries of Brisley, &c.,* pp. 17, 21.

BEESTON REGIS, NORFOLK, ALL SAINTS' CHURCH.
Portion of rood screen painted and gilt in the vestry' 15th cent.
Figures of the Apostles formerly depicted on the panels. *Hart, Antiq. of Norfolk*, p. 65.

BEIGHTON CHURCH, NORFOLK.
Rood screen with panel paintings of Saints and Apostles. *Removed.*

BELAUGH CHURCH, NORFOLK.
Rood screen; the Apostles, omitting SS. Philip and Matthias, SS. Paul and John the Baptist, the faces all destroyed. *Hart, Antiq. of Norfolk*, p. 65.

BELEIGH ABBEY, MALDON, ESSEX.
On the interior of the W. doorway of chapter house; decorative painting. 13th cent. *Hadfield's Ecclesiastical, Castellated, and Domestic Architecture; or, Churches of Essex*, pl. lxxv. fig. 1; *Builder*, 1876, p. 813; *Murray's Handbook of Essex. Spurrell, Notes on the present state of Beleigh Abbey*, p. 16.

BELTON CHURCH, SUFFOLK.
N. wall of nave; Les Trois Vifs, &c. St. Christopher and St. James Major. 15th cent. *Archæol. Journ.*, xxi. 218., xxx. 193. *East Anglian Notes and Queries*, ii. 326.

BEMPTON CHURCH, YORKSHIRE.
Chancel roof; rudely painted flowers on some of the beams. *Prickett's Priory Church of Bridlington*, p. 53.

BENGEO CHURCH, HERTFORDSHIRE.
E. wall of nave, S. side of chancel arch; an ecclesiastic, perhaps St. Leonard, preaching, and scene from the history of St. Catherine. Circ. 1300.
S. side of chancel; on splays of lancet windows, masonry pattern. *Cussans, Hist. of Hertfordshire*, vol. ii., pt. ii., p. 37.

BENTLEY, GREAT, CHURCH, ESSEX.
Remains of colouring on two niches in the E. wall of the chancel, and on the entrance to the roodloft on the N. side of the chancel arch. 15th cent.

BEPTON CHURCH, SUSSEX.
Over chancel arch; remains of decorative colour,

BERE REGIS CHURCH, DORSETSHIRE.

The Crucifixion or the Trinity.

Remains of decorative colouring throughout the church.

BERKELEY CASTLE CHAPEL, GLOUCESTERSHIRE.

Painted roof.

On the wall under the arched passage; traces of black letter texts from the book of Revelation. Date about 1400. *J. H. Cooke, F.S.A., A Sketch of the History of Berkeley*, 2nd ed., p. 15. *Bristol and Gloucestershire Archæol. Soc. Trans.*, 1876, p. 138.

BERKELEY CHURCH, GLOUCESTERSHIRE.

Over chancel arch; part of a Doom.

E. end of N. aisle; The Martyrdom of a Saint.

Within the splay of a window in N. aisle; figure of a Saint or Angel.

Remains of colour; wall and decorative patterns were found on all the walls, round all the windows, on the nave piers, round all the arches, and on the chancel screen. Ranging from the 13th to 15th cents. Most of it has been renewed. *British Archæol. Assoc. Journ.*, xxi. 352. *J. H. Cooke, F.S.A., A Sketch of the History of Berkeley*, 2nd ed., p. 20.

On the sills of the S. aisle windows; three small effigies which bear traces of painting and gilding. *British Archæol. Assoc. Journ.*, xxiv. 79.

S. side of nave; remains of gilding on monument, and effigies of Thomas eighth Lord Berkeley and his Lady. Late 14th cent.

BERKHAMPSTEAD ST. MARY'S. *See* NORTHCHURCH.

BERKHAMPSTEAD, GREAT, HERTFORDSHIRE, ST. PETER'S CHURCH.

N. Transept; traces of colour on the monument and effigies of a Torrington, or Incent, and Lady. Late 14th cent. *Cussans, Hist. of Hertfordshire*, vol. iii., pt. i., p. 64. *Clutterbuck's Hist. of Hertfordshire*, i. 306.

On nave walls; the Apostles, and St. George and the Dragon. *Destroyed. J. W. Cobb, Hist. of Berkhamsted*, pp. 44, 46.

BERKHAMPSTEAD, GREAT, HERTFORDSHIRE.

Old farm house at Hucksters End.

Beneath some old panelling some curious paintings, one of three serving men. Circ. 1550. *Cussans, Hist. of Hertfordshire*, vol. iii., pt. i., p. 55.

BERRY-POMEROY CHURCH, DEVONSHIRE.

Rood screen ; on the panels, the four doctors, SS. James Minor, Thomas, Stephen, Jude, Matthias, Mary Magdalene, Barbara, and Gudule. *Building News*, 1870, p. 429. *Lysons' Magna · Britannia, Devonshire*, p. cccxxvii. *C. Worthy, Ashburton and its Neighbourhood*, p. 120. *Worth, Tourist's Guide to S. Devon*, p. 57.

BERSTED, SOUTH, CHURCH, SUSSEX.

On E. wall of chancel; portions of a winged figure.

On a pillar of the nave ; St. Christopher, Whitewashed over. *Sussex Archæol.*, xxiv. 168. *Now destroyed.*

On a pillar, N. of nave ; painting in compartments, with several figures. Subject uncertain.

Decorative painting round the capitals, and on various parts of the church.

BERWICK BASSETT CHURCH, WILTSHIRE.

Rood screen.

BERWICK ST. JAMES' CHURCH, WILTSHIRE.

Within the splay in the head of the E. window ; The Ascension. 13th cent.

BERWICK ST. JOHN'S CHURCH, WILTSHIRE.

Wilts Archæol. and Nat. Hist. Soc. Mag., vii. 246.

BESFORD CHURCH, WORCESTERSHIRE.

Painted roodloft. *Ecclesiologist*, xxiii. (xx. new series) 291. *Noakes, Rambles in Worcestershire*, 2nd series, p. 122. *Associated Architect. Societies' Repts.*, xiii. 274.

BEVERLEY MINSTER, YORKSHIRE.

Painted canopy of niche from altar screen, restored. *Colling, Gothic Ornaments*, ii. pl. 27.

Part of original altar screen richly coloured and gilt. *Long Ago*, 1873, vol. i., p. 252.

" 'The roof of the choir has been coloured partly from indications of former painting." *Murray's Handbook of Yorkshire.*

Numerous richly carved and coloured fragments found in a well close to the high altar. *Yorkshire Archæol. and Topog. Journal*, v. 126.

The decoration of the groining of the nave is a reproduction of the design and colouring found under modern yellow washes.

BEVERLEY, YORKSHIRE, ST. MARY'S CHURCH.

Chancel ceiling panelled and painted with figures of English kings. Date 1445. Panels repainted.

Transept ceilings, also painted. *Murray's Handbook of Yorkshire.*

N. transept; inscriptions on roof.

Nave ceiling; before 1829 represented a serene sky with stars of gold.

S. aisle; over capitals of piers; heads, &c., with remains of colour and gilding.

N. wall of nave, behind the Minstrels' Pillar; two sepulchral recesses ornamented with mural colouring, and with inscriptions now nearly obliterated.

S. porch; remains of colour and gilding on vaulting and bosses. *Associated Architect. Societies' Repts.,* viii. 104, 105, 110.

N. side of nave, on Minstrels' Pillar; coloured statuettes of the minstrels. *Archæologia,* xxi. 554. *Sheahan and Whellan, Hist. and Topog. of City of York, &c.,* ii. 267, 268, 269, 271. *Ashby De La Zouch, Anastatic Drawing Soc.,* 1855, p. 2, pl. x.

Ceiling of S. aisle; the history of St. Catherine in 14 compartments. *Destroyed.*

S. cross on ceiling of Chantry Chapel; St. John the Baptist, St. John the Evangelist, the Annunciation, St. John of Beverley, a king, queen, and ecclesiastic, all with inscriptions. *Destroyed. Gent, Hist. of Rippon,* pp. 79, 81. *Oliver, Hist. of Beverley,* pp. 351, 353, 355.

BEVERSTON CHURCH, GLOUCESTERSHIRE.

"The literal Transubstantiation of the Wafer." Discovered in 1844, and, after drawings had been made, recovered with yellow wash. *Society of Antiquaries' Proceedings,* i. 55. *J. M. Neale, Hierologus,* p. 295. *Neale and Webb, Durandus,* p. 57.

BIBURY CHURCH, GLOUCESTERSHIRE.

Opposite the S. door; St. Christopher. Whitewashed over. *Rudders' History of Gloucestershire,* p. 286. *Blackburne, Decorative Painting,* p. 16. *Antiquarian Cabinet,* vol. v.

BIDDENDEN, KENT, ST. MARY'S CHURCH.

Painted ceiling. About 1500. *Ecclesiologist,* xvi. 319.

S. chancel chapel; coloured bosses on ceiling. *Glynne, Churches of Kent,* p. 222.

BIDDENHAM CHURCH, BEDFORDSHIRE.
Over S. doorway, back of a Norman window; figure
of a saint. *Whitewashed over.*

BIDEFORD CHURCH, DEVONSHIRE.
Rood-screen. *Ecclesiologist,* xxviii. (xxv. new series),
p. 308.

BIGGLESWADE CHURCH, BEDFORDSHIRE.
E. bays of aisle roofs; scroll and ornamental patterns.
15th cent. Only the S. aisle colouring now remains.

BILDESTONE CHURCH, SUFFOLK.
Chamber over porch; *destroyed;* traces of painting.
East Anglian Notes and Queries, i. 33.

BILLINGFORD CHURCH, NORFOLK.
Rood screen.
Mural painting with a number of figures; the subject
uncertain. *Norfolk Archæol.,* VI., 2nd annual report, p. ii.
Over N. door; St. Christopher. *Antiquarian and
Architect. Year Book,* 309.
E. wall; painted niche.

BILLINGFORD CHURCH, SUFFOLK.
Nave, S. wall; St. Peter at the gate of Heaven (?)
Painted rood screen; whitewash partly removed.

BILLINGHAY CHURCH, LINCOLNSHIRE.
Perpendicular roof; painted. *Trollope: Sleaford
Flaxwell, Aswardhurn,* p. 495.

BINHAM ABBEY CHURCH, NORFOLK.
Portions of screen; figures of saints on the panels;
obscured by white paint and Scripture texts. *Gent.
Mag.,* 1847, xxviii., new series, 264. *Proceedings of
the Royal Archæol. Institute,* 1847, Norwich vol., p. 186.
Viz.; on N. side E. face; SS. Agnes, Agatha, Sebastian,
and Thomas of Canterbury.
On S. side W. face; St. Catherine, Henry VI., and
St. Christopher.

BINSTEAD CHURCH, SUSSEX.
On jambs of a window.
N. side of chancel; St. Margaret and another subject.
N. wall of chancel; diaper pattern.
S. wall of chancel; ? the Entombment, and Our Lord
in Glory. 13th cent. *Sussex Archæol.,* xx. 233.

BIRCHAM, NORFOLK, ST. ANDREW'S CHURCH.
Two Dedication Crosses.

BIRCHINGTON, KENT, ALL SAINTS' CHURCH.
North chancel chapel; remains of a mural painting.
W. Miller, Jottings of Kent, p. 148.
Remains of colouring on the screens and walls. *? Destroyed. Ecclesiologist*, xxv. (xxii. new series,) 204, 290.

BIRMINGHAM, WARWICKSHIRE, ST. MARTIN'S CHURCH.
On E. wall of chancel, and N. jamb of E. window, paintings of St. Martin, (i.) as an archbishop, (ii.) dividing his cloak with a beggar, (iii.) cutting down a sacred tree, and (iv.) a representation of his shrine. Time of Richard II. *Long Ago*, 1873, vol. i., pp. 21, 49.
Colour and gilding on effigy of Sir William de Bermingham the 2nd. Time of Edward II.
In crypt at W. end; a band of fleurs de lis, painted in distemper.
On beam over chancel arch; Our Lord in Judgment.
In chancel, a diaper of white roses on a chocolate ground.
Indications of colour, concealed by texts within scroll borders, in various parts of the church. *J. T. Bunce, Old St. Martin's, Birmingham*, pp. 11, 12, 15, 23, 24, 27, *and* pl. viii.
Coloured effigy of an Ecclesiastic. *Hollis, Monumental Effigies*, pt. vi., pl. 9.

BISHAM ABBEY, BERKSHIRE.
E. wall of hall; St. Peter. *Sheahan, Hist. and Topog. of the County of Buckingham*, p. 901.

BISHOP'S CANNINGS. *See* CANNINGS, BISHOP'S.

BISHOP'S CLEEVE. *See* CLEEVE, BISHOP'S.

BISHOP'S LYDEARD. *See* LYDEARD, BISHOP'S.

BISHOP'S STORTFORD. *See* STORTFORD, BISHOP'S.

BISHOP'S TAWTON. *See* TAWTON, BISHOP'S.

BISHOP'S WILTON. *See* WILTON, BISHOP'S.

BISLEY CHURCH, GLOUCESTERSHIRE.
N. wall; St. Michael subduing the evil angels. Discovered in 1771.

BLACKFORD CHURCH, SOMERSETSHIRE.
N., S., and W. walls of nave; decorative painting. *Destroyed.* Statuette of (?) St. Michael, with traces of gold and colour.

BLACKMORE, ESSEX, ST. LAWRENCE CHURCH.
Coloured bosses of roof. *Suckling's Antiquities and Architecture of Essex*, p. 25. *Murray's Handbook of Essex.*

BLAKENHAM, LITTLE, CHURCH, SUFFOLK.
On E. side of chancel; St. John the Baptist. *East Anglian Notes and Queries*, iv. 11.
Painted panels at E. end of chancel. *Parker, Eccles. and Architect. Topog. of England, Suffolk*, No. 8.

BLEADON CHURCH, SOMERSETSHIRE.
Over inner doorway of porch; coloured niche, with Cross and figures of the Virgin and Child. *Pooley, Old Crosses of Somerset*, p. 68. *J., L. E. H., Visitor's Handbook to Weston-super-Mare*, p. 256 (*note*).

BLEDINGTON CHURCH, GLOUCESTERSHIRE.
Roof of nave; remains of scroll painting. 15th cent.
S. wall of S. aisle; remains of texts. 15th cent.

BLETSOE CHURCH, BEDFORDSHIRE.
N. wall of nave; a knight on horseback.

BLEWBURY CHURCH, BERKSHIRE.
N. wall of S. aisle; remains of colour showing through the whitewash.

BLISLAND CHURCH, CORNWALL.
Lower part of rood screen. *Maclean, Hist. of the Deanery of Trigg Minor*, i. 54.

BLOFIELD CHURCH, NORFOLK.
Rood screen; the Apostles. *Hart, Antiq. of Norfolk*, p. 66. Restored. *Eastern Counties Collect.*, *p.* 96.
N. wall of N. aisle; a consecration cross.

BLOXHAM CHURCH, OXFORDSHIRE.
N. aisle; St. Christopher.
Over the chancel arch; part of a Doom; with the inscription "Carne comburemer" (?).
Chapel, S. side of nave; our Lord in Glory, and in the Judgment Hall.
Round S. nave arcade; scroll pattern.

BLOXHAM CHURCH, OXFORDSHIRE—*cont.*

Rood screen; "the lower panels have been richly painted with figures of Saints," viz., SS. Matthew, Mark, and John, their evangelistic emblems, and portrait of Cardinal Wolsey. *Ecclesiologist*, xxviii. (xxv. new series,) 374. *British Archæol. Assoc. Journ.*, xxxvi. 129.

BLUNDESTON CHURCH, SUFFOLK.

Rood screen; with figures of St. Peter, Angels and Saints on the panels. *Suckling's History of Suffolk*, i. 318. *Parker, Eccles. and Architect. Topog. of England, Suffolk*, No. 222. *East Anglian Notes and Queries*, iii. 316.

On the walls; St. Christopher and other subjects. *Whitewashed over.*

BLUNHAM CHURCH, BEDFORDSHIRE.

Sculptures of the Virgin and Child, Our Saviour bearing the Cross, and the Descent from the Cross, richly gilt and coloured, and probably portions of a reredos.

Found in 1849, in the wall under the E. window, and now preserved at the Rectory.

BLUNTISHAM, HUNTINGDONSHIRE, ST. JOHN'S CHURCH.

Rood screen. *Ecclesiologist*, iv. 239.

BLYBOROUGH CHURCH, LINCOLNSHIRE.

N. wall of chapel; remains of decorative colouring. Time of Henry VIII. *Associated Architect. Societies' Repts.*, xiv. p. x.

BLYTH CHURCH, NOTTINGHAMSHIRE.

Nave walls, upper part; masonry patterns. 12th cent.

On vault of nave; gold stars and flowers on an azure ground.

Screen; cresting of painted alabaster.

Panels of screen; S.S. Barbara, Stephen, Euphemia, Edmund, and Ursula. *Murray's Handbook of Nottinghamshire.* *J. Raine, Hist. of Blyth*, p. 54 *and* pl. *Associated Architect. Societies' Repts.*, xv. 155.

BLYTHBURGH, SUFFOLK, HOLY TRINITY CHURCH.

On the beams of the ceiling; the sacred Monogram and floral patterns, with angels at the intersections holding shields, and richly painted and gilt. *Cromwell, Excursions through Suffolk*, ii. 119.

Portion of rood screen; with painting in the lower panels; partly whitewashed over. Date about 1450.

BLYTHBURGH, SUFFOLK, HOLY TRINITY CHURCH—*cont.*
Bench Ends; SS. Anthony, Bartholomew, and Matthias.
Painting and gilding on the font. *Paley's Introduction to Illustrations of Baptismal Fonts.* .*Van Voorst*, 1844, p. 23.
Painted reliquary, used as an alms box.
E. wall of chancel, exterior; consecration crosses with traces of colour.

BOLSOVER CHURCH, DERBYSHIRE.
In the S. aisle; bas relief representing the Nativity. Retains much of its original colouring. Date 14th cent. *Builder*, 1878, p. 748. *J. C. Cox, Churches of Derbyshire,* i. 102, and iv. 451.

BOLTON ABBEY, YORKSHIRE.
Nave roof; painted about 1513, recently renewed in a different style. *Murray's Handbook of Yorkshire. Whitaker's Hist. and Antiq. of Craven,* 3rd ed., p. 486.
Within a niche over the Early English W. door exterior; faint traces of a painting of Our Lord and two angels. *Whitaker's Hist. and Antiq. of Craven,* 3rd ed., p. 492.

BOLTON-ON-SWALE CHURCH, YORKSHIRE.
Fronting the entrance; St. Christopher. *W. Hylton Longstaffe, Richmondshire, Its Ancient Lords and Edifices,* p. 47.

BONCHURCH CHURCH, ISLE OF WIGHT.
Paintings which appear to represent the Glory of the Righteous and the Condemnation of the Wicked. *British Archæol. Assoc. Journ.,* xi. 320. *W. H. D. Adams, The Hist. Topog. and Antiq. of the Isle of Wight,* p. 196.

BORDESLEY ABBEY, WORCESTERSHIRE.
A head, fragments of tabernacle work, mouldings, &c., coloured and gilt, dug up on the site of the chapel. *J. M. Woodward, The Hist. of Bordesley Abbey,* pp. 93, 102, 103.

BOROUGH GREEN CHURCH, CAMBRIDGESHIRE.
N. wall of chancel; traces of colour on various portions of the central monument. *Archæol. Journ.,* xxxiv. 123.

BORTHWICK CASTLE, EDINBURGHSHIRE.
Remains of painting on walls and ceiling of Great Hall. *Billing's Antiquities of Scotland,* vol. i.

BOSHAM CHURCH, SUSSEX.
Wall painting of the Virgin and child. *Destroyed.*

BOSTON CHURCH, LINCOLNSHIRE.
Painting on a tie beam of the nave roof. *Thompson's History of Boston*, p. 183.
Aisle roofs; formerly panelled and ornamented with scriptural and historic paintings. *Antiquarian Itinerary*, vol. vi. *Lincolnshire Churches*, 1843, *Boston*, p. 37.

BOSTON, LINCOLNSHIRE, THE ROCHFORD TOWER.
Mural paintings representing the Annunciation, St. Anne instructing the Virgin, St. Michael, St. Anthony, and ? the Rochford coat of arms. Early 16th cent. *Associated Architect. Societies' Repts.*, v. lxxvii.

BOTTESFORD, LEICESTERSHIRE, ST. MARY'S CHURCH.
Over chancel arch; paintings discovered during the restoration. *Ecclesiologist*, ix. 268. viz., the Doom.
Chancel; colour and gilding on the monuments, and effigies of the Earls of Rutland. The earliest, date 1543. *Associated Architect. Societies' Repts.*, vii. 208.

BOTTISHAM CHURCH, CAMBRIDGESHIRE.
Inner S. doorway ; painted mouldings.
On the outside, a niche; the interior "decorated with chocolate coloured crosses upon a vermilion ground." *Cambridge Antiq. Soc. Proceedings, Bottisham*, p. 26.

BOVEY TRACEY CHURCH, DEVONSHIRE.
Les Trois Morts et les Trois Vifs, the Agnus Dei, and St. Michael weighing Souls. (*Engraving in Art Library, South Kensington Museum*). *Exeter Diocesan Architect. Soc.*, vi. 309, and pl. 39.
Remains of colour on the chancel screen, pulpit, and some panels of the roof. 15th cent. *Ecclesiologist*, xix. 135.
Painted font. *Lysons, Magna Britannia, Devonshire*, p. 329.
On panels of pulpit; plaster figures of the Evangelists and SS. George, Margaret, Peter, Paul, Andrew, and James. *Repainted.* On panels of screen ; Apostles and Prophets, alternately. *Worth, Tourist's Guide to S. Devon*, p. 75.

BOVINGDON CHURCH, HERTFORDSHIRE.
Under the tower; coloured effigy of a knight. Circ. 1360. *Cussans, Hist. of Hertfordshire*, vol. iii., pt. i., p. 186.

BOWDEN, LITTLE, CHURCH, NORTHAMPTONSHIRE.

On the N. wall, E. end of N. aisle ; the Ascension, and some decorative painting. 13th cent.

BOWNESS CHURCH, WESTMORELAND.

Scriptural texts with comments upon them, explanatory of certain doctrines of the reformers ; time of Edward VI. or Elizabeth. *Gent. Mag.*, 1849, xxxii. new series, 586.

BOXFORD CHURCH, SUFFOLK.

E. end of S. aisle ; Edward the Confessor, kneeling figure, &c. *Suffolk Archæol.*, iii. 204.

BOXGROVE CHURCH, SUSSEX.

Ceiling of nave and chancel. Said to have been painted by Theodore Bernardi about 1530. *Murray's Handbook of Sussex. M. A. Lower, History of Sussex,* i. 71.

De la Warr monumental chapel. Circ. 1532. " Displays numerous devices and heraldic decorations, richly coloured and gilded." *Proceedings of the Royal Archæol. Institute, Chichester* vol., p. 36.

BOXTED CHURCH, SUFFOLK.

E. bay of nave ; painted, perpendicular period. *Parker, Eccles. and Architect. Topog. of England, Suffolk,* No. 463.

BOYTON CHURCH, WILTSHIRE.

South chapel ; altar tomb, formerly richly painted and gilt. *Bristol and West of England Archæol. Mag.,* p. 29.

BOZEAT CHURCH, NORTHAMPTONSHIRE.

Late decorated rood screen, " retains marks of painting and gilding." *Churches of the Archdeaconry of North-ampton,* p. 200.

And figures of Our Saviour and the Dove, an Apostle, nude figures kneeling to the Virgin, &c., on the panels, covered with brown paint. *Associated Architect. Societies' Repts.,* ix. xliii., x. lxxxvii.

BRABOURNE CHURCH, KENT.

Within the splays of original E. windows (now walled up); floral ornament. Perhaps 12th cent.

Round an arch leading from the S. aisle to the Scott chapel ; roses. Early 14th cent.

On N. wall, E. end of south aisle ; floral decorations within an oblong wall pattern.

BRADENSTOKE PRIORY, WILTSHIRE.

Prior's room; carved and painted chimney-piece. Time of Henry VI.

Ceiling of principal room; painted boss. *E. Kite, Hist. Notes on the Places of Interest to be visited by the British Archæol. Assoc. in* 1880, p. 73.

BRADFIELD CHURCH, BERKSHIRE.
Ecclesiologist, xii. 287.

BRADFIELD CHURCH, NORFOLK.

E. end of aisles; roofs "curiously painted with the history of the Saints, whose chapels were there." *Blomefield, (Parkin,) Hist. of Norfolk,* ed. 1810, xi. 7. *Chambers, Hist. of Norfolk,* ii. 950.

BRADFIELD-COMBUST CHURCH, SUFFOLK.

N. wall of nave; St. George, St. Christopher, and an angel. About 1400.

BRADFIELD HOUSE, DEVONSHIRE.

In the hall; "two huge figures are painted on the " wall over the dais, with the words 'vivat E(dwardus) " Rex' above them." *Worth, Tourist's Guide to N. Devon,* p. 84.

BRADFORD ABBAS CHURCH, DORSETSHIRE.

Nave roof; beams decorated with red and white roses, and supported on painted angels holding armorial shields.

N. aisle roof; rafters ornamented · with armorial shields. About 1500. *Murray's Handbook of Dorsetshire. Hutchins, Hist. of Dorset,* 3rd ed., iv. 123.

BRADFORD-ON-AVON, WILTSHIRE, TRINITY CHURCH.

Within a recess on N. side of nave; coloured panelling, &c. Late 15th cent. Remains of colour round the chancel arch. On the chancel walls.; Traces of illumina-. tion; Sentences from the Creed, &c. *Wilts. Archæol. and Nat. Hist. Soc. Mag.,* v. 212, 215, 217.

S. porch wall; portion of the effigy of a lady richly coloured. First quarter of the 14th cent. Found during restorations in 1865. Remains of colour on a Norman capital found at the same time. *Archæol. Journ.,* xxii. 85. *British Archæol. Assoc. Journ.,* xxi. 192.

BRADNINCH CHURCH, DEVONSHIRE.

Rood screen. Date 15th cent. Painted, and with figures of Saints and Martyrs depicted on the panels.

BRADNINCH CHURCH, DEVONSHIRE—*cont.*

Exeter Diocesan Architect. Soc., 2nd series, ii. 96. *Ecclesiologist*, xxviii. (xxv. new series), p. 308.

Viz., the doctors of the Church, the Sybils bearing their emblems, the Annunciation, Visitation, the temptation and expulsion from Paradise, Samson, the Infant Christ, and numerous other figures.

On panels of screen at W. end, formerly at N.E. corner of nave; ? SS. Bridget, Christopher, Giles, the Crucifixion, SS. Francis, Michael and Satan, George and the Dragon, Gabriel, Sebastian, and other figures.

Painting on panel of the Crucifixion, formerly in N. aisle. *Murray's Handbook of Devonshire. Black's Guide to Devonshire. Worth, Tourist's Guide to N. Devon*, p. 83.

BRADWELL PRIORY, BUCKINGHAMSHIRE.

Small chapel, now converted into a stable; on the ceiling and walls, paintings of clouds, angels, &c. *Sheahan, Hist. and Topog. of the County of Buckingham,* p. 495.

BRAILES CHURCH, WARWICKSHIRE.

Nave roof. On some of the beams traces of decoration, one with heads of Our Lord and the Apostles. *Church Builder,* 1879, No. lxxi. p. 148.

BRAINTREE CHURCH, ESSEX.

Canopy over the vestry door and string course. Early English. *Destroyed. Builder,* 1864, p. 724.

BRAMDEAN CHURCH, HAMPSHIRE.

Walls of chancel, diaper pattern. 13th cent. Chancel arch, remains of colour. *British Archæol. Assoc. Journ.,* viii. 155.

BRAMFIELD CHURCH, SUFFOLK.

Between the four arms of a cross, which was fixed to the wall beneath an arched recess, N. wall of nave, are nimbed angels issuing from clouds, with scrolls, and bearing chalices.

Conversion of St. Paul, two angels, &c.

Rood screen; figures of the Evangelists, St. Mary Magdalene, and three Saints effaced. *British Archæol. Assoc. Journ.,* xxv. 79. *Parker, Eccles. and Architect. Topog. of England, Suffolk,* No. 80. *Archæol. Journ.,* xxx. 193. *Suckling's History of Suffolk,* vol. ii. frontispiece.

N. wall, W. end; St. George, St. Michael, &c.

BRAMFORD CHURCH, SUFFOLK.
Mural painting, representing a Cross with angels. *Archæol. Journ.,* xxix. 194.

BRAMLEY CHURCH, HAMPSHIRE.
On S. wall of nave: the Martyrdom of St. Thomas à Becket. 13th cent. And some other indistinct subjects.
On the N. wall of nave; St. Christopher. 14th cent.
On the E. and N. walls of chancel; decorative floral painting.
On the N. wall of chancel; a dedication Cross.

BRANCEPETH CHURCH, DURHAM.
Nave roof; painted bosses. *Ornsby, Sketches of Durham,* p. 184.
Over the chancel arch; numerous illuminated panels formerly canopy of rood screen, some charged with the instruments of the Passion and other devices.
Billing's Geometrical Tracery of Brancepeth Church. Murray's Handbook of Durham. Ecclesiologist, xxv. (xxii. new series), p. 6. *British Archæol. Assoc. Journ.,* xxii. 278.
Chancel; Effigies of Ralph Lord Neville and his Lady. Circ. 1484. Formerly coloured. *British Archæol. Assoc. Journ.,* xxii. 276. *Durham and Northumberland Architect. and Archæol. Soc. Trans.,* 1862–63, pp. 74, 78.

BRANDON CHURCH, SUFFOLK.
Remains of painted rood screen. *Parker, Eccles. and Architect. Topog. of England, Suffolk,* No. 425.

BRATTON CLOVELLY CHURCH, DEVONSHIRE.
Wall of N. aisle; figures of Moses and the Prophets, and scripture texts, probably post reformation.
Colouring on chancel arch, on E. bay of nave roof, and on remaining portion of rood screen.

BRAUGHING CHURCH, HERTFORDSHIRE.
Eastern bay of nave roof; repainted and gilt. The original was 15th cent. work.
Mural paintings of St. George and the Dragon, the Virgin and child, &c. Not now visible.

BRAXTED, LITTLE, CHURCH, ESSEX.
Three series of paintings, of different dates, were discovered on the walls; the earliest of the Norman period. Also several consecration Crosses. *Builder,* 1864, p. 688. *Essex Archæol.,* iv. 138, 139.

BRAY CHURCH, BERKSHIRE.
On S. wall; various figures of Saints. *Destroyed.*
Diapers and sacred subjects on the walls.
On mouldings of nave arches; red spiral bands.
Chapel of All Saints, E. end of S. aisle; Our Lord appearing to St. Mary Magdalene. Circ. 1500.
Above arches on N. of chancel; black letter texts. Time of the Reformation. *Kerry, Hist. and Antiq. of the Hundred of Bray*, p. 28.

BREADSALL CHURCH, DERBYSHIRE.
A "Pieta" sculptured in alabaster, and painted and gilt. 15th cent. Discovered in 1877. *J. C. Cox, Churches of Derbyshire*, iii. 522.

BREAMORE CHURCH, HAMPSHIRE.
Traces of paintings, (?) the Crucifixion, on the walls of a room over the S.W. porch.

BRECKLES CHURCH, NORFOLK.
Rood screen. *The Ecclesiologist's Guide to the Deaneries of Brisley, &c.*, p. 79.

BRECON, BRECKNOCKSHIRE, ST. MARY'S CHURCH.
"Traces of stencilling under an arch." *Archæologia Cambrensis, 3rd series*, iii. 427.

BREDHURST CHURCH, KENT.
E. wall of S. chapel; masonry patterns. 13th cent. *Church Builder*, 1869, No. xxix., p. 12.

BREDON, WORCESTERSHIRE, ST. GILES' CHURCH.
Painted and gilt rood loft; now removed. *Ecclesiologist*, xvi. 211. *Associated Architect. Societies' Repts.*, iii. 337.

BREMHILL CHURCH, WILTSHIRE.
Canopy of screen; painted and powdered with stars. *Bowles, Hist. of Bremhill*, p. 171.

BRENT, SOUTH, CHURCH, DEVONSHIRE.
Rood and parclose screens.
Fragments of a fine effigy and high tomb, with the original colouring and gilding on them. Discovered built into the sedilia and piscina recesses. Date 15th cent. *Exeter Diocesan Architect. Soc.*, 2nd series, iii. 207. *W. H. H. Rogers, The Ancient Sepulchral Effigies, &c. in Devon*, p. 58.

BRENTWOOD, ESSEX, CHAPEL OF ST. THOMAS THE MARTYR.
Pulled down.
In the chancel; decorative patterns. 13th cent.
S.E. corner of nave ; the Sacred Monograms IHC, XPC.
Date about 1500.
In the E. splay of an adjoining window; an Arch-
bishop, (?) St. Thomas of Canterbury.
On opposite splay; two courses of colouring.
On W. face of the chancel arch ; black letter inscrip-
tions. Time of Edward VI.
Essex Archæol., v. 99.

BREWOOD CHURCH, STAFFORDSHIRE.
Altar tombs of the Giffords, richly painted and gilt.
The earliest circ. 1556. *Garner, Natural History of the
County of Stafford*, p. 133. *J. H. Smith, The Brewood
Chancel*, pp. 1–9, *and, Brewood, a resumé, Hist. and.
Topog.*, pp. 14–19.

BRICETT, GREAT, CHURCH, SUFFOLK.
Wall painting, now covered with whitewash.

BRICKHILL, GREAT, CHURCH, BUCKINGHAMSHIRE.
Window in N. chancel wall; scroll masonry patterns.
13th cent. *Church Builder*, xxxv. 101.

BRIDFORD CHURCH, DEVONSHIRE.
Rood and parclose screens, and pulpit ; painted and gilt.
Date 1508. *Oliver's Ecclesiastical Antiquities of Devon*,
ii. 132. *Exeter Diocesan Architect. Soc.*, iv. 166.
*Murray's Handbook of Devonshire. W. H. H. Rogers,
The Ancient Sepulchral Effigies, &c. in Devon*, p. 208.

BRIDGE CHURCH, KENT.
On the tympanum of a doorway walled up on the
N. side (interior) of the chancel; remains of blue colour-
ing, and a black letter inscription on the lintel.

BRIDGHAM, NORFOLK, ST. MARY'S CHURCH.
"Scenes from the Life of Our Saviour," re-covered with
whitewash. *Ecclesiologist*, iii. 94.
Lower part of painted rood screen. 15th cent.
Remains of colour on the font. 15th cent.

BRIGHTLINGSEA CHURCH, ESSEX.
Remains of colouring on a pedestal. *Essex Archæol.*,
v. 97.

BRIGHTON, SUSSEX, ST. NICHOLAS CHURCH.
Rood screen. 15th cent. *Murray's Handbook of Sussex.*

BRIGSTOCK CHURCH, NORTHAMPTONSHIRE.

On arches, between the chancel and Lady Chapel; decorative colouring. Early 13th century.

Lady Chapel; traces of mural paintings on the N. wall, and of decorative colouring on a canopied niche, and round E. and N.E. windows. 15th cent.

Remains of colour on lower portions of the panels of the pulpit. 15th cent.

On central arch, N. side of nave; bold foliage pattern. Late 12th or early 13th cent.

On central arch, S. side of nave; pattern of stars and scroll foliage. Circ. 1260.

Builder, 1877, p. 41. *Associated Architect. Societies' Repts.*, xiii. 242, 245.

BRIMPTON CHURCH, BERKSHIRE.

Window N. side of chancel; remains of colour on the jambs. 12th or 13th cent. *British Archæol. Assoc. Journ.*, xvi. 89.

BRINGTON, GREAT, CHURCH, NORTHAMPTONSHIRE.

Bench ends; stencilled patterns. *Associated Architect. Societies' Repts.*, ix. 250.

N. side of chancel; remains of colour on the monument of Sir John Spencer and Lady, painted shields, &c. Date about 1522. *Blore's Monumental Remains of Noble and Eminent Persons.*

Richly coloured monuments, with painted effigies, shields, &c. of Sir John Spencer and Lady, circ. 1586, of Sir Robert Spencer and Lady, circ. 1599, and of Sir John Spencer and Lady, circ. 1599.

Painted shields on the altar tomb of Sir William Spencer. Circ. 1532.

F. Whellan, Hist. Topog. and Directory of Northants, 1874, p. 297.

E. bay of nave roof; remains of decoration. Early 16th cent.

On a pew, on a panel probably of a screen; figure of St. Margaret.

BRINSOP CHURCH, HEREFORDSHIRE.

Over the S. door; the Crucifixion.

On S. wall of nave; Martyrdom of King Edmund.

On splay of window, S. side of chancel; the Salutation.

On S. wall of chancel; Our Lord in Glory (?), or the martyrdom of a bishop. Very indistinct.

BRINSOP, THE COURT HOUSE, HEREFORDSHIRE.

Here " there is some of the finest timber work with polychrome in a very perfect state." *Havergal, Fasti Herefordenses*, p. 157. *Associated Architect. Societies' Repts.*, viii. xlii.

BRISLEY CHURCH, NORFOLK.

On S. wall of nave; St. Christopher between SS. Andrew and Bartholomew. *British Archæol. Assoc. Journ.*, iii. 324. *Dawson Turner, &c.*, (*see heading of Appendix*,) iii. 113, i., new series, 202.

Over S. door; the Ascension.

Screen originally painted and gilded. *Carthew's Hundred of Launditch*, ii. 649, iii. 66.

The Assumption of the Virgin, and some consecration crosses. *The Ecclesiologist's Guide to the Deaneries of Brisley, &c.*, p. 21.

BRISTOL CATHEDRAL, GLOUCESTERSHIRE.

N. and S. walls, E. end of choir; ball flower string-course, repainted and regilt. Circ. 1320.

S. choir aisle; remains of colouring on effigies of Thomas lord Berkeley, circ. 1243; and of the 2nd Maurice lord Berkeley, circ. 1281. *Murray's Handbook of Somersetshire.*

S. side of choir; remains of a painting at the back of monumental recess occupied by effigy of Abbot Newland.

Lavatory S. side of choir; gilding on bosses restored.

Berkeley chapel to the E. of lavatory; within the splay of two E. windows. 14th cent. painting and gilding restored.

N. choir aisle; remains of colour on arcading and sedilia. Early 13th cent.

Lady Chapel, E. end of N. choir aisle; reredos with remains of colour. 15th cent.

BRISTOL, GLOUCESTERSHIRE, ST. AUGUSTINE'S MONASTERY.

New Testament subjects on the walls. Time of Queen Mary. *Society of Antiquaries' Proceedings*, iii. 267.

BRISTOL, GLOUCESTERSHIRE, ST. JAMES'S CHURCH.

Nave arches; decorative painting. 12th cent. *Destroyed.*

Remains of colour on corbels. 15th cent.

Figures of saints. Discovered on the walls in 1877, and *destroyed*.

BRISTOL, GLOUCESTERSHIRE, ST. JOHN'S CHURCH.

Paintings discovered at the W. end; the Destruction of the Seven Deadly Sins. Our Lord crowned with thorns, between St. Peter and an archbishop, &c. Date middle of 15th cent. *Coloured drawings in the Society of Antiquaries' Library.*

BRISTOL, GLOUCESTERSHIRE, ST. MARK'S (THE MAYOR'S) CHAPEL.

Roof and bosses painted. *Murray's Handbook of Gloucestershire.*

In wall of aisle; coloured effigy of William de Gaunt. Circ. 1268.

BRISTOL, GLOUCESTERSHIRE, ST. MARY REDCLIFFE CHURCH.

N. porch; 15th cent. bosses of outer porch re-gilt.

Within the arcade of the inner portion; figures of saints. 13th cent. *Destroyed.*

BRISTOL, GLOUCESTERSHIRE, ST. PETER'S CHURCH.

On N.W. pillar; painted and gilt niche. Late perpendicular period. *Pryce, Notes on the Ecclesiastical and Monumental Architecture and Sculpture of the Middle Ages in Bristol, p. 203.*

BRISTOL, GLOUCESTERSHIRE, CHURCH OF ST. PHILIP AND ST. JACOB.

Numerous painted and gilt fragments of capitals, cornices, &c. Discovered within the rood loft staircase, and now (?) preserved in the chancel. *Churches of Bristol, p. 185. Bristol and Gloucestershire Archæol. Soc. Trans., 1878–9, p. 24.*

BRISTOL, GLOUCESTERSHIRE, ST. STEPHEN'S CHURCH.

N. aisle; remains of colour on the weepers of a 15th cent. monument. *Archæol. Journ., iii. 82. Antiquarian and Architect. Year Book, 1844, p. 114.*

Also coloured shield. *Ashby De La Zouch Anastatic Drawing Soc., 1860, p. 6. pl. xxxiv.*

BRISTOL, GLOUCESTERSHIRE, HOUSE ADJOINING THE MAYOR'S CHAPEL.

Oratory discovered; adorned with scriptural paintings. *J. Willis, Ecclesiæ Bristolianæ. Churches of Bristol, p. 63.*

BRITFORD CHURCH, WILTSHIRE.

Romanesque arch in wall of nave; ornamented with scroll work, picked out with colour. *Archæol. Journ.,* xxx. 201.

BRIXWORTH CHURCH, NORTHAMPTONSHIRE.

S. side of chancel arch, within a pointed arched recess, a painted " Gloria." *Ecclesiologist,* xxvii. (xxiv. new series), p. 53.

BROADCLIST CHURCH, DEVONSHIRE.

Chancel screen painted and gilt; our Saviour with the woman of Samaria, and other subjects, painted on the panels. *Destroyed.*

Paintings on the walls, and decoration round the arches. Whitewashed over.

Exeter Diocesan Architect. Soc., iii. pt. ii., p. 55.

BROADWAS CHURCH, WORCESTERSHIRE.

Mural paintings on N. walls of nave and chancel. *Noakes' Rambles in Worcestershire,* 2nd series, p. 361; *and Guide to Worcestershire,* p. 65.

BROADWATER CHURCH, SUSSEX.

Monument of Thomas, Lord La Warre; originally enriched with gold and colour. Date 1526. *M. A. Lower, History of Sussex,* i. 86.

BROADWAY CHURCH, WORCESTERSHIRE.

Traces of colour on nave roof. Early 15th cent.

Walls of nave formerly painted.

Columns of nave painted with the zigzag ornament. *British Archæol. Assoc. Journ.,* xxxii. 436.

BROCKDISH CHURCH, NORFOLK.

Painted rood screen; remains of colour on the roof and walls. Discovered during the restoration of the church. *Ecclesiologist,* xiv. 372.

BROCKLEY CHURCH, SUFFOLK.

Remains of painted screen.

BROMHAM CHURCH, WILTSHIRE.

Roof of chancel aisle; painted and gilt. About 1520. *Murray's Handbook of Wiltshire. British Archæol. Assoc. Journ.,* xxxvii. 171.

BROMSGROVE CHURCH, WORCESTERSHIRE.

Ancient colouring on one bay of roof, renewed. *Civil Engineer and Architect's Journ.*, 1858, p. 378.

Painted effigies of Margaret and Elizabeth, wives of Sir John Talbot. Circ. 1550. *Hollis, Monumental Effigies*, pt. vi. pl. 10.

Over chancel arch; the Doom. *Destroyed.* *W. A. Cotton, Bromsgrove Church, its Hist. and Antiq.*, pp. 12, 71.

BROOK CHURCH, KENT.

Oratory in the tower; over the altar, our Lord giving the benediction.

On chancel walls; scenes from the life of Christ.

On nave walls; the history of a saint.

Four consecration crosses. Decorated period.

BROOKE CHURCH, NORFOLK.

W., N., and S. walls; the Prodigal Son. 14th cent. The Seven Deadly Sins. Expulsion from Paradise. St. Christopher, &c. 15th cent. *Norfolk Archæol.*, iii. 62. *British Archæol. Assoc. Journ.*, xiv. 28.

Painted font. *British Archæol. Assoc. Journ.*, xiv. 53.

BROOKE CHURCH, RUTLANDSHIRE.

N. wall of N. aisle; figure of Our Saviour and other subjects. *Destroyed.*

BROOME CHURCH, NORFOLK.

Painted font.

BROUGHTON, BUCKINGHAMSHIRE, ST. LAWRENCE'S CHURCH.

Space between windows N. side of nave; the Virgin with the body of our Lord.

Over the N. doorway; the Day of Judgment. 15th cent.

Over the S. doorway; St. George and the Dragon. 15th cent.

Space between windows, S. side of nave; an Archbishop or Bishop? St. Dunstan, and a female Saint ? St. Helena. Below, horseshoes, hammers, and various implements.

Remains of decorative patterns.

A series of tracings are in the Library of the *Royal Archæol. Institute.*

Archæol. Journ., vi. 176. *Builder*, 1864, p. 725, and 1881, vol. xl., p. 747. *Gent. Mag.*, 1849, xxxi. new series, 405. *Ecclesiologist*, ix. 314. *Sheahan, Hist. and Topog. of the County of Buckingham*, p. 508.

BROUGHTON CHURCH, HUNTINGDONSHIRE.
Remains of colour on a pillar on the N. and on the S. sides of the nave; also decorative painting round the arch of the chancel doorway (? old).

BROUGHTON CHURCH, NORTHAMPTONSHIRE.
In N. aisle; the Virgin.
S. side of nave, above the main arcade; numerous figures. Discovered in 1854, and again whitewashed over.

BROUGHTON, OXFORDSHIRE, ST. MARY'S CHURCH.
N. wall of chancel; the Five Joys of the Virgin.
Over chancel arch and on N. wall of nave; subjects concealed by whitewash.
Coloured shields on the founder's monument, renewed.

BROUGHTON GIFFORD CHURCH, WILTSHIRE.
On inner W. wall of S. porch; round the heads and on jambs of two doorways, remains of decorative colour.

BROUGHTON-IN-AIREDALE CHURCH, YORKSHIRE.
Sculptures of the Virgin and Child, and another subject; with remains of colour and gilding. Found in 1871. *Whitaker, Hist. and Antiq. of Craven*, 3rd ed., p. 113.

BROUGHTON, BRANT, CHURCH, LINCOLNSHIRE.
Painted roof. 15th cent. *Associated Architect. Societies' Repts.*, ix. 254, xiii. lxvi.
Portion of a sculpture of the Trinity; richly painted and gilt.

BRUNSTEAD CHURCH, NORFOLK.
S. wall; Seven Deadly Sins. *Destroyed.*

BRUTON CHURCH, SOMERSETSHIRE.
E. bay of nave roof; decorated with gold and colour.
Aisle roofs; painted shields, &c.
Somerset. Archæol. and Nat. Hist. Soc. Proceedings, xxiv. pt. i., p. 34.

BRYMPTON D'EVERCY CHURCH, SOMERSETSHIRE.
Painted rood beam, with shields, &c. 15th cent.

BUCKENHAM, NEW, CHURCH, NORFOLK.
Rood screen; diapers.

BUCKENHAM FERRY, NORFOLK, ST. NICHOLAS CHURCH.
Sculpture representing the Martyrdom of St. Erasmus, with remains of colour and gilding. Late 14th cent. Discovered in 1840. *Norfolk Archæol.*, i. 243.

BUCKLAND CHURCH, GLOUCESTERSHIRE.

Nave roof; has remains of colour, time of Henry VII. Wall paintings in nave whitewashed over. *British Archæol. Assoc. Journ.*, xxxii. 97, 442.

On nave walls; Our Saviour on the Cross, St. Michael and various other figures on pedestals showing through the whitewash. Powdering of the Rose en Soleil and texts.

Round the windows and on the pillars; decorative colour.

BUCKLAND CHURCH, HERTFORDSHIRE.

S. wall of Lady Chapel; decorative pattern.

S. side of chancel, on splays of a low side window; the Virgin and child, and a female Saint.

Cussans, Hist. of Hertfordshire, vol. i., pt. ii., p. 49. The stem of Jesse. *Building News*, 1868, p. 177.

BUCKLAND-IN-THE-MOOR CHURCH, DEVONSHIRE.

Rood screen; illuminated mouldings.

On the panels; the Adoration of the Magi, the Annunciation and St. Simon; (on the doors,) SS. Philip, Bartholomew, Andrew, and James Minor; SS. Matthias and Thomas, and six figures (? of the other Apostles), effaced.

On inner side a king, &c. *C. Worthy, Ashburton and its Neighbourhood*, p. 53.

BUGBROOKE CHURCH, NORTHAMPTONSHIRE.

Rood screen; rich perpendicular with remains of colour and gilding. *Churches of the Archdeaconry of Northampton*, p. 274. *Associated Architect. Societies' Repts.*, ix., cii.

BUNBURY CHURCH, CHESHIRE.

St. Christopher and altar-piece. *Archæol. Journ.*, xxiv. 67.

Screen between chancel and chantry; grotesque figures, flowers, &c., with date 1527. Screen between nave and S. aisle; the Annunciation, Sancta Jubana ? Juliana, &c., on the lower portion. *Lysons' Magna Britannia, Cheshire*, p. 443.

In the centre of chancel; Monument and effigy of Sir Hugh Calveley, formerly adorned with a profusion of colour and gilding. *Ormerod's History of Cheshire*, ii. 142. *Stothard's Monumental Effigies*, p. 77, pl. 99.

BURES, SUFFOLK, ST. MARY'S CHURCH.
Wooden effigy, time of Henry III., formerly painted.
British Archæol. Assoc. Journ., xxxii. 416.
Private chapel, now used as a barn; stencilled walls,
and one or two consecration crosses. 13th cent.

BURES, MOUNT, CHURCH, ESSEX.
S. wall, E. end of nave; (?) the meeting of the Virgin
and Elizabeth.
Early coloured decoration on the nave arcade.
Destroyed.
Essex Archæol., i., new series, p. 131.

BURFORD CHURCH, OXFORDSHIRE.
N. wall of nave; St. Christopher. *Bloxam's Princi-
ples of Architecture,* 10th ed., p. 411; 11th ed., ii. 201.
In niche at E. end, and round the E. window; remains of
colour.. In S. transept; floral pattern. Chantry Chapel;
S. side of nave; floral patterns. Early 15th cent.
Painted pulpit.

BURFORD CHURCH, SHROPSHIRE.
N. wall of chancel; wood panelling, on which are
paintings of the Twelve Apostles; in the centre panels
Richard Cornwall and Janet his wife. Executed 1517.
Murray's Handbook of Herefordshire.

BURGATE CHURCH, SUFFOLK.
Painted chest; two knights tilting. Time of Richard II.
Suffolk Archæol., i. 212. *Parker, Eccles. and Architect.
Topog. of England, Suffolk,* No. 131. *Murray's Hand-
book of Suffolk.*

BURGH CHURCH, SUFFOLK.

BURGH CASTLE CHURCH, SUFFOLK.
St. Christopher, &c. *Suckling's History of Suffolk,*
i. 338.

BURGH ST. PETER CHURCH, NORFOLK.
(?) Martyrdom of St. Thomas à Becket. *Destroyed.
Norfolk Archæol.,* vii. 374.
N. wall of nave; St. Christopher.
S. wall of nave; the death of the Virgin.

BURLESCOMBE CHURCH, DEVONSHIRE.
Screen, late 15th cent. *Repainted. Ecclesiologist,*
xxii. (xix. new series), 123; and xxviii. (xxv. new series),
202

BURLINGHAM, ST. ANDREW'S CHURCH, NORFOLK.

Rood screen; SS. Thomas of Canterbury, Edward the Confessor, Benedict, Withburgha, John the Baptist, Cecilia, Walstan, Catherine, Edmund, Edward King and Martyr, and Etheldreda. *East Anglian Notes and Queries*, iii. 290. *Norfolk Archæol.*, iii. 19. Date, 1536.

Hexagonal wooden stand, curiously ornamented with paintings. Early 15th cent. Formerly in the church. *Proceedings of the Royal Archæol. Institute*, Norwich vol., p. xxxix.

BURLINGHAM, ST. EDMUND'S CHURCH, NORFOLK.

S. wall of chancel; Murder of Becket. Late 14th cent. *Norfolk Archæol.*, v. 185.

Rood screen; powdered panels, tracery, cresting, &c. 15th cent.

Pulpit; panels, tracery, cresting, powder of stars and flowers, &c. Early 15th cent.

Blackburne, Decorative Painting, pp. 81–86; and *Colling, Gothic Ornaments*, ii., pl. 102. *Cotman, Archi- tect. Etchings*, 3rd series, pl. vii., p. 5.

BURNHAM NORTON CHURCH, NORFOLK.

Painted screen, with figures of King Ethelbert, St. Gre- gory, the Virgin, and the donors, depicted on the panels Late 15th cent.

On panels of pulpit the Four Doctors of the Church, and portraits of John Goldale and Katharine his wife. Restored.

Blomefield, (Parkin,) Hist. of Norfolk, ed. 1807, vii. 17. *Chambers, Hist. of Norfolk*, i. 24.

BURNHAM OVERY CHURCH, NORFOLK.

Over chancel doorway; St. Christopher. *Illustrations of Norfolk Topography*, p. 27.

Whitewashed over.

BURNSALL CHURCH, YORKSHIRE.

Wall of S. aisle; Black letter texts. Circ. 1550.

Sculpture representing the Adoration of the Magi, with remains of colour and gilding. Discovered in 1858.

Whitaker's Hist. and Antiq. of Craven, 3rd ed., pp. 504, 505. *Bristol and Gloucestershire Archæol. Soc. Transactions*, 1877–8, pt. i., p. 166.

BURROW-ON-THE-HILL CHURCH, LEICESTERSHIRE.

"On scraping the arcade arches, the remains of elaborate decorations in colours were discovered, and the timbers of

BURROW-ON-THE-HILL CHURCH, LEICESTERSHIRE—*cont.*
the roof were found to have been similarly ornamented."
Associated Architect. Societies' Repts., v. cvii. *J. H. Hill, Hist. of Market Harborough, &c.,* p. 77. *Leicester Architect. and Archæol. Soc. Trans.,* ii. 34. *White's Gazetteer of Leicestershire. All destroyed.*

BURTON AGNES CHURCH, YORKSHIRE.
Chapel E. end of N. aisle; remains of colour and gilding on the monument and effigies of Sir Walter Griffith and his Lady. Date about 1481.

BURTON LATIMER CHURCH, NORTHAMPTONSHIRE.
Between the spandrils of the nave arches, the Twelve Patriarchs. 16th cent.
Above the chancel arch; probably two series of paintings, some medallions, and figures on N. side.
On the wall of the N. aisle; the Judgment and Martyrdom of St. Catherine. 13th cent.
Painted font cover. ? Gone.
Chancel screen painted. Early 15th cent.
Churches of the Archdeaconry of Northampton, p. 147. *Ecclesiologist,* xxviii. (xxv. new series) p. 244. *Associated Architect. Societies' Repts.,* viii. cxiii. *Leicester Architect. and Archæol. Soc. Trans.,* iii. 270.

BURTON-UPON-STATHER CHURCH, LINCOLNSHIRE.
Nave arches have apparently been painted. *W. Andrew, The Hist. of Winterton, &c.,* p. 61.

BURY CHURCH, HUNTINGDONSHIRE.
On shaft on N. side of chancel arch; traces of a cable pattern. 12th cent.

BURY ST. EDMUNDS, SUFFOLK, ST. JAMES'S CHURCH.
On W. wall an inscription recording a bequest to the Grammar School by King Edward VI. Circ. 1553.

BURY ST. EDMUNDS, SUFFOLK, ST. MARY'S CHURCH.
Ceiling of E. compartment of S. aisle; legend, and diaper of stars and monograms. 15th cent. *Colling, Gothic Ornaments,* i. pl. 40; and *Tymms, Hist. of the Church of St. Mary,* p. 173. *Antiquarian Repertory,* new ed., iii. 330.
In S. aisle; remains of painting on the monument of John Barrett. Within a piscina close to the monument the sacred Monogram within a garter of SS.

Q 3254.   D

BURY ST. EDMUNDS, SUFFOLK, ST. MARY'S CHURCH—*cont.*

W. end of N. aisle; remains of a painting of the Descent from the Cross.

One bay at E. end of the nave roof, repainted.

Painted ceiling of chancel.

Remains of colouring on shields, and gilt roses on the monument of Sir William Carew and his Lady, on the S. side of the chancel. Late 15th cent.

Painted and gilt shields on the font.

On chancel aisle walls; remains of texts and paintings.

On S. wall of S. chancel aisle; " a cross patonce in red."

Tymms, Hist. of the Church of St. Mary, pp. 27, 95, 96, 169, 173, 175, and 185. *Tymms, Handbook of Bury St. Edmunds,* pp. 17, 21, 23.

BUTTINGTON CHURCH, MONTGOMERYSHIRE.

Traces of mural paintings.

BUXTON CHURCH, NORFOLK.

Rood screen; colour and gilding on the mouldings, figures of Saints on the panels, painted over, the panels have now been removed.

E. wall of S. aisle; powdering of " M "s and crowns.

Round a window and along wall of S. aisle; decorative pattern.

BYCKNACRE PRIORY CHURCH, ESSEX.

On one of the tower arches; remains of a chevron pattern. *Antiquarian Cabinet,* vol. iv.

BYFLEET CHURCH, SURREY.

Over N. door; diaper pattern, with seated figure, believed to be Edward II.

W. of N. door; consecration cross.

BYTHAM, CASTLE, CHURCH, LINCOLNSHIRE.

Chancel screen; figures of Saints painted on the panels. *Associated Architect. Societies' Repts.,* iv. lxxiv.

CADBURY, NORTH, CHURCH, SOMERSETSHIRE.
E. end of chancel; two niches, the original painting and gilding restored.
Traces of colour on the effigies of Lord Botreaux and Lady. Circ. 1462. *W. H. H. Rogers, The Ancient Sepulchral Effigies, &c. in Devon,* p. 389.
On vestry wall; three black letter alphabets.

CADBURY, SOUTH, CHURCH, SOMERSETSHIRE.
S. wall of S. aisle; large figures. *Destroyed.*
E. end of S. aisle; colouring on a piscina.
By N. window; running foliage pattern. Traces of colour on the chancel arch. Four figures projecting from the wall-plate, formerly painted, now varnished over.

CADDINGTON CHURCH, BEDFORDSHIRE.
Decorative colouring, and figures of Time and Death. Discovered on the walls and destroyed.

CAERLEON CHURCH, MONMOUTHSHIRE.
Side of arch; painted Greek cross. Discovered during the restoration of the church. *Murray's Handbook of South Wales.*

CALDECOTE CHURCH, CAMBRIDGESHIRE.
Rood screen. *F. A. Paley, The Ecclesiologist's Guide to the Churches . . . . . round Cambridge,* p. 17.

CALDEY ISLAND, PEMBROKESHIRE.
An alabaster reliquary, dug up at, with remains of colouring. Latter half of 15th cent. Now in the possession of E. K. Bridger, Esq. *Archæologia Cambrensis,* 4th series, i. 125. *Archæol. Journ.,* xxv. 166, xxvi. 211.

CALLINGTON CHURCH, CORNWALL.
Monument of Lord Willoughby de Broke. "Still bears considerable marks of polychrome." Date about 1502. *Exeter Diocesan Architect. Soc.,* iii. 192, and vi. 330. *Hutchison, Monograph of Callington Church,* p. 24.

CAMBRIDGE, CAMBRIDGESHIRE, JESUS COLLEGE CHAPEL.
Panels of nave roof; formerly coloured. Renewed in a different style.

CAMBRIDGE, CAMBRIDGESHIRE, KING'S COLLEGE CHAPEL.
S. side of nave; Provost Hacombleym's chantry, painted pendant and portion of fan tracery roof, painted and gilt screen work.

CAMBRIDGE, CAMBRIDGESHIRE, PEMBROKE COLLEGE CHAPEL.
On E. wall; a pattern of foliage and two dedication crosses. Circ. 1400.

CAMBRIDGE, CAMBRIDGESHIRE, QUEEN'S COLLEGE CHAPEL.
Painted roof. About 1450. *Ecclesiologist*, iv. 142.

CAMBRIDGE, CAMBRIDGESHIRE, ST. ANDREW THE LESS CHURCH, BARNWELL.
Original polychrome. Discovered on the walls and restored. *Ecclesiologist*, xix. 133.
Splays of windows; decorated with colour. Early 13th cent.
Rood screen, with remains of colour. *Removed.*

CAMBRIDGE, CAMBRIDGESHIRE, ST. BOTOLPH'S CHURCH.
Diaper patterns on two columns. Early 15th cent.

CAMBRIDGE, CAMBRIDGESHIRE, GREAT ST. MARY'S CHURCH.
St. Andrew's Chapel, E. end of N. aisle; traces of gilding and colour on the stringcourses. Late 15th cent. *Cambridge Antiq. Soc. Publications, Hist. and Architect' Notes on Gt. St. Mary's Ch., Cambridge*, 1869, p. 38.

CAMBRIDGE, CAMBRIDGESHIRE, ST. SEPULCHRE'S CHURCH.
Paintings in red and black. Discovered during the restoration in 1841. *Ecclesiologist*, i. 30, 111, 203.

CAMBRIDGE CAMBRIDGESHIRE, TRINITY CHURCH.
N. transept; painted niche.
Statuette of a bishop, ? St. Erasmus or Amator, richly coloured and gilt.
Cambridge Antiq. Soc. Journ., iv. pt. iv., pp. xii., xiii., 314, 328.

CAMEL, WEST, CHURCH, SOMERSETSHIRE.
E. bay of nave roof; painting renewed.

CAMPSALL CHURCH, YORKSHIRE.
On rood screen; inscription, and within roundels, the words "I.H.S.," and "M." 15th cent. *Murray's Hand-book of Yorkshire.*

CANEWDON CHURCH, ESSEX.
On the right side of the doorway; St. Christopher. Formerly existing, discovered in 1711. *Morant, Hist. and Antiq. of Essex*, i. 317 (note). *Wright, Hist. of Essex*, ii. 624 note). *Blackburne, Decorative Painting*, p. 17.

CANFIELD, GREAT, CHURCH, ESSEX.

Over altar on E. wall of chancel; the Virgin and Child.
Consecration cross and floriated ornament.

CANNINGS, BISHOP'S, CHURCH, WILTSHIRE.

On panel of a carrel or stall; large hand, with inscriptions. 15th cent. *Wilts Archæol. and Nat. Hist.
Soc. Mag.*, vi. 149. *Ecclesiologist*, v. 150. *Hist. of
Devizes*, H. Bull, 1859, p. 577. *British Magazine for
April*, 1835. *E. Kite, Hist. Notes on the Places of Interest
to be visited by the British Archæol. Assoc. in* 1880, p. 53.

CANTERBURY CATHEDRAL, KENT.

N. transept; remains of colour and gilding on the
canopy of the monument of Archbishop Peckham. About
1292.

Chapel of the Virgin, or the Dean's Chapel; decorative
painting. 15th cent.

The choir:—N. side; the colouring on the monument of
Archbishop Chicheley has lately been renewed.

S. side, above the former altar of St. Dunstan; rich
diapered panelling with remains of colour.

On existing woodwork of screen near the E. end;
remains of colour.

On old screen, whole length figures of the Apostles,
&c., with traces of the former blue and gold decorations.
Cromwell, Excursions through Kent, p. 52.

On portions of Prior Eastry's screen; a pattern of
lions and lilies. Date about 1304.

Archæol. Cantiana, x. 72.

On a projection above St. Michael's or the Warrior's
Chapel; paintings on panels of SS. Gregory and Augustine.
Removed.

On ceiling of chapel above; remains of colour on the
bosses and groining.

S. side of S. choir aisle; remains of colour on shields,
&c., on the monuments of Archbishops Walter Reynolds
and Hubert Walter.

Trinity Chapel or Retrochoir; monument of Edward
the Black Prince. Remains of gilding on the effigy.

On canopy above; remains of colour and gilding on
the parapet and shields, and on the under side "The
Trinity," with the emblems of the Four Evangelists at the
corners. Date about 1376. *Blore's Monumental Remains
of Noble and Eminent Persons. Stothard's Monumental
Effigies*, pl. 85.

CANTERBURY CATHEDRAL, KENT—*cont.*

Monument of Henry IV. and Joan of Navarre; on the canopy above, the mottoes "Soverayne" and "a temperance," repeated many times, and considerable remains of heraldic and decorative colouring. *Stothard's Monumental Effigies*, p. 82. *Blore's Monumental Remains of Noble and Eminent Persons. Gostling, "A Walk in and about Canterbury." J. Brent, Canterbury in the Olden Time*, pp. 292, 294.

On a panel at the head of the monument; the Martyrdom of Thomas à Beckett. On a panel at the foot of the monument, an angel holding a shield. Date about 1437. *Dart, Hist. and Antiq. of Canterbury Cathedral.*

Chapel, N. of Trinity Chapel; Remains of paintings. *Dart, Hist. and Antiq. of Canterbury Cathedral.*

*Becket's crown :—*N. side; two angels holding a cardinal's hat. S. side; St. Christopher, and various representations of a Phœnix rising from the flames. *All destroyed.*

St. Andrew's Chapel; decorative painting. Late 12th cent.

N. choir aisle; within a recessed arch on the N. side, the legend of St. Eustace.

The Adoration of the Magi. *Destroyed. Lower, Curiosities of Heraldry*, p. 9.

The crypt; on some of the piers and arches, texts within scroll borders. Time of Elizabeth.

In the centre of the vault of several of the bays; a .Tudor rose.

On the eastern portion of the ceiling of the chapel of St. Mary Undercroft; paintings of the angelic choir, patterns of suns and stars, &c. End of 14th cent.

On the walls; numerous armorial shields.

Remains of colour on the reredos, and a black letter inscription at the back. Time of Henry VII.

Chapel under St. Andrew's tower; remains of colour.

Chapel under Becket's crown; the initials "I" and "M" and crowns on the groining. 15th cent.

Chapel under the Trinity Chapel; on S.W. face of a pier, S. side, a Bishop.

Archæol. Cantiana, xiii. 522–539.

Chapel of St. Gabriel (commonly called St. John's) :—

S. side of crypt on ceiling of western portion or nave; Seraphim holding scrolls. Various subjects within medallions and decorative painting. Mainly late 12th cent.

CANTERBURY CATHEDRAL, KENT—*cont.*

The Norman pillar, supporting the arches between the nave and chancel. Retains its original colouring.

On a buttress strip on N. and S. sides of inner chapel or chancel; an angel with six wings full of eyes and the feet resting on a winged wheel. (*See* Isaiah vi. and Ezekiel i.).

On N. side; a tree and domes, &c. above.

On the vault of the ceiling; our Lord within a vesica, supported by four angels, in the act of benediction.

On the N. wall; the events connected with the nativity and naming of St. John the Baptist.

On the S. wall; the Annunciation, Salutation, and Birth of our Saviour.

On the E. wall; within the splay of a recessed arch, St. John writing the Apocalypse, and the angels of the seven churches, each with a candlestick (only four remain), and the seven stars, within medallions.

Over western arch; a seraph holding a scroll; a tree, &c.

Decorative colour and inscriptions on scrolls in various parts of this chapel. Date probably late 12th cent.

These paintings have recently been preserved from further decay.

See description and illustrations in *Archæol. Cantiana*, xiii. 48–80. *Dart, Hist. and Antiq. of Canterbury Cathedral. Wright's Archæological Album. Antiquarian and Architect. Year Book*, 1844, p. 174. *J. Brent, Canterbury in the Olden Time*, p. 284.

Chapter House; remains of colour on the canopies at the E. end. Middle of the 14th cent.

On E. wall; the Coronation of the Virgin.

Ceiling; painted mouldings.

Cloisters; bosses of roof formerly coloured. Texts painted on the walls in 1472.

Winkle's English Cathedrals, i. 36, 37. *Cromwell, Excursions through Kent*, p. 66.

For an account of all the paintings, *see Archæol. Journ.*, xxxv. 275–288.

In the library; panel painting of Queen Edyve.

CANTERBURY, KENT, ST. ALPHEGE CHURCH.

Remains of diaper painting in niche.

CANTERBURY, KENT, EAST BRIDGE HOSPITAL.

The Martyrdom of Thomas à Becket. *J. Brent, Canterbury in the Olden Time*, p. 240 (note).

CARBROOKE CHURCH, NORFOLK.
Panel of rood screen; angel under canopy and diaper pattern. 15th cent. *Colling, Gothic Ornaments,* i. pl. 88.
Ceilings of nave and aisles, original colouring. *Chambers, Hist. of Norfolk,* ii. 980, 981. *The Ecclesiologist's Guide to the Deaneries of Brisley, &c.,* p. 78.

CARDINGTON CHURCH, BEDFORDSHIRE.
On monument, N. of chancel; two coloured armorial shields. Circ. 1500.

CARDYNHAM CHURCH, CORNWALL.
Chancel; decayed paintings. *Journ. Royal Inst. Cornwall,* 1872, p. 57..

CARLISLE CATHEDRAL, CUMBERLAND.
Aisle screens; Our Saviour and the Twelve Apostles, &c. About 1500. *Scott, Antiquarian Gleanings,* pls. xxx. and xxxi. *Gough, Sepulchral Monuments,* i. p. 3, *Introduction.*
Back of the stalls; legends of St. Augustine, St. Anthony, and St. Cuthbert. *Harcourt, Legends of St. Augustine, &c., Carlisle,* 1868. *Whellan, Hist. and Topog. of the Counties of Cumberland and Westmoreland,* p. 104. *Hist. and Antiq. of Carlisle,* 1838, pp. 173–177. *Gough, Sepulchral Monuments,* vol. i., pt. i., p. cxxvi.
Choir roof; painted and gilt. Restored. *Whellan, Hist. and Topog. of the Counties of Cumberland and Westmoreland,* p. 102.
On choir pillars; diaper of the sacred monogram. Late 15th cent.
Remains of painting everywhere discovered in the choir.
On tower piers; legendary subject. *Archæol. Journ.,* xvi. 374.
N.E. pier of central tower; the Death of St. Aidan, as revealed to St. Cuthbert while tending his flocks on the distant hills. *Society of Antiquaries' Proceedings,* iii. 86.
Wall pattern; Norman period. *Builder,* 1864, p. 686.

CARLISLE, CUMBERLAND, THE DEANERY.
Ceiling of principal chamber panelled and painted. Date 1507. *Archæol. Journ.,* xvi. 372.

CARLTON-IN-LINDRICK CHURCH, NOTTINGHAMSHIRE.
Painted sculpture in alabaster of the Trinity, now in the possession of Mr. Ramsden. *Associated Architect. Societies' Repts.,* v. lxx., x. 168.

CARLTON RODE CHURCH, NORFOLK.
. Painted rood screen. *Paley's Manual of Gothic Architecture*, p. 246.

CARTMEL, LANCASHIRE, THE PRIORY CHURCH.
Shields on Harington monument, colour apparent in 1818. *J. Stockdale, Annales Caermoelenses*, p. 142.
Canopy of Harington monument; painted boards, the emblems of SS. Mark and Luke, &c. 14th cent.

CARTMEL FELL, LANCASHIRE, ST. ANTHONY'S CHAPEL.
N. side of nave; Comer Hall pew, figures of saints on the panels, and various remains of colouring.
Remains of colour on a wooden figure of Our Saviour, (?) part of the rood; and on a panel of the rood screen, now destroyed.
Cumberland and Westmoreland Antiq. and Archæol. Soc. Transactions, ii. 396.

CASHEL CATHEDRAL, TIPPERARY, IRELAND.
Cormac's Chapel:—" The whole of the vaulted roof as well as the sides of the chancel appear to have been richly painted in fresco, in which the prevailing colours used were red, yellow, brown, and white. In the small side recesses curtains were represented, and arches were depicted on the ceiling. These frescoes were obviously contemporary with the building." Date 1134. *Dr. Petries' Round Towers of Ireland*, p. 296. *Brash's Ecclesiastical Architecture of Ireland*, p. 97. *Lord Dunraven, Notes on Irish Architecture*, ii. 73, 74.
Martyrdom of St. Sebastian (?).

CASSINGTON CHURCH, OXFORDSHIRE.
On the soffit of the W. tower arch; a series of circular wreaths, enclosing the Agnus Dei and various crosses and emblems, the spaces between being filled up with foliage.
Over the face of the arch; the Last Judgment.
Within the jamb of an adjoining window; St. Barbara.
Over the S. doorway; an angel with the implements of the Passion.
On S. wall of chancel; the Annunciation.
The dates of these paintings are late 15th cent.
Whitewashed over in 1842. Sketches existing in the possession of the Oxford Society for Promoting the Study of Gothic Architecture.

CASSINGTON CHURCH, OXFORDSHIRE—*cont.*

Parker's Architectural Guide to the Neighbourhood of Oxford, p. 152. *Gent. Mag.*, 1842, xviii. (new series), 304. *Archæol. Journ.*, iv. 259. *Hist. Gazett. and Directory of the County of Oxford*, p. 667.

CASTLE ACRE. *See* ACRE, CASTLE.

CASTLE ASHBY. *See* ASHBY, CASTLE.

CASTLE BYTHAM. *See* BYTHAM, CASTLE.

CASTLE COMBE. *See* COMBE, CASTLE.

CASTLE EATON. *See* EATON, CASTLE.

CASTLE HEDINGHAM. *See* HEDINGHAM, CASTLE.

CASTLE RISING. *See* RISING, CASTLE.

CASTON CHURCH, NORFOLK.

Painted roof. *Associated Architect Societies' Repts.*, x. 91.

CASTOR, NORTHAMPTONSHIRE, ST. KYNEBURGA'S CHURCH.

West end of north aisle; the Descent from the Cross. Sale of Joseph by his Brethren. Martyrdom of St. Catherine, &c. *Ecclesiologist*, iii. 56., ix. 192. *F. A. Paley, Notes on Twenty Parish Churches round Peterborough*, p. 95. *Sweeting, Parish Churches in and around Peterborough*, pp. 18, 19. *F. Whellan, Hist. Topog. and Directory of Northants*, 1874, p. 655.

St. Christopher. Martyrdom of St. Agatha. The Entombment. Early 14th cent. *Gent. Mag.*, 1846, xxv., new series, 631.

Only three scenes in the history of St. Catherine now (1880) remain.

CATFIELD CHURCH, NORFOLK.

On N. wall of the nave; the Wheel of Fortune, the Tree of the Seven Deadly Sins, the Seven Virtues, the Seven Sacraments of the Church, Our Saviour and the Woman of Samaria, and (?) Nathan and David.

On S. wall of nave; the Adoration of the Shepherds, The Magi before Herod, and presenting their offerings; Martyrdom of St. Lawrence, Martyrdom of St. Catherine, The Resurrection, with Mary Magdalene at the Sepulchre, St. John the Evangelist before the Latin Gates, and the History of St. John the Baptist. Time of Edward III.

CATFIELD CHURCH, NORFOLK—*cont.*

Norfolk Archæol., i. 133 and 365. *British Archæol. Assoc. Journ.*, xiv. 27. *Exeter Diocesan Architect. Soc.*, iv. 46. *Illustrations of Norfolk Topography*, p. 32. *The Ecclesiologist's Guide to the Deaneries of Brisley, &c.*, p. 96. *Hart, Antiq. of Norfolk*, p. 63.

Whitewashed over.

Rood screen; on lower panels are 16 figures of Kings, including St. Edmund, with ermine and gilt crowns.

CAWSTON CHURCH, NORFOLK.

E. wall of S. transept; the Dedication of the Church to St. Agnes. 15th cent. *Norfolk Archæol.*, iii. 37.

On N.E. column of nave; a pattern of roses and two-headed eagles.

Rood screen; on the doors, the Four Doctors of the Church. Sir John Shorne, The Apostles, SS. Paul, Helena, and Agnes on the panels. About 1400. *British Archæol. Assoc. Journ.*, xxiii. 263, 376, xxxvii. 135. *East Anglian Notes and Queries*, iii. 291. *Blomefield, Hist. of Norfolk*, ed. 1807, vi. 266.

CAYTHORPE, LINCOLNSHIRE, ST. VINCENT'S CHURCH.

Over arch opening into tower; Last Judgment. *Associated Architect. Societies' Repts.*, ix. 30.

CERNE ABBAS, DORSETSHIRE.

Portions of a shrine richly painted and gilt, dug up on the site of the Abbey Church. *Hutchins' Hist. of Dorset*, 3rd ed., iv. 27.

CERNEY, NORTH, GLOUCESTERSHIRE, ALL SAINTS' CHURCH.

Remains of frescoes discovered on the walls. *Dollman, Antient Pulpits*, p. 20.

CERRIGYDRUIDION CHURCH, DENBIGHSHIRE.

Traces of wall paintings. *Thomas, Hist. of the Diocese of St. Asaph*, p. 534. *All destroyed.*

CHADDESDEN CHURCH, DERBYSHIRE.

E. end of N. aisle; figures painted on the reredos, representing Our Saviour on the Cross, &c. *J. C. Cox, Churches of Derbyshire*, iii. 309.

CHADDESLEY CORBET CHURCH, WORCESTERSHIRE.

Over the chancel arch; the Last Judgment. Now concealed by whitewash. Indications of colour on the walls. *Bowman's Ecclesiastical Architecture*, p. 12.

CHAGFORD CHURCH, DEVONSHIRE.

N. side of nave; colouring on the arches, and remains of large subject above them.

CHALDON CHURCH, SURREY.

W. wall of nave; Ladder of the Salvation of the Human Soul, and the Road to Heaven. End of 12th cent. *Surrey Archæol.*, v. 275 *et seq.*, and vii. 295. *Archæol. Journ.*, xxx. 35.

CHALFIELD, GREAT, CHURCH, WILTSHIRE.

Walls of Tropenel Chantry; figures of saints, subjects from the bible, &c., time of Henry VIII., whitewashed over, once existed. *Walker, Hist. and Antiq. of the Manor House and Church of Great Chalfield, Wilts*, pp. 11–24. *Pugin, (T. L. Walker,) Examples of Gothic Architecture,* pt. ii., pp. 11, 24. *Builder,* 1881, vol. xli., p. 251. *Devizes and Wiltshire Gazette,* August 18th, 1881.

CHALFIELD, GREAT, MANOR HOUSE, WILTSHIRE.

Hall screen; painted and gilt. Circ. 1530. *Walker, Hist. and Antiq. of the Manor House and Church of Great Chalfield, Wilts,* pp. 22, 24. *Pugin, (T. L. Walker,) Examples of Gothic Architecture,* pt. ii., p. 22, pls. xvii., xviii.

CHALFONT ST. GILES' CHURCH, BUCKINGHAMSHIRE.

S.E. corner of S. aisle; two scenes from the history of St. Catherine.

S. wall of S. aisle; the Crucifixion, Herod's feast, and the Beheading of St. John the Baptist.

Over chancel arch; decorative painting, battlements, &c. All 14th cent.

CHALGROVE CHURCH, OXFORDSHIRE.

N. wall of chancel; the Stem of Jesse and the Life of Christ.

Within the window splays; SS. Mary Magdalene, Helena, Gabriel, and the Virgin.

S. wall of chancel; the Death of the Virgin, and the Day of Judgment.

Within the window splays; SS. John the Baptist, John the Evangelist, Lawrence, and Bartholomew.

E. wall of chancel; the Descent into Hell, Resurrection and Ascension, and the Assumption and Coronation of the Virgin.

Within the window splays; SS. Peter and Paul. 13th and 14th cents.

CHALGROVE CHURCH, OXFORDSHIRE—*cont.*

Archæologia, xxxviii. 431. *Gent. Mag.,* 1837, viii., new series, 547. *Ecclesiologist,* xx. 279. *Archæol. Journ.,* xxxviii. 84.

CHARD CHURCH, SOMERSETSHIRE.

Some indistinct paintings discovered on the walls of the chancel.

Vermilion colouring round the nave arches.

CHARLTON HORETHORNE CHURCH, SOMERSETSHIRE.

N. chantry chapel; remains of polychrome on two niches. *Ecclesiologist,* xii. 153.

CHARLTON ON OTMOOR CHURCH, OXFORDSHIRE.

Rood-loft with original painting and gilding. Date about 1500. *Parker's Architectural Guide to the Neighbourhood of Oxford,* p. 11. *Dunkin, Hist. and Antiq. of the Hundreds of Bullington and Ploughley,* vol. i., p. 207.

CHARLWOOD CHURCH, SURREY.

S. aisle; the legend of St. Margaret, (?) of St. Eulalia, and the story of St. Nicholas. 13th cent.

The Martyrdom of St. Sebastian or Edmund. 14th cent. And " Les Trois Vifs et les Trois Morts."

Archæol. Journ., xvi. 89, and xxi. 209.

N. chancel, on either side of E. window; richly coloured niches, found in 1844. *Brayley's Hist. of Surrey,* 2nd ed., iv. 60.

CHARWELTON CHURCH, NORTHAMPTONSHIRE.

Gilding and painting, nearly obliterated, on the monument of Sir Thomas Andrew and his two wives. Date about 1450. *Baker's Hist. and Antiq. of Northamptonshire,* p. 303.

CHATHAM CHURCH, KENT.

Sedilia richly painted and gilt. Date late 13th cent. Discovered and *destroyed* in 1788. *Vetusta Monumenta,* iii. pl. 4.

CHAWLEIGH CHURCH, DEVONSHIRE.

Rood screen. 15th cent. *Ecclesiologist,* xxviii. (xxv. new series), 308. *Exeter Diocesan Architect. Soc.,* 2nd series, ii. 96.

CHECKENDON, OXFORDSHIRE, ST. MARY'S CHURCH.

Wall and vault of apse; Our Saviour and the Twelve Apostles. About 1300. Restored 1869. Other paintings have been discovered much obliterated.

Building News, 1868, p. 708, and 1869, p. 261. *Church Builder*, 1869, No. xxxi., p. 95.

The series of Apostles includes St. Paul. Date 12th cent. *Proceedings of Oxford Architect. and Historic. Soc.*, new series, No. xvi., p. 75.

Remains of colour on arch and capital of a Norman doorway.

CHECKLEY CHURCH, STAFFORDSHIRE.

"Ancient and curious paintings beautified."

Emblems of mortality, time, and eternity, with black letter texts, one from Hosea, xiii. 14.

Redfern, Hist of Uttoxeter, p. 348. *Garner, Nat. Hist. of the County of Stafford*, supp., p. 9. *Murray's Handbook for Staffordshire*.

CHEDDAR, SOMERSETSHIRE, ST. ANDREW'S CHURCH.

Painted pulpit. About 1500. *Dollman, Antient Pulpits*, p. 27. Restored.

On E. pier of arch opening to S. chapel; coloured niches. About 1500.

Nave roof repainted. Late 15th cent. *Builder*, 1873, p. 413.

On N. of chancel; monument of Sir Thomas de Cheddar and Lady. 1443. Repainted.

Under the tower; part of a large subject, (?) St. George and the Dragon, discovered and *destroyed*.

CHEDDINGTON CHURCH, BUCKINGHAMSHIRE.

Remains of painting discovered in 1855–56, and *destroyed*. *Sheahan, Hist. and Topog. of the County of Buckingham*, p. 658.

CHELLESWORTH CHURCH, SUFFOLK.

Over chancel arch; Day of Doom. This painting has undergone "restoration."

Over great western arch; part of a painting of St. George and the Dragon.

In the S. aisle; St. Christopher, and other fragments of painting.

15th cent.

Suffolk Archæol., i. 146. *Archæol. Journ.*, vii. 87. *Parker, Eccles. and Architect. Topog. of England, Suffolk*, No. 452. *Illustrated London News*, Sept. 15th, 1849, p. 187.

CHELMORTON CHURCH, DERBYSHIRE.
   N. wall of N. aisle; various figures and some black letter texts. *J. C. Cox, Churches of Derbyshire*, ii. 83. S. wall of S. transept; ornamental texts. 15th cent.

CHELMSFORD MUSEUM, ESSEX. *See* LATCHINGDON.

CHELTENHAM CHURCH, GLOUCESTERSHIRE.
   S. wall of chancel, and N. jamb of chancel arch; dedication crosses. *Bristol and Gloucestershire Archæol. Soc. Trans.*, 1878–79, p. 71. *Destroyed.*

CHELTENHAM, GLOUCESTERSHIRE, OLD HOUSE AT.
   Panel painting of Edward the Black Prince conferring a crest of five ostrich feathers on Sir Richard de la Bere. *Bigland's, Gloucestershire*, i. 312. *Lower, Curiosities of Heraldry*, p. 172.

CHENIES CHURCH, BUCKINGHAMSHIRE.
   Tombs of the Earls of Bedford; richly painted and gilt. *Parker, Eccles. and Architect. Topog. of England, Bucks*, No. 48.

CHERITON. *See* STACKPOLE ELIDUR.

CHERRY HINTON CHURCH, CAMBRIDGESHIRE.
   On the rood screen; Our Lady of Pity, St. Mary Magdalene, and other Saints. Now painted over.
   Over the N. doorway; St. Christopher. Whitewashed over.
   Churches of Cambridgeshire, pp. 23 and 30. *Lysons' Magna Britannia, Cambridgeshire*, p. 59.

CHESHAM CHURCH, BUCKINGHAMSHIRE.
   On S. wall of S. aisle; St. Christopher.
   On N. wall of N. aisle; St. Michael weighing Souls. *Destroyed.* 14th cent. On N. W. tower pier; a head. Consecration Cross. *Records of Buckinghamshire*, iv. 27–28.

CHESHAM BOIS CHURCH, BUCKINGHAMSHIRE.
   St. Christopher. Whitewashed over.
   Chancel roof; the original 15th cent. painting. *Restored.*

CHESTER CASTLE, CHESHIRE.
   Chantry of St. Mary, formerly on the wall; a picture of Moses receiving the tables of the law. *Thomas' Visitors' Guide to Chester*, 1853, p. 23.

CHESTER CATHEDRAL, CHESHIRE.
Lady Chapel; colouring on the walls and the bosses of the ceiling. *Chester Architect. Archæol. and Historic. Soc.*, ii. 140, 264.
N. aisle; altar tomb. 15th century. *Murray's Handbook of Cheshire.*

CHESTER, CHESHIRE, ST. JOHN'S CHURCH.
Painting on pillar adjoining the N.W. pier of the tower; subject uncertain. *Archæologia Cambrensis*, 3rd series, xv. 196.
Remains of colouring and masonry patterns on the walls of the S. transept. *Chester Architect. Archæol. and Historic. Soc.*, ii. 345.

CHESTER, CHESHIRE, CHURCH OF ST. MARY-ON-THE-HILL.
On S. wall, in a line with the pulpit; the Crucifixion, with the Virgin, St. John, and an Archbishop on a groundwork of foliage. Above, a crowned figure, probably King Henry VI.
On jamb of adjoining window; the Resurrection. Late 15th cent.
Chester Architect. Archæol. and Historic. Soc., i. 400.

CHESTER, CHESHIRE, ST. PETER'S CHURCH.
On a pillar near S. door; the Annunciation to the Shepherds. *The Artisan*, January, 1848.
Grooves of the pillars, painted. *Builder*, 1847, p. 596.

CHESTER, CHESHIRE, ST. WERBURGA'S CHURCH.
St. Werburgh. *Archæologia Cambrensis*, 3rd series, xiv. 450.

CHESTERFIELD CHURCH, DERBYSHIRE.
On either side of the transept arch; the Crucifixion and another subject. Over the N.W. door; two series of paintings. *J. C. Cox, Churches of Derbyshire*, i. 135. All whitewashed over.

CHESTERTON CHURCH, CAMBRIDGESHIRE.
Over chancel arch and the E. nave arches; the Last Judgment.
Within the splays of the E. window, N. side of N. aisle; painting in compartments, subject uncertain, perhaps the seven acts of mercy. Circ. 1300.
Remains of paintings in the nave, within the spandrels of the arches and elsewhere.
A. G. Hill, Churches of Cambridgeshire, p. 175.

CHESTERTON CHURCH, CAMBRIDGESHIRE—*cont.*

Found on a block of stone used to fill up a window; painting of St. Dorothy. About 1350. Now in the Fitzwilliam Museum, Cambridge. *Cambridge Antiq. Soc. Journ.,* iv. 1.

CHETWODE CHURCH, BUCKINGHAMSHIRE.

N. of chancel, back of arched recess; bold foliaged pattern.

CHEVELY CHURCH, CAMBRIDGESHIRE.

In N. transept; Arabesque patterns, and powdering of "fleur de lis." *Suffolk Archæol.,* i. 244.

A pattern of "fleur de lis" within the splay of the W. window, figured in *Fairlie's Illustrations of Cheveley Church.*

CHEVENING CHURCH, KENT.

Painted font. *Blackburne, Decorative Painting,* p. 72.

CHEW MAGNA CHURCH, SOMERSETSHIRE.

Wooden effigy of Sir John Hautville. 13th cent. Repainted. *Murray's Handbook of Somersetshire. British Archæol. Assoc. Journ.,* xxxii. 415.

CHICHESTER CATHEDRAL, SUSSEX.

Nave and choir ceilings; paintings executed in 1520, erased in 1817 or 1829. Coloured engraving existing. *Proceedings of the Royal Archæol. Institute, Chichester Vol.,* p. 99. *British Archæol. Assoc. Journ.,* i. 257. *Antiquarian Cabinet,* vol. vi.

W. wall of S. transept; a series of shields within quatrefoils, with inscriptions below. 14th cent. .

S. side of S. transept; remains of colouring on effigy of Bishop Langton. Circ. 1338.

Choir; stalls of Bishop Sherborne gilt, and with the names of the Prebendaries, &c. painted over them in antique characters.

S. choir aisle; monument and effigy of Bishop Sherborne, died 1536. Have been regilt and repainted.

Back of stalls, S. choir aisle; Ceadwalla bestowing the monastery of Selsey on St. Wilfrid, and the confirmation of the grant by Henry VIII. to Bishop Sherborne. Painted by Theodore Bernardi. Circ. 1520.

On N. wall of N. transept; portraits of the Monarchs of England and the Bishops of Selsey and Chichester. Painted by Theodore Bernardi. Circ. 1520.

CHICHESTER CATHEDRAL, SUSSEX—*cont.*

On the pier of the arch opening from N. transept into the library ; a Bishop on a diapered ground.

Above, within the splay of the arch ; the lower portion of two other figures. Late 12th cent.

N. wall of Lady Chapel, within a recess ; remains of bold foliated ornament. Remains of colour on the groining of the ceiling, and capitals of the groining shafts in the Lady Chapel. Partly *restored.*

Murray's English Cathedrals, pp. 303 and 310. *Murray's Handbook of Sussex. Black's Guide to Sussex. Ecclesiologist,* xxix. (xxvi. new series), 208. *M. A. Lower, History of Sussex,* i. 105. *Antiquarian Cabinet,* vol. vi. *Cromwell, Excursions through Sussex,* p. 15.

CHICHESTER, SUSSEX, ST. OLAVE'S CHURCH.

E. wall of chancel ; the Coronation of the Virgin, 16 figures of Saints under canopies, 2 consecration Crosses, decorative patterns, &c. 12th and 13th cents. *Destroyed. Sussex Archæol.,* v. 213, 222, viii. 321. *Proceedings of the Royal Archæol. Institute, Chichester vol.,* p. 97.

CHICHESTER, SUSSEX, THE BISHOP'S PALACE.

Domestic chapel of the Bishops ; the Virgin and Child. Time of Henry III. *Gent. Mag.,* 1835, iii. new series, 197. *Proceedings of the Royal Archæol. Institute, Chichester vol.,* p. 99.

Two consecration crosses.

Ceiling of Great Hall ; panel paintings with armorial bearings and devices of Bishop Sherborne, and the nobility and gentry of the county. *Winkles' English Cathedrals,* ii. 37.

CHICHESTER, SUSSEX, HOUSE BELONGING TO MR. MASON.

Paintings discovered on the walls, representing a row of houses, and figures of birds and flowers. 16th cent. *Archæol. Journ.,* i. 165. *British Archæol. Assoc. Journ.,* iv. 199. *Archæologia,* xxxi. 483.

CHICKERELL, WEST, CHURCH, DORSETSHIRE.

St. Christopher. Whitewashed over in 1759. *Hutchins' History of Dorset,* i. 424 ; 3rd. ed., ii. 496. *Blackburne, Decorative Painting,* p. 16.

CHIDDINGLY CHURCH, SUSSEX.

Recess in S. chancel wall ; masonry pattern. *Sussex Archæol.,* xviii. 186.

CHILDERDITCH CHURCH, ESSEX.

Scripture texts. *British Archæol. Assoc. Journ.*, i. 313.

CHILLINGHAM CHURCH, NORTHUMBERLAND.

S. aisle; altar tomb of Sir Ralph Grey and his wife, Elizabeth Fitzhugh, has been sumptuously coloured. Perpendicular period. *Wilson's Churches of Lindisfarne,* p. 76.

CHILTINGTON, WEST, CHURCH, SUSSEX.

N. wall of nave under trefoil headed arches; the Annunciation, Salutation, Nativity, Angels appearing to the Shepherds, and Adoration of the Magi. Seraphim between the heads of the arches. 13th cent.

Also St. Christopher.

E. splay of E. window, N. of nave; Christ showing the wounds and surrounded by certain implements.

On pillars between nave and S. aisle; ? St. Michael weighing Souls; and other subjects, mixed up with texts.

Round, and on the soffits of, the arches, and on S. wall of nave; masonry, star, intersecting arched, lozenge, and zigzag patterns. 12th and 13th cents.

S. wall of nave under trefoil headed arches; the Triumphal Entry into Jerusalem, ? the Last Supper, ? the Betrayal, the Scourging, Christ bearing his Cross, the Crucifixion, the Maries at the Sepulchre, and the Resurrection. 13th cent.

In S.E. corner; foliage decoration.

Within an arch between S. aisle and chancel chapel; figures of the Apostles, and part of a vesica held by seraphim, probably enclosing a figure of Our Lord in Glory. Late 12th cent. Over this has been painted a bold scroll pattern, angels blowing trumpets, &c.

Archæol. Journ., xxxviii. 82, 92, 95.

Within the splay of a decorated window in S. aisle; Painted niche.

CHILTON CHURCH, BERKSHIRE.

Remains of rood-loft painted in gaudy colours. *Hewett, Hist. of the Hundred of Compton*, p. 18.

CHILTON CANTELO CHURCH, SOMERSETSHIRE.

N. transept; diaper pattern, and the death, burial, assumption, and coronation of the Virgin. *Destroyed. Somerset Archæol. and Nat. Hist. Soc. Proceedings*, xx. 71.

CHIPCHASE CASTLE, NORTHUMBERLAND.

"Traces of the ordinary mediæval decoration of the interior walls of castellated residences, may still be seen in the tattered fragments of Mural Gothic paintings, especially in the third story or family chambers." *Revd. G. R. Hall, Memoir on Chipchase Castle, p. 9. Mackenzie, View of the County of Northumberland,* ii. 222.

CHIPPENHAM CHURCH, CAMBRIDGESHIRE.

Screen and rood-loft. *Lysons' Magna Britannia, Cambridgeshire,* p. 59.

CHIPPENHAM CHURCH, WILTSHIRE.

South chancel chapel; painted roof and cornices. Late 15th cent.

CHIPPING ONGAR. *See* ONGAR, CHIPPING.

CHISELHURST, KENT, ST. NICHOLAS CHURCH.

Wall paintings from 1442–1460.

N. aisle, the Scadbury Chantry; S. side, a red and white rose with date, 1422, and a falcon on a fetter lock with date, 1460.

Screen "with moulded cornice ornamented with small gilded estoiles." *Archæol. Cantiana,* xiii. 388.

CHISHILL, GREAT, CHURCH, ESSEX.

Over chancel arch; portion of a Doom.

On N. wall; St. Lawrence. Remains of texts, &c. *All destroyed.*

CHOLESBURY CHURCH, BUCKINGHAMSHIRE.

N. and S. walls of nave; various figures. *Destroyed.*

CHRISTCHURCH PRIORY CHURCH, HAMPSHIRE.

Remains of colour and gilding on the rood screen. Time of Edward III. *Archæol. Journ.,* v. 73, 142, 144.

Pilasters supporting the choir roof. Painted about 1310.

In a chapel E. end of N. choir aisle; effigies of Sir John Chydioke and his Lady retain traces of their original colouring. Early 15th cent. *Murray's Handbook of Hampshire.*

Bosses of choir retain their original polychrome. *Proceedings of the Royal Archæol. Institute, Winchester vol.*

CHULMLEIGH CHURCH, DEVONSHIRE.

Rood screen. *Ecclesiologist,* xxviii. (xxv. new series) p. 308.

CHURSTON FERRARS CHURCH, DEVONSHIRE.
Screens, richly painted. *Builder*, 1865, p. 212.

CIRENCESTER CHURCH, GLOUCESTERSHIRE.
Chancel, band of quatrefoils. Restored.

ST. KATHARINE'S CHAPEL.
E. end of N. wall; St. Christopher, on diaper background.
W. end of N. wall; medallion with two figures.
S. wall; St. Katherine with emblems, on diaper background. *F. G. Baylis, Ancient Churches of Gloucestershire*, p. 30.

ST. JOHN'S CHAPEL.
On rib of arch, S. aisle; wall pattern. Restored.
In S.E. angle; painted and gilt screen work.

LADY CHAPEL.
On spandrel on S. wall; a Purgatory.

TRINITY CHAPEL.
N. wall; Martyrdom of St. Erasmus. 14th cent. *Archæologia*, xv. 405.
Portrait and arms of William Prelatte, and black letter text below. *Hist. and Antiq. of Cirencester*, pp. 65, 67, 69, 73.
Fragments in other parts of the church.

CLACTON, GREAT, CHURCH, ESSEX.
Coloured decorations on the walls. 15th cent. *Essex Archæol.*, iv. 86.

CLAPHAM CHURCH, BEDFORDSHIRE.
Traces of early decoration of nave walls. *D. G. C. Elwes, Bedford and its neighbourhood*, p. 112.

CLAPHAM CHURCH, SUSSEX.
E. end of S. aisle; painted decoration on the splay of a lancet window. *Sussex Archæol.*, xxvi. 276.

CLAPTON IN GORDANO CHURCH, SOMERSETSHIRE.
N. of nave; female Saint beneath a canopy, holding a cross.
N. of chancel; consecration cross.

CLATFORD, GOODWORTH, CHURCH, HAMPSHIRE.
Side walls of nave. Middle of 15th cent. *British Archæol. Assoc. Journ.*, vii. 431. *Destroyed.*
On the E. pillar, N. side of nave; remains of black letter inscription.

CLAUGHTON CHURCH, LANCASHIRE.
Fine rood screen, painted and gilt. 16th cent. Destroyed. *Whitaker's History of Richmondshire*, ii. 244.

CLAVERDON CHURCH, WARWICKSHIRE.
E. wall; remains of scroll painting. *Warwickshire Churches, Deanery of Warwick*, ii. 32.

CLAYHANGER CHURCH, DEVONSHIRE.
Screen; painted panels. *Murray's Handbook of Devonshire. Introduction.*

CLAYWORTH CHURCH, NOTTINGHAMSHIRE.
Coloured mouldings found in the churchyard wall. *Associated Architect. Societies' Repts.*, xiii. xi.

CLEEVE, BISHOP'S, CHURCH, GLOUCESTERSHIRE.
Remains of painting under N.W. window of N. aisle, and elsewhere.
Colouring on a cross-legged effigy in S. transept, and on the effigy of a nun.
Bristol and Gloucestershire Archæol. Soc. Trans., 1878–79, pp. 262, 265, 1879–80, p. 24.

CLEEVE, OLD, ABBEY, SOMERSETSHIRE.
E. wall of refectory, now part of farm; the Crucifixion, with SS. Mary and John. 15th cent. *Somerset Archæol. and Nat. Hist. Soc. Proceedings*, vi. 95. *British Archæol. Assoc. Journ.*, xxxi. 410. *Worth, Tourist's Guide to N. Devon,* p. 10.
Photograph in the Art Library, S.K.
Painted chamber, leading out of the refectory; SS. Margaret Katherine, and Thecla.
British Archæol. Assoc. Journ., xxxi. 411.
Vault of vestibule to chapter house; traces of painting. *British Archæol. Assoc. Journ.*, xxxi. 408. *Builder*, 1875, p. 801. *Somerset. Archæol. and Nat. Hist. Soc. Proceedings*, vi. 91.
E. wall of buttery; three human figures, with monsters, and fishes. *Somerset. Archæol. and Nat. Hist. Soc. Proceedings*, xxi. 40.

CLEY, NORFOLK, ST. MARGARET'S CHURCH.
Remains of colour on brackets on each side of the nave. Early 14th cent.

CLIFFE-AT-HOO CHURCH, KENT.
N. transept; masonry patterns.

CLIFFE-AT-HOO CHURCH, KENT—*cont.*

E. wall of N. transept ; the Martyrdom of St. Edmund, with arcades, borderings and floral patterns. Late 13th cent. *Archæol. Cantiana*, xi. 148, 158.

E. wall of S. transept; the Day of Judgment, &c. *Archæol. Cantiana*, xi. 148. *Glynne, Churches of Kent* p. 348. *Ecclesiologist*, iv. 196.

CLIFTON CHURCH, BEDFORDSHIRE.

Panels of screen, now fixed to the N. and S. walls of the tower; on N. side, St. John, the Annunciation, SS. Peter and Paul. On S. side, SS. James Major, Jude, Bartholomew, and Thomas. Each Apostle has a duplicate figure, perhaps the corresponding Prophet, holding a scroll on the adjoining panel. *Parker, Eccles. and Architect. Topog. of England, Bedford*, No. 110.

Colour and gilding on effigies and shields on tomb of Sir Michael Fisher and Lady. Circ. 1500.

CLIFTON REYNES CHURCH, BUCKINGHAMSHIRE.

N. side of chancel; colouring on wooden effigy of a lady. Early 14th cent. *Archæol. Journ.*, xi. 152.

Over chancel arch ; the Day of Judgment.

CLIMPING CHURCH, SUSSEX.

On S. wall of tower ; a consecration cross. Late 12th cent. *Archæologia*, xlvii. 165.

Remains of painting discovered during the restoration of the church. *Destroyed.*

CLYFFE PYPARD CHURCH, WILTSHIRE.

Faint traces of paintings on the walls.

Screens restored and partially repainted. 15th cent.

CLYST ST. GEORGE CHURCH, DEVONSHIRE.

Scrolls with texts, discovered beneath the plaster. reproduced. *H. T. Ellacombe, Hist. of the Parish of Clyst St. George*, pp. 18, 28.

CLYST ST. LAWRENCE CHURCH, DEVONSHIRE.

Remains of painting on rood screen. *Exeter Diocesan Architect. Soc.*, 2nd series, i. 15.

COBHAM CHURCH, KENT.

Heads of images, &c., parts of a reredos, with considerable remains of colour, found in the S.E. wall of the chancel. *Ecclesiologist*, xxii. (xix. new series), 110.

COBHAM, KENT, HENHURST MANOR.
Painting on the wall of a room now destroyed, viz., a pomegranate pattern, two angels holding a shield, &c. Late 15th cent.

COCKERINGTON, SOUTH, CHURCH, LINCOLNSHIRE.
Seven crosses painted on walls of nave, and one on wall of chancel. *Associated Architect. Societies' Repts.*, xii. 0.

COCKINGTON CHURCH, DEVONSHIRE.
Remains of colour on the font.
Painted pulpit brought from Tor Mohun Church.

CODFORD ST. MARY'S CHURCH, WILTSHIRE.
Chancel arch, sprinkled with dark red colouring, and enriched with a kind of running scroll work, probably 12th cent.
Memorials of the Parish of Codford St. Mary, p. 9.

COGGESHALL, GREAT, CHURCH, ESSEX.
The Nativity and Crucifixion, and figures of saints. *Ecclesiologist*, xxv. 177.
Wall decoration. Perpendicular period. *Builder* 1864, p. 734.
Eight consecration crosses. *Essex Archæol.*, iv. 139.

COGGESHALL, LITTLE, CHAPEL, ESSEX.
On the walls; masonry patterns. 13th cent.
Within the space between the eastern lancets and the containing arch; decorations of flowing foliage.
At the back of one of the sedilia; a cruciform nimbus. Part of a painting of Our Saviour. *Essex Archæol.*, i. 174. and iii. 48. *Builder*, 1864, p. 724. *Ecclesiologist*, xxv. (xxii. new series), p. 177. *B. Dale, The Annals of Coggeshall*, p. 73.

COGGESHALL ABBEY, ESSEX.
Walls and groining of the ambulatory and of another room; remains of masonry patterns. *Essex Archæol.*, i. 180, 181.

COLCHESTER, ESSEX, ST. LEONARD-AT-HYTHE CHURCH.
"The roof of the chancel is wainscotted, and on the boards are painted the Patriarchs or ancestors of Jesus Christ, according to his genealogy in St. Matthew and St. Luke." *Morant Hist. and Antiq. of Essex*, i. 129. *Cromwell, Hist. of Colchester*, i. 235; *and, Excursions through Essex*, i. 80 *Wright Hist. of Essex*, i. 328.

COLCHESTER, ESSEX, ST. LEONARD-AT-HYTHE CHURCH—
cont.

N. wall of chancel; part of a subject visible; supposed
to have been " the Ascension."

On E. wall of S. chancel aisle; crowned M's found under
the tower. 15th cent.

COLERIDGE CHURCH, DEVONSHIRE.

Rood screen. 15th cent. *Exeter Diocesan Architect.
Soc.*, ii. p. 167, plate 5.

COLERNE CHURCH, WILTSHIRE.

" In the course of these repairs and alterations it became
evident that the church had once been literally covered
with polychromatic decoration, but this it was not
thought advisable to retain." *Wilts Archæol. and Nat.
Hist. Soc. Mag.*, iii. 366.

COLKIRK CHURCH, NORFOLK.

Screen, three painted shields. *Carthew's Hundred of
Launditch*, ii. 656.

COLLINGHAM, NORTH, CHURCH, NOTTINGHAMSHIRE.

Panels of screen; gilding and colour. *E. G. Wake,
The Hist. of Collingham*, p. 28.

COLMER CHURCH, HAMPSHIRE.

On piers of transept arch; floriated border.

On splays of E. window; the early block pattern and
masonry containing six-leaved roses.

Hervey, Hist. of Colmer and Priors Dean, pp. 22, 36.

COLTISHALL CHURCH, NORFOLK.

N. wall; a burial, probably intended to represent the
Seventh Act of Mercy. *Destroyed.*

COLTON CHURCH, STAFFORDSHIRE.

S. chancel wall; St. Nicholas and the miracle of the
three children, also the Salutation. Time of Richard II.

S. wall of S. chancel aisle, " Tasting the Forbidden
Fruit, and the Expulsion from Paradise." Also " the
Resurrection."

On W. wall of S. aisle of nave; figures of bishops and
saints.

Within the jamb of the W. window; two saints, one
perhaps St. Christopher.

Discovered during the rebuilding of the church, and
destroyed. Date about 1320. *Ecclesiologist*, xii. 374.

COLTON CHURCH, STAFFORDSHIRE—*cont.*
Ashby De La Zouch Anastatic Drawing Soc., 1865,
p. 4, pl. xxiii. *Some Account of Colton and the De*
Wasteneys family, pp. 105–107.

COMBE CHURCH, WILTSHIRE.
The Day of Judgment. *Duke's Prolusiones Historiæ*,
p. 545.

COMBE MARTIN CHURCH, DEVONSHIRE.
Rood screen; paintings of Our Lord, the Virgin, St.
Paul, and the Apostles in the lower panels. 15th cent.
Exeter Diocesan Architect. Soc., ii. 83. *Worth, Tourist's*
Guide to N. Devon, p. 29. *Stewart's N. Devon Hand-*
book, pp. 28, 180.
W. face of pier between the screens; double niche with
painted and gilt canopies.

COMBE, CASTLE, CHURCH, WILTSHIRE.
Chancel and chancel chapel ceilings, richly painted
and gilt. *G. P. Scrope, Hist. of Castle Combe*, p. 364.

COMBERTON CHURCH, CAMBRIDGESHIRE.
Screen and rood loft. *Lysons' Magna Britannia,*
Cambridgeshire, p. 59.
E. bay of nave roof, decorated with colour. *F. A.*
Paley, The Ecclesiologist's Guide to the Churches . . . . .
round Cambridge, p. 21.

COMPTON BASSETT CHURCH, WILTSHIRE.
Rood screen.

COMPTON, EAST, CHURCH, DORSETSHIRE.
N. wall of nave; a large 14th cent. painting dis-
covered and *destroyed* in 1838. *Hutchins' Hist. of*
Dorset, 3rd. ed., ii. 295.

COMPTON MARTIN CHURCH, SOMERSETSHIRE.
St. Anne instructing the Virgin. *J. M. Neale,*
Hierologus, p. 295.

COMPTON WYNYATE CHURCH, WARWICKSHIRE.
Roof; representation of the firmament.

CONISBOROUGH CHURCH, YORKSHIRE.
Paintings of figures, 13th cent.; and of decorative
patterns of the 15th cent. Discovered on the walls, and
destroyed. *Ecclesiologist*, xxviii. (xxv. new series),
282, 345.
Over N. door; St Christopher.

COOLING CHURCH, KENT.
Archæol. Journ., xx. 407.

COPFORD CHURCH, ESSEX.

Apsidal chancel; on the ceiling, our Lord in Glory, surrounded by angels, and with a background of towers signifying the New Jerusalem.

Over N. S. and E. windows; angels.

Within the splay of the E. window; St. Michael and Satan.

On chancel walls; figures of St. Peter, and nine other Saints,? the apostles, under canopies.

On the soffit of the chancel arch; the signs of the zodiac within medallions.

On chancel arch; frette and other Norman patterns.

This series of paintings probably dates from the 12th cent., but seems to have been partly renewed in the 14th. They have been recently restored.

Building News, 1876, xxxi. pp. 138, 149. *Society of Antiquaries' Proceedings*, 2nd series, vii. 72. *Builder*, 1876, p. 778. *Church Builder*, 1877, No. LXI. p. 51. *Archæol. Journ.*, xxxiii. 423, xxxiv. 272, xxxv. 285.

Crucifixion, Peter's wife's mother lying sick of a fever, and Mary Magdalen. Whitewashed over. *Wright's Hist. of Essex*, i. 406. *Antiquary*, 1871, i. 158, 184. *Cromwell, Excursions through Essex*, i. 57.

COPLE CHURCH, BEDFORDSHIRE.

Roof, S. aisle; remains of painting and gilding. *Parker, Eccles. and Architect. Topog. of England, Bedford*, No. 8.

Chancel screen; faint traces of colour. Red earth colour on the shields, on brass of Sir Walter Luke and Lady, 1536, on N. of chancel; and on those of Robert and Joan Bulkeley, 1550, and 1556, on S. wall of S. chancel aisle.

CORRINGHAM CHURCH, ESSEX.

Traces of colour on a head on the keystone of the Romanesque arch opening into the tower. Scraped off in 1864. *Rev. W. Palin, Stifford and its Neighbourhood*, p. 128.

CORRINGHAM CHURCH, LINCOLNSHIRE.

Lower part of rood screen; enriched with colour and gilding. *Associated Architect. Societies' Repts.*, viii. 236.

CORSHAM CHURCH, WILTSHIRE.
Tomb of Thomas Tropenell and Agnes his wife, painted and gilt mouldings, date 1490. *Walker, Hist. and Antiq. of the Manor House and Church of Great Chalfield, Wilts,* p. 25. *Pugin, (T. L. Walker,) Examples of Gothic Architecture,* 3rd series, pt. ii., pl. viii., and p. 26.

CORSTON CHURCH, SOMERSETSHIRE.
Arches and porch. *Destroyed.*

COTHELSTONE CHURCH, SOMERSETSHIRE.
Painting and gilding on the font. *Ecclesiologist,* i. 126. *Blackburne, Decorative Painting,* p. 72.

COTON CHURCH, CAMBRIDGESHIRE.
Remains of ancient painting on chancel screen. *F. A. Paley, The Ecclesiologist's Guide to the Churches . . . . . . round Cambridge,* p. 17.
The colouring has recently been twice renewed in different styles.

COTTENHAM CHURCH, CAMBRIDGESHIRE.
Faint traces of painting on the chancel arch. *Cambridge Antiq. Soc. Report for* 1854, p. 8.

COTTON CHURCH, SUFFOLK.
S. door: "the original colouring, only partially faded." *Cotton Church, Brief Account of,* p. 3.

COVE, NORTH, CHURCH, SUFFOLK.
N. wall of the chancel; scenes from the Passion, with foliated bordering.
S. wall of the chancel; the Ascension and the Day of Judgment. Date about 1300.
Remains of colour on the shields of the font. Early 14th cent.

COVE, SOUTH, CHURCH, SUFFOLK.
Head of a painted panel.

COVEHITHE CHURCH, SUFFOLK.
Painted font.

COVENTRY, WARWICKSHIRE, ST. MICHAEL'S CHURCH.
Panels of roof; painted and studded with gilt stars. *Blackburne, Decorative Painting,* p. 43.
N. side of nave, St. Andrew's Chapel; figures of two saints painted on the wall, within an ornamented recess. *W. Smith, Hist. of County of Warwick,* p. 213.

COVENTRY, WARWICKSHIRE, ST. MICHAEL'S CHURCH—*cont.*
Mercer's Chapel, E. end of S. aisle; carved and richly
coloured bracket. *Sharp's Coventry Antiquities*, pp.
28, 33.

COVENTRY, WARWICKSHIRE, TRINITY CHURCH.
Tower arch; the Doom. *Associated Architect. So-
cieties' Repts.*, i. 220.
Nave roof repainted from traces of the original colour-
ing on the beams. *Ecclesiologist*, xviii. 320. *Asso-
ciated Architect. Societies' Repts.*, iv., lvi.
Remains of colour and gilding on the font. 15th cent.
Illustrations of baptismal fonts, Van Voorst, 1844.
Sharp's Coventry Antiquities, pp. 100, 103.

COVERHAM ABBEY, YORKSHIRE.
Black letter texts. Date 1508. *Hardcastle, Wanderings in Wensleydale*, p. 37.

COWDRAY HOUSE, MIDHURST, SUSSEX.
On walls of dining parlour; subjects of English
history during the reigns of Henry VIII. and Edward VI.,
a head of Henry VIII., &c.
On walls of Great Hall; the twelve Apostles; also
Diana and her nymphs, and the story of Actæon. Time
of Edward VI. *Sussex Archæol.*, v. 183. *Antiquarian
Cabinet*, vol. vii. *Cromwell, Excursions through Sussex*,
p. 114.

COWLEY CHURCH, GLOUCESTERSHIRE.
About the windows in the chancel; shafts, capitals,
bases, and masonry patterns. 13th cent.

COWLEY CHURCH, OXFORDSHIRE.
N. and S. walls of nave; masonry patterns. Circ. 1300.
E. wall of nave; diaper of cinquefoils.
S. spandrel of chancel arch; two female figures, one
presenting a church to the other.
E. wall of chancel, S. side; Our Saviour in the act of
Benediction.
N. Side; the Virgin and Child, and the Presentation
in the Temple.
Over E. window; the Trinity.
On containing arches of E. window; masonry pattern.
N. wall of chancel; row of Saints.
S. wall of chancel; the Descent from the Cross.
Colouring on Norman shafts of chancel arch.
Building News, 1867, p. 157.

COWLING, SUFFOLK, ST. MARGARET'S CHURCH.
Painted screens. 15th cent. *Parker, Eccles. and Architect. Topog. of England, Suffolk*, No. 399.

COYCHURCH, GLAMORGANSHIRE, ST. GRALLO'S CHURCH.
E. end of S. transept, on jamb of a window and on the walls, remains of painting were discovered, which could not be deciphered.
On southern arch of the tower; rich arabesque patterns.
Ecclesiologist, viii. 253. *Archæologia Cambrensis*, 3rd series, iii. 113.

CRAIGMILLAR CASTLE, EDINBURGHSHIRE.
Remains of old painting on vault of hall. *Billing's Antiquities of Scotland*, vol. i.

CRANBORNE CHURCH, DORSETSHIRE.
On the walls of the chancel; the Crucifixion, with portraits of the Earl and Countess of Gloucester, the designer of the painting, and others. *Builder*, 1875, p. 1071.
Effigy of a warrior with remains of colour and gilding, found in the chancel wall.
The Antiquary, 1881, iv. 38.

CRANLEY CHURCH, SURREY.
Paintings over chancel arch and nave arcade. *Destroyed. Surrey Archæol.*, vi. 31. *Brayley's History of Surrey*, v. 175, and 2nd ed., iv. 267.

CRANOE CHURCH, LEICESTERSHIRE.
Windows and arches.

CRANSLEY CHURCH, NORTHAMPTONSHIRE.
Remains of colour on the nave roof. *Brandon, Parish Churches*, ii. 23. *Associated Architect. Societies' Repts.*, x. 88, 89.

CRATFIELD CHURCH, SUFFOLK.
Roof over rood loft. *Civil Engineer and Architect's Journ.*, 1860, p. 5. *Gorham, Hist. and Antiq. of Eynesbury and St. Neots*, ii. cxxxi.
Church chest; painted inscription on a scroll.

CRAWLEY, NORTH, CHURCH, BUCKINGHAMSHIRE.
Rood screen, on the panels, N. side; Jeremiah, David, Isaiah, Daniel, Hosea, Amos.

CRAWLEY, NORTH, CHURCH, BUCKINGHAMSHIRE—*cont.*

S. side; Zephaniah, Joel, Micah, Malachi, Daniel, Ezekiel. All holding scrolls.

On N. door; SS. Blaise and Martin.

On S. door; SS. Edward the Confessor and Edmund.

Painting on roof.

Parker, Eccles. and Architect. Topog. of England, Bucks, No. 106. *Lipscomb, Hist. and Antiq. of Bucks,* iv. 131. *Gent. Mag.,* 1849, xxxi., new series, 158.

CREAKE, NORTH, CHURCH, NORFOLK.

Painted roof. *Brandon, Parish Churches,* ii. 63

On four panels in the vestry, paintings of "Temperancia." "Fortitudo," "Justicia," and ? the emblem of "St. Veronica." 15th cent.

CREAKE, SOUTH, CHURCH, NORFOLK.

Painted rood screen. *Brandon, Parish Churches,* ii. 64.

Remains of colour on the roof, on an arch on N. side of screen, on one panel of the pulpit, and on the font.

CREDITON CHURCH, DEVONSHIRE.

On the effigy of Sir John Sully, three red chevrons painted on the breast. Date about 1387. *Exeter Diocesan Architect. Soc.,* 2nd series, ii. 52. *W. H. H. Rogers, The Ancient Sepulchral Effigies, &c. in Devon,* pp, 18, 29, 332.

On the sedilia and a monumental recess at the back, remains of rich colour and gilding. Date about 1410. *Exeter Diocesan Architect. Soc.,* 2nd series, iv. 104.

CREECH, ST. MICHAEL'S CHURCH, SOMERSETSHIRE.

On E. pier of arch opening from chancel to S. chapel; remains of colour on pier and two niches. About 1500.

CREETING, SUFFOLK, ST. PETER'S CHURCH.

N. wall of nave; mural painting, partly visible. *Parker, Eccles. and Architect. Topog. of England, Suffolk,* No. 307.

This painting no longer exists. *Suffolk Archæol.,* v. 118.

CRESSINGHAM, GREAT, CHURCH, NORFOLK.

Chancel screen, curiously painted. E. bay of chancel roof; stars, &c. *Blomefield, Hist. of Norfolk,* ed. 1807, vi. 101. *Cromwell, Excursions through Norfolk,* ii. 118.

CRICK CHURCH, NORTHAMPTONSHIRE.
Remains of mural paintings. *Churches of the Archdeaconry of Northampton*, p. 204. *W. Whellan, Hist. Gazett. and Directory of Northants*, p. 357.

CRINGLEFORD CHURCH, NORFOLK.
Font with remnants of its original painting and gilding. *Illustrations of Norfolk Topography*, p. 37.

CROFT CHURCH, LINCOLNSHIRE.
Richly painted screen; the upper part repainted. *Oldfield, Topog. and Hist. Account of Wainfleet*, p. 136.

CROMER CHURCH, NORFOLK.
Faint suspicion of colour on the walls, where the loft joined the rood turret.
"The old pews were found placed on beams of oak and horse chestnut, richly painted and gilt, probably part of the old screen or roof."
W. Rye, An Account of the Churches of Shipden and Cromer, p. 24 (note).

CROPREDY CHURCH, OXFORDSHIRE.
On the chancel walls; foliage and interlacing patterns. Over and near the N. door of N. aisle; the Seven Deadly Sins, and Seven Acts of Mercy; also some Black-letter texts, almost obliterated. *Builder*, 1876, p. 939.
Over chancel arch; the Day of Judgment.

CROSTHWAITE CHURCH, CUMBERLAND.
N. aisle; three concentric circles with parts of inscriptions. Circ. 1550. Concealed by a modern tablet.
E. end of S. aisle; remains of colour on effigies of Sir John de Derwentwater and Lady. Time of Henry IV.
Gent. Mag., 1849, xxxi. new series, 254, 374. *Hist. of the Church of Crosthwaite, J. B. Nicholls*, 1853, pp. 35, 62. *Corner, Rural Churches*, p. 30.

CROSTWICK CHURCH, NORFOLK.
S. wall of nave; St. Christopher. *Kelly's Post Office Directory for Norfolk.*

CROSTWIGHT CHURCH, NORFOLK.
On N. wall; Tree of the Seven Deadly Sins; a Soul rescued by the Patron Saint; St. Christopher; our Lord before Pilate; and the Crucifixion.
On pier S. side of chancel screen; St. Michael and Satan. Late 14th cent. *Norfolk Archæol.*, ii. 352. *British Archæol. Assoc. Journ.*, iii. 171.

CROYDON CHURCH, SURREY.

S. wall; St. George. 14th cent. St. Christopher. 15th cent. *Destroyed.* Engraved in *Anderson's Croydon Church,* pp. 7 and 8, and *J. C. Anderson, Croydon, Past and Present,* pp. 37-39. *Archæol. Journ.,* ii. 92, 194, 267. *British Archæol. Assoc. Journ.,* i. 65, 139. *Gent. Mag.,* 1846, xxv. new series, 77. *Society of Antiquaries' Proceedings,* iv. 120.

CROYLAND CHURCH, LINCOLNSHIRE.

Portion of screen, with remains of colouring and gilding. *Ecclesiologist,* v. 128. *Hist. of the County of Lincoln,* 1834, p. 323. *Sweeting, Parish Churches in and around Peterborough,* p. 126.

CUCKFIELD CHURCH, SUSSEX.

Bosses of nave roof, coloured. 15th cent. *Sussex Archæol.,* xviii. 184.

CUDDESDEN CHURCH, OXFORDSHIRE.

Archæol. Journ., ii. 368.

CUDHAM, KENT, SS. PETER AND PAUL CHURCH.

Paintings discovered over chancel arch and *destroyed. Ecclesiologist,* v. 266.

CULFORD CHURCH, SUFFOLK.

Splays, soffits, and jambs of windows in E. wall; passages from the life of St. Vincent (?). *Destroyed;* church pulled down in 1855.

CULLOMPTON CHURCH, DEVONSHIRE.

On N. wall of N. aisle; St. Christopher; St. Michael weighing Souls; and St. Bridget.

Over the rood loft on N. wall; St. Clara.

On S. wall of nave, between the clerestory windows; St. Catherine, and traces of other figures.

These are all probably early 15th cent.

Round the arches of the nave; decorative patterns.

Shields and arabesque patterns fill up spaces between the arches.

Nave roof, and rood screen, richly painted and gilt.

The paintings were discovered in 1849, and whitewashed over again.

The screen has been repainted.

Exeter Diocesan Architect. Soc., iii. 58, 59, 61, 260. *Ecclesiologist,* vii. 106, and x. 226. *Murray's Handbook of Devonshire. Black's Guide to Devonshire.*

CURRY-RIVELL CHURCH, SOMERSETSHIRE.
Crockets and mouldings of an early English tomb; and figure of a knight.

CURRY, NORTH, CHURCH, SOMERSETSHIRE.
Groined roofs; painted and gilt decorations. *The Antiquary*, 1881, iii. 236.

CURY CHURCH, CORNWALL.
Sculptured heads of Our Saviour blessing the cup, and the Apostles. Coloured and gilt. Probably portions of an altar piece. *A. H. Cummings, Churches and Antiq. of Cury and Gunwalloe*, pp. 19, 24. *Long Ago*, 1873, vol. i., p. 205.

DALE ABBEY, DERBYSHIRE.
Traces of red colouring in grooves of an incised slab found in the Chapter House. *Derbyshire Archæol. and Nat. Hist. Soc. Journ.*, i. 109.

DALHAM CHURCH, SUFFOLK.
Under the clerestory; one of the Seven Deadly Sins, and one of the Seven Acts of Mercy.
Over chancel arch; Last Judgment.
About 1480.

DALLING, FIELD, CHURCH, NORFOLK.
An interesting series of mural paintings. *Norfolk Archæol.*, vi. 1st Annual Report, p. ii.

DANBURY CHURCH, ESSEX.
E. end of N. aisle; band of interlacing ornament and foliage. 13th cent.

DARENT CHURCH, KENT.
S. side of chancel; remains of painting on a walled-up capital. *Glynne, Churches of Kent*, p. 307.
N. aisle; St. George, *destroyed*. Masonry patterns on the windows.

DARESBURY CHURCH, CHESHIRE.
On walls and one of the arches; decorative patterns, also black letter inscriptions. *Beamont, Hist. of Halton and Norton, Cheshire*, p. 155.

DARSHAM CHURCH, SUFFOLK.
Spandrils of the roof principals; sacred Monogram.
15th cent.

DARTFORD CHURCH, KENT.
E. wall of S. aisle; St. George and the Dragon. Late
15th cent. *Gent. Mag.*, 1836, ·vi. new series, 134.
Dunkin's History of Dartford, p. 51.

DARTINGTON CHURCH, DEVONSHIRE.
Screen; painted panels. *Murray's Handbook of
Devonshire, Introduction.*

DARTMOUTH, DEVONSHIRE, ST. SAVIOUR'S CHURCH.
Painted wooden pulpit. About 1530.
Painted rood screen.
Dollman, Antient Pulpits, pl. xxvii.
Galleries and panelling painted and emblazoned with
coats of arms. *Murray's Handbook of Devonshire.*

DAVIDSTOW CHURCH, CORNWALL.
Remains of screen, with one figure of a saint in one of
the panels. *Exeter Diocesan Architect. Soc.*, iv. 289.
Scrolls and texts of three different dates discovered
and *destroyed.*

DEAN CHURCH, BEDFORDSHIRE,
Some decorative painting, a fleur de lis pattern, &c., was
found on the walls, and *destroyed.*

DEDDINGTON CHURCH, OXFORDSHIRE.
W. end of N. aisle; figures in armour. 13th cent.
Archæol. Journ., xvi. 182.
E. end of N. aisle; remains of colour on a niche and
piscina. *North Oxon. Archæol. Soc. Trans.*, 1878, *Ded-
dington*, p. 30.

DEEPING, MARKET, CHURCH, LINCOLNSHIRE.
E. end of chancel; painted shields charged with crosses,
on lower part of two canopied niches. 15th cent.
Remains of colour and texts discovered on the walls.

DEERHURST CHURCH, GLOUCESTERSHIRE.
Saxon period. *British Archæol. Assoc. Journ.*, ii. 390.
Society of Antiquaries' Proceedings, 2nd series, i. 375.
Painting in S. aisle; an altar and numerous heads.
Ashby de la Zouch Anastatic Drawing Soc., 1862, p. 4.
Ecclesiologist, xxiii. (xx. new series), 97.

DENE CHURCH, NORTHAMPTONSHIRE.
Remains of colour and gilding on the recumbent figures of Sir Robert Brudenell and his two wives. Circ. 1532. *Hyett, Sepulchral Memorials of the County of Northampton*, p. 21.

DENFORD CHURCH, NORTHAMPTONSHIRE.
E. end of N. aisle; late perpendicular screen work " with shields painted with the instruments of the Passion, and much painting and gilding remaining, especially a good gilded crest of the Tudor flower." *Churches of the Archdeaconry of Northampton*, p. 79.

DENHAM CHURCH, BUCKINGHAMSHIRE.
Panels of the roof painted with the arms of the Bowyers. Time of Henry VIII. *Lipscomb, Hist. and Antiq. of Bucks*, iv. 449. *Sheahan, Hist. and Topog. of the County of Buckingham*, p. 859. Not now existing.
S. aisle, over S. door.; the Doom. 15th cent.

DENNINGTON CHURCH, SUFFOLK.
Painted screens. *British Archæol. Assoc. Journ.*, xxi. 178.

DENTON CHURCH, NORFOLK.
Rood screen; SS. Edward The Confessor, Edmund, Mary Magdalen, Sitha, Walstan or James Major, Agnes, Dorothy, Jude, Clement, Barbara, and Paul. Circ. 1500. These panels now form the side of the church chest.

DENVER CHURCH, NORFOLK.
On the splay of a window; a painting, subject uncertain. Date about 1360. *Norfolk Archæol.*, vii. 358.

DEOPHAM CHURCH, NORFOLK.
Back of screen ; foliated diaper.

DERBY, DERBYSHIRE, St. PETER'S CHURCH.
E. end of N. aisle ; portions of mural paintings.
E. window of S. aisle ; scroll work on the jambs.
Remains of colour on the capitals of the columns.
J. C. Cox, Churches of Derbyshire, iv. 153.

DEREHAM, EAST, NORFOLK, CHURCH OF ST. NICHOLAS.
Ceiling, N. aisle ; two-headed eagle, and the letter T with martyr's crown. *Armstrong, Parish Church of East Dereham*, 1864, p. 34. *Gent. Mag.*, 1847, xxviii., new series, 480.

DEREHAM, EAST, NORFOLK, CHURCH OF ST. NICHOLAS—*cont.*
Ceiling of S. aisle; painted and gilt mouldings, and on the panels, the Agnus Dei. *Chambers, Hist. of Norfolk,* ii. 824.
Rood screen. *Destroyed.*
Font with remains of colour visible under a modern coating of white paint; the Seven Sacraments, and the Crucifixion. Date about 1400. *Murray's Handbook of Norfolk.*

DEREHAM, WEST, ABBEY, NORFOLK.
Paintings representing Saul's entry into Jerusalem, and Saul arming David. *Illustrations of Norfolk Topography,* p. 41.

DEREHAM, WEST, CHURCH, NORFOLK.
Traces of paintings. *Hart, Antiq. of Norfolk,* p. 66.

DERSINGHAM CHURCH, NORFOLK.
Rood screen, with figures of the Virgin, SS. Denis, Juliana, &c. on the panels. *Sacristy,* iii. 152.
Painted pulpit.

DERWENT CHAPEL, DERBYSHIRE.
Remains of decorative colouring discovered on the walls when the church was pulled down in 1867. *Reliquary,* x. 29.

DEVIZES, WILTSHIRE, ST. JOHN'S CHURCH.
Nave roof; originally painted.
N.E. chapel; black letter inscription. 15th cent.
Some paintings were discovered in the nave, and were *destroyed.*
Wilts Archæol. and Nat. Hist. Soc. Mag., ii. 225, 228, 231.
E. end of chancel; an arcade of Norman arches was discovered during the restoration of the church, with traces of colouring on the mouldings. *Archæol. Journ.,* xxxiv. 277.

DEVIZES, WILTSHIRE, ST. MARY'S CHURCH.
Nave roof; originally painted; Black-letter inscription on it. Date 1435.
On a stone taken from the E. chancel wall; a foliated pattern. Probably late 12th cent.
On N. wall of nave; the Assumption of the Virgin; St. Christopher; and St. George and the Dragon.
On S. wall of nave; texts and flowers, of Queen Mary's time, with traces of earlier paintings below.

DEVIZES, WILTSHIRE, ST. MARY'S CHURCH—*cont.*
Over chancel arch; remains of a large subject, ? the
Doom. 15th cent. *Destroyed.*
Wilts Archæol. and Nat. Hist. Soc. Mag., ii. 230, 244.
Hist. of Devizes, H. Bull, 1859. p. 570.

DICKLEBURGH CHURCH, NORFOLK.
Panels of rood screen; quatrefoil ornament. 15th cent.
Colling, Gothic Ornaments, i. pl. 18.
N. wall of chancel; Christ bearing the Cross, and
probably, the Resurrection. Partly renewed.
Blomefield, Hist. of Norfolk, ed. 1805, i. 200.

DILWYN CHURCH, HEREFORDSHIRE.
Numerous traces of wall decoration, discovered and
destroyed. British Archæol. Assoc. Journ., xxvii. 153.
Lady Chapel; 13th cent. painting.
S. aisle and N. transept; stencilling, 15th cent.
Screens of Lady Chapel and N. transept, vermilion
freely used on.
Archæologia Cambrensis, 3rd series, xiv. 136.

DITCHEAT, SOMERSETSHIRE, ST. MARY'S CHURCH.
Remains of painting and gilding on roof. *Ecclesio-
logist,* vi. 184. *Somerset Archæol. and Nat. Hist. Soc.
Proceedings,* xxiv., pt. 1, p. 40.

DITCHINGHAM CHURCH, NORFOLK.
N. wall of nave; les Trois Vifs et les Trois Morts, and
the Final Judgment. 14th cent. *Archæol. Journ.,* v. 69.
Norfolk Archæol., ii. 405. *Gent. Mag.,* 1847, xxviii. new
series, 525.

DITTERIDGE CHURCH, WILTSHIRE.
N. wall, E. end of nave; St. Christopher, and St. Michael weighing Souls. *Archæol. Journ.,* xii. 195. *Wilts
Archæol. and Nat. Hist. Soc. Mag.,* iv. 147. *Tunstall,
Rambles about Bath and its neighbourhood,* 7th ed.,
p. 407. Whitewashed over. Copied in glass in a modern
window, S. side of nave.
On W. wall of nave; two consecration crosses. 12th
cent. *Archæologia,* xlvii. 165.
On tympanum of S. doorway; part of a semicircular
arch, and other remains of colouring. 12th cent.

DITTISHAM CHURCH, DEVONSHIRE.
Rood screen.

DITTON, FEN, CHURCH, CAMBRIDGESHIRE.
Chancel, on either side of E. window; painted niche.
Late 14th cent.

DITTON, WOOD, CHURCH, CAMBRIDGESHIRE.
Screen and rood-loft. *Lysons' Magna Britannia,
Cambridgeshire*, p. 59.

DODDINGTON CHURCH, KENT.
Painted woodwork. *Murray's Handbook of Kent.*

DODDINGTON CHURCH, NORTHAMPTONSHIRE.
On the S. side of the chancel arch; the Crucifixion.
Murray's Handbook of Northants, p. 27. *Building
News*, 1871, p. 37. *F. Whellan, Hist. Topog. and Di-
rectory of Northants*, 1874, p. 876.

DODFORD CHURCH, NORTHAMPTONSHIRE.
N. wall of N. aisle, within the arch and at the back of
the tomb of Hawise and Wentiliana de Keynes; the departed soul being carried away by angels; and five coats
of arms. Date about 1340.
On S. side; remains of painting and gilding on the
tomb of Sir John Cressy. Circ. 1447. *Baker's Hist.
and Antiq. of Northamptonshire*, p. 360. *Archæol.
Journ.*, xxxv. 258.
On walls of N. aisle; decorative colouring. 14th cent.

DONCASTER, YORKSHIRE, ST. GEORGE'S CHURCH.
Panels of nave roof; representations of the Apostles,
Twelve Tribes of Israel, various coats of arms, &c.
Destroyed in 1853. *Hatfield, Memorials of St. George's
Church, Doncaster*, p. 38. *J. Wainwright, Yorkshire*, i. 82.

DONCASTER, YORKSHIRE, ST. MARY MAGDALEN'S CHURCH
(now destroyed).
Arches; scroll patterns, &c. Norman period. *Builder*,
1864, p. 688, and a work on the church by the Rev. J.
E. Jackson.

DONINGTON CHURCH, LINCOLNSHIRE.
Within a niche over W. door; statuette of Our Lord,
once coloured and gilt. *Associated Architect. Societies'
Repts.*, x. 202.

DORCHESTER CHURCH, OXFORDSHIRE.
· E. wall of S. transept; the Crucifixion.
Diaper work and other traces of colour discovered on
the back of the sedilia, on mouldings of S. chancel window,

DORCHESTER CHURCH, OXFORDSHIRE—*cont.*

and below the Jesse (N. chancel) window. *Ecclesiologist,* v. 24.

S. aisle; head of a female Saint, &c. Colour on the effigy of a Bishop, 14th cent., and on other monuments. *Dorchester Church, Oxon, J.H. Parker,* 1845, pp. 12, 13, 36.

DORMINGTON CHURCH, HEREFORDSHIRE.

On the W. wall; Our Lord in Glory, and two other subjects, one, perhaps, the Martyrdom of St. Margaret.

Masonry pattern on wall and window splays.

Builder, 1877, p. 249. *Hereford Times,* Feb. 17th, 1877.

DORNEY COURT, BUCKINGHAMSHIRE.

On panels of several rooms; coats of arms with inscriptions below, too far gone to be restored. *Sheahan, Hist. and Topog. of the County of Buckingham,* p. 846.

DOUGLAS CHURCH, LANARKSHIRE, SCOTLAND.

On N. side of chapel; remains of colour on the monument of Archibald, Fifth Earl of Douglas. Date about 1438. *Blore's Monumental Remains of Noble and Eminent Persons.*

DOULTING CHURCH, SOMERSETSHIRE.

Transept roofs; formerly had colouring and metal stars studded on the panels. Late 15th cent.

DOVEBRIDGE CHURCH, DERBYSHIRE.

N. aisle roof; scroll pattern. *J. C. Cox, Churches of Derbyshire,* iii. 120.

DOVER CASTLE, KENT.

Mural decoration in one of the rooms. 13th or 14th cent.

DOVER, KENT, ST. MARTIN'S ABBEY.

Refectory, E. end wall; Christ and the Apostles. The Last Supper. Probably 13th cent.

On one of the side walls; decorative colour.

Archæol. Cantiana, iv. 16. *Murray's Handbook of Kent. J. T. Perry, An Account of the Priory of St. Martin, Dover,* p. 17.

DOWNE, WEST, CHURCH, DEVONSHIRE.

Colouring on the effigy of a Judge. Date about 1310. *Exeter Diocesan Architect. Soc.,* 2nd series, iii. 197. *W. H. H. Rogers, The Ancient Sepulchral Effigies, &c. in Devon,* pp. 47, 367.

DOWNHAM MARKET CHURCH, NORFOLK.
On S. wall of S. transept; consecration cross. 13th cent.

DOWSBY CHURCH, LINCOLNSHIRE.
Traces of colour on the effigy of Dame Margaret Ashton Remains of colour and gilding found over S. nave arcade.

DRAYTON CHURCH, BERKSHIRE.
Painted rood-loft.
Remains of alabaster reredos in the parish chest. Early 15th cent.
Parker, Eccles. and Architect. Topog. of England, Berkshire, No. 4. Builder, 1873, p. 13.

DRAYTON CHURCH, NORFOLK.
N. wall of nave; St. Christopher, St. Thomas, St. George, Our Lord, and St. Mary Magdalene.
Over chancel arch; Our Lord in Glory. *Destroyed.*
On chancel arch; diaper and scroll patterns. *Destroyed.*
Three consecration crosses. *Norfolk Archæol.* iii. 24.

DRAYTON CHURCH, OXFORDSHIRE.
"Some old painting."
Parker, Eccles. and Architect. Topog. of England, Oxford, No. 130.
N. of chancel; remains of painting on side of monument of Ludovic Grevile and his Lady. Circ. 1438.
Beesley, Hist. of Banbury, p. 117.

DRAYTON BEAUCHAMP CHURCH, BUCKINGHAMSHIRE.
S. side of nave, on two E. arches; scroll pattern. 13th cent.

DRAYTON, WEST, CHURCH, MIDDLESEX.
Vestiges of paintings and black letter texts. *J. H. Sperling, Church Walks in Middlesex,* pp. 28, 64. Not now visible.

DROITWICH, WORCESTERSHIRE, ST. PETER'S CHURCH.
E. compartment of nave roof; illuminated with red and gold stars on a blue ground. Circ. 1500. *Associated Architect. Societies' Repts.,* v. 177.

DUNHAM, LITTLE, CHURCH, NORFOLK.
Colouring on sedile and piscina within sill of S. chancel window. *Carthew's Hundred of Launditch,* ii. 676.

DUNSTER CHURCH, SOMERSETSHIRE.

Font formerly coloured. *Ecclesiologist*, ii. 64.

Effigy of Sir Hugh Luttrell, circ. 1428; traces of gilding. *Archæol. Journ.*, xxxvii. 172.

DUNTISBOURNE ROUSE CHURCH, GLOUCESTERSHIRE.

E. wall; four fragmentary figures under canopies, background powdered with stars, below, three crosses in circles.

Wall patterns on N. wall of chancel and other places, also in the Norman crypt. 15th cent.

Traces of earlier work.

DURHAM CATHEDRAL, DURHAM.

Recess in eastern wall of the Galilee; the folds of a curtain. Two full length figures supposed to represent Richard I. and Bishop Pudsey, about 1185, and to have formed part of a painting of the Crucifixion, now destroyed. *W. B. Scott, Antiquarian Gleanings*, pls. vii. and viii. *Archæol. Journ.*, xxxiv. 275. *British Archæol. Assoc. Journ.*, xxii. 221. *Perry and Henman, Illustrations of the Mediæval Antiq. of the County of Durham*, pl. i.

Coloured drawings in the Society of Antiquaries' Library.

Above the altar of Our Lady; the Passion of Our Lord. Date between 1406 and 1437.

P. Sanderson, The Antiquities of the Abbey or Cathedral Church of Durham, p. 47.

On piers of W. doorway, "pattern of tracery and flowers of vermilion upon a ground of pure white."

Remains of colouring on the chevron mouldings of the arches of the Galilee and the nave.

In the choir; the monument of Bishop Hatfield has traces of colour. *Murray's Handbook of Durham.*

Tomb of John, Lord Nevile, circ. 1388, traces of colour and gilding.

S. transept, fragments of richly decorated screen work, now in the Galilee.

Ornsby, Sketches of Durham, pp. 39, 51, 83, 87, 101.

Remains of colouring in the Nevile Chapel. *Society of Antiquaries' Proceedings*, 2nd series, vi. 176.

Frater house, above the wainscotting; the Crucifixion, with the Virgin and St. John visible beneath the whitewash.

DURHAM CATHEDRAL, DURHAM—*cont.*

P. Sanderson, *The Antiquities of the Abbey or Cathedral Church of Durham*, p. 72. *Ornsby, Sketches of Durham*, p. 123.

Chancery court; on lid of Chancery chest, heraldic and other paintings, time of Richard II.

Parker, Domestic Architecture, ii. 113.

DURHAM, ST. GILES' CHURCH, DURHAM.

During the restoration, was discovered on S. side of the nave a richly coloured sculpture of the Deity seated, with the emblems of the Evangelists. This had been used as a step for the pulpit. Date early 13th cent. *Surtees' Hist. and Antiq. of Durham*, iv. 164.

Wooden effigy; painting and gilding renewed. *Ornsby, Sketches of Durham*, p. 170.

DURHAM, ST. MARGARET'S CHURCH, DURHAM.

On buttress supporting the chancel arch; painting, of a date prior to 1153; subjects uncertain. *The Antiquary*, 1880, i. 186.

DURHAM, ST. OSWALD'S CHURCH, DURHAM.

The eastern compartment of the nave roof has been painted blue, sprinkled with stars. *Surtees' Hist. and Antiq. of Durham*, iv. 74.

DURRINGTON CHURCH, WILTSHIRE.

On the N. wall; St. Christopher. *Destroyed. Duke's Prolusiones Historiæ*, p. 560.

DURWESTON CHURCH, DORSETSHIRE.

Sculpture with remains of colour. *Hutchins' Hist. of Dorset*, 3rd ed., i. 266.

DUXFORD, CAMBRIDGESHIRE, ST. JOHN'S CHURCH.

On piers of E. tower arch; scroll pattern. Late 12th cent.

EARDISLEY CHURCH, HEREFORDSHIRE.

"When this church was rebuilt some very fine mural decoration was discovered," and *destroyed. Havergal, Fasti Herefordenses*, p. 157.

EASBY ABBEY CHURCH, YORKSHIRE.

N. wall of chancel; two sepulchral recesses, still
retaining traces of colour. *W. Hylton Longstaffe, Richmondshire, Its Ancient Lords and Edifices*, p. 3.

EASBY CHURCH, YORKSHIRE.

On nave arcades, remains of colouring, of two periods.
S. side of chancel on the back of the sedilia; paintings of Archbishops seated. Restored.

On N. wall of chancel; the Creation and Fall of Man,
with zigzag border above and scroll below.

Within the splays of the windows, representations of the
Seasons; viz., Winter and Spring.

On S. wall of chancel; the Annunciation, Nativity,
Offerings of the Magi; Descent from the Cross; Entombment; and The Marys at the Sepulchre. Partially restored. Date about 1250.

Associated Architect. Societies' Repts., ix. 252, xiii. 66.

EASTON CHURCH, HAMPSHIRE.

Effigy of St. John the Baptist; richly coloured. Late
15th cent. *Archæol. Journ.*, xxix. 92.

EASTON CHURCH, HUNTINGDONSHIRE.

Various coats of paint, including the original painting
removed from the 15th cent. rood screen.

EASTON CHURCH, NORFOLK.

Murder of St. Thomas à Becket. 14th cent. *Archæol.
Journ.*, xviii. 269.

EASTON CHURCH, SUFFOLK.

Walls of nave; the Nativity; Martyrdom of St. Edmund
or St. Sebastian; a king, bishop, &c. *British Archæol.
Assoc. Journ.*, x. 180.

EASTON, LITTLE, CHURCH, ESSEX.

On the S. wall; scenes from the Passion, with Latin
sentences in Old German text letters below. Figure of
the Patron Saint; and the Temptation of Eve.

EASTRY CHURCH, KENT.

Over the chancel arch; Seven medallions containing
foliage and (? animals). 13th cent. *Memorials of Eastry*,
p. 80. *Archæol. Journ.*, xv. 79.

EATINGTON, LOWER, CHURCH, WARWICKSHIRE.

Colouring on the effigies of Sir Ralph Shirley, circ. 1336,
and a Lady. *Lower Eatington, its Manor-house and
Church*, 1869. pp. 62, 63.

EATON CHURCH, NORFOLK.

On S. wall of Nave; a Soul being rescued by the Patron Saint. The Martyrdom of Thomas à Becket. Early 15th cent. And two consecration crosses.

On N. wall of nave; within the splay of a window,
· SS. Helen, and Jane of Valois. Also some other remains of painting, and a consecration cross.

On N. wall of chancel; St. John the Evangelist.

On S. wall of chancel; St. John the Baptist and a consecration cross.

At E. end of chancel on either side of E. window; a saint on a diapered ground, with a censing angel below.

Remains of painting on the chancel roof.

Norfolk Archæol. vi. 161.

EATON BISHOP CHURCH, HEREFORDSHIRE.

Faint traces of paintings of saints, &c. on columns in the nave. 13th cent.

EATON BRAY CHURCH, BEDFORDSHIRE.

Lower part of rood screen. Early 15th cent.

EATON SOCON CHURCH, BEDFORDSHIRE.

Rood screen ; varnished over.

EATON, CASTLE, CHURCH, WILTSHIRE.

Mural paintings representing "Scripture History or Saintly Legends." 14th cent. *Hall, The Book of the Thames*, p. 29.

The Virgin and Child.

ECCLES CHURCH, NORFOLK.

Mural painting of St. Nicholas. *Barr's Anglican Church Architecture*, p. 202. *Blomefield, Hist. of Norfolk*, ed. 1805, i. 410.

EDDLESBOROUGH CHURCH, BUCKINGHAMSHIRE.

Wall of N. aisle ; within a niche, the Virgin. 15th cent.

EDGCOTT CHURCH, NORTHAMPTONSHIRE.

S. aisle; two painted monuments of the Chauncy family. (I.) Date 1571–85, (II.) date 1579. *Lecsley, Hist. of Banbury*, p. 130.

EDGFIELD CHURCH, NORFOLK.

Rood screen ; panel paintings. *Hart, Antiq. of Norfolk*, p. 66.

On screen enclosing Chapel, figures of the donors, their family, and an inscription. Date 1526. *Blomefield, (Parkin,) Hist. of Norfolk*, ed. 1808, ix. 387.

EDINBURGH, SCOTLAND, ST. GILES' CATHEDRAL CHURCH.
Chepman's aisle; on a corbel, the eagle of St. John, with black letter inscription, " in principium." *W. Chambers, Story of St. Giles' Cathedral Church, Edinburgh,* p. 31.

EDINGTHORPE CHURCH, NORFOLK.
Rood screen; painted mouldings, &c. 14th cent.
On the panels; figures of SS. Bartholomew, Andrew, Peter, Paul, (?) Matthew, John the Evangelist, and James Major. 15th cent.
Ashby de la Zouch Anastatic Drawing Soc., 1859, p. 4, pl. xxiii.

EDINGTON CHURCH, WILTSHIRE.
S. transept; monument of an ecclesiastic, with richly coloured canopy. *Murray's Handbook of Wiltshire.*
Niche; traces of paint and gold.
On rood-loft; short sentences from the Proverbs, painted in black letter. Time of Edward VI.
E. Kite, Hist. Notices on the Places of Interest to be visited by the British Archæol. Assoc. in 1880, p. 39.
Painted roofs. 14th cent.

EDITH WESTON. *See* WESTON, EDITH.

EDLINGTON CHURCH, YORKSHIRE.
On piers of chancel arch; cable bands at intervals. 12th cent.; not now existing.

EDMONDTHORPE CHURCH, LEICESTERSHIRE.
Painted screen. *Ecclesiologist,* xxi., (xviii. new series), 292.
Chancel; paintings of Moses and Aaron, shortly after the Reformation. *Associated Architect. Societies' Repts.,* viii., lxiii.
Now placed in the S. aisle; screen varnished over.

EDSTASTON CHAPEL, WEM, SHROPSHIRE.
On W. wall of nave; the Virgin and Child.
Traces of mural paintings and coloured decorations everywhere apparent. *Proceedings of British Archæol. Association, Gloucester Vol.,* p. 309. *British Archæol. Assoc. Journ.,* ii. 389.

EGGINGTON CHURCH, BEDFORDSHIRE.
On the wall above the chancel arch, above the present late ceiling, Our Lord in Majesty, with two censing angels. Date about 1400. *Destroyed.*

EGLETON CHURCH, RUTLANDSHIRE.
Traces of colour on the chancel screen, now placed at
W. end. 15th cent.

EGLWYSCUMMIN CHURCH, CARMARTHENSHIRE.
On chancel arch; the Creed and Lords Prayer. Dated
time of Edward VI. *Whitewashed over.*
"Sketches of figures" on the walls.
M. Curtis, The Antiq. of Laugharne, &c., pp. 318, 324.

ELFORD CHURCH, STAFFORDSHIRE.
In S. chancel chapel; remains of colour and gilding on
the monuments, shields, and effigies of Sir Thomas Arderne
and Lady, circ. 1400; on that attributed to Sir John
Stanley, circ. 1474, but really a century earlier, and on
that of Sir William Smythe and Lady, circ. 1525..
On N. side of altar; effigy of (? William Staunton),
circ. 1500, highly coloured.
E. Richardson, The Elford Church Effigies, &c.
On a panel (formerly part of a screen); "The Eagle and
Child," the badge of the Stanleys.
On S. wall of chancel; the temptation and fall of man.
14th cent. Nave roof, remains of colouring. Bosses of
S. aisle roof, enriched with gilding.
P. E. Paget, Some Account of Elford Church, pp. 18,
22, 25, 33, 35–47.

ELGIN CATHEDRAL, MORAYSHIRE, SCOTLAND.
Vault of Bishop Winchester's tomb; angels bearing
the bishop's soul to Heaven. Circ. 1458. *Black's Guide
to Scotland.*

ELHAM CHURCH, KENT.
N. side of nave, between two eastern pillars; painted
canopy. *Archæol. Cantiana*, x. 62.

ELLESBOROUGH CHURCH, BUCKINGHAMSHIRE.
Remains of chancel screen; carved and gilt. *Lipscomb,
Hist. and Antiq. of Bucks*, ii. 183.
Not now in the church.

ELMHAM, NORTH, CHURCH, NORFOLK.
Parclose screen, E. end of S. aisle, on the panels;
SS. Barbara, Cecilia, Dorothea, Sitha, Juliana, Petronilla,
Agnes, and Christina.
On screen, N. side of chancel; SS. Giles, Jude, James
Minor, Philip, John, and Paul.

ELMHAM, NORTH, CHURCH, NORFOLK—*cont.*

Against a pillar, N. side of chancel, on a panel; St. Clement and a monk.

On panels of screen, W. end of S. aisle; SS. Benedict Thomas, Mathias, an ecclesiastic, and two other saints.

Carthew's Hundred of Launditch, ii. 537. *British Archæol. Assoc. Journ.,* xxv. 262. *East Anglian Notes and Queries,* iii. 291.

On doors of chancel screen; the four Doctors of the Church and an inscription.

Blomefield, (Parkin,) Hist. of Norfolk, ed. 1808, ix. 494. *Cromwell, Excursions through Norfolk,* i. 185. *Chambers, Hist. of Norfolk,* ii. 824. *The Ecclesiologist's Guide to the Deaneries of Brisley, &c.,* p. 21.

Date. Circ. 1500. ·

All the panels are now placed in the N. aisle.

Plastering of the walls, originally drawn in masonry patterns, with arabesque decoration at intervals.

Carthew's, Hundred of Launditch, ii. 536, note, and iii. 102.

ELMHAM, SOUTH, SUFFOLK, CHURCH OF ST. JAMES.

Either side of window in N. wall; St. Christopher. Left side of E. window; the Virgin and Child. *Destroyed.*

On N. wall of chancel, and over chancel doorway; remains of other paintings. *Archæol. Journ.,* vii. 297.

ELMLEY CASTLE CHURCH, WORCESTERSHIRE.

Painted wall decorations. *Associated Architect. Societies' Repts.,* xiv. xciii.

ELSING CHURCH, NORFOLK.

On S.E. wall; paintings discovered representing events in the life of St. John the Baptist. 14th cent. *Norfolk Archæol.* vi. 201, and 2nd Annual Report ii. *East Anglian Notes and Queries,* i. 100.

Painted font cover. *Civil Engineer and Architects' Journ.,* 1860, p. 5.

On panels of screen; the Apostles. *Antiquarian and Architect. Year Book,* 1844, p. 304.

ELSING HALL, NORFOLK.

Remains of painting on the walls of the chapel, and of a solar or chamber adjoining it. *Norfolk Archæol.,* vi. 191.

ELSTOW CHURCH, BEDFORDSHIRE.

Round and on the soffits of the three eastern arches; decorative patterns. Late 12th or early 13th cent.

ELSTOW CHURCH, BEDFORDSHIRE—*cont.*

On N. wall of chancel; imitation zigzag stringcourse. Late 12th or early 13th cent.

On soffits of two western arches, N. side of nave; foliated patterns. 13th cent.

On the splay of the W. window and W. wall of N. aisle; masonry pattern. 13th cent.

On E. wall of N. and S. choir aisles; scroll pattern. 15th cent.

On lower part of rood screen, and spandrils of the roof; remains of colour. 15th cent.

On N. wall of S. choir aisle; St. Michael and Satan.

Traces of colour are everywhere visible through the whitewash.

ELY CATHEDRAL, CAMBRIDGESHIRE.

Formerly had paintings, alluded to by Barclay in an eclogue written about 1514.

Lady Chapel, range of niches on exterior of W. wall; remains of colouring.

"The whole of the interior of the Lady Chapel has been elaborately painted and gilded." *J. K. Colling.*

See Gothic Ornaments, ii. pls. 1, 5, 16, and 18.

Viz., on the roof, the Nativity, Crucifixion, and the history of the Virgin, sculptured and once beautifully painted and gilt. Traces of colour and gilding on the walls, arcading, niches, &c.

Paintings of W'lstan, Osmund, Alwin, Elfgar, Ednod, and Athelstan, bishops of Ely, and duke Brithnoth, time of Edward III., formerly on N. wall of choir. *Stevenson, Supplement to* 2nd ed. *of Bentham's Hist. and Antiq. of Ely Cathedral,* p. 23, and *notes,* p. 144.

Gough, Sepulchral Monuments, vol. i., pt. i., p. clvi.

The font lid and rose are coloured.

Round the arches at the Eastern end of the nave and on the vault of the S. aisle; cable, zigzag and floral ornaments. Late 12th cent.

In a chapel on the E. side of the N. transept; the Martyrdom of St. Edmund.

Also in the same and adjoining chapel; numerous circles and other ornaments.

In the vestry in the S. transept; scroll and floral patterns; partly restored. Late 12th cent.

Roofs of transepts repainted.

Vault of octagon; original decoration and outline quite clear. Discovered in 1850.

ELY CATHEDRAL, CAMBRIDGESHIRE—*cont.*

Civil Engineer and Architect's Journ., 1859, p. 114.

Remains of colour in Bishop West's Chapel, about 1530; in Bishop Alcock's Chapel, about 1500; on the monument of Bishop de Luda (restored), 14th cent; and of Sir Mark Stewart, 16th cent.

Ecclesiologist. xii. 333. *Murray's Handbook of Cambridgeshire.*

The Choir and Presbytery; mouldings and bosses of the vaulting originally coloured and gilded.

Antiquarian Itinerary, vol. iv.

W. part of Choir; two corbels coloured and gilded.

Tomb of Bishop Hotham, richly decorated.

Arch on N. of Choir aisle leading to the Lady Chapel; mouldings formerly gilt and coloured. *Stevenson, Supplement to 2nd ed. of Bentham's Hist. and Antiq. of Ely Cathedral*, pp. 62, 70, 75, and *notes*, p. 15. *Millers, Description of Ely Cathedral*, pp. 70, 74, 95, 97. *Archæol. Guide to Ely Cathedral*, 1851, pp. 2, 3, 4. *Handbook to the Cathedral Church of Ely*, 1852, pp. 22, 28, 30, 34, 37, 43, 46, 47, and 9th ed. [1874], pp. 38, 48, 49, 50, 52, 58, 63, 73, 74, 78, 84, 85. *A Companion to the Cathedral Church of Ely*, 1854, pp. 17, 23, 24, 28. *Stewart, On the Architect. Hist. of Ely Cathedral*, pp. 104, 113, 141–43. *Hewett, A Brief Hist. and Description of the Conventual and Collegiate Church of the Holy Trinity, Ely*, pp. 18, 22.

ELY, CAMBRIDGESHIRE, PRIOR CRAUDEN'S CHAPEL.

The Crucifixion. *Blackburne, Decorative Painting*, p. 10. *Stewart, On the Architect. Hist. of Ely Cathedral*, p. 246. *Handbook to the Cathedral Church of Ely*, 1852, p. 61, and 9th ed. [1874], p. 101.

EMNETH CHURCH, NORFOLK.

Remains of colouring on the rood screen. *Ecclesiologist*, xxviii. (xxv. new series), p. 7. *The Fen and Marshland Churches*, i. 16.

EMPINGHAM CHURCH, RUTLANDSHIRE.

N. transept roof; coloured, 16th cent. *Associated Architect. Societies' Repts.*, ix. 250.

Painted chest. *Paley's Manual of Gothic Architecture*, p. 247.

Nave roof; remains of colour on the E. beam, and on wooden brackets of figures holding shields, &c. 15th cent.

On nave arches; decorative patterns whitewashed over.

ENBORNE CHURCH, BERKSHIRE.
Traces of painting on belfry wall, and on the jambs and arch of a western Norman window. *Newbury District Field Club,* 1872-1875, p. 79.

ENFIELD CHURCH, MIDDLESEX.
On a panel, now *destroyed*; the Day of Judgment. Figured in *Gent. Mag.,* vol. xciii. part i. p. 631. *Blackburne, Decorative Painting,* p. 21. *Tuff, Historical Notices of Enfield,* p. 109.
Window jamb, S. side of chancel; masonry pattern. 13th cent. *Building News,* 1867, p. 121.

ENFORD CHURCH, WILTSHIRE.
St. Christopher. *Hoare's Hist. of Wiltshire,* vol. ii., pt. ii., p. 21.

ENGLEFIELD CHURCH, BERKSHIRE.
Coloured effigy of a lady of the Englefield family. *Hollis, Monumental Effigies,* pt. vi., pl. 1.

ENGLISHCOMBE CHURCH, SOMERSETSHIRE.
Window of S. chapel; panelled in the splay, and with remains of colour. About 1500.

EPWORTH CHURCH, LINCOLNSHIRE.
Painted boards forming part of the panelling of the chancel screen, with the badges of Mowbray, Earl of Norfolk, and Richard II. End of the 14th cent. *Associated Architect. Societies' Repts.,* x., xiv.

ERISWELL CHURCH, SUFFOLK.
Painting of the Miraculous Draught of Fishes can be seen through the whitewash. *Parker, Eccles. and Architect. Topog. of England, Suffolk,* No. 429.

ERPINGHAM CHURCH, NORFOLK.
Rood screen; panel paintings of St. Robert Confessor, and other Saints, formerly at. *Blomefield, (Parkin,) Hist. of Norfolk,* ed. 1807, vi. 412. *Husenbeth, Emblems of Saints.*

ERWARTON, SUFFOLK, ST. MARY'S CHURCH.
Effigy of Sir Bartholomew Davillers the 2nd; retains traces of colouring. Date about 1330. *Parker, Eccles. and Architect. Topog. of England, Suffolk,* No. 278.

ETON COLLEGE CHAPEL, BUCKINGHAMSHIRE.

On S. wall, upper row, the Assumption and miracles of the Virgin, and various figures. On lower row, the story of the Roman Empress, and, on pedestals, SS. Catherine, Barbara, Apollonia, Dorothy, ?, Juliana, and Agnes or Agatha.

On N. wall, the miracles of the Virgin, and, on pedestals, SS. Sidwell, ? Sira, Martha, or Ulph, Etheldreda, Margaret, Theodosia or Jean of Valois, and other Saints. Time of Edward IV.

H. C. Maxwell-Lyte, Eton College, pp. 86–94, 166–168, and 431. *Notes and Queries*, 4th series, i. 341, ii. 474. *Ecclesiologist*, viii. 242, xi. 247. "*The Times*," July 17th, 1847. *Gent. Mag.*, 1847, vol. xxviii. new series, 187. *Tighe and Davis, Annals of Windsor*, ii. 660 (note).

Panelled over; drawings existing.

Painted lectern. *Blackburne, Decorative Painting*, p. 73.

Painting of a converted Jew receiving the Holy Communion through a low side window. *Archæol. Cantiana*, ix. 239.

[This is clearly an erroneous interpretation of one of the miracles of the Virgin.]

ETTON CHURCH, NORTHAMPTONSHIRE.

E. wall of S. aisle; the Stem of Jesse. 13th. cent. *Ecclesiologist*, iii. 56. *Brandon, Parish Churches*, i. 21.

EVERCREECH CHURCH, SOMERSETSHIRE.

Nave roof; ancient colouring restored. *Somerset Archæol. and Nat. Hist. Soc. Proceedings*, xxiv., pt. i., p. 48.

EVERSDEN CHURCH, CAMBRIDGESHIRE.

S. Wall of nave; St. Christopher. *Destroyed.*
N. wall of nave; St. George and St. Anthony. *Destroyed.*
Over chancel arch; The Doom.

EVESHAM ABBEY, WORCESTERSHIRE.

Numerous fragments, richly coloured and gilt, found on the site of the Abbey Church. *Vetusta Monumenta*, vol. v., pl. lxix.

EWELME CHURCH, OXFORDSHIRE.

Walls; diaper of the sacred Monogram.
Back of one of the monuments; the Assumption of the Virgin.

EWELME CHURCH, OXFORDSHIRE—*cont.*

Civil Engineer and Architect's Journal, 1851, pp. 197 and 208.

Monument of the Duchess of Suffolk. On ceiling of lower portion; the Annunciation and other painting. Date about 1475. *Napier, Historical Notices of Swyncombe and Ewelme*, p. 103.

EXETER CATHEDRAL, DEVONSHIRE.

N.E. corner of N. transept; the Resurrection. Our Lord and St. Mary Magdalene, and the three Maries at the sepulchre. Date about 1350. Discovered in 1852. *Archæol. Journ.*, x. 71 and 171. *Exeter Diocesan Architect. Soc.*, v. pl. 9. *Black's Guide to Devonshire.*

Series of paintings on the panels of the organ screen, descriptive of various Old and New Testament subjects, viz.; the Creation, Adam and Eve in the Garden of Eden, the Deluge, the children of Israel crossing the Red Sea, the destruction of Solomon's Temple, the building of the second temple, the Angel appearing to Zacharias, the Nativity, baptism of Christ, descent from the Cross, Resurrection, Ascension, and day of Pentecost. Said to be time of Edward III., but really not earlier than the reign of Henry VII. *Murray's Handbook of Devonshire. Black's Guide to Devonshire.*

Choir roof; rich colouring partly renewed.

Bishop's throne; white and gold decoration. On the enclosure, portraits of four bishops. *Revived.*

S. Choir aisle; three painted bosses. Time of Edw. III.

On the canopy above Bishop Stapledon's tomb; painting of our Saviour. Circ. 1326.

Exeter Diocesan Architect. Soc., iv. 45, 330, and vi. 53.

Lady Chapel; ribs and bosses of the ceiling repainted, traces of the original painting and gilding having been discovered. *Exeter Diocesan Architect. Soc.*, 2nd series, ii. 318. *Sir G. G. Scott, Personal and Professional Recollections*, p. 348.

Behind the tomb of Bishop Simon de Apulia; bishop seated. Early 14th cent.

On the walls; traces of heads and running foliage.

Central compartment of reredos; painted and gilt. 14th cent.

Colling, Gothic Ornaments, vol. ii. pl. 93.

EXETER CATHEDRAL, DEVONSHIRE—*cont.*

E. wall of W. aisle; Virgin in Glory surrounded by kings, queens, angels, and the Heavenly hierarchy. *Antiquary*, 1871, i. 158.

Near the entrance of the Lady Chapel; a king and bishop.

Between the Lady Chapel and chantry of St. Gabriel; the piers are painted black, with an alternate diaper of the letter " E " and a fleur-de-lis.

Colour and gilding on the parclose screens round the chantries of SS. Paul, Mary Magdalene, and Gabriel.

In the Chapel of St. Gabriel; diaper pattern at the back of the arcade. Painting and gilding on the vault. *renewed.*

Traces of colour on the back of the sedilia, S. side of Choir; recently whitewashed over.

Remains of colour on monuments of Bishops Stapledon, 1326; Stafford, 1419; and Oldham, 1519; also on the effigy of a Crusader, ? Humphrey de Bohun, died 1321, in S. Choir aisle.

Exeter Diocesan Architect. Soc., vol. iii., pt. ii., pp. 94–96.

Effigy of Bishop Bronescombe; coloured. End of 13th cent. Canopy above it coloured and gilt. Early 15th cent. *Exeter Diocesan Architect. Soc.*, iv. 228–237, and plates. *Ecclesiologist*, xiv. 45. *W. H. H. Rogers, The Ancient Sepulchral Effigies, &c. in Devon*, pp. 44, 45, 103.

Back of the monument, St. John the Evangelist, between SS. James and Jude. *Gough, Sepulchral Monuments*, vol. i., pt. i., p. 61.

Monument of Bishop Leofric; portrait of the bishop between Edward the Confessor and his Queen. *Gough, Sepulchral Memorials of Great Britain*, vol. i., pt. i., p. 60. *Archæologia*, x. 313.

A side Chapel; Apostles and Prophets holding scrolls; much damaged. *Destroyed (?).*

Wm. Silkes' chantry; a mural painting, lately discovered.

Nave; minstrels gallery and corbels of the vaulting shafts, remains of colour.

Bosses of nave roof; repainted and regilt.

Murray's Handbook of Devonshire.

Remains of mural paintings over the N. door, and on the W. wall at each side of the main entrance.

EXETER CATHEDRAL, DEVONSHIRE—*cont.*

Builder, 1877, p. 1084. *T. B. Worth, Exeter Cathedral and its Restoration,* pp. 8, 24, 26, 31, 35, 41, 43. *Worth, Tourist's Guide to S. Devon,* pp. 26, 31, *and to N. Devon.* p. 110.

Chapter house ; painted and gilt ceiling. About 1427. *Exeter Diocesan Architect. Soc.,* iv. 330. Or, 1465–78. *T. B. Worth, Exeter Cathedral and its Restoration,* p. 52.

EXETER, DEVONSHIRE, ST. MARY MAJOR'S CHURCH.

On S. wall of tower ; lower portion of St. Christopher.

Painted and gilt niche in N. window of chancel, and fragments of other coloured sculptures worked into the walls.

On E. wall of chancel ; figures of heroes, saints, and angels ; perhaps the Day of Judgment. |Discovered during the demolition of the church in 1865.

Exeter Diocesan Architect. Soc., 2nd series, ii. 27.

EXETER, DEVONSHIRE, BEDFORD CIRCUS (site of the Dominican Convent).

"At various periods fragments of sculpture, enriched " with painting and gilding, have been brought to " light." *Archæol. Journ.,* ix. 188.

EXETER, DEVONSHIRE, THE BISHOP'S PALACE.

Bosses of ceiling of one of the rooms ; painted and gilt. Time of Bishop Grandisson, 1327–1369. *Archæol. Journ.,* v. 225.

EXETER, DEVONSHIRE.

Roof in one of the residentiary houses ; original colour on the bosses and shields. Date about 1400. *Exeter Diocesan Architect. Soc.,* ii. 165.

EXTON CHURCH, HAMPSHIRE.

Five consecration crosses. *Beale Post, History of the College of All Saints, Maidstone,* p. 78. *British Archæol. Assoc. Journ.,* iii. 260. *Proceedings of the British Archæol. Assoc., Winchester vol.,* p. 409.

EXTON CHURCH, RUTLANDSHIRE.

Under the tower ; colouring on the effigies of Sir John Haryngton and Lady. Circ. 1524.

EYAM CHURCH, DERBYSHIRE.

Between the clerestory windows of the nave ; two distinct series of the Banners of the Tribes of Israel, and some earlier paintings on the original surface of the wall. *Destroyed. J. C. Cox, Churches of Derbyshire.* ii. 193.

EYE, SUFFOLK, CHURCH OF ST. PETER AND ST. PAUL.

Over chancel arch ; the Doom. *Destroyed.* A copy of it at the vicarage.

Division of nave roof over the rood-loft ; restored, the sacred monogram within a wreath.

Coloured bosses in the S. aisle.

Painted rood screen ; saints in the panels. On the Epistle side ; SS. Agatha, Blaise, Lucy, William of Norwich,* Catherine, and John the Evangelist. On the Gospel side ; SS. Edward King and Confessor, Agnes, Barbara, Dorothea, King Henry VI.; SS. Ursula, Edmund or Christina, Helen, and Paul. Date about 1450.

Suffolk Archæol., ii. 133–136. *East Anglian Notes and Queries,* iii. 317. *Murray's Handbook of Suffolk. British Archæol. Assoc. Journ.,* xxviii. 126, xxxvi. 432.

* Figured in *Goulburn. The Ancient Sculptures in the Roof of Norwich Cathedral, plate facing* p. 83.

FAIRFORD CHURCH, GLOUCESTERSHIRE.

The Day of Judgment.

N. wall ; St. Christopher. *Destroyed.*

Inside of tower piers ; four figures. 15th cent.

FAKENHAM CHURCH, NORFOLK.

Rood screen.

FANGFOSS CHURCH, YORKSHIRE.

Remains of colouring on the walls. *Gent. Mag.,* 1848, xxx., new series, 632.

FARLEIGH HUNGERFORD CASTLE CHAPEL, SOMERSETSHIRE.

E. wall ; stencilled patterns. Remains of colour on monument and effigies of Sir Thomas Hungerford and Joan his lady. Circ. 1398. *Somerset Archæol. and Nat. Hist. Soc. Proceedings,* vol. iii. pp. 119, 120. *J. E. Jackson, Farleigh Hungerford,* pp. 28, 35.

FAVERSHAM CHURCH, KENT.

On a Pillar; events in the life of Our Saviour; and of the Virgin, in three tiers, viz., on the lower, the Annunciation, Salutation, and Adoration of the Magi; on the middle, the Nativity, announcement to the shepherds, and the presentation in the temple; on the upper, the Crucifixion, with the Virgin and St. John, and the Maries at the tomb. 13th cent.

S. wall of N. chancel aisle; in the spandrils of the easternmost arch, King Edward and the Pilgrim; below, under a canopy, a civilian (? judge), with an inscription on a scroll proceeding from his mouth. 14th cent.

Archæol. Cantiana, i. 150. *Society of Antiquaries' Proceedings*, 2nd series, i. 40. *Giraud and Donne, Guide to Faversham*, pp. 49–51.

N. transept; rude painting.

S. transept; colouring on back of niche.

S. chancel aisle; St. Paul.

Antiquary, 1873, iii. 42, 183.

St. Thomas à Becket's Chapel, N. wall; murder of Thomas à Becket. *Glynne, Churches of Kent*, p. 15. *Archæol. Cantiana*, ix., lxi.

Organ diapered. 16th cent.

FAWSLEY CHURCH, NORTHAMPTONSHIRE.

S. side of nave; altar tomb with coloured effigies of Sir Richard Knightley and Lady. Date 1534. *Murray's Handbook of Northants.*

FEERING CHURCH, ESSEX.

N. door; St. Christopher, &c. *British Archæol. Assoc. Journ.*, ii. 86 *note*, and 190.

Walls; powder of roses and fleurs-de-lys, on a slate ground. *Builder*, 1864, p. 725.

Spandrils of N. aisle arcade; painted shields of arms.

FELMERSHAM CHURCH, BEDFORDSHIRE.

Considerable remains of painting, of early character. Perpendicular rood-loft; richly painted.

Parker, Eccles. and Architect. Topog. of England, Bedford, No. 23. *D. G. C. Elwes, Bedford and its Neighbourhood*, p. 108.

N. aisle; formerly numerous paintings. *W. M. Harvey, Hist. of Willey Hundred*, p. 292.

FEN DITTON. *See* DITTON, FEN.

FENITON CHURCH, DEVONSHIRE.

Rood screen; panel paintings of Saints.

FERSFIELD CHURCH, NORFOLK.
Painted effigy of Sir Robert Du Bois. Circ. 1311. *Stothard's Monumental Effigies*, p. 52, and of William Du Bois, priest, founder of the chancel. *Blomefield, Hist. of Norfolk*, ed. 1805, i. 104. *Cromwell, Excursions through Norfolk*, i. 72. *Chambers, Hist. of Norfolk*, i. 124.
Painted chest. *Paley's Manual of Gothic Architecture*, p. 247.

FETCHAM CHURCH, SURREY.
Mural paintings discovered in 1857, and *destroyed*. Drawings existing. *Surrey Archæol.* vol. ii. *Repts.*, p. xxiv. Viz.: in N. transept; the Coronation of the Virgin, les Trois Morts et les Trois Vifs, the Sacrament of Extreme Unction, and a Purgatory.
Chancel walls; a decorative pattern, a copy of that found in 1857.

FIELD DALLING. *See* DALLING, FIELD.

FILBY CHURCH, NORFOLK.
Rood screen; SS. Cecilia, George, Catherine, Peter, Paul, Margaret, Michael weighing Souls, and Barbara. *British Archæol. Assoc. Journ.*, xxviii. 126, xxxv. 435, xxxvi. 92, xxxvii. 136. *Brandon, Parish Churches*, i. 45. *East Anglian Notes and Queries*, iii. 291. *The Ecclesiologist's Guide to the Deaneries of Brisley, &c.*, p. 141.

FINCHALE PRIORY, DURHAM.
Lower part of the rood screen, found in situ; of stone, " covered in plaster, diapered, the ground yellow, the " pattern, some of five foils, gules." *Ornsby, Sketches of Durham*, p. 188. *Gibson, Notices of Northumbrian Castles, Churches, &c.*, 1st series, p. 28.

FINCHAM CHURCH, NORFOLK.
Painted screen.

FINCHLEY CHURCH, MIDDLESEX.
St. George and the Dragon.

FINDON CHURCH, SUSSEX.
N. wall of nave.

FISHLAKE CHURCH, YORKSHIRE.
Chancel arch; various decoration.
Remains of decorative colouring on the eastern portion of the nave roof. *Associated Architect. Societies' Repts.*, iv. 97., xii. 93, 94.

FLAMBOROUGH CHURCH, YORKSHIRE.

Screen and rood-loft; once richly painted and gilt. Early 16th cent. *Murray's Handbook of Yorkshire. Prickett's Priory Church of Bridlington*, p. 52. *Sheahan and Whellan, Hist. and Topog. of City of York, &c.,* ii. 471. *Ashby De la Zouch Anastatic Drawing Soc.,* 1856, p. 5, pl. xxvi.

FLAMSTEAD CHURCH, HERTFORDSHIRE.

On S. wall of the nave above the arches; two large figures, probably part of a subject covering the whole of the S. wall.

On each side of the eastern arch on the S., and round the eastern arch on the N. side of the nave; floral decorations. 13th cent. Remains of colour on the chancel screen. Early 15th cent.

FLAWFORD CHURCH, NOTTINGHAMSHIRE.

Effigy of St. Peter, richly painted and gilt. Originally belonged to the church here, and is now in the possession of Edward Percy, Esq., of Nottingham. *Reliquary*, xv. 6.

FLEMPTON CHURCH, SUFFOLK.

Chancel roof; red and white roses. *Gage, Hist. of Suffolk, Thingoe Hundred*, p. 65.

FLOORE CHURCH, NORTHAMPTONSHIRE.

N. of chancel arch; colouring on the arch and jambs of rood-loft doorway.

Chancel screen; painted panels and mouldings. 15th cent.

FLYFORD-GRAFTON CHURCH, WORCESTERSHIRE.

Painted ceiling. *Associated Architect. Societies' Repts.,* v., xcvi., vi. 241.

FOLKINGHAM CHURCH, LINCOLNSHIRE.

Two coloured decorated niches. *Associated Architect. Societies' Repts.,* iv. 247.

FORDINGTON CHURCH, DORSETSHIRE.

Painted and gilt chancel stalls, removed in 1750. *Hutchins' Hist. of Dorset*, 3rd ed., ii. 798.

S. doorway, sculptured tympanum; St. George slaying his enemies, traces of red colouring. *Ashby De la Zouch Anastatic Drawing Soc.,* 1857, p. 8, pl. xlvii.

FOULDEN CHURCH, NORFOLK.

Rood screen; lower panels. *Blomefield, Hist. of Norfolk*, ed. 1807, vi. 31. *Chambers, Hist. of Norfolk*, ii. 626.

FOULSHAM CHURCH, NORFOLK.
Interior of font cover; painting of the Evangelists. *Destroyed. Quarles, Hist. of Foulsham,* p. 31. *Chambers, Hist. of Norfolk,* i. 222.

FOUNTAINS ABBEY, YORKSHIRE.
Round cloister court doorway; chevron pattern in three colours. *Builder,* 1864, p. 686.

FOWLIS EASTER CHURCH, PERTHSHIRE, SCOTLAND.
Painted panels of rood screen. *Murray's Handbook of Scotland,;* viz., the Crucifixion, with the thieves on either side, and numerous other figures; also panel paintings of Saints.

FOXLEY CHURCH, NORFOLK.
Rood screen; St. Louis, the four doctors of the Church, &c. *Hart, Antiq. of Norfolk,* p. 66.

FOXTON CHURCH, CAMBRIDGESHIRE.
Paintings on panels, formerly part of rood screen, *Ecclesiologist,* i. 59.
E. wall of S. aisle; foliage patterns. Early 14th cent.
E. bay of nave roof; traces of colour.

FRAMLINGHAM CHURCH, SUFFOLK.
Tomb of the Earl of Surrey. Circ. 1546. *Cromwell, Excursions through Suffolk,* ii. 69.

FRAMPTON CHURCH, DORSETSHIRE.
Panels of the nave roof; painted with the " Rose en Soleil," time of Edward IV. *Hutchins' Hist. of Dorset,* 3rd ed., ii. 301.

FRATING CHURCH, ESSEX.
Masonry pattern.

FRECKENHAM CHURCH, SUFFOLK.
Painted bas-relief of St. Eligius, discovered in the wall in 1776. *Gent. Mag.,* xlvii. 416.

FREETHORPE CHURCH, NORFOLK.
Rood screen.

FRIESTON CHURCH, LINCOLNSHIRE.
Font cover; once enriched with colour and gilding. *Associated Architect. Societies' Repts.,* xi. xvii.

FRING CHURCH, NORFOLK.
Curious mural paintings, much obliterated. *Kelly's Post Office Directory of Norfolk.*

FRISKNEY CHURCH, LINCOLNSHIRE.

Nave roof above the rood loft, richly coloured. On the panels are two angels swinging censers, a priest kneeling before an altar. Numerous painted panels incorporated with modern pews. *Church Builder*, 1879, No. lxxi. p. 160.

Above and between the nave arches :—S. side; the Last Supper. N. side; the Nativity, the Adoration of the Magi, and the Shepherds, and the Assumption of the Virgin. St. John the Baptist. The Resurrection. Colouring round, and large figure above, the chancel arch.

FRITTON CHURCH, NORFOLK.

N. wall; St. Christopher and St. George. *Norfolk Archæol.*, iv. 345.

Rood screen; on the panels; SS. Simon and Jude, the Doctors of the Church, and portraits of Sir John Bacon, wife and family. Circ. 1510. *See* published account by Revd. R. Hart. *Norfolk Archæol.*, vol. vii. 2nd Annual Rept., p. ii. *East Anglian Notes and Queries*, iii. 291. *Parker's Calendar of the Prayer Book*, p. 120.

FRITTON CHURCH, SUFFOLK.

N. wall; St. Christopher. Round one of the Norman windows in apse, original colouring. *Quarterly Journ. of Suffolk Inst. for.* 1869, p. 15. *British Archæol. Assoc. Journ.*, xxxv. 438, xxxvi. 102.

FRODINGHAM, NORTH, CHURCH, YORKSHIRE.

Poulson's Hist. and Antiq. of Holderness, i. 303.

FROME CHURCH, SOMERSETSHIRE.

Richly coloured piscina found in the tower wall on the nave side, once in the rood loft. *Ecclesiologist*, xxvii. (xxiv. new series), p. 65.

E. part of nave roof; colour on beams. *Restored.* W. J. E. Bennett, *The Old Church of St. John of Froome*, pp. 15, 121.

FULBECK CHURCH, LINCOLNSHIRE.

Remains of late rood screen, with powdering of roses, &c.

FULBOURN, CAMBRIDGESHIRE, ALL SAINTS' CHURCH.

Pulled down. Two panels of a screen, formerly at. Paintings of Our Saviour and St. Elizabeth of Hungary, now in the Library of Trinity College, Cambridge *Archæol. Journ.*, xxxi. 421, xxxii. 133. *Cambridge Antiq. Soc. Journ.*, iv. 5.

FULBOURN, CAMBRIDGESHIRE, ST. VIGOR'S CHURCH.

Many traces of mural decoration, too imperfect to be preserved. *Cambridge Antiq. Soc. Journ.*, iii. 222.

Remains of a painting in the sacristy. *Parker, Eccles. and Architect. Topog. of England, Cambridge*, No. 70.

Roof of nave and chancel. *Murray's Handbook of Cambridgeshire. A. G. Hill, Churches of Cambridgeshire*, p. 30. *Notes on Cambridgeshire Churches*, 1827, p. 75. *F. A. Paley, The Ecclesiologist's Guide to the Churches . . . . round Cambridge*, p. 43.

FUNDENHALL CHURCH, NORFOLK.

Rood screen, with armorial bearings, &c., removed. *Blomefield, Hist. of Norfolk*, ed. 1806, v. 174. *Cromwell, Excursions through Norfolk*, i. 36. *Chambers, Hist. of Norfolk*, i. 105.

FURNESS ABBEY CHURCH, LANCASHIRE.

S. side of presbytery; remains of gilding on the sedilia, piscina, &c., and on numerous fragments dug up in the Choir and elsewhere. *Tweddell: Furness, Past and Present*, ii. 120, 129. *Beck, Annales Furnesienses*, 381.

Clustered column of transept; masonry pattern, 12th cent.

FYFIELD CHURCH, BERKSHIRE.

N. side of chancel; monument of Lady Catherine Gordon richly painted and gilt. Circ. 1537. *Archæologia*, xxxii. 448. *Ashmole's Antiquities of Berkshire*, i. 99. *Parker, Eccles. and Architect. Topog. of England, Berkshire*, No. 24.

GADDESBY CHURCH, LEICESTERSHIRE.

E. wall of chancel, S. side of E. window; decorative pattern. 14th cent.

GADDESDEN, LITTLE, HERTFORDSHIRE, THE MANOR HOUSE.

On panel of a door in an upper room; portrait of the Princess Elizabeth being summoned by Lord Howard to repair to London in 1554. The painting is apparently of this date. *Cussans, Hist. of Hertfordshire*, vol. iii., pt. i., p. 138.

GAINSBOROUGH, LINCOLNSHIRE, THE MANOR HOUSE.

On wall of room adjoining the hall ; a falcon. Other paintings discovered behind the wainscot in the hall, and *destroyed. Sir C. Anderson, The Lincoln Pocket Guide,* p. 73.

GARBOLDISHAM CHURCH, NORFOLK.

Nave roof, painted. *Destroyed. Chambers, Hist. of Norfolk,* ii. 703.

Over altar in vestry ; the Last Judgment. *Blomefield, Hist. of Norfolk,* ed. 1805, i. 267.

Painted screen, with figures of SS. William of York, Mary Magdalene, Margaret, and a Bishop. *Destroyed.*

GARVESTONE, NORFOLK, ST. MARGARET'S CHURCH.

Niches on each side of altar have remains of colour, and other mural paintings, discovered during the restoration of the church. *Ecclesiologist,* xvii. 460.

Niches stopped up and paintings destroyed.

GATELY CHURCH, NORFOLK.

Rood screen, on the panels :—

N. side ; St. Audria, Elizabeth, the Virgin, and St. Puella Ridibowne.

S. side ; St. Louis, King Henry VI., (?) St. Augustine, Master John Schorn. Date circ. 1480.

British Archæol. Assoc. Journ., xxiii. 273, 376, xxiv. 72. *Norfolk Archæol.,* ii. 280. *East Anglian Notes and Queries,* iii. 291. *Carthew's Hundred of Launditch,* ii. 774. *The Ecclesiologist's Guide to the Deaneries of Brisley, &c.,* p. 21.

GAWSWORTH CHURCH, CHESHIRE.

Over chancel arch ; the Day of Judgment. Circ. 1495.

N. wall of nave ; St. Christopher and St. George and the Dragon. Circ. 1450. *Destroyed. Hist. and Antiq. Notes on Gawsworth Church, near Macclesfield, &c., by Joseph F. A. Lynch. Earwaker's East Cheshire,* ii. 573–575. *Norfolk Archæol.,* v. 222. *Archæol. Journ.,* ix. 101. *Society of Antiquaries' Proceedings,* ii. 190. *Gent. Mag.,* 1851, xxxvi., new series, 628. *Builder,* 1853, p. 119. *J. Croston, Nooks and Corners of Lancashire and Cheshire,* p. 139. *W. H. Massie, The Paintings in Gawsworth Church.*

Traces of other paintings discovered. Remains of colour and gilding on nave roof, about 1500. *Earwaker's East Cheshire,* ii. 573–575.

Chancel roof ; painted panels.

GIDLEIGH CHURCH, DEVONSHIRE.
Painted screen, with figures of St. George, St. Louis, the Evangelists,&c., in lower panels. 15th cent. Restored. *Murray's Handbook of Devonshire.* *Worth, Tourist's Guide to S. Devon,* p. 79.

GILLINGHAM CHURCH, KENT.
The pillars seem to have been "painted red, while a red and black tracing ran round the arches." *J. H. Leach, Memoir of . . . . Gillingham,* p. 12.

GILLINGHAM, NORFOLK, ST. MARY'S CHURCH.
Rood screen, elaborately coloured. 15th cent. *Archæol. Journ.,* vii. 145.
Only two panels now remain.

GISLEHAM CHURCH, SUFFOLK.
Lower part of rood screen; paintings of the Apostles. *Suckling's History of Suffolk,* i. 248. *Parker, Eccles. and Architect. Topog. of England, Suffolk,* No. 229.

GLASTONBURY ABBEY, SOMERSETSHIRE.
St. Joseph's Chapel; remains of chromatic decorations on many portions of the interior arcade. *British Archæol. Assoc. Journ.,* xii. 384.
Also on the arcade of the basement. *Somerset Archæol. and Nat. Hist. Soc. Proceedings,* i. 113.
Remains of colour on a portion of the Easter Sepulchre. ? Now in the Yeovil Museum. Early 15th cent. *British Archæol. Assoc. Journ.,* xix. 147.

GLASTONBURY, SOMERSETSHIRE, ST. JOHN THE BAPTIST'S CHURCH.
S. wall, W. end of S. aisle; coloured monument and effigy of Campbell, a bursar to the Abbot of Glastonbury, said to have been brought from the Abbey. 15th cent.
On either side of the chancel; table tombs of a knight and lady, with colouring on the panels. Date about 1500.
Painted shields on chest. 14th cent.

GLATTON CHURCH, HUNTINGDONSHIRE.
On jamb of chancel arch; Mary Magdalen in arched recess, the ground *semé* with crowns.

GLINTON CHURCH, NORTHAMPTONSHIRE.
Paintings of figures, &c. discovered in 1855 on N. wall of N. aisle, and whitewashed over.

GLODDAETH MANOR HOUSE, LLANDUDNO, CARNARVONSHIRE.

Two wall paintings; each pourtraying two angels
supporting a shield, charged, the upper one, with a
Maltese cross, and the five wounds; the lower, with the
instruments of the Passion. Early 16th cent.

GLOUCESTER CATHEDRAL, GLOUCESTERSHIRE.

Lady Chapel. Backs of niches in the screen; diaper
patterns. 1457–99. *Blackburne, Decorative Painting,*
p. 78; and *Civil Engineer and Architect's Journal,* 1851,
p. 197.

In the triforium; panel painting of the Last Judgment.
Time of Henry VIII. or Edward VI. *Archæologia,*
xxxvi. 370.

St. Andrew's Chapel, E. side of S. transept; back of
niche, a saltire on a diapered ground. *Building News,*
1868, p. 708.

S. side, in a chapel; on back of stalls; portraits of
Saints.

In a chapel on S. side; a reredos, and on back of
stalls, painted niches, a powdering of crowns, &c.

Nave piers; powdering of large roses.

In niches above door from N. aisle to W. ambulatory
of cloisters; small figures of Saints.

On N. side of Abbot Sebroke's Chapel; panelling, with
small figures of Saints.

Capitals of great piers of Choir, by monument of
Edward II.; the badge of Richard II.
Murray's Handbook of Gloucestershire.

The chapter house; inscriptions on the walls, in Lom-
bardic characters. Supposed to date from the 13th cent.
*Murray's Handbook of Gloucestershire. Ashby De La
Zouch Anastatic Drawing Soc.,* 1859, p. 10, pl. li.

GLOUCESTER, GLOUCESTERSHIRE, CHURCH OF ST. MARY
DE CRYPT.

Paintings in chancel and on the back of the sedilia,
viz. the lifting up the brazen serpent in the wilderness, &c. *Ecclesiologist,* iv. 44. *Murray's Handbook of
Gloucestershire.*

Paintings of a nobleman and his lady;? of James Lord
Berkeley and his Lady. Date about 1450. Discovered
in 1827. *Gent. Mag.,* vol. xcviii. pt. i. p. 65.

Stonework of sedilia and Easter sepulchre, once gilt
and painted.

On N. wall of chancel;? the prophecy of Simeon.

GLOUCESTER, GLOUCESTERSHIRE, CHURCH OF ST. MARY
DE CRYPT—*cont.*

On S. wall; the Adoration of the Magi, the Marys at
the Sepulchre, and the Resurrection.

F. G. Baylis, Ancient Churches of Gloucestershire,
p. 49.

On the groining of the ceiling below the tower; the
emblems of the Evangelists. *Power's Handbook for
Gloucester,* p. 44.

The Visit of the Queen of Sheba to King Solomon.
15th cent. *British Archæol. Assoc. Journ.,* ii. 275.

Back of sedile; consecration cross.

GLOUCESTER, GLOUCESTERSHIRE, LLANTHONY ABBEY.

Various painted mouldings dug up in 1852. *Archæologia Cambrensis,* 2nd series, iii. 157.

GODALMING CHURCH, SURREY.

S. chancel aisle, within two window splays; St. John
the Baptist, and a diaper of imitation dog-tooth ornament.
13th cent. *Archæol. Journ.,* xxxviii. 92.

Norman windows in chancel, on the splays, the
original colouring. *Surrey Archæol.,* vii. 279, 280.

GODSHILL CHURCH, ISLE OF WIGHT.

Christ on the Cross, and the Stem of Jesse. *British
Archæol. Assoc. Journ.,* ii. 143. *Archæol. Journ.,* i. 67
and 165. *Society of Antiquaries' Proceedings,* i. 51.
Archæologia, xxxi. 483. *Antiquarian and Architect.
Year Book,* 1844, p. 166.

GONALSTON CHURCH, NOTTINGHAMSHIRE.

Effigies of two cross-legged knights and a lady, with
traces of the original colouring. *Archæol. Journ.,* vi. 11.

GOODERSTONE CHURCH, NORFOLK.

Rood screen; the Twelve Apostles and four Doctors of
the Church, with Archangels above, in the panels.

Blomefield, Hist. of Norfolk, ed. 1807, vi. 63. *Cromwell, Excursions through Norfolk,* ii. 132. *Chambers,
Hist. of Norfolk,* ii. 627.

GOOSEY CHURCH, BERKSHIRE.

"Over the altar is a flat perpendicular tester, painted
with emblems of the Crucifixion, &c.; and above this,
on the E. wall, a painting of the Crucifixion." *Parker,
Eccles. and Architect. Topog. of England, Berkshire,*
No. 61.

GORLESTON, SUFFOLK, ST. ANDREW'S CHURCH.

N. chancel aisle, under the canopy of a tomb; the Trinity, and figures below; two shields bearing the emblems of the Crucifixion and the Trinity banner.

In the splays of two N. windows in N. chancel Chapel; Angels embowered in the foliage and fruit of the vine. Also paintings of figures and foliage on S. arcade of the N. chancel chapel, on E. wall of chancel, on the walls of the S. chancel chapel, W. wall of S. aisle, and in various parts of the nave. *Builder*, 1873, p. 52.

On S.W. side of S. chancel arch pillar; St. Anne instructing the Virgin, and St. Etheldreda or Catherine.

On N. wall; mural paintings of St. Christopher, "Les " Trois Morts et les Trois Vifs," &c., *destroyed. British Archæol. Assoc. Journ.*, xxxvi. 229, 437–439. *Antiquary*, 1872, ii. 184.

Painted and gilt font; the Seven Sacraments of the Church, and the Resurrection. 15th cent. *Suckling's History of Suffolk*, i. 375. *Paley's Manual of Gothic Architecture*, p. 248. *British Archæol. Assoc. Journ.*, xxxvi. 228. *East Anglian Notes and Queries*, ii. 325.

GORLESTON, SUFFOLK, ST. NICHOLAS PRIORY CHURCH.

Pulled down in 1786.
In the S. wall; mouldings with remains of colouring. Under the floor; joists of original roof richly gilt.
East Anglian Notes and Queries, i. 300.

GRADE CHURCH, CORNWALL.

Roofs of chancel and transepts; painting on the principals. Date 1486. *Exeter Diocesan Architect. Soc.*, vi. 149. *Archæol. Journ.*, xviii. 236.

GRAFTON REGIS CHURCH, NORTHAMPTONSHIRE.

Rood screen, formerly at, with figures of St. Denis, &c. depicted on the panels. *Schnebbelie, The Antiquaries' Museum.*

GRANTCHESTER CHURCH, CAMBRIDGESHIRE.

N. wall of nave; St. Christopher. Late 15th cent. *Cambridge Antiq. Soc. Journ.*, iv. 63. *Destroyed.*

GRAVENHURST, LOWER, CHURCH, BEDFORDSHIRE.

Decorated rood screen, with remains of the original painting. *Parker, Eccles. and Architect. Topog. of England, Bedford*, No. 68.

GRENDON CHURCH, NORTHAMPTONSHIRE.

Wall paintings of St. Roche, St. Martin, an entombment, decorative patterns, &c. Time of Edward IV.
Destroyed.

GRENDON UNDERWOOD CHURCH, BUCKINGHAMSHIRE.

Over the chancel arch; the sacred Monogram, and the
representation of the firmament.

"The walls of the nave formerly displayed texts of
scripture and emblematical paintings."

*Sheahan, Hist. and Topog. of the County of Bucking-
ham,* p. 385.

GRESHAM CHURCH, NORFOLK.

Painted font; the seven sacraments. *Paley's Manual
of Gothic Architecture,* p. 248.

GRESSENHALL CHURCH, NORFOLK.

Rood screen; the Doctors of the Church, SS. Leonard,
Margaret, Anthony, &c. *Blomefield, (Parkin), Hist. of
Norfolk,* ed. 1808, ix. 518. *The Ecclesiologist's Guide to
the Deaneries of Brisley, &c.,* p. 21. *Carthew's Hundred
of Launditch,* ii. 449.

GREYSTOKE CHURCH, CUMBERLAND.

Choir screen. *Cumberland and Westmoreland Antiq.
and Archæol. Soc. Transactions,* i. 325.

GRIMSBY, GREAT, CHURCH, LINCOLNSHIRE.

Effigy of Sir Thomas Haslerton "said to have been
originally gilded, but no traces of this decoration now
remain." *Oliver, Antiq. of Great Grimsby,* p. 102.

GRIMSTONE CHURCH, NORFOLK.

Lower portion of screen; painted panels.

GRUNDISBURGH CHURCH, SUFFOLK.

Screen between nave and chancel; richly coloured
and gilt. Foliated designs on the panels. Late 14th
cent.

Screen between S. aisle and S. chancel Chapel; remains
of painting. Circ. 1500.

GUERNSEY, PARISH CHURCH OF STE. MARIE DU CHASTEL.

On N. vault of original chancel; the Supper in the
house of Simon the Leper, with Mary of Bethany at the
feet of Jesus.

On flat vaulting rib of same chancel; ? the martyrdom
of an ecclesiastic.

Between the last painting and the tower; Les Trois
Morts et Les Trois Vifs.

GUERNSEY, PARISH OF ST. SAVIOUR'S, LA CHAPELLE STE. APOLLINE, otherwise LA CHAPELLE DE NOTRE DAME DE LA PERRELLE.
The Nativity, and the Flight into Egypt.

GUILDEN MORDEN CHURCH, CAMBRIDGESHIRE.
Rood screen; St. Edmund and St. Erkenwold, with flowers, &c. 15th cent. *Lysons' Magna Britannia, Cambridgeshire*, p. 59. 14th cent. *Ecclesiologist*, xxi. (xviii. new series), 172. *Notes on Cambridgeshire Churches*, 1827, p. 37.

GUILDFORD, SURREY, ST. MARY'S CHURCH.
St. John the Baptist's Chapel, E. end of N. chancel aisle:—
On the ceiling of the apse between the groining ribs, our Lord in Glory; and within medallions, the Tortures of the Wicked after death, with our Lord pleading on the Souls' behalf. Foliage around the medallions. Conjectured to be the work of William the Florentine, but more probably late 12th cent.
On the arch opening from the chancel aisle, a scroll pattern; above it on left, St. Michael weighing a Soul; on right, Demons carrying a Soul to Hell. Probably 14th cent.
Colling, Gothic Ornaments, pls. 37–40 and 44. *Archæologia*, xxvii. 413. *Archæol. Journ.*, xxix. 178, xxxiv. 277. *Civil Engineer and Architect's Journal*, 1851, p. 59. *Builder*, 1864, p. 724. *Society of Antiquaries' Proceedings*, 2nd series, ii. 298. *Murray's Handbook of Surrey. Figured in Brayley's History of Surrey*, i. 352, and 2nd ed., i. 145.
Within the splays of two (?) Saxon windows on N. and S. sides of the tower; portions of large figures, with inscriptions on a red ground. Perhaps 11th cent.
S. chapel, oak screen formerly the reredos, retaining traces of colour.

GUILDFORD, SURREY, ST. NICHOLAS CHURCH.
Within a chapel on S. side of nave; coloured effigy of Arnold Brocas. Date circ. 1395. *T. Cromwell, Excursions through the County of Surrey, &c.*, No. i., p. 24. *Brayley's Hist. of Surrey*, 2nd ed., i. 152.

GUILSFIELD CHURCH, MONTGOMERYSHIRE.
Chancel roof; carved and formerly coloured; said to have been brought from the Abbey of Ystrad Marchell. *Collections of Powys Land Club*, iv. 3. *Thomas, Hist. of the Diocese of St. Asaph*, p. 735.

GUISBOROUGH PRIORY, YORKSHIRE.

Portions of a shrine, richly painted and gilt; dug up
on the site of the church. *Archæol. Journ.*, xxv. 249.

GUIST CHURCH, NORFOLK.

On inner N. wall; a large figure. ? Moses. Discovered
in 1827, and again whitewashed over. *Gent. Mag.*, 1836,
v. new series, 218.

GULVAL. *See* ST. GULVAL.

GUMFRESTON CHURCH, PEMBROKESHIRE.

Lower portion of a mural painting, viz., the feet of a
figure, surrounded by a purse, brush, comb, knives, &c.
Notes and Queries, 4th series, xii. 268. *Archæologia
Cambrensis*, 4th series, xi. 335.

GUNWALLOE CHURCH, CORNWALL.

Panels of rood screen; paintings of the Apostles.
Blight's Churches of West Cornwall, p. 35. *Parochial
History of Cornwall*, ii. 125.

Divided, and now forming the doors to each of the
entrances. *A. H. Cummings, Churches and Antiq. of
Cury and Gunwalloe*, pp. 126, 128.

GUY'S CLIFF CHAPEL, WARWICKSHIRE.

Effigy of Earl Guy still retains traces of gilding and
colour. *Cooke's Guide to Warwickshire*, 12th ed., p. 185.

GYFFYLIOG CHURCH, DENBIGHSHIRE.

S. wall; paintings of the Coronation of the Virgin by
the Blessed Trinity or, more probably, the Presentation
in the Temple. Remains of painting on the N. wall;
with earlier colouring beneath it. All *destroyed.*
Archæologia Cambrensis, 4th. series, vii. 75.

HACCOMBE CHURCH, DEVONSHIRE.

Remains of colour on the effigy of Sir Stephen de
Haccombe, date about 1250; on the two effigies of ladies,
dates between 1250 and 1310; and on a small effigy,
date about 1350. *Murray's Handbook of Devonshire.
Exeter Diocesan Architect. Soc.*, 2nd series, i. 65, 66, 67,
ii. 42, 51, 52. *British Archæol. Assoc. Journ.*, xviii.
179. *W. H. H. Rogers, The Ancient Sepulchral Effigies,
&c., in Devon.* pp. 17, 18.

HADDENHAM CHURCH, CAMBRIDGESHIRE.

S. transept roof; rafters, black and white decoration.

HADDISCOE CHURCH, NORFOLK.

N. wall; St. Christopher. *Murray's Handbook of Norfolk. Quarterly Journ. of Suffolk Inst. for* 1869, p. 15.

HADDON HALL, DERBYSHIRE. THE CHAPEL.

Arches of N. arcade, and jamb of E. window S. aisle; running pattern. 1310.

W. wall of nave; running pattern of rose branches, &c. 1427.

S. wall of chancel; diaper of red and green, enclosing the Presentation of the Virgin, Virgin learning to read, Holy Family, and the Flight into Egypt. 1425.

Reliquary, xii. 1–4. *J. C. Cox, Churches of Derbyshire*, ii. 93. *L. Jewitt and S. C. Hall, The Stately Homes of England*, i. 247.

HADDON, WEST, CHURCH, NORTHAMPTONSHIRE.

E. beam of nave roof; scroll pattern. On nave walls; paintings have been seen through the whitewash.

HADHAM, MUCH, CHURCH, HERTFORDSHIRE.

Within the splay of a window, N. side of chancel; decorative painting.

HADLEIGH CHURCH, ESSEX.

N. and S. walls; a foliated stringcourse.

N. wall; Virgin and Child under a canopy, and a female.

Splays of window in N. wall; two angels.

W. splay of window, E. end of N. nave wall; St. Thomas à Becket.

S. aisle, on W. wall; a colossal figure, probably St. Michael, &c.

This series of paintings is of four different periods; the earliest late 13th cent.

S. wall; St. George.

Builder, 1864, pp. 724 and 734. *Essex Archæol.*, i. 161. *Murray's Handbook of Essex*.

Niche in window near rood screen; enriched with tabernacle work, highly decorated and painted. *Buckler's Churches of Essex*, p. 83.

HADLEIGH CHURCH, SUFFOLK.

Colouring on chancel roof. Various texts on the walls. *Suffolk Archæol.*, vol iii. preface pp. iv. and v. *H. Pigot, Hadleigh, the Town, Church, &c.*, p. v.

HAGBOURNE CHURCH, BERKSHIRE.
Painted shields on font. Circ. 1400.

HAINTON CHURCH, LINCOLNSHIRE.
N. chancel chapel; monuments of John and Anne Heneage, circ. 1559, and of Sir George Heneage, 1593, richly coloured and gilt. *Associated Architect. Societies' Repts.*, vi. 169.

HALESOWEN CHURCH, SHROPSHIRE.
The Legend of King Kenelm. *Destroyed. Noake's Rambles in Worcestershire*, 1st series, p. 200.
Within the splay of a window; masonry pattern, 12th cent. *Archæol. Journ.*, xxxiv. 277.
On or near the chancel arch; the Crucifixion and Resurrection. *Destroyed. Associated Architect. Societies' Repts.*, xiv. 94.

HALESWORTH CHURCH, SUFFOLK.
N. side of chancel, over the vestry door; black letter inscription recording the builders of the vestry. *Suckling, History of Suffolk*, ii. 340. Date 1506.

HALIFAX CHURCH, YORKSHIRE.
On S. side of chancel; painting of a bishop. Perpendicular period. Discovered in 1874 and *destroyed. The British Architect*, i. 409.
Fragments of decoration on the walls, and of scrolls on the pillars. *Associated Architect. Societies' Repts.*, vii. 116.

HAM, EAST, CHURCH, ESSEX.
On E. wall of chancel, on arch opening to the apse; life-sized figures of saints, one St. Etheldreda. 15th cent.
On soffit of chancel arch; in the centre, a figure; on either side, foliage.
Wall of apse; masonry patterns. Norman and Early English periods. *Essex Archæol.*, i. 72, ii. 106. *Builder*, 1864, p. 686. *Murray's Handbook of Essex.*

HAM, WEST, CHURCH, ESSEX.
E. end of S. clerestory wall; the Reward of the Righteous, part of a Doom. Late 15th cent.
Various remains of diapers and other patterns discovered and *destroyed.*
Essex Archæol., iv. 45. *Archæol. Journ.*, xxiii. 63.

HAMPSTEAD NORRIS CHURCH, BERKSHIRE.
Over S. door; "Some writing in Saxon characters." *Hist. and Antiq. of Newbury*, 1839, p. 216.

HAMPSTHWAITE CHURCH, YORKSHIRE.
Paintings and texts discovered on the walls in 1820, and *destroyed. Grainge, Hist. of Harrogate and the Forest of Knaresborough*, p. 394.

HAMPTON COURT PALACE, MIDDLESEX.
Roofs of hall and chapel, enriched with polychrome. Early 16th cent. *J. H. Sperling, Church Walks in Middlesex*, pp. 17, 44. *A. Wood, Eccles. Antiq. of London*, pp. 302, 305.
Charles I.'s Chapel, painted and gilt ceiling.
On one side paintings on panels, probably time of Henry VIII., viz.: The Last Supper, Scourging, Christ bearing His Cross, Crucifixion, Resurrection, and other subjects.
F. Summerly, A Handbook for Hampton Court, p. 39.

HAMPTON LOVETT CHURCH, WORCESTERSHIRE.
On N. wall; traces of painting and Scripture sentences. *Noake's Rambles in Worcestershire*, 2nd series, p. 388.
Rood screen; enriched with colour and gilding. *Associated Architect. Societies' Repts.*, v. 161. *J. Severn Walker, Architect. Sketches, &c., in Worcestershire*, pt. i., p. 7.

HAMPTON POYLE CHURCH, OXFORDSHIRE.
Effigies of a cross-legged knight and lady retain traces of their original colouring. *Hist. Gazett. and Directory of the County of Oxford*, p. 757.

HANBURY CHURCH, STAFFORDSHIRE.
S. aisle wall; diapered in colours. *Destroyed Archæol. Journ.*, iv. 153.

HANDBOROUGH CHURCH, OXFORDSHIRE.
Rood screen; richly painted and gilt. Date about 1460. *Parker's Architectural Guide to the Neighbourhood of Oxford*, p. 146. *Hist. Gazett. and Directory of the County of Oxford*, p. 677.

HANNEY CHURCH, BERKSHIRE.
Lower part of rood screen; remains of painting.

HANSLOPE CHURCH, BUCKINGHAMSHIRE.
On a beam in the nave; painted quatrefoils. *Shealan, Hist. and Topog. of the County of Buckingham*, p. 542.

HANSLOPE CHURCH, BUCKINGHAMSHIRE—*cont.*

At N.E. corner of S. aisle; remains of painting.

The walls are covered with paintings, now concealed by white and yellow wash.

HANWELL CHURCH, OXFORDSHIRE.

E. wall of chancel; figures of Saints, &c. *Destroyed. Beesley, Hist. of Banbury,* p. 612.

HAPPISBURGH CHURCH, NORFOLK.

Rood screen, with paintings of Saints on the panels. Circ. 1429. *Destroyed.*

HARBERTON CHURCH, DEVONSHIRE.

Pulpit and rood screen; painted and gilt. (The screen has been restored.) Early 15th cent. *Murray's Handbook of Devonshire. Antiquary,* 1871, i. 51.

HARBLEDOWN HOSPITAL CHAPEL, KENT.

Panels of chancel roof; "ornamented with stars and Gothic roses upon a dark ground." *Antiquarian Itinerary,* vol. i.

Numerous indistinct subjects on the walls.

HARBOROUGH, MARKET, CHURCH, LEICESTERSHIRE.

Mural decorations.

HARDHAM CHURCH, SUSSEX.

In chancel; the Apostles, probably part of a subject of Our Lord in Glory; in nave, Seven Ages of Man (?).

Over C. arch, ? the Doom.

On S. wall of nave; the Nativity, Ascension, and Our Lord in Glory.

Over N. door; the Flight into Egypt.

On N. wall, W. end of nave; St. George and the Dragon.

Within the window splays; ornamental patterns. All 12th cent.

The walls are covered with paintings; all very indistinct.

Building News, 1866, p. 294. *Archaeol. Journ.,* xxxviii. 82, 95.

HARDWICK CHURCH, CAMBRIDGESHIRE.

S. wall of nave; Six Acts of Mercy, and Legend of St. Cyriac. Over N. door; St. Christopher. End of 15th cent. *Destroyed.* Drawings existing. *Ecclesiologist,* xx. 316.

HARDWICK CHURCH, NORFOLK.
On N. wall of nave; St. Christopher, with part of inscription above.
Painted panels of screen.
East Anglian Notes and Queries, iii. 23.

HARDWICK CHURCH, NORTHAMPTONSHIRE.
Traces of paintings on nave walls; discovered and *destroyed*.

HAREFIELD, MIDDLESEX, MOOR HALL.*
E. walls of granary, upper storey; masonry pattern, with roses of five and six leaves. *London and Middlesex Archæol.*, iii. 23.

HAREWOOD CHURCH, YORKSHIRE.
S. of chancel, on monument of Sir John Neville, of Womersley, blazoned shields. Circ. 1482. *J. Jones, Hist. of Harewood*, p. 108.
Several other monuments, all retaining traces of colour. *Ashby De la Zouch Anastatic Drawing Soc.*, 1858, p. 5.

HARGRAVE CHURCH, NORTHAMPTONSHIRE.
Over N. door; St. George and the Dragon (now covered). 15th cent. *Churches of the Archdeaconry of Northampton*, p. 40.
On the nave walls; some of the Twelve Patriarchs. *Ecclesiologist*, xxviii. (xxv. new series), 244. *Associated Architect. Societies' Repts.*, vi. cxiii.
On N. wall of nave; St. Christopher.

HARLING, EAST, NORFOLK, SS. PETER AND PAUL'S CHURCH.
E. end of S. aisle; parclose screen. On the panels, quatrefoil ornaments, and the monogram I.H.C. in a quatrefoil. Date about 1465. *Colling, Gothic Ornaments*, i. pl. 66. *Ecclesiologist*, iv. 229. *Cromwell, Excursions through Norfolk*, ii. 163. *Chambers, Hist. of Norfolk*, ii. 706.
On N. wall of nave; portion of a Doom. 15th cent.

HARLINGTON CHURCH, MIDDLESEX.
S. side of chancel, on E. splay of E. window; female Saint with inscription.

---

* Formerly a Camera of the Knights Hospitallers.

HARMONDSWORTH CHURCH, MIDDLESEX.
Black letter texts from the book of Wisdom. Circ.
1580. *J. H. Sperling, Church Walks in Middlesex*, p. 66.
Not now visible.

HARNHAM, WEST, CHURCH, WILTSHIRE.
Within a recess on the S. side of the chancel arch; a
female figure kneeling at the feet of our Saviour.
Probably 13th cent.

HARPLEY CHURCH, NORFOLK.
Rood screen; repainted.
On the N. door; St. Lawrence and the Virgin and
Child.
On the S.; St. Joacim, and St. Anne instructing the
Virgin.
On the panels of the screen; the Prophets, omitting
Habakkuk, Nahum, Zephaniah, and Haggai. 15th cent.
Norfolk Archœol., viii. 35.

HARPTREE, EAST, SOMERSETSHIRE.
Remains of colour on the drapery of figures sculptured
on the head of a churchyard cross, found built up in the
chimney stack of an old cottage. Date early 13th cent.
Now in the Taunton Museum. *Somerset Archœol. and
Nat. Hist. Soc. Proceedings*, xv. pt. i. p. 34.

HARROW CHURCH, MIDDLESEX.
Niche and ceiling of small room over porch. 15th
cent. *Blackburne, Decorative Painting*, p. 88. *J. H.
Sperling, Church Walks in Middlesex*, p. 92. *T. Smith,
Handbook to Harrow-on-the-Hill*, p. 29.

HARTING CHURCH, SUSSEX.
Mural paintings of St. Helena, St. Anne, and St.
Lawrence. 14th cent. Now concealed. *Archœol. Journ.*,
xix. 91.

HARTINGTON CHURCH, DERBYSHIRE.
Various remnants of old painting on the walls; dis-
covered in 1858, and *destroyed*. *J. C. Cox, Churches of
Derbyshire*, ii. 482.

HARTLAND ABBEY, DEVONSHIRE.
"Richly ornamented gilded mouldings," dug up on the
site. *Polwhele, Hist. of Devon*, i. 236 (*note*). *W. H. H.
Rogers, The Ancient Sepulchral Effigies, &c. in Devon*,
p. 220.

HARTLAND, OR STOKE ST. NECTAN'S, CHURCH, DEVONSHIRE.
Roofs of nave and N. chancel aisle; gilt bosses and painted panels. *Exeter Diocesan Architect. Soc.,* ii. 43. *Murray's Handbook of Devonshire.*
. .Rood screen; remains of gold and colour. *Stewart's N. Devon Handbook,* p. 201. *Worth, Tourist's Guide to N. Devon,* p. 70.

HARTLEPOOL, DURHAM, ST. HELEN'S CHAPEL.
Fragment of a coloured image found at. *Archæol. Journ.,* xii. 149 *note.*

HARTLEY WINTNEY CHURCH, HAMPSHIRE.
Wall paintings of figures under canopies, covered up. *Ecclesiologist,* ii. 25.

HARTY CHURCH, KENT.
Considerable remains of painting found built up in E. wall on niches and tracery—of figures which cannot be made out.

HASELEY, GREAT, CHURCH, OXFORDSHIRE.
Chancel roof; formerly panelled and painted with clouds, the sun, moon, stars, &c.
E. end of S. aisle; reredos with remains of original colouring.
Weare, Church of Gt. Haseley, Oxon, 2nd ed., pp. 17, 27.

HASTINGLEIGH CHURCH, KENT.
N. aisle; the Annunciation, 15th cent.

HASTINGS, SUSSEX, ALL SAINTS' CHURCH.
Over chancel arch; fragments of the Last Judgment, 15th cent., and other remains.
On the S. wall; the Decollation of John the Baptist.
On the N. wall; a fleet and black-letter texts. 16th cent.
Sussex Archæol., xxiii. 192.
Colour on groining beneath the tower.
Moss, Hist. of Hastings, p. 99.

HATHERLEIGH CHURCH, DEVONSHIRE.
Mural paintings, whitewashed over, tracings existing.
Coloured roof.

HAUXTON CHURCH, CAMBRIDGESHIRE.
On S. side of chancel arch; St. Thomas à Becket and scroll work. 13th cent. *Ecclesiologist,* xxii. (xix. new series), 383. *Archæol. Journ.,* xxxv. 278. *A. G. Hill, Churches of Cambridgeshire,* p. 45.

HAVANT CHURCH, HAMPSHIRE.
S. transept, on the jambs of a lancet window; the
burning of a Virgin Martyr (? St. Lucia) in a cauldron,
and another subject. 13th cent. *Kelly's County Topography*, and *Kelly's Post Office Directory, Hampshire.*

HAVERHILL CHURCH, SUFFOLK.
Sculptured stones, with remains of colour, found in
1851. *Suffolk Archæol.*, iv. 103.

HAWKCHURCH CHURCH, DORSETSHIRE.
S. aisle; screen richly painted and gilt.
Hutchins' Hist. of Dorset, 3rd ed., iv. 52.
Walls of chancel.

HAWKEDON CHURCH, SUFFOLK.
Traces of mural painting. *Parker, Eccles. and Archi-
tect. Topog. of England, Suffolk*, No. 407.
Opposite the S. door; St. Christopher. *Destroyed.*
Two paintings partially hidden by tablets, one St.
Paul preaching. *Destroyed.*
Over E. window; Our Saviour preaching to the spirits
in prison.
Lower part of screen; traces of colour.

HAYES, CHURCH OF ST. MARY THE VIRGIN, MIDDLESEX.
N. wall of N. aisle; St. Christopher.
N.E. and E. wall of N. aisle; decorative pattern.
Late 15th cent.
On two columns, N. of nave; remains of painting.
E. wall of S. aisle; colouring on two brackets.
T. Mills, History of Hayes, p. 21. *Long Ago*, 1873,
vol. i., p. 349.

HAZELBURY BRYAN CHURCH, DORSETSHIRE.
Chancel; painted shields. Early 15th cent. *Hutchins'
Hist. of Dorset*, 3rd ed., i. 277.

HEADBOURN WORTHY. *See* WORTHY, HEADBOURN.

HEADINGTON CHURCH, OXFORDSHIRE.
On the sides of the windows; the Nativity, Flight
into Egypt; Slaughter of the Innocents; Triumphal
Entry into Jerusalem; St. Christopher; the Virgin; a
Bishop (?) St. Nicholas; the heads of SS. Peter and
Paul, &c. Late 13th cent. *Society of Antiquaries' Pro-
ceedings*, 2nd series, ii. 316: and *Builder*, 1864, p. 733.

HEADINGTON CHURCH, OXFORDSHIRE—*cont.*
Over the chancel arch; Our Lord in Majesty. 13th cent.
Wall decoration. Tudor period.
Builder, 1864, pp. 733 and 734.

HEAVITREE CHURCH, DEVONSHIRE.
Lower part of screen; formed into pews.
In panels; SS. Dunstan, Agatha, and Catherine.
Lysons' Magna Britannia, Devonshire, p. cccxxviii
Oliver's Ecclesiastical Antiquities of Devon, i. 44.

HECKFIELD CHURCH, HAMPSHIRE.
Dedication cross. *Destroyed.*

HEDINGHAM, CASTLE, CHURCH, ESSEX.
S. wall of chancel; bishop in pontificals; whitewashed
over. Late Norman period. *Builder,* 1864, p. 724.

HEIGHAM, POTTER, CHURCH, NORFOLK.
Over the door; St. Christopher.
S. aisle; Works of Piety and Mercy. Latter part of
14th cent. *Norfolk Archæol.,* ii. 358 *note. Chambers,
Hist. of Norfolk,* ii. 727.
Rood screen; three of the Evangelists, omitting St.
Matthew, St. Eligius, and the four Fathers of the Church.
15th cent.
Antiquary, 1872, ii. 200. *The Ecclesiologist's Guide
to the Deaneries of Brisley, &c.,* pp. 83, 95.
Paintings on N. wall and over chancel arch; white-
washed over.

HELLAND CHURCH, CORNWALL.
Under the tower; painted wall plate of former roof.
Maclean, Hist. of the Deanery of Trigg Minor, ii. 15.

HEMESBY CHURCH, NORFOLK.
Painted roof. *Illustrations of Norfolk Topography,*
p. 61.

HEMINGBOROUGH CHURCH, YORKSHIRE.
Painting on nave roof, and on a beam under the tower.
15th cent.
Bench ends with remains of colour.

HEMINGFORD ABBAS CHURCH, HUNTINGDONSHIRE.
Nave; painted roof. *Parker, Eccles. and Architect.
Topog. of England, Huntingdon,* No. 67.

HEMPSTEAD, NORFOLK, ST. MARY'S CHURCH.

Rood screen; on S. side; St. George, St. Erasmus, St. Stephen, St. Laurence, St. Blase, St. Francis, St. Leonard, and St. Eligius. *The Ecclesiologist's Guide to the Deaneries of Brisley, &c.*, p. 94.

Formerly on N. side, but now incorporated with a prayer desk; SS. Theobald, Dionysius, John of Burlington or Beverley, Egidius, Juliana, Edmund, and Edward the Confessor. Date circ. 1493.

HEMPSTON, LITTLE, CHURCH, DEVONSHIRE.

Rood screen.

HENFIELD CHURCH, SUSSEX.

S. wall of chancel. *Sussex Archæol.*, xxiii, 213.

HENGRAVE CHURCH, SUFFOLK.

Over N. door; St. Christopher. Has perished from damp. *Gage, Hist. of Hengrave*, p. 64. *Suffolk Archæol.*, i. 339. *British Archæol. Assoc. Journ.*, i. 139. *Murray's Handbook of Suffolk.* Date circ. 1450.

Over S. door; black letter inscription, recording the name of the founder, and two shields of arms above.

Coloured effigies of the Countess of Bath and her husbands. Circ. 1561.

Gage, Hist. of Hengrave, p. 65, *and Hist. of Suffolk, Thingoe Hundred*, pp. 226, 228, 229.

HENHURST MANOR. *See* COBHAM.

HENLEY IN ARDEN CHURCH, WARWICKSHIRE.

Roof of nave, E. end; traces of colouring. *Ecclesiologist*, xv. 436.

Canopy of rood loft; gilt and highly coloured. *J. Hannett, The Forest of Arden*, p. 40.

HENSTRIDGE CHURCH, SOMERSETSHIRE.

St. Christopher. *Builder*, 1873, p. 475. *Surrey Archæol.*, vi. 209.

Remains of colour on the monument and effigies of William and Margaret Carent. About 1460. *Somerset Archæol. and Nat. Hist. Soc. Proceedings*, xvi. pt. i. p. 43. *Hutchins' Hist. of Dorset*, 3rd ed., iv. iii.

HEREFORD CATHEDRAL, HEREFORDSHIRE.

On arch opening from S. transept to S. aisle of nave; various decorative designs. Discovered between the years

1842 and 1846, and *destroyed.* Dates 12th, 14th, and
15th centuries. Figured in *Havergal, Fasti Herefordenses,* pl. xv.

N. transept; remains of colour on canopy over the
monument and on the effigy of Bishop d'Aqua Blanca.
1239.

" N. wing "; portrait of Bishop Cantelupe.
Ashby De La Zouch Anastatic Drawing Soc., 1855,
p. 5, pl. xxx.

S. side of N. chancel aisle; gilding on monument of
Bishop Stanbery. About 1450.

N. E. transept; walls covered with painting, very faint.
Over and round the arch opening into the aisle; (?) Our
Lord in Glory.

Many beautiful designs in the Lady Chapel.
Dallaway's Anecdotes of the Arts, p. 422.

On N. side of Lady Chapel; coloured monument of
Joanna de Bohun, Countess of Hereford. Within the
canopy the Countess presenting a church to the Virgin.
Date 1331.

On S. side of Lady Chapel, Bishop Audley's chantry
Chapel; on the exterior 33 figures of saints, bishops, &c.;
in the interior, fan tracery, ceiling, &c., richly coloured.
Late 15th cent. *Duncumb, Hist. of County of Hereford,*
i. 565.

Murray's Handbook of Herefordshire.

On the S. side of the Lady Chapel; within the canopy
of the monument of a Dean commonly ascribed to Dean
Borew, who died in 1462, but really a century earlier, is
a painting of the Dean kneeling to St. 'Anne instructing
the Virgin. *See Archæol. Journ.,* xxxiv. 409 and 419.

Remains of colour on the monuments of Bishop Booth,
about 1530; Sir R. Pembridge, 1375; and Sir R. Denton,
1566. *Hollis' Monumental Effigies,* pt. v. pl. 8.

Traces of rich vermilion and gold colouring were found
on the canopies of the stalls and the Bishop's chair; also
on the groining of the S. transept, and on the wooden
ceiling of Bishop Booth's porch.
Archæologia Cambrensis, 3rd series, xiii. 414.

On the exterior, N. side of Lady Chapel; red ground
colour within the medallions.
Havergal, Fasti Herefordenses, pp. 155 and 156.

In S. Transept; an image of St. John the Baptist, with
traces of ancient colour, discovered when the old church

HEREFORD CATHEDRAL, HEREFORDSHIRE—*cont.*

of St. Nicholas was taken down. *Havergal, Fasti Herefordenses,* p. 199.

On a pedestal against a pier on the S. side of the sacrarium, remains of colour and gilding on an effigy of King Ethelbert. Date 14th cent. *Havergal, Fasti Herefordenses,* p. 110.

Chapter House, pulled down, within the panelling at the back of the seats; portraits of King Milfrid, Ethelbert, Bishop Athelstan, Wulwive, and Godiva, Our Saviour, the Apostles and early Saints, SS. George, David, Edward, Winifred, Ceadda, and four representations of the Virgin and Child. *Duncumb, Hist. of the County of Hereford,* i. 583. *Stukeley's Itinerarium Curiosum,* ed. 1776, i. 71. *Ashby De La Zouch Anastatic Drawing Soc.,* 1855, p. 6, pl. xxxi.

HEREFORD, ALL SAINTS' CHURCH, HEREFORDSHIRE.

Decorative colouring. *Havergal, Fasti Herefordenses,* p. 157.

HEREFORD, ST. NICHOLAS' OLD CHURCH, HEREFORDSHIRE.

Havergal, Fasti Herefordenses, p. 157.

HEREFORD, THE BISHOP'S PALACE, HEREFORDSHIRE.

Remains of colour " on the plaster adjacent to the ancient timber arcade." *Havergal, Fasti Herefordenses,* p. 157.

HEREFORD COLLEGE, HEREFORDSHIRE.

Remains of colour still to be seen on the timber walls. *Havergal, Fasti Herefordenses,* p. 157.

HEREFORD, LITTLE, CHURCH, HEREFORDSHIRE.

Within a recess over the chancel arch; the Crucifixion. *British Archæol. Assoc. Journ.,* xxiv. 194. *Murray's Handbook of Shropshire.*

HERN-HILL CHURCH, KENT.

Remains of ancient colouring on the walls. *Builder,* 1878, p. 335.

HERRINGFLEET CHURCH, SUFFOLK.

N. wall of nave; St. Christopher. *" The Times,"* August 15th, 1879.

Painting on panel of an ecclesiastic. Brought from St. Olave's Priory. *British Archæol. Assoc. Journ.,* xxxvi. 120.

HESSETT CHURCH, SUFFOLK.

On S. wall of S. aisle ; St. Christopher and St. Etheldreda.

On N. wall of N. aisle; the Tree of the Seven Deadly Sins, and Representative Christian triumphing. Figure surrounded with various instruments.* Date about 1460.

Rood screen repainted.

Suffolk Archæol., v. 21, 25, 26, 29. *Quarterly Journ. of Suffolk Institute for* 1869, p. 22. *Rectangular Review*, October 1870, p. 281. *Archæol. Journ.*, xxvi. 398. *Ecclesiologist*, xxix. (xxvi. new series), 87. *Society of Antiquaries' Proceedings*, 2nd series, iv. 87.

HESTON CHURCH, MIDDLESEX.

Remains of colour on arch opening from N. aisle to N. chancel aisle. *Destroyed. Ecclesiologist*, xxvi. (xxiii. new series), 334.

HETHERSETT CHURCH, NORFOLK.

E. wall ; mural decoration. Partly 15th cent. *Destroyed. Norfolk Archæol.*, vii. 353.

HEVENINGHAM CHURCH, SUFFOLK.

Niche in the chancel wall, coloured and gilt.

HEXHAM, NORTHUMBERLAND, ST. ANDREW'S CHURCH.

Prior Richard's shrine ; SS. Andrew, Peter, Paul, and the Crucifixion. About 1320.

Roof above Prior Richard's shrine, on a boss, a red rose.

Rood screen ; painted figures on panels, on both faces, on W., St. Cuthbert, in heads of doorways, pictures of the Annunciation and Salutation ; ceiling of loft coloured and gilt ; above, 24 panels, which do not belong, with paintings from the Dance of Death, Our Lord, the Apostles, the Virgin, &c. Date about 1500.

In passage leading to the cloister ; remains of screen of the Ogle shrine ; the Crucifixion, with the Virgin in a scarlet robe, and St. John, with a background of hexagonal rosettes bearing the sacred monogram on a crimson ground. About 1500.

Murray's Handbook of Northumberland. Ecclesiologist, viii. 30., xxi. (xviii. new series), 347. *Society of Antiquaries' Proceedings*, 2nd series, ii. 157. *British Archæol. Assoc. Journ.*, xix. 58.

---

* *See* notice of Stedham Church.

HEXHAM, NORTHUMBERLAND, ST. ANDREW'S CHURCH—*cont.*

Painted panels worked up into the pulpit. *Archæologia Æliana*, new series, v. 157.

On litany desk, painted panels, with St. Peter, Our Lord in the act of Benediction, the Virgin and Child, &c. Late 15th cent.

On vestry screen, formerly over litany desk ; SS. Wilfrid, John of Beverley, Acca, Fridbert, Eilfrid, Alcmund, and Eata.

Wright, Hist. of Hexham, pp. 68, 69, 71, 72, 76, 78, 79. *Hutchinson's Tour to the Lakes*, p. 306. *Hutchinson's View of Northumberland*, ii. 95. *Mackenzie, View of the County of Northumberland*, ii. 276, 277. *J. Hewitt, A Handbook to Hexham Abbey Church*, pp. 17, 18, 27, 28, 37. *Durham and Northumberland, Architect. and Archæol. Soc. Trans.*, 1862–63, pp. 25, 27. *Gibson, Notices of Northumbrian Castles, Churches, &c.*, pp. 77, 86.

HEYFORD, NETHER, CHURCH, NORTHAMPTONSHIRE.

E. end of S. aisle ; coloured monument of Francis Morgan, Justice of the King's Bench, with painted shields, &c. Date 1558. *Murray's Handbook of Northamptonshire*, p. 110.

HEYFORD, LOWER, CHURCH, OXFORDSHIRE.

Mural paintings.
N. wall ; the Commandments. Time of Elizabeth.

HEYTESBURY CHURCH, WILTSHIRE.

Over the W. tower arch ; ? the Doom. *Destroyed.*

HICKLING CHURCH, NORFOLK.

Rood screen ; figures covered over with a coat of white paint.

HIGHAM FERRERS CHURCH, NORTHAMPTONSHIRE.

Under the E. arch, between the chancel and Lady chapel ; painting in compartments of red and green on the canopy of an altar tomb. 14th cent. *Murray's Handbook of Northants*, p. 30. *Churches of the Archdeaconry of Northampton*, p. 11. *Gent. Mag.*, ci. pt. ii., p. 497.

Colour and gilding on " backs of turn-up seats " in the Choir. *J. Cole, Hist. of Higham Ferrers*, pp. 46, 60.

HIGHAM FERRERS, NORTHAMPTONSHIRE, THE SCHOOL HOUSE.
Wooden roof, formerly painted. *J. Cole, Hist. of Higham Ferrers*, p. 91.

HIGHAM, COLD, CHURCH, NORTHAMPTONSHIRE.
E. end of chapel; painted shields of arms, figures of knights, helmets, &c. Discovered about 1857, and re-covered with whitewash.

HIGHWORTH CHURCH, WILTSHIRE.
St. Dunstan and inscriptions. *Wilts Archæol. and Nat. Hist. Soc. Mag.*, vii. 243, 246.

HILDERSHAM CHURCH, CAMBRIDGESHIRE.
N. side of chancel; red colour on the cross of a coffin lid. 13th cent.
S. chancel chapel; traces of painting on the wooden effigies of a cross-legged knight and his lady. 13th cent.

HILGAY CHURCH, NORFOLK.
Roof of S. aisle; curiously painted with the arms of benefactors. *Cromwell, Excursions through Norfolk*, ii. 149. *Chambers, Hist. of Norfolk*, i. 56.

HILLESDEN CHURCH, BUCKINGHAMSHIRE.
Chancel; round the N.E. and S. walls, beneath the roof; a series of sculptures of angels holding musical instruments and scrolls, richly coloured and gilt.
On either side of E. window; painted angel bracket. About 1493.
Within the stone panelling; two shields of the Dentons. Date about 1550.
N. chancel chapel; monument and effigies of the first of the Dentons. Date 1560. Have been richly coloured and gilt.

HILLMORTON CHURCH, WARWICKSHIRE.
Remains of colour on the effigy of Dame Margerie Astley. Latter part of 14th cent. *Society of Antiquaries' Proceedings*, 2nd series, iv. 264.

HILTON CHURCH, DORSETSHIRE. *See* MILTON ABBAS.

HINGHAM CHURCH, NORFOLK.
S. wall of chancel; murder of St. Thomas à Becket (now concealed). *Norfolk Archæol.*, vi. 167.

HINTON, CHERRY. *See* CHERRY HINTON.

HISTON CHURCH, CAMBRIDGESHIRE.
Behind the pulpit ; the Annunciation.
S. transept, jambs of window ; lozenges of yellow, scored in black lines on a dark-red ground.
Ecclesiologist, v. 270.
Traces of colour on the chancel arch, tower arch, and transept walls.
Coloured fragments removed to Madingley from the destroyed church of St. Etheldreda, Histon, and now brought back and placed in the chancel.
A. G. Hill, Churches of Cambridgeshire, pp. 8, 21.

HITCHAM CHURCH, SUFFOLK.
Panels of rood screen ; cherubim bearing implements of the Passion.

HITCHIN CHURCH, HERTFORDSHIRE.
S. chancel aisle ; painted roof. 15th cent.

HOCKERING CHURCH, NORFOLK.
Wall painting of St. Christopher. *Gent. Mag.*, 1843, xix. new series, 384. *Hart, Antiq. of Norfolk*, p. 66. *The Ecclesiologist's Guide to the Deaneries of Brisley, &c.*, p. 39.

HOLCOMBE BURNELL CHURCH, DEVONSHIRE.
Gilding on roof at E. end of nave.

HOLCOMBE ROGUS CHURCH, DEVONSHIRE.
Screen ; formerly painted. *Builder*, 1865, p. 212.

HOLDENBY CHURCH, NORTHAMPTONSHIRE.
Scripture texts from the bishop's Bible. Date about 1575.

HOLM CULTRAM ABBEY CHURCH, CUMBERLAND.
Transept walls ; traces of colour. *Cumberland and Westmoreland Antiq. and Archæol. Soc. Transactions*, i. 272.

HOLNE CHURCH, DEVONSHIRE.
Rood screen ; figures of saints. *Murray's Handbook of Devonshire.*
Across N. chancel aisle ; SS. Sativola, Sebastian, Barbara, Pancras, Mary Magdalene, Bartholomew, Simon, and three other Saints.
Chancel screen, N. side ; SS. Matthew, Thomas, James Major, Peter, Jerome, Gregory, Luke, and John.

HOLNE CHURCH, DEVONSHIRE—*cont.*

On the doors; the Virgin as Queen of Heaven, Our Saviour, and angels.

S. side; SS. Matthew, Mark, Ambrose, Augustine, Paul, Andrew, John, and John the Baptist.

Across N. chancel aisle; SS. Jude, Philip, Agatha, Catherine, Nicholas, Lawrence, Roche, Margaret, and two other Saints.

Painted pulpit.

On the panels; eight heraldic shields.

Gent. Mag., xcviii. pt. ii. p. 115. *Blackburne, Decorative Painting,* p. 73. *C. Worthy, Ashburton and its Neighbourhood,* p. 126. *Worth, Tourist's Guide to S. Devon,* p. 83.

HOLT CHURCH, WORCESTERSHIRE.

In the chancel; painted effigy of a lady.

HOMINGTON CHURCH, WILTSHIRE.

Wall opposite N. door; St. Christopher.

HONING CHURCH, NORFOLK.

Ornamental painting on a beam. *Illustrations of Norfolk Topography,* p. 67.

HONITON CHURCH, DEVONSHIRE.

Rood screen. 15th cent. *Ecclesiologist,* xxviii. (xxv. new series), p. 308. *Exeter Diocesan Architect. Soc.,* new series, ii. 96.

HONNINGTON, SUFFOLK, ALL SAINTS' CHURCH.

On N. wall; indication of a large painting, disguised by whitewash. *Parker, Eccles. and Architect. Topog. of England, Suffolk,* No. 371.

HOOE CHURCH, SUSSEX.

N. wall of nave; paintings of an angel, &c. have been seen through the whitewash.

HOOTON ROBERTS CHURCH, YORKSHIRE.

Traces of several quaint old paintings, a crowned figure &c., discovered on the removal of the plaster. *Builder,* 1876, p. 324. *Destroyed. Tomlinson, From Doncaster into Hallamshire,* p. 199.

HOPTON, SUFFOLK, ALL SAINTS' CHURCH.

Nave roof painted. Perpendicular period. *Parker, Eccles. and Architect. Topog. of England, Suffolk,* No. 372.

HORBLING CHURCH, LINCOLNSHIRE.
N. transept; remains of colour on a monument and on a sculptured representation of the Resurrection above it. Late 15th cent.

HORHAM CHURCH, SUFFOLK.
Painted and gilt font cover. *Harrod's Suffolk Directory*, 1864. *Kelly's Post Office Directory for Suffolk.*

HORKESLEY, LITTLE, CHURCH, ESSEX.
Traces of colour on the N. wall of the chancel and on a niche within the splay of a window on the N. side of the nave.

HORLEY CHURCH, OXFORDSHIRE.
A Weighing of Souls.
Wall of N. aisle; St. Christopher. 15th cent.
Archæol. Journ., xiii. 416. *Beesley, Hist. of Banbury*, pp. 109, 124.

HORNBY CHURCH, YORKSHIRE.
Painted parclose screen. *Murray's Handbook of Yorkshire.* *W. Hylton Longstaffe, Richmondshire, its Ancient Lords and Edifices*, p. 58.

HORNCHURCH CHURCH, ESSEX.
Nave wall; story of St. George.
S. wall of chancel; the Raising of Lazarus, and remains of other paintings, discovered in the body of the church in 1826, and ? destroyed. *Gent. Mag.*, xcviii. pt. i. p. 306. *Blackburne, Decorative Painting*, p. 22.
Paintings of figures with scrolls, at the back of the sedilia. *Essex Archæol.*, v. 245.

HORNDON-ON-THE-HILL CHURCH, ESSEX.
Numerous mural paintings and texts discovered and destroyed. *Rev. W. Palin, Stifford and its Neighbourhood*, p. 137.

HORNINGSEY CHURCH, CAMBRIDGESHIRE.
Decorative painting on nave pillars.
S. aisle; coloured niche and piscina. About 1300. *Parker, Eccles. and Architect. Topog. of England, Cambridge*, No. 73. *Cambridge Antiq. Soc. Publications, Horningsey*, pp. 38, 40.
Lower panels of screen, curiously painted. *F. A Paley, The Ecclesiologist's Guide to the Churches . . . . . round Cambridge*, p. 3.

HORNINGTOFT CHURCH, NORFOLK.

Traditional paintings. *The Ecclesiologist's Guide to the Deaneries of Brisley, &c.,* p. 21.

HORNTON CHURCH, OXFORDSHIRE.

Remains of painting. 14th cent. *Parker, Eccles. and Architect. Topog. of England, Bucks,* No. 16.

N. aisle; St. George and the Dragon.

S. aisle; "walls, roof, and screen, painted in brilliant party colours and gilt."

On S. aisle walls; the Virgin and Child with St. Joseph, and kneeling figure of a bishop. 14th cent.

Chancel, in sill of E. window; colour on some Norman carving.

On transitional Norman font, early colouring.

Beesley, Hist. of Banbury, pp. 125, 126.

HORSHAM, SUSSEX, ST. MARY'S CHURCH.

W. wall of nave; the Annunciation and Last Supper, repainted.

Within the splay of two windows in the S. aisle; foliated patterns.

Remains of sacred subjects, diaper patterns and texts, found on various portions of the walls.

Rood screen; richly coloured. *Destroyed* in 1825.

Ribs and bosses of roof; the original colouring restored.

Horsham, its History and Antiquities, pp. 42, 48, 51, 56, 57.

HORSHAM ST. FAITH'S CHURCH, NORFOLK.

On panels of pulpit; St. Christopher, St. John the Baptist, the Virgin and Infant Saviour, St. John the Evangelist, St. Stephen, St. Andrew, (?) St. Benedict, St. Faith, St. Thomas of Canterbury, and an armorial shield. Date 1488.

On panels of screen; SS. Catherine of Siena, Etheldreda, Oswald, Michael, Apollonia, George, Anne, Bridget, ? Genevieve, Wandragesilas, and other Saints. Date 1528

Builder, 1874, pp. 483, 755. *Church Builder,* 1874, No. lii. p. 150.

On either side of chancel; three ancient shields in wood, painted beneath the roof. *Blomefield, (Parkin,) Hist. of Norfolk,* ed. 1809, x. 439.

HORSTEAD CHURCH, NORFOLK.

Roof; ornamented with black eagles. *Blomefield, (Parkin,) Hist. of Norfolk,* ed. 1809, x. 445.

HORSTED KEYNES CHURCH, SUSSEX.
N. side of chancel; small effigy coloured. Circ. 1270.
Archæol. Journ., iv. 155. *Sussex Archæol.*, i. 131.

HORTON CHURCH, BUCKINGHAMSHIRE.
Numerous mural paintings, Saints, the Virgin Mary,
&c., discovered in 1827. *G. W. J. Gyll, Hist. of Wrays-
bury, Colnbrook, and Horton*, p. 244.

HORTON, MONK'S, PRIORY, KENT.
Upper room on N. of staircase; ceiling panelled and
painted with the sacred Monogram within a crown of
thorns. Time of Edward III. These panels were removed about the year 1840. *Archæol. Cantiana*, x. 88.

HORWOOD CHURCH, DEVONSHIRE.
Remains of colour and gilding on the effigy of a lady.
Early 15th cent. *Exeter Diocesan Architect. Soc.*, vi. 204.

HOUGHTON CONQUEST CHURCH, BEDFORDSHIRE.
Over chancel arch; Our Lord in Glory, and angels and
shields bearing the emblems of the Passion. 14th cent.
Archæol. Journ., xxxviii. 85.
N. wall of aisle over the N. door; St. Christopher.
15th cent.
E. wall of S. aisle; double triangles containing mono-
grams.
S. wall of S. aisle; St. George and the Dragon, and
(?) part of a Doom.
Over S. door and on N. wall; remains of texts. 16th
cent.
Associated Architect. Societies' Repts., x. xcvi. *D. G.
C. Elwes, Bedford and its Neighbourhood*, p. 82.
Chancel screen; 15th cent. decoration, partly restored.

HOUGHTON-LE-DALE CHURCH, NORFOLK.
Rood screen; on the twelve panels, figures of Saints,
viz.: on N.; ? St. Monica, with St. Augustine, St.
Salome, with SS. James and John, the Virgin and Child,
St. Mary Cleopas, with SS. James, Joses, Simon, and
Judas, St. Elizabeth, with St. John the Baptist, and St.
Anne instructing the Virgin.
On S.; the four doctors, St. Sylvester, with kneeling
figure of a lady with scroll, and St. Clement. 15th cent.

HOUND CHURCH, HAMPSHIRE.
" When the walls are damp, the traces of ancient paintings appear." *Collectanea Archæologica*, ii. 91.

HOVINGHAM CHURCH, YORKSHIRE.
Numerous layers of paintings discovered and *destroyed,* the lowest probably dating from the 12th cent. *Archæol. Journ.,* xxxiv. 277.

HOXNE CHURCH, SUFFOLK.
David and Goliath, St. Paul confined in the Stocks, the Crucifixion, Resurrection from the Dead, &c. *Gent. Mag.,* 1835, iii. new series, 420.

HUBBERHOLME CHAPEL, YORKSHIRE.
Painted rood screen. Date 1558. *Murray's Handbook of Yorkshire. Whitaker's Hist. and Antiq. of Craven,* 3rd ed., p. 586.

HUCKNALL, AULT, CHURCH, DERBYSHIRE.
N. wall of nave; chocolate-coloured diapered patterns. *J. C. Cox, Churches of Derbyshire,* i. 248.

HUISH EPISCOPI CHURCH, SOMERSETSHIRE.
Nave roof; painting on the ribs reproduced. *Builder,* 1873, p. 974.

HULL, YORKSHIRE, HOLY TRINITY CHURCH.
S. wall of nave; monument with sculptures of the Trinity, a priest, &c., with remains of gilding and colouring. Circ. 1484. *Antiquary,* 1871, i. 133.

HULLAVINGTON CHURCH, WILTSHIRE.
On arches and capitals, N. side of nave; masonry and scroll patterns. End of 12th cent. *Archæol. Journ.,* xxxviii. 92.
Across the N. aisle; painted screen. Lower part 13th cent., upper 15th cent.

HUNMANBY CHURCH, YORKSHIRE.
Above nave arches; eleven shields of arms, with the emblazoned bearings of the ancient Lords of Hunmanby, recoloured. *Cole, Hist. and Antiq. of Filey,* p. 150. *G. A. Poole, Churches of Scarborough, &c.,* p. 132. *Sheahan and Whellan, Hist. and Topog. of City of York, &c.,* ii. 479.

HUNSTANTON CHURCH, NORFOLK.
Pillars; chevron pattern. 13th cent. *Associated Architect. Societies' Repts.,* ix. 253.
Rood screen; St. Paul, and the Apostles, omitting Matthew, on the panels. Drawing in the South Kensington Musuem.

HUNTINGDON, HUNTINGDONSHIRE, ALL SAINTS' CHURCH.
Chancel ceiling; 15th century colouring discovered; repainted. *Ecclesiologist*, xxiii. (xx. new series), 201.

HUNTINGFIELD CHURCH, SUFFOLK.
Chancel, at the back of the Easter sepulchre; Christ sitting in Judgment, and other figures. *Suckling's History of Suffolk*, ii. 417.
Below, Our Lord in the sepulchre, surrounded by angels.

HURSTMONCEUX CHURCH, SUSSEX.
N. side of chancel, gilding on the Dacre monument. Early 16th cent.

HURSTPIERPOINT CHURCH, SUSSEX.
Danny chancel; remains of colour and gilding on the effigy of a knight. 14th cent. *Sussex Archæol.*, xi. 77.

HUSBORNE CRAWLEY CHURCH, BEDFORDSHIRE.
Roof of N. aisle, on a beam; powdering of the words "Jhu Mercy" between flowers. *Fisher's Collections for Bedfordshire*.

IBSLEY CHURCH, HAMPSHIRE.
Representations of Heaven and Hell, (?) parts of a Doom.

ICKBURGH CHURCH, NORFOLK.
On cornice of chancel screen; shields of Benefactors, the Trinity banner, and the five wounds. *Blomefield, Hist. of Norfolk*, ed. 1805, ii. 236. *Cromwell, Excursions through Norfolk*, ii. 127.

ICKENHAM CHURCH, MIDDLESEX.
On wall-plate, N. of nave; decorative colouring.
S. of nave, on a piscina, and the jambs of a window; traces of vermilion.

ICKLESHAM, SUSSEX, ST. NICHOLAS' CHURCH.
N. chantry chapel; remains of colour on an early English arcade. 13th cent. *Ecclesiologist*, vi. 181.

ICKLETON CHURCH, CAMBRIDGESHIRE.
   Old wall paintings much obscured by time. *Kelly's Post Office Directory of Cambridgeshire.*
   Tower ceiling painted.
   On jambs of clerestory windows; various figures.

ICOMB CHURCH, WORCESTERSHIRE.
   Chancel arch; picked out with colour. Circ. 1220.
   Gilding on the effigy of Sir John Blaket. About 1431.
   Associated Architect. Societies' Repts., x. 96, 98.

ICOMB PLACE, GLOUCESTERSHIRE.
   Refectory; red colour on linen panelling. 16th cent.
   In a room in the attic story; a ship painted in distemper.
   Associated Architect. Societies' Repts., x. 107.

IDMISTON CHURCH, WILTSHIRE.
   On S. wall of nave; St. Christopher. *Wilts Archæol. and Nat. Hist. Soc. Mag.,* x. 38.

IDSWORTH CHAPEL, CHALTON, HAMPSHIRE.
   N. wall of chancel; St. Hubert and the Decollation of St. John the Baptist. Late 13th cent.
   Figures of St. Peter and St. Paul on jambs of east window.
   Archæol. Journ., xxi. 184, 185.

IFFLEY CHURCH, OXFORDSHIRE.
   Vault of chancel; decorative patterns. 12th cent.
   Whitewashed over. *Archæol. Journ.,* iv. 224.

IFIELD CHURCH, SUSSEX.
   Remains of colour and gilding on the effigy of Sir John de Ifield. Circ. 1317. *Stothard's Monumental Effigies,* p. 53. *Cartwright's Rape of Bramber,* p. 386. *Sussex Archæol.,* viii. 267.

IFORD CHURCH, SUSSEX.
   Remains of painting on N. wall.
   Sussex Archæol., xxix. 150.

IGHTHAM MOTE CHAPEL, KENT.
   Ceiling; painted with the Tudor devices. About 1500.
   Wright's Archæological Album, p. 189. *Murray's Handbook of Kent.*

ILFORD, LITTLE, CHURCH, ESSEX.
   Much painting.

ILFRACOMBE CHURCH, DEVONSHIRE.

Roof over the place of the rood. *Civil Engineer and Architect's Journ.,* 1860, p. 5.

ILKETSHALL, ST. MARGARET, CHURCH, SUFFOLK.

N. wall; St. Christopher, and King Henry VI.
S. wall; the Crucifixion and Descent from the Cross.

ILSINGTON CHURCH, DEVONSHIRE.

Rood screen and aisle roofs. *Exeter Diocesan Architect. Soc.,* v. 87, 88.

IMPINGTON CHURCH, CAMBRIDGESHIRE.

N. wall of nave; St. Christopher. Circ. 1400. *Parker, Eccles. and Architect. Topog. of England, Cambridge,* No. 82. *Ecclesiologist,* iii. 31, and xxi. (xviii. new series), 203. *Blackburne, Decorative Painting,* p. 17. *F. A. Paley, The Ecclesiologist's Guide to the Churches ...... round Cambridge,* p. 8.

Painted roof. *Blackburne, Decorative Painting,* p. 48.
S. wall of chancel; imitative niches and canopies enclosing figures, one St. Peter; also cherubim bearing shields.

INGATESTONE CHURCH, ESSEX.

Seven Deadly Sins, in the form of a wheel. About 1400. Whitewashed over.

Coloured drawing in the Art Library, South Kensington Museum.

Essex Archæol., iv. 140. *Reliquary,* x. 217. *Rectangular Review,* October 1870, p. 281. *Building News,* 1867, p. 101.

And Seven Virtues. *Murray's Handbook of Essex.*
St. Christopher. *Essex Archæol.,* iv. 140.

INGHAM CHURCH, NORFOLK.

Three paintings on panel formerly at; now in the possession of Mr. Dawson Clarke; representing scenes in the Life of St. Nicholas. 14th cent. *Norfolk Archæol.,* viii. 208. *Archæol. Journ.,* xiv. 285.

At the back of the tomb of Sir Oliver de Ingham; (?) St. Hubert hunting *Destroyed. Stothard's Monumental Effigies,* plate 67. *J. P. Neale and J. Le Keux, Views of the most interesting Collegiate and Parochial Churches in Great Britain,* vol. i. *Chambers, Hist. of Norfolk,* ii. 733.

INGHAM CHURCH, NORFOLK—*cont.*

Remains of colouring on the canopy of the tomb, also on the stone chancel screen, and on the panels of the monument and the effigies of Sir Roger de Bois and his Lady at the E. end of the S. aisle.

INWORTH CHURCH, ESSEX.

Scenes from the Life of St. Nicholas, discovered during the recent (1877) restorations.

In nave, fragments of colour remaining and preserved, but not intelligible.

IPPLEPEN CHURCH, DEVONSHIRE.

Rood screen and pulpit, the former with figures of Saints on the panels, defaced. *C. Worthy, Ashburton and its Neighbourhood,* p. 84.

IPSWICH, SUFFOLK, ST. MARGARET'S CHURCH.

N. side of the nave; St. Anthony preaching to the Fishes, St. Christopher, and several texts. *Archæol. Journ.,* xxx. 96. *Antiquary,* 1872, ii. 232. *Wodderspoon, Memorials of Ipswich,* p. 398.

Coloured roof. 16th cent. *Associated Architect. Societies' Repts.,* ix. 250. *Wodderspoon, New Guide to Ipswich,* 1842, p. 99.

Colouring on the rafters of the S. chantry ceiling.

IPSWICH, SUFFOLK, ST. MATTHEW'S CHURCH.

Panels from screen now attached to a cupboard in the vestry; figures of bishops, one St. Nicholas or Eligius, and the lady and daughters of the donor. 15th cent.

IPSWICH, SUFFOLK, ST. NICHOLAS' CHURCH.

Behind a tomb; some curious paintings, ? St. Michael, &c. *Wodderspoon, New Guide to Ipswich,* 1842, p. 100.

Three very early, ? Saxon, sculptures of bishops, found worked into the walls. "All the figures had been rudely " coloured, red, blue (or green), and portions of a purple " tint remain." *Wodderspoon, Memorials of Ipswich,* pp. 333, 334.

One of the sculptured figures may be St. James the Less.

The whole church, including piscinæ, niches, &c. "had " once been rubricated, and the colouring in many parts " contained a considerable degree of freshness."

H. P. Drummond, Church of St. Nicholas, Ipswich, pp. 24, 25.

IRSTEAD CHURCH, NORFOLK.
> N. wall of chancel; part of the Heavenly Hierarchy.
> On jambs of chancel window; six angels.
> Rood screen; the Twelve Apostles.
> N. wall; fragment of painting.
> *Illustrations of Norfolk Topography,* p. 74. *East Anglian Notes and Queries,* iii. 292. *Hart, Antiq. of Norfolk, p.* 66. *The Ecclesiologist's Guide to the Deaneries of Brisley, &c.,* p. 122. *Norfolk Archæol.,* iii. 19.

IRTHLINGBOROUGH CHURCH, NORTHAMPTONSHIRE.
> Over chancel arch; two series of texts and portions of a Doom.
> S. wall of S. chancel chapel; SS. Anthony and Sebastian. (?) End of 14th cent.
> S. wall of S. transept; large figure, probably St. Christopher, and numerous texts.
> N. transept, within a window splay; female figure handing a jug through a grating to another figure. *Destroyed.* Drawings existing. (?) One of the Acts of Mercy.
> Remains of colour on E. wall of N. transept, also of colour and texts on all the walls of the church.

ISFIELD CHURCH, SUSSEX.
> S. chapel, E. wall; painted armorial shields on monument of Thomas Shurley, died 1579.

ISLEHAM CHURCH, CAMBRIDGESHIRE.
> N. wall of chancel; the Virgin and Child, covered over,
> N. transept; coloured piscina. *Suffolk Archæol.,* iv. 368. *Parker, Eccles. and Architect. Topog. of England, Cambridge,* No. 190.

ISLIP CHURCH, OXFORDSHIRE.
> S. wall of S. aisle; the Nativity and Adoration of the Magi, St. Michael weighing Souls, and the Resurrection. Date about 1360.
> Other paintings in the N. aisle. *Archæol. Journ.,* iv. 259. *British Archæol. Assoc. Journ.,* ii. 146, and v. 45. *Blackburne, Decorative Painting,* p. 22. *Skelton's Antiquities of Oxfordshire. Archæologia,* xxix. 420. *Halliwell, Hist. Notes of Islip,* pp. 9, 10.

IXWORTH CHURCH, SUFFOLK.
> Lower panels of rood screen with remains of colour. Braces and principal rafters of the roof over the rood-loft also painted. *Suffolk Archæol.,* i. 100, 101.

JERSEY, PARISH CHURCH OF GROUVILLE.
Western nave, N. wall; 2 figures, (?) The Annunciation. S. wall; traces of colour.

JERSEY, PARISH CHURCH OF THE HOLY TRINITY.
Centre of nave; the Massacre of the Innocents. (?)14th cent.

JERSEY, PARISH CHURCH OF ST. CLEMENT.
S. transept; Les Trois Morts et les Trois Vifs. *Archæol. Journ.*, xxxvii. 106.
N. transept; St. Margaret or Martha, and St. Barbara.
N. side of nave; St. Michael and Satan.
On the splays of a window, N. side, E. end of nave; St. Mary Magdalene, and Virgin and Child. Latter half of 15th cent. *Société Jersiaise, Cinquième Bulletin Annuel*, p. 194.

JERSEY, PARISH CHURCH OF ST. MARTIN.
S. wall of chancel; painting of an Ecclesiastic. *Destroyed.*

JERSEY, ST. BRELADE'S, "LA CHAPELLE ÉS PÊCHEURS" OR "NOTRE DAME DES PAS."
W. wall; part of a Doom.
S. wall; the Annunciation, Offering of the Magi, and part of a Doom.
N. wall; Our Lord before Herod, &c.
E. wall; the Assumption of the Virgin.
Drawings existing. 15th cent.
Archæol. Journ., xvi. 89. *Builder*, 1864, p. 733.
H. D. Inglis, The Channel Islands, i. 76.

JERSEY, HERMITAGE OF ST. HELIER.
The Triumphal Entry into Jerusalem.

JERVAULX ABBEY, YORKSHIRE.
The chapter house; remains of vermilion colour on springers of the roof. *Murray's Handbook of Yorkshire. W. Hylton Longstaffe, Richmondshire, Its Ancient Lords and Edifices*, p. 73.

KEEVIL, WILTSHIRE, HOUSE NEAR THE CHURCH.
On front of gallery of hall, coats of arms, repainted.
Ceiling of parlour, figures of angels.
On the walls some rude distemper paintings.
E. Kite, Hist. Notes on the Places of Interest to be visited by the British Archæol. Assoc. in 1880, p. 46.

KELHAM CHURCH, NOTTINGHAMSHIRE.
Over the chancel arch; the Resurrection, *now lost.*
Associated Architect. Societies' Repts., xi. x.

KELLS ABBEY, KILKENNY, IRELAND.
Traces.

KELSHALL CHURCH, HERTFORDSHIRE.
Nave and aisle roofs; colouring restored.
Chancel screen; figures of SS. Edward, Edmund, and two Bishops on the panels. Late 15th cent.
Church Builder, 1876, No. lx. p. 190. *Cussans, Hist. of Hertfordshire,* vol. i., pt. iii., pp. 133, 136.

KELSTON CHURCH, SOMERSETSHIRE.
Our Lord within a Vesica, showing the wounds, and with a censing angel on either side. Below, within niches on either side of a window, a female saint and a lamb. Date late 15th cent. *Society of Antiquaries' Proceedings,* 2nd series, v. 294. *Lithograph in Soc. Antiquaries' Library.*

KELVEDON CHURCH, ESSEX.
Wall border. Tudor period. *Builder,* 1864, p. 734.

KELVEDON, ESSEX.
Room of an old inn; panelled with the linen pattern with remains of colouring. Early 16th cent. *Essex Archæol.,* i., new series, 157.

KEMPLEY, GLOUCESTERSHIRE, ST. MARY'S CHURCH.
W. wall of nave; blue-letter texts. 15th or early 16th cent
S. side of nave, remains of more than one painting; one perhaps the Conversion of St. Paul, or the History of Constantine.

KEMPLEY, GLOUCESTERSHIRE, ST. MARY'S CHURCH—*cont.*

S. aisle of the nave, within the splay of a window; figure of an Archbishop. 15th cent. .

On N. wall of nave; a Wheel of Fortune. 13th cent.

Within the splay of a window on N. side of the nave; on one side an Archangel weighing a Soul, the Blessed Virgin interceding, on the other St. Anthony; above a pattern of roses. 12th cent.

On S. side of chancel arch; large figure of a saint under a semicircular arched canopy. 12th cent.

Mouldings of chancel arch have been coloured in red, white, and yellow.

On the soffit of the chancel arch; alternate squares of red and white. 12th cent.

Above the W. side of the chancel arch; a diaper pattern. 12th cent. Above this an indistinct subject, perhaps the Day of Judgment.

On the vault of the chancel; Our Lord in Glory giving the Benediction, surrounded by the emblems of the four Evangelists, with two cherubim at His head and feet, also St. Peter and the Virgin; around Him, are the seven candlesticks, the Sun, Moon, Earth, and Stars.

At the E. and W. ends; a border of chevrons in red, yellow, and white.

On the chancel walls, between the chancel arch and N. and S. windows; the Twelve Apostles, six on each side, under semicircular-headed canopies.

Within the soffits of the N. and S. windows is a pattern of semicircles, above the windows are turrets representing the Heavenly Jerusalem.

On S. side of chancel, between the window and the E. end (?) the Virgin.

On N. side of chancel, between the window and the E. end; St. James.

On either side of E. window; a bishop giving the Benediction, and a consecration cross.

Within the splay of the E. window; chequered pattern.

Above the E. window; three angels within medallions, holding scrolls.

On the E. face of the chancel arch; an embattled "Tau" pattern in red, white, and yellow. On inner course, 10 medallions. All the paintings in the chancel probably date from about the year 1130.

Discovered at the restoration of the church in 1872.

Archæol. Journ., xxxiv. 270, xxxviii. 84. *Archæologia.* xlvi. 186. xlvii. 165. *Builder.* 1873, p. 649.

KEMPLEY, GLOUCESTERSHIRE, ST. MARY'S CHURCH—*cont.*
Norris, Gloucestershire Directory. Church Builder,
1873, No. L p. 75. Associated Architect. Societies' Repts.,
xii., xlviii. Bristol and Gloucestershire Archæol. Soc.
Trans., 1879–80, p. 10.

KEMPSTON CHURCH, BEDFORDSHIRE.
In the vestry, panels of screen, on which are depicted
the presentation of Eve to Adam, the temptation,
curse, and expulsion from Paradise.

KENDERCHURCH CHURCH, HEREFORDSHIRE.
Coloured screen. *Havergal, Fasti Herefordenses,* p. 157.

KENILWORTH CASTLE, WARWICKSHIRE.
Early wall pattern in one of the "Domi" (now
glazed).

KENN CHURCH, DEVONSHIRE.
Rood screen; on the panels, SS. Andrew, James, John,
Simon, Thomas, Stephen, and Lawrence, with the four
Doctors of the Church on the doors.
Screen across the S. aisle; on the panels, the Cruci-
fixion, the Virgin, St. Sidwell, the four Evangelists, SS.
Scholastica, Veronica, Mary Magdalene, and Catherine.
Oliver's Ecclesiastical Antiquities of Devon, i. 27.
Polwhele, Hist. of Devon, iii. 183.

KENNET CHURCH, CAMBRIDGESHIRE.
Painted rood screen. *Lysons, Magna Britannia.*
Cambridgeshire, p. 50.

KENNINGHALL CHURCH, NORFOLK.
Rood screen; traces of large decorative pattern.
Paintings of the Apostles on the panels. *Blomefield,*
Hist. of Norfolk, i. 148. *Destroyed.*
Screen across N. aisle; painted diapers.

KENSWORTH CHURCH, HERTFORDSHIRE.
W. wall of chancel, S. side of chancel arch; masonry
pattern, and a portion of a text above it. Whitewashed
over.

KENTISBEARE CHURCH, DEVONSHIRE.
Rood screen. *Ecclesiologist,* xxviii. (xav. new series),
p. 308.

KENTON CHURCH, DEVONSHIRE.

Rood screen, with figures of Saints depicted on the panels; viz. :—SS. Appollonia, Agnes, Cecilia, Helena, Anthony, George, Edmund, and another Royal Saint. Then the 12 Apostles and Prophets (Jonah, Nahum, Micah, and Habakkuk being omitted) alternately, each with a sentence from the Creed. Then SS. Lawrence, Barbara, Stephen, a female Saint, the Virgin, SS. Mary Magdalene, Dorothy, and Catherine. Date 15th cent. *Oliver's Ecclesiastical Antiquities of Devon,* i. 14–16. *Exeter Diocesan Architect. Soc.,* 2nd series, ii. 96. *Murray's Handbook of Devon. Polwhele, Hist. of Devon,* iii. 165.

Painted pulpit.

KERSEY CHURCH, SUFFOLK.

Rood screen; figures of kings, one St. Edmund, and ecclesiastics.

Arches originally painted.

Kersey, Account of the Austin Friars, &c., pp. 7, 8, and pl. frontispiece.

KETTERING CHURCH, NORTHAMPTONSHIRE.

N. aisle; St. Roche. Wrongly described by all the authorities as St. James the Greater. *Churches of the Archdeaconry of Northampton,* p. 156. *J. P. Neale and J. le Keux, Views of the most interesting Collegiate and Parochial Churches in Great Britain,* vol. i. *Leicester Architect. and Archæol. Soc. Trans.,* iii. 247. *F. Whellan, Hist. Topog. and Directory of Northants,* 1874, p. 761. Date late 15th cent.

Round the chancel arch; decorative painting. About 1300.

KETTON CHURCH, RUTLANDSHIRE.

E. tower arch; running pattern. *Associated Architect. Societies' Repts.,* ix. 253. 13th cent.

N. wall of nave; St. Christopher. Discovered in 1844 and *destroyed. White's Gazetteer of Rutlandshire.*

KEWSTOKE CHURCH, SOMERSETSHIRE.

Stone reliquary, with remains of colouring. 13th cent. Found in the church, and now in the Taunton Museum.

KEYMER CHURCH, SUSSEX.

Apse and chancel arch; various figures. *Sussex Archæol.,* xvii. 249

KEYMER CHURCH, SUSSEX—*cont.*
W. face of chancel arch; three figures.
Soffit of chancel arch; lozenge pattern.
Walls of apse; ornamental diaper, and figures of four Saints approaching a female Saint.
On S. side; figures carrying a bier.

KEYNSHAM ABBEY, SOMERSETSHIRE.
Traces of red colouring very apparent on the walls. *British Archæol. Assoc. Journ.*, xxxi. 203.
Numerous fragments of carved and tabernacle work dug up retaining traces of colour. Date 15th cent. *Society of Antiquaries' Proceedings*, 2nd series, v. 83.

KEYSOE CHURCH, BEDFORDSHIRE.
N. aisle; remains of a painted ceiling. *Parker, Eccles. and Architect. Topog. of England, Bedford*, No. 89.

KILLALOE CATHEDRAL, COUNTY CLARE, IRELAND.
Round one of the arches; a dog-tooth pattern painted in red. *Kilkenny Archæol. Soc. Transactions*, iii. 344.

KILMELCHEDOR CHURCH, COUNTY KERRY, IRELAND.

KILWORTH, NORTH, CHURCH, LEICESTERSHIRE.
Perpendicular pulpit; diaper ornament.

KILWORTH, SOUTH, CHURCH, LEICESTERSHIRE.
16th cent. *Associated Architect. Societies' Repts.*, ix. 250.

KIMBLE, GREAT, CHURCH, BUCKINGHAMSHIRE.
On bowl of Norman font, traces of red colouring.

KIMBLE PARVA CHURCH, BUCKINGHAMSHIRE.
N. wall of nave; St. George. 14th cent.
In N.W. corner; ? the Crucifixion, or torture of some Saint.
Over S. door; a burial with angels.
By S. door; a gigantic figure holding a closed book.
Other remains of ancient paintings on the nave walls and window splays.

KIMBOLTON CHURCH, HUNTINGDONSHIRE.
Chancel roof; painted bosses.
S. chancel chapel; panels of ceiling painted and with a powdering of metal stars. The cornice is also richly painted. Date 15th cent.

KIMPTON CHURCH, HERTFORDSHIRE.

Over chancel arch, within medallions, the Seven Acts of Mercy. *Church Builder,* 1865, No. xvi., p. 167.

Within a recess on either side of the E. window; painting of a saint. That on the N. side seems to be an archangel, that on the S. a female figure, or perhaps a priest, much defaced. The two subjects may represent the Annunciation.

Traces of a large subject, ? St. Christopher, above the main arcade N. side of nave, facing the principal entrance.

KINGSCLERE CHURCH, HAMPSHIRE.

Two coats of paintings discovered and *destroyed. Newbury District Field Club,* 1870–1871, p. 203.

KINGSTON, SOMERSETSHIRE, ST. MARY'S CHURCH.

S. aisle; remains of colour on the shields of a monument to the family of the Warres of Hestercombe. Time of Edward III. *Somerset Archæol. and Nat. Hist. Soc. Proceedings,* iv. 37.

KINGSTON DEVERILL CHURCH, WILTSHIRE.

Rood screen; painted and gilt. *Hoare's Hist. of Wiltshire,* vol. i. pt. i. p. 139.

KINGSTON-ON-THAMES CHURCH, SURREY.

Paintings discovered in 1835 and *destroyed. Gent. Mag.,* 1835, iv. new series, 106.

On respond of arch between S. transept and the Chapel of St. James; St. Blaise. *Surrey Archæol.,* viii. 60.

KINGTON CHURCH, HEREFORDSHIRE.

S.E. angle of Vaughan's Chapel; monument of Thomas Vaughan, emblazoned shields. Circ. 1469. *Hist. o Kington,* p. 98.

KIRBY HILL CHURCH, YORKSHIRE.

Nave arches; decorative painting, 13th and 15th cents. *Associated Architect. Societies' Repts.,* x. 240, 242, 243.

KIRDFORD CHURCH, SUSSEX.

E. wall; the Crucifixion.

On other walls; St. Nicholas, St. Catherine, a king between a good counsellor and a demon, and (apparently) the Adoration of the Magi. Mostly plastered over. Drawings existing.

M. A. Lower, History of Sussex, ii. 8. *Archæol. Journ.,* ii. 89.

KIRKBY LONSDALE CHURCH, WESTMORELAND.

A stone painted with a cable pattern, dug up in the chancel. *Cumberland and Westmoreland Antiq. and Archæol. Soc. Transactions*, i. 191.

KIRTON-IN-LINDSEY CHURCH, LINCOLNSHIRE.

Wall of N. aisle; Crucifixion, with SS. Mary and John, and Sacraments, and shield of donor below. Late 14th cent. *Society of Antiquaries' Proceedings*, 2nd series, i. 419. *Associated Architect. Societies' Repts.*, v. 200, vi. xxxv., viii. 233. *Destroyed.* Lithographed in *Peacock, Church Furniture*, frontispiece, and p. 24.

KNAPTON CHURCH, NORFOLK.

Painted roof; figures under canopies, angels, &c. 15th cent. *Colling, Gothic Ornaments*, i. pl. 27, and *Brandon, Open Timber Roofs*, p. 77. *Sacristy*, iii. 154.

KNOCKMOY ABBEY CHURCH, COUNTY GALWAY, IRELAND.

N. wall of chancel; Les Trois Rois Vifs et les Trois Rois Morts, and the martyrdom of St. Sebastian, or (?) of St. Christopher.

At the back of the monument of O'Connor, the founder of the Abbey; the Crucifixion.

Date 14th cent.

Ledwich's Antiquities of Ireland, 1st. ed., p. 281, 2nd ed., p. 520. *Dublin Penny Journal*, i. 227–229. *Archæol. Journ.*, xx. 180. *Murray's Handbook for Ireland.*

KNOWLE CHURCH, WARWICKSHIRE.

Over the rood-loft; the Virgin Mary, another saint, and an angel. *W. Smith, Hist. of County of Warwick*, p. 377.

Roof of nave; painted, and with a powdering of metal stars. *Archæol. Journ.*, xxii. 30.

LAMBETH PALACE, SURREY.

Colouring in Chapel, (?) restored.

LANCHESTER CHURCH, DURHAM.

Colouring on the stonework above the modern ceiling. *Perry and Henman, Illustrations of the Mediæval Antiq. in the County of Durham*, p. 8.

LANDBEACH CHURCH, CAMBRIDGESHIRE.
Painted panels over the altar. *Parker, Eccles. and Architect. Topog. of England, Cambridge*, No. 82. *Murray's Handbook of Cambridgeshire.*
Paintings discovered and re-covered with yellow wash. *Ecclesiologist*, xvii. 150.
E. beam of nave roof; colour and gilding on a seraph and foliage set within a hollow of the wall-plate. 15th cent.
On S. wall, E. end of nave; scroll foliage. Circ. 1300.
On arch opening from N. aisle to N. chancel chapel; pattern of squares in three colours. 13th cent.
Chancel, on the under side of two miserere stalls; emblazoned shields.
There were numerous other painted decorations which were destroyed in 1857. *Cambridge Antiq. Soc. Journ.*, iv. 258.

LANDKEY CHURCH, DEVONSHIRE.
At the back of the monumental recess; the Crucifixion.
Colouring on the effigies of cross-legged knight and two ladies.
Exeter Diocesan Architect. Soc., 2nd series, iii. 197.
W. H. H. Rogers, The Ancient Sepulchral Effigies, &c., in Devon, p. 47.

LANERCOST PRIORY, CUMBERLAND.
The banqueting hall; various cinque-cento patterns, an armed figure, &c. *Cumberland and Westmoreland Antiq. and Archæol. Soc. Transactions*, i. 131. *Ferguson, A Short Hist. and Architect. Account of Lanercost*, p. 42.

LANGFORD CHURCH, NOTTINGHAMSHIRE.
On nave wall; painting of arms, *whitewashed over again.* E. G. Wake, The Hist. of Collingham, p. 83.

LANGFORD, STEEPLE, CHURCH, WILTSHIRE.
Let into N. aisle wall; panels of a monument with coloured shields. Date about 1500.

LANGHAM CHURCH, RUTLANDSHIRE.
Walls everywhere decorated with paintings. *All destroyed.*

LANGLEY, KING'S, CHURCH, HERTFORDSHIRE.
S. aisle; painting discovered and whitewashed over.

LANGLEY, KIRK, CHURCH, DERBYSHIRE.
Wall of S. aisle; two series of inscriptions. *J. C. Cox,
Churches of Derbyshire*, iv. 273.

LANGPORT CHURCH, SOMERSETSHIRE.
Painted ceiling. *Somerset Archæol. and Nat. Hist. Soc.
Proceedings*, xi. pt. i. p. 16.

LANIVET CHURCH, CORNWALL.
S. aisle; representative Christian triumphing; figure
surrounded with various instruments,* also several other
paintings. *Suffolk Archæol.*, v. 30.
The Descent of Our Lord into Hades. *Ecclesiologist*,
xxv. (xxii. new series), 384.
Our Saviour with the blood flowing from His side into
two hands open to receive it.
A royal personage; ? St. Ursula holding (?) a chaplet
of beads, and a crowned figure, also group of warriors
fighting.
N. aisle; several figures.
· In splay of a window, a female Saint, with inscription,
S. Vede or S. Crede,† above; other remains of painting in
porch and elsewhere.
Parochial Hist. of Cornwall, iii. 15, 16. *Journ. Royal
Inst., Cornwall*, Oct. 1865, pp. 76–80, and April 1870,
p. 172.

LAPFORD CHURCH, DEVONSHIRE.
Rood screen. *Ecclesiologist*, xxviii. (xxv. new series),
p. 308.

LAPWORTH CHURCH, WARWICKSHIRE.
Painting on a sub-arch.

LASSINGTON CHURCH, GLOUCESTERSHIRE.
On E. wall of chancel; decorative painting. 13th cent.
Builder, 1874, p. 578.

LASTINGHAM CHURCH, YORKSHIRE.
On E. wall of N. aisle; St. Catherine, the Crucifixion,
and (?) the three Marys. *Eastmead, Historia Rieval-
lensis*, p. 441.

LATCHINGDON CHURCH, ESSEX.
Panels of screen; figures of saints, viz.; SS. Jerome,
James Major, ? Catherine, a King, &c. In the Chelms-
ford Museum.

---

* *See* notice of Stedham Church.
† Probably St. Etheldreda.

LATHBURY CHURCH, BUCKINGHAMSHIRE.

On the walls of the nave and round the arches dividing the nave and aisles, and in the splays of the clerestory windows; a bold floral pattern. 15th cent.

On S. wall of nave; "Penance," "Extreme Unction," and "Burial;" the remaining sacraments are obliterated.

On N. wall of nave; St Michael weighing Souls, and the Virgin. Over the chancel arch; "The Doom."

On the capitals on N. side of nave and in the aisles; faint remains of colouring. *Records of Buckinghamshire*, iv. 37–42.

LATTON CHURCH, ESSEX.

In N. chantry chapel, now the vestry; on the monument of Peter Arderne, a series of paintings representing St. Anne instructing the Virgin, the Nativity, and (?) scenes in the early Life of our Lord, the Trinity, St. Dunstan, two Bishops, &c. Over the W. doorway; St. Christopher. Date about 1460.

Gough, Sepulchral Memorials of Great Britain, ii. pl. 86.

LAUGHARNE CHURCH, CARMARTHENSHIRE.

Roof, "formerly decorated with gold, crimson, and azure." *M. Curtis, The Antiq. of Laugharne, &c.*, p. 96.

LAUNCELLS CHURCH, CORNWALL.

Screen, lower part; figures of the Apostles. *Lysons, Magna Britannia, Cornwall*, p. ccxxxii.

LAUNCESTON CHURCH, CORNWALL.

St. Roche, &c. *Journ. Royal. Inst., Cornwall*, 1872, p. 57.

Colouring on Norman pillar and capital.

Chequered panelling. Circ. 1550. Below, "the rich colouring and flowing outlines of the original decoration." *J. R. Pattison, Some Account of the Church of St. Mary Magdalene, Launceston*, pp. 11, 23.

Pulpit, said to have been brought from North Petherwin; panel paintings of Saints.

LAUND PRIORY CHAPEL, LEICESTERSHIRE.

Painted roof. *Nicholls, History of Leicestershire*, iii. 326.

LAVANT, MID, CHURCH, SUSSEX.

Sacraments and services of the Church. Late 15th cent. Now *destroyed*.

On S. wall; St. George. Time of Henry VII.

Archæol. Journ., iii. 265. *Hussey, Churches of Kent, Sussex, and Surrey*, p. 248.

LAVENDON CHURCH, BUCKINGHAMSHIRE.
Over chancel arch ; the Day of Judgment.

LAXFIELD CHURCH, SUFFOLK.
· Painted screen, removed to W. end. *Parker, Eccles. and Architect. Topog. of England, Suffolk,* No. 175.

LAYCOCK ABBEY, WILTSHIRE.
Remains of painting on the doorway opening from the sacristy to the cloisters.
Sacristy ; decorative painting within and round a recess on the N. side and on an adjacent arch, also on the surface of the vaulting.
" Sir William Sherrington's " room ; masonry pattern on vaulting ribs.
Sketch of (?) St. Joseph on the wall.
Remains of Early English masonry patterns on jambs of Early English arches at the N. end of E. walk and W. end of N. walk of cloisters.
Wilts Archæol. and Nat. Hist. Soc. Mag., xii. 223, 224, 227, 230.
Chapter house ; decorative colour on groining ribs. 13th cent.
Colour and gilding on bosses of cloisters. Late 15th cent.

LAYCOCK CHURCH, WILTSHIRE.
N. chancel chapel ; ceiling, walls, niches, piers, and arches richly painted and gilt. Late 15th cent.
Monument of Sir William Sherrington. Date 1561. Painted and gilt.

LAYER MARNEY CHURCH, ESSEX.
N. wall ; St Christopher. *Essex Archæol.,* i., new series, 62.

LEAKE CHURCH, YORKSHIRE.
Painted screen ; (?) decorated period. *Blackburne, Decorative Painting,* p. 51.

LEAKE, WEST, CHURCH, NOTTINGHAMSHIRE.
A branch of a tree and other remains of mural painting discovered during the restoration.

LEASINGHAM CHURCH, LINCOLNSHIRE.
Remains of gilding on the font. *Sketches illustrative of the Topography and History of New and Old Sleaford,* p. 294.

LECKHAMPSTEAD CHURCH, BUCKINGHAMSHIRE.

On tympanum of S. dooorway; decorative colour. Late
12th cent. *Archæologia*, xlvii. 178.

On nave piers; scroll and zigzag patterns, a cross, and
inscriptions. Late 12th cent.

LECKHAMPTON CHURCH, GLOUCESTERSHIRE.

Coloured effigies of Sir John Gifford and Lady. Circ.
1330. *Bristol and Gloucestershire Archæol. Soc. Trans.*
1879–80, p. 15.

LEEDS, KENT, BATTLE HALL.

Painted panel; supposed to have been the reredos of
an altar. *Archæol. Journ.*, xx. 391.

LEEDS CHURCH, YORKSHIRE.

S. of communion table; effigies of Thos. Hardwicke
and family, 1577. *Whitaker, Hist. of Leeds*, i. 41.

Walls originally covered with Scripture subjects.
*Destroyed. R. W. Moore, A Hist. of the Parish Church
of Leeds*, pp. 3, 8.

LEEK, STAFFORDSHIRE, CHURCH OF ST. EDWARD THE
CONFESSOR.

On either side of E. window; painting of an angel.
Sleigh, History of Leek, p. 72.

LEICESTER, LEICESTERSHIRE, ST. MARGARET'S CHURCH.

Part of an angel; originally a roof corbel, enriched
with colour and gilding. *British Archæol. Assoc. Journ.*,
xix. 247.

E. wall; the Annunciation and two painted niches.
Builder, 1848, p. 7.

LEICESTER, LEICESTERSHIRE, ST. MARTIN'S CHURCH.

Roof of chancel aisle; richly coloured and gilt.

Under the tower; St. Catherine. *Destroyed*, tracing
existing.

*Figured in North's Chronicle of St. Martin's Church,
Leicester, p. 46, and at the end of the Publications of the
Cambridge Antiq. Soc., vol. ii., quarto series. British
Archæol. Assoc. Journ., xix. 116. Gent. Mag., 1847,
xxviii. new series, 526.*

S. aisle roofs; taken down, and found to have been
richly coloured. *Brandon's Analysis of Gothic Architecture*, i. 94 (note).

LEICESTER, LEICESTERSHIRE, ST. MARY'S CHURCH.

Roof of N. aisle ; diaper of quatrefoils on the principal timbers. *Civil Engineer and Architect's Journal*, 1851, p. 196.

LEICESTER, LEICESTERSHIRE, OLD BLUE BOAR INN.

Roof of a room on the second storey ; painted scroll work on the principal beams and other portions. *Destroyed. British Archæol. Assoc. Journ.*, xix. 120. *Antiquarian Cabinet*, vol. ix. *Leicester Architect. and Archæol. Soc. Trans.*, ii. 134.

LEIGH, WORCESTERSHIRE, ST. EDBURGH'S CHURCH.

Painted rood-loft, restored. 15th cent. *Ecclesiologist*, xxiii. (xx. new series), 291.

LEIGH, NORTH, CHURCH, OXFORDSHIRE.

Over chancel arch ; the Day of Judgment. Of the same date and almost exactly similar to that at South Leigh. *Antiquary*, 1872, ii. 130.

LEIGH, SOUTH, CHURCH, OXFORDSHIRE.

Over chancel arch and on N.E. wall of nave ; the Day of Judgment. Early 15th cent.

S. wall of nave ; St. Michael weighing Souls. Early 15th cent.

N. aisle ; St. Clement vested. Late 15th cent.

W. end of N. aisle : Hell and the Vices (?) possibly the descent into Limbus.

Window in nave: floral pattern.

S. side of E. chancel window ; full-length figure of the Virgin.

Various other wall patterns.

Archæol. Journ., xxx. 52. *Church Times*, Jan. 5th, 1872. *Church Builder*, 1872, No. xliv. 290. *Antiquary*, 1872, ii. 17, 75, 83, 207, 248.

LEIGHTON BUZZARD CHURCH, BEDFORDSHIRE.

Lectern with remains of painting. *Parker, Eccles. and Architect. Topog. of England, Bedford*, No. 47. *Varnished over.*

LENHAM CHURCH, KENT.

St. Michael weighing Souls. 14th cent. *Archæol. Journ.*, i. 270, 274., ii. 73. *British Archæol. Assoc. Journ.*, i. 47, 60. *Gent. Mag.*, 1851, xxxvi., new series, 24. *Antiquarian and Architect.—Year Book*, 1844, p. 173.

Canterbury chancel ; Vision of St. Hubert. *Blackburne, Decorative Painting*, p. 23. *Destroyed.*

LENTON, NOTTINGHAMSHIRE, HOLY TRINITY CHURCH.
Norman font; the sculptures appear to have been painted. *Illustrations of Baptismal Fonts, Van Voorst,* 1844.

LEOMINSTER, PRIORY CHURCH, HEREFORDSHIRE.
On S. side of original Norman nave; within and round the triforium arches, chevron, scallop, and other Norman ornamentation. 12th cent.
At W. end of original Norman N. aisle; a Wheel of Fortune, and scroll painting. 13th cent.
Archæol. Journ., xxxiv. 271, 277. *Archæologia Cambrensis*, 2nd series, iv. 20.

LESSINGHAM CHURCH, NORFOLK.
Rood screen; the Apostles omitting St. Thomas, and St. Paul. 14th cent. The Four Fathers of the Church and St. Giles, upon paper, pasted over some of the figures of the Apostles, probably in the 16th cent.
Four female saints, viz.; SS. Catherine, Apollonia, Mary Magdalene, and Margaret, upon the doors of the rood screen, now detached. *East Anglian Notes and Queries,* iii. 292. *The Ecclesiologist's Guide to the Deaneries of Brisley, &c.,* p. 94. *Norfolk Archæol.,* iii. 19.

LETHERINGSETT, NORFOLK, ST. ANDREW'S CHURCH.
Remains of decorative painting were found on the walls, but were too imperfect to be preserved.

LEWES MUSEUM, SUSSEX. *See* ROBERTSBRIDGE ABBEY.

LEWES PRIORY, SUSSEX.
Effigy of a de Braose, richly painted and gilt; dug up in 1846, and now in Southover Church, Lewes. 13th cent. *British Archæol. Assoc. Journ.,* ii. 106. *Archæol. Journ.,* iii. 79.

LEYLAND CHURCH, LANCASHIRE.
Nave roof; pulled down in 1816. Painted blue and studded with gilt stars. *Historic Society of Lancashire and Cheshire,* vii. 18.

LICHFIELD CATHEDRAL, STAFFORDSHIRE.
Colour and gilding on roofs. Early 16th cent. *Civil Engineer and Architect's Journ.,* 1860, p. 30. *Sir G. G. Scott, Personal and Professional Recollections,* p. 203.
At E. end of S. choir aisle; the arcades and bosses retain traces of painting and gilding.
Within a piscina recess in the E. wall; the Crucifixion. 13th cent.

LICHFIELD CATHEDRAL, STAFFORDSHIRE—*cont.*
On the jambs of the windows, and on the niches between the windows in the Lady Chapel; remains of colouring.
Over the doorway to the chapter house, on the inner (E.) side; indistinct subject.

LIMINGTON, SOMERSETSHIRE, ST. MARY'S CHURCH.
Painted roof; whitewashed over. Mural paintings obliterated. *Ecclesiologist,* iii. 64.

LIMPENHOE CHURCH, NORFOLK.
N. wall; Martyrdom of St. Catherine. Late 14th cent. *Norfolk Archæol.,* v. 221.

LIMPSFIELD CHURCH, SURREY.
S. side of chancel, on jambs of two lancet windows; decorative painting. (?) 13th cent.
On inner jambs of E. window; three courses of painting. From 13th to 15th cents. *Surrey Archæol.,* vi. 72, 74. *Brayley's Hist. of Surrey,* 2nd ed., iii. 360.

LINCOLN CATHEDRAL, LINCOLNSHIRE.
Ceiling of N. transept; painting and gilding restored.
Ceiling of S. transept; paintings visible through the whitewash.
On vault of Angel Choir; "a great quantity of painted ornament was discovered and *destroyed.*" *Associated Architect. Societies' Repts.,* x. 87.
Remains of colour on ceiling of passage leading to the cloisters, restored; on the back of the stalls S. side of the choir, on the chancel screen, and on the shrine of Bishop Hugh.
West front exterior; remains of colour on two of the Norman sculptures. Perhaps end of 11th century.
Archæol. Journ., xxv. 13. *Associated Architect. Societies' Repts.,* viii. 287, 288.

LINCOLN, LINCOLNSHIRE, CHURCH OF ST. MARY-LE-WIG-FORD.
Decorative colouring on the arch of a walled-up doorway, and diaper patterns on the walls. *Antiquary,* 1871, i. 120.

LINDFIELD CHURCH, SUSSEX.
E. wall of S. transept; St. Michael weighing Souls, and St. Margaret. 15th cent. *Sussex Archæol.,* ii. 129. *M. A. Lower, History of Sussex,* ii. 31. *Black's Guide to Sussex. Murray's Handbook of Sussex.*

LINGFIELD CHURCH, SURREY.
Mural paintings, of SS. Clement, Margaret, Michael weighing Souls, and a Bishop. 15th cent. *Surrey. Archæol.*, i. 71. *Now gone.*

LITCHAM CHURCH, NORFOLK.
Rood screen. 1430. *Antiquary*, 1871, i. 153.
Richly painted, and with figures depicted on the panels, viz., on N. side, SS. Petronilla, Ursula, &c.; on S., SS. Gregory, Edmund, Edward King and Martyr, King Henry VI., SS. Hubert and William of Norwich. *Carthew, Hundred of Launditch*, ii. 419.

LITTLEBURY CHURCH, ESSEX.
Lectern. 15th cent. *Blackburne, Decorative Painting*, p. 87.

LLANABER CHURCH, MERIONETHSHIRE.
E. wall of chancel; (?) portrait of Queen Elizabeth, with inscription. *Archæologia Cambrensis*, 3rd series, v. 143.

LLANARMON-IN-YALE CHURCH, DENBIGHSHIRE.
S. aisle; colour on 14th cent. monument and effigy. *Lloyd-Williams and Underwood, Churches of Denbighshire*, plate 25.

LLANARTH CHURCH, MONMOUTHSHIRE.
Archæologia Cambrensis, 4th series, vii. 352.

LLANBADARN FAWR CHURCH, CARDIGANSHIRE.
W. wall; large figures, St. Peter, a man in armour, inscriptions, &c. *Archæologia Cambrensis*, 3rd series, xiv. 449, and xv. 196.

LLANDAFF, GLAMORGANSHIRE.
Bishop's palace; painting on board, the Coronation of the Virgin, formerly in the chapter house. *Murray's Handbook of South Wales.*

LLANDANWG CHURCH, near HARLECH, MERIONETHSHIRE.
Roof; four Evangelists, cherubim, &c. 15th cent. In ruins. *British Archæol. Assoc. Journ.*, ii. 339, iii. 84.
Roof over the altar; panel painting of the Doom. *J. M. Neale, Hierologus*, p. 295. *Neale and Webb, Durandus*, p. 57. *Archæologia Cambrensis*, 3rd series, ii. 173.

LLANDAWKE CHURCH, CARMARTHENSHIRE.
In the chancel; coloured effigy of a lady. 14th cent. *Gent. Mag.*, 1838, ix., new series, 44.

Q 3254.   L

LLANDUDNO, CARNARVONSHIRE, ST. TUDNO'S CHURCH.
Many beautiful paintings discovered beneath the whitewash and *destroyed*. *Antiquary*, 1873, iv. 202. *J. Smith, Jun., The Archæology of the Great Orme's Head*, pp. 12, 13

LLANEILIAN CHURCH, ANGLESEY.
St. Eilian's Chapel; principals of roof and splay of E. window, decorative colour. *Archæologia Cambrensis*, 3rd series, vii. 128.

LLANELIAN CHURCH, DENBIGHSHIRE.
Roof of chancel, over altar; the sacred Monogram.
E. end of N. aisle; roof painted blue, and with gilt bosses.
Thomas, Hist. of the Diocese of St. Asaph, p. 384.

LLANFIHANGEL YNG NGHWNFA CHURCH, MONTGOMERY-SHIRE.
Shields of arms, of the family of Vaughan of Llwy-diarth, painted on 30 oak panels. Date 1577. Formerly part of a pew. *Collections of Powys Land Club*, iii. xxx.

LLANGURIG CHURCH, MONTGOMERYSHIRE.
· Painted rood screen. *Destroyed* in 1836. *Collections of Powys Land Club*, ii. 253. *Hamer and Lloyd, Hist. of the Parish of Llangurig*, pl. facing p. 31.

LLANGWM ISAF CHURCH, MONMOUTHSHIRE.
Painted rood screen. Late 15th cent. *Ecclesiologist*, iii. 91. *British Archæol. Assoc. Journ.*, xxxi. 506.

LLANGWM UCHA CHURCH, MONMOUTHSHIRE.
Over chancel arch; Our Lord in the Act of Benediction.
N. wall of nave; paintings which have perished. Remains of colour and gilding on the rood screen. *Archæologia Cambrensis*, 4th series, viii. 46–49. *Church Builder*, 1876, No. lvii. 35.

LLANIDAN CHURCH, ANGLESEY.
Early texts and traces of red colouring. *Archæologia Cambrensis*, i. 433.

LLANIDLOES CHURCH, MONTGOMERYSHIRE.
N. aisle; wall paintings representing Scriptural sub-jects, and texts. Obliterated in 1816. *Collections of Powys Land Club*, vi. 163, 169.

LLANRHAIADR IN KINMERCH CHURCH, DENBIGHSHIRE.
Portions of rood screen.

LLANTWIT MAJOR, GLAMORGANSHIRE, THE OLD CHURCH.
Several mural paintings. *Murray's Handbook of South Wales.*
On N. wall of chancel; one of the Marys.
On S. wall of chancel; floral pattern. 13th cent.
Round a niche, E. end of S. aisle ; scroll work and a stem of Jesse, rich colour and gilding. *Archæologia Cambrensis,* 3rd series, iv. 40, 43, and xv. 436.

LLANWYDDYN CHURCH, MONTGOMERYSHIRE.
N. wall; two lines of painting, upper one defaced, lower one represents Our Lord and the Apostles, the Massacre of the Innocents, Christ washing the Disciples' Feet, the Last Supper, scenes from the Passion, and the Crucifixion. *Archæologia Cambrensis,* 4th series, v. 95. *Collections of Powys Land Club,* vii. 75. *Thomas, Hist. of the Diocese of St. Asaph,* p. 751.

LOCKING CHURCH, SOMERSETSHIRE.
Pulpit. 15th cent. Colouring restored.

LODDON CHURCH, NORFOLK.
Lower panels of rood screen ; Crucifixion of St. William of Norwich,* the Annunciation, Nativity, Circumcision, Offerings of the Magi, Ascension, and other subjects. *Archæol. Journ.,* ix. 113.
Painting and gilding on the font.
On S. wall of S. aisle ; a framed painting of Sir James Hobart and his Lady, the founders of the church and St. Olave's Bridge. Date 1496.

LONDON. CARPENTERS' HALL.
W. wall; Noah building the Ark, Josiah ordering the repair of the Temple, Christ assisting Joseph as a Carpenter, and Christ preaching in the Synagogue, also the arms of the Company. Date about 1540. *British Archæol. Assoc. Journ.,* i. 275. *Society of Antiquaries' Proceedings,* 2nd series, ii. 81. *A. Wood, Eccles. Antiq. of London,* p. 37.

LONDON. CROSBY PLACE.
Ceilings of the throne room and great parlour ; painted and gilt mouldings. *Blackburne, Hist. of Crosby Place,* p. 37. *Carlos, Account of Crosby Place.*

---

* Figured in Goulburn, The Ancient Sculptures in the Roof of Norwich Cathedral, plate facing p. 83.

LONDON. ST. BARTHOLOMEW'S, SMITHFIELD.

Painted and gilt font cover. 14th cent. *Ecclesiologist*, xiii. 3.

E. wall; diaper of black stars on a red ground. *Blackburne, Decorative Painting*, p. 37. *Ecclesiologist*, xxvi. (xxiii. new series), 119. *Civil Engineer and Architect's Journal*, 1851, p. 197.

S.E. pier of tower; remains of colour.

N. side of Choir; remains of colour on the canopy, and (restored) on the lower part of the monument and effigy of an ecclesiastic. Circ. 1500. *J. H. Sperling, Church Walks in Middlesex*, p. 158. *A. Wood, Eccles. Antiq. of London*, p. 23.

S. Choir aisle; colour and gilding on monument of Walter Mildmay. Circ. 1589. Restored.

LONDON. GREAT ST. HELEN'S CHURCH.

Red colouring on pillars on S. of present chancel.
Monument brought from St. Martin Outwich.

LONDON. ST. LAURENCE'S CHURCH, JEWRY.

LONDON. ST. MARTIN'S-IN-THE-FIELDS.

LONDON. ST. MARTIN OUTWICH.

"Triple canopied altar tomb, circ. 1500, with remains of its ancient gilding." *J. H. Sperling, Church Walks in Middlesex*, p. 150.

Traces of colour on the effigies of John and Mary de Oteswich. Time of Henry IV. These have been moved to Great St. Helen's Church.

LONDON. ST. MARY-LE-STRAND.

LONDON. ST. MATTHEW, FRIDAY STREET.

Painted female head, time of Henry III. or Edward I., discovered during some excavations close to the church. *Archæol. Journ.*, i. 253.

LONDON. ST. SEPULCHRE'S CHURCH.

Sculptured fragment found in the wall with original colour and gilding. 15th cent. *Gent. Mag.*, 1837, viii. new series, 580.

LONDON. THE TEMPLE CHURCH.

Traces of colour and gilding on some of the cross-legged effigies. *Archæol. Journ.*, i. 50.
Colouring on the Choir roof. Renewed.

LONDON. THE TEMPLE CHURCH—*cont.*
Between the Round and Choir; painted and gilt corbel heads.
E. Richardson, The Temple Church, Ancient Coffins, p. 23.

LONDON. THE TOWER, ST. PETER'S CHAPEL.
N. side, E. end of N. aisle ; remains of colour and gilding on effigies of Sir William Cholmondeley and Lady. Circ. 1522.
N. wall of chancel ; coloured monument of Sir Richard Blount. Circ. 1564.
D. C. Bell, " The Chapel in the Tower," pp. 32, 33.

LONGHAM CHURCH, NORFOLK.
Screen repaired, all traces of painting obliterated. *Carthew's Hundred of Launditch,* iii. 270.

LONGSTONE, GREAT, CHURCH, DERBYSHIRE.
During the demolition of the church, in 1872, the walls were found to be covered with paintings.

LOSTWITHIEL CHURCH, CORNWALL.
Over N. door ; alto relievo of the flaying of St. Bartholomew. Colouring restored. *Archæologia Cambrensis,* 3rd series, viii. 322. .

LOUGHBOROUGH CHURCH, LEICESTERSHIRE.
St. Christopher, and Time and Death. *Nicholls, History of Leicestershire,* iii. 898.

LOUTH, LINCOLNSHIRE, ST. JAMES' CHURCH.
A mural painting was discovered on the wall of the S. aisle.
S. chancel aisle ; a quatrefoil panel enriched with . gold and colour.
Associated Architect. Societies' Repts., xii. 3.

LOUTH PARK ABBEY, LINCOLNSHIRE.
Remains of decorative colour on walls and columns of chapel, and on walls of chapter house. Partly 13th cent. *Associated Architect. Societies' Repts.,* xii. 24.

LOWESTOFT CHURCH, SUFFOLK.
N. wall, near the . doorway; faint traces. *British Archæol. Assoc. Journ.,* xxxvi. 38.

LOXTON CHURCH, SOMERSETSHIRE.
On N. wall of nave ; St. Christopher. *Destroyed.*

LUDBOROUGH CHURCH, LINCOLNSHIRE.

N. side of the chancel, within the sill of the western window; scroll painting. 13th cent. *Associated Architect. Societies' Repts.*, v. xix., xii. 11. *Kelly's Post Office Directory of Lincolnshire. Civil Engineer and Architect's Journ.*, 1860, p. 169.

LUDGERSHALL CHURCH, WILTSHIRE.

Between nave and S. transept; monument and effigies of Sir Richard Brydges and Lady, partly repainted. Date circ. 1558.

LUDGVAN CHURCH, CORNWALL.

St. Christopher and the Hermit. *Journ. Royal Inst., Cornwall*, 1872, p. 50.

LUDHAM CHURCH, NORFOLK.

Painted rood screen, dated 1493; on the 12 panels, SS. Mary Magdalene, Stephen, Edmund, Henry VI., the Doctors of the Church, S.S. Edward the Confessor, Walstan, Lawrence, and Apollonia. *Proceedings Royal Archæol. Institute*, Norwich vol., p. xxxix. *Colling, Gothic Ornaments*, i. pl. 3. *The Ecclesiologist's Guide to the Deaneries of Brisley, &c.*, p. 95. *British Archæol. Assoc. Journ.*, xxxvii. 139.

Rood-beam figures, on panels, of Our Lord, the Virgin, and St. John; found in the rood-loft staircase. *British Archæol. Assoc. Journ.*, xxxvi. 93–95.

Traces of colour on the font, with the Evangelistic emblems.

LUDLOW CHURCH, SHROPSHIRE.

On S. tower piers and windows of S. aisle; large figures of Saints, Angels holding shields, &c. *Whitewashed over*.

On beams under tower, colour restored.

Roof of nave; gilt bosses. 15th cent.

Roof of nave and aisles had been magnificently coloured.

Roof of Choir; painted 15th cent.

Wall above arch from S. chapel to chancel, and on E. end of chapel; a powdering of red roses.

E. wall of N. transept; traces of a large subject.

Walls of N. chancel aisle; colouring.

N. chancel aisle, canopy over altar; painted angels.

Screen across St. John's Chapel.

S. porch; fragments of wall painting, and gilded boss. *Murray's Handbook of Shropshire.*

LUDLOW CHURCH, SHROPSHIRE—*cont.*

Reredos, with remains of colour, discovered during the restoration. 15th cent. *Ecclesiologist*, ix. 314. *Wright's History of Ludlow*, p. 463. *British Archæol. Assoc. Journ.*, v. 166.

Fragments of a decorated tomb with painted figures in the panels; found in the Church. Now in the town museum.

Other coloured fragments still visible in the wall. *Irvine, Historical Sketches of Ludlow Church*, pp. 10, 15, 17, 20, 23, 25, 26, 28, 29, 30, 40, 53, 54, 60. *British Archæol. Assoc. Journ.*, xxxii. 354.

LUFFENHAM, NORTH, CHURCH, RUTLANDSHIRE.

Painted roof. *Associated Architect. Societies' Repts.*, x. 89.

Arches, S. side of nave; masonry patterns, and scroll ornament on the soffits.

LURGASHALL CHURCH, SUSSEX.

On the plaster; three coats of arms. 14th cent. *M. A. Lower, History of Sussex*, ii. 36.

LUTON CHURCH, BEDFORDSHIRE.

Portion of chancel screen; repainted. Date 15th cent. *Davis, Hist. of Luton*, p. 54.

LUTTERWORTH CHURCH, LEICESTERSHIRE.

Pillars and arches; running pattern. Late 13th cent. S. wall of S. aisle; Les Trois Vifs. 14th cent. *Associated Architect. Societies' Repts.*, ix. cxviii., 252, 253, 293.

Over chancel arch; the General Resurrection. *Leicester Architect. and Archæol. Soc. Trans.*, iii. 361, iv. 151.

LYDD CHURCH, KENT.

S. aisle; a crowned king seated within a roundel, &c. *Archæol. Cantiana*, xiii. 435.

LYDEARD, BISHOP'S, CHURCH, SOMERSETSHIRE.

Screens; repainted.

LYMPSTONE CHURCH, DEVONSHIRE.

N. aisle of nave; St. Christopher, and several layers of texts.

Other remains of mural painting.

Painted roofs.

Remains of decoration on the shafts and capitals on the N. nave arcade; also on the jambs of the doorway opening to the rood-loft staircase. *Destroyed.*

Exeter Diocesan Architect. Soc., 2nd series, i. 166.

LYNEHAM CHURCH, WILTSHIRE.
Screen ; repainted.

LYNN, KING'S, NORFOLK, ST. NICHOLAS' CHAPEL.
Remains of colour and gilding on the mutilated canopies of the sedilia, on a fragment of the rood screen, and on the roof.

On a panel to a cupboard in the vestry ; a priest kneeling to St. Peter, with the motto "Aperi mihi portas justiciæ confitebor Dño." All early 15th cent.
Taylor, Antiq. of King's Lynn, p. 83, and pl. facing p. 66.

LYNN, SOUTH, CHURCH, NORFOLK.
Screen. *Destroyed.* On the panels were the Twelve Apostles. Some are still preserved in the vestry. Date 15th cent. *Taylor, Antiq. of King's Lynn*, p. 105.

MABE CHURCH, CORNWALL.
Painted and gilt sculptures, one representing the martyrdom of a bishop. *Journ. Royal Inst. Cornwall,* April 1872, p. c.

MADLEY CHURCH, HEREFORDSHIRE.
Over the chancel arch ; Our Lord in Glory, and in Humiliation. Traces of painting elsewhere throughout the church. Probably about 1300.

MADRON CHURCH, CORNWALL.
Part of the rood screen. Also some figures carved in alabaster and gilt; deciphered as representing a portion of the Heavenly Hierarchy. *British Archæol. Assoc. Journ.,* xxxiii. 211. *Blight's Churches of West Cornwall,* p. 20. *Parochial History of Cornwall,* iii. 217.

MAGOR CHURCH, MONMOUTHSHIRE.
Figures of the Apostles depicted on the panels of the roof. *British Archæol. Assoc. Journ.,* x. 290.

MAIDSTONE, KENT, ALL SAINTS' CHURCH.
On N. of chancel; richly painted screen. Circ. 1390.
S. chancel aisle, above the monument of Master John Wotton ; the Annunciation and kneeling figure of John

MAIDSTONE, KENT, ALL SAINTS' CHURCH—*cont.*

·Wotton. On either side, SS. Catherine, Mary Magdalene or Margaret, Thomas à Beckct, and Richard de la Wych.

Gilding on the cresting, &c. Circ. 1417.

Weale's Quarterly Papers, vol. iv. *Archæologia,* xxxi. 512. *Blackburne, Decorative Painting,* p. 84. *Murray's Handbook of Kent. Archæol. Cantiana,* iv. xli.

N. piers of chancel ; the sacred Monogram.

On the wall to the W. of the vestry door ; a consecration cross.

Beale Post, History of the College of All Saints, Maidstone, pp. 77, 78. *British Archæol. Assoc. Journ.,* iii. 260.

MALLING, EAST, CHURCH, KENT.

Chapel at the E. end ; bosses retaining their gilding. About 1300. *Murray's Handbook of Kent. Glynne, Churches of Kent,* p. 154.

MALMESBURY ABBEY CHURCH, WILTSHIRE.

On the tympanum of the S. doorway ; remains of colour and gilding on sculpture of Our Lord in Glory. *Cockerell, Sculptures of Wells Cathedral,* Appendix, p. 45.

MALPAS CHURCH, CHESHIRE.

Brereton chancel ; monument of Sir Randle Brereton, died 1522, formerly painted and gilt. *Ormerod's History of Cheshire,* ii. 343, and, 2nd ed. ii. 614.

MALVERN, GREAT, ABBEY CHURCH, WORCESTERSHIRE.

Oak ceiling ; panel decoration. *Civil Engineer and Architect's Journal,* 1851, p. 196, and *Blackburne, Decorative Painting,* p. 79.

S. chancel wall ; dedication cross.

MAMHEAD CHURCH, DEVONSHIRE.

Panels of screen ; forming a pew with paintings of SS. James, John, Andrew, Paul, and Peter. *Oliver's Ecclesiastical Antiquities of Devon,* iii. 65.

MANATON CHURCH, DEVONSHIRE.

Screens ; richly decorated and with figures of saints and martyrs depicted on the panels. Date 15th cent. *Exeter Diocesan Architect. Soc.,* iv. 164; and 2nd serie ii. 96. *Worth, Tourist's Guide to S. Devon,* p. 77.

Across N. aisle ; eight panels defaced, SS. Helen, Blaise, Dorothy, and Cosmos.

MANATON CHURCH, DEVONSHIRE—*cont.*

Chancel screen, N. side ; SS. Ursula, Nicholas, Andrew, Luke, Matthias, James the Great, Bartholomew, and Paul.

On the doors; the Doctors of the Church, and St. Catherine replacing St. Ambrose.

On S. side ; SS. Peter, Thomas, Olave, Simon, Philip, John Evangelist, John the Baptist, and Barbara.

Across S. aisle ; St. Agatha, the Virgin and Child, St. Mary Magdalene, a bishop, SS. Catherine, George, Margaret, and five panels defaced.

Round the central doors; carved figures of SS. Paul, Stephen, and the Apostles, omitting John, James Major, and Simon.

C. Worthy, Ashburton and its Neighbourhood, p. 76.

MANCHESTER CATHEDRAL, LANCASHIRE.

Nave roof; painted and gilt. *Murray's Handbook of Lancashire. Murray's Handbook of the Northern Cathedrals,* pt. ii. 419.

MANNINGFORD BRUCE CHURCH, WILTSHIRE.

E. wall of apse; consecration crosses, perhaps pre-Norman.

Over N. door ; the Doom. *Destroyed.*

MAPLEDURHAM CHURCH, OXFORDSHIRE.

Roof of chancel ; gilt metal stars on a blue ground. *Ecclesiologist,* xi. 271.

MAPPOWDER CHURCH, DORSETSHIRE.

Small effigy with remains of the original colouring. *Archæol. Journ.,* iv. 156. *Hutchins' Hist. of Dorset,* 3rd ed., iii. 732.

MARCLE, MUCH, CHURCH, HEREFORDSHIRE.

Under the central tower ; coloured effigy of Joan Lady Mortimer. About 1450.

MARESFIELD CHURCH, SUSSEX.

Round all the windows ; festoon bordering of birds and flowers.

On splays of windows ; Scripture sentences within scroll borders.

On S. side of nave; (?) Martyrdom of St. Bartholomew.

On N. side of nave ; Baptism of the Ethiopian Eunuch.

MARESFIELD CHURCH, SUSSEX—*cont.*

On each side of chancel arch ; two angels with expanded wings holding a chaplet of palm branches.
On chancel ceiling ; the sun, moon, and stars.
All re-covered with whitewash.
Sussex Archæol., xiv. 142.

MARGARET MARSH CHURCH, DORSETSHIRE.

N. wall ; St. Christopher. *Destroyed. Hutchins' Hist. of Dorset*, 3rd ed., iii. 550.

MARGARETTING CHURCH, ESSEX.

Nave roof has the original colouring. *Essex Archæol.*, iv. 102.

MARHOLME CHURCH, NORTHAMPTONSHIRE.

S. of nave ; altar tomb with coloured effigies of Sir W. Fitzwilliam and Lady. Date 1529. *Murray's Handbook of Northamptonshire*, p. 86.
On N. of chancel ; coloured armorial bearings on the monument of Sir William Fitzwilliam. Circ. 1534. *Gibson and Gough, Hist. of Castor*, p. 156. On W. wall ; figures of St. Catherine, another female Saint, and St. Andrew. 14th cent. *F. A. Paley, Notes on Twenty Parish Churches round Peterborough*, pp. 86, 89. *Sweeting, Parish Churches in and around Peterborough*, pp. 7, 8, 209.

MARNHULL CHURCH, DORSETSHIRE.

In little S. aisle ; remains of gilding on alabaster effigies of a knight and his two wives. *Hutchins' Hist. of Dorset*, 3rd ed., iv. 322.

MARSHAM CHURCH, NORFOLK.

Painted screen. *British Archæol. Assoc. Journ.*, xiv. 27. *Blomefield, Hist. of Norfolk*, ed. 1807, vi. 287.
Figures of the Apostles, St. Paul, a Bishop, St. Faith, &c. depicted on the panels.

MARSTON MONTGOMERY CHURCH, DERBYSHIRE.

On the pillars of the N. aisle ; cinquefoils. stencilled in red.
Black-letter texts and other remains of colour discovered on the walls.
J. C. Cox, Churches of Derbyshire, iii. 103.

MARSTON MORETAINE CHURCH, BEDFORDSHIRE.

Painted roof.

Lower part of rood screen remains, painted and gilt, with figures of prophets.

Parker, Eccles. and Architect. Topog. of England, Bedford, No. 75. Lysons' Magna Britannia, Bedfordshire, p. 31.

Nave roof; the bosses, and brackets in the form of archangels, have been regilt and repainted.

Only a portion of the rood screen has been preserved, with figures of David, Isaiah, Daniel, and Hosea, all holding scrolls, on the panels.

Over chancel arch ; the Doom.

N. wall of N. aisle back and arch of altar recess ; decorative colouring. Circ. 1500.

E. wall of chancel; female figure on a pedestal under a rich canopy. Circ. 1500.

N. wall of S. chancel chapel; an armorial shield, and text from i. Samuel, ii., 30. Circ. 1560.

MARSTON ST. LAWRENCE CHURCH, NORTHAMPTONSHIRE.

Chancel screen. *Baker's Hist. and Antiq. of Northamptonshire,* page 644.

MARSTON, LONG, CHURCH, HERTFORDSHIRE.

Traces of rude drawings on the walls, one supposed to represent St. Christopher. *A Guide to Hertfordshire,* 1881, p. 423.

MARSTON, NORTH, CHURCH, BUCKINGHAMSHIRE.

Chancel screen. *Lipscomb, Hist. and Antiq. of Bucks,* i. 345.

MARSWORTH CHURCH, BUCKINGHAMSHIRE.

S. wall of S. aisle, within a canopied recess ; text from Psalm xliii. About 1550.

MARTHAM CHURCH, NORFOLK.

Over chancel arch ; a large subject, (?) part of a Doom.

Rood beam, with diaper and coloured mouldings, removed.

Painted font. Date about 1460.

Norfolk Archæol., v. 170, 171.

MARTINHOE CHURCH, DEVONSHIRE.

Compartment of nave roof over the rood screen painted.

Exeter Diocesan Architect. Soc., 2nd series, iii. 35.

MARTOCK CHURCH, SOMERSETSHIRE.
Back of niches on each side of nave; paintings of the
Apostles. Circ. 1550.

MASSINGHAM, GREAT, CHURCH, NORFOLK.
? On screen; a diaper of foliage and flowers on alternate red and green grounds.

MATTISHALL CHURCH, NORFOLK.
Painted roofs of nave and N. aisle, and screen.
Brandon, Open Timber Roofs, p. 79.
On screen; panel paintings of the Apostles with scrolls,
inscribed with sentences from the Creed.
Hart, Antiq. of Norfolk, p. 66. *The Ecclesiologist's
Guide to the Deaneries of Brisley, &c.*, pp. 24, 39.

MAUTBY CHURCH, NORFOLK.
Painted screen.

MAWNAN CHURCH, CORNWALL.
On screen; well painted figures. *Parochial History
of Cornwall*, iii. 362.

MAYFIELD CHURCH, SUSSEX.
E. end of S. aisle; coloured niche. *British Archæol.
Assoc. Journ.*, xxiii. 360.

MEARS ASHBY, *see* ASHBY, MEARS.

MEDBOURN MANOR HOUSE, LEICESTERSHIRE.
"Some rather fine mural decorations discovered" at.
Associated Architect. Societies' Repts., xiv. ciii.

MEIFOD CHURCH, MONTGOMERYSHIRE.
Over E. chancel window; figures of saints, 13th cent.
Destroyed.

MELBOURNE CHURCH, CAMBRIDGESHIRE.
On E. arch, N. side of nave; pattern of chevrons and
decorative colour. 14th cent.
E. wall of S. transept; two tabernacle niches with
remains of colour and gilding. 14th cent.

MELBOURNE CHURCH, DERBYSHIRE.
N. pillar of central tower; one of the Vices. 14th
cent. *British Archæol. Assoc. Journ.*, xvi. 286. *Reliquary*, i. 31.
On a pillar in the nave; the Death of Queen Osthrid,
and other subjects.
Numerous paintings discovered in 1842.

MELBOURNE CHURCH, DERBYSHIRE—*cont.*

Melbourne Church, by Rev. J. Deans, p. 19. *British Archæol. Assoc. Journ.*, ii. 207, 210, vii. 353. *Murray's Handbook of Derbyshire. Bemrose, Guide to Derbyshire,* p. 308. *J. C. Cox, Churches of Derbyshire,* iii. 406. *Leicester Architect. and Archæol. Soc. Trans.*, i. 155. *Briggs, Hist. of Melbourne*, 2nd ed., p. 51.

MELCOMBE-HORSEY CHURCH, DORSETSHIRE.

N. side of nave; St. Christopher, and St. Michael weighing Souls. Early 15th cent. *Destroyed. Archæol. Journ.*, iii. 265. *Hutchins' Hist. of Dorset*, 3rd ed., iv. 378.

MELDRETH CHURCH, CAMBRIDGESHIRE.

E. beam of nave roof and wall plate, N. side, E. end; various decorations. 15th cent.

On piers of chancel arch; scroll foliage on a red ground. 15th cent.

MELFORD, LONG, CHURCH, SUFFOLK.

N. side of chancel; Clopton chantry: on the monument of John Clopton, Esq., on the under side of the canopy, (?) the Resurrection, painted scrolls, diapers, escutcheons, &c.; at the head of the monument, portraits of Sir John and his Lady, and at the foot, portraits of their children. *Colling, Gothic Ornaments*, i. pls. 36, 37. *Cromwell, Excursions through Suffolk*, i. 57.

The walls have been nearly covered with Scripture legends and prayers.

N. wall; the Entombment.

J. P. Neale and J. Le Keux, Views of the most interesting Collegiate and Parochial Churches in Great Britain, vol. ii.

MELLIS CHURCH, SUFFOLK.

Rood screen. Repainted.

MELLS CHURCH, SOMERSETSHIRE.

N. wall of a chantry chapel adjoining the chancel; Aquila and Priscilla, or, more probably, St. Winifred, and texts. Time of Edward VI.

Over N. door; St. Christopher.

Arabesque patterns on the pillars, and painted decorations on upper walls of S. aisle and elsewhere.

Gent. Mag., 1846, xxvi., new series, 189. *Archæol. Journ.*, ii. 391. *Blackburne, Decorative Painting*, p. 17.

MELTON MOWBRAY CHURCH, LEICESTERSHIRE.

N.E. transept arcade; 14th cent. decoration. *Leicester Architect. and Archœol. Soc. Trans.,* iii. 290.

MENDHAM PRIORY, SUFFOLK.

Discovered on the walls of the present mansion a portion of 13th cent. painting, with a later pattern above; also the arms of Mary Queen Dowager of France, and some decorative work of the middle of the 16th cent. *Gent. Mag.,* 1836, vi., new series, 603.

MENDLESHAM CHURCH, SUFFOLK.

Roof over rood-loft. *Civil Engineer and Architect's Journ.,* 1860, p. 5.
Roof of chantry chapel; E. end of N. aisle. *Ecclesiologist,* v. 200.
Within a niche at E. end of N. aisle; painting of the Virgin. *Destroyed.*
Roof of parvise over N. porch; painted blue. *Destroyed. British Archœol. Assoc. Journ.,* xxx. 92.

MENTMORE CHURCH, BUCKINGHAMSHIRE.

Wall of S. aisle; Martyrdom of Thomas à Becket, below, St. Anne instructing the Virgin, the Virgin and Child, St. Margaret and other Saints. 13th cent. *Society of Antiquaries' Proceedings,* iv. 148. *Whitewashed over.*

MEON, EAST, CHURCH, HAMPSHIRE.

St. Christopher. *Archœol. Journ.,* ii. 201.
Chancel arch; on S. pier a crowned head, on N. pier the Crucifixion, under a trefoil-headed canopy.

MEREVALE ABBEY CHAPEL, WARWICKSHIRE.

Remains of colour on fragments found during excavations in 1849. *Ecclesiologist,* x. 309.

MERSTHAM CHURCH, SURREY.

W. pillar, S. side of nave; a Bishop.
S. wall of chancel; the Virgin and Child. Early 15th cent.
On wall of S. aisle; (?) Martyrdom of Thomas à Becket. Discovered in 1861, and *destroyed.* Also, the Virgin and Child, and (?) two scenes from the history of St. Catherine.
Surrey Archœol., iii. 7 and 8. *Murray's Handbook of Surrey,* ed. 1876. *R. F. D. Palgrave, Handbook to Reigate,* pp. 128, 129.

MERSTHAM CHURCH, SURREY—*cont.*
Coloured effigy, (?) of Alderman Janys or Sir John Danett. 15th cent. *Brayley's Hist. of Surrey*, 2nd ed., iv. 100.

MERTHYR CYNOG CHURCH, BRECKNOCKSHIRE.
Chancel screen. 15th cent. *Ecclesiologist*, xxi. (xviii. new series), 116.

MERTON ABBEY, SURREY.
Sculptured female head painted and gilded. Found embedded in the abbey wall. *Archæologia*, xiv. 282.

MERTON CHURCH, NORFOLK.
Painted font. Rood screen with diaper on the panels. *Norfolk Archæol.*, vi. 304.
Font cover; formerly gilt. *Chambers, Hist. of Norfolk*, ii. 989.

MERTON CHURCH, OXFORDSHIRE.
Nave roof; remains of colouring. 15th cent. *Parker's Architectural Guide to the Neighbourhood of Oxford*, p. 16. *Dunkin, Hist. and Antiq. of the Hundreds of Bullington and Ploughley*, ii. 4.

METHLEY CHURCH, YORKSHIRE.
Roof of Waterton chantry. About 1424. *Murray's Handbook of Yorkshire. Yorkshire Archæol. Journ.*
Effigies of Lionel, Lord Welles, and Cicely his wife have been richly gilt and coloured. About 1461. *Murray's Handbook of Yorkshire.*

MICHAELCHURCH ESKLEY CHURCH, HEREFORDSHIRE.
Havergal, Fasti Herefordenses, p. 157.
N. wall of nave; Our Saviour surrounded by the implements of the Passion.

MICHAELCHURCH-ON-ARROW CHURCH, RADNORSHIRE.
Chancel roof; formerly painted.

MICHELDEVER CHURCH, HAMPSHIRE.
Parts of a stone screen or reredos of large dimensions, decorated with colour and gold.
Builder, 1881, vol. xli, p. 375.

MICKFIELD CHURCH, SUFFOLK.
Painted screen, perforated panels.

MIDDLETON CHURCH, NORFOLK.
Rood screen, on the panels; the Apostles.

MILCOMB, OXFORDSHIRE, ST. LAURENCE'S CHURCH.
Opposite N. door; Martyrdom of St. Laurence.
N. wall; Seven Deadly Sins and Works of Mercy.
Destroyed. Builder, 1864, p. 734.
Lower part of screen, painted and gilt.
Beesley, Hist. of Banbury, p. 137.

MILDENHALL CHURCH, SUFFOLK.
At E. end of S. aisle; rough painting, of which a
tracing remains in the possession of J. Read, Esq.,
Mildenhall.
At E. end of N. aisle; colouring on a piscina.
Suffolk Archæol., iv. 348.

MILLOM CHURCH, CUMBERLAND.
S. aisle; altar tomb of a knight and lady. 15th cent.
The effigies appear to have been painted and gilded.
Jefferson, Hist. and Antiq. of Cumberland, ii. 168.

MILTON ABBAS, DORSETSHIRE, THE ABBEY CHURCH.
Let into the stalls on either side of the entrance to the
Choir; two painted panels representing Athelstan and his
Queen, the founders of the Abbey. Date 12th or 13th
cent. *Archæol. Journ.,* xxxiv. 278.
Also panel painting of the Annunciation. :
N. transept, under N. window; the Resurrection and
Ascension. *Whitewashed over.*
S. transept; E. wall, painted and gilt cornices. S. wall,
the Seven Deadly Sins and the Seven Acts of Mercy.
Remains of colour and gilding on altar screen. Date
1492.
Panel paintings of St. Paul and the Apostles, omitting
St. Bartholomew, formerly belonging to a screen, now
removed to Hilton Church, Dorsetshire.
Formerly similar panel paintings of the Virgin, SS.
Bartholomew, Martin, Nicholas, Benedict, and Sampson,
also existed, but these have now disappeared.
Hutchins' Hist. of Dorset, 1st ed., ii. 445; 3rd ed., iv.
358, 401–405, and 410.

MILTON CHURCH, CAMBRIDGESHIRE.
N. wall of nave; St. Christopher. *Ecclesiologist,* xx.
317.
E. end of S. aisle; painted niche. *Cambridge Antiq.
Soc. Publications, Milton,* p. 51.
Found built into the wall; alabaster figure of St.
Leonard, coloured and gilt. *Ecclesiologist,* xxiv. (xxi.

Q 3254.   M

MILTON CHURCH, CAMBRIDGESHIRE—*cont.*
new series), p. 195. *F. A. Paley, The Ecclesiologist's
Guide to the Churches . . . . . round Cambridge,*
p. 5.

MILTON, GREAT, CHURCH, OXFORDSHIRE.
The Virgin and Child. *Archæol. Journ.,* ii. 368.
Ecclesiologist, xi. 60.

MIMMS, NORTH, CHURCH, HERTFORDSHIRE.
N. chancel chapel; colouring on a shield of a 15th cent.
monument.
Remains of colouring found on N. wall of chancel, too
faint to be worth preserving.

MINEHEAD CHURCH, SOMERSETSHIRE.
The doors of the screen retain their original colour and
gilding. *Bristol and West of England Archæol. Mag.,*
p. 107.

MINSTER CHURCH, CORNWALL.
S. aisle; figure of a man and other mural decorations.
Maclean, Hist. of the Deanery of Trigg Minor, i. 606.

MINSTER CHURCH, ISLE OF SHEPPEY, KENT.
S. side of S. aisle; coloured effigy of Sir Robert de
Shurland. Early 14th cent. *Stothard's Monumental
Effigies,* p. 39. *Antiquary,* 1873, iii. 108.
Mural painting of an Archbishop.

MINSTER LOVEL CHURCH, OXFORDSHIRE.
Roof E. end of Choir; panelled and painted. 15th cent.
Ecclesiologist, xviii. 251.

MITCHELDEAN CHURCH, GLOUCESTERSHIRE.
On a set of panels, above the chancel arch; the Day of
Judgment, and scenes in the Life of Our Lord. Time of
Edward IV.
Painted pulpit. Time of Henry VII.
Gent. Mag., ci. pt. ii. 409, 410. *Blackburne, Deco-
rative Painting,* pp. 20, 73.

MOCCAS CHURCH, HEREFORDSHIRE.
Havergal, Fasti Herefordenses, p. 157. *Destroyed.*

MOLD CHURCH, FLINTSHIRE.

E. end of N. aisle ; "richly carved and coloured niche."
Thomas, Hist. of the Diocese of St. Asaph, p. 600.

MOLTON, NORTH, CHURCH, DEVONSHIRE.

Pulpit painted and gilt. 15th cent. *Murray's Handbook of Devonshire.*

MONKTON FARLEIGH PRIORY, WILTSHIRE.

Portions of a cross-legged effigy with remains of colour,
dug up in 1841. *Wilts Archæol. and Nat. Hist. Soc. Mag.,*
iv. 284. *J. E. Jackson, Hist. of the Priory of Monkton
Farley*, p. 20.

MORBORNE CHURCH, HUNTINGDONSHIRE.

St. Christopher. *Bloxam's Principles of Architecture,*
10th ed., p. 411 ; 11th ed., ii. 201.

MORDIFORD CHURCH, HEREFORDSHIRE.

Over W. window ; "painting of the famous Mordiford
dragon." *Destroyed in 1811. Archæologia Cambrensis*, 3rd series, xiii. 414. *Duncumb, Hist. of the County
of Hereford*, iii. 81.

MORETON HALL CHAPEL, CHESHIRE.

Scripture texts, nearly effaced. *Blackburne, Decorative
Painting*, p. 31.

MORETON, MAID'S, CHURCH, BUCKINGHAMSHIRE.

"Here were some paintings on the chancel walls, but
they have been also defaced ; an unskilful dauber has
frightfully attempted to draw over again Our Saviour
sitting at the Last Supper, &c." *Browne Willis, Hist. of
the Hundred of Buckingham*, p. 231.

N. wall of chancel ; the Crucifixion.

S. wall of chancel, back of sedilia ; the Last Supper.
*Parker, Eccles. and Architect. Topog. of England,
Bucks.*, No. 19. *Kelly's Post Office Directory of Bucks.*

Chancel roof, E. bay ; painted panels and metal stars
at the intersections, colouring on the wall pieces and wall
plate. Late 15th cent. *Sheahan, Hist. and Topog. of
the County of Buckingham*, p. 290.

MORLEY CHURCH, DERBYSHIRE.

N. pier of chancel arch ; autograph of Gregory Hawkes-
well painted in chocolate letters. (?) Time of Queen Mary.
Repainted in 1850. *J. C. Cox, Churches of Derbyshire*,
iv. 345.

MORLEY, NORFOLK, ST. BOTOLPH'S CHURCH.

Over chancel screen; old drawing of Thomas Warde, Rector, with the Churches of St. Botolph's and St. Peter's on either side. Circ. 1480.

Blomefield, Hist. of Norfolk, ed. 1805, ii. 477. *Cromwell, Excursions through Norfolk*, ii. 159. *Chambers, Hist. of Norfolk*, i. 349.

MORSTON, NORFOLK, ALL SAINTS' CHURCH.

Lower portion of rood screen; the four Evangelists and four Doctors of the Church.

MUCHELNEY ABBEY, SOMERSETSHIRE.

A splendid canopy, with remains of colour and gilding. Dug up in 1879. *Builder*, 1879, p. 1078.

Now in the parish church. Numerous painted bosses dug up on the site of the abbey church. *Somerset Archæol. and Nat. Hist. Soc. Proceedings*, xix. 124, xxiv., pt. ii., p. 71.

Coloured and gilt sculpture of the Trinity, (?) portion of the tomb of an abbot.

Builder, 1881, xli. 833.

MUCHELNEY CHURCH, SOMERSETSHIRE.

Roof of nave; Angels with scrolls bearing the Doxology.

MUNDEN, LITTLE, CHURCH, HERTFORDSHIRE.

N. of chancel; gilding on the effigy of Sir John Thornbury. *Cussans, Hist. of Hertfordshire*, vol. ii. pt. iii., p. 152.

MYLOR CHURCH, CORNWALL.

N. wall of nave; St. Christopher. *Destroyed*. Drawings existing.

N. wall of nave; on original surface a female Saint, also numerous layers of paintings and texts.

Portions of rood screen; painted and gilded, and with figures of Saints, inscriptions in the Cornish language, &c. Painted figure of an Angel holding a St. George's Cross.

Parochial History of Cornwall, iii. 394. *Journ. Royal Inst., Cornwall*, 1870, pp. 168–170, 1872, p. 53.

NARBURGH CHURCH, NORFOLK.

In the nave; various emblazoned armorial shields.
E. end of N. aisle, within a sepulchral recess; monumental inscription in golden letters. Circ. 1293.
Blomefield, Hist. of Norfolk, ed. 1807, vi. 154, 162.

NAVENBY CHURCH, LINCOLNSHIRE.

On corbels supporting the wall plates of the nave roof; heraldic bearings distinctly visible.
Associated Architect. Societies' Repts., xiii. lxiii.

NAWORTH CASTLE, CUMBERLAND.

Wainscoting of the oratory adjoining the library; powdering of escallop shells and cross crosslets.
Ceiling of chapel; portrait pictures of prophets, patriarchs, &c., forming a stem of Jesse. Date 1512.
Ceiling of great hall; heads of kings of England from the Saxon times to the union of the houses of York and Lancaster, said to have been brought from Kirkoswald Castle.
Lysons' Magna Britannia, Cumberland, p. cciv.
Sharpe's London Magazine, Nov. 22nd 1845, p. 51.
Whellan, Hist. and Topog. of the Counties of Cumberland and Westmoreland, p. 663.

NEATISHEAD CHURCH, NORFOLK.

On screen; the Apostles.
Blomefield, (Parkin,) Hist. of Norfolk, ed. 1810, xi. 51.

NECTON CHURCH, NORFOLK.

Painted and gilt figures supporting the nave roof; viz. on N., Our Saviour and six Apostles, and on S., the Virgin, and six other Apostles. *Blomefield, Hist. of Norfolk*, ed. 1807, vi. 49. *Cromwell, Excursions through Norfolk*, ii. 62. *Chambers, Hist. of Norfolk*, ii. 652.

NEEN SAVAGE CHURCH, SHROPSHIRE.

N. and S. walls and window splays; decorative colouring. 12th cent.

NETHERBURY CHURCH, DORSETSHIRE.

N. wall; St. Michael weighing Souls, Seven Acts of Mercy and Seven Deadly Sins. Time of Hen. IV. *Destroyed*. Tracings remain.
Ecclesiologist, xi. 251, and xii. 59. *Somerset Archæol. and Nat. Hist. Soc. Proceedings*, i. 69.

NETLEY ABBEY, HAMPSHIRE.

Traces of decorative colouring on the capitals and bases of the columns in the chapel, also on the walls of a chapel in the S. transept of the refectory and of a room over the sacristy. *Collectanea Archæologica*, ii. 75, 79, 83.

NETTLEDEN CHURCH, BUCKINGHAMSHIRE.

"The screen that separated the nave from the chancel was ornamented with gilding and portraits of Saints on panels."

Sheahan, Hist. and Topog. of the County of Buckingham, p. 702.

NEWARK, NOTTINGHAMSHIRE, ST. MARY MAGDALENE'S CHURCH.

Rood-loft. *A. Billing, Mural Painting*, 1872, p. 22.

S. side of Choir, on panels of the monument of Robert Markham ; the Dance of Death. Date about 1520.

Brown, Annals of Newark, pp. 38, 299. *Gent. Mag.*, 1846, xxvi. new series, p. 37. *Associated Architect. Societies' Repts.*, xi. 5. *Shilton, Hist. of Newark*, p. 222.

E. end, behind the high altar ; coloured shields on the monument of Thomas Brown. Date 1532. Restored.

E. end of N. aisle ; remains of decorative pattern at the back of a niche. Circ. 1500.

NEWBOURNE, SUFFOLK, ST. MARY'S CHURCH.

Lower part of rood screen ; retaining its original gilding and painting. *Parker, Eccles. and Architect. Topog. of England, Suffolk*, No. 40.

NEWDIGATE CHURCH, SURREY.

N. wall ; remains of St. Christopher.

Round a window ; diaper of fleur-de-lis. 15th cent. *Surrey Archæol.*, vi. 57, 293. *All destroyed*.

NEWINGTON BY SITTINGBOURNE CHURCH, KENT.

Beneath the whitewash some effective wall painting has been discovered around the N. doorway. *Glynne, Churches of Kent*, p. 6.

E wall of N. aisle ; the Day of Judgment. *Archæol. Journ.*, xxxviii. 85, 87.

N. wall of N. aisle; the Nativity, and other indistinct subjects, also scroll patterns. 14th cent.

N. aisle within the window splays ; large figures of SS. Paul, Andrew, &c.

Traces of paintings in many other parts of the church.

NEWINGTON, SOUTH, CHURCH, OXFORDSHIRE.

Traces of colour on N. pier of chancel arch.

North Oxon. Archæol. Soc. Trans., 1877, *Gt. Tew and South Newington*, p. 37. *Beesley, Hist. of Banbury*, pp. 109, 136.

NEWMINSTER ABBEY, NEAR MORPETH, NORTHUMBERLAND.

During excavations made in 1878 were discovered :—

In the N. transept, on three separate stones of a pillar or pier, a painting of a Saint.

Decorative colour on the walls and groining ribs of the chapter house.

Builder, 1878, p. 1181.

NEWNHAM CHURCH, NORTHAMPTONSHIRE,

Rood screen. *Baker's Hist. and Antiq. of Northamptonshire*, p. 260.

NEWNHAM REGIS CHURCH, WARWICKSHIRE.

Walls of nave; paintings of the Evangelists.

N. wall of chancel; the Offerings of the Magi.

S. wall of chancel; the Descent from the Cross.

Destroyed at the end of the last century.

Thorne, Rambles by Rivers, p. 58.

NEWPORT CHURCH, ESSEX.

Over the chancel arch; the Day of Judgment. *Destroyed. Ecclesiologist*, xxi. (xviii. new series), 196.

Church chest. Interior of lid; paintings of the Crucifixion, St. Peter, the Virgin, St. John, and St. Paul. Late 13th cent. *British Archæol. Assoc. Journ.*, iii. 204, and xxviii. 225.

NEWPORT, ISLE OF WIGHT, ST. THOMAS'S CHURCH.

On either side of window in S.E. chapel; paintings of King David, female figure, symbolical of the Jewish law, or St. Osyth. 13th cent. Tracings existing in the Newport Museum. *British Archæol. Assoc. Journ.*, xi. 270.

On S. side of chancel arch; text from Deuteronomy, xxviii.

Nave; The Expulsion from Paradise. Numerous other paintings in nave and aisles. *All destroyed.*

Colour and gilding on monument of Sir Edward Horsey. Circ. 1582.

S. B. Beal, The Church of St. Thomas, Newport, Isle of Wight, pp. 7, 8, 20.

NEWPORT CHURCH, PEMBROKESHIRE.

"There was a rood-loft in the memory of some old people handsomely wrought and gilt."
Fenton's Tour in Pembrokeshire, p. 545.

NEWTON, CAMBRIDGESHIRE, ST. JAMES'S CHURCH.

Nave roof. Remains of gilding. *History of Wisbech and the Fens*, p. 532. *Watson, Historical Account of Wisbech*, p. 480.

NEWTON BROMSWOLD CHURCH, NORTHAMPTONSHIRE.

Walls of chancel; decorative painting 15th cent.
N. wall of chancel, over Easter sepulchre: a crucifix and angels descending with scrolls. *All destroyed.*

NEWTON LONGUEVILLE CHURCH, BUCKINGHAMSHIRE.

Remains of gilding on the roofs. *Lipscomb, Hist. and Antiq. of Bucks*, iv. 268.

NEWTON SOLNEY CHURCH, DERBYSHIRE.

Angels supporting the head of an effigy, coloured and gilt. Time of Richard II. *Archæol. Journ.*, vii. 367. *Bigsby, Hist. of Repton*, p. 354.

NEWTON TRACY CHURCH, DEVONSHIRE.

"A good deal of mural painting is still to be found in the chancel." Three courses of paintings mentioned. *Exeter Diocesan Architect. Soc.*, iii. 59, and 2nd series ii. 19.

NEWTON, WATER, CHURCH, HUNTINGDONSHIRE.

Beam over rood-loft; painted decorations.
F. A. Paley, Notes on Twenty Parish Churches round Peterborough, p. 104.

NEWTOWN CHURCH, MONTGOMERYSHIRE.

Rood screen, with remains of gilding and colour. Now forming a reredos to the new church. Date 1st half of the 14th cent. (? 15th cent.) *Collections of Powys Land Club*, iii. 213. *British Archæol. Assoc. Journ.*, i. 259.

NORBURY CHURCH, DERBYSHIRE.

N. and S. sides of chancel; remains of colour on the monuments of Nicholas and Ralph Fitzherbert. 15th cent. *Bowman's Ecclesiastical Architecture*, p. 12. *British Archæol. Assoc. Journ.*, vii. 338. *J. C. Cox, Churches of Derbyshire*, iii. 236. *Ashbourn and the Valley of the Dove*, pp. 231, 232.

NORBURY CHURCH, STAFFORDSHIRE.
Traces of painting on the walls. *Garner, Natural History of the County of Stafford*, supplement, p. 20.

NORTHAMPTON, ST. SEPULCHRE'S CHURCH, NORTHAMPTONSHIRE.
On the N. side of the rounded portion; remains of a mural painting. *Murray's Handbook of Northants*, p. 9.
On arch, N. side of nave; remains of decorative colour.

NORTHAMPTON, HOSPITAL OF ST. JOHN THE BAPTIST, NORTHAMPTONSHIRE.
The Master's house, *destroyed*; on wall of parlour, a large painting. *Associated Architect. Societies' Repts,,* xii. 229.

NORTHCHURCH, OR BERKHAMPSTEAD ST. MARY'S, CHURCH, HERTFORDSHIRE.
Coloured mouldings found in the walls.

NORTHENDEN CHURCH, CHESHIRE.
Traces of black-letter inscriptions and mural paintings on walls and pillars. *Destroyed. Earwaker's East Cheshire,* i. 272.

NORTHOLT CHURCH, MIDDLESEX.
St. Christopher, and other paintings. *Whitewashed over.*

NORTHWOLD CHURCH, NORFOLK.
Nave; painted roof, recoloured. *Associated Architect. Societies' Repts.,* x. 90.
Screen; various Saints.
Blomefield, Hist. of Norfolk, ed. 1805, ii. 215.
Chambers, Hist. of Norfolk, ii. 690, 691.

NORTHWOOD CHURCH, ISLE OF WIGHT.
Last Judgment. Re-whitewashed. *British Archæol. Assoc. Journ.,* v. 362.

NORTON CHURCH, DERBYSHIRE.
Monument of the parents of Bishop Blythe, with painted mouldings. Circ. 1524. *Addy, Hist. Memorials of Beauchief Abbey,* p. 129.
Traces of mural decorations recently discovered.

NORTON FITZWARREN CHURCH, SOMERSETSHIRE.
Screen. Late 15th cent. The original colouring covered with a layer of oak paint in 1825. *Somerset Archæol. and Nat. Hist. Soc. Proceedings,* xviii. pt. i. 43.

NORWICH CATHEDRAL, NORFOLK.

N. Choir aisle; ceiling of sacrist's room, three out of four original groups. (I.) The Virgin, SS. Catherine and Margaret. (II.) SS. Andrew, Paul, and Peter as an Archbishop. (III.) St. Richard of Chichester. Late 13th cent.

Remains of foliated and decorative painting on the arches and caps at the E. end of the Choir, in the Choir aisles, on the ceiling of the sacrist's room, and of St. Luke's Chapel, also (restored) on the E. side of the chancel arch and on the ceiling of the Jesus Chapel. 12th and 13th cents.

Colling, Mediæval Foliage. Archæol. Journ., xxxiv. 276.

Painted and gilt bosses on roof of nave and Choir (restored), representing scenes from the Creation to the time of Solomon, and from the birth of Christ to the final Judgment.

Illustrated and described in Goulburn, The Ancient Sculptures in the Roof of Norwich Cathedral.

Gilt bosses on roof of the Beaucarne Chapel.

S. wall of S. aisle; SS. Wulstan and Edward the Confessor, and SS. (?) Etheldreda and (?) Nicholas. Late 14th cent.

Norfolk Archæol., vi. 272. East Anglian Notes and Queries, i. 287.

In the S. Choir aisle; the former reredos from the Jesus Chapel. Date about 1370. Supposed to be the work of the Siennese School. Subjects: the Scourging, Bearing the Cross, Crucifixion, Resurrection, and Ascension. *Catalogue, Fine Arts Exhibition, 1871, No. 4066. Murray's Handbook of Norfolk. Ecclesiologist, xiii. 347. Proceedings of the Royal Archæol. Institute, Norwich vol., p. 198.*

S. aisle, over Dean Gardiner's monument; decorative colour.

S. wall of Beauchamp Chapel; cross lines enclosing quatrefoils.

On Norman capital, and groining of aisle over E. door of cloister; pattern of chevrons, &c.

East Anglian Notes and Queries, i. 302, 347.

On S. wall of chamber over the dark entry; mural decoration. 13th cent.

On S. wall of chamber over S.E. angle of cloisters a circle with a lion.

Norfolk Archæol., viii. 330.

NORWICH CATHEDRAL, NORFOLK—*cont.*

Arches formerly standing in the lower close, (?) of the Infirmary chapel; chevron pattern and diapers.

Drawings by Mr. Repton.

East Anglian Notes and Queries, i. 302.

Walls of Norman refectory; decorative painting, Norman period.

Antiquary, 1873, iv. 158.

NORWICH, NORFOLK, ST. CLEMENT'S CHURCH.

N. and S. walls of chancel; emblems of the Passion. *Illustrations of Norfolk Topography,* p. 135.

NORWICH, NORFOLK, ST. EDMUND'S CHURCH.

Painted ornament on the roof. *Illustrations of Norfolk Topography,* p. 133.

NORWICH, NORFOLK, ST. ETHELDRED'S CHURCH.

N. wall; St. Christopher, &c. *Norfolk Archæol.,* v. 120.

Destroyed since the publication of the first list.

NORWICH, NORFOLK, ST. GEORGE'S TOMBLAND CHURCH.

St. George and the Dragon, formerly an altar piece.

NORWICH, NORFOLK, ST. GILES' CHURCH.

Over N. door; St. Christopher. *Blomefield, Hist. of Norfolk,* ed. 1806, iv. 239. *Norfolk Archæol.,* vi., second annual report, p. iii.

NORWICH, NORFOLK, ST. GREGORY'S CHURCH.

W. end of N. aisle; St. George and the Dragon. About 1450. *Archæol. Journ.,* xix. 81.

Three panels of screen, with paintings of SS. Barbara, John the Baptist, and an angel.

NORWICH, NORFOLK, ST. HELEN'S CHURCH.

South transept; painted bosses of roof. *British Archæol. Assoc. Journ.,* xiv. 76. *Proceedings of the Royal Archæol. Institute,* Norwich vol., p. 165.

Chancel roof panelled and painted.

NORWICH, NORFOLK, ST. JAMES'S CHURCH.

Rood screen. *Destroyed;* some of the panels are in private possession with figures of SS. Oswald, Sitha, Walstan, Blaise, Blida, Helen, Joan of Valois (with date 1505), Jude, Martin, Simon, Agnes, &c.

Coats of arms painted on the walls near the altar.

Illustrations of Norfolk Topography, p. 134.

NORWICH, NORFOLK, ST. JOHN'S MADDERMARKET CHURCH.

Figures of SS. William of Norwich,* Agatha, Appollonia, and Leonard, in private possession and removed from the church ; the rest of the rood screen *destroyed.*

* *Figured in Goulburn, The Ancient Sculptures in the Roof of Norwich Cathedral,* plate facing p. 83.

Ceiling over E. end of N. aisle ; angels holding labels with sentences from the "Te Deum," and the name of "Jesus" within a crown of thorns.

Ceiling over E. end of S. aisle; angels bearing the "Ave Maria" and the name "Maria," crowned. Date 15th cent.

Murray's Handbook of Norfolk. British Archæol. Assoc. Journ., xiv. 76. *Hart, Antiq. of Norfolk,* p. 63.

W. wall of N. aisle ; St. George. *Destroyed.*

NORWICH, NORFOLK, ST. JOHN DE SEPULCHRE CHURCH.

Consecration crosses on the walls.

Part of rood screen, with paintings of SS. James or Jerome, Blaise, Ursula, George, Etheldreda, and Gregory. 1st half of 15th cent.

Norfolk Archæol., vii. 354. *Antiquary,* 1872, ii. 124.

NORWICH, NORFOLK, CHURCH OF ST. JOHN THE BAPTIST, TIMBERHILL.

Paintings of the crucifixion, and St. John the Baptist.

NORWICH, NORFOLK, ST. MICHAEL-AT-PLEA CHURCH.

Detached panel paintings now in the vestry, probably from a parclose, or the stations of the Cross representing a head of the Virgin, Pietà, the Annunciation, Betrayal, Crucifixion, and Resurrection. *East Anglian Notes and Queries,* iv. 282. *Hart, Antiq. of Norfolk,* p. 63.

Panel painting of St. Erasmus, formerly part of a screen at.

Proceedings of the Royal Archæol. Inst., Norwich vol, p. xxxix.

On panels of screen ; the Annunciation, Salutation, Crucifixion, a Bishop, Martyr, and St. Margaret. *Illustrations of Norfolk Topography,* p. 130. *Blomefield, Hist. of Norfolk,* ed. 1806, iv. 321.

NORWICH, NORFOLK, ST. PAUL'S CHURCH.

Rood screen. *Destroyed.*

NORWICH, NORFOLK, ST. PETER HUNGATE CHURCH.

Colouring on the sedilia.

NORWICH, NORFOLK, ST. PETER MANCROFT CHURCH.

"Alabaster carving, painted, representing nine female Saints," viz. SS. Mary Magdalene, Hildegarde, Justine (?), Ursula, Margaret, Helena, Etheldreda, Barbara, &c. 15th cent. *British Archæol. Assoc. Journ.*, xiv. 70. *Proceedings of the Royal Archæol. Institute*, Norwich vol., p. 173. *Carter's Sculpture and Painting*, pl. 77. *Blomefield, Hist. of Norfolk*, ed. 1806, iv. 210. *Hart, Antiq. of Norfolk*, p. 64.

Panels in the vestry, with figures of SS. John Evangelist, James Minor, Thomas, Simon, and James Major; also Joel, Habakkuk, Hosea, Isaiah, Nahum, Moses, and Micah.

NORWICH, NORFOLK, ST. PETER PER MOUNTERGATE CHURCH.

On screen; St. Michael. *Blomefield, Hist. of Norfolk*, ed. 1806, iv. 96.

Dedication crosses surrounded by texts. *Norfolk Archæol.*, vi., 2nd annual report, p. iii.

NORWICH, NORFOLK, ST. SAVIOUR'S CHURCH.

E. wall of chancel; two consecration crosses with inscriptions. *Norfolk Archæol.*, vii. 352.

NORWICH, NORFOLK, SS. SIMON AND JUDE'S CHURCH.

On the altar screens are paintings of the Assumption of the Virgin, the Passion of Our Saviour, divers Evangelists, &c.

Blomefield, Hist. of Norfolk, ed. 1806, iv. 356.

NORWICH, NORFOLK, ST. STEPHEN'S CHURCH.

Alabaster tablet with figures of SS. John the Baptist, Simon, Matthias, &c.; part of a reredos. *Hart, Antiq. of Norfolk*, p. 64.

NORWICH, NORFOLK, ST. SWITHIN'S CHURCH.

Figure of St. Edmund in the vestry; the remainder of the rood screen *destroyed*; or St. Edward the Confessor. *Proceedings of the Royal Archæol. Institute*, Norwich vol., p. 175. *Hart, Antiq. of Norfolk*, p. 63.

Painting (?) of St. Swithin, said to have belonged to the screen at. *Illustrations of Norfolk Topography*, p. 124.

NORWICH CASTLE, NORFOLK.

Within the walls of an oratory; sculptures of the Trinity, (? of the Virgin and Child), St. Catherine, St.

NORWICH CASTLE, NORFOLK—*cont.*

Christopher, St. Michael and the Dragon, and another
figure, with remains of colouring. *Woodward, Hist.
and Antiq. of Norwich Castle,* p. 21, and pl. xiii.
British Archæol. Assoc. Journ., xiv. 68.

NORWICH, NORFOLK, HUBY'S YARD, ST. SAVIOUR'S.

Panel paintings found at, representing several scenes
of the Crucifixion. Formerly parts of a reredos. *Norfolk
Archæol.,* viii. 326. *Antiquary,* 1872, ii. 124.

NORWICH, NORFOLK, ST. GILES' HOSPITAL.

Ceiling of S. transept of the ancient chapel ; painted
with spread eagles. *Gent. Mag.,* 1847, xxviii., new series,
480.

NOTGROVE CHURCH, GLOUCESTERSHIRE.

E. wall of chancel ; lower portion, the Crucifixion, St.
Mary Magdalene anointing our Saviour's feet, and five
other subjects. Above, under richly gilt canopies, the
Annunciation, Nativity or Adoration of the Magi, and
the Coronation of the Virgin, above again six Saints
under canopies, and a row of battlements.

S. side of chancel ; masonry and foliated patterns, and
figure of a saint within the splay of the E. window.

N. side of chancel ; masonry pattern and richly
coloured niche and figure.

Church Builder, 1872, No. xli. 151.

On arches of the nave ; scroll patterns and masonry
decoration on the soffits. 13th cent. *Church Builder,*
1873, No. xlv. 21. *Gloucestershire Notes and Queries,*
vol. i., pp. 367–369, No. ccclxii.

NOTTINGHAM, NOTTINGHAMSHIRE, ST. MARY'S CHURCH.

S. wall of chancel ; tablet representing a pope inaugurating a bishop, richly coloured and gilt. *Gent. Mag.,*
1846, xxvi., new series, 516. *J. P. Briscoe, Old Nottinghamshire,* p. 31.

NOTTINGHAM, NOTTINGHAMSHIRE, ST. PETER'S CHURCH.

"A beautiful flowered diapering laid bare in many
places." *Gent. Mag.,* 1846, xxvi., new series, 516.

OAKINGTON CHURCH, CAMBRIDGESHIRE.
Painted panels of screen. *F. A. Paley, The Ecclesiologist's Guide to the Churches . . . . . round Cambridge*, p. 14.

OAKLEY CHURCH, BEDFORDSHIRE.
Rood screen; powdering of flowers on the panels. *Parker, Eccles. and Architect. Topog. of England, Bedford*, No. 19. *Ecclesiologist*, iv. 47.
Across the N. aisle; screen with painted canopy, on which is a figure of Our Lord showing the wounds, an Angel holding the instruments of the Passion, and a diaper of stars on a red ground.
Across the S. aisle; upper part of screen with painted and gilt mouldings.
Nave walls; floral decorations.
Whitewashed over.

OAKLEY, LITTLE, CHURCH, NORTHAMPTONSHIRE.
N. wall of N. aisle; part of a large subject and inscription.
E. wall of S. aisle; remains of colour.

OCKHAM CHURCH, SURREY.
Coloured floral decoration on the walls and over the chancel arch. 14th cent. *Brayley's Hist. of Surrey*, 2nd ed., i. 307.

ODELL CHURCH, BEDFORDSHIRE.
Painted screen; E. end of N. aisle. *W. M. Harvey, Hist. of Willey Hundred*, p. 368.

OGWELL, WEST, CHURCH, DEVONSHIRE.
Screen; painted panels. *Murray's Handbook of Devonshire, Introduction.*

OLNEY CHURCH, BUCKINGHAMSHIRE.
Paintings of scripture history and sentences in old English characters. *Whitewashed over. Antiquarian Cabinet*, vol. viii.
Panels of screen; Elijah fed by ravens, &c. *Destroyed* in 1854. *Sheahan, Hist. and Topog. of the County of Buckingham*, p. 587.

ONGAR, CHIPPING, CHURCH, ESSEX.
N. wall; St. Christopher. *Destroyed.*
On lancet windows in chancel; masonry patterns. *Destroyed.*

ONGAR, HIGH, CHURCH, ESSEX.
Painted roof of chancel, plastered over. *Wright, Hist. of Essex*, ii. 335.

ORCHESTON, ST. MARY CHURCH, WILTSHIRE.
Nave ceiling; fragments of painted woodwork. *Hoare's Hist. of Wilts*, ii. pt. i. 41.

ORLETON CHURCH, HEREFORDSHIRE.
Rude paintings discovered, which could not be preserved. *Kelly's Post Office Directory of Herefordshire.*
On W. wall; Jacob feeding his flock, (or, the Annunciation to the Shepherds), and a decorative pattern. 14th cent. Later decoration painted over them.
Lower walls of chancel; subjects or texts within oblong borders.

ORMSKIRK CHURCH, LANCASHIRE.
N. side of chancel; remains of colour on splays and outside jamb mouldings of a Norman window. *Historic Society of Lancashire and Cheshire*, xxx., 3rd series vi., 147.

ORSETT CHURCH, ESSEX.
Painted screen at E. end of N. aisle. *Rev. W. Palin, Stifford and its Neighbourhood*, p. 154.

ORTON LONGUEVILLE. *See* OVERTON LONGUEVILLE.

ORWELL CHURCH, CAMBRIDGESHIRE.
Chancel roof; colour on shields and figures at intersections. *Parker, Eccles. and Architect. Topog. of England, Cambridge*, No. 14.

OSMASTON CHURCH, DERBYSHIRE.
N. side of chancel; painting round a recess discovered in 1878. *J. C. Cox, Churches of Derbyshire*, iv. 168.

OTTERY ST. MARY CHURCH, DEVONSHIRE.
The chancel; series of niches with remains of statues and sculpture retaining traces of gilding and colouring.
Remains of colour visible through the whitewash and at the back of the reredos.
Exeter Diocesan Architect. Soc., i. 34, 61, and iv. 202–204. *Ecclesiologist*, xiii. 83, 85.

OULTON, SUFFOLK, ST. MICHAEL'S CHURCH.
Arms of Fastolf painted on the ceiling. *Parker, Eccles. and Architect. Topog. of England, Suffolk*, No. 240. *Cromwell, Excursions through Suffolk*, ii. 153.

OUNDLE CHURCH, NORTHAMPTONSHIRE.

On the arch opening from the chancel to the S. aisle "remains of ancient colouring, a good pattern in red." *Murray's Handbook of Northants*, p. 48.

OUTWELL CHURCH, NORFOLK.

Over arch from N. aisle to N. transept; the Salutation. N. transept; painted roof. Circ. 1420. *Blomefield, (Parkin,) Hist. of Norfolk*, ed. 1807, vii. 472. *Chambers, Hist. of Norfolk*, i. 70. *The Fen and Marshland Churches*, ii. 23. *Brandon's Parish Churches*, ii. 47. *Brandon, Open Timber Roofs*, p. 63.

Chapel to N. of chancel; painted and gilt roof. 15th cent.

Chancel screen.
History of Wisbech and the Fens, p. 519.

OVERBURY CHURCH, WORCESTERSHIRE.

E. end of chancel; reredos painted red and blue. 15th cent.

OVERTON LONGUEVILLE CHURCH, HUNTINGDONSHIRE.

N. wall of N. aisle; St. Christopher. *F. A. Paley, Notes on Twenty Parish Churches round Peterborough*, p. 56. *Sweeting, Parish Churches in and around Peterborough*, p. 138.

OVERTON, COLD, CHURCH, LEICESTERSHIRE.

S. wall of S. aisle; St. John the Baptist and (?) the Virgin; below, the burial (?) of St. John the Baptist. 14th cent.

Farther E.; the Flight into Egypt, *whitewashed over*. All the other walls were also covered with subjects which have been again whitewashed over.

OXBURGH CHURCH, NORFOLK.

Rood screen; SS. Audrey, Mary Magdalene, ? Willebrod, Thomas of Canterbury, John the Baptist, and Withburgha.

Cornice of sedilia, S. of chancel; figures of angels, gilt.

Roof of N. porch has been painted.
Blomefield, Hist. of Norfolk, ed. 1807, vi. 184, 185. *Cromwell, Excursions through Norfolk*, ii. 135. *Chambers, Hist. of Norfolk*, ii. 652.

OXFORD, OXFORDSHIRE, CHRIST CHURCH CATHEDRAL.

Beneath the arches between N. Choir aisle and N. chapel; effigy of a prior with remains of colouring. Circ. 1330.

OXFORD, OXFORDSHIRE, CHRIST CHURCH CATHEDRAL—*cont.*
Monument and effigy of Elizabeth Lady Montacute, richly painted and gilt.
Archæol Journ., ix. 151. *Proceedings of Royal Archæol. Institute*, Oxford vol., p. 222. *Gent. Mag.*, 1850, xxxiv., new series, 260. *Hollis, Monumental Effigies*, pt. ii. pl. 5, pt. iii. pls. 5, 6.
Lady Chapel; painted shields on the monument of Sir G. Nowers.
S. Choir aisle; remains of colour on a pillar.
Parker's Handbook for Oxford, 17, 18.

OXFORD, OXFORDSHIRE, ST. ALDATE'S CHURCH.
Coloured effigy of John Noble. Circ. 1522. *Hollis, Monumental Effigies*, pt. iii. pl. 9.

OXFORD, OXFORDSHIRE, ALL SOULS' COLLEGE CHAPEL.
Panel paintings attached to the roof; angels with trumpets, &c. *Builder*, 1871, p. 953. *Antiquary*, 1871, i. 197.
Reredos richly coloured. Circ. 1440. *Antiquary*, 1872, ii. 155.

OXFORD, OXFORDSHIRE, COLLEGE OF ST. MARY MAGDALENE.
Chambers within the gate tower; painted and gilt bosses, restored. *Parker's Handbook for Oxford*, 143.
See also Theale *and* Wainfleet.

OXFORD, OXFORDSHIRE, MERTON COLLEGE CHAPEL.
On wall near the altar; a series of figures. *Dallaway's Anecdotes of the Arts*, p. 424.

PADBURY CHURCH, BUCKINGHAMSHIRE.
N. aisle, near E. end; a Wheel of Fortune.

PAIGNTON CHURCH, DEVONSHIRE.
Stone pulpit, painted, with sculpture of the Crucifixion, with the Virgin and St. John, and ? the Evangelists. 15th cent. *Murray's Handbook of Devonshire*.
Portions of richly coloured Norman sedilia, discovered during the restoration of the Church. *J. T. White, Hist. of Torquay*, p. 381.
S. transept; remains of colour on the jambs of W. window.

PAKEFIELD CHURCH, SUFFOLK.

Niches in the walls; the Virgin and Child, &c., portions of richly painted screens. *Suckling's History of Suffolk*, i. 283. *Parker, Eccles. and Architect. Topog. of England, Suffolk*, No. 241.

PALGRAVE CHURCH, SUFFOLK.

Painted roof. *Brandon, Open Timber Roofs*, p. 61. *Ecclesiologist*, iii. 106. *Parker, Eccles. and Architect. Topog. of England, Suffolk*, No. 139.

PARHAM CHURCH, SUFFOLK.

Rood screen; about 1380, repainted. *Suffolk Archæol.*, iii. 407. *Parker, Eccles. and Architect. Topog. of England, Suffolk*, No. 219. *Murray's Handbook of Suffolk. Builder*, 1877, p. 555.

PARTRICIO CHURCH, BRECKNOCKSHIRE.

Walls covered with texts, &c. *R. Stephenson, Hist. of Llanthony Abbey, &c.*, p. 20. *Archæologia Cambrensis*, 3rd series, ii. 286.

PASTON CHURCH, NORFOLK.

Rood screen. Varnished over.

PATCHAM CHURCH, SUSSEX.

N. wall of nave; figures of Saints. *Destroyed.*

Over the chancel arch; the Day of Judgment. Late 12th or early 13th cent.

Archæol. Journ., xxxvii. 205, xxxviii. 80. *British Archæol. Assoc. Journ.*, xxxvi. 118. *Archæologia*, xlvii. 164 note, 169.

PATELEY BRIDGE OLD CHURCH, YORKSHIRE.

Three courses of black letter texts on the walls. *W. Grainge, Nidderdale*, p. 20.

PATRISHOW. *See* PARTRICIO.

PAYHEMBURY CHURCH, DEVONSHIRE.

Screen and parclose; painted and gilt. *Murray's Handbook of Devonshire. Ecclesiologist*, xxviii. (xxv. new series), 308. *Polwhele, Hist. of Devon*, iii. 268.

Figures of Saints on the panels; painted over.

E. bay of nave roof; painted blue and studded with gilt stars.

PEAKIRK CHURCH, NORTHAMPTONSHIRE.

Paintings discovered in 1845. *Archæol. Journ.*, i. 158.

Traces of painting on the S.W. column of the nave, and at the E. end of N. chancel chapel.

Lettern; fragments of painting.

Sweeting, Parish Churches in and around Peterborough, p. 67.

PEMBRIDGE CHURCH, HEREFORDSHIRE.

Round a walled-up arch on each side of the chancel: remains of scroll painting. 13th cent.

PENALLY CHURCH, PEMBROKESHIRE.

Mural paintings near the chancel arch. *Archæologia Cambrensis,* 2nd series, ii. 81.

PENMYNYDD CHURCH, ANGLESEY.

On an ancient stone let into the wall, armorial bearings of the Tudors, properly blazoned. *Archæologia Cambrensis,* 3rd series, xv. 279.

PENNANT MELANGELL CHURCH, MONTGOMERYSHIRE.

In front of W. gallery, screen work probably from rood-loft, coloured mouldings and carvings representing the story of St. Melangell or Monacella. *Archæologia Cambrensis,* iii. 226.

On panels of front of "Galilee," the Apostles. *Destroyed.*

On chancel wall, an armorial shield. Various texts.

Collections of the Powys Land Club, xii. 63, 64.

PENSAX CHURCH, WORCESTERSHIRE.

Behind the pulpit; the Temptation of Our Saviour in the Wilderness. *Destroyed. Noake's Rambles in Worcestershire,* 2nd series, p. 164.

PENTRICH CHURCH, DERBYSHIRE.

On pillars of chancel arch and elsewhere; traces of the original red colouring. *J. C. Cox, Churches of Derbyshire,* iv. 359.

PERSHORE ABBEY CHURCH, WORCESTERSHIRE.

Remains of colour on lower portions of the string-courses of the tower. *Styles, Hist. of Pershore Abbey Church,* p. 25, note.

On S. pier; remains of painting.

PERTENHALL CHURCH, BEDFORDSHIRE.

Perpendicular rood screen. *Parker, Eccles. and Architect. Topog. of England, Bedford,* No. 91.

PETERBOROUGH CATHEDRAL, NORTHAMPTONSHIRE.

Nave ceiling; various figures within lozenge-shaped medallions, viz., the "Agnus Dei," SS. Peter, Paul, Edward King and Martyr, Edward King and Confessor, (?) Moses, and several other kings, archbishops, bishops, and allegorical and grotesque figures. 12th cent. *Archæologia*, ix. 146. *Strickland, The Ancient Painted Ceiling in the Nave of Peterborough Cathedral.*

S. transept roof; plainer and earlier than that in nave.

Bosses of Choir roof; originally gilt, and now restored.

O. W. Davys, Guide to Peterborough Cathedral, 3rd ed., pp. 51, 54, 56.

Painted shields, &c. round the apse. On the S. wall of N. Choir aisle; a scroll border. 13th cent.

PEVENSEY CHURCH, SUSSEX.

S. wall of chancel; a consecration cross.

PICKERING CHURCH, YORKSHIRE.

N. wall of nave; St. George and the Dragon, St. Christopher, Herod's Feast, the Coronation of the Virgin, the Martyrdom of St. Thomas of Canterbury, and the Martyrdom of St. Sebastian or St. Edmund.

S. wall of nave; series of subjects from the life of St. Catherine, (?) SS. Cosmo and Damian, two of the Sacraments, viz. Extreme Unction and Burial, and the Passion and Crucifixion of Our Lord, the Descent from the Cross, Entombment and Descent into Limbus. Dates about 1450. *Whitewashed over.*

[The subject of the Descent from the Cross has again been uncovered.]

S. wall of N. transept; the Last Judgment. 15th cent. *Destroyed.* Soffit of arches, N. side of nave; traces of figures under trefoil-headed canopies and foliated patterns. End of 12th cent.

On the splays of the clerestory windows; figure of Saints and Apostles. All destroyed or whitewashed over. Drawings existing.

Archæol. Journ., xi. 66. *Murray's Handbook of Yorkshire. Associated Architect. Societies' Repts.,* ii. 279.

On W. wall of nave; St. George or St. Michael. *Destroyed.*

S. transept; painting on the splay of a lancet window.

PICKHILL CHURCH, YORKSHIRE.

The Day of Judgment. *Builder,* 1876, p. 962.

St. George and the Dragon, &c.

PICKHILL CHURCH, YORKSHIRE—*cont.*
> W. Hylton Longstaffe, *Richmondshire, Its Ancient Lords and Edifices*, p. 48.

PIDDLETOWN CHURCH, DORSETSHIRE.
> S. aisle; on monument of a knight and lady. Circ. 1480. Traces of much painting and gilding. *Hutchins' Hist. of Dorset*, 3rd ed., ii. 622.

PILTON CHURCH, SOMERSETSHIRE.
> Upper part of screen found to be painted; now varnished over. E. bay of nave roof; repainted.

PINCHBECK CHURCH, LINCOLNSHIRE.
> Armorial bearings formerly emblazoned on shields borne by angels, in roof of nave. "Covered over and redone." *Lincolnshire Churches*, 1843, *Pinchbeck*, p. 6.

PINHOE CHURCH, DEVONSHIRE.
> Traces of colour on rood screen.

PINVIN CHURCH, WORCESTERSHIRE.
> S. side of nave; five coats of paintings, one over the other, the two lowermost representing St. Edburga with an angel, or, the Annunciation and Salutation, and the Adoration of the Magi, the Crucifixion, with the Virgin and St. John, Resurrection, and Ascension.
> Sketches in the Art Library, South Kensington Museum.
> *Notes and Queries*, 3rd series, x. 482.
> E. wall of nave, S. of chancel arch; the Trinity, and angels adoring.
> Over chancel arch; the Day of Judgment.
> The Virgin and Child, and St. Roche.
> *Ashby De La Zouch Anastatic Drawing Soc.*, 1856, p. 7, pls. xlv., xlvi., and 1860, p. 12, pl. lxvii.

PIRFORD CHURCH, SURREY.
> Chancel N. and S. wall, and S. side of W. wall; consecration cross. *Archæologia*, xlvii. 165.
> S. wall of nave; Jezebel at her toilet, and Jezebel looking out at the window (?), or part of the legend of St. Nicholas.
> N. wall of nave; a scroll with figures above it, and beneath it two angels welcoming a soul to Paradise. Early 12th cent. Part of the legend of St. Nicholas.
> Painting on the roof. *Surrey Archæol.*, vii. 57–59. *Brayley's Hist. of Surrey*, 2nd ed., i. 337.

PITTINGTON CHURCH, DURHAM.

On the jambs of the Norman clerestory; scenes in the life of St. Cuthbert, viz., his consecration as Bishop, and his vision at Aelflæde's table. *Perry and Henman, Illustration of the Mediæval Antiq. of the County of Durham,* p. 6, and pls. i. 46.

PLUMPTON CHURCH, SUSSEX.

E. wall of nave : E. face, the Flight into Egypt; W. face, the Doom, and the Company of the Archangels.

On the soffit of the chancel arch; the "Agnus Dei." Time of Richard II.

Sussex Archæol., xx. 198. *Whitewashed over.*

PLUMSTEAD, GREAT, CHURCH, NORFOLK.

Rood screen; detached figures of St. Egidius St. Dunstan, St. Benedict, and St. Martin. *Hart, Antiq. of Norfolk,* p. 66.

PLUSCARDINE PRIORY CHAPEL, MORAYSHIRE, SCOTLAND.

Lady Chapel; decorative painting.

On N. side of chancel arch, an angel, pattern of stars, clouds, &c.

Black's Guide to Scotland.

There were also formerly to be seen :—

On the Sanctuary arch; St. John writing the Apocalypse.

On the sacristy walls; Our Lord, the Virgin and St. John, also the Evangelists, Apostles, and various allegorical figures.

Cordiner, Remarkable Ruins, &c. of N. Britain, vol. i.

PLYMSTOCK CHURCH, DEVONSHIRE.

Upper part of font cover; remains of gilding. 15th cent. *Illustrations of Baptismal Fonts, Van Voorst,* 1844.

Screen; painted panels. *Murray's Handbook of Devonshire, Introduction.*

PLYMTREE CHURCH, DEVONSHIRE.

Rood screen; figures of saints and martyrs depicted on the panels. Date 15th cent. *Exeter Diocesan Architect. Soc.,* 2nd series, ii. 96. *Ecclesiologist,* xxviii. (xxv. new series), p. 308. *Builder,* 1865, p. 212. *Polwhele, Hist. of Devon,* iii. 264. *Worth, Tourist's Guide to N. Devon,* p. 82.

PLYMTREE CHURCH, DEVONSHIRE—*cont.*

On chancel screen; SS. Paul. Thomas, James the Greater, John the Baptist, Our Saviour, John, the Annunciation, Visitation, Adoration of the Magi,* ? Bishop Fox, SS. Clara or Catherine, Roche, an angel, Margaret, John the Baptist, Lucia, and ? Odilo.

S. aisle screen; St. Petronilla, a Bishop, SS. Cyr, Dorothy, Michael and Satan, Sidwell, Sebastian, ? Etheldreda or Bridget, Romuald, Agnes, Edward the Confessor, and Catherine. *T. Mozley, " Henry VII., Prince Arthur, and Cardinal Morton,"* pp. 39 and 44 folio, and 147, 165, quarto ed.

*The Magi are portraits of Henry VII., Prince Arthur, and Cardinal Morton.

PODYMORE MILTON CHURCH, SOMERSETSHIRE.

N. wall of nave; the three Magi, and Christ before Pilate.

E. wall of nave; decorative pattern.

POLESWORTH CHURCH, WARWICKSHIRE.

Effigy of an Abbess, retains much painting and gilding.

POOL, SOUTH, CHURCH, DEVONSHIRE.

At the back of the Easter Sepulchre; remains of colour on a " bas-relief " of the Resurrection.

Traces of gilding and red colour on the effigy of a priest. Date late 15th cent.

Exeter Diocesan Architect. Soc., 2nd series, xi. 51, 52.

Coloured effigy of a lady. *W. H. H. Rogers, The Ancient Sepulchral Effigies, &c. in Devon,* pp. 17, 18.

PORINGLAND CHURCH, NORFOLK.

Rood screen; with figures on the panels, of the Apostles, the Fall of Man, and Expulsion from Paradise, Moses, St. Peter, David, Isaiah, Daniel, Haggai, figure with text from Judges xx. i., Malachi, Zechariah, Jeremiah, and other prophets, kings, and confessors. Date circ. 1473. *Blomefield, Hist. of Norfolk,* ed. 1806, v. 440. *Chambers, Hist. of Norfolk,* ii. 757.

PORTBURY CHURCH, SOMERSETSHIRE.

Parts of figures, &c. discovered on the walls in 1871, not now existing.

PORTISHAM CHURCH, DORSETSHIRE.

N. wall, W. end of nave; St. Christopher (twice), St. Michael weighing Souls, a king, and a portion of another subject. Dates, circ. 1460 and 1500. *Whitewashed over.*

PORTLEMOUTH CHURCH, DEVONSHIRE.

Painted and gilt screen, with the Coronation of the Virgin, and the choir of angels, SS. Cornelius, (?) Leonard, (?) Machutus, Bruno, Christina, Catherine of Siena or Bridget, the Doctors of the Church, &c. in the panels. Date about 1500.

PORTSLADE CHURCH, SUSSEX.

S. wall of nave; the Day of Judgment. 15th cent. Painted over an earlier decorative painting.

On S. wall of S. aisle; the Adoration of the Magi.

Remains of two courses of painting on N. wall of nave. *Sussex Archæol.*, i. 161. *M. A. Lower, History of Sussex*, ii. 104. *Gent. Mag.*, 1848, xxix., new series, 291. *Archæologia*, xxxvi. 385.

All destroyed.

POSTWICK CHURCH, NORFOLK.

Beams of chancel roof; painted. *Illustrations of Norfolk Topography*, p. 147.

POTTER HEIGHAM. *See* HEIGHAM, POTTER.

POTTERNE CHURCH, WILTSHIRE.

E. end of chancel; painted cross.

Masonry and floral patterns of the 13th and 15th cents. found on the walls and stringcourse and *renewed*. *Wilts. Archæol. and Nat. Hist. Soc. Mag.*, xvi. 278.

Oak pulpit; traces of original colour. 15th cent. *E. Kite, Hist. Notes on the Places of Interest to be visited by the British Archæol. Assoc. in* 1880, p. 24.

POUGHLEY PRIORY, CHADDLEWORTH, BERKSHIRE.

Coloured effigy of a priest, circa 1500, and other fragments, with remains of colouring, dug up on the site of the chapel. *Newbury District Field Club*, 1872–1875, p. 58.

POUNDSTOCK CHURCH, CORNWALL.

Portion of screen, with painted figures. *Parochial History of Cornwall*, iv. 89.

POYNTINGTON CHURCH, SOMERSETSHIRE.

On E. face of a pier between nave and aisle; the Virgin.

On another pier; the Virgin and Child, St. Christopher and two other Saints.

Remains of paintings on the other piers, with inscriptions; (?) the names of the saints on the capitals. *Somerset. Archæol. and Nat. Hist. Soc. Proceedings*, xvi. pt. ii. 70.

PRESTON, KENT, ST. CATHERINE'S CHURCH.

N. side of nave; running floral ornament. 13th cent. Tracing in Art Library, South Kensington Museum.

Wall by W. door; decorative painting. Colouring on the back of the sedilia. *Antiquary*, 1873, iii. 113.

PRESTON CHURCH, RUTLANDSHIRE.

N. side of nave; traces of decorative colour on two late Norman arches.

PRESTON CHURCH, SUFFOLK.

Over chancel arch; St. George and the Dragon (twice) and St. Christopher. Martyrdom of St. Edmund.

PRESTON CHURCH, BRIGHTON, SUSSEX.

E. wall of nave and both sides of arch opening to the chancel; Murder of St. Thomas à Becket, Incredulity of St. Thomas, *Noli me Tangere*, St. Katherine, St. Margaret, bishop, and a female figure under a canopy, and St. Michael weighing Souls. 13th cent. *Archæologia*, xxiii. 311, and *Builder*, 1864, p. 725. *Black's Guide to Sussex*. M. A. Lower, *History of Sussex*, ii. 110. *Nibbs' Churches of Sussex*, No. 10. *Brighton in the Olden Time*, p. 381.

N. wall of nave; St. Sebastian. *Destroyed*.

J. M. Neale, *Hierologus*, p. 309.

N. wall of nave; the Last Supper, the Nativity, and three Magi. All the paintings have been restored.

PRESTON BISSETT CHURCH, BUCKINGHAMSHIRE.

N. wall; portion of a large subject.

On N. and S. walls of aisles and chancel; remains of two series of paintings, the earlier 14th cent., discovered and *destroyed*.

PRESTON IN HOLDERNESS CHURCH, YORKSHIRE.

Found under the floor of the nave, fragments of an Easter Sepulchre, Reredos, &c., with painted and gilt sculptures of The Adoration of the Magi, The Resurrection (twice), The Ascension, The Coronation of the Virgin, The Sacraments of Baptism, Confession, and the Holy Eucharist, and figures of SS. Anthony and Agatha or Agnes. Date circ. 1350. *The Antiquary*, 1881, iv. 81.

PRITTLEWELL CHURCH, ESSEX.

Traces of mural painting have been found. *Essex Archæol.*, 1, new series, 162.

PUCKINGTON·CHURCH, SOMERSETSHIRE.
    On the sedilia; paintings of Elias and other subjects, probably the Transfiguration.
    Blackburne, Decorative Painting, p. 73. Gent. Mag., lvii. 755. Archæologia, x. 313.

PUDDIMORE MILTON, *see* PODYMORE MILTON.

PULHAM CHURCH, DORSETSHIRE.
    N. wall of chancel; painted niche.
    Within a hagioscope, on either side of the chancel arch; painted and gilded screen work.
    N. aisle roof; richly coloured. Late 15th cent.
    Hutchins' Hist. of Dorset, 3rd ed., iii. 738.

PULHAM ST. MARY MAGDALENE CHURCH, NORFOLK.
    E. bay of nave; painted with angels, sacred Monograms, and other devices. Repainted during the restoration of the church. *Builder*, 1873, p. 1036.

PULHAM ST. MARY THE VIRGIN CHURCH, NORFOLK.
    Screen, painted and gilt mouldings. On the panels; SS. Jude, Simon, James Major, Andrew, John, James Minor, and other figures defaced or painted over.

PUTNEY CHURCH, SURREY.
    Masonry patterns on N. chancel wall and on the semipier at the E. end of the S. aisle. Late 15th cent. *Destroyed. Gent. Mag.*, 1836, v. new series, 378.

PUTTENHAM CHURCH, HERTFORDSHIRE.
    E. bay of nave roof; painted and gilt shield. Late 15th cent.

PYRFORD. *See* PIRFORD.

PYTCHLEY CHURCH, NORTHAMPTONSHIRE.
    W. arch, N. side of nave; remains of scroll ornament on the inner course, and of lozenge pattern on the soffit. Late 12th cent. *Archæol. Journ.*, xxxviii. 92.
    Painting on a beam, and within the splay of a window, in the S. aisle, and on the nave roof. 15th cent.
    Remains of colour visible through the whitewash in various parts of the church.

QUAINTON CHURCH, BUCKINGHAMSHIRE.

On lower part of rood screen; paintings of the Evangelists or Apostles. *Lipscomb, Hist. and Antiq. of Bucks,* i. 425. *Murray's Handbook of Bucks. Sheahan, Hist. and Topog. of the County of Buckingham,* p. 421.

QUAT CHURCH, SHROPSHIRE.

The Seven Acts of Mercy, and the Day of Judgment. On vellum nailed to a board, the Resurrection. Found in 1763. *C. Hulbert, The Hist. and Description of the County of Salop,* p. 338.

QUINTON CHURCH, GLOUCESTERSHIRE.

On N. nave arcade; remains of early colouring. *Ecclesiologist,* xxvi. (xxiii. new series), p. 317.

QUY CHURCH, CAMBRIDGESHIRE.

Walls of nave, and within a recess in the chancel wall; remains of decorative colour.
Building News, 1880, vol. xxxix., p. 659. *Builder,* 1880, vol. xxxix., p. 681.

RAINHAM CHURCH, ESSEX.

Colouring on the nave piers. *Rev. W. Palin, More about Stifford,* p. 133.

RAINHAM CHURCH, KENT.

Over the rood loft, the panels of the roof painted with the " Rose en soleil," the badge of Edward IV. *Glynne, Churches of Kent,* p. 173.
Painted chest. 14th cent.

RAINHAM, SOUTH, CHURCH, NORFOLK.

Screen; panel paintings of Saints. Removed. Portions in private possession. *Builder,* 1847, p. 535. *Hart, Antiq. of Norfolk,* p. 66.

RAMPTON CHURCH, CAMBRIDGESHIRE.

Coloured effigy of a de L'Isle. Circ. 1300. *Stothard's Monumental Effigies,* p. 23.

RANDWORTH CHURCH, NORFOLK.

S. wall; St. Christopher. *Destroyed.*

Rood screen.

N. retable; SS. Etheldreda (or Withburgha), John the Baptist (twice), and Barbara, all with archangels above.

N. wing; a Bishop, ? St. Felix, St. George and the Dragon, and St. Stephen.

On screen; St. Paul and the Apostles, omitting St. Matthias.

S. wing; an Archbishop, probably St. Thomas à Becket, St. Lawrence, and St. Michael and Satan.

S. retable; St. Salome with SS. James and John, the Virgin and Child, St. Mary, the mother, of and with, SS. James, Joses, Simon and Judas, and St. Margaret, all with archangels above. 15th cent.

Colling, Gothic Ornaments, ii. pls. 98 and 101–103. *Illustrations of Norfolk Topography,* pp. xi. and 148. *East Anglian Notes and Queries,* iii. 303. *Norfolk Archæol.,* iii. 19.

Described by Rev. J. Gunn, with lithographs of the saints by C. Winter. *Illustrations of Norfolk Topography,* pp. xiv. and 148.

Painted Lettern; Eagle of St. John and texts.

Two consecration crosses.

RAUCEBY CHURCH, LINCOLNSHIRE.

N. wall of aisle; St. Matthew and Satan. Probably contemporary with the aisle. Date about 1320. *Archæol. Journ.,* xi. 68, 69, and *Associated Architect. Societies' Repts.,* vii. 24. Or St. Anthony and a panther, with powdering of red stars. *Society of Antiquaries' Proceedings,* iii. 54. *Trollope: Sleaford, Flaxwell, Aswardhurn,* p. 282.

RAUNDS CHURCH, NORTHAMPTONSHIRE.

N. wall of nave; the Purging of the Seven Deadly Sins, St. Christopher, and " Les Trois Morts and les Trois Vifs." 15th cent.

Over tower arch, E. side, painted clock-face, with numerals of the 24 hours, supported by angels and kneeling figures of the donors on either side. Date 15th cent.

Over the chancel arch; a cross and an angel supporting the instruments of the Passion.

N. aisle; story of St. Catherine. Early 15th and 16th cents.

Over N. door; St. George and the Dragon.

Archæol. Journ., xxxiv. 219.

RAVENSTHORPE CHURCH, NORTHAMPTONSHIRE.
Rood screen. *Baker's Hist. and Antiq. of Northamptonshire*, p. 218.

RAVENSTON CHURCH, BUCKINGHAMSHIRE.
St. Christopher.

RAYNHAM MARTIN. *See* RAINHAM, SOUTH.

READING, BERKSHIRE, ST. LAURENCE'S CHURCH.
E. wall of chancel; five series of paintings, one beneath the other : first, Ten Commandments, &c.; second, floriated texts of Scripture; third, the Annunciation ; fourth, on the splays of the window, floral ornament and angels, mouldings, &c.; fifth, wall pattern of six-leaved flowers.
Above the window ; the Transfiguration.
St. John's chapel, E. wall ; flowing pattern, and between the arches of the window, an animal.
Civil Engineer and Architect's Journal, 1851, p. 195.
Hist. and Antiq. of Reading, 1835, p. 139.

READING, BERKSHIRE, ST. MARY'S CHURCH.
N. chapel; diaper of flowers. *Civil Engineer and Architect's Journal*, 1851, p. 197.
Back of sedilia. *English Churchman*, July 13th, 1843.

READING. BERKSHIRE, CHURCH OF THE FRANCISCAN MONASTERY.
Walls of nave; remains of paintings. *British Archæol. Assoc. Journ.*, xvi. 193.

RECULVER, OLD CHURCH, KENT.
Figures of the Apostles and a lion, richly gilt, discovered during the demolition of the church in 1811. *W. Miller, Jottings of Kent*, p. 144.
N. wall of chancel; painted canopy.
Portions of the painted effigy formerly within the recess are now in Hilborough Churchyard.
Archæol. Cantiana, xii. 260.

REDENHALL CHURCH, NORFOLK.
Rood screen ; on the panels, the twelve Apostles.
E. bay of N. aisle; painted roof with spread eagles on the panels. 15th cent.
Blomefield, Hist. of Norfolk, ed. 1806, v. 364.

REEPHAM CHURCH, NORFOLK.

Remains of colouring on the weepers on the monument of Sir Roger de Kerdiston. Circa 1337. *Stothard's Monumental Effigies*, p. 54, pl. 64. *Chambers, Hist. of Norfolk*, i. 229.

REIGATE CHURCH, SURREY.

E. wall of chancel; reredos and niches richly coloured and gilt. 15th cent. Discovered in 1845. *Gent. Mag.*, 1846, xxvi., new series, 490. *British Archæol. Assoc. Journ.*, i. 365. *Ecclesiologist*, v. 162. *Proceedings of the British Archæol. Association*, Winchester vol., p. 456. *R. F. D. Palgrave, Handbook to Reigate*, p. 61.

REPPS, NORTH, CHURCH, NORFOLK.

On exterior walls; twelve dedication crosses painted on stucco. *Destroyed.*

REPTON CHURCH, DERBYSHIRE.

Remains of painting. *Bentley's Miscellany*, October, 1845.

REWE CHURCH, DEVONSHIRE.

Rood screen.

RHOS CHAPEL, CARNARVONSHIRE.

Walls found to be covered with paintings of sacred subjects.

RHUABON. *See* RUABON.

RIBBESFORD CHURCH, WORCESTERSHIRE.

E. end of S. aisle; painted niche. *Church Times*, October 17th, 1868, p. 383.

RICHMOND, YORKSHIRE, ST. MARY'S CHURCH.

E. bay of chancel roof; painted armorial shields and other devices. *C. Clarkson, Hist. and Antiq. of Richmond, Yorks.*, p. 142.

RICHMOND, OLD. *See* BARFORTH.

RIDLINGTON CHURCH, RUTLANDSHIRE.

St. Christopher. *Destroyed.*

RINGLAND CHURCH, NORFOLK.

Rood screen; the Apostles, with labels containing parts of the Creed. *Hart, Antiq. of Norfolk*, p. 66.

RINGSFIELD CHURCH, SUFFOLK.

Remains of rood screen, with figures on the panels.

RINGSHALL CHURCH, SUFFOLK.

Over S. door of nave; (?) the Seven Acts of Mercy. *East Anglian Notes and Queries*, i. 77, 110.

RINGSTEAD CHURCH, NORTHAMPTONSHIRE.

N. of chancel, chantry wall; female Saint. Late 15th cent. *Churches of the Archdeaconry of Northampton*, p. 71. *Murray's Handbook of Northants*, p. 33.

Painting on S. wall of nave. *Leicester Architect. and Archæol. Soc. Trans.*, iii. 278.

RIPON MINSTER, YORKSHIRE.

S, transept, round the head of a Transition Norman window; " Christ coming to Judgment."

On N. wall of S. transept aisle; " The Offerings of the Wise Men."

Murray's Handbook of Yorkshire.

RISBOROUGH, MONK'S, CHURCH, BUCKINGHAMSHIRE.

Rood screen; panel paintings of the Prophets. *Parker, Eccles. and Architect. Topog. of England, Bucks.*, No. 197. *Sheahan, Hist. and Topog. of the County of Buckingham*, p. 186. Circ. 1500.

E. beam of nave over rood-loft. Circ. 1500.

RISBY CHURCH, SUFFOLK.

Screen, highly painted and gilt. *Gage, Hist. of Suffolk, Thingoe Hundred*, p. 80.

RISING, CASTLE, CHURCH, NORFOLK.

Sanctuary arch; various decoration. *Associated Architect. Societies' Repts.*, iii. 361.

On the soffit of the arch opening from the tower to the nave; a defaced inscription in large letters and a pattern of stars.

At the back of small arch on N. side of W. tower arch; the Crucifixion. 13th cent.

RISSINGTON, GREAT, CHURCH, GLOUCESTERSHIRE.

N.E. corner of N. transept; traces of colour on a niche and piscina and round a window.

ROBERTSBRIDGE ABBEY, SUSSEX.

Mutilated effigy of Sir Edward Dalingruge, with remains of colour and gilding. Circ. 1400. Now in the Lewes Musuem. *Sussex Archæol.*, xii. 223.

ROCHE ABBEY CHURCH, YORKSHIRE.

N. transeptal chapels; masonry patterns and decorative colouring. *R. White, Photographic Handbook of the Antiquities of Worksop and its Neighbourhood.*

On N. of Choir; rich tabernacle work, coloured red. *Eddison, Hist. of Worksop and Neighbourhood,* p. 236.

ROCHESTER CATHEDRAL, KENT.

The whole of the Norman work in the nave has been coloured.

Blackburne, Decorative Painting, p. 40. *British Archæol. Assoc. Journ.,* x. 38.

The colour is only visible now on the E. bay, triforium story, on each side.

E. wall of S. transept, on the soffit of the central arch; remains of colouring, (?) foliage, and medallions.

On N. side of arch; figures under canopies.

On S. side; a kneeling female figure.

S.E. pier of nave; diaper pattern. 15th cent. *Blackburne, Decorative Painting,* p. 77.

Ornamental painting on walls of Choir, viz., a pattern of lions and fleur-de-lis. Restored. Time of Edward III. *Archæol. Cantiana,* x. 70.

Supporting the back row of desks in the Choir are a series of trefoil-headed arches with the original early 13th cent. colouring.

Painting on screen, partly 13th cent., repainted in the renaissance style. *Sir G. G. Scott, Personal and Professional Recollections,* p. 350.

On N.E. pier of Choir; the Wheel of Fortune. 13th cent. *British Archæol. Assoc. Journ.,* ii. 143. *Proceedings of British Archæol. Assoc., Gloucester vol.,* p. 179.

S. Choir aisle, on a buttress strip; the Virgin and Child. *Destroyed. Miller, Jottings of Kent,* p. 38. *Phippen, Sketches of Rochester,* p. 115.

N. wall of N. Choir transept; St. William's Chapel, at the back of the monument of St. William, scroll pattern. 13th cent. *Archæologia,* xxxi. 512. *Murray's Handbook of Kent.*

N. side of presbytery; effigy of Bishop John de Sheppey richly coloured and gilt. Date circ. 1360. Found within the wall in 1825. Also coloured statuettes of the Virgin and Child, Moses, &c., formerly on the canopy of the monument.

Archæologia, xxv. 122, pls. vii., viii. *Glynne, Churches of Kent,* p. 318.

ROCHESTER CATHEDRAL, KENT—*cont.*

S. side of presbytery; remains of gilding and painted shields on the sedilia.

S. Choir transept; a portion of the original painting from the Choir screen, within a frame, showing two series of 13th and 14th cents. respectively.

Crypt, N.E. bay, between the groining ribs; figures within medallions, and shields; on other portions of the vault and groining, scroll and foliated patterns. 13th cent.

Numerous fragments, statuettes, &c., with rich colour and gilding, preserved in the crypt.

ROCHESTER, KENT, ST. BARTHOLOMEW'S CHAPEL.

S. wall of nave, E. end; within a recess, masonry pattern. 12th cent. *Antiquary,* 1873, iv. 146.

ROCHESTER, KENT.

Remains of colouring found on the walls of the Lepers' Hospital, erected by Gundulph in the 12th cent. *Builder,* 1873, p. 790.

ROCHESTER, KENT.

On wall of a room at the Crown Inn, decorative painting. 16th cent. *Destroyed.*

ROGATE CHURCH, SUSSEX.

A large figure, (?) St. Christopher, and other painting. *Destroyed.*

ROLLWRIGHT, GREAT, CHURCH, OXFORDSHIRE.

Rood screen; richly painted and gilt. Upper part now placed above the chancel arch, E. side. 15th cent.

ROMFORD CHURCH, ESSEX.

Aisle wall; story of St. Edward the Confessor. *Destroyed.*

ROMSEY, HAMPSHIRE, ABBEY CHURCH.

Ceiling; emblazoned shields. *Civil Engineer and Architect's Journal,* 1851, p. 196.

At the E. end, on one of the piers of the arches opening into the Lady Chapel; various subjects within medallions, with painting representing the folds of a curtain. Late 12th cent.

On the pier of the W. arch S. side of chancel; decorative colouring. Late 12th cent.

Panel of screen, with painting of a monk kneeling and the inscription "Jhu. fili Dei miserere mihi." 15th cent.

ROMSEY, HAMPSHIRE, ABBEY CHURCH—*cont.*

Part of a reredos discovered behind the high altar, with paintings of the four Doctors of the Church, SS. Francis, Sebastian, (?) Scholastica, Roche, and Anthony on the panels. Below is the Resurrection. Date about 1500.

There were formerly two tiers of paintings above these, with the Deity seated in the upper, and the choir of angels in the lower.

Gent. Mag., xcix., pt. ii., p. 584. *C. Spence, An Essay descriptive of the Abbey Church of Romsey,* p. 69, *and, The Abbey Church of Romsey,* p. 55.

ROPSLEY CHURCH, LINCOLNSHIRE.

Portion of painted rood screen. *Associated Architect. Societies' Repts.,* xiii. 3.

ROTHERFIELD CHURCH, SUSSEX.

Near the pulpit; Martyrdom of St. Laurence. *Murray's Handbook of Sussex.* M. A. Lower, *History of Sussex,* ii. 128.

ROTHERFIELD PEPPARD CHURCH, OXFORDSHIRE.

E. end of chancel, on two walled-up Norman windows; remains of 13th cent. decoration. *Builder,* 1875, p. 265.

ROTHERHAM CHURCH, YORKSHIRE.

At the end of the S. chancel aisle was the Lady Chapel, the roof of which was richly coloured, and retains many striking and unusual devices, all relating to the Blessed Virgin. *Murray's Handbook of Yorkshire.*

On walls of Lady Chapel; remains of painting.

Over chancel arch; Our Lord surrounded by the Apostles and other Saints in act of adoration.

J. Guest, *Historic Notices of Rotherham,* p. 300.

ROTHERSTHORPE CHURCH, NORTHAMPTONSHIRE.

E. end of S. aisle; coloured decoration on two beams of the roof. Late 15th cent.

ROTHWELL CHURCH, NORTHAMPTONSHIRE.

Arch on S. side of chancel; decorative painting. Date about 1200. *Associated Architect. Societies' Repts.,* ix. 253. *Gent. Mag.,* 1849, xxxi., new series, 196.

At E. end of crypt under the S. aisle; (?) the Resurrection. About 1300. *Archæol. Journ.,* xxxvi. 58. *Leicester Architect. and Archæol. Soc. Trans.,* iii. 178.

N. of chancel, E. end of Lady Chapel; walls have been painted in arabesque patterns. *Cypher, Hist. of the Hundred of Rowell,* p. 26.

ROTTINGDEAN CHURCH, SUSSEX.

Stone, with remains of colouring, found in 1855. *Sussex Archæol.*, ix. 68.

ROUGHAM CHURCH, SUFFOLK.

Over chancel arch; the Day of Judgment. *Suffolk Archæol.*, ii. 215. *Archæologia*, xxxvi. 387.

ROWNER CHURCH, HAMPSHIRE.

Within the splay of the E. window; (?) the Ascension.

N. wall of chancel; (?) part of a subject representing the Offerings of the Magi.

On walls of chancel; traces of diaper patterns.

Over chancel arch; letters, &c. Date, time of Edward III. *Destroyed.* Drawings remain in the possession of M. Snape, Esq., *Forton.*

ROWLSTONE CHURCH, HEREFORDSHIRE.

A " figure with a nimbus, very fine." *Havergal, Fasti Herefordenses*, p. 157.

ROXTON CHURCH, BEDFORDSHIRE.

Remains of the rood screen, painted and gilt, with figures depicted on the panels, viz., on N., a Saint, a Bishop, ? St. Erasmus, Lazarus, SS. Christopher, Sebastian, and Dorothy. On S., the Doctors of the Church, ? St. Helena, and another Saint. *Parker, Eccles. and Architect. Topog. of England, Bedford*, No. 95.

ROYSTON CHURCH, HERTFORDSHIRE.

N. side of chancel, within the splay of a window; masonry patterns. 13th cent.

ROYSTONE CHURCH, YORKSHIRE.

Over the chancel arch; large figures of Moses, Aaron, and Joshua. Traces of paintings, texts, &c. on all the walls. *Hatton and Fox, Churches of Yorkshire*, i. 97, 98.

RUABON CHURCH, DENBIGHSHIRE.

S. wall of nave; apparently the Seven Acts of Mercy. *Society of Antiquaries' Proceedings*, 2nd series, iv. 517. *Lloyd-Williams and Underwood, Churches of Denbighshire*, plate 40. *Thomas, Hist. of the Diocese of St. Asaph*, p. 836.

RUCKINGE CHURCH, KENT.

Between S. aisle and chantry; perpendicular screen work, bearing traces of colour. *Archæol. Cantiana*, viii. 311, xiii. 228.

RUDHAM, NORFOLK, ST. PETER'S CHURCH.

Rood screen; saints of the Old Testament.

RUISHTON CHURCH, SOMERSETSHIRE.

On N. wall of chancel; fragment of foliated pattern. About 1500.

RUISLIP CHURCH, MIDDLESEX.

On the N. side of the E. window, on the N. wall of the chancel, and within the splays of 2 windows, N. side of chancel; decorative painting. 15th cent.

Between two windows on N. of chancel; a large subject, almost entirely concealed by a 17th cent. tablet, the "Assumption of the Virgin." 15th cent.

Above the nave arcade, on both sides; a series of paintings, probably illustrating the life of St. Martin, also some decorative painting.

At the E. end of the N. aisle, over the entrance to the rood-loft; St. Michael weighing Souls, and St. Laurence. Date 15th cent.

A large subject over the N. door and on the wall of the S. aisle.

RUSCOMBE, BERKSHIRE, CHURCH OF SS. PETER AND PAUL.

Figures of SS. Matthew (?), Stephen, Peter, and Paul, on jambs of early lancet E. window.

Drawing and tracings in Art Library, South Kensington Museum.

Painted screen.

RUSHALL CHURCH, NORFOLK.

On S. wall; two Bishops consecrating a third, with female figure standing by, (?) a scene in the life of St. Nicholas. Date 13th cent.

Norfolk Archæol., vi. 381, and second report, p. ii.

RUSHDEN CHURCH, NORTHAMPTONSHIRE.

Remains of colour on capitals of columns of chancel arch and in the nave, also on a reredos E. end of N. Choir aisle. 14th and 15th cents.

Numerous paintings were discovered during the late restoration, and were *destroyed.*

RUSHMERE, SUFFOLK, ST. MICHAEL'S CHURCH.

A painting of St. Christopher was discovered over the N. door and re-covered with whitewash.

RUSHTON HALL, NORTHAMPTONSHIRE.

Walled up in one of the bedrooms was found a representation in plaster of the Crucifixion retaining its ancient
colouring. Date 1579. *Leicester Architect. and Archæol.
Soc. Trans.*, iii. 252.

RUSTON, EAST, CHURCH, NORFOLK.

Rood screen; the four Evangelists and the four Fathers
of the Church. 15th cent. *East Anglian Notes and
Queries*, iii. 315. *Norfolk Archæol.*, iii. 19. *The Ecclesiologist's Guide to the Deaneries of Brisley, &c.*, pp. 83, 95.

RUTHIN CHURCH, DENBIGHSHIRE.

Mural decorations. Time of Henry VII. *Archæologia
Cambrensis*, 3rd series, v. 143.

RYCOTE CHAPEL, OXFORDSHIRE.

Roof painted to represent the sky. Late 15th cent.
Weare, Church of Gt. Haseley, Oxon., 2nd ed., p. 133.

RYE CHURCH, SUSSEX.

Screen between S. transept and S. chancel aisle;
original colouring on the panels. 15th cent.

SAFFRON WALDEN CHURCH, ESSEX.

Roofs of nave and aisles. Circ. 1500. *Cromwell, Excursions through Essex*, ii. 125. *Wright, Hist. of Essex*,
ii. 113.

ST. ALBANS CATHEDRAL, HERTFORDSHIRE.

On inner arches of N.W. and S.W. porches; remains
of colour.

On a pillar S. side of nave; the Adoration of the
Magi, twice. 15th cent.

N. side of nave :—

On W. faces of two W. Norman piers; the Crucifixion
with the Virgin and St. John; and below, the Virgin and
Child.

On W. face of third Norman pier; the Crucifixion
with the Virgin and St. John; below, the Annunciation.

On W. face of fourth Norman pier; the Crucifixion;
below, the Annunciation. Early to late 13th cent.

215

ST. ALBANS CATHEDRAL, HERTFORDSHIRE—*cont.*

On W. face of fifth Norman pier; the Crucifixion with the Virgin and St. John above, and the Coronation of the Virgin below. Late 12th or early 13th cent.

On W. face of sixth Norman pier; "Christ in Glory."

On S. faces of the four W. Norman piers; SS. Christopher, Thomas à Becket, Citha, and St. Edward and the Pilgrim, all with inscriptions below. Late 14th cent.

Builder, 1864, p. 725. *The Antiquary*, 1880, ii. 245.

Nave roof; remains of colouring on braces, &c. 15th cent.

Remains of colour and gilding on screen between nave and Choir. About 1360.

Round and within the Norman arches on N. side of nave, on N. and S. sides of the Choir, supporting the tower, on the E. side of the transepts, also on the groining of the Choir and presbytery aisles and within and round the windows of the N. transept, masonry, zigzag, cable, floral, and other Norman decorative patterns. Mostly late 12th century.

Archæol. Journ., xxxiv. 276.

Choir ceiling, on the panels; Angels holding shields of benefactors, surrounded by scrolls on which are sentences from the "Te Deum." Also the sacred Monogram, the Coronation of the Virgin, and shields charged with the instruments of the Passion, and the Trinity banner. Date 1390 or 1440–1460. *Restored. See* frontispiece to *Neale's Abbey Church of St. Alban's. G. G. Scott, An Essay on the Hist. of English Church Architecture*, p. 119.

On a pier, N. side of Choir; the Trinity. 14th cent.

In the Choir, between the clerestory windows; large figures of saints.

On piers in the Choir; remains of blue-letter texts. 16th cent.

In S. Choir aisle, and elsewhere; early English masonry patterns.

Portion of the cresting of the rood screen, richly gilt and coloured. Now in the retrochoir.

Within an arch, E. side of N. transept; pattern of fleur-de-lis and lions. 14th cent.

N. transept, on a buttress strip, E. side of; the Incredulity of St. Thomas, with an inscription below.

Archæol. Journ., ii. 386, and *British Archæol. Assoc. Journ.*, i. 318, and ii. 146.

ST. ALBANS CATHEDRAL, HERTFORDSHIRE —*cont.*

Roof of presbytery and retrochoir; Agnus Dei and the Eagle of St. John in alternate compartments, the groining ribs also painted and gilt. 15th cent.

Neale's Abbey Church of St. Alban's, pls. 33, 35, 36, 38. *Colling, Gothic Ornaments,* i. pl. 54.

S. wall of presbytery; band of scroll and dogtooth ornament. 13th cent. *Archæol. Journ.,* xxxviii. 92.

Remains of colour and gilding on high altar screen. Late 15th cent.

Ceiling of N. presbytery aisle; sacred Monogram. 15th cent.

Within the spandril of the arch opening from the S. transept to the S. presbytery aisle; a seraph holding a scroll. 12th cent.

Archæol. Journ., xxxiv. 276.

E. wall of retrochoir; diaper of roses on a crimson ground.

In N. E. corner; St. William of York, and armorial shield below.

Shrine of St. Alban, with remains of rich colour and gilding.

Back of high altar; lower part of effigy of St. Erasmus, richly painted and gilt.

On splay of great E. window; diaper of roses.

Neale's Abbey Church of St. Alban's, pls. 40 and 41.

Ceiling of antechapel or sanctuary; painted bosses. 15th cent. *Neale's Abbey Church of St. Alban's,* pls. 37, 46.

Shrine of St. Amphibalus; on capitals E. side, traces of colour and gilding.

On N. wall of sanctuary; diaper of roses. *Neale's Abbey Church of St. Alban's,* pl. 42.

On each side of entrance to Lady Chapel; canopied niches, richly gilt.

Within the splays of the Lady Chapel windows; rich arabesque patterns. 15th cent.

Remains of painted roof to Lady Chapel. 15th cent.

Numerous fragments with remains of colour and gilding have been found during the restoration.

J. W. Comyns Carr, The Abbey Church of St. Alban's, frontispiece, pp. 16, 17, 28, &c. *Nicholson, The Abbey of St. Alban,* 6th ed., pp. 48, 60, 62, 70, 71, 76, 77, 78, 100, 102.

See also the *Hertfordshire Standard,* Dec. 28th, 1878, and Jan. 4th, 1879.

St. Albans Cathedral, Hertfordshire—*cont.*

Eastern extremity of S. aisle; remains of decorative colouring on the mullions of two windows opened out in 1845. Date about 1470. *Archæol. Journ.*, iii. 84.

N. side of nave, on the site of St. Andrew's Church; portions of richly coloured sedilia, dug up in 1880. Date late 14th cent.

St. Albans, Hertfordshire, St. Michael's Church.

Over the chancel arch and partly on a panel filling in the head of the arch; the Day of Judgment, with Crucified Saviour in the centre.

On a panel; a king, probably Henry VI. Date about 1450.

Drawings in the Society of Antiquaries' Library.

Drawings and the panel are preserved in the church; the upper part of the painting has been destroyed.

Within the splay of a clerestory window, S. side of nave; figure of a saint, and decorative pattern. 13th cent.

Within a splay of a window, E. end of N. aisle; early decorative ornament.

Nave roof, E. tie beam; pattern of chevrons. 15th cent.

On S. wall of S. chapel; armorial shields and bearings of the Maynard family. Circ. 1556.

Clutterbuck's History of Hertfordshire, i. 103.

St. Albans, Hertfordshire, St. Peter's Church.

S. wall of S. aisle; oak leaf pattern on vaulting shafts. Circ. 1500.

St. Albans, St. Stephens Church. *See* St. Stephens.

St. Anthony in Roseland Church, Cornwall.

On the walls; old paintings, chiefly in black and red. *Parochial History of Cornwall*, i. 38. *Architect*, 1849, p. 489.

St. Asaph Cathedral, Flintshire.

St. Bartholomew's Chapel, Oxfordshire.

"On each side of the W. door is a cross patée in a circle painted in dark fresco, and traces of painting may be found in other parts of the chapel." *Parker's Architectural Guide to the Neighbourhood of Oxford*, p. 396.

St. Bees Church, Cumberland.

N. transept; "some remains of colouring have been discovered." *Whellan, Hist. and Topog. of the Counties of Cumberland and Westmoreland*, p. 428.

St. Budoc Church, Cornwall.

Remains of screen; upper part painted in polychrome, lower part having 27 paintings of saints within niches. *Ecclesiologist*, xii. 436.

St. Buryan Church, Cornwall.

Remains of rood screen, richly painted and gilt. Late 15th cent. *Blight's Churches of West Cornwall*, pp. 5, 128, and, *A week at the Land's End*, p. 158. *Ecclesiologist*, xvi. 396, xx. 376. *Builder*, 1876, p. 847. *Parochial History of Cornwall*, i. 160.

St. Catherine Church, Somersetshire.

Pulpit; repainted and regilt. 15th cent. *Tunstall, Rambles about Bath and its Neighbourhood*, 7th ed., p. 352.

St. Clement's Church, near Truro, Cornwall.

N. wall of nave; paintings discovered and whitewashed over, viz., large painting (?) of St. Christopher.

On E. splay of aisle windows; a female Saint, the Triumphal Entry into Jerusalem, or the Flight into Egypt, and the Crucifixion.

Parochial History of Cornwall, i. 213. *Ecclesiologist*, xii. 79.

Principals of roof, painted. *Journ. Royal Inst., Cornwall*, April, 1866, pp. 44–46.

Drawing of a figure preserved.

St. Columb Major Church, Cornwall.

Remains of painting discovered during restorations. *Ecclesiologist*, ii. 58, iv. 141.

Lower part of rood screen. *Ecclesiologist*, vii. 108. *Archæol. Journ.*, x. 323.

St. Cross. *See* Winchester, St. Cross.

St. David's Cathedral, Pembrokeshire.

On pillar, S. of nave; ? the Virgin within a vesica, accompanied by censing angels; also a crowned figure, ? portrait of King Henry IV.

On corresponding pillars N. and S. of nave; achievements of arms.

On the interior of the rood screen; foliage and scroll work, the Crucifixion with the Virgin and St. John, the emblems of the Evangelists, grotesque figures, &c.

Archæologia Cambrensis, iii. 80. *Ecclesiologist, Guide to St. Davids*, p. 29.

ST. DAVID'S CATHEDRAL, PEMBROKESHIRE—*cont.*
Painted boss from roof of presbytery now in chapter house.
W. B. Jones and E. A. Freeman, Hist. and Antiq. of St. Davids, pp. 127, 128.
Choir roof; "of wood is curiously painted and enriched with the arms of the different benefactors of the Church." *Fenton's Tour in Pembrokeshire*, p. 76.

ST. DONAT'S CHURCH, GLAMORGANSHIRE.
Stradling chapel; panel paintings, commemorating different members of the Stradling family. 16th cent. *Murray's Handbook of South Wales. Archæologia Cambrensis*, 3rd series, xv. 435.

St. ENDELLION CHURCH, CORNWALL.
Distemper paintings discovered on the walls. Subjects uncertain. *Exeter Diocesan Architect. Soc.*, v. 116.

ST. ENODOC CHURCH, CORNWALL.
Remains of painting and gilding on panels of roof. *Murray's Handbook of Cornwall.*

ST. FEOCK CHURCH, CORNWALL.
Texts and colour discovered on the walls at the restoration, and restored. *Ecclesiologist*, iv. 242.

ST. GERMAN'S CHURCH, CORNWALL.
"The venerable history of Our Saviour's life from His " Nativity to His Crucifixion, on 14 tablets, 12 on boards, " and two on canvas." (?) *Destroyed. Whitaker, Ancient Cathedrals of Cornwall*, ii. 294.

ST. GULVAL CHURCH, CORNWALL.
S. side of nave ; on the moulding of the third arch are traces of ancient painting. *Blight's Churches of West Cornwall*, p. 81.

ST. JUST IN PENWITH CHURCH, CORNWALL.
N. wall of N. aisle ; St. George and the Dragon, and a large figure surrounded by quaint devices. *Blight's Churches of West Cornwall*, p. 103. *Murray's Handbook of Cornwall. Parochial History of Cornwall*, ii. 291. *Journ. Royal Inst., Cornwall*, October, 1865, p. 81.

ST. KENELM'S CHAPEL, SHROPSHIRE.
The legend of King Kenelm. *Destroyed. Noake's Rambles in Worcestershire*, 1st series, p. 199.

St. Lawrence Church, Isle of Thanet, Kent.
At E. end of N. chancel aisle; wooden screen with panels on which may be traced the outlines of three figures of saints. *Archæol. Cantiana*, iii. 371.

St. Levan's Church, Cornwall.
Roof of S. aisle; remains of rich painting and gilding. Lower part of rood screen; traces of painting. 15th cent. *Exeter Diocesan Architect. Soc.*, 2nd series, ii. 217. *Blight's Churches of West Cornwall*, pp. 11, 14, 114 *Archæol. Journ.*, ii. 237.

St. Madron. *See* Madron.

St. Minver Church, Cornwall.
Rood screen; painted and gilt. Removed in 1837. *Maclean, Hist. of the Deanery of Trigg Minor*, iii. 23.

St. Minver, Cornwall. St. Enodoc's Chapel.
Rood screen; repainted and gilt. *Maclean, Hist. of the Deanery of Trigg Minor*, iii. 34.

St. Neots Church, Huntingdonshire.
Painting on the E. bay of the nave roof. Restored. 15th cent.

St. Sennen. *See* Sennen.

St. Stephen's Church, Hertfordshire.
Round two arches on S. side of the nave; faint traces of decorative ornament in vermilion.
Red masonry patterns discovered on the walls of the S. aisle.

St. Teath Church, Cornwall.
Within the E. window of S. aisle; painted effigy of a civilian. *Maclean, Hist. of the Deanery of Trigg Minor*, iii. 109.

St. Thomas by Launceston Church, Cornwall.
Traces of elaborate painting recently (1872) discovered. *Exeter Diocesan Architect. Soc.*, 2nd series, iii. 60.
S. aisle; paintings "representing the life and crucifixion of St. Roch." *Parochial History of Cornwall*, iv. 221.

St. Winnow Church, Cornwall.
Screen. *Builder*, 1848, p. 272.

Salhouse Church, Norfolk.
Rood screen; painted panels.
Traces of figure subjects discovered on the walls. Very fragmentary, probably 14th cent.

SALISBURY CATHEDRAL, WILTSHIRE.

Consecration crosses over W. door and in the N. and S. transepts.

W. wall of S. transept; remains of arcading.

On walls of two E. transepts; bold scroll patterns. 13th cent.

N.E. transept; remains of rich gilding and colour on the arcading, formerly part of the Choir screen removed by Wyatt.

Choir roof; painting of the Prophets, Evangelists, &c. and the symbols of the months, also the "Majesty." Date about 1270. *Society of Antiquaries' Proceedings*, 2nd series, vi. 477. *Builder*, 1876, p. 127.

Arches and walls of Choir and Presbytery.

Lady Chapel roof, repainted in 1870–1871. *Sir G. G. Scott, Personal and Professional Recollections*, pp. 304, 305.

Altar piece in the Lady Chapel; richly painted. The central part was the altar piece of the Beauchamp chapel, date 1481. The remainder, from the entrances to the Beauchamp and Hungerford chapels, dates 1470, *destroyed* by Wyatt. *Murray's Handbook of Wiltshire.*

Remains of colour on the monuments of Sir John de Montacute, circ. 1389, N. side of nave;* William Longespée, Earl of Salisbury, circ. 1227, S. side of nave;* on the ceiling of the monument, and on the effigy of Bishop Bligh, 1499, N. side of N. transept; on a shield on the monument of Bishop Mitford, S. side of S. choir aisle; on Bishop Audley's chantry, date 1424, N. side of Choir; also in the N. Choir aisle, on the groining ribs of the S. Choir aisle, and on the effigy of Robert Lord Hungerford, circ. 1459.*

Stothard's Monumental Effigies, p. 21, and pls. 94 and 129.

W. H. H. Rogers, *The Ancient Sepulchral Effigies, &c. in Devon*, p. 47.

Back of the monument of Precentor Bennet; portrait of the Precentor kneeling, and scrolls. Circ. 1558. *Schnebbelie, The Antiquaries' Museum.*

Groining of passage leading to the chapter house; floriated ornament. *Colling, Gothic Ornaments*, i. pl. 79.

The groining is of wood, 14th cent., and has been previously painted in an earlier style, which can still be partially seen through the later work.

The groining of chapter house has painting of a similar character, now restored.

SALISBURY CATHEDRAL, WILTSHIRE—*cont.*

HUNGERFORD CHAPEL :—

S. wall ; Death and a Gallant, a Man and Death, St. Christopher, the Salutation, and numerous inscriptions. Second half of 15th cent. *Destroyed;* drawings existing. *Hoare's Hist. of Wiltshire,* vi. 542. *Hutchins' Hist. of Dorset,* 3rd ed., iv. 176, 177.

SALISBURY, WILTSHIRE, ST. EDMUND'S CHURCH.

Arch in S. aisle wall, coloured mouldings.

SALISBURY, WILTSHIRE, ST. MARTIN'S CHURCH.

Numerous paintings, discovered in 1849 and again whitewashed over.

SALISBURY, WILTSHIRE, ST. THOMAS' CHURCH,

Over chancel arch ; the Day of Judgment. Late 15th cent. *Destroyed. Hoare's Hist. of Wiltshire,* vi. 589. *Archæologia,* xxxvi. 458.

S. wall of nave ; St. George and the Dragon. *Destroyed. Duke's Prolusiones Historiæ,* p. 545. *British Archæol. Assoc. Journ.,* xxxiii. 496.

S. chancel aisle, Swayne chantry, Spandrils of pier arches on N. side ; the Annunciation, Salutation of Elizabeth, and Adoration of the Magi, with diaper ground-work, and St. George's shields on a red ground. Late 15th cent. *Destroyed.* Drawings in the Salisbury Museum. Painted ceiling.

Remains of colour on an early English pillar and capital in the S. chancel wall.

SALISBURY, WILTSHIRE, HOUSE IN NEW STREET.

Annunciation, and the Adoration of the Magi. Latter half of 15th cent. *British Archæol. Assoc. Journ.,* iv. 91.

SALISBURY MUSEUM, WILTSHIRE.

Norman reliquary in stone with remains of colour and gilding ; found at Old Sarum.

SALL, NORFOLK, SS. PETER AND PAUL CHURCH.

Lower part of rood screen ; the four Doctors of the Church, St. James Minor, St. Bartholomew, and St. Thomas ; partly painted over.

Roof of nave ; monogram of foliage, and angels holding scrolls.

Remains of colour on the ringers' gallery ; font cover and beam whence the font cover was suspended.

SALTASH CHURCH, CORNWALL.
Painted bosses of roof. *Exeter Diocesan Architect. Soc.*, iii. 180.

SALTFLEETBY, ALL SAINTS' CHURCH, LINCOLNSHIRE.
S. chantry chapel; crowned rose. *Associated Architect. Societies' Repts.*, xii. 16.

SALTFLEETBY, ST. PETER'S CHURCH, LINCOLNSHIRE.
Decorative painting and texts on S. aisle arcade and wall of N. aisle. *Associated Architect. Societies' Repts.*, xii. 13.

SALTHOUSE CHURCH, NORFOLK.
· Chancel and aisle screens, now forming the sides of a pew.
On the panels of the former; SS. Andrew, James Major, James Minor, Matthias, Simon, Matthew, and four other Saints. *Hart, Antiq. of Norfolk*, p. 66.
On panels of aisle screen; powdering of flowers and mitred "N"s.

SALTON CHURCH, YORKSHIRE.
Fragments of early painting, brought to light during recent repairs. *Associated Architect. Societies' Repts.*, xv. 221.

SALWARPE CHURCH, WORCESTERSHIRE.
S. side of chancel; remains of colour on the sedilia. *Noake's, Rambles in Worcestershire*, 2nd series, p. 24.
On one of the pillars; a Bishop, (?) St Dunstan.
Various other remains of colour on the walls.
Associated Architect. Societies' Repts., v. 185.

SANCREED CHURCH, CORNWALL.
Remains of the rood screen preserved in the vestry, with traces of colouring. *Builder*, 1876, p. 849. *Archæol. Journ.*, xviii. 327. *Blight's Churches of West Cornwall*, p. 25.

SANDFORD, OXFORDSHIRE, ST. ANDREW'S CHURCH.
Sculpture representing the Assumption of the Virgin; with remains of the original gilding. Dug up in the churchyard. Late 15th cent. *Parker's Architectural Guide to the Neighbourhood of Oxford*, p. 356.

SANDRIDGE CHURCH, HERTFORDSHIRE.
Over the S. doorway a mural painting was discovered, and re-covered with whitewash.

SANDWICH, KENT, ST. CLEMENT'S CHURCH.
S.E. pier of tower; remains of colour and gilding on a niche. Perpendicular period. *Glynne, Churches of Kent,* p. 41.

SANDWICH, KENT, ST. MARY'S CHURCH.
Coloured wall pattern round W. window and doorway. Fragments of tower columns with vermilion colouring on them.
Antiquary, 1873, iii. 127, 128.

SANDWICH, KENT, ST. PETER'S CHURCH.
On the back of a monument on the N. side of the nave, within the canopy; portions of a black-letter inscription. *British Archæol. Assoc. Journ.,* ii. 335 *(note).*

SANDY CHURCH, BEDFORDSHIRE.
" Some interesting alabaster figures coloured and gilt " have been found, and are now in the possession of the Rector. ? Portions of a monument or reredos. *D. G. C. Elwes, Bedford and its Neighbourhood,* p. 108.

SARRATT CHURCH, HERTFORDSHIRE.
Walls of chancel and greater part of church found to have been covered with paintings illustrative of the life of Our Saviour, viz., on walls of S. transept, the Nativity, Message, Shepherds watching their flocks, the Resurrection, Ascension, &c. *Herts Advertiser and St. Alban's Times,* May 22nd 1880. *Cussans, Hist. of Hertfordshire,* vol. iii., pt. ii., p. 114.

SARUM, OLD. *See* SALISBURY MUSEUM.

SAWLEY CHURCH, DERBYSHIRE.
Against the screen, at the back of the altar; "An " intersecting set pattern, painted in chocolate on a " plate of zinc," being a reproduction of that found here in 1865. *J. C. Cox, Churches of Derbyshire,* iv. 390.

SAXHAM, LITTLE, CHURCH, SUFFOLK.
On a column, N. side of nave; a floral pattern. 15th cent.

SAXTHORPE CHURCH, NORFOLK.
Rood screen; painted and gilt mouldings and diapered panels.

SCARNING CHURCH, NORFOLK.
Rood screen ; diapered panels, part of rood-loft.
The Ecclesiologist's Guide to the Deaneries of Brisley,
&c., p. 17.

SCROPTON CHURCH, DERBYSHIRE.
Pulled down.
N. wall of nave, on a 15th cent. monument, coloured
shields within niches.
Ashby De La Zouch Anastatic Drawing Soc., 1855, p. 9.

SCULTHORPE CHURCH, NORFOLK.
In the roof of the S. aisle ; a half effaced painting.
Norfolk Archæol., vii. 335.

SEATON CHURCH, DEVONSHIRE.
Screens across N. transept ; red and white roses.
Removed ; portions to Bovey House. *W. H. H. Rogers,*
The Ancient Sepulchral Effigies, &c. of Devon, p. 186.

SEATON CHURCH, RUTLANDSHIRE.
N. wall of N. aisle ; fragments of texts. 15th cent.

SEDGBERROW CHURCH, WORCESTERSHIRE.
Remains of rood screen. *Murray's Handbook of*
Worcestershire.

SEDGBROOK, LINCOLNSHIRE, ST. LAWRENCE CHURCH.
S. chancel chapel ; traces of colour on piscina and
niches. *Ecclesiologist,* vii. 198.

SEDGFORD CHURCH, NORFOLK.
S. wall of nave ; St. Christopher, with inscription, and
other paintings. *Gent. Mag.,* 1843, xix. new series, 381.
Surrey Archæol., vi. 296.

SEETHING CHURCH, NORFOLK.
Over or by N. door ; Les Trois Morts et les Trois Vifs,
St. Christopher. *Destroyed.*

SEFTON CHURCH, LANCASHIRE.
Traces of vermilion and gilding on the screen work.
Bridgen's Antiquities of Sefton Church.

SELBY ABBEY CHURCH, YORKSHIRE.
Interior of altar screen ; 15th cent. Oak panelling
powdered over with lead stars gilt.
Brought from some other part of the Church.
Associated Architect. Societies' Repts., xiii. 149.

SELBY, YORKSHIRE.

On wall, N. side of a room adjoining the Abbey Church; portrait figures in compartments and inscription. Time of Abbot Deeping, early 16th cent. *Gough's Sepulchral Monuments*, vol. i., pt. i., p. cxxvi.

'SENNEN CHURCH, CORNWALL.

On the S. aisle wall; 15th century painting. *British Archæol. Assoc. Journ.*, xxxiii. 200. *Builder*, 1876, p. 828.

On E. wall; two embattled and canopied towers. *Parochial History of Cornwall*, iv. 143.

SHAFTESBURY ABBEY, DORSETSHIRE.

On the site numerous coloured fragments have been found. *Wilts Archæol. and Nat. Hist. Soc. Mag.*, vii. 261, 277.

SHARNBROOK CHURCH, BEDFORDSHIRE.

Walls formerly decorated with colouring of a white fleur de lis on a maroon ground. *D. G. C. Elwes, Bedford and its Neighbourhood*, p. 116.

SHAWELL. *See* SHORWELL.

SHEBBEAR CHURCH, DEVONSHIRE.

Coloured effigy of a lady in the S. aisle. Date between 1350 and 1450. *Exeter Diocesan Architect. Soc.*, 2nd series, iii. 197. *W. H. H. Rogers, The Ancient Sepulchral Effigies, &c. in Devon*, p. 47.

SHELDWICH CHURCH, KENT.

S. doorway, Norman, with colouring on the jambs. *Antiquary*, 1873, iii. 102.

SHELFORD, LITTLE, CHURCH, CAMBRIDGESHIRE.

Panels of stalls. Circ. 1370. Powdering of ermine spots and crescents re-coloured. *Murray's Handbook of Cambridgeshire*.

N. side of nave, on splays of Norman window; scroll pattern.

Remains of colour on arch from nave to de Freville Chantry.

A. G. Hill, Churches of Cambridgeshire, p. 66.

SHELTON CHURCH, BEDFORDSHIRE.

Remains of colour on rood screen. 15th cent.

SHENFIELD CHURCH, ESSEX.

Remains of colour on the timbers supporting the tower, also on the pillars on the N. side of nave and the screens between the chancel and chancel chapel. *Essex Archæol.*, iv. 115. *Buckler's Churches of Essex*, p. 75.

SHENINGTON CHURCH, GLOUCESTERSHIRE.

On walls and arches; extensive remains of early paintings. *Beesley, Hist of Banbury*, pp. 109, 141.

SHENLEY MANSELL CHURCH, BUCKINGHAMSHIRE.

S. transept; Adam and Eve after the expulsion from the Garden of Eden, Noah looking out of the Ark, and traces of other paintings.

S. side of nave, on soffit of W. arch; scroll foliage. About 1200.

N. side of nave, W. arch; remains of crimson colouring. About 1300.

SHEPRETH CHURCH, CAMBRIDGESHIRE.

On N. pier of chancel arch; traces of decorative colour.

SHERBORNE ABBEY, DORSETSHIRE.

W. bay of Lady Chapel; rich painted and gilded carving, and bosses of roof. *Somerset Archæol. and Nat. Hist. Soc. Proceedings*, xx. 53. *Archæol. Journ.*, xiv. 72. *Hutchins' Hist. of Dorset*, 3rd ed., iv. 244.

SHERBORNE, DORSETSHIRE, CHAPEL OF THE ALMSHOUSE.

Painting on oak, probably the original altar piece, with representations of Our Lord's five principal miracles, and the emblems of the Evangelists. 15th cent. *Hutchins' Hist. of Dorset*, 3rd ed., iv. 295.

SHERBORNE, MONKS, CHURCH, HAMPSHIRE.

On the jambs of two of the chancel windows; remains of paintings.

Original colouring on the capitals of the Norman chancel arch.

British Archæol. Assoc. Journ., xxxii. 265.

Dedication cross.

SHERINGHAM CHURCH, NORFOLK.

Painted beam across the nave whence the font cover was formerly suspended. Traces of colour on the font. 15th cent.

SHEVIOCKE CHURCH, CORNWALL.

Under a canopy in the S. transept; effigies of Sir Edward Courtenay and his Lady richly gilt. Date about 1370. *Exeter Diocesan Architect. Soc.*, v. 3, and (2nd series) iii. 197, 514. *W. H. H. Rogers, The Ancient Sepulchral Effigies, &c. in Devon*, pp. 47, 365.

SHILLINGTON CHURCH, BEDFORDSHIRE.

Remains of painting on the screens and on the roof of the N. aisle. *Parker, Eccles. and Architect. Topog. of England, Bedford*, No. 123.

SHIMPLING CHURCH, NORFOLK.

Found in a hole in the chancel wall; sculpture of the Virgin and Child, coloured and gilt. 15th cent. *Norfolk Archæol.*, viii. 336.

SHINGHAM CHURCH, NORFOLK.

Painted screen; scroll work in the panels. 15th cent.

SHIPLEY CHURCH, SUSSEX.

Reliquary; enamelled and gilt. 12th cent. *Gent. Mag.*, 1836, v., new series, 369.

Painted ceiling. *Murray's Handbook of Sussex. Black's Guide to Sussex. M. A. Lower, History of Sussex*, ii. 156.

SHORNCOTE CHURCH, WILTSHIRE.

Masonry pattern, and scroll ornament round the chancel arch. Early English. *Builder*, 1864, p. 724.

SHORWELL CHURCH, ISLE OF WIGHT.

Over N. door; legend of St. Christopher.

Over S. door; Last Judgment. *Destroyed.*

Decorative colouring and stencilled patterns on the pillars, splays, and mullions of the windows, &c. 14th cent. *British Archæol. Assoc. Journ.*, iii. 85, 92, and xi. 317. *Gent. Mag.*, 1847, xxviii., new series, p. 188. *Moody, Notes and Essays, Hants and Wilts*, p. 188. *W. H. D. Adams, The Hist. Topog. and Antiq. of the Isle of Wight*, p. 196.

SHOTTESWELL CHURCH, WARWICKSHIRE.

St. Christopher. 14th cent. *Builder*, 1876, p. 669.

SHREWSBURY, SHROPSHIRE, ST. CHAD'S OLD CHURCH.

Back of altar piece; colouring belonging to an earlier reredos.

Colour and gilding on mouldings, &c., disclosed by the falling away of the whitewash. *Destroyed. Owen and Blakeway, Hist. of Shrewsbury*, i. 193, 248.

SHURDINGTON CHURCH, GLOUCESTERSHIRE.
On exterior E. chancel wall; sculptured consecration crosses with traces of colour.

SHUTFORD CHURCH, OXFORDSHIRE.
Perpendicular rood screen. *Parker, Eccles. and Architect. Topog. of England, Oxford,* No. 146.
Extensive remains of early wall paintings. *Beesley, Hist. of Banbury,* p. 141.

SIBTON CHURCH, SUFFOLK.
Fragment of rood screen, removed to W. end.

SIDDINGTON CHAPEL, CHESHIRE.
" A richly carved oak screen formerly painted and gilt separates the Nave from the Chancel."
G. Y. Osborne, A Sketch of the Parish of Prestbury, p. 28. *Ormerod, Hist. of Cheshire,* 2nd ed., iii. 729.

SILCHESTER CHURCH, HAMPSHIRE.
S. wall at the back of a monumental recess; remains of painting of the lady whose effigy is below in the attitude of prayer. *Wright's Archæological Album,* p. 154. *British Archæol. Assoc. Journ.,* xvi. 95.
Decorative painting. *Destroyed.*

SITTINGBOURNE CHURCH, KENT.
N.E. corner of chancel; Head (?) of the Virgin. *Destroyed. Phippen, Sketches of Rochester,* p. 253.

SKIPTON CHURCH, YORKSHIRE.
Painted screen. *Whitaker's Hist. and Antiq. of Craven,* 3rd ed., p. 586.

SLAPTON CHURCH, NORTHAMPTONSHIRE.
Nave; St. Christopher, St. George, Our Lady of Pity.
In the splay of a window; St. Michael weighing souls.
On jamb supporting arches; St. Gregory's Mass, the Ecstasy of St. Francis, and an unknown subject, probably representing the founders.
In the N. aisle; the Annunciation and " Les Trois Morts et les Trois Vifs," the Martyrdom of St. Edmund.
Beneath these, some earlier paintings; (?) the story of St. Nicholas, St. Anne teaching the Virgin.
Many of the subjects are palimpsest, the earlier 15th, the later 16th cents.
Archæol. Journ., xxxiv. 233. *Builder,* 1875, p. 289. *Associated Architect. Societies' Repts.,* xii. lxxv.

SLAUGHAM CHURCH, SUSSEX.

N. wall; Last Supper, &c., and the passage of a soul to Heaven.* *Sussex Archæol.*, xiii. 237. *M. A. Lower, History of Sussex,* ii. 166.

* This subject has been apparently retouched.

SLEAFORD CHURCH, LINCOLNSHIRE.

Several consecration crosses. 14th cent. *Associated Architect. Societies' Repts.*, v. ix., vii. 5. *Trollope: Slea-ford, Flaxwell, Aswardhurn,* p. 150.

SLINDON CHURCH, SUSSEX.

S. side of nave; decorative patterns. 12th cent.

On other parts of the church, 13th and 15th cents. decorations.

On E. wall of chancel; three consecration crosses. *Sussex Archæol.,* xix. 130.

SLINGSBY CHURCH, YORKSHIRE.

Consecration cross.

SLOLEY CHURCH, NORFOLK.

On N. side of chancel window; painting of a man with a staff.

On E. wall of S. aisle; three nude females, (?) part of a Doom. Middle of 15th century. *Norfolk Archæol.,* iii. 89.

SLYMBRIDGE CHURCH, GLOUCESTERSHIRE.

Over chancel arch; the Day of Judgment. Date about 1485.

Remains of decorative colour on the chancel arch on the labels of the soffits of the arches N. side of nave, and on the piers and capitals of the arches S. side of nave, also on a fragment discovered in the chancel.

Notes, Hist. and Arch. on Church of St. John the Baptist, Slymbridge, pp. 49, 50, 59, 60. *Ecclesiologist,* iv. 41. *Archæol. Journ.,* xxxviii. 89.

SMALLBURGH CHURCH, NORFOLK.

Rood screen; SS. Anthony, Benedict, George, Giles, Lawrence, and three other saints covered over with a fresh coat of paint. *Illustrations of Norfolk Topography,* p. 166. *Hart, Antiq. of Norfolk,* p. 66.

SNAITH CHURCH, YORKSHIRE.

Traces of colour round an Early English arch. *Murray's Handbook of Yorkshire.*

SNETTERTON CHURCH, NORFOLK.

Over the rood-loft; defaced painting of the Day of Judgment. *Blomefield, Hist. of Norfolk*, ed. 1805, i. 419. *Chambers, Hist. of Norfolk*, ii. 882.

SNETTISHAM CHURCH, NORFOLK.

Painted pulpit. *Kelly's Post Office Directory of Norfolk.* Repainted. *Sacristy*, iii. 152.

SOBERTON CHURCH, HAMPSHIRE.

N. wall of chantry chapel; diaper pattern. *British Archæol. Assoc. Journ.*, vi. 442.

SOHAM CHURCH, CAMBRIDGESHIRE.

N. chancel aisle; a bishop. *Ecclesiologist*, xiv. 374. *Gent. Mag.*, 1850, xxxiii., new series, 70.

Screen, richly gilt. *Notes on Cambridgeshire Churches,* 1827, p. 56.

SOMERBY CHURCH, LINCOLNSHIRE.

Portion of painted rood screen. *Associated Architect. Societies' Repts.*, xiii. 2.

SOMERCOTES, SOUTH, CHURCH, LINCOLNSHIRE.

Remains of colour on chancel screen. *Associated Architect. Societies' Repts.*, xii. 19.

SOMERFORD KEYNES CHURCH, WILTSHIRE.

N. wall; large figure of St. Christopher. *Hall, the Book of the Thames*, p. 25.

SOMERLEYTON CHURCH, SUFFOLK.

Rood screen of 16 panels; SS. Michael, Edmund, William of Norwich or Robert of Bury, Lawrence, Simon, Thomas of Canterbury, Anne instructing the Virgin, Andrew, John, Mary Magdalene, Zeno, Sitha, Nicholas, Cecily, Edward the Confessor, and George. 15th cent. *British Archæol. Assoc. Journ.*, xxxvii. 140.

SOMERTON, WEST, CHURCH, NORFOLK.

S. wall of nave; the Day of Judgment.

N. wall of nave; the Entry into Jerusalem, Flagellation, and Resurrection. Time of Edward III. *Norfolk Archæol.*, vii. 256, and viii. 336. *Murray's Handbook of Norfolk. Sacristy*, iii. 155.

On a narrow thick piece of deal, suggested to have been part of a rood; painting of the Virgin and Child. *Norfolk Archæol.*, viii. 336.

SOTBY CHURCH, LINCOLNSHIRE.

Chancel, within the window splays; Our Lord and St. Mary Magdalene, and (?) Belshazzar's feast, apparently 14th cent. *Destroyed. Associated Architect. Societies' Repts.,* iv. lxxiii.

SOTTERLEY CHURCH, SUFFOLK.

Painted screen; the Twelve Apostles. Date about 1470. Partly restored (?). Only SS. Simon, Thomas, Paul, and Peter remain.

On N. wall of chancel; heraldic shields, the arms and alliances of the Playters.

SOUTHACRE. *See* ACRE, SOUTH.

SOUTHAM, WARWICKSHIRE, ST. JAMES'S CHURCH.

Remains of polychromatic decoration discovered during repairs, but now entirely obliterated. *Ecclesiologist,* xvii. 127.

SOUTHAMPTON, HAMPSHIRE, ST. MICHAEL'S CHURCH.

Monument of Sir Richard Lyster; remains of colouring. Date about 1567. *British Archæol. Assoc. Journ.,* xi. 323. *Moody, Notes and Essays, Hants and Wilts,* p. 84.

SOUTHFLEET CHURCH, KENT.

Painting and gilding on monument of Sir John Sedley. 1561. *Glynne, Churches of Kent,* p. 308.

Traces of early painting.

Several consecration crosses.

SOUTHWARK, SURREY, CHURCH OF ST. MARY OVERIE, OR ST. SAVIOUR.

Wooden cross-legged effigy, time of Edward I.; formerly painted. *British Archæol. Assoc. Journ.,* xxxii. 415.

SOUTHWELL, NOTTINGHAMSHIRE.

SOUTHWOLD CHURCH, SUFFOLK.

Ceiling over rood screen; angels with scrolls and implements of the Passion. *British Archæol. Assoc. Journ.,* xxi. 352, and xxv. 282. *Cromwell, Excursions through Suffolk,* ii. 128.

Roofs of nave and N. aisle; traces of colouring.

Chancel roof; panelled and painted.

Pulpit restored.

Chancel screen; the Apostles, omitting Matthew or Matthias, and St. Paul, depicted on the panels.

SOUTHWOLD CHURCH, SUFFOLK—*cont.*
Screen across N. aisle; the Heavenly Hierarchy.
Screen across S. aisle; David, Amos, Isaiah, Jonah, Ezekiel, Moses, Elias, Jeremiah, Nahum, Hosea, and Baruch.
Civil Engineer and Architect's Journ., 1859, p. 383, and 1860, p. 5. *Sacristy*, iii. 156.

SOUTHWOLD, SUFFOLK.
Panel painting representing the entombment of Christ, formerly part of a reredos, found in a cottage. *Norfolk Archæol.*, viii. 326. *Antiquary*, 1872, ii. 123.

SPALDING CHURCH, LINCOLNSHIRE.
On N.E. pier of S. transept; part of a St. Christopher (a head, and hand holding a staff), and some floral decoration.

SPALDWICK CHURCH, HUNTINGDONSHIRE.
On the jamb of the chancel arch; some scroll painting. 13th cent.

SPARHAM CHURCH, NORFOLK.
Rood screen; Dance of Death, SS. Thomas of Canterbury, Walstan, and various saints. *Gent. Mag.*, 1846, xxvi., new series, 135. *East Anglian Notes and Queries*, iii. 315.

SPILSBY CHURCH, LINCOLNSHIRE.
Colour and gilding on monument and effigies of Richard Bertie, and Catherine, Duchess of Suffolk. Circ. 1580. *Associated Architect. Societies' Repts.*, viii. 11.

SPORLE CHURCH, NORFOLK.
S. aisle wall; legend of St. Catherine of Alexandria. About 1400. *Society of Antiquaries' Proceedings*, 2nd series, iii. 386. *Norfolk Archæol.*, vii. 303. *Antiquary*, 1871, i. 154.
Painted font cover. *Civil Engineer and Architect's Journ.*, 1860, p. 5.

SPRATTON CHURCH, NORTHAMPTONSHIRE.
On N. side of chancel; traces of colour on the shields on the monument of Sir John Swinford. Date about 1370.

SPROTBOROUGH CHURCH, YORKSHIRE.
Beneath the clerestory windows; "scrolls of varied colours." *J. G. Fardell, Sprotborough*, p. 39.

SPROUGHTON CHURCH, SUFFOLK.
N. aisle; St. George and the Dragon, and St. Christopher.
Various other paintings.
S. aisle, back of piscina; the Virgin.
Antiquarian and Architect. Year Book, 1844, p. 172.

SPROXTON CHURCH, LEICESTERSHIRE.
Traces of painting on the font. *White's Gazetteer of Leicestershire.*

STACKPOLE ELIDUR OR CHERITON CHURCH, PEMBROKESHIRE.
E. wall of S. transept; painted niche, with representations of a cross and a figure holding a St. George's shield. *Archæologia Cambrensis*, 4th series, xi. 339.

STAGSDEN CHURCH, BEDFORDSHIRE.
Near N. door of nave; mural painting, plastered over.
W. M. Harvey, Hist. of Willey Hundred, p. 134.

STAINDROP CHURCH, DURHAM.
In S. wall; colour and gilding on 14th cent. effigy.
Colouring on monument and effigies of Ralph Neville, Earl of Westmoreland, and his two wives, circ. 1426, and of Henry, fifth Earl of Westmoreland, and his two wives, date 1560. *Antiquarian Repertory*, new ed., iii. 302, and pl. 62. *Lipscomb, Hist. of Staindrop Church*, pp. 9, 13, 18. *W. Whellan, Hist. Gazett. and Directory of Durham*, p. 466.

STALHAM CHURCH, NORFOLK.
Rood screen; six figures remain in the vicarage, St. Andrew, St. Thomas of Canterbury, St. Edward, St. Sebastian or Edmund, St. Roch, and St. Francis. These only have survived the "restoration" of the church. *East Anglian Notes and Queries*, iii. 315. *Norfolk Archæol.*, iii. 19. *The Ecclesiologist's Guide to the Deaneries of Brisley, &c.*, p. 95.
A small portion of the old screen with gilding on it is incorporated in a modern one.
Painted font.

STAMFORD, LINCOLNSHIRE, ALL SAINTS' CHURCH.
Principals of nave roof; roses and a running pattern, 15th cent.

STAMFORD, LINCOLNSHIRE, ST. GEORGE'S CHURCH.
Chancel roof, and lower panels of screen, 15th cent. Repainted.

STAMFORD, LINCOLNSHIRE, ST. JOHN'S CHURCH.
Nave roof; coloured red and black. 15th cent.
Murray's Handbook of Northants, p. 95.
Chancel and aisle screens; remains of colour and
gilding. *Drakard's Hist. of Stamford*, p. 298.

STAMFORD, LINCOLNSHIRE, ST. MARY'S CHURCH.
. N. side of chancel; roof of St. Mary's chapel, coloured
and powdered with stars. Date 1467. *Murray's Handbook of Northants*, p. 93. *Drakard's Hist. of Stamford*,
p. 242. *Nevinson, Hist of Stamford*, p. 25.

STAMFORD, LINCOLNSHIRE, HOUSE NEAR THE HIGH STREET.
Over a fireplace; a decorative pattern stencilled on
the walls. *Antiquary*, 1872, ii. 81.

STANDON CHURCH, HERTFORDSHIRE.
S. side of chancel; monument of Sir Ralph Sadleir,
richly coloured and gilt. Date 1587.

STANFIELD CHURCH, NORFOLK.
Chancel screen; once painted and gilded, with the
sacred Monogram on the panels. *Carthew's Hundred of
Launditch*, ii. 476.

STANFORD CHURCH, NORTHAMPTONSHIRE.
S. aisle, on splay of a window; decorative colour.
Screen work, now worked up into the pulpit, formerly
gilt and painted, now varnished over.
N. side of nave; monument of Sir Thomas Cave and
Lady, circ. 1550, painted effigies and shields.
N. wall of N. aisle; coloured mouldings and shields on
monument of Sir Ambrose Cave. Circ. 1568.

STANFORD DINGLEY CHURCH, BERKSHIRE.
N. side of nave, round the eastern arch; masonry
pattern and part of a Doom. The former late 12th cent.
Archæol. Journ., xxxiv. 277.
Within the splay of the arch; a scroll pattern, on the
W. side, St. Edmund, King and Martyr, on the E. the
head of a Bishop.
S. side of nave, on the side of the eastern arch; the
vision of a monk, an angel, and another figure above.
At E. end of aisles; scroll and flower patterns.

STANFORD LE HOPE CHURCH, ESSEX.
W. wall of S. chantry chapel; early mural painting.
Essex Archæol., i., new series, 202.
Painted parclose screen. *Rev. W. Palin, Stifford and
its Neighbourhood*, p. 120.

STANION CHURCH, NORTHAMPTONSHIRE.
On E. piers of nave; rich early 15th cent. colouring.
Discovered and *destroyed.*

STANLEY, ST. LEONARD, CHURCH, GLOUCESTERSHIRE.
On window jamb, N. side; figures in armour (?) receiving a cross from an ecclesiastic.
On S. side; large subject, with numerous figures, animals, and fishes.
Antiquary, 1872, ii. 232.

STANNINGFIELD CHURCH, SUFFOLK.
Over chancel arch; the Day of Judgment.
Colouring on mouldings of chancel arch.

STANTON CHURCH, SUFFOLK.
Rood screen; angels with emblems of the Passion.

STANTON HARCOURT CHURCH, OXFORDSHIRE.
S. wall of nave; Our Lord washing His disciples' feet, the Last Supper, and probably scenes from the Passion.
N. wall of nave; the Descent from the Cross, Entombment and Descent into Limbus.
On the wall beneath, diamond panelling. Circ. 1400. *Destroyed;* engravings existing.
Archæol. Journ., ii. 365, and *Builder,* 1864, p. 725.
N. side of chancel; remains of colouring on the canopy of the monument of Isabel, daughter of Richard de Camvil, also used as an Easter Sepulchre. Date about 1300.
S. side of chancel; effigy of Maud, daughter of John Lord Grey of Rotherfield. Painted and gilt. Date about 1392.
Parker's Architectural Guide to the Neighbourhood of Oxford, pp. 176, 177.

STANTON HARCOURT, OXFORDSHIRE, THE MANOR HOUSE CHAPEL.
Arch between inner and outer chapel "retains much of the ancient red and blue colouring." Perpendicular period. *Parker's Architectural Guide to the Neighbourhood of Oxford,* p. 184.

STANTON, ST. JOHN'S CHURCH, OXFORDSHIRE.
N. aisle; "Beautiful oak screen work, which retains many traces of its former brilliant colouring." "The wall above the altar was covered with painting."
S. aisle; paintings of angels on some woodwork.
Parker's Architectural Guide to the Neighbourhood of Oxford, pp. 229, 230.

STANTON, ST. QUINTIN'S CHURCH, WILTSHIRE.
Over S. door; St. Christopher. *Ashby De La Zouch Anastatic Drawing Soc.*, 1860, p. 2.
S. wall of chancel; remains of large painting, mainly concealed by a tablet. 13th cent.

STAPLEFORD CHURCH, WILTSHIRE.
On the soffit of the two eastern arches, S. side of nave; scroll and foliated pattern. Late 12th cent. *Archæol. Journ.*, xxxviii. 92.

STAPLEHURST CHURCH, KENT.
S. chancel chapel; ceiling painted with crowns, &c. *Glynne, Churches of Kent*, p. 89. *Cambridge Antiq. Soc. Report for* 1845, p. 12.
Date, early 16th cent., a few panels only preserved and now inserted beneath the tower. *Archæol. Cantiana*, ix. 197.

STAPLETON CHURCH, CUMBERLAND.
Fragments of paintings where the whitewash has peeled off; figures of David, Samson, Amos, and Baruch.

STARSTON CHURCH, NORFOLK.
Within an arched recess in the N. wall of the nave; an entombment, and the Soul being received into Paradise. Date about 1300. *Coloured drawing by C. J. W. Winter, and lithograph. Norfolk Archæol.*, vii. 301. *Notes and Queries*, 4th series, vi. 542, 577, vii. 40, 172, 245, 368, 410, 497, 517, viii. 10, 96, 228, 272. *Archæol. Journ.*, xxviii. 162, 172.

STAVELY CHURCH, DERBYSHIRE.
N. aisle, back of monumental recess; (?) the Resurrection. *J. C. Cox, Churches of Derbyshire*, i. 351.

STAVERTON CHURCH, DEVONSHIRE.
Screen, remains of painting. *Worth, Tourist's Guide to S. Devon*, p. 81.

STEDHAM CHURCH, SUSSEX.
S. wall; St. George and the Dragon, the three Maries, &c.
N. wall; St. Ursula, figure of Our Saviour on a chariot surrounded by various implements, St. Christopher, the Last Judgment, &c. 14th cent.
Sussex Archæol., iv. 1 and 19. *M. A. Lower, History of Sussex*, ii. 176. *Gent. Mag.*, 1850, xxxiv., new series, 308.

STEEPLE ASTON. *See* ASTON, STEEPLE.

STEETLY CHAPEL, DERBYSHIRE.
Colour on the groining ribs of the apse. *J. C. Cox, Churches of Derbyshire,* i. 401. *White: Worksop, The Dukery and Sherwood Forest,* p. 127. *British Archæol. Assoc. Journ.,* xxx. 114.

STEVENAGE CHURCH, HERTFORDSHIRE.
Effigy of a lady, time of Edward I.; richly coloured. *Archæologia,* xxi. 499.
E. end of chancel; remains of colour on reredos. *Cussans, Hist. of Hertfordshire,* vol. ii., pt. iii., p. 91.

STEVINGTON CHURCH, BEDFORDSHIRE.
Remains of a painted rood screen. *Parker, Eccles. and Architect. Topog. of England, Bedford,* No. 33. Now placed at W. end of N. aisle. *W. M. Harvey, Hist. of Willey Hundred,* p. 161.

STEWKLEY CHURCH, BUCKINGHAMSHIRE.
Chancel roof; scroll patterns, copied from remains found during the restoration of the church. The original painting dated from the 12th cent.
Let into the N. wall of the chancel; a portion of sculpture in alabaster of "the Virgin and Child," richly gilt. Date about 1300.

STEYNING CHURCH, SUSSEX.
N. side of nave, on a pillar; a figure in the act of benediction.

STIFFORD CHURCH, ESSEX.
E. end of S. nave arcade; corbel, painted, and with a diaper pattern, also a consecration cross.
N. wall of nave; St. Dunstan.
E. wall of chantry; the Angel appearing to Zacharias. *Rev. W. Palin, Stifford and its Neighbourhood,* pp. 53, 60.

STILLINGFLEET CHURCH, YORKSHIRE.
Traces of colour, and 16th cent. texts on nave walls. *Destroyed. Associated Architect. Societies' Repts.,* xiv. 76.

STOCKLAND CHURCH, DORSETSHIRE.
Rood screen. Restored. *Ecclesiologist,* iv. 237.

STOCKTON CHURCH, WILTSHIRE.
Decorative painting and Scriptural texts. *Destroyed. Wilts Archæol. and Nat. Hist. Soc. Mag.,* xii. 113.

STOKE ASH CHURCH, SUFFOLK.
Splays of E. window; S. Paul and another figure.
Destroyed.

STOKE BY CLARE, SUFFOLK, ST. AUGUSTINE'S CHURCH.
Painted roof, perpendicular period. *Parker, Eccles.
and Architect. Topog. of England, Suffolk,* No. 415.

STOKE BY NAYLAND CHURCH, SUFFOLK.
Over the chancel arch; (?) the Day of Judgment.
In St. Edmund's chapel; two paintings, of which copies
have been made.
Suffolk Archæol., iv. 187.
Wall of N. aisle; SS. Ursula and Lucy. *Destroyed.*
Cambridge Antiq. Soc. Report for 1849, p. 8. *Archæol.
Journ.,* vi. 211. *Torlesse, Account of Stoke by Nayland,*
pp. 12, 13.

STOKE CHARITY CHURCH, HAMPSHIRE.
N. wall of N. Chancel Chapel; gilding on the cresting
and spandrils of a monument, also emblazoned shields,
and painted on two of the lower panels figures of Thomas
à Becket, and the Virgin and Child. *British Archæol.
Assoc. Journ.,* x. 74.
Sculpture representing St. Gregory's Mass. Richly
coloured. *British Archæol. Assoc. Journ.,* vi. 80.
Archæol. Journ., vi. 192.

STOKE D'ABERNON CHURCH, SURREY.
Murder of Becket. *Records of Buckinghamshire,* iii.
273.

STOKE DRY CHURCH, RUTLANDSHIRE.
St. Christopher.
S. chancel chapel; the Martyrdom of St. Edmund and
other subjects. *Murray's Handbook of Northants,* p. 226.

STOKE FLEMING CHURCH, DEVONSHIRE.
Blue colouring on the effigy of a lady. Late 13th cent.
Exeter Diocesan Architect. Soc., 2nd series, ii. 51. *W. H.
H. Rogers, The Ancient Sepulchral Effigies, &c. in Devon,*
p. 17.

STOKE GABRIEL CHURCH, DEVONSHIRE.
Rood screen.

STOKE HAMMOND CHURCH, BUCKINGHAMSHIRE.
Nave roof; painted panels. *Lipscomb, Hist. and
Antiq. of Bucks,* iv. 363.

STOKE IN TEIGNHEAD CHURCH, DEVONSHIRE.

Rood screen; remains of colour and figures of saints and martyrs depicted on the panels. Date, late perpendicular period. *Exeter Diocesan Architect. Soc.*, 2nd series, ii. 96.

These panels have been *destroyed*.

STOKE NEWINGTON CHURCH, MIDDLESEX.

Alabaster tomb with painted effigies of John Dudley and his wife, 1580. *J. H. Sperling, Church Walks in Middlesex*, p. 126.

STOKE ST. NECTANS. *See* HARTLAND.

STOKE-SUB-HAMDON CHURCH, SOMERSETSHIRE.

Over chancel arch, W. side; figures of angels. (?) Part of a Doom. Late 15th cent. *Somerset Archæol. and Nat. Hist. Soc. Proceedings*, xvii. 56.

Chancel arch; various decorations. (? *Destroyed*).

On N. and S. sides of nave, within the splay of Norman window; masonry pattern and diaper of stars and roses. 12th cent.

E. wall of chancel; painting on back of niche.

STOKESBY CHURCH, NORFOLK.

S. wall of nave; St. Edward, King and Martyr, or more probably a portion of "Les trois Vifs et les Trois Morts."

N. wall of nave; St. Christopher, and the Seven Deadly Sins. *Norfolk Archæol.*, v. 291.

STONE, KENT, ST. MARY'S CHURCH.

N. aisle wall; two paintings of the Virgin and Child. Date about 1300.

On chancel arch; remains of a coloured border, and colouring on two sculptured crosses above it.

S. aisle; running pattern. 13th cent.

E. wall of chancel; painted crosses.

Archæol. Cantiana, iii. 118, 120, 121, 126. *Ecclesiologist*, xxi. (xviii. new series), 300.

STONE BY FAVERSHAM CHURCH, KENT.

Remains of painting on the walls. 13th cent. *Builder*, 1875, p. 817. *British Archæol. Assoc. Journ.*, xxxi. 251, 254.

STONELEIGH CHURCH, WARWICKSHIRE.

(?) The martyrdom of St. Thomas à Becket, St. Christopher, Time and Death, and many passages of Scripture in old arabesque borders. Discovered in 1822. *Stoneleigh Abbey*, p. 38.

STONHAM ASPALL CHURCH, SUFFOLK.
Roof with remains of colour. *Suffolk Archæol.*, v. 116.
Interior compartment of chest painted red. 15th cent.
British Archæol. Assoc. Journ., xxviii. 228.
Coloured fragments of the founder's effigy. *Antiquary*, 1873, iii. 249.

STONHAM, EARL, CHURCH, SUFFOLK.
Over the chancel arch ; the Last Judgment.
On the E. wall of the N. transept; "the Nativity," "Message to the Shepherds," and "Offerings of the Magi."
On the W. wall of the N. transept ; numerous heads, part of a subject destroyed.
On the E. wall of the S. transept ; the Martyrdom of St. Catherine.
On the W. wall of the S. transept; St. George and the Dragon.
Discovered during the restoration of the church.
Builder, 1874, p. 934. Copied from *The Suffolk Chronicle. British Archæol. Assoc. Journ.*, xxx. 433, xxxi. 217.
Screen now *destroyed.* Fragments in the possession of *Mr. H. Watling.*

STORTFORD, BISHOP'S, CHURCH, HERTFORDSHIRE.
On N. wall; a winged figure holding a "tau" cross, and a diaper of the Sacred Monogram. *Cussans, Hist. of Hertfordshire*, vol. i., pt. i., p. 123.

STOTFOLD CHURCH, BEDFORDSHIRE.
St. Michael weighing Souls, St. George and the Dragon, &c. *Whitewashed over. Gent. Mag.*, xcvii., pt. ii., p. 401, and *Parker, Eccles. and Architect. Topog. of England, Bedford*, No. 124.

STOURTON CANDEL CHURCH, DORSETSHIRE.
Painted pulpit. *Hutchins' Hist. of Dorset*, 3rd ed., iii. 667, 669.

STOW, LINCOLNSHIRE, ST. MARY'S CHURCH.
In a recess over altar, E. wall of N. transept; in the centre Thomas à Becket, on either side his Supper with Ecclesiastics, and his Murder. *Associated Architect. Societies' Repts.*, viii. x. and 249.

STOW BARDOLPH CHURCH, NORFOLK.
On N. and S. walls of nave; diaper of the Sacred Monogram.

STOW BARDOLPH CHURCH, NORFOLK—*cont.*

On N. wall of nave; St. Christopher, about 1500, and (?) the Annunciation.

Over S. door; St. Christopher, with scrolls. Date about 1400. Painted over the Martyrdom of St. Edmund.

On each side of chancel arch; a figure, (?) part of a Doom.

Above the chancel arch; two angels holding a shield on which are the implements of the Passion. Also a shield with the arms of Beaufort and two others. Also a diaper of " XP."

Round the windows of the chancel and the sedilia; decorative patterns.

On E. wall of chancel, S. of altar; a consecration cross.

All *destroyed.*

Norfolk Archæol., iii. 134.

STOW-CUM-QUY. *See* QUY.

STOWLANGTOFT, SUFFOLK, ST. GEORGE'S CHURCH.

N. wall; St. Christopher.

Painted screen. About 1375.

Murray's Handbook of Suffolk. Parker, Eccles. and Architect. Topog. of England, Suffolk, No. 386.

STRADBROKE CHURCH, SUFFOLK.

Nave roof; painted bosses, and in E. bay, painted panels with the Sacred Monogram and figures of Angels and Cherubim.

STRATA FLORIDA, CARDIGANSHIRE.

Painting in panel of Temptation, formerly belonging to the abbey, and now in a neighbouring farmhouse. *Murray's Handbook of South Wales.*

STRATFORD-UPON-AVON, WARWICKSHIRE, HOLY TRINITY CHURCH.

N. side of chancel; monument of Dean Balsall. Circ. 1491, formerly painted. *J. P. Neale and J. le Keux, Views of the most interesting Collegiate and Parochial Churches in Great Britain,* vol. ii.

STRATFORD-UPON-AVON, WARWICKSHIRE, CHAPEL OF THE GUILD OF THE HOLY CROSS.

Walls of chancel; the legend of the Holy Cross. Visit of the Queen of Sheba to King Solomon, (?) Vision of St. Francis, &c. *Destroyed.*

STRATFORD-UPON-AVON, WARWICKSHIRE, CHAPEL OF THE GUILD OF THE HOLY CROSS—*cont.*

Over chancel arch, W. face; the Day of Judgment.

Walls of nave; St. George and the Dragon. The Martyrdom of Thomas à Becket, and two allegorical subjects.

Within niches at W. end of nave; SS. Modwenna and Ursula. *Whitewashed over.* Late 15th cent.

The series published by T. Fisher, London, 1807–1821. *W. Smith, Hist. of County of Warwick,* p. 262. *F. Smith, Warwickshire Delineated,* p. 257.

Figure of St. Modwenna re-discovered in 1875. *British Archæol. Assoc. Journ.,* xxxii. 91.

STRELLEY CHURCH, NOTTINGHAMSHIRE.

Rood-loft. *A. Billing, Mural Painting,* 1872, p. 22.

STRENSHAM CHURCH, WORCESTERSHIRE.

W. end of nave; remains of rood-loft with 23 paintings on panel, of Our Lord, the Apostles, SS. Paul, Stephen, Lawrence, Anthony, John the Baptist, Edmund, Edward King and Martyr, Blaize, ? Thomas of Canterbury, &c. *Associated Architect. Societies' Repts.,* vi. 240.

STRETTON GRANDISON CHURCH, HEREFORDSHIRE.

Over the S. door; part of a mural figure. *Havergal, Fasti Herefordenses,* p. 157.

On S. wall; traces of decoration.

STROXTON CHURCH, LINCOLNSHIRE.

N. side of nave; remains of painting on the pillars and arches. *Associated Architect. Societies' Repts.,* xiii. xiv. and 27.

STRUMPSHAW CHURCH, NORFOLK.

Rood screen; diapered. 15th cent. *Colling, Gothic Ornaments,* ii. pl. 102.

STUDLAND CHURCH, DORSETSHIRE.

"Traces of painting in distemper remain on the outside of the chancel arch." *Hutchins' Hist. of Dorset,* 3rd ed., i. 653.

STURMINSTER MARSHALL CHURCH, DORSETSHIRE.

St. Michael and other fragments. (?) *Destroyed. Ecclesiologist,* xxix. (xxvi. new series), p. 266. *Hutchins' Hist. of Dorset,* 3rd ed., iii. 363.

STURMINSTER NEWTON CHURCH, DORSETSHIRE.
> E. bay of roof; painted and gilt. Destroyed in 1827. *Hutchins' Hist. of Dorset*, 3rd ed., iv. 342.

STYDD CHAPEL, LANCASHIRE.
> On mullions of E. window; " painting in polychromy now hardly visible."
> On tie beam of roof; a gilt star. *G. Latham, The Hist. of Stydd Chapel and Preceptory*, pp. 8, 11.

SUDBURY, SUFFOLK, ALL SAINTS' CHURCH.
> Nave roof; painted. Early 15th cent.
> On E. wall of N. chancel chapel; numerous shields and armorial bearings. About 1500.

SUDBURY, SUFFOLK, ST. GREGORY'S CHURCH.
> Font cover. *Murray's Handbook of Suffolk. J. P. Neale and J. Le Keux, Views of the most interesting Collegiate and Parochial Churches in Great Britain*, vol. ii. Repainted.
> In S. aisle chapel; a consecration cross.

SUDBURY, SUFFOLK, ST. PETER'S CHURCH.
> Roof of nave; painted. Late 15th cent. *Parker, Eccles. and Architect. Topog. of England, Suffolk*, No. 488.
> Paintings of figures in the panels of the rood screen. *Suffolk Archæol.*, i. 230.

SUDBURY, SUFFOLK.
> Panel of screen with paintings of Sir John Schorn and St. Audree. Late 15th cent. or 1550. *In the possession of Mr. Gainsborough Dupont. Suffolk Archæol.*, i. 222. *British Archæol. Assoc. Journ.*, xxiii. 376.

SUFFIELD CHURCH, NORFOLK.
> Rood screen; Sir John Schorn, St. Julian Hospitator, the four Evangelists, and four Doctors of the Church, or (?) SS. Longinus, Geron, and Louis, depicted on the panels. *British Archæol. Assoc. Journ.*, xxiii. 266, 376, xxiv. 72.
> The upper part of the screen has been destroyed, and the panels, with figures of SS. Matthew and Mark, lost.

SUTTON, CAMBRIDGESHIRE, ST. ANDREW'S CHURCH.
> In a niche over the chancel piscina; a carved figure, richly painted and gilt. *Parker, Eccles. and Architect. Topog. of England, Cambridge*, No. 105.

SUTTON BINGHAM CHURCH, SOMERSETSHIRE.
Chancel; Coronation of the Virgin, late 14th cent., and a bishop, the background powdered with cinquefoils.

SUTTON COURTENAY CHURCH, BERKSHIRE.
Remains of paintings. *Parker, Glossary of Gothic Architecture*, 4th ed., p. 204.

SUTTON ST. MARY'S CHURCH, LINCOLNSHIRE.
On N. wall of S. aisle; floral pattern. 13th cent.

SUTTON, KING'S, CHURCH, NORTHAMPTONSHIRE.
Screen across the S. aisle. *Baker's Hist. and Antiq. of Northamptonshire*, p. 699.
On walls and arches; extensive remains of early paintings. *Beesley, Hist. of Banbury*, pp. 109, 112.

SUTTON, LONG, SOMERSETSHIRE, HOLY TRINITY CHURCH.
Painted rood screen, and E. bay of nave roof.
Painted wooden pulpit; canopy ornament, &c. About 1530. *Dollman, Antient Pulpits*, frontispiece and p. 29.

SWAFFHAM CHURCH, NORFOLK.
Screen, E. end of N. aisle; Saints on the panels.
N. of chancel; effigy of John Bolewright, D.D., formerly painted.
Blomefield, Hist. of Norfolk, ed. 1807, vi. 215. *Chambers, Hist. of Norfolk*, ii. 673. *Murray's Handbook of Norfolk*.
S. wall of nave; Scripture texts. Early 16th cent.
Panel paintings of Saints no longer exist.

SWAFFHAM BULBECK CHURCH, CAMBRIDGESHIRE.
Painted chest. *Paley's Manual of Gothic Architecture*, p. 247.

SWAFIELD CHURCH, NORFOLK.
Rood screen; remains of colour and gilding, and with figures of SS. Andrew, Peter, Jude, Simon, James Major, John, Thomas, and James Minor, depicted on the panels.
Hart, Antiq. of Norfolk, p. 66. *The Ecclesiologist's Guide to the Deaneries of Brisley, &c.*, p. 122.

SWALCLIFFE CHURCH, OXFORDSHIRE.
Screen. *Parker, Eccles. and Architect. Topog. of England, Oxford*, No. 144. *Beesley, Hist. of Banbury*, p. 140.

SWANBOURNE CHURCH, BUCKINGHAMSHIRE.
N. wall; various conditions of the soul. *Records of Buckinghamshire*, iii. 136.

SWANSCOMBE CHURCH, KENT.

Within two recessed niches on either side of the chancel arch ; St. James and the Virgin. *Destroyed.* 14th cent.

Beneath these were found two earlier coats of colour.

Round the soffit of an arch on N. side; flowing tracery.

Within the soffit of a window ; various floral and leaf patterns.

Painted screen. About 1260.

Society of Antiquaries' Proceedings, 2nd series, vi. 233. *J. A. Sparvel-Bayly, Hist. of Swanscombe*, pp. 39, 40. *Long Ago*, 1874, vol. ii., p. 58.

SWANSEA, GLAMORGANSHIRE, ST. MARY'S CHURCH.

Monument of Sir Matthew Cradock, formerly painted and gilt. Early 16th cent. *Archæologia*, xxxii. 448.

SWANTON MORLEY, CHURCH, NORFOLK.

Traces of colour on the font. *Carthew's Hundred of Launditch*, ii. 743.

SWATON CHURCH, LINCOLNSHIRE.

Over chancel arch; passages in the life of Our Lord. *Associated Architect. Societies' Repts.*, ii. 143. *Trollope: Sleaford, Flaxwell, Aswardhurn*, p. 450.

SWIMBRIDGE CHURCH, DEVONSHIRE.

Roof over rood screen ; painted blue, with gilded metal stars. *Stewart's N. Devon Handbook*, p. 204.

SWINCOMBE CHURCH, OXFORDSHIRE.

On walls of apse; Our Lord in Glory between two angels, three consecration crosses, and a powdering of stars. Perhaps pre-Norman. *Archæologia*, xlvii. 165.

W. side of chancel arch ; crosses ragulé.

N. wall of nave; various ornamental borders. 12th and 13th cents.

S. side of nave ; incised forms in plaster of a zigzag character.

Napier, Historical Notices of Swyncombe and Ewelme pp. 222, 223.

SWINDERBY CHURCH, LINCOLNSHIRE.

Painting discovered on one of the walls, very imperfect. *E. G. Wake, The Hist. of Collingham*, p. 77.

TADMARTON CHURCH, OXFORDSHIRE.
On walls and arches; extensive remains of early paintings. *Beesley, Hist. of Banbury*, pp. 109, 139.

TALATON CHURCH, DEVONSHIRE.
Rood screen, richly painted.
N. wall of nave; St. Christopher. *Destroyed.*

TALLAND CHURCH, CORNWALL.
On N. wall: two series of paintings, discovered during
the restoration of the church and *destroyed.*
Lower series; Our Lord and the woman of Samaria,
miraculous draught of fishes, the Crucifixion, &c. 13th
cent.
Upper series; a demon, &c.
*Murray's Handbook of Cornwall. Exeter Diocesan
Architect. Soc.,* iv. 50. *Ecclesiologist,* x. 251. *Parochial
History of Cornwall,* iv. x. *Couch, Hist. of Polperro,*
pp. 66–69.
Painted screen.

TAMERTON CHURCH, CORNWALL.
Canopy of pulpit; gilt ornaments on a blue ground.
Lysons' Magna Britannia, Cornwall, p. ccxxxii.

TAMWORTH, STAFFORDSHIRE, ST. EDITH'S CHURCH.
E. wall of S. transept, St. Nicholas' chapel; St.
Nicholas raising the Three Students to Life, and kneeling
figures of the three ladies who caused the paintings to
be executed. Time of Edward III.
The Crucifixion with the Virgin and St. John, and a
scene (?) from the life of St. Edith. Late 15th cent.
Scripture texts painted over them, and now *destroyed.*
The earlier paintings again whitewashed over.
On wall of crypt; a painting, now lost, over which has
been inscribed a text and the Sacred Monogram.
Under an arch between the choir and chantry chapel;
monument and effigy of Sir John Ferrers and his Lady
died 1512, with remains of colouring.
Palmer, Hist. and Antiq. of Tamworth Church, pp. 77,
90. *Blackburne, Decorative Painting,* pp. 78, 79.
Reliquary, xvii. 60.

TANSOR CHURCH, NORTHAMPTONSHIRE.
S. wall; painting representing a range of arches.
Patterns on the arcades of the nave.

TANWORTH, WARWICKSHIRE, ST. MARY MAGDALENE'S CHURCH.
Bracket on S. side of E. window; gilt and painted panels. About 1300. *Warwickshire Churches, Deanery of Warwick*, ii. 10.

TAUNTON, SOMERSETSHIRE, ST. MARY MAGDALENE'S CHURCH.
Eastern bays of chancel roof; repainted. Late 15th cent.

TAUNTON MUSEUM. *See* WELLINGTON (SOMERSET), AND KEWSTOKE.

TAVERHAM CHURCH, NORFOLK.
Rood screen; painted panels, figures of Saints. *Hart, Antiq. of Norfolk*, p. 66.

TAVISTOCK CHURCH, DEVONSHIRE.
Rood screen; the Heavenly Hierarchy, &c. (?) still existing. *Civil Engineer and Architect's Journ.*, 1860, p. 7.

TAVY, PETER, CHURCH, DEVONSHIRE.
Remains of screen; painted and with figures of SS. Peter, Joseph, Mary Magdalene, Paul, Andrew, &c. on the panels. *Exeter Diocesan Architect. Soc.*, iv. 171.

TAWSTOCK CHURCH, DEVONSHIRE.
Colour on panelling about a small window in the roof over the rood-loft, the Bourchier knot introduced.
Under an arch in the N. chancel; coloured effigy of a lady. Date about 1335. *Exeter Diocesan Architect. Soc.*, 2nd series, iii. 197. *W. H. H. Rogers, The Ancient Sepulchral Effigies, &c. in Devon*, p. 47.
S.W. tower pier; figures? of S.S. Anthony and Erasmus.

TAWTON, BISHOP'S, CHURCH, DEVONSHIRE.
N. aisle; St. Christopher and St. Michael weighing Souls, also Joseph and Potiphar's Wife. *Exeter Diocesan Architect. Soc.*, 2nd series, i. 196, iv. 50. *Worth, Tourist's Guide to N. Devon*, p. 44.

TEALBY CHURCH, LINCOLNSHIRE.
A good deal of old wall painting found during the restoration of the Church. *Associated Architect. Societies' Repts.*, xi. lxxix.

TEIGNTON, KING's, CHURCH, DEVONSHIRE.
Panels of screen; SS. Catharine, Denys, Barbara,
Helen, Geneviève, &c. *Oliver's Ecclesiastical Antiquities
of Devon,* i. 178. *Stirling's Newton,* p. 124.

TEMPSFORD CHURCH, BEDFORDSHIRE.
N. wall of nave; St. Catherine. *Builder,* 1874, p. 20.

TETTENHALL CHURCH, STAFFORDSHIRE.
Chancel; les Trois Morts. *Archæol. Journ.,* xxi. 219,
and *Gent. Mag.,* 1842, xviii. new series, 199.

TEW, GREAT, CHURCH, OXFORDSHIRE.
Over the S. door; the Doom. *Blackburne, Decorative
Painting,* p. 21. *Skelton's Antiquities of Oxfordshire.*
W. end of N. aisle; Christ feeding the Hungry.
Destroyed. North Oxon. Archæol. Soc., 1875, *Gt. Tew,*
p. 17.

TEWKESBURY, ABBEY CHURCH, GLOUCESTERSHIRE.
Chantry chapel of Robert Fitzhamon; remains of
painting. *Blackburne, Decorative Painting,* p. 60.
Roof formerly painted and gilt. Circ. 1397.
Trinity chapel; on E. wall a painting of the Trinity.
Below it portraits of Edward le Despencer, Earl of
Gloucester, and Elizabeth his wife. Date about 1400.
See note to plate lxxix. of *Lysons' Antiquities of
Gloucestershire. Gent. Mag.,* 1849, xxxii., new series,
472. *Civil Engineer and Architect's Journal,* 1851,
p. 197. *A new Handbook and Guide to Tewkesbury
Abbey Church,* pp. 22, 24. *A Guide to Tewkesbury and
Neighbourhood,* pp. 90, 91.
Walls of the Warwick chapel; countercharged pattern.
Blackburne, Decorative Painting, p. 77. *Builder,* 1877,
p. 393.
Also, formerly painted, the Apostles, St. Christopher,
two Angels worshipping the Cross, &c. *J. G. Nichols,
Description of the Church of St. Mary, Warwick, &c.,*
p. 27.
Decorative colour on the canopy of the monument and
on the effigy of Sir Guy de Brien. Circ. 1391. *Builder,*
1877, p. 393. *Stothard's Monumental Effigies,* pl. 90.
Colour on monument of Lord Despencer. *Gent. Mag.,*
xcvii., 122.
Walls of Spencer Chapel; portraits of Our Lord and
the Apostles. *Dyde's History of Tewkesbury,* p. 50.

TEWKESBURY, ABBEY CHURCH, GLOUCESTERSHIRE—*cont.*

Stone stalls on S. of high altar; the canopies and backs have been richly painted and gilt with a diaper of fleur-de-lis and flowers. Circ. 1300. Figured in *Lysons' Antiquities of Gloucestershire*, pl. lvi. *Blackburne, Decorative Painting*, p. 39.

Nave roof shows traces of original colouring.

Choir roof repainted.

Numerous statues with remains of colouring discovered. *Builder*, 1877, p. 394.

12th cent. colouring. *Archæol. Journ.*, xxxiv. 277.

TEY, MARK'S, CHURCH, ESSEX.

Wooden font, with remains of polychrome painting. *Essex Archæol.*, iv. 117. *Murray's Handbook of Essex.*

THAME CHURCH, OXFORDSHIRE.

Wall paintings.

THEALE CHURCH, BERKSHIRE.

Chantry, N. side of altar, brought from Magdalene College Chapel, Oxford, remains of colour on doorways, &c. 15th cent. *Newbury District Field Club*, 1872–75, p. 119.

THERFIELD CHURCH, HERTFORDSHIRE.

Mural paintings, much decayed. Discovered beneath the whitewash.

THETFORD, NORFOLK, ST. CUTHBERT'S CHURCH.

On the screens, "were painted several saints, and the "history of Our Saviour's passion, but they are now "much defaced."

On N. wall of chancel; "many historical pieces out of "the New Testament." *Whitewashed over. Blomefield, Hist. of Norfolk*, ed. 1805, ii. 65. *J. Wilkinson, The Architect. Remains of Thetford*, p. 5. *A. L. Hunt, The capital . . . of East Anglia*, p. 91.

THETFORD, NORFOLK, ST. PETER'S CHURCH.

On the screens; the Apostles with sentences from the Creed. *Blomefield, Hist. of Norfolk*, ed. 1805, ii. 62. *A. L. Hunt, The Capital . . . . of East Anglia*, p. 107.

THETFORD, NORFOLK, BENEDICTINE NUNNERY OF ST. GEORGE.

Portions of images which had been painted found in the ruins. *Blomefield, Hist. of Norfolk*, ed., 1805, ii. 94.

THETFORD, NORFOLK, THE PRIORY CHURCH.

Chapel on N. side of nave; E. wall painted red, also many mutilated fragments of perpendicular screen work richly gilt and painted. Discovered during excavations made by Mr. Harrod in 1851. *Norfolk Archæol.,* iii. 116.

THIRSK CHURCH, YORKSHIRE.

Between the clerestory windows; the Twelve Apostles. *Ripon and Richmond Chronicle,* March 1st, 1878. *Builder,* 1876, p. 444.

THORINGTON CHURCH, ESSEX.

Masonry foliated and diaper patterns. Early 13th cent. *Essex Archæol.,* v. 97.

THORNFORD CHURCH, DORSETSHIRE.

Chancel roof; original colour and gilding. *Hutchins' Hist. of Dorset,* 3rd ed., iv. 301.

THORNHAM CHURCH, NORFOLK.

Rood screen of 16 panels; David, the Prophets, omitting Obadiah, Jonah, Nahum, Habakkuk, and Haggai, SS. Paul, Barbara, Mary Magdalene, and Lazarus. Early 15th cent. *Sacristy,* iii. 153.

THRIGBY CHURCH, NORFOLK.

On chancel walls; a diaper pattern with monograms, and three consecration crosses. Date 15th cent. *Norfolk Archæol.,* vi. 386. *East Anglian Notes and Queries,* ii. 126.

THROWLEY CHURCH, DEVONSHIRE.

Lower part of screen; biblical subjects. 1544. *Lysons' Magna Britannia, Devonshire,* p. cccxxviii.
The panels have been removed.

THURGARTON CHURCH, NOTTINGHAMSHIRE.

E. end of chancel; remains of canopy, richly painted and gilt. Time of Edward II. *British Archæol. Assoc. Journ.* viii. 250.

THURLOW CHURCH, SUFFOLK.

Screen; diapers.

THURNBY CHURCH, LEICESTERSHIRE.

E. end of S. aisle; recess decorated with a margin of scroll work in black and red, containing four lines in old English character, coloured.
On under side of chancel arch; scroll work in red.
Over W. tower arch; some lettering.

THURNBY CHURCH, LEICESTERSHIRE—*cont.*

On W. front of N.W. tower column, old English writing, and under the capital semi-circular pattern.

Mural paintings of early English date. *Associated Architect. Societies' Repts.*, xi., 185, 188. *Antiquary*, 1871, i. 202. *J. H. Hill, Hist. of Market Harborough,* &c., p. 292.

THURSBY CHURCH, CUMBERLAND.

Sculpture representing the Flagellation of Christ found under the flagstones; richly coloured and gilt. *British Archæol. Assoc. Journ.*, iv. 196.

TICHBORNE CHURCH, HAMPSHIRE.

N. wall of nave; St. Christopher. *Proceedings of the British Archæol. Association*, Winchester vol., p. 411. *Proceedings of the Royal Archæol. Institute*, Winchester vol., p. 28.

TIDMARSH CHURCH, BERKSHIRE.

On jambs of windows; portraits of Saints. *Ecclesiologist*, iii. 70, xii. 287.

TILBROOK CHURCH, BEDFORDSHIRE.

Painted rood screen; on lower panels, St. Margaret, the Virgin and Child, ? St. Helen, and St. Mary Magdalene. 15th cent. *Colling, Gothic Ornaments*, ii. pls. 65 and 69.

Over the chancel arch; under several layers of paintings was discovered the Last Judgment, now whitewashed over or *destroyed.*

TILNEY, NORFOLK, ALL SAINTS' CHURCH.

Screen, E. end of N. aisle; shields of arms, "roses, mullets, and stars."

On walls of Chapel, E. end of S aisle; "are painted several shields, now much obscured by length of time." *Blomefield, (Parkin,) Hist. of Norfolk*, ed. 1808, ix. 81, 82.

TILTON-ON-THE-HILL CHURCH, LEICESTERSHIRE.

N. wall of nave; decorative colouring, whitewashed over.

Traces of colour on the cross-legged effigy of a Digby, and part of a blue letter inscription on the slab; also traces of painting on the effigy of his lady.

TIMWORTH CHURCH, SUFFOLK.

Chancel, scriptural subjects; the Annunciation, Salutation, Adoration of the Magi, and the Shepherds, and

TIMWORTH CHURCH, SUFFOLK—*cont.*

decorative patterns. 13th cent. *Destroyed.* Rough sketch in the possession of Rev. F. Sutton. Above these was another system of colouring. 15th cent. *Associated Architect. Societies' Repts.*, ix. 252, 253. *Quarterly Journ. of Suffolk Inst. for* 1869, p. 22.

TINTAGEL, CORNWALL, ST. SYMPHORIAN'S CHURCH.

Numerous paintings were found, one set painted over another, during the restoration, the lowest being in bold zigzag patterns of the Norman period. They are now again covered with yellow wash. *Ecclesiologist*, xii. 234.

Square oak shouldered doorway from chancel to Lady Chapel, once painted a deep red. *Journ. Royal Inst., Cornwall*, 1872, p. 47.

TIVERTON CHURCH, DEVONSHIRE.

Rood screen; richly painted. Early 15th cent.

N. wall of nave; two tiers of foliage and geometrical patterns of the Geometrical and Renaissance periods. *Exeter Diocesan Architect. Soc.*, iii. pt. ii. 4, and vi. 43.

Buttresses of tower and wall of N. aisle; flowers and foliage.

Roof of S. aisle; remains of colour.

British Archæol. Assoc. Journ., xviii. 235, 236.

Greenway's Chapel; screen, *removed*, roof, &c. *Harding, Hist. of Tiverton*, iv. 7, 10.

TODDINGTON CHURCH, BEDFORDSHIRE.

N. and S. walls of nave; figures of ecclesiastical personages, with scroll inscriptions.

Over N. door; large figure between two trees, (?) St. Christopher, and a scroll border.

TOFT CHURCH, CAMBRIDGESHIRE.

Fragments of the reredos, richly coloured and gilt, discovered built up in the walls. *Ecclesiologist*, xxiv. (xxi. new series), 180, 246.

TOFT MONKS CHURCH, NORFOLK.

Screen, with panel paintings of Saints. *Removed.*

TOFTS, WEST, CHURCH, NORFOLK.

Chancel screen. *Kelly's Post Office Directory of Norfolk.*

TONG CHURCH, SHROPSHIRE.

S. aisle (Golden) Chapel; over the effigy of Sir H. Vernon, remains of painting, (?) the Crucifixion.

TONG CHURCH, SHROPSHIRE—*cont.*

Painting and gilding on the ceiling and on the canopy of the monument of Arthur Vernon. Date about 1517.
Archæol. Journ., ii. 8, 9. *British Archæol. Assoc. Journ.*, xvii. 149. *Antiquary*, 1871, i. 145.

Over screen between chancel and chapel; four tabernacle niches with remains of colour and gilding. *Kelly's Post Office Directory of Shropshire.*

TOR BRYAN CHURCH, DEVONSHIRE.

Rood screen and pulpit painted and gilt. About 1430. *Murray's Handbook of Devonshire. Lysons' Magna Britannia, Devonshire*, p. cccxxviii.

On panels of screen; the Evangelists and Apostles, omitting SS. James Minor and Matthias, The Virgin as Queen of Heaven, and St. Gabriel, and SS. Veronica, Laurence, Cecilia, Barbara, Apollonia, Dorothy, Helena, and Agatha. *C. Worthy, Ashburton and its Neighbourhood*, p. 155.

TOR MOHUN CHURCH, DEVONSHIRE. *See* COCKINGTON.

TOTHAM, GREAT, CHURCH, ESSEX.

N. side, next the chancel arch, between the ashlar upright sides of the nave roof; paintings of archangels and angels in adoration [towards the Passion which probably existed over the chancel arch.]

TOTNES CHURCH, DEVONSHIRE.

Stone rood screen, painted and gilt, and decorated with heraldic shields. Traces of figures on the panels. *Lysons' Magna Britannia, Devonshire*, p. cccxxvii. *Cotton, Antiquities of Totnes*, p. 41. *Worth, Tourist's Guide to S. Devon*, p. 53.

In S. Chantry Chapel; altar tomb coloured and gilt. Circ. 1555. *C. Worthy, Ashburton and its Neighbourhood*, p. 111.

On panels of pulpit; traces of figures found beneath two other courses of colouring.

TOTNES, DEVONSHIRE, THE GUILDHALL.

On wall of Hall; arms of Edward VI. *East Anglian Notes and Queries*, i. 46.

TOTTINGTON CHURCH, NORFOLK.

Screen; carved and gilded. *Chambers, Hist. of Norfolk*, ii. 998.

TREDINGTON CHURCH, WORCESTERSHIRE.
Remains of painting on the props of the roof. *Ecclesiologist*, xxvi. (xxiii. new series), 372.

TREETON CHURCH, YORKSHIRE.

TRENT CHURCH, SOMERSETSHIRE.
Chapel N. side of nave; coloured effigy (?) of Roger Wyke. Late 14th cent. *Somerset Archæol. and Nat. Hist. Soc. Proceedings*, xx. 134.

TRENTISHOE CHURCH, DEVONSHIRE.
Compartment of the nave roof above the rood screen painted. *Exeter Diocesan Architect. Soc.*, 2nd series, iii. 34.

TREVALGA CHURCH, CORNWALL.
Diaper and other wall decorations. 13th cent. *Notes and Queries*, 4th series, ix. 52. *Maclean, Hist. of the Deanery of Trigg Minor*, iii. 291. *Antiquary*, 1871, i. 190.

TREYFORD CHURCH, SUSSEX.
E. end of chancel; decorative colouring on the splays of the E. triple lancet window. 13th cent. *Society of Antiquaries' Proceedings*, ii. 19. *Sussex Archæol.*, ii. x. and iii. ix.
Several consecration crosses.

TRIMMINGHAM CHURCH, NORFOLK.
Rood screen. Painted and gilt, and with SS. Edmund, Clare, Clement, James the Greater, Petronilla, Cicely, Barbara, and Edward, King and Martyr, depicted on the panels.

TROSTON, SUFFOLK, ST. MARY'S CHURCH.
Painted screen. Perpendicular period. *Parker, Eccles. and Architect. Topog. of England, Suffolk*, No. 389.
Wall paintings of St. George and the Dragon, St. Christopher, and martyrdom of St. Edmund.

TRUMPINGTON CHURCH, CAMBRIDGESHIRE.
Original gilding and diaper work on panels of chancel screen; carefully restored. *Ecclesiologist*, xviii. 197.

TRUNCH, NORFOLK, ST. BOTOLPH'S CHURCH.
Rood screen; dated 1502, St. Paul and eleven of the Apostles, omitting St. Matthew, tracery, panels, &c. *East Anglian Notes and Queries*, iii. 316.
Canopy of font; the Crucifixion, &c. *Ecclesiologist*, vi. 31. *Blackburne, Decorative Painting*, p. 80. *Hart, Antiq. of Norfolk*, p. 31.
Remains of painting on the ringers' gallery.

TRUSHAM CHURCH, DEVONSHIRE.

On screen ; painted figures of SS. Peter, Paul, Andrew, James, Simon, George, and Helen. *Oliver's Ecclesiastical Antiquities of Devon,* i. 192. *Lysons' Magna Britannia, Devonshire,* p. cccxxviii.

TUDDENHAM, NORTH, CHURCH, NORFOLK.

On panels of rood screen ; N. side ; SS. Agnes, Gregory, Dorothy, and Jerome, or Geron.

S. side ; SS. Catherine, Sebastian, (or Edmund,) Etheldreda, and Roche.

TUNSTEAD CHURCH, NORFOLK.

On panels of rood screen; St. Paul, the Apostles, omitting St. Matthew, and the four Doctors of the Church. Date about 1500. *Civil Engineer and Architect's Journal,* 1851, p. 196. *Society of Antiquaries' Proceedings,* i. 103. *The Ecclesiologist's Guide to the Deaneries of Brisley, &c.,* p. 122.

Three beams across the nave, with a foliated monogram and other painting.

TURRIFF CHURCH, ABERDEENSHIRE, SCOTLAND.

Paintings of St. Ninian and other ecclesiastics discovered on the walls. *Murray's Handbook of Scotland. Black's Guide to Scotland.*

TURVEY CHURCH, BEDFORDSHIRE.

S. wall of S. aisle, back of monumental recess ; the Crucifixion. 13th cent.

Above the recess, a large painting was discovered and destroyed.

W. M. Harvey, Hist. of Willey Hundred, p. 206.

TWYFORD CHURCH, LEICESTERSHIRE.

Nave roof; remains of colour and gilt bosses. 15th cent.

TYWARDRETH CHURCH, CORNWALL.

Screen ; figures in white robes holding the symbols of the Crucifixion. *Lysons' Magna Britannia, Cornwall,* p. ccxxxii.

UFFCULME CHURCH, DEVONSHIRE.
Painted screen. '*Lysons' Magna Britannia, Devonshire*, p. cccxxviii. *J. Davidson, Hist. of Axminster Church*, p. 57, note.

UFFINGTON CHURCH, LINCOLNSHIRE.
E. wall of chancel; large figures. *Destroyed.*

UFFORD CHURCH, SUFFOLK.
Painted font cover. About 1450. *Colling, Gothic Ornaments*, ii. pls. 51, 52, and 58.
Rood beam and roof of chancel. *Colling, Gothic Ornaments*, ii. 61.
Lower part of rood screen, with figures depicted on the panels, those on the N. side defaced.
On S. side; SS. Agnes, Cecilia, Agatha, Fides, Brigida, and Florentia.
Suffolk Archæol., v. 124. *Parker, Eccles. and Architect. Topog. of England, Suffolk*, No. 356.
N. wall of nave; scroll patterns whitewashed over, and St. Christopher.
Nave roof; richly painted and with powdering of the monograms Ihc and M. 15th cent.

UGBOROUGH CHURCH, DEVONSHIRE.
Rood screen; figures of saints and martyrs depicted on the panels, viz., on N.; SS. Appollonia, Margaret, the Annunciation, the Adoration of the Magi, the Virgin, two Angels, St. John the Baptist, the martyrdom of St. Sebastian, and a doubtful subject.
On S.; twelve female figures bearing the emblems of the Passion, (? the Sybils), SS. Agnes, Agatha, and (?) an executioner and the daughter of Herodias, part of the martyrdom of St. John the Baptist. Date 15th cent.
Exeter Diocesan Architect. Soc., 2nd series, ii. 96.

UGGESHALL CHURCH, SUFFOLK.
Chancel wall; a dedication cross.

ULCOMB CHURCH, KENT.
Lazarus and Dives; the Crucifixion. St. Michael and Satan. 14th cent.
Pattern of chevrons and masonry. Late 12th cent.

ULLENHALL CHURCH, WARWICKSHIRE.
"Three distinct coats of decoration, one an ornamental design, the other two consisting of sentences from Scripture." *Associated Architect. Societies' Repts.*, xiii. xciv.

Q 3254. R

UPCHURCH CHURCH, KENT.

Within a recess E. end, N. side of nave; an archbishop, (?) St. Thomas à Becket. 13th cent.

S. wall, E. end of S. aisle; the history of a bishop. Early 13th cent.

On E. wall of S. chancel chapel; two priests, two knights in combat, &c. 14th cent.

Archæol. Cantiana, xi. 42. *Glynne, Churches of Kent*, p. 176.

UPHILL CHURCH, SOMERSETSHIRE.

On E. wall of chancel; three figures. 13th cent. *J., L E. H., Visitor's Handbook to Weston-super-Mare*, p. 233.

UPMINSTER CHURCH, ESSEX.

Screen across N. aisle; " of the age of Henry VI., " finely carved and finished in colours and gold, still " brilliant." *T. L. Wilson, Sketches of Upminster*, p. 44.

UPPINGHAM CHURCH, RUTLANDSHIRE.

Arches; running pattern. *Associated Architect. Societies' Repts.*, ix. 253.

UPTON CHURCH, BERKSHIRE.

On both sides of chancel arch ; scripture texts.

Remains of colouring on walls of nave.

UPTON CHURCH, BUCKINGHAMSHIRE.

Capitals of columns, &c. coloured. 13th cent. *Associated Architect. Societies' Repts.*, iii. 360.

N. wall of nave; an Angel carrying a Soul up to Heaven.

Gent. Mag., 1846, xxvi., new series, 607.

E. wall of nave; nook shafts and capitals of arched recess painted. Early 13th cent. *Gent. Mag.*, 1847, xxviii., new series, 489.

Sculpture in alabaster of the Trinity coloured and gilt. 14th cent. Found embedded in the N. wall. *Archæol. Journ.*, vii. 388.

Chancel vaulting ; not in original condition.

UPTON CHURCH, NORFOLK.

Rood screen; the Fathers of the Church, SS. Helena, Etheldreda, Agatha, and Joan of Valois. *East Anglian Notes and Queries*, iii. 316. *Norfolk Archæol.*, iii. 19.

UPTON BISHOP CHURCH, HEREFORDSHIRE.
"Early scroll pattern about lancet windows of the chancel." *Havergal, Fasti Herefordenses,* p. 157.

UPTON GRAY CHURCH, HAMPSHIRE.
Traces of masonry patterns occur on the walls in several parts.

UPWELL CHURCH, NORFOLK.
Roof of nave. *Brandon, Parish Churches,* ii. 48.
Rood screen; Christ bearing His Cross, the Ascension, the Descent of the Holy Ghost upon the Apostles, an altar with the Cup and Wafer, supported by two bishops, the Trinity, and several female Saints, on the panels. Removed circ. 1820. *Blomefield, (Parkin,) Hist. of Norfolk,* ed. 1807, vii. 466. *Watson, Historical Account of Wisbech,* p. 543.

UPWOOD CHURCH, HUNTINGDONSHIRE.
Remains of colouring on the E. column, S. side of nave.

VALLE CRUCIS ABBEY, DENBIGHSHIRE.
Remains of coloured decoration still visible on the sheltered portions of the chapel walls. *Builder,* 1877, p. 914.

WACTON MAGNA CHURCH, NORFOLK.
Over N. door; St. Christopher. *Blomefield, Hist. of Norfolk,* ed. 1806, v. 301. *Cromwell, Excursions through Norfolk,* i. 55. *Chambers, Hist. of Norfolk,* i. 115.

WADDINGTON CHURCH, LINCOLNSHIRE.
Ornamental colouring on pillar shafts, capitals, and font. *Associated Architect. Societies' Repts.,* ix. xii.

WAINFLEET, ALL SAINTS (OLD) CHURCH, LINCOLNSHIRE.
Monument of Richard Patten; coloured shield on, and figure of bishop Wainfleet at the head of, his effigy. Now in the Chapel of Magdalen College, Oxford. *Oldfield, Topog. and Hist. Account of Wainfleet,* p. 39.

WAKEFIELD, YORKSHIRE, ALL SAINTS' CHURCH.
S. spandrel, W. side of chancel arch; figure of an
angel. About 1470. *Society of Antiquaries' Proceedings,*
2nd series, iv. 28. *Ecclesiologist,* xxix. (xxvi. new series)
135. *Banks' Walks in Yorkshire, Wakefield and
Neighbourhood,* p. 20.
Remains of colour on roof of nave and chancel. About
1470. *Society of Antiquaries' Proceedings,* 2nd series,
vi. 139.

WAKEFIELD, YORKSHIRE, THE BRIDGE CHAPEL.
N. side of E. window; niche with remains of colouring.
British Archæol. Assoc. Journ., xx. 117.

WAKERING, LITTLE, CHURCH, ESSEX.
N. side of chancel, within the splay of a window; the
Nativity. Probably late 12th cent. *Essex Archæol.,*
i., new series, 276.

WALBERSWICK, SUFFOLK, ST. ANDREW'S CHURCH.
Rood screen panels at W. end.

WALCOT CHURCH, NORFOLK.
Rood screen. Circ. 1429.

WALDEN, KING'S, CHURCH, HERTFORDSHIRE.
Chancel screen; repainted. *Cussans, Hist. of Hertfordshire,* vol. ii., pt. i., p. 124.

WALDEN, SAFFRON. *See* SAFFRON WALDEN.

WALGRAVE CHURCH, NORTHAMPTONSHIRE.
Chancel roof; painted boss.

WALLINGFORD, BERKSHIRE, ST. LEONARD'S CHURCH.
Over first inner arch; a flower pattern.
On S. of chancel; various figures.
Hedges, Hist. of Wallingford, ii. 393.

WALPOLE, ST. PETER'S CHURCH, NORFOLK.
Fronts of the book boards and panels of screen; Saints
under canopies, viz., SS. Dorothy, Catherine, The Virgin
and Child, SS. Margaret, Helena, Peter, Paul, Andrew,
John the Evangelist, James, Thomas, Barbara, Mary Magdalene, and Gudule. Time of Henry VI. *Illustrations
of Norfolk Topography,* p. 187. *Associated Architect.
Societies' Repts.,* ix. 250. *Husenbeth, Emblems of Saints.*
Over rood stair, on N. pier; the Virgin, and on opposite

WALPOLE, ST. PETER'S CHURCH, NORFOLK—*cont.*

S. pier, St. John the Evangelist. *Schnebbelie, The Anti-quaries' Museum. Blomefield, (Parkin,) Hist. of Norfolk,* ed. 1808, ix. 114. *Cromwell, Excursions through Norfolk,* ii. 94. *Chambers, Hist. of Norfolk,* i. 493. *Watson, Historical Account of Wisbech,* p. 622.

Over S. door; traces of a St. Christopher.

WALSHAM CHURCH, SUFFOLK.

Paintings exist under the whitewash. *British Archœol. Assoc. Journ.,* i. 339.

St. Barbara, St. Margaret, St. Mary Magdalene.

WALSHAM, NORTH, CHURCH, NORFOLK.

Richly painted screen, with figures depicted on the panels; viz., the Apostles, omitting St. Matthias, the Virgin, an Archangel, and SS. Mary of Egypt or Wilgefortis, Catherine, Paul, Barbara, Margaret, and Mary Magdalene. *Archœol. Journ.,* i. 258. *The Ecclesiologist's Guide to the Deaneries of Brisley, &c.,* p. 122.

Painted font cover.

WALSHAM, SOUTH, CHURCH, NORFOLK.
Rood screen.

WALSHAM-LE-WILLOWS CHURCH, SUFFOLK.

Painted screen and roof of nave and aisles. Perpendicular period. *Parker, Eccles. and Architect. Topog. of England, Suffolk,* No. 390.

Within the spandrils of the chancel arch; paintings of angels or cherubim.

On the E. wall of the S. aisle; diaper and panelled work. *Builder,* 1878, p. 1024.

WALSINGHAM, NEW, CHURCH, NORFOLK.

Ceiling, E. end of aisles; painted panels.

Rood screen; traces of colour, and formerly figures of Saints on the panels. *Hart, Antiq. of Norfolk,* p. 66.

Traces of colour on the pulpit. Font formerly painted and gilt; the seven Sacraments and the Crucifixion.

WALSOKEN CHURCH, NORFOLK.

On the chancel arch; a foliated pattern. About 1200, *Archœol. Journ.,* xxxviii. 92.

Remains of colour and gilding on the roof of the nave and on the screens between the aisles and chancel aisles. 15th cent.

WALTHAM, GREAT, CHURCH, ESSEX.
Chancel arch; Our Lord in Glory, and on the spandrils St. Michael weighing Souls, and Death on the Pale Horse.
Fragments of other paintings in various parts of the church. 14th cent.
British Archæol. Assoc. Journ., iii. 92, *Builder,* 1864, p. 725. *Gent. Mag.,* 1847, xxviii., new series, 188.

WALTHAM ABBEY CHURCH, ESSEX.
N. side of nave. *British Archæol. Assoc. Journ.,* ii. 197.
In S. aisle; masonry patterns on S. wall, and traces of colour on the chevron mouldings of the windows and on the S. doorway; also an inscription in Old English within a border. *Essex Archæol.,* ii. 42.

WALTHAM ABBEY, ESSEX.
House of Mr. E. H. Kearley. Stone chimney piece, with remains of colour and gilding. 15th cent. *Antiquary,* 1871, i. 50.

WALTON, SUFFOLK, ST. MARY'S CHURCH.
Lower part of rood screen. *Parker, Eccles. and Architect. Topog. of England, Suffolk,* No. 74.

WALTON, WEST, NORFOLK, ST. MARY'S CHURCH.
Clerestory, S. side; representations of tapestries, various diapers.
Spandrel between arches of nave, N. side; circular ornament.
13th cent.
Colling, Gothic Ornaments, i. pls. 58, 62, and 63; and *Builder,* 1864, p. 724. *The Fen and Marshland Churches,* i. 8.

WANGFORD, SUFFOLK, CHURCH OF SS. PETER AND PAUL.
S. wall of nave; St. Christopher. Between 1450–1480.
Portions of the panelling of the roof, decorated with the Sacred Monogram.

WANTAGE CHURCH, BERKSHIRE.
Coloured effigy of Amicia, Lady Fitz Warine. *Hollis, Monumental Effigies,* pt. iii. pl. 7.

WARBLINGTON CHURCH, HAMPSHIRE.
Nave walls; a series of Our Saviour's miracles, one His miraculous intervention on behalf of Shadrach,

WARBLINGTON CHURCH, HAMPSHIRE—*cont.*
Meschach, and Abednego. He is also twice depicted bearing His Cross. Powdering of crimson stars.
Behind the pulpit, a coat of arms. All 14th cent. found in 1852, and again whitewashed over.
Longcroft, A Topog. Account of the Hundred of Bosmere, &c., p. 115.

WARDEN ABBEY CHURCH, BEDFORDSHIRE.
" Fragments of carved work, bosses, &c., on which the " painting and gilding retained its original brightness," dug up on the site in 1838. *Parker, Eccles. and Architect. Topog. of England, Bedford, No.* 127, *note.*

WARDEN, OLD, CHURCH, BEDFORDSHIRE.
On each of the two nave pillars ; a crowned " M."

WARDLEY CHURCH, RUTLANDSHIRE.
On inner W. wall of S. porch; outlines of figures visible through the whitewash.

WARE CHURCH, HERTFORDSHIRE.
Painted roofs. *Antiquarian Itinerary,* vol. i.

WARE-GIFFORD. *See* WEAR-GIFFORD.

WARFIELD CHURCH, BERKSHIRE.
Figure of Henry VI. 15th cent. *Archæologia,* xv. 405.

WARKWORTH CHURCH, NORTHAMPTONSHIRE.
On walls and arches; extensive remains of early paintings. *Beesley, Hist. of Banbury,* pp. 109, 120.

WARLINGHAM CHURCH, SURREY.
On N. wall ; St. Christopher. *Surrey Archæol.,* vii. *Repts.* p. xviii.

WARMINGTON CHURCH, NORTHAMPTONSHIRE.
Lower part of screen ; painted mouldings and diapers on the panels.
Pulpit ; panel paintings of Our Saviour and various Saints.

WARMINSTER, WILTSHIRE, ST. DENIS' CHURCH.
On N. wall of an oratory within the tower; painting of ? St. Denis. *Destroyed. J. J. Daniell, Hist. of Warminster,* p. 153.

WARTNABY CHURCH, LEICESTERSHIRE.

On arches; devices, zigzag and foliated patterns. Late 12th or early 13th cent. *Associated Architect. Societies' Repts.*, ix., lxxi. *Leicester Architect. and Archæol. Soc. Trans.*, iii. 336.

WARTON CHURCH, LANCASHIRE.

Painted panels; the Virgin, Ecclesiastics, &c. . *Whitaker's History of (Lonsdale) Richmondshire*, ii. 296.

WARWICK, WARWICKSHIRE, ST. MARY'S CHURCH.

Roof of choir; painted and gilt shields. About 1400.

BEAUCHAMP CHAPEL.

E. window; canopied niches painted and gilt, containing coloured effigies of the Heavenly Hierarchy, also SS. Barbara, Catherine, Margaret, and Mary Magdalene. *Antiquarian and Architect. Year Book*, p. 318. About 1450.

Roof; painted and gilt bosses.

Warwickshire Churches, Deanery of Warwick, i. 42, 71, 73. *J. G. Nichols, Description of the Church of St. Mary, Warwick, &c.*, pp. 3, 5. *Cooke's Guide to Warwickshire*, 12th ed., p. 133.

WATERBEACH CHURCH, CAMBRIDGESHIRE.

Decorative painting on nave pillars. *Cambridge Antiq. Soc. Publications, Horningsey*, p. 38.

WATFORD CHURCH, HERTFORDSHIRE.

Pillars between nave and N. aisle; St. Christopher and St. Dunstan. *British Archæol. Assoc. Journ.*, iv. 71. Not now visible.

WATH, YORKSHIRE, ST. MARY-THE-VIRGIN'S CHURCH.

Chapel S. side of nave; remains of colour and gilding on the canopy of a monument. *Associated Architect. Societies' Repts.*, xiii. 78.

WATH, YORKSHIRE, THE RECTORY.

Coloured decoration on walls of parlour. Late 16th cent. *Associated Architect. Societies' Repts.*, xiii. 218.

WATTISFIELD CHURCH, SUFFOLK.

Traces of paintings on the walls. *Quarterly Journ. of Suffolk Inst. for 1869*, p. 23.

Rood screen.

WATTON CHURCH, YORKSHIRE.

Traces of colour on the roofs. Circ. 1500. *Associated Architect. Societies' Repts.*, vi. cxiii.

WEAR-GIFFORD CHURCH, DEVONSHIRE.
Martyrdom of St. Sebastian. *Exeter Diocesan Architect. Soc.*, iv. 51.

WEATHERSFIELD CHURCH, ESSEX.
Screen, formerly painted, now varnished over.

WEDMORE CHURCH, SOMERSETSHIRE.
Behind the pulpit; three representations of St. Christopher. *Builder*, 1881, vol. xl. p. 742. *The Antiquary,* 1881, iv. 79.

WEETING, NORFOLK, ALL SAINTS' CHURCH.
Screen; saints on the panels. *Blomefield, Hist. of Norfolk*, ed. 1805, ii. 168. *Cromwell, Excursions through Norfolk*, ii. 141. *Chambers' Hist. of Norfolk*, ii. 697.

WELBOURNE CHURCH, LINCOLNSHIRE.
Said to have a painted roof under the plaster ceiling. *Associated Architect. Societies' Repts.*, ix. 254.

WELLINGBOROUGH CHURCH, NORTHAMPTONSHIRE.
Roof of chapel, S. side of S. aisle; principals painted, and on the panels between, the Sacred Monogram, emblems of the Evangelists, shields with the instruments of the Passion, and other devices. Late 15th cent. *J. Cole, Hist. of Wellingborough*, p. 50. *F. Whellan, Hist. Topog. and Directory of Northants*, 1874, p. 888.

WELLINGHAM CHURCH, NORFOLK.
Rood screen; figures of Saints on the panels, and spiral mouldings. *Hart, Antiq. of Norfolk*, p. 67. *The Ecclesiologist's Guide to the Deaneries of Brisley, &c.*, p. 17.

WELLINGTON CHURCH, SOMERSETSHIRE.
Portions of richly gilt and painted reredos, with the Crucifixion, SS. Christopher, Catherine, Michael, &c. End of 14th cent. Now in the Taunton Museum.
Some Norman fragments with polychromatic decoration. *Somerset Archæol. and Nat. Hist. Soc. Proceedings*, vol. i. pt. ii. p. 30.

WELLOW CHURCH, HAMPSHIRE.
Window at E. end of church; two crowned heads and scroll ornament. 13th cent. *British Archæol. Assoc. Journ.*, vii. 69. *Archæol. Journ.*, ix. 117.
HUNGERFORD CHAPEL.
Our Saviour and the Apostles. *Murray's Handbook of Hampshire. Moody, Sketches of Hampshire*, p. 216.

WELLOW CHURCH, SOMERSETSHIRE.

Painted screens. 15th cent.

Nave roof with remains of colouring. 15th cent.

N. CHANCEL CHAPEL.

Eastern bay of roof, painted, with gilt stars on the panels. Late 15th cent.

Over E. window ; Our Lord in Glory.

On either side of the E. window and on the N. wall ; large figures of saints, the Virgin, SS. Stephen, Thomas, Margaret, Bartholomew, and others. Late 15th cent.

Fragments of painted woodwork. Late 15th cent.

Antiquary, 1871, i. 38. *Tunstall, Rambles about Bath and its Neighbourhood*, pp. 197, 352.

WELLS CHURCH, NORFOLK.

Over S. door ; St. Christopher, with inscriptions painted over it.

Between the aisle windows ; pots of flowers and scroll work. 16th cent.

Lower part of rood screen repainted.

Norfolk Archæol., v. 85. *Murray's Handbook of Norfolk.*

" Over the S. door in the Church, the history of the " flood is painted, and over the N. door, that of Jonas." *Blomefield, (Parkin,) Hist. of Norfolk*, ed. 1808, ix. 286. *Chambers, Hist. of Norfolk*, ii. 612.

[This interpretation of the subjects is clearly erroneous, the first being St. Christopher, the second, probably, a Doom.]

WELLS CATHEDRAL, SOMERSETSHIRE.

On tympanum of central W. porch ; sculpture of the Virgin and Child, displaying remains of colour. *Murray's Handbook of Somerset.*

Upper wall of S. aisle ; powder of yellow stars on a red ground. *Builder*, 1864, p. 725.

Remains of colour round the great W. window. 13th cent.

Bubwith chantry, S. side of nave ; painted shield.

N. transept ; painted clock, brought from Glastonbury Abbey, and originally made in 1334.

S. transept ; cornice on S. wall, painted with heads, roses, &c.

Rich colouring, diaper patterns, &c., on monuments of Bishop de la Marchia, died 1303 ; and of Joanna, Viscountess Lisle. Circ. 1464.

Painted font. 13th cent.

WELLS CATHEDRAL, SOMERSETSHIRE—*cont.*

In E. aisle of S. transept; Bishop Beckington's shrine; painted groining, diapered panels, cornices, &c.   15th cent.

Colling, Gothic Ornaments, vol. ii. pls. 73, 77, 82, and 86.

Nave roof; repainted in imitation of the original colouring.   Date about 1450.   Discovered during the restoration in 1842. *Murray's Handbook of Somersetshire.*

S. side of chancel; colouring on Bishop's throne *Destroyed.*

S. choir aisle; remains of colour on the effigy and table-tomb of Bishop Beckington.   1464.

Colour and gilding on monument and effigy of Bishop William Button, died 1279, on S. side of retrochoir; on shields on the monument of Dean Gunthorpe, died 1498; and on capitals in St. Catherine's and the Lady Chapel. Some restored.

Chapter house, on central arch, E. side; within and above the canopy, a saltire and other painting.   Circ. 1300.

In crypt below the chapter house; numerous remains of screen work and other fragments with traces of gilding and colour.

WELLS, SOMERSETSHIRE, ST. CUTHBERT'S CHURCH.

St. Winifred.   *Destroyed.   Blackburne, Decorative Painting,* p. 40.

[This is probably an error, the painting of St. Winifred being at Mells, which see.]

N. aisle; Our Saviour in the act of Benediction. *Destroyed. Gent. Mag.,* 1851, xxxvi., new series, 522.

Chapel of the Virgin, N. transept; richly painted and gilt reredos.

E. wall of S. transept; reredos, with the Stem of Jesse, and numerous statuettes, richly painted and gilt.   Date 1470.

Somerset Archæol. and Nat. Hist. Soc. Proceedings, i. 69, and ii. 93. *Archæol. Journ.,* vi. 283. *British Archæol. Assoc. Journ.,* xii. 388, 389. *Gent. Mag.,* 1848, xxx., new series, 636, and 1849, xxxii., new series, 184. *Murray's Handbook of Somersetshire.*

Nave roof; painted angels.

N. chapel roof; panels painted blue, and studded with metal stars.   Date about 1500.

WELLS, SOMERSETSHIRE, BUBWITH'S ALMSHOUSES.
Painted chest. 15th cent. *Somerset Archæol. and Nat. Hist. Soc. Proceedings*, vol. xii. pt. ii., p. 35. *Ecclesiologist*, xxiv. (xxi. new series) 312.

WELLS, SOMERSETSHIRE, ST. JOHN'S PRIORY.
Portions of an altar screen, richly gilt and illuminated, dug up in the ruins. *Somerset Archæol. and Nat. Hist. Soc. Proceedings*, vol. ix. pt. 1, p. 17, and vol. xii. pt. 1, p. 60. *Civil Engineer and Architect's Journ.*, 1858, p. 315.

WELSHPOOL CHURCH, MONTGOMERYSHIRE.
Numerous stones, with traces of colour and diaper patterns. Discovered during the restoration of the church. *Collections of Powys Land Club*, iv. xxvii.

WENDLING CHURCH, NORFOLK.
Lower part of chancel screen; painted and gilt diaper on the panels. *Carthew's Hundred of Launditch*, ii. 686. *The Ecclesiologist's Guide to the Deaneries of Brisley, &c.*, p. 17.

WENHAM, GREAT, CHURCH, SUFFOLK.
Scroll and masonry pattern. Early English. *Builder*, 1864, p. 724.
Remains of rood screen.

WENHAM, LITTLE, CHURCH, SUFFOLK.
N. side of E. window; the Virgin and Child.
S. side of E. window; SS. Margaret, Catherine, and Mary Magdalene.

WESENHAM, NORFOLK, ST. PETER'S CHURCH.
Rood screen, figures of saints on the panels, defaced by recent paint.
Painting on board of King Henry VI. *Destroyed.* *Blomefield, (Parkin,) Hist. of Norfolk*, ed. 1809, x. 80. *Chambers, Hist. of Norfolk*, ii. 836.

WESTBURY-ON-TRYM CHURCH, GLOUCESTERSHIRE.
In sepulchral chamber of Bishop Carpenter; mural paintings representing the funeral of the Bishop, with the town of Worcester, &c. Date about 1476.
Various alabaster figures, gilt and coloured.
Chester Architect. Archæol. and Historic. Soc., i. 352. *Ashby De La Zouch Anastatic Drawing Soc.*, 1855, p. 11, pl. lxi.

269

Westcott Barton Church, Oxfordshire.

Lower portion of painted screen. 15th cent. *Parker's Architectural Guide to the Neighbourhood of Oxford,* p. 93. *Ecclesiologist,* iii. 140. *Hist. Gazett. and Directory of the County of Oxford,* p. 664.

Westfield Church, Norfolk.

Over N. door of nave ; St. Christopher.

Westfield Church, Sussex.

S. wall of nave ; a knight on horseback, ? St. George, &c., very faint. *Whitewashed over.*

Westhall Church, Suffolk.

Eight central panels of rood screen; on N., St. James Major, St. Leonard, St. Clement, St. Michael, Moses, Our Lord, Elias, and St. Anthony. On S., SS. Etheldreda, Sitha, Agnes, Brigida, Katherine, Dorothy, Margaret, and Apollonia. *British Archæol. Assoc. Journ.,* xxviii. 190.

Painted font ; the Seven Sacraments of the Church.

The corbels of the roof are in the form of angels holding painted shields.

All of the 15th cent.

Westley Church, Suffolk.

Nave roof, painted with the "rose en soleil." *Gage, Hist. of Suffolk, Thingoe Hundred,* p. 96.

Westmeston Church, Sussex.

E. wall of nave, over the chancel arch ; the "Agnus Dei." 12th cent.

On N. side ; the Scourging, and part of the Offering of the Magi. 12th cent. And below, part of a 13th cent. subject.

On S. side ; "The Descent from the Cross," "Our Lord " delivering the Key to St. Peter, and a book to St. Paul." 12th cent. Below, the Crucifixion. 13th cent.

On soffit of the chancel arch ; the Signs of the Zodiac ; and on a panel below, a Demon threatening a figure in a shroud.

On N. wall of the nave ; ? the Betrayal, and St. Peter cutting off the ear of Malchus; the History and Martyrdom of St. Vincent ; and ? part of a Doom. 12th cent.

All *destroyed.*

Sussex Archæol., xiv. x. and xvi. 1. *Archæol. Journ.,* xx. 73, 168, xxxviii. 94. *Builder,* 1862, p. 699. *M. A. Lower, History of Sussex,* ii. 244.

WESTMINSTER ABBEY, MIDDLESEX.

NAVE;

Within the arcading in N. and S. aisles; painted shields.
13th cent.

N. transept; E. side, colour on a stone screen.

PRESBYTERY;

Remains of colour on the effigies of Edmund Crouchback, Earl of Lancaster, circ. 1296; and Aymer · de
Valence, Earl of Pembroke, circ. 1323.

Stothard's Monumental Effigies, pp. 40, 46.

Rich colouring on the canopies, &c. of the monuments
of the Countess of Lancaster, and of Aymer de Valence.
Vetusta Monumenta, vol. ii. pls. xxix., xxxi., pp. 5, 6.

Sedilia, St. Peter, King Sebert, Henry III., an
Ecclesiastic, and King Edward and the Pilgrim. Circ.
1300.

*Harding and Moule, Antiquities of Westminster
Abbey*, pls. 1, 2, 3. *Civil Engineer and Architect's
Journ.*, 1851, p. 197. *Vetusta Monumenta*, vol. ii.
pls. xxxii.–xxxiv., pp. 10–14. *Schnebbelie, The Antiquaries' Museum.*

RETROCHOIR;

On canopy of Richard II.'s tomb; four compartments,
with paintings of Our Lord in Glory; the Coronation of
the Virgin and two angels holding shields. Date about
1400.

Remains of colour on canopy above the effigy of Queen
Philippa, also of gilding on the effigies of Edward III.
and Richard II. and his Queen.

Painting and gilding on shrine of Edward the Confessor.

Reredos now placed in S. choir aisle; Our Lord, St.
Peter, the Adoration of the Magi, and raising of Lazarus.

Sir Gilbert Scott, Mediæval Architecture, i. 181.

N. choir aisle; painting on lower part of monument of
Queen Eleanor. *Blore's Monumental Remains of Noble
and Eminent Persons.*

S. choir aisle; on monument of Edward III.; painted
shields.

CHAPEL OF ST. EDMUND.

S. side of choir; remains of gilding and colour on effigy
of William de Valence. Circ. 1296.

Stothard's Monumental Effigies, p. 42.

Painted shields, &c. on the monument of Sir Richard
Pecksall. Circ. 1572.

WESTMINSTER ABBEY, MIDDLESEX—*cont.*

CHAPEL OF ST. NICHOLAS.

Painted shields on monument, and colour on effigy of Philippa, Duchess of York, 1430. *W. H. H. Rogers, The Ancient Sepulchral Effigies, &c. in Devon,* p. 47.

Colour and gilding on monuments of the Duchess of Somerset, circ. 1587; Lord Burleigh, circ. 1588; the Marchioness of Winchester, circ. 1586; and Elizabeth Brooke, wife of Sir John Cecil, 1591.

Portion of the reredos, with remains of colour, found within an aumbrye.

CHAPEL OF ST. PAUL.

N. side of choir; tomb of Lord Bourchier; panels and canopy. 1431.
Blackburne, Decorative Painting, pp. 82 and 83.

Remains of colour on effigies of Sir Giles Daubeny and Lady, circ. 1507; on the monuments of the Countess of Sussex, 1589; and of Sir Thomas Bromley, 1587.

CHAPEL OF ST. JOHN THE BAPTIST.

Coloured shields on the monument of Abbot Fascet, circ. 1500; and painting on effigy of Abbot William de Colchester, circ. 1420.

CHAPEL OF ST. ERASMUS.

Panelling of W. wall; tracery, &c. About 1500. *Blackburne, Decorative Painting,* p. 77. *Also,* a powder of flowers and fleurs-de-lys upon the other walls. *Civil Engineer and Architect's Journ.,* 1851, p. 197.

W. wall of Henry VII.'s chapel; three consecration crosses. End of 15th cent.

Gilding on effigies of Henry VII. and his Queen.

S. Lady Chapel aisle; colour and gilding on the monument of the Countess of Lennox. Circ. 1577.

Revestry, S. side of S. transept; round the eastern arch, pattern of chevrons. Within the arch, St. Faith. Below, the Crucifixion, and a monk kneeling.
Scott, Westminster Abbey, 2nd ed., p. 48. *Sir Gilbert Scott, Mediæval Architecture,* ii. 206. *A. Wood, Eccles. Antiq. of London,* p. 259.

The chapter-house; the Second Coming of Christ, and History of St. John the Evangelist, and the Apocalypse. Partly 14th and partly 15th cents.
Church Builder, 1872, No. xlii. p. 195. *Antiquary,* 1872, ii. 128, 142. *London and Middlesex Archæol.*

WESTMINSTER ABBEY, MIDDLESEX—*cont.*

Soc., iv. 371. *A. Wood, Eccles. Antiq. of London,* pp. 254–56. *Wrongly described in Eastlake's Hist. of Oil Painting,* i. 179, 180.

Muniment room; painting of the " White Hart." Time of Richard II.

Cloisters; remains of painting over refectory doorways, and passage to Abbot's house.

WESTMINSTER, ST. MARGARET'S CHURCH.

N. aisle, at the back of a recess; the Annunciation. Circ. 1499.

Within a recess in the S. chancel aisle; effigy of St. Margaret, richly coloured and gilt.

Part of another small coloured effigy. Discovered during the restoration of the church. *Builder,* 1878, pp. 509, 510.

WESTMINSTER, ST. STEPHEN'S CHAPEL.

E. wall; Edward III., his Queen and family, St. George, and the histories of Job and Tobit. *Dallaway on Architecture in England,* pp. 50, 63.

The Adoration of the Shepherds, and of the Magi Presentation in the Temple, &c. *A. Wood, Eccles. Antiq. of London,* p. 261. 14th cent. *Destroyed.* Drawings and tracings existing in the rooms of the Society of Antiquaries.

WESTMINSTER HALL, THE PAINTED CHAMBER.

History of Joab and Abner; Martyrdom of the Mother and her seven sons, and the sacrifice of Antiochus; (?) History of Antiochus; Story of Abimelech; Story of Hezekiah; Captivity of Jehoiachin; and of the Jews; Elijah and Ahaziah; Miracles of Elisha; Flight of Syrian Host, ii. Kings, v.; Acts of Judas Maccabeus; History of Matthias, i. Maccabees, ii.; Coronation of Edward the Confessor; Warriors on Horseback; the Virtues overcoming the Vices; King Edward and the Pilgrim; The Triumph of a Virtue; and ornamental patterns. 13th cent. *Vetusta Monumenta,* vol. vi.

THE HALL.

Painted and gilt fragments used again in the walls. An upper early Norman arcade has bright colouring on the columns and imposts, and masonry patterns on the wall within the arcade. Probable date about 1100. The walls above and below the arches were also ornamented with rich and minute painting, probably of some subsequent date. *Archæologia,* xxvi. 407–409.

WESTMINSTER, CANON LEIGHTON'S RESIDENCE.

Wall painting; oval shield, France and England quarterly, and arabesque and scroll work. Time of Henry VIII. *Antiquarian Mag. and Bibliographer*, i. 213, 279.

WESTON CHURCH, STAFFORDSHIRE.

Two wooden painted effigies. Time of Edward I. *British Archæol. Assoc. Journ.*, xxix. 222, xxxii. 415.

WESTON BAGGARD CHURCH, HEREFORDSHIRE.

Under the arch of a tomb; painting of the Virgin between two censing angels. *Blackburne, Decorative Painting*, p. 60. *Goughs' Sepulchral Memorials of Great Britain*, vol. i. pt. i. p. 198.

WESTON IN GORDANO CHURCH, SOMERSETSHIRE.

N. wall of nave; colour and gilding on the monument of Sir Richard Percivale. Restored. Date about 1483.

Remains of colour on the nave roof and on the chamfered edges of the original altar stone. *Ecclesiologist*, xxvi. (xxiii. new series) 72–74.

Remains of colour on a wooden platform within the S. porch. Perpendicular period. *Ecclesiologist*, xxi. (xviii. new series) 294.

Also on niche above the S. doorway.

WESTON LONGVILLE CHURCH, NORFOLK.

Lower part of screen; panel paintings of the Apostles, with sentences from the Creed. *Antiquarian and Architect. Year Book*, 1844, p. 305. *Chambers, Hist. of Norfolk*, ii. 1335. *Hart, Antiq. of Norfolk*, p. 67.

WESTON, EDITH, CHURCH, RUTLANDSHIRE.

St. Christopher. *Kelly's Post Office Directory of Rutlandshire. Destroyed.*

E. arch of S. transept; early decoration on the soffit.

WESTWICK CHURCH, NORFOLK.

Rood screen; St. Paul and the Apostles, omitting St. Matthew. Injured by restoration and repainting. *Hart, Antiq. of Norfolk*, p. 67.

WESTWOOD CHURCH, WILTSHIRE.

Roof of N. aisle. About 1500.

WHADDON CHURCH, BUCKINGHAMSHIRE.

Murder of St. Thomas à Becket. 14th cent. *Norfolk Archæol.*, vi. 167. *Archæol. Journ.*, xxiii. 78.

Les Trois Morts, &c.

WHADDON CHURCH, BUCKINGHAMSHIRE—*cont.*

Splays of window in S. wall of chancel; King Edmund and a bishop. *Records of Buckinghamshire*, iii. 270-73.

On either side of E. window; symbolical figures of the Evangelists. *Sheahan, Hist. and Topog. of the County of Buckingham*, p. 770.

All whitewashed over.

WHAPLODE CHURCH, LINCOLNSHIRE.

Indistinct subject over the chancel arch. *The Fen and Marshland Churches*, iii. 63. *Archæol. Journ.*, xxxviii. 84, note.

WHEATHAMPSTEAD CHURCH, HERTFORDSHIRE.

S. transept; on the shields and effigies on the monument of Sir John Brocket and his lady, remains of colouring. Date about 1550. *Cussans, Hist. of Hertfordshire*, vol. iii., pt. i., p. 339.

On the walls of the upper sacristy; remains of mural paintings. *British Archæol. Assoc. Journ.*, xxvi. 262.

WHIMPLE CHURCH, DEVONSHIRE.

On N. wall of nave; St. Christopher and St. George. *Exeter Diocesan Architect. Soc.*, iv. 51.

WHISSENDINE CHURCH, RUTLANDSHIRE.

Reredos; the Crucifixion with the Virgin and St. John, on either side, SS. Andrew and Margaret and the emblems of the Evangelists. 15th cent. Traces of an older design beneath.

Portions of another reredos, with remains of gilding, and a hand grasping a drawn sword, and the heads of two female Saints.

Richly painted bracket.

These all are placed in N. transept.

E. window of S. transept; marble pattern round the arch.

On the wall; traces of an old man with a scythe, and a crowned Saint. *Destroyed.*

On a niche in E. pillar, S. side of nave; red colouring.

(?) Paintings on the spandrils of the nave arches.

Associated Architect. Societies' Repts., viii. lxiv., lxxiii. *Gent. Mag.*, 1866, i., new series, 61. *Leicester Architect. and Archæol. Soc. Trans.*, iii. 96.

WHISSONSETT CHURCH, NORFOLK.
Texts and inscriptions. *The Ecclesiologist's Guide to the Deaneries of Brisley, &c.,* p. 21.

WHITCHURCH CANONICORUM CHURCH, DORSETSHIRE.
N. transept; remains of painting on a tomb, dating from the 12th cent. *Society of Antiquaries' Proceedings,* 2nd series, iv. 510. *Gent. Mag.,* 1850, xxxiii., new series, 70.

WHITTINGTON CASTLE, SHROPSHIRE.
On wall of room over gateway; figure of knight on horseback, a portrait of "Syr ffoulke Gwarine," with inscription below. *Ashby De La Zouch Anastatic Drawing Soc.,* 1861, p. 9.

WHITTLESEA, CAMBRIDGESHIRE, ST. MARY'S CHURCH.
On a panel of the screen; large "I.H.S." in the original colouring. *F. A. Paley, Notes on Twenty Parish Churches round Peterborough,* p, 34.

WHITTLESFORD CHURCH, CAMBRIDGESHIRE.
E. wall of chancel; traces of a painting.
E. wall of S. chancel chapel; richly coloured niche. 15th cent.
Portions of one or more altar pieces, coloured and gilt, with sculptured fragments of the Virgin, St. Anne instructing the Virgin, Our Saviour on the Cross, St. Citha, a bishop, and parts of canopies, &c. Now in the possession of the parish clerk.

WHITWELL CHURCH, ISLE OF WIGHT.
Martyrdom of St. Erasmus. 15th cent. *Archæol. Journ.,* xxii. 79. *Society of Antiquaries' Proceedings,* 2nd series, vii. 36.

WICKEN BONANT CHURCH, ESSEX.
Round the splay of a window in the nave; decorative ornament. *Destroyed. Ecclesiologist,* xx. 213.

WICKHAM CHURCH, ESSEX.
Decorative colouring. *Essex Archæol.,* iv. 138.

WICKHAM, CHILD'S, CHURCH, WORCESTERSHIRE.
St. Christopher. *Antiquary,* 1871, i. 76.

WICKHAM, EAST, CHURCH, KENT.
Walls of chancel; St. Michael and Satan, the Salutation, the Offering of the Magi, and other subjects in our Lord's

WICKHAM, EAST, CHURCH, KENT—*cont.*

life, under trefoil-headed arches. Late 13th cent. *Destroyed.*
Proceedings of British Archæol. Assoc., Canterbury vol., p. 155. *British Archæol. Assoc. Journ.,* i. 139, ii. 146. *Archæol. Journ.,* i. 165, 274, 400. *Society of Antiquaries' Proceedings,* i. 74. *Antiquarian and Architect. Year Book,* 1844, p. 170.

WICKHAM MARKET CHURCH, SUFFOLK.

Painted font. Late decorated period. *Suffolk Archæol.,* v. 123.

WICKHAMPTON CHURCH, NORFOLK.

N. wall; three consecration crosses.
Over N. door; St. Christopher.
On N. wall of nave; Les Trois Vifs et Les Trois Morts. Early 15th cent.
Proceedings of the Royal Archæol. Institute, Bristol vol., p. lxxxii. *Norfolk Archæol.,* vii. 2.

WICKMERE CHURCH, NORFOLK.

Rood screen; panel paintings. *Hart, Antiq. of Norfolk,* p. 67.

WIDECOMBE-IN-THE-MOOR CHURCH, DEVONSHIRE.

Lower part of screens; on the panels, SS. Apollonia, John the Evangelist, Sebastian, Philip, Matthew, Jude, and Thomas. *C. Worthy, Ashburton and its Neighbourhood,* p. 66.

WIDFORD CHURCH, HERTFORDSHIRE.

E. wall of chancel; a Bishop and another figure.
N. wall of chancel; Our Lord in Judgment. Circ. 1500.
Cussans, Hist. of Hertfordshire, vol. i., pt. i., p. 57. *Neale and Webb, Durandus,* p. 57. *J. M. Neale, Hierologus* p. 295.

WIDWORTHY CHURCH, DEVONSHIRE.

"Walls appeared to have been painted throughout." *Polwhele, Hist. of Devon,* iii. 319.

WIGGENHALL, ST. MARY MAGDALEN CHURCH, NORFOLK.

Rood screen; the Evangelistic symbols; St. Agatha. *Brandon, Parish Churches,* ii. 44. *Blomefield, (Parkin,) Hist. of Norfolk,* ed. 1808, ix. 170.

WIGGENHALL, ST. MARY THE VIRGIN CHURCH, NORFOLK.
Lower panels of screen; the Virgin and Child, St. John the Baptist, St. Mary Magdalene, St. Barbara, St. Margaret, (?) St. Anne, St. Catherine, and St. Dorothy. 14th cent.

WIGGINTON CHURCH, OXFORDSHIRE.
Nave and aisle roofs; formerly painted and gilt.
On walls and arches; extensive remains of early paintings. *Whitewashed over. Beesley, Hist. of Banbury,* pp. 109, 138.

WIGHTON CHURCH, NORFOLK.
Screen; panel paintings of Saints.

WILBURTON CHURCH, CAMBRIDGESHIRE.
N. wall of nave; St. Blase, St. Leodegar, St. Christopher, &c. *Parker, Eccles. and Architect. Topog. of England, Cambridge,* No. 113. *Ecclesiologist,* xxi. (xviii. new series) 203.

WILBY CHURCH, SUFFOLK.
Roof, E. end of S. aisle; remains of painted mouldings.

WILLEY CHURCH, SHROPSHIRE.
N. side of nave, on jambs and splay of a Norman window; decorative painting. Late 12th cent.

WILLINGHAM CHURCH, CAMBRIDGESHIRE.
Remains of colour on decorated rood screen, and on roofs of nave and N. aisle, of the perpendicular period. *A. G. Hill, Churches of Cambridgeshire,* pp. 78, 79. *Parker, Eccles. and Architect. Topog. of England, Cambridge,* No. 91.
Traces of colour visible through the whitewash, on the nave walls and arcade and over the chancel arch.

WILLINGTON CHURCH, BEDFORDSHIRE.
During the recent restorations, painting, texts, &c., were found over the chancel door, on the nave walls, and elsewhere, and *destroyed.*
On sides of monuments of the Gostwicks, on N. of chancel, and N. wall of N. Chancel Chapel, painted armorial shields and crests. Circ. 1550.

WILMINGTON CHURCH, SUSSEX.
Coloured image of a Bishop, found in chancel wall *Sussex Archæol.,* iv. 61.

WILMSLOW CHURCH, CHESHIRE.

Beams of roof; escutcheons and stars. ? Early 16th cent. *Historic Society of Lancashire and Cheshire,* i. 133.

S. aisle; black-letter inscription. Date 1523. *Earwaker's East Cheshire,* i. 66.

WILSFORD AND LAKE CHURCH, WILTSHIRE.

Two paintings of St. Christopher; the later one painted over the earlier. Figured in *Duke's Prolusiones Historiæ,* p. 561. *Fosbrooke's Encyclopædia of Antiquities,* vol. i. *Blackburne, Decorative Painting,* pp. 16 and 38.

St. Michael and Satan, and St. George and the Dragon. *Duke's Prolusiones Historiæ,* p. 568.

WILSHAMPSTEAD CHURCH, BEDFORDSHIRE.

Roof painted over the space for the rood-loft. *Parker, Eccles. and Architect. Topog. of England, Bedford,* No. 15.

WILTON CHURCH, NORFOLK.

On panels at back of altar; St. John the Evangelist, St. John the Baptist, two priests kneeling at an altar, and armorial shields. *Blomefield, Hist. of Norfolk,* ed. 1805, ii. 175. *Cromwell, Excursions through Norfolk,* ii. 142. *Chambers, Hist. of Norfolk,* ii. 686.

WILTON, BISHOP'S, CHURCH, YORKSHIRE.

Remains of colouring on the Norman chancel arch.

WIMBORNE MINSTER, DORSETSHIRE.

Side of E. window, S. chancel aisle; last scenes of the Life of the Virgin. 14th cent.

On walls of crypt; painting in fresco of King Edward receiving a model of the church from the architect, or a model of the Church between SS. Edmund and Edward, King and Martyr. *Hutchins' Hist. of Dorset,* 3rd ed., iii. 203, 204.

Vaulting of sacristy decorated with flower patterns. *History of Wimborne Minster, Bell and Daldy,* 1860, pp. 45, 52, 133. *Yeatman, Historical Description of Wimborne Minster,* p. 43. *Archæol. Journ.,* xiii. 103.

On S. side of the choir; remains of gilding on the monument of John Beaufort, Duke of Somerset. Date about 1444. *Blore's Monumental Remains of Noble and Eminent Persons.*

WIMBOTSHAM CHURCH, NORFOLK.

S. wall of nave; St. Christopher. 15th cent. *Norfolk Archæol.*, ii. 136. *Destroyed.*.

Traces of colour and gilding on bosses of nave roof.

WIMMINGTON. *See* WYMINGTON.

WINCHELSEA, SUSSEX, ST. THOMAS' CHURCH.

S. chancel aisle; colouring on .the monuments and effigies of Gervase Alard, circ. 1310, and of Stephen Alard, circ. 1340. *Blore's Monumental Remains of Noble and Eminent Persons. Cooper's History of Winchelsea*, pp. 133, 135. *B. Champneys, A Quiet Corner of England*, p. 21.

Also on the sedilia, and effigy of a Saint.

N. chancel aisle; traces of colour on the canopies of three monuments. Early 14th cent.

WINCHESTER CATHEDRAL, HAMPSHIRE.

N. TRANSEPT :—

Figure of a king. 13th cent. *Winchester Vol. of the British Archæol. Assoc.*, p. 268.

On E. wall; St. Christopher. *Savage's Guide to Winchester. Gough's Sepulchral Monuments*, vol. i., pt. 1., p. cxxvi.

Above; the Adoration of the Magi. *Destroyed.*

On the walls; two male figures, probably Prophets, SS. Catherine, Agatha, &c. *Schnebbelie, The Antiquaries' Museum.*

Round the arches and on their soffits; various decorative patterns; medallions containing roses, beaded lozenge, scroll, &c. Norman period. *Weale's Quarterly Papers*, vol. iv. *British Archæol. Assoc. Journ.*, x. 37.

Transept roofs; formerly flat and painted in Tudor style. *Moody, Sketches of Hampshire*, p. 52.

SILKSTEADE CHAPEL.

E. wall, Christ upon the Water. *British Archæol. Assoc. Journ.*, iii. 340.

CHAPEL OF THE HOLY SEPULCHRE.

Annunciation, Birth of Christ, &c., demi-figure of Christ. Entry into Jerusalem. Raising of Lazarus. Descent from the Cross. Lamentation over the Tomb. Descent into Limbus. Appearance to Mary Magdalene. Story of St. Catherine, &c. 13th cent. *Winchester Vol. of the British Archæol. Assoc.*, p. 264 *et seq.*

WINCHESTER CATHEDRAL, HAMPSHIRE—*cont.*

THE CHOIR :—

Remains of colour and gilding, visible through the whitewash which covers the great screen, and on sculptures of the Visitation and Annunciation, on the spandrils, above the two doorways. Date late 15th cent.

On Foxe's screen round the choir; painted and gilt chests. Date about 1520.

Vaulting richly coloured and gilt.

Ceiling of Bishop Foxe's chantry; arms of Tudor and Bishop Foxe properly blazoned. Gilded niches over altar.

CHAPEL BEHIND THE HIGH ALTAR.

Above the Holy Hole; fragments of a stone, on which are painted portions of the subject of the Coronation of the Virgin. 13th cent.

On the floor; a panelled piece of wood, (?) a retable, on which are depicted SS. George, Peter, James Major, a Bishop, a Majesty with the four Evangelists, four angels holding the instruments of the Passion, the Virgin and Child, the Coronation of the Virgin, Crucifixion, St. John the Baptist, kneeling figures of knight and lady, and several armorial shields. 13th cent.

THE RETROCHOIR :—

Colour on the effigies of Bishop Waynflete and Cardinal Beaufort, renewed.

CHAPEL OF THE GUARDIAN ANGELS.

Wall patterns, and medallions with demi-figures of angels on the ceiling, &c. 13th cent. *Winchester Vol. of the British Archæol. Assoc.*, p. 268.

LANGTON'S CHAPEL, S. side of Lady Chapel :—

On the reredos; paintings of Saints, defaced; also remains of colour and gilding.

Colour on the bosses of the ceiling. Date about 1500.

LADY CHAPEL.

Miracles wrought by the Virgin, &c. About 1490. *Winchester Vol. of the British Archæol. Assoc.*, p. 268 *et seq. Antiquarian Repertory*, new ed., iii. 189, pl. 26.

On S. wall; portrait of Bishop Langton, within piscina recess portrait of Prior Silkstede.

Bosses of ceiling and cornice painted and gilt; also ornamental colouring round the Early English windows.

Milner, Hist. of Winchester, ii. 42, 44, 45, 56, 57, 59, 64, 73, 74. *Milner, Historical Account of Winchester*

WINCHESTER CATHEDRAL, HAMPSHIRE—*cont.*

Cathedral, 12th ed., pp. 66, 69, 71, 86, 87, 88, 92, 99, 101, 112, 113, 169. *Ball, Historical Account of Winchester,* pp. 120, 130. *Moody, Sketches of Hampshire,* pp. 32–35. *Moody, Notes and Essays, Hants and Wilts,* pp. 91, 189–194.

WINCHESTER CASTLE, HAMPSHIRE.

W. wall of Banqueting Hall; traces of the original coloured decorations. 13th cent. *Archæol. Journ.,* xxix. 392.

WINCHESTER, HAMPSHIRE, ST. BARTHOLOMEW'S CHURCH, HYDE.

N. wall of nave; fragment of painting.

WINCHESTER, HAMPSHIRE, ST. JOHN'S CHURCH.

N. wall of N. aisle; the Day of Judgment. Our Lord in Glory. The Crucifixion, with St. Francis of Assissium, and Isaias. The Martyrdom of St. Andrew. The Virgin and Child. Consecration crosses and decorative patterns. Late 13th cent.

Richly coloured niche.

Scroll borders and texts. Circ. 1550.

British Archæol. Assoc. Journ., ix. i. and x. 85. *Archæol. Journ.,* xxxviii. 89.

S. wall of N. aisle; the Martyrdom of St. Thomas à Becket; and the Seven Acts of Mercy. Late 13th cent.

Painted over these; SS. Walburge, or Mary Magdalene, (?) John the Evangelist, and other figures of Saints. Early 15th cent.

British Archæol. Assoc. Journ., x. 53–70.

S. aisle; St. Christopher. Late 14th cent. *British Archæol. Assoc. Journ.,* x. 80. *Builder,* 1853, p. 524.

WINCHESTER, HAMPSHIRE, ST. LAWRENCE'S CHURCH.

S.W. wall; St. Christopher. *Destroyed. Gent. Mag.,* 1849, xxxi. new series, 522. *Society of Antiquaries' Proceedings,* i. 306. *Archæol. Journ.,* vi. 184. *British Archæol. Assoc. Journ.,* iv. 387. *Moody, Notes and Essays, Hants and Wilts,* p. 189.

WINCHESTER, HAMPSHIRE, ST. SWITHIN'S CHURCH.

Diaper of the Sacred Monogram. 15th cent. *British Archæol. Assoc. Journ.,* ix. 198.

WINCHESTER, HAMPSHIRE, THE COLLEGE CHAPEL.

Remains of colour and gilding on cornice and panels of the original reredos.

WINCHESTER, HAMPSHIRE, MAGDALEN HOSPITAL CHAPEL.

The mouldings of the arches were decorated with a variety of patterns painted in black and brown ; such as running sprigs, flowers, stars, birds, quatrefoils, and zigzag ornaments. Partly late 12th cent.

Over E. window have been painted five shields, and on each side, flowers, a niche, &c.

On N. side of altar ; St. Peter, with pontifical robes, holding a church ; also two other figures, one in pontificals and the other in mail. Date about 1300.

On the S. side of altar; St. Paul and an Archbishop. Date about 1300.

On the spandrils of the arch over the altar ; paintings of angels.

On the soffit of the easternmost arch in the N. aisle ; three tiers of subjects; the middle one perhaps the Martyrdom of Thomas à Becket.

Blue consecration crosses on various portions of the walls.

The chapel was pulled down in 1788.

Vetusta Monumenta, iii. pls. 1, 2, 3. *Coloured drawings in the Society of Antiquaries' Library. Milner, Hist. of Winchester, p. 204. Ball, Historical Account of Winchester, p. 177.*

WINCHESTER, HAMPSHIRE, CHAPEL OF THE HOSPITAL OF ST. CROSS.

Clerestory of nave :—within the splay of a window on S. side; the Virgin and St. John. Within the splay of a window on N. side; SS. Swithin and Catherine.

On W. face of N.W. tower pier ; Christ with the Rabbi.

N. transept, E. wall ; St. Nicholas restoring the three children to life ; also a canopied niche, with traces of a figure painted within it.

S. transept, S. wall ; a pietà; below, a consecration cross ; and remains of painting within an arched recess.

E. wall ; within an arched recess, the Crucifixion ; and above, under a series of trefoil-headed arches, events in the life, and the martyrdom, of St. Thomas à Becket. 13th cent. Fragments of a richly painted reredos. Late 14th or early 15th cent.

Choir; Norman decorations, diaper patterns, &c., mostly renewed.

On S. side ; St. Anne instructing the Virgin.

On N. side ; stone screen, with outlines of figures on the panels.

WINCHESTER, HAMPSHIRE, CHAPEL OF THE HOSPITAL OF
ST. CROSS—*cont.*
S. choir aisle ; S. wall, decorative patterns. N.E. corner,
remains of red colouring on the shafts.
E. wall ; the Crucifixion, with the Virgin and St. John.
N. choir aisle ; within splay of E. window, St. John
the Evangelist. In S.E. corner ; St. Simeon.
E. wall ; the Crucifixion, and four other subjects on
each side.
All round the walls figures of bishops and saints under
canopies. 13th cent.
On S. wall ; decorative patterns.
On N. and E. walls ; consecration crosses.
On the ceiling between the groining ribs and on a
cross arch, remains of foliage and decorative colouring.
Late 12th cent.
British Archæol. Assoc. Journ., vi. 79, ix. 444, and
xx. 77. *Reliquary,* x. 219. *Moody, Sketches of Hamp-
shire,* p. 61.

WINCHFIELD CHURCH, HAMPSHIRE.
S. side of nave ; head of a Queen. 14th cent.
N. wall ; Christ walking on the sea.
S. wall ; Lazarus and Dives. 13th cent.
W. wall ; Last Judgment.
British Archæol. Assoc. Journ., vi. 76.
Outer W. wall of the tower ; dragons with label
moulding below. About 1160. *Archæol. Journ.,* xxxiv.
277. The mural paintings named in the previous edition
are not now visible.

WINDSOR, BERKSHIRE, ST. GEORGE'S CHAPEL.
Bosses on the roofs of. the nave and aisles ; original
colouring discovered and restored.
S. aisle, the Oxenbridge Chapel ; three scenes in the
history of St. John the Baptist. Circ. 1522.
N. aisle ; Hastings Chapel, four incidents in the history
of St. Stephen. About 1490.
S. choir aisle, back of stalls ; full length paintings on
panel of Prince Edward, son of Henry VI., Edward IV.,
Edward V., and Henry VII. Circa 1490.
*Harrington, St. George's Chapel, Windsor. Ecclesio-
logist,* iii. 152. *Willement's St. George's Chapel. Colling,
Details of Gothic Architecture,* vol. i. (Early English), pl. 9.
Tighe and Davis, Annals of Windsor, ii. 657.
Chantry of Oliver King ; wall diaper. *Antiquarian
and Architect. Year Book,* 1844, p. 374.

WINDSOR, BERKSHIRE, ST. GEORGE'S CHAPEL—*cont.*
Dean's cloister, wall on S. side; head of a king,
Henry III. 13th cent.

WINDSOR, OLD, CHURCH, BERKSHIRE.
Various floral and decorative patterns copied from
traces of paintings discovered during the restoration of
the church.

WINFIELD, NORTH, CHURCH, DERBYSHIRE.
N. wall of N. aisle; St. George and the Dragon. *J. C.
Cox, Churches of Derbyshire,* i. 425.

WINFRITH NEWBURGH CHURCH, DORSETSHIRE.
S. wall of nave; St. Christopher; plastered over.
Hutchins' Hist. of Dorset, i. 164; 3rd ed., i. 442. *Black-
burne, Decorative Painting,* p. 16.

WING CHURCH, BUCKINGHAMSHIRE.
N. aisle, monument of Robert Dormer and Lady, 1541–
52. "Shields of arms in brass, with the tinctures
" indicated by white metal and coloured pigments."
Archæol. Journ., xxxviii. 442.
E. beam of nave roof; remains of decorative colour.
Late 15th cent.
N. side of chancel; monument and effigies of Sir
William Dormer and Lady, richly coloured and gilt.
Completed October 20th, 1590, and recently restored.

WING CHURCH, RUTLANDSHIRE.
Traces of painting over chancel arch and on all the walls.

WINGFIELD CHURCH, SUFFOLK.
Bay of nave roof over the rood-loft; Sacred Monogram
painted on the panels. *Suffolk Archæol.,* iii. 332. *Paley's
Manual of Gothic Architecture,* p. 139.
Perpendicular rood screen; figures of SS. Peter and
Paul depicted on the panels. *British Archæol. Assoc.
Journ.,* xxxvi. 212.
Fragments of carved and painted stone work.
N. side of chancel, above the monument of John de la
Pole, Duke of Suffolk. Crest and supporters of the De La
Poles, carved in wood and painted. *Suffolk Archæol.,*
iii. 333, 339.
In the vestry; carved and coloured representations of
a fight between a lion and a dragon. *East Anglian
Notes and Queries,* i. 11.

WINGFIELD CHURCH, SUFFOLK—*cont.*

Colouring on an effigy, circ. 1380; and on the effigies of John de la Pole, Duke of Suffolk, and his Lady, circ. 1491. *Stothard's Monumental Effigies*, p. 71, and pl. 139.

WINGRAVE CHURCH, BUCKINGHAMSHIRE.

Lower part of chancel screen. *Lipscomb, Hist. and Antiq. of Bucks*, iii. 537.

W. wall of N. aisle; painted text. 16th cent.

WINSHAM CHURCH, SOMERSETSHIRE.

On a panel formerly over the rood screen, now placed on the N. wall of the tower; the Crucifixion. *Gent. Mag.*, cii., pt. 1, p. 310. *Blackburne, Decorative Painting*, p. 10. *Pulman's " Book of the Axe,"* p. 375. *Antiquary*, 1873, iv. 278. *J. Davidson, Hist. of Axminster*, p. 57, *note.*

Traces of paintings visible through the whitewash.

WINSTONE CHURCH, GLOUCESTERSHIRE.

Traces of early colouring and several courses of decoration on the chancel arch and the surrounding walls. *Builder*, 1876, p. 324. *Gloucestershire Notes and Queries*, vol. i., p. 211. No. ccxxiv.

WINTERBOURNE DAUNTSEY CHURCH, WILTSHIRE.

N. side of nave, on wall and window splays; the Annunciation, Nativity, Adoration of the Magi, Angel appearing to Joseph in a dream, Massacre of the Innocents, Flight into Egypt, and a knight in armour. 13th cent. Also of later date, St. Christopher.

S. side of nave; the Anointing of Our Lord by Mary Magdalene, Last Supper, Agony in the Garden, Mocking and Scourging, and Our Lord bearing the Cross.

W. wall; the Crucifixion, Descent into Limbus, the Maries at the Sepulchre, Resurrection, and Our Lord in Glory. 13th cent., with rich scroll borders. *Destroyed.* Photographs taken, and tracings made by Mr. Zillwood, of Salisbury.

Salisbury and Winchester Journal, June 1st, 1867.

WINTERBOURNE EARLS CHURCH, WILTSHIRE.

W. wall of nave; the Holy Trinity. Circ. 1200.

N. wall of nave; St. Christopher, also St. Michael and Satan. Date about 1553.

N. window of chancel; (?) the Temptation.

All destroyed. Drawings made by Mr. Zillwood, of Salisbury.

Salisbury and Winchester Journal, June 1st, 1867.

WINTERTON CHURCH, LINCOLNSHIRE.

Ancient remains of paintings. *Destroyed. Antiquary,*
1872, ii. 126.

On N. of nave, "an ancient piece of writing."

On S. of nave, "a nun with her hands closed, as if in
prayer."

W. Andrew, The Hist. of Winterton, &c., p. 29.

WINTHORPE CHURCH, LINCOLNSHIRE.

N. chantry; roof and panels of screen have remains of
colour and gilding. *Associated Architect. Societies'
Repts.,* viii. 75. *Oldfield, Topog. and Hist. Account of
Wainfleet,* p. 287.

WINWICK CHURCH, NORTHAMPTONSHIRE.

Over the chancel arch; the Doom.

On N. wall of nave; head of a royal personage. 15th
cent. Very indistinct, and probably *destroyed. Ecclesiologist,* xvii. 441. *Associated Architect. Societies' Repts.,*
iv. xl.

WIRKSWORTH CHURCH, DERBYSHIRE.

Rich wall paintings. *Antiquary,* 1872, ii. 145.

WISBOROUGH-GREEN CHURCH, SUSSEX.

Within a recess, S. side of chancel arch; St. James
introducing pilgrims to Our Lord in Heaven; and below,
the Crucifixion. Late 12th or early 13th cent.

On wall of tower; the Purging of the Seven Deadly
Sins. *Destroyed. Archæol. Journ.,* xxx. 48, xxxviii. 95.
Sussex Archæol., xxii. 134. *Building News,* 1867, p. 101.

WISSETT CHURCH, SUFFOLK.

Abraham frightening the birds from the Sacrifice. *Destroyed.*

WISTON CHURCH, SUFFOLK.

N. wall; incidents in the life of John the Baptist, and
a Franciscan friar, &c.

S. wall; Annunciation, Nativity, Annunciation to the
Shepherds, Adoration of the Magi, the Virgin, Magi
warned in a dream, &c.

S. respond of the chancel arch; saint holding a cross,
and a diaper of trellis work and quatrefoils.

W. wall; the Last Judgment.

Various scroll works about the church, and a painting
upon the tympanum of the N. door.

All probably late 13th cent. *Builder,* 1864, p. 725.

On N. wall of nave; a consecration cross. *Archæologia*
xlvii. 165.

WISTON CHURCH, SUSSEX.
S. chancel chapel; N. wall, remains of colour on a 15th cent. monument.
Painting found on various portions of the walls and *destroyed.*

WITCHINGHAM, GREAT, CHURCH, NORFOLK.
Painted font. *British Archæol. Assoc. Journ.,* xiv. 52.

WITHERSFIELD CHURCH, SUFFOLK.
Screen, perpendicular period; repainted and gilded. *Suffolk Archæol.,* iv. 107.

WITHYAM CHURCH, SUSSEX.
Within a niche over the doorway; St. Michael and Satan.
Over the chancel arch; the Day of Judgment.
On E. wall of chancel; Our Lord in Glory.
History of Withyam, pp. 31, 34, 37.

WITHYBROOK CHURCH, WARWICKSHIRE.
Chancel; colour on a receptacle for the Easter sepulchre. Date about 1450. *Associated Architect. Societies' Repts.,* xi. 81.

WITNEY CHURCH, OXFORDSHIRE.
E. side of N. transept; back of niche, floral pattern. 15th cent.

WITTENHAM, LONG, CHURCH, BERKSHIRE.
S. wall of nave; texts showing through the whitewash. 15th cent.

WITTERING, WEST, CHURCH, SUSSEX.
Sussex Archæol., xxvi. 212.

WITTON CHURCH, NORFOLK.
N. wall of nave; St. Christopher, 14th cent. St. George and the Dragon, early 15th cent. King Henry VI. and St. John the Baptist, late 15th cent. Various black letter texts, early 16th cent. *Norfolk Archæol.,* vi. 42.

WIVELSFIELD CHURCH, SUSSEX.
Reredos or recess, E. end of S. chancel chapel; diaper and lozenge pattern. 13th cent. *Sussex Archæol.,* xxii. 54.

WIVETON, NORFOLK, ST. MARY'S CHURCH.
Clerestory, N. side of nave; traces of a floral pattern. Late 15th cent.

WOKING CHURCH, SURREY.
Faint traces of painting on the wall of the S. aisle.

WOLSTON CHURCH, GLOUCESTERSHIRE.
On interior walls; three painted consecration crosses.
On exterior walls; several consecration crosses, the colour scraped away.

WOLSTON CHURCH, WARWICKSHIRE.
Painted font About 1320. *Illustrations of Baptismal Fonts, Van Voorst,* 1844.

WOLVERHAMPTON, STAFFORDSHIRE, ST. PETER'S CHURCH.
S. aisle; on monument of Thomas Lane, date 1582, tinctures remain on some of the shields. *G. Oliver, Account of the Collegiate Church of Wolverhampton,* p. 112.

WOODBRIDGE CHURCH, SUFFOLK.
Rood screen; SS. Paul, Edward, Kenelm, Oswald, Cuthbert, Blaize, Quintin, Leodegare, Barnaby, and Jerome. *East Anglian Notes and Queries,* iii. 317.
Traces of colour on the font. 15th cent.

WOODCHURCH, OR WEST ARDSLEY, CHURCH, YORKSHIRE.
Gilding and painted floral decorations, and black letter texts, on the walls. *Destroyed. Banks, Walks in Yorkshire, Wakefield, and Neighbourhood,* p. 521. *R. V. Taylor, Ecclesiæ Leodienses,* pp. 120, 122. *W. Smith, Old Yorkshire,* i. 9.

WOODFORD CHURCH, NORTHAMPTONSHIRE.
N. aisle; remains of painting and vermilion on the effigies of Sir Walter Trailli and Alianora his wife. Date about 1290. *Murray's Handbook of Northants,* p. 34. *Churches of the Archdeaconry of Northampton,* p. 91.
Colouring on a pillar and shrine stone. *Leicester Architect. and Archæol. Soc. Trans.,* iii. 279.
On an arch, N. side of nave; a diaper of roses.

WOODFORD HALSE CHURCH, NORTHAMPTONSHIRE.
Nave walls; St. Christopher, &c. *Associated Architect. Societies' Repts.,* xiv. 259.

WOOLBOROUGH CHURCH, DEVONSHIRE.
Screens; painted and gilt, and with figures of saints depicted in the lower panels. Restored. *Exeter Diocesan Architect. Soc.,* v. 42. *Murray's Handbook of Devonshire.* Viz.:—W. end of N. transept; Jacob, St. Thomas of Canterbury, two Bishops, and another figure.

WOOLBOROUGH CHURCH, DEVONSHIRE—*cont.*

S. side of N. transept; SS. James the greater, Stephen, Paul, Bartholomew, Andrew, Jude, Philip, Matthew, Simon, and Thomas.

N. chantry; a Bishop, SS. Aidan, ? Gertrude, Ursula, ? Wulstan, Sidwell, Pancras, and Dorothy.

Chancel screen; Sir John Shorn, SS. Damien, Jude (?), Irenæus, ? Isaac and Abraham, the Four Doctors, SS. Appollonia, Eligius, Edward the Confessor, ? John the Baptist, Moses, &c.

S. chantry; SS. Barbara, Helena, Veronica, &c.

S. transept, N. side of; SS. Jerome, ? Ambrose, ? the Annunciation, St. Roche, &c.

S. transept, W. end; ? St. George, ? St. Leonard, a Bishop, &c.

WOOLPIT CHURCH, SUFFOLK.

On either side of E. chancel window; tracings of paintings.

Rood screen; figures much defaced.

WOOTTON CHURCH, NORTHAMPTONSHIRE.

N. wall of chancel, within the splay of a lancet window; remains of paintings. 15th cent. *Associated Architect. Societies' Repts.,* ix., c.

Two paintings discovered on chancel walls in 1844. *Hist. Gazett. and Directory of Northants, by W. Whellan,* p. 274, and ed. 1874, by *F. Whellan,* p. 285.

WOOTTON BASSETT CHURCH, WILTSHIRE.

Roof panelled and painted. *Murray's Handbook of Wiltshire.*

S. wall of nave; the Martyrdom of Thomas à Becket. *Archæol. Journ.,* xxxv. 279. *Kelly's Post Office Directory of Wiltshire.*

WOOTTON WAWEN CHURCH, WARWICKSHIRE.

E. wall of nave; New Testament subjects. Numerous mural paintings discovered in 1855. *J. Hannett, The Forest of Arden,* p. 52.

WORCESTER CATHEDRAL, WORCESTERSHIRE.

Round the arch opening from N. transept to N. Choir aisle; pattern of roses. 14th cent.

Round Norman arch in S. transept; cable and other ornaments. 12th cent.

Archæol. Journ., xxxiv. 276.

WORCESTER CATHEDRAL, WORCESTERSHIRE—cont.

Prince Arthur's Chantry Chapel; sculpture of the Descent from the Cross with remains of colour and gilding. Late 15th cent. *Green, Hist. and Antiq. of Worcester,* i. 101, 103.

In S. E. transept; coloured effigy of Sir William Harcourt. *Archæol. Journ.,* xx. 347.

In the crypt, St. Oswald's chapel; figures, &c. under canopies. Date about 1300.

On head and jamb of window in passage leading from the crypt; an angel swinging a thurible. 11th or 12th cent. *Destroyed. Archæol. Journ.,* xix. 382, xx. 91. *Associated Architect. Societies' Repts.,* v. xcvi.

Remains of colour are visible in the S. E. transept and the chapter house.

Coloured effigy of King John. *British Archæol. Assoc., Report of Proceedings at Worcester,* p. 52. *Stothard's Monumental Effigies,* p. 15. *Archæol. Journ.,* xx. 345.

Coloured effigies of a lady of the Clifford family; of Bishop Giffard, circ. 1301; and of Lady Beauchamp of Holt, late 14th cent. *Hollis, Monumental Effigies,* pt. v., pl. 2, pt. vi. pls. 2 and 4.

Wall arcades of the E. transepts and the chapter house; faint traces of the figures of Saints.

Guesten Hall; Adoration of the Magi. Early. *British Archæol. Assoc. Journ.,* iv. 95. *Destroyed.*

Ceiling in the Deanery; panel and rib decoration, &c. 16th cent. *Destroyed.* Lithographed in *Blackburne, Decorative Painting,* p. 80.

WORCESTER, WORCESTERSHIRE.

E. end of the refectory of the Monastery; sculpture with remains of gilding and colouring. ? Late 12th cent. *Builder,* 1873, pp. 532 and 555. *Church Builder,* 1873, No. xlviii. p. 139. *Long Ago,* 1873, vol i., p. 251.

WORFIELD CHURCH, SHROPSHIRE.

On roofs; "real decorated painted timber." *S. B. James, Worfield on the Worfe,* p. 54. *The Wolverhampton Chronicle,* October 22nd, 1862.

WORKSOP CHURCH, NOTTINGHAMSHIRE.

Sculptures of the Virgin, an Angel, &c., with remains of colouring. *Archæol. Journ.,* iv. 155.

WORLABY CHURCH, LINCOLNSHIRE.

On tower arch; figure of "Death" on one side, and a winged figure on the other. Numerous scroll and diaper patterns and texts discovered on the walls, and? *destroyed. Builder,* 1874, p. 675.

WORLINGWORTH CHURCH, SUFFOLK.

Painted font-cover reaching to the ceiling.

W. side of priest's door; a dedication cross.

S. pier of chancel arch; a fleur de lis and crown. Time of Henry VI.

On rood stair door; diaper pattern.

Parker, Eccles. and Architect. Topog. of England, Suffolk, No. 186.

WORSTEAD CHURCH, NORFOLK.

Wall painting of St. George and the Dragon. *Norfolk Archæol.,* iii. 20, note.

Painted screen across the chancel arch and the aisles, on the lower panels, 24 in number; the Apostles, "Vir Doloris," the four Doctors of the Church, SS. Margaret, Paul (twice), John the Baptist, Joseph, William of Norwich, Wilgefortis, Lawrence, and Thomas of Canterbury. *Colling, Gothic Ornaments,* ii. 16. *East Anglian Notes and Queries,* iii. 316. *Chambers, Hist. of Norfolk,* ii. 981. *The Ecclesiologist's Guide to the Deaneries of Brisley, &c.,* p. 122.

At the E. end of N. aisle, painted and gilt frame for the reredos, and remains of colouring below. Also on N. wall of N. aisle, a pattern of "Ts."

On S. side of central portion of rood screen; a painted canopy. All 14th cent. (late).

On the walls are numerous consecration crosses, 14th cent.; and scripture texts of about the middle of the 16th cent.

WORTH MATRAVERS CHURCH, DORSETSHIRE.

S. side of chancel; 15th cent. stone screen work brought from a neighbouring farm-house, and retaining some of its original colouring. *Hutchins' Hist. of Dorset,* 3rd ed., i. 700.

WORTHING CHAPEL, NORFOLK.

Coloured niche. Late perpendicular period. *Carthew's Hundred of Launditch,* ii. 743.

WORTHY, HEADBOURN, CHURCH, HAMPSHIRE.

Within the Galilee or Baptistery at the W. end of the church ; remains of colour on the figures of Our Lord and the Virgin and St. John, which form the rood.

Diaper of the sacred monograms χρc and IHC on the walls in black letter. 15th cent. *Proceedings of the British Archæol. Association, Winchester vol.*, p. 412.

WOTTON, GLOUCESTERSHIRE, CHURCH OF ST. MARY MAGDALENE.

On splay of N. chancel window ; the Virgin.

WRAXALL CHURCH, SOMERSETSHIRE.

N. side of chancel ; colour and gilding renewed on monument and effigies of Sir E. and Lady Ann Gorges. Circ. 1512.

WREXHAM CHURCH, DENBIGHSHIRE.

On the wall facing the main entrance ; Our Saviour bound before Pilate, and surrounded by the evidences of His Passion.

Over the chancel arch ; the Doom.

On the walls of the E. end of N. aisle ; a powdering of fleur-de-lis and other devices.

Builder, 1867, p. 824 ; 1873, p. 809 ; and 1877, p. 905. *Archæologia Cambrensis*, 3rd series, xv. 196. *Thomas, Hist. of the Diocese of St. Asaph*, p. 852.

WRITTLE CHURCH, ESSEX.

Nave roof ; painted tie-beams. 15th cent. *Buckler, Churches of Essex*, p. 207.

WROTHAM, GREAT, OR EAST, CHURCH, NORFOLK.

On panels of screens ; SS. Augustine, Ambrose, &c. *Blomefield, Hist. of Norfolk*, ed. 1805, i. 468.

WROXETER CHURCH, SHROPSHIRE.

N. side of chancel ; coloured effigies of Sir Thomas Bromley and his Lady. Date about 1555. *British Archæol. Assoc. Journ.*, xvii. 91.

WYCOMBE, HIGH, CHURCH, BUCKINGHAMSHIRE.

Painted roofs ; restored. *Church Builder*, 1876, No. lvii. p. 51.

WYFORDBY CHURCH, LEICESTERSHIRE.

On chancel walls ; scroll work. 15th cent. *Leicester Architect. and Archæol. Soc. Trans.*, iii. 84.

WYMINGTON CHURCH, BEDFORDSHIRE.

A painting in the Lady Chapel, and colouring on the capitals of the pillars. *Associated Architect. Societies' Repts.*, x. 1. *W. M. Harvey, Hist. of Willey Hundred*, p. 437.

WYMONDHAM CHURCH, NORFOLK.

S. side of nave, within three triforium arches; floral pattern or (?) imitation of a rose window, les Trois Morts et les Trois Vifs, and a knight on horseback. *Archæologia*, xxvi. 290, note. Probably 13th cent.

N. aisle, over door, "is an old piece of painting repre-
" senting naked people in a boat in great danger, and
" several others suffering for righteousness' sake, on the.
" right hand; and on the left, the devils, some offering
" a can of drink, others, a purse of money, encouraging
" sinners to their own destruction." *Blomefield, Hist. of Norfolk*, ed. 1805, ii. 528. *Chambers, Hist. of Norfolk*, i. 360.

Nave; painted roof.

On space filling up the present eastern arch; the Day of Judgment. *Destroyed.*

WYMONDHAM, NORFOLK, CHAPEL OF ST. THOMAS À BECKET.

Fragments of a mural painting. *Antiquary*, 1872, ii. 207.

WYSALL CHURCH, NOTTINGHAMSHIRE.

E. bay of chancel roof; boarded and painted. *Bloxam's Principles of Architecture*, 10th ed., p. 226, 11th ed., i. 196.

YARDLEY. *See* ARDELEY.

YARDLEY HASTINGS CHURCH, NORTHAMPTONSHIRE.

Three distemper paintings, discovered in 1859, and *destroyed. Ecclesiologist*, xix. 402. *Associated Architect. Societies' Repts.*, iv. xc.

YARMOUTH, GREAT, NORFOLK, ST. NICHOLAS' CHURCH

On N. wall of chancel; paintings of knights in chain armour, (?) the murder of Thomas à Becket.

YARMOUTH, GREAT, NORFOLK, ST. NICHOLAS CHURCH—*cont.*
S. chancel aisle, back of sedilia; remains of painting, viz., the upper part of an angel, &c.

Fragments of reredos of high altar; richly painted and gilt.

S. aisle; scroll pattern.

Palmer, Continuation of the Hist. of Yarmouth, p. 119. *Norfolk Archæol.,* vii. 220 and 221. *Ecclesiologist,* i. 202. *British Archæol. Assoc. Journ.,* xxxvi. 224.

S. aisle; colour and gilding on the canopy of the monument ? of Sir John Fastolfe. *Archæol. Journ.,* iv. 151.

Corbel heads at the termination of the hoodmould of the E. window of N. chancel aisle, pourtraying Edw. I. and Bishop Middleton; retain their original colour. Circ. 1286. *Gent. Mag.,* 1849, xxxi., new series, 403.

Ceiling of N. aisle; original colouring. *J. P. Neale and J. Le Keux, Views of the most interesting Collegiate and Parochial Churches in Great Britain,* vol. i. *Chambers, Hist. of Norfolk,* i. 266.

YARMOUTH, GREAT, NORFOLK.
The Hutch or Corporation Chest (probably originally a church chest) has been painted in colours in the mediæval style, a bright diaper pattern being introduced between the bands. Probable date early 15th cent. *Norfolk Archæol.,* vi. 176.

YATELEY CHURCH, HAMPSHIRE.
Royal figure. Whitewashed over.

Rude mural paintings, probably 14th cent. Too mutilated to be preserved. *Society of Antiquaries' Proceedings,* 2nd series, iv. 449.

YATTON CHURCH, SOMERSETSHIRE.
N. transept; remains of gilding and colour on the monument and effigies of Lord Chief Justice Newton and his Lady. Late 15th cent.

YAXLEY, HUNTINGDONSHIRE, ST. MARY'S CHURCH.
N.E. walls of N. transept; the torments of the damned.

N. chapel; figures of pilgrims, of early date. Re-whitewashed; drawings existing. *Ecclesiologist,* iii. 55.

All the walls formerly covered with paintings. *F. A. Paley, Notes on Twenty Parish Churches round Peterborough,* p. 28.

Above arches to chancel; a pilgrim, and Our Lord and St. Mary Magdalene, "Noli me tangere." *Sweeting, Parish Churches in and around Peterborough,* p. 190.

YAXLEY, SUFFOLK, ST. MARY'S CHURCH.

Chancel arch; the Doom. 14th or 15th cent.

Splays of window above the chancel arch; two angels bearing emblems of the Passion.

Over doorway in the W. wall leading to the parvise of the porch; traces of a scroll diaper. The eastern bay of nave has been enriched with colour.

On panels of the screen; SS. Ursula, Catherine, Mary Magdalene, Barbara, Dorothy, and Cecilia. Late 15th cent. *Ecclesiologist*, xxviii. (xxv. new series), 369. *British Archæol. Assoc. Journ.*, xxv. 262, xxvi. 248.

Cornice of nave roof; painted mouldings and Angels and Cherubim in the hollow.

YELDHAM, GREAT, CHURCH, ESSEX.

Painted figures on screen. *East Anglian Notes and Queries*, iii. 29.

YELVERTON CHURCH, NORFOLK.

Chancel screen. Circ. 1500.

YEOVIL, SOMERSETSHIRE, THE MUSEUM.

See GLASTONBURY ABBEY.

YETMINSTER CHURCH, DORSETSHIRE.

Nave columns; remains of colour.

Nave roof, on the beams; the Sacred Monogram and circles charged with stars.

Aisle roofs; painted bosses.

Hutchins' Hist. of Dorset, 3rd ed., iv. 454. *Archæol. Journ.*, xxii. 346. *Antiquary*, 1873, iv. 273.

YORK MINSTER.

Retable below E. window of Choir; subjects from the Passion. 15th cent. *Browne, St. Peter's Church, York*, i. 291.

The sculptured bosses at the intersection of the groining ribs in the nave have been painted and gilt. *Civil Engineer and Architect's Journ.*, 1851, p. 197. *A Description of York*, 1809, p. 24.

S. transept; remains of coloured decorations on the E. wall. *Church Builder*, 1875, No. liv. p. 73.

Colour on the ceiling, restored.

Remains of colour on the monument of Archbishop Walter Gray, died 1255, in S. transept; on effigy and monumental recess of William of Hatfield, died 1344, in N. Choir aisle; and on the E. wall, below the Lady Chapel window.

YORK MINSTER—*cont.*

Vestibule to chapter-house; remains of decorative painting on the vaulting ribs, with shields, roses, &c. on the walls. 14th cent. Also of decorative colour on W. doorway of chapter-house. Over the entrance were formerly painted figures of saints, kings, and prelates, now washed over. *Visitor's Guide to Cathedral and City of York,* 7th ed., p. 45.

Three portions of the chapter-house roof, with paintings of an Archbishop and Justice, are preserved in the vestibule.

Chapter-house; painting and gilding, obliterated in 1845. Before this date, " the roof was richly painted with " the effigies of kings, bishops, &c., and large silver knots " of carved wood at the uniting of the timbers; all much " defaced and sullied by time." *Gent, History of York, &c.,* pp. 50–52. *Murray's Handbook of Yorkshire Gough, Sepulchral Monuments,* vol. i., pt. i., p. cxxvi.

YORK, ST. MARTIN'S CHURCH, YORKSHIRE.

Bosses and painted roof. 15th century. *Murray's Handbook of Yorkshire.*

YORK, ST. MARY'S ABBEY, YORKSHIRE.

Dug up on S. of the church; seven statues, one of St. John the Baptist, all formerly painted and gilded. Now placed in the City Museum. *Sheahan and Whellan, Hist. and Topog. of the City of York, &c.,* i. 487.

YOUGHAL, COUNTY CORK, IRELAND, ST. MARY'S CHURCH.

Remains of decorative painting on a window in the gable between the nave and choir. 13th cent. Nave roof, painted and powdered with gold stars. *Kilkenny Archæol. Soc. Transactions,* iii. 344.

YOULGRAVE CHURCH, DERBYSHIRE.

Monument and effigy of Sir John Cokayne. Cir. 1504. Retains its original colouring. *British Archæol. Assoc. Journ.,* vii. 326.

YOXFORD CHURCH, SUFFOLK.

On fragments of screen worked into pews; remains of a Dance of Death (?). 16th cent.

Mural and other Paintings of later Date.

BARKING, ESSEX, EASTBURY HOUSE.

"In a room in the right wing, painted in fresco, are some military figures in niches, of the time of James I., almost obliterated."

In another room are some ship pieces and a coat of arms. *Ogborne's Hist. of Essex,* p. 49.

BRATOFT CHURCH, LINCOLNSHIRE.

Over the chancel arch; the Destruction of the Spanish Armada. Early 17th cent. *Associated Architect. Societies' Repts.,* viii. 89. *Oldfield, Topog. and Hist. Account of Wainfleet,* p. 124.

EXETER CATHEDRAL, DEVONSHIRE.

Under the window of the S. aisle; various heraldic bearings, all much decayed. Date early 17th cent. Discovered during the restoration. *Builder,* 1877, p. 1084. *T. B. Worth, Exeter Cathedral and its Restoration,* p. 34. *Worth, Tourist's Guide to S. Devon,* p. 31.

FARLEIGH HUNGERFORD, CASTLE CHAPEL, SOMERSETSHIRE.

E. wall; St. George and the Dragon, &c.

St. Anne's chapel; on walls and ceiling, coats of arms, figures of angels, apostles, &c. Circ. 1650.

Somerset. Archæol. and Nat. Hist. Soc. Proceedings, iii. 119, 120. *J. E. Jackson, Farleigh Hungerford,* p. 29. *Tunstall, Rambles about Bath and its Neighbourhood,* 7th ed., pp. 402, 404.

HADLEIGH CHURCH, SUFFOLK.

W. wall; painting of a Church. Early 17th cent. Obliterated in 1834. *H. Pigot, Hadleigh, the Town, Church, &c.,* p. 47.

HADLEY, MONKEN, MIDDLESEX.

Buckskin Hall or Dacre Lodge.

On wall of upper chamber, a Stag Hunt. Time of James I. *F. C. Cass, Monken Hadley,* p. 8.

LONDON. ST. ANDREW UNDERSHAFT.
Roof of Sacrarium; the Angelic Choir in Adoration.
Between nave arches; scenes from the life of Christ.
Between clerestory windows; whole length figures of Apostles and other Saints. Circ. 1630.
J. H. Sperling, Church Walks in Middlesex, pp. 28, 146.

LONDON. GREAT ST. HELEN'S CHURCH.
Over the Choir; a series of paintings of Apostles and Saints. Circ. 1630. *Destroyed. J. H. Sperling, Church Walks in Middlesex*, p. 148.

LYTES CARY MANOR HOUSE, SOMERSETSHIRE.
Walls of chapel; shields of arms. Time of Charles I.

NORTON, CHIPPING, CHURCH, OXFORDSHIRE.
Painting of "Time and Death." Early 17th cent. *Bloxam's Companion to Gothic Architecture*, 11th ed., p. 122.

SHULBREDE PRIORY, FARNHURST, SUSSEX.
Prior's chamber; Nativity, &c. Time of James 1st. *M. A. Lower, Hist. of Sussex*, ii. 157. *Murray's Handbook of Sussex. Black's Guide to Sussex. Cromwell, Excursions through Sussex*, p. 116.

STEVINGTON CHURCH, BEDFORDSHIRE.
Over S. door; a judge and two other figures, with text from James v. 9, and date, 1633. *W. M. Harvey, Hist. of Willey Hundred*, p. 161. *D. G. C. Elwes, Bedford and its Neighbourhood*, p. 122.

STOW, WEST, HALL, SUFFOLK.
Upper chamber in the gatehouse.
Ages of Man. Early 17th cent.
East Anglian Notes and Queries, i. 7.

TERRINGTON, ST. CLEMENT'S CHURCH, NORFOLK.
Richly decorated tabernacle font cover, with paintings on the inside panels, viz., the Baptism of Our Lord, two scenes from the Temptation, the Evangelistic emblems, &c. Date 1635. *Blomefield, (Parkin,) Hist. of Norfolk*, ed. 1808, ix. 93. *Cromwell, Excursions through Norfolk*, ii. 95. *Chambers, Hist. of Norfolk*, i. 488. *Watson, Historical Account of Wisbech*, p. 637. *The Fen and Marshland Churches*, i. 41. *Murray's Handbook of Norfolk*.

WOODFORD, ESSEX, OLD HOUSE ON THE COMMON.

Twelve paintings, exhibiting as many subjects of rural life. Date 1617. *British Archæol. Assoc. Journ.*, iv. 100.

WOOLBOROUGH CHURCH, DEVONSHIRE.

Panel paintings of the Evangelists. Time of James I.

WYE, KENT, THE COLLEGE.

On walls of a staircase; figures of Truth, Justice, Charity, &c.

On the balustrade; several coloured sculptured effigies of warriors, &c. Date 1622.

Additional examples received too late for insertion in their proper alphabetical places.

N.B.—Full title of work from which (i.) the Norfolk examples have been obtained, "*Dawson Turner, drawings, engravings, &c., illustrating Blomefield's History of Norfolk.*" British Museum Library, press mark 23,024–23,062. (ii.) The Shropshire examples, "*Revd. E. Williams, drawings, &c., in Shropshire,* 1792–1803." British Museum Library, press mark 21,236, 21,237.

ACLE CHURCH, NORFOLK. (Additional, *see* p. 2.)
The original painted decorations on the rood screen remained until 1865, when it was grained and varnished. " I could detect under the groining that the panels had " been originally diapered with the letters ' M ' and ' E,' " the latter pierced with two arrows in saltire, the " church being dedicated to St. Edmund, K. and M." *Eastern Counties Collectanea,* 1872–73, p. 61.

ADISHAM CHURCH, KENT.
N. side of nave, on jambs of a window; figures of St. Edmund and a bishop.
In a recess, S. transept; mediæval frame work, with paintings of the four Evangelists. Brought from Canterbury Cathedral.
Archæol. Cantiana, xiv. 158, 159.

ALBRIGHTON CHURCH, SHROPSHIRE.
On monument of John Talbot of Grafton; coloured armorial shields. Circ. 1555. *Revd. E. Williams,* ii. 179.

ALKHAM CHURCH, KENT.
E. end of S. aisle; traces of colour on a bracket, and the adjoining pillar.

ALLINGTON, EAST, CHURCH, DEVONSHIRE.
Painted oak pulpit.

AMESBURY CHURCH, WILTSHIRE.

On a pillar; a figure. In the transepts; masonry patterns.

N. wall of nave; traces of painting. *All destroyed.*

On screen, now in the possession of Mr. Job Edwards, traces of the original colouring were found.

ANSTEY CHURCH, HERTFORDSHIRE.

On piscina, S. side of chancel; painted armorial shield, and traces of a second one.

ARDELEY CHURCH, HERTFORDSHIRE. (Additional.)

E. beam of nave roof; a pattern of chevrons. 15th cent.

ASHBURTON CHURCH, DEVONSHIRE. · (Add.)

On a piscina, traces of colour.

Pulpit and lectern. *See* Bigbury.

ASHENDON CHURCH, BUCKINGHAMSHIRE.

Roodloft painted and gilt. *Destroyed.*

On stone effigy of late 13th or early 14th cent., in N. wall of chancel, green, gold, scarlet, and blue colouring discovered under the whitewash. *Records of Buckinghamshire,* i. 137.

ASHWELL CHURCH, HERTFORDSHIRE.

E. wall of S. aisle; painted bracket.

ASPENDEN CHURCH, HERTFORDSHIRE.

S. side of S. Chantry Chapel; gilding on brass effigies of Sir Robert Clifford and Lady, and on their armorial shields. Early 16th cent.

ASTBURY CHURCH, CHESHIRE. (Add.)

On a pillar; "diaper of the royal monogram, crown, and stars."

In S. aisle; decorative colouring. *Ormerod's History of Cheshire,* 2nd ed., iii. 29.

ASTON CHURCH, HERTFORDSHIRE.

S. wall of nave; considerable remains of painting. *Whitewashed over.*

ATTLEBOROUGH CHURCH, NORFOLK. (Add.)

Over W. tower arch; the Adoration of the Cross, with figures of Isaiah, Jeremiah, cherubim, &c. *Dawson Turner,* i., new series, p. 29.

On lower panels of screen, the instruments of the Passion, St. Edward the Confessor, &c. *Husenbeth,*

BABINGLEY CHURCH, NORFOLK. (Additional.)

Additional figures on panels of former screen; SS. Gertrude, Veronica, Bridget or Genevieve, Winifred, Blida, Barbara, Etheldreda or Clare, Apollonia, and Ursula.

[The emblems are unusual, and as there are no names the two last can alone be identified with certainty.]

Dawson Turner, i., new series, 56–77.

BADBY CHURCH, NORTHAMPTONSHIRE.

Painted roodscreen. *Destroyed.*

BARTON TURF CHURCH, NORFOLK. (Add.)

In spandril of third arch, N. side of nave; the torments of the damned, part of a Doom. *Dawson Turner*, ii. 14.

BASING, OLD, CHURCH, HAMPSHIRE.

On partition of the Poulet Chapel; inscription with date, 1488. *Gough, Sepulchral Memorials of Great Britain*, ii. cclxiv.

BEAUMARIS CHURCH, ANGLESEY.

Monument in white marble "painted and guilded" to a knight and his lady in the middle of the chancel. *Dingley's Beaufort Progress*, p. 68.

Now preserved in the vestry. *Archæologia Cambrensis*, 4th series, iv. 238.

BELAUGH CHURCH, NORFOLK. (Add.)

On miserere seats; blazoned shields. *Dawson Turner*, ii. 109, 110.

BENGEO CHURCH, HERTFORDSHIRE. (Add.)

S. of chancel, on splay of window, forming a sedile recess; diaper of lions, 13th cent., and masonry patterns, 14th cent.

BENNINGTON CHURCH, HERTFORDSHIRE.

N. side of chancel; traces of red colour on the angel and pillow supporting the head of the effigy of a lady. Late 15th cent.

BIDEFORD CHURCH, DEVONSHIRE. (Add.)

A beautifully modelled and painted representation of St. John the Baptist by Donatello. Early 15th cent. Formerly in the church, and now in the possession of Mr. Friendship, of Bideford. *Exeter and Plymouth Gazette*, Dec. 14th, 1880.

BIGBURY CHURCH, DEVONSHIRE.

Eagle lectern of oak gilt.

Old oak pulpit formerly painted.

Originally belonging to, and brought from, Ashburton Church.

BOURN CHURCH, CAMBRIDGESHIRE.
Screen; original colour scraped off.

BRABOURNE CHURCH, KENT. (Additional.)
Rood beam. 15th cent.

BRAMALL HALL, CHESHIRE.
Banqueting hall; "the sides are timber and plaister, painted with figures and foliage in imitation of tapestry." *Ormerod's History of Cheshire*, 2nd ed., iii. 829.

BRECON, BRECKNOCKSHIRE, ST. JOHN'S CHURCH.
On each side of nave; wooden partitions, on which emblematical devices illustrative of the trades of the several guilds were formerly partly carved and partly painted. *Lewis' Topographical Dictionary of Wales*, vol. i.

BRIDESTOW CHURCH, DEVONSHIRE.
Rood screen; traces of colour.

BRISLEY CHURCH, NORFOLK. (Add.)
By N. door; St. Christopher. *Blomefield, (Parkin,) Hist. of Norfolk*, ed. 1809, ix. 469.

BROOK CHURCH, KENT. (Add.)
On walls of chancel, within medallions; on S., the Annunciation, the Magi journeying to Jerusalem and before Herod, Christ among the doctors, &c.
On E.; ? Christ casting out a devil, the Last Supper, ? Judas receiving the Betrayal money, the triumphal Entry into Jerusalem, ? the Agony in the Garden, Christ bearing His cross, ? a pietà, ? the Entombment, and ? the Marys at the Sepulchre, &c.
On N. wall; Christ in Majesty, &c. All late 12th cent.

BROOKE CHURCH, NORFOLK. (Add.)
On bowl of font; sculptured representations of the seven Sacraments and the Crucifixion. *British Archæol. Assoc. Journ.*, xiv. 53.

BROXBOURNE CHURCH, HERTFORDSHIRE.
Above the chancel arch; painting on board of the Royal arms (time of Edward VI. or Elizabeth), with black letter inscription below, recording the gifts of Master John Bayce.
Beneath the E. arch S. of chancel, on monument of Sir John Say and lady; painted shields and decorative colouring on the panels. Late 15th cent. *Cussans, Hist. of Hertfordshire*, ii. pt. ii., p. 183.

BUCKLAND MONACHORUM CHURCH, DEVONSHIRE.

S. transept roof; bosses carved in the form of foliage, and one or two grotesque heads, formerly coloured.

Nave roof; coloured bosses, on one the Coronation of the Virgin, on others figures of angels.

BUNBURY CHURCH, CHESHIRE. (Additional.)

On S. wall of nave; St. Christopher.

On sides of great E. window; on N. an angel, on S. " a child in arms (the body defaced), and a hammer, " pincers, &c., hanging up, either the ordinary emblems " of the Crucifixion, or of the trade of Joseph the " Carpenter."

Spurstow altar piece; paintings of the Resurrection, with the two Marys and a bishop on either side. "The " background is red, powdered with stars or some such " ornaments in green."

Screen, twelve painted panels in the possession of Mr. Lowe, figures of SS. Catherine, Appollonia, and [Michael] Juliana, can be made out. *Ormerod's History of Cheshire*, 2nd ed., ii. 263, 266.

BURFORD CHURCH, SHROPSHIRE. (Add.)

N. side of chancel; (i.) painted effigy, and shields on monument of Elizabeth, Lady Cornwall, circ. 1426. (ii.) Painted wooden effigy and shield, circ. 1508. *Revd. E. Williams*, ii. 236.

BURNHAM OVERY CHURCH, NORFOLK. (Add.)

N. wall of nave; St. Christopher. *Dawson Turner*, iii. 189, 190.

BUSHLEY, WORCESTERSHIRE, PAYNES PLACE.

On walls of sitting room; couplets of verse on a white ground, circ. 1550. *British Archæol. Assoc. Journ.*, xxxviii. 180.

CAMBRIDGE, CAMBRIDGESHIRE, KING'S COLLEGE CHAPEL. (Add.)

By S. door; on brass of John Stokes, 1559, tinctures on the armorial shields in dry earth colours.

CAMBRIDGE, CAMBRIDGESHIRE, ST. JOHN'S COLLEGE.

The walls of the old chapel "were decorated with " fresco paintings in the time of the hospital. Traces " of them were found in various places, and especially " the remains of a large and elaborate painting of St. " Christopher, which existed behind the wainscot in the " secularized part of the nave." *C. C. Babington, Hist. of . . . . . . the Hospital and College of St. John the Evangelist at Cambridge*, p. 20.

CAMBRIDGE, CAMBRIDGESHIRE, ST. BENET'S CHURCH.
On either side of former chancel arch, on the splays of two arched recesses; scroll patterns. 13th cent.

CAMPTON CHURCH, BEDFORDSHIRE.
E. wall of chancel, S. of altar; decorated niche. Circ. 1330.
Paintings have been noticed beneath the whitewash.

CANFIELD, GREAT, CHURCH, ESSEX. (Add.)
Date of paintings, circ. 1360, or late 13th cent. *Academy*, 1882, p. 456. *Athenæum*, 1882, p. 852. *Antiquarian Magazine*, 1883, iii. 90. *The Antiquary*, 1883, vii. 74.

CANTERBURY, KENT, ST. MARTIN'S CHURCH.
S. side of chancel, on arch of a very early walled-up doorway; remains of colouring, perhaps pre-Norman.
On the arch of a tomb in N. chancel chapel traces of decoration.

CANTERBURY, KENT, EASTBRIDGE HOSPITAL. (Add.)
On wall of the hall; Christ in Majesty, surrounded by the emblems of the Evangelists, the Last Supper, and the murder of St. Thomas of Canterbury. 13th cent.

CAPEL CHURCH, SURREY.
Over S. door; "a cross within a circle having a star." *Winchester Diocesan Calendar*, 1867, p. 88.
Monumental tablet with coloured effigies of John Cowper, serjeant-at-law, and his lady. Circ. 1590.

CAPEL LE FERNE CHURCH, KENT.
N. wall of nave, within the splays of a Norman window; scroll foliage. Perhaps 12th cent.

CARLISLE CATHEDRAL, CUMBERLAND. (Add.)
Effigy, and canopy of monument, of Bishop Barrow, died 1420, "evidently richly painted and gilt." *Billings, Carlisle Cathedral*, p. 66.

CASSINGTON CHURCH, OXFORDSHIRE. (Add.)
On the splays of. windows; (i.) on S. of nave, St. Margaret; (ii.) on N. of nave, a bishop.

CATERHAM CHURCH, SURREY.
N. wall, W. end of N. aisle; decorative colouring.

Q 3254. U

CATTON CHURCH, NORFOLK.
E. end of chancel; ornamental decoration, restored. *Dawson Turner*, iv. 178.

CHALDON CHURCH, SURREY. (Additional.)
Portions of main subject on W. wall; Our Lord in Majesty, the Descent into Limbus, St. Michael weighing Souls, the Torments of the Wicked, angels, demons, &c., also a consecration cross.

CHALE CHURCH, ISLE OF WIGHT.
Remains of mural painting over the vestry door. *The Antiquary*, 1882, vi. 224.

CHALGRAVE CHURCH, BEDFORDSHIRE.
N. and S. of nave; remains of colour on shields on the monuments of two knights of late 14th cent. date.

CHARLTON ON OTMOOR CHURCH, OXFORDSHIRE. (Add.)
Round the nave arches; scrolls, crescents, stars, and roses. Circ. 1300.
On splay of E. window; scroll pattern.
On N. clerestory wall; crowned "I" s. *Proceedings of Oxford Architect. and Historic. Soc.*, new series, No. xvii., p. 201.

CHEPSTOW CHURCH, MONMOUTHSHIRE.
Monument of Henry Somerset, Earl of Worcester, and his lady (he died in 1549, she in 1565), "painted and guilded." *Dingley's Beaufort Progress*, p. 220.

CHESTER CATHEDRAL, CHESHIRE. (Add.)
" On the north outside the quire westward, is a curious
" ancient piece of painting and guilding against ye wall,
" of Symon Ryppley Abbot made kneeling praying to
" the Virgin with a glory about her head, standing be-
" tween Moses and Elias, at her feet St. Peeter kneeling
" with the keyes and St. John." *Dingley's History from Marble*, pp. 132, cccxcix.
On N. side of N.E. pillar, supporting the central tower, was painted the history of the Transfiguration. An imperfect sketch preserved in Harleian MS. 2151. *Ormerod's History of Cheshire*, i. 215, and 2nd end., i. 253. [These two accounts refer to the same painting.] Abbot Ryppley died in 1492.
Shrine of St. Werburgh, time of Edward III., painted and gilt.

CHESTER CATHEDRAL, CHESHIRE. (Additional.)—*cont.*

On it, within niches, are 30 statues of kings and saints of the royal line of Mercia, of which the following can be identified by the name on a scroll : Rex Crieda, Rex Penda, Rex Wolpherus, Rex Ceolredus, Rex Offa, Rex . Egfertus, St. Kenelm, St. Milburga, Rex Benora, Rex Colwulphus, St. Erminilda, Rex Ethelredus, St. Keneburga (or Withburga), Rex Kenredus (?), Baldredus, Merwaldus, Rex Wiglaff, Rex Bertwulph, Rex Burghredus, St. Etheldreda, Rex Ethelbertus, and St. Mildrida. *Ormerod's History of Cheshire*, 2nd ed., i. 298, 299.

CHESTER, CHESHIRE, ST. JOHN'S CHURCH. (Add.)

On a pillar at end of N. aisle by chancel arch ; fine early painting of St. John the Baptist. *Ormerod's History of Cheshire*, 2nd ed., i. 318.

CHIPSTEAD CHURCH, SURREY,

S. wall of S. aisle, on edge of recess ; pattern of six-leaved roses.

CHIVELSTON CHURCH, DEVONSHIRE.

Screen and wooden pulpit ; much colour remaining.

CHRISTCHURCH PRIORY CHURCH, HAMPSHIRE. (Add.)

N. aisle ; oratory ceiling painted in panels ornamented with red and white roses.

Wooden screen with inscription in gold letters on the top. *Warner's Hampshire*, ii. 197.

CHUDLEIGH CHURCH, DEVONSHIRE.

On panels of screen ; the Apostles and Prophets alternately. *Murray's Handbook for Devonshire.*

CLAVERLEY CHURCH, SHROPSHIRE.

On monument to Robert Brooke, circ. 1558, and on alabaster slab to William and Helen Gatacre, circ. 1577, armorial shields, properly blazoned. *Revd. E. Williams*, ii. 305.

CLOCAENOG CHURCH, DENBIGHSHIRE.

On E. wall of chancel ; an ecclesiastic and warrior.

On N. wall ; an armorial shield. *Archæologia Cambrensis*, 4th series, xiii. 238.

COLLINGBOURN KINGSTON CHURCH, WILTSHIRE.

On E. respond of S. nave arcade ; traces of colour.

COMPTON CHURCH, HAMPSHIRE.
"On the interior splay of one of the Norman arches,
" discovered behind the monuments in the north wall of
" the chancel, was a fresco of an ecclesiastic with a
" crozier in one hand and a book in the other." *Winchester Diocesan Calendar*, 1881, p. 94.

COURTEENHALL CHURCH, NORTHAMPTONSHIRE.
Octagon pillar on S. side of nave ; heads and shoulders
very imperfect, of three figures, two being apparently
female saints.
Above the capital and on the soffit of the arch ; rude
decorative patterns.
Tracings taken by Sir Henry Dryden, Bart.

COVENTRY, WARWICKSHIRE, ST. MICHAEL'S CHURCH.
(Add.)
Wooden pulpit, circ. 1400, remains of gilding and
colour. *Dollman, Antient Pulpits*, p. 17. *Removed.*

COVINGTON CHURCH, HUNTINGDONSHIRE.
Traces of colour found on the walls in 1882.

CROSTWIGHT CHURCH, NORFOLK. (Add.)
The Baptism of Our Lord.
N. wall of nave ; the Descent from the Cross.
On S. side ; a consecration cross, figure carrying a
banner, and a bishop.
On E. wall, N. of nave ; a crowned figure with cup,
? St. Edward, king and martyr.
On S. wall ; two nimbed male Saints.
Diapering on boards, &c., probably parts of screen.
Dawson Turner, ii., new series, 100–122, *and* 125,
126.

DALLING, WOOD, CHURCH, NORFOLK.
Traces of colour and gilding on remains of a screen.
Dawson Turner, xxvi. 17.

DARTMOUTH, DEVONSHIRE, ST. PETROX CHURCH.
Galleries and panelling painted and emblazoned with
coats of arms. *Murray's Handbook for Devonshire.*

DENNINGTON CHURCH, SUFFOLK. (Add.)
Colour and gilding on effigies of William Lord Bardolf
and lady. Circ. 1438. *Gough, Sepulchral Memorials of
Great Britain*, ii. 362.

DENTON CHURCH, NORFOLK. (Additional.)
Figures on panels of former screen; add, a bishop and SS. Cecily and Edward king and martyr.
[The doubtful figure is St. Walstan, not St. James Major.]
Dawson Turner, ii., new series, 147.

DEVIZES, WILTSHIRE, ST. JOHN'S CHURCH. (Add.)
Remains of figures and other carvings, portions of a reredos, painted and gilt in very rich colours. Found in S. wall of arcade.

DEVIZES, WILTSHIRE, ST. MARY'S CHURCH. (Add.)
On E. end, N. wall of chancel, on original plaster, part of a figure in royal robes.

DISS CHURCH, NORFOLK.
Painted roof. Circ. 1500. *Dawson Turner*, vi. 5.

DITTON CHURCH, KENT.
"Remains of an old mural painting." *Canterbury Diocesan Church Calendar*, 1861, pt. ii., p. 59.

DUNFERMLINE ABBEY CHURCH, FIFESHIRE, SCOTLAND.
"Fragments of a marble monument, which has been carved and gilt." *Sir W. Scott, Border Antiquities*, p. 177.

DURHAM CATHEDRAL, DURHAM. (Add.)
Bishop's throne; colour and gilding. Circ. 1350. *Billings, Durham Cathedral*, p. 41.

DUSTON CHURCH, NORTHAMPTONSHIRE.
"Two frescoes discovered on the tower, one of them being an historical one, the other being a crucifix of a Byzantine character." *Peterborough Diocesan Calendar*, 1867, p. 117.

EASTWICK CHURCH, HERTFORDSHIRE.
On W. wall of tower; shield in brass, 'the azure tincture painted on it. Early 16th cent.

EDINGTHORPE CHURCH, NORFOLK. (Add.)
Two E. bays of nave roof, richly coloured.
On N. wall; decorated niche.
Dawson Turner, ii., new series, 257.

EDWORTH CHURCH, BEDFORDSHIRE.
On S. wall, E. end of N. aisle; two kings, probably a portion of the subject "Les trois rois vifs, &c." 14th cent. These only have been preserved of numerous paintings discovered on the walls.

EFENECHTYD CHURCH, DENBIGHSHIRE,
N. wall of chancel; portion of Commandments in black letter in Welsh. Late 16th or early part of 17th cent.

EVENLEY CHURCH, NORTHAMPTONSHIRE.
On wall of nave; St. George and the Dragon, some skeletons standing (? Les trois rois morts), scrolls and inscriptions.
On jamb of a window; a perfect figure.

EXETER, DEVONSHIRE, ALL HALLOWS CHURCH.
Two wooden candlesticks, with remains of colour and gilding, formerly in the church chest.

EXETER, DEVONSHIRE, COLLEGE OF PRIESTS VICARS.
W. end of hall; screen with figures of the ancient bishops on the upper panels. *Murray's Handbook for Devonshire.*

EYNSHAM CHURCH, OXFORDSHIRE.
Colouring found on N.E. pier of nave.

FAKENHAM CHURCH, NORFOLK. (Add.)
Pillar on S. of nave; rich decoration, the "IHC" within an ornamental border.
On N. of nave; portion of a St. Christopher.
Dawson Turner, iii., new series, 5, 6, 7.

FARNBOROUGH CHURCH, HAMPSHIRE.
N. wall of nave, W. end; SS. Eugenia, Agnes, and Mary Magdalene, and a consecration cross. Date circ. 1330.
On W. wall; a consecration cross. *Notes and Queries*, 6th series, vi. 468, 539. *The Antiquary*, 1883, vii. 130.

FERNHURST CHURCH, SUSSEX.
On N. wall of nave; "An interesting fresco of a very early date." *Chichester Diocesan Calendar*, 1882, p. 158.

FLAUNDEN OLD CHURCH, HERTFORDSHIRE.
Chancel, in N.E. corner, pattern of roses; on S. wall, a consecration cross.
S. transept; on S. wall, a consecration cross; on E. wall, lozenge decoration, and colouring on back of reredos recess.

FLAUNDEN OLD CHURCH, HERTFORDSHIRE—*cont.*

N. transept, on N. wall, decorative patterns. On E. splay of N. window, an angel. On E. wall, (?) the Crucifixion with the Virgin and St. John, a consecration cross, and ornamental designs.

14th and 15th cents.

FREETHORPE CHURCH, NORFOLK. (Additional.)

S. wall of nave ; St. Christopher.

N. wall of nave; a Saint.

Dawson Turner, iii., new series, 75, 76.

FRING CHURCH, NORFOLK. (Add.)

On N. wall; St. Christopher.

On side of window in S. wall; ? St. Faith.

FRISKNEY CHURCH, LINCOLNSHIRE. (Add.)

On S. wall of nave ; the Children of Israel gathering the Manna in the Wilderness, and Moses. Early 15th cent. *The Antiquary*, 1883, vii. 119.

FURNEAUX PELHAM CHURCH, HERTFORDSHIRE.

E. bay of nave roof; rich colouring. On N. wall plate ; two figures playing musical instruments. On S. two holding armorial shields.

S. chapel; pattern of chevrons on the rafters. All 15th cent.

GADDESDEN, GREAT, CHURCH, HERTFORDSHIRE.

E. wall of S. aisle ; painted bracket. 15th cent.

GRAVENHURST, LOWER, CHURCH, BEDFORDSHIRE. (Add.)

Over N. door: St. Christopher. *Whitewashed over.*

GRAVENHURST, OVER, CHURCH, BEDFORDSHIRE.

E. beam of nave roof, over roodloft ; pattern of stars, &c., circ. 1500.

GYFFIN CHURCH, CARNARVONSHIRE.

Roof of chancel; the Twelve Apostles and the four evangelistic emblems.

HANNINGTON CHURCH, NORTHAMPTONSHIRE.

N. and S. of chancel, on splays of two low side windows; decorative pattern. 13th cent. Restored.

On central arcade of nave ; traces of red colouring were discovered.

On screen in N.E. corner of nave ; slight remains of the original decoration. Circ. 1500.

HARLINGTON CHURCH, BEDFORDSHIRE.

On arch mouldings of E. window of N. aisle; pattern of roses and chevrons, early 14th cent. Above, a kneeling figure, and faint outlines of a mural painting.

On E. bay of nave roof; (?) traces of decorative colouring.

HARRINGWORTH CHURCH, NORTHAMPTONSHIRE.

Rood screen; "once painted in blue, red, white, and gold." *Leicester Architect. and Archæol. Soc. Trans.,* iv. 101.

HARTHILL CHURCH, CHESHIRE.

Restored "in 1863, and some rude wall decorations were discovered under the plaster at the W. end." *Ormerod's History of Cheshire,* 2nd ed., ii. 714.

HASTINGLEIGH CHURCH, KENT. (Add.)

On E. wall of S. aisle; figure beneath a canopy.

On N. wall of nave, within a recess; 13th cent. painting.

HEMBLINGTON CHURCH, NORFOLK.

Nave and chancel roofs; diaper of "M," "IHC," and roses on the rafters, also painted and gilt spandrils. *Dawson Turner,* viii. 125, 127–29.

HEMPSTEAD CHURCH, NORFOLK. (Add.)

On additional panels of screen; SS. Helena, and Agnes or Agatha. *Eastern Counties Collectanea,* 1872–73, pp. 133, 134.

HENNOCK CHURCH, DEVONSHIRE.

Roof over roodloft; painted and gilt.

On panels of screen; SS. John the Evangelist, Peter, Jude, Paul, Stephen, Philip, Matthias, Lawrence, Gertrude, Margaret, Anastasia, the Annunciation, an abbot, bishop, &c.

HEREFORD CATHEDRAL, HEREFORDSHIRE. (Add.)

N. aisle; figures of SS. Thomas of Canterbury and Thomas Cantilupe of Hereford. *Dingley's History from Marble,* pp. 84, 85, 163, clxxxix.

HEREFORD, HEREFORDSHIRE, ST. PETER'S CHURCH.

Painting of the Last Judgment, initials, and inscriptions, formerly at. *Dingley's History from Marble,* pp. 49, 165, ccxxi

HERRINGFLEET CHURCH, SUFFOLK. (Additional.)
On screen; St. Stephen. *Husenbeth, Emblems of Saints*, 3rd ed.

HETHERSETT CHURCH, NORFOLK. (Add.)
Lower part of screen; richly coloured mouldings, and on the panels, stars with busts of kings or archangels above. *Dawson Turner*, viii. 153.

HIGHAM, COLD, CHURCH, NORTHAMPTONSHIRE. (Add.)
In Totcote Chapel; Saint, probably St. John the Baptist on the jamb of E. window. Female Saint with female child and book (probably St. Anne instructing the Virgin) on N. jamb.
In another place, two ecclesiastics.

HINXWORTH CHURCH, HERTFORDSHIRE.
On E. splay of E. window, N. and S. sides of nave; a tabernacle niche with traces of decoration.
N. W. corner of nave; remains of colour.

HOLNE CHURCH, DEVONSHIRE. (Add.)
Additional figures on screen; SS. Appollonia, Dunstan, Cecilia, Thomas of Canterbury, and Helena.

HOLYWELL, FLINTSHIRE, ST. WINIFRED'S WELL.
On the wall was painted the legend of the Saint, now almost defaced. *D. Parkes, Drawings of Remains of Antiquity, &c. British Museum Library*, No. 21,011.

HOPE MANSEL CHURCH, HEREFORDSHIRE.
"Portions of a painted screen, curiously carved, which served as the roodloft." *Duncumb, Hist. of the County of Hereford*, ii. 376.

HORLEY CHURCH, SURREY.
Painting discovered on S. wall of chancel, and *destroyed*.
E. pier of nave arcade, decorative patterns. 14th cent.

HORNCHURCH CHURCH, ESSEX. (Add.)
A king preaching, probably St. Oswald. *Husenbeth, Emblems of Saints*, 3rd ed.

HOUGHTON REGIS CHURCH, BEDFORDSHIRE.
In S. wall of nave; coloured shields on a monument. Late 14th cent.

HOUSTON CHURCH, RENFREWSHIRE, SCOTLAND.

On S. wall of aisle ; paintings of John Houston and his lady. Circ. 1400. *Gough, Sepulchral Memorials of Great Britain*, ii. 381.

HUNSDON CHURCH, HERTFORDSHIRE.

Over chancel arch ; the mottoes "IHC" and "Maria," 15th cent., also portions of a later text.

On N. wall of chancel ; on monument of Robert Poyntz, two painted shields. Circ. 1526

HUNTINGDON, HUNTINGDONSHIRE, ALL SAINTS CHURCH. (Add.)

Above the chancel arch ; large painting of the Last Judgment, traceable in 1859, which fell to pieces on the removal of the whitewash.

ICKLEFORD CHURCH, HERTFORDSHIRE.

Decorative patterns discovered during the restoration of the church.

ILSINGTON CHURCH, DEVONSHIRE. (Add.)

Within image tabernacles supporting the nave roof, figures carved in oak representing SS. Dunstan, James Major, Thomas, Helena, Lawrence, Jude, and Michael ; the whole still bears traces of illumination. *C. Worthy, Ashburton and its Neighbourhood*, p. 102.

IRSTEAD CHURCH, NORFOLK. (Add.)

Early texts. *Dawson Turner*, x. 60, 61.

KEMSING CHURCH, KENT.

Painted crosses and other fragments.

KERSWELL, ABBOTS, CHURCH, DEVONSHIRE.

Coloured effigy of a lady, found in S. chancel wall. *The Antiquary*, 1882, vi. 34. *Builder*, 1882, vol. xliii., pt. ii., p. 315.

KETTERINGHAM CHURCH, NORFOLK.

Gilding and enamel on brass of Sir Thomas Hevening-ham and Lady. Early 16th cent. *Dawson Turner*, x. 99, iv., new series, 41.

KIDLINGTON CHURCH, OXFORDSHIRE.

N. transept, on N. and E. walls, several figures, &c.

KIMBOLTON CHURCH, HUNTINGDONSHIRE. (Additional.)
Over the chancel arch; fragments of a mural painting
(? the Last Judgment) under the whitewash were discovered in 1882. The arch itself was coloured, and on
the wall near was a scroll pattern. *Destroyed.*
On the panels of the S. parclose; figures of the Apostles
were apparently painted.

KNAPTON CHURCH, NORFOLK. (Add.)
Painted corbels of roof, in the form of angels, one
holding a shield, another a crown of thorns.
Sculptured figure of St. Edmund, terminating one of
the principals.
Dawson Turner, iv., new series, 56, 57.

KNEBWORTH CHURCH, HERTFORDSHIRE.
Under arch between chancel and N. chapel, on a brass;
a shield on which the tinctures have been painted.

LANREATH CHURCH, CORNWALL.
On panels of the screen; the Doctors of the Church,
SS. Elizabeth of Hungary, Barbara, and Catherine. *The
Antiquary,* 1882, vi. 220.

LEIGHTON CHURCH, SHROPSHIRE.
S. E. corner of chancel; painted effigy of a crusader,
arms on his shield properly blazoned. *Revd. E. Williams,*
i. 152.

LENHAM CHURCH, KENT. (Add.)
S. of chancel, on splay of lancet window; a bishop.

LEVENS HALL, WESTMORELAND.
Shields of arms in plaster, with tinctures properly
blazoned. Time of Queen Elizabeth.

LICHBOROUGH CHURCH, NORTHAMPTONSHIRE.
S. wall of S. aisle; heads and shoulders of a bishop and
of several other figures, recently found and *destroyed.*
Tracings taken by Sir H. Dryden, Bart.

LICHFIELD CATHEDRAL, STAFFORDSHIRE. (Add.)
" Had before the fire, pictures of the kings of Collen "
(Cologne). *Dingley's History from Marble,* pp. 128,
cclxviii. cclxix.

LIMPENHOE CHURCH, NORFOLK. (Add.)
On N. wall; St. Christopher. Whitewashed over again.
Dawson Turner, iv., new series, 81.

LIMPENHOE CHURCH, NORFOLK. (Add.)
"Les Trois Rois Morts et les Trois Rois Vifs." *Archæol. Journ.*, xxi. 219.

LODDON CHURCH, NORFOLK. (Additional.)
On bowl of font; sculptured representations of the seven Sacraments, and the Virgin and Child.

LONDON, ST. JAMES' PALACE, THE CHAPEL ROYAL.
Painted and gilt beams dividing the ceiling into numerous plaster panels, on which are delineated the Royal arms, the monograms "H. R." and "H. A.," and numerous other devices, and the date 1540. The ceiling has been restored.

LONDON, THE SAVOY, THE CHAPEL ROYAL.
"On the front of the gallery, which had occupied the southern end, were formerly 12 panels painted with figures of the Apostles, and other similar representations were at either side of the chancel window."
Roof panelled and painted; shields, surrounded by the crown of thorns, charged with the instruments of the Passion, the emblem of St. Veroncia, &c., the Salutation of Judas, heads of Peter and Malchus, and of Pilate and Caiaphas, &c., also various armorial shields. Destroyed by fire in 1864. *Loftie, Memorials of the Savoy*, pp. 228, 231.

LUSTLEIGH CHURCH, DEVONSHIRE.
On 24 panels of screen; figures, one St. Barbara, carved in relief and coloured.

LYDDINGTON CHURCH, RUTLANDSHIRE.
Rood screen; painted panels, and diaper of roses and crowns. Late 15th cent.

LYDDINGTON, RUTLANDSHIRE, THE BEDE HOUSE.
Cornice in the hall; remains of decorative colour. 15th cent.

MARTHAM CHURCH, NORFOLK. (Add.)
Rood screen; painted panels and mouldings. *Dawson Turner*, xii. 33.

MEAVY CHURCH, DEVONSHIRE.
Bosses of S. chantry chapel, with traces of colour; representing a head of our Saviour, a female head, with mask, coming out of her car, a dying stag, lioness, &c.

MEDBOURNE CHURCH, LEICESTERSHIRE.
N. transept; scroll patterns, yellow-washed over.

MELFORD, LONG, CHURCH, SUFFOLK. (Additional.)
Bas-relief of the Offerings of the Magi, gilt and coloured. *Suffolk Archæol.,* ii. 81. *Carter, Specimens of Ancient Sculpture,* ii., pl. 8. *Archæologia,* xii. 93.
In side wall of squint from Clopton aisle to chancel; mural painting of the Virgin and Child.
On ceiling, painted blue with leaden stars gilt, moulded rafters painted red with white scrolls, the sacred monogram, coloured shields of arms of the Clopton alliances, &c. *Sir W. Parker, Bart., The Hist. of Long Melford,* pp. 127, 129–135, 139.

MELFORD, LONG, SUFFOLK, CHAPEL OF ST. JAMES.
" The original waggon roof and the panelled ceiling,
" with cornice and beams carved with rich and bold
" foliage, remain still perfect, with the bright paint of
" various colours upon them." *Sir W. Parker, Bart., The Hist. of Long Melford,* p. 348.

MEON, EAST, CHURCH, HAMPSHIRE. (Add.)
Remains of a painting of the Last Judgment, too decayed for preservation. *Winchester Diocesan Calendar,* 1871, p. 85.

MIDDLETON CHENEY CHURCH, NORTHAMPTONSHIRE.
Colouring on screen, pulpit, and some timber.
On next beam to chancel arch; a row of busts, probably the Saviour and His Apostles.

MILSTON CHURCH, WILTSHIRE.
On N. wall of nave; traces of subjects.
On E. respond of N. nave arcade; an angel.

MITCHELDEAN CHURCH, GLOUCESTERSHIRE. (Add.)
The paintings on panel represent, The Betrayal, Christ before Pilate, the Scourging, Crowning with Thorns, Descent from the Cross, Entombment, Descent into Limbus, and Ascension. *Bristol and Gloucestershire Archæol. Soc. Trans.,* vi. 262, 274.

MONMOUTH CHURCH, MONMOUTHSHIRE.
"On the right hand entring the great south door," a monument of marble " anciently guilt and painted," which is said to represent John of Monmouth, who died in 1234. *Dingley's Beaufort Progress,* pp. 231, 232.
The effigy is cross-legged.

MORETON CORBET CHURCH, SHROPSHIRE.'
    S. aisle; blazoned shields on monument of Robert
Corbet and Lady.   Circ. 1513.   *Revd. E. Williams*, i. 204.

MOULTON CHURCH, NORFOLK.
    Panel of screen; diaper of " M "s.
    Roof over rood-loft, richly illuminated.
    Dawson Turner, iv., new series, 191.

MULBARTON CHURCH, NORFOLK.
    Two grotesque carvings in wood, coloured and gilt.
    Dawson Turner, iv., new series, 205, 206.

MUNDEN, GREAT, CHURCH, HERTFORDSHIRE.
    N. wall of nave; painted canopied niche.

NORTHALLERTON CHURCH, YORKSHIRE.
    S. transept, within a niche; a diamond pattern in
black and red.   12th or 13th cent.

NORTHOLT CHURCH, MIDDLESEX.   (Add.)
    E. window N. of nave, on the splay; pattern of fleurs
de lis and roses.   14th cent.
    Traces of colouring on the font.

NORWICH CATHEDRAL, NORFOLK.   (Add.)
    Beneath the tower; painted shields.
    S. of choir; effigy of Bishop Goldwell, richly coloured.
    Dawson Turner, xiv. 130, 136.

NORWICH, NORFOLK, ST. HELEN'S CHURCH.   (Add.)
    Bosses of chapel roof painted and gilt, and with
sculptured representations of The Coronation of the
Virgin, The Annunciation, Nativity, Resurrection, and
Ascension, SS. Mary the Virgin, Catherine, Edmund,
Edward the Confessor, Paul, and the Apostles, and angels
holding blazoned shields.
    Chancel roof; coloured bosses, and a diaper of black
eagles on the panels.
    Dawson Turner, v., new series, 86–112.

NORWICH, NORFOLK, ST. MARY IN COSLANY CHURCH.
    S. wall of chancel; figures painted on back of monu-
ment of Martin Van · Kurnbeck.   Circ. 1579.   *Dawson
Turner*, v., new series, 160.

NORWICH, NORFOLK, ST. PETER MANCROFT CHURCH.   (Add.)
    On W. wall of Lady Chapel; painted decorations.
    Whitewashed over.   *Dawson Turner*, xvii. 48, 51, 52, 50.

NORWICH, NORFOLK, ST. PETER MANCROFT CHURCH—*cont*
Wooden baptistery with remains of gilding and colour.
Early 16th cent.

NORWICH, NORFOLK, ST. SIMON'S CHURCH. (Additional.)
Gilt cornices and mouldings of screen. *Dawson
Turner*, xvii. 93.

NORWICH, NORFOLK, ST. STEPHEN'S CHURCH. (Add.)
Gilt and painted cornice to roof. On ceiling, the
letters " T," " M," and " J " within medallions, and painted
and gilt mouldings. *Dawson Turner*, xvii. 104, vi., new
series, 94.

NORWICH, NORFOLK, ST. SWITHIN'S CHURCH. (Add.)
The figure represented on panel is St. Edward the
Confessor.
Portion of screen; painted and gilt spandrils and two
shields on panels.
On misereres, the Trinity banner and two other shields.
Dawson Turner, xvii. 121, 127, 128, 133–35.

NORWICH, NORFOLK, THE BISHOP'S PALACE.
In the centre of the roof of a vaulted apartment; the
arms and supporters of bishop Lyhart, well carved and
painted and gilt. *Norfolk Archæol.*, vi. 29.

NORWICH, NORFOLK, CARROW ABBEY.
"Traces of colouring of very bright colours still remain
on many of the moulded stones that have been found."
British Archæol. Assoc. Journ., xxxviii. 174.

NORWICH, NORFOLK, ST. MILES, OLD HOUSE AT.
Linen panelling, with heads of kings, monograms,
merchants' marks, &c., decorated with colour and gilding. *Dawson Turner*, v., new series, 171.

NOTTINGHAM, NOTTINGHAMSHIRE, ST. MARY'S CHURCH.
(Add.)
Wall painting of St. Christopher, visible as late as the
year 1800. *Lincoln Diocesan Calendar*, 1882, frontispiece.

NOTTINGHAM, NOTTINGHAMSHIRE, ST. PETER'S CHURCH.
(Add.)
Crest of the Strelleys, painted on bosses of nave roof.
Time of Henry VII. *Lincoln Diocesan Calendar*, 1876,
pt. ii., p. 76.

NUNEATON CHURCH, WARWICKSHIRE.

On an arch: the scroll and chevron ornament. 15th cent. "Time and Death." Late 16th cent. *Bloxam's Companion to Gothic Architecture*, 11th ed., p. 122.

NYMPTON ST. GEORGE CHURCH, DEVONSHIRE.

Ancient colour and stencilled ornament found on all the walls. *Exeter and Plymouth Gazette*, Dec. 1st, 1882.

OAKWOOD CHURCH, SURREY.

On the splays and jambs of all the windows; scroll and ornamental designs. 13th, 14th, and 15th cents.

On N. wall; two pairs of large figures. 14th cent. *Destroyed.* Tracings in the possession of the vicar.

On E. wall; two single figures.

On S. wall near E. end; two large figures, (?) the Annunciation. 14th cent.

Over S. chancel door; two figures and ornamental patterns.

On S. wall near W. end; portion of a St. George and the Dragon. 15th cent.

At W. end, on N., W., and S. walls; numerous small figures, parts of a large subject. 15th cent. *Winchester Diocesan Calendar*, 1881, p. 83.

ORLINGBURY CHURCH, NORTHAMPTONSHIRE.

N. of chancel; traces of colour on the alabaster effigy of a warrior. End of 14th cent.

ORMESBY, ST. MARGARET'S CHURCH, NORFOLK.

Nave roof; painted and gilt bosses. *Dawson Turner*, xviii. 6.

OTTERY ST. MARY CHURCH, DEVONSHIRE. (Add.)

In the S. transept " were discovered, walled up in the " frame of an old window, some fragments of canopies, " of middle pointed character, elaborately carved, and " richly painted and gilded." *Bristol and West of England Architect. Soc. Repts.*, 1848, p. 30.

Gilded stone lectern. 14th cent. *Murray's Handbook for Devonshire.*

OXFORD, OXFORDSHIRE, CHRIST CHURCH CATHEDRAL. (Add.)

On ceiling above the tomb of Lady Montacute; angels swinging censers, &c. 14th cent.

On arch opening to the Latin Chapel; decorative colour.

OXFORD, OXFORDSHIRE, CHRIST CHURCH CATHEDRAL.
(Add.)—*cont.*
On portions of shrine of St. Frideswide. 13th cent.
Remains of gilding.
The Chapter House :—
On ceiling of E. bay, masonry patterns, and within
medallions, SS. Peter, Paul, and two other figures. In
the second bay; an angel swinging a censer, and a
portion of a scroll pattern.

OXFORD, OXFORDSHIRE, CHURCH OF ST. MARY THE
VIRGIN.
On E. wall of chancel; seven richly canopied niches
with remains of colouring. Circ. 1500.

PENGERSICK CASTLE, CORNWALL.
Upper apartment in tower; "on the wainscot round
" the upper part of the room are pictures in miniature,
" proverbs divided, and betwixt the divisions, verses; all
" serving to illustrate each other, and to enforce some
" moral instruction." *Borlase's MS. Collection.*
"These are at present much decayed." *Lysons, Magna
Britannia, Cornwall,* p. ccxliii. Time of Henry VIII.
Polwhele, Hist. of Cornwall, iv. 117.

PERSHORE ABBEY CHURCH, WORCESTERSHIRE. (Add.)
Screen, now a partition between church and chapel;
"richly carved and guilded. 6th of Henry VI." *Dingley's
History from Marble,* pp. 105, cclxxi., cclxxii.

PETERBOROUGH CATHEDRAL, NORTHAMPTONSHIRE. (Add.)
"Operations in the morning chapel in the north
" transept have led to the discovery of an ancient door,
" with some old frescoes." "*The Globe,*" January 27th,
1883.

PIRTON CHURCH, HERTFORDSHIRE.
On N. wall of nave; portion of a Doom. *Destroyed.*

PITTON CHURCH, WILTSHIRE.
N. wall of nave; St. George and the Dragon. *Hoare,
Hist. of Wilts.,* v. 207. *Destroyed.*

POLING CHURCH, SUSSEX..
Several consecration crosses.
Mural paintings under a window in the Fitzalan Chapel.
All destroyed.

PORLOCK CHURCH, SOMERSETSHIRE.
Canopy of monument and effigies of Lord Harington of Aldingham and his lady. Date circ. 1450. *M. Halliday, The Porlock Monuments,* pts. vi., ix. *British Archæol. Assoc. Journ.,* xxxviii. 245.

POSTLING CHURCH, KENT.
Rood beam. 15th cent.

PULHAM, ST. MARY MAGDALENE CHURCH, NORFOLK. (Add.)
Lower panels of screen; rich colouring. *Dawson Turner,* vii., new series, 89.

RACKHEATH CHURCH, NORFOLK.
On panel of screen; St. Edmund. *Husenbeth, Emblems of Saints,* 3rd ed.

RANDWORTH CHURCH, NORFOLK. (Add.)
On under side of miserere stall; two shields and part of a scroll. *Dawson Turner,* xix. 70.
Font cover, dated 1505. *Destroyed,* probably in 1811. Nave roof, exceedingly rich in carving and gilding. *Destroyed* in 1811. *Norfolk Archæol.,* v. 268, vii. 180.

REDENHALL CHURCH, NORFOLK. (Add.)
On screen; St. Paul and the Apostles, omitting St. Matthew. *Dawson Turner,* vii., new series, 141–54.

REPPS CHURCH, NORFOLK.
On panels of screen; SS. Thomas, Andrew, Ursula, Gregory, Helena, Bartholomew, Francis, Edward the Confessor, Mary Magdelene, Agnes, Francis, Margaret, John the Evangelist, and John the Baptist, painted over. *Dawson Turner,* vii., new series, 204–17.

RICKMANSWORTH, HERTFORDSHIRE, BATCHWORTH HOUSE.
Various wall decorations. Late 16th cent.

RICKMANSWORTH, HERTFORDSHIRE, THE BURY.
Wall of S. wing; found beneath the whitewash, decorative patterns in red, white, and black. Late 16th cent.

RIDGE CHURCH, HERTFORDSHIRE.
N. wall of nave; St. Christopher, with (?) figure of the person who defrayed the expense of the painting, scrolls, and ornamental diaper.

RINGMORE CHURCH, DEVONSHIRE.
Over chancel arch; a diaper of conventual flowers, 13th cent., also the Commandments in black letter within arabesque borders.
On the walls, the Crucifixion, St. Christopher, &c., too decayed to be capable of being preserved.

ROSS CHURCH, HEREFORDSHIRE.
Altar tomb of marble once variously coloured, with effigies of William Rudhale and Ann his wife. He died in the year 1530. *Duncumb, Hist. of the County of Hereford*, iii. 123.

RUSHALL CHURCH, NORFOLK. (Additional.)
Two portions of screen; diapered panels. *Dawson Turner*, vii., new series, 248.

RUSHDEN CHURCH, HERTFORDSHIRE.
E. beam of nave roof; pattern of chevrons. 15th cent.

ST. MICHAEL'S MOUNT CHAPEL, CORNWALL.
Rood loft; " carved and painted with the history of the Passion, and not inelegantly for former times." *Polwhele, Hist. of Cornwall*, ii. 188.

ST. TWINNEL'S CHURCH, PEMBROKESHIRE.
Decorative colouring. 13th cent.

SALISBURY CATHEDRAL, WILTSHIRE. (Add.)
Additional figures on choir roof; the Apostles, Abraham, Isaac, Jacob, Moses, David, Job, Zacharias, and St. John the Baptist. *Brown, The Illustrated Handbook to Salisbury Cathedral*, No. 1, pp. 35–37.

SALISBURY, WILTSHIRE, ST. EDMUND'S CHURCH. (Add.)
Back of arch in S. wall of S. aisle; traces of nimbed figures, (?) Christ and the Apostles.
On E. wall of S. chancel chapel; niches with remains of colouring.

SALISBURY, WILTSHIRE, ST. THOMAS CHURCH. (Add.)
The paintings over chancel arch, and in S. chancel chapel, have been again uncovered and divested of the new coat of whitewash.
On the spandrils of the chancel arch; on N. St. James Major, on S. a bishop.
On the vaulting shafts of the nave; shields charged with the instruments of the Passion.
On E. splay of N.E. window in N. aisle; richly coloured niche.

Sandringham Church, Norfolk.
Nave roof; richly painted and gilt. *Dawson Turner,* xx. 110.

Sandwich, Kent, St. Peter's Church. (Additional.)
N. wall of nave, back of monumental recess; painting of the Crucifixion.

Sco-Ruston Church, Norfolk.
A crowned "M," &c., on panelling with remains of colour. *Dawson Turner,* xxiii. 148.

Selborne Church, Hampshire.
On jambs of E. window; remains of decorative colour. *Winchester Diocesan Calendar,* 1878, p. 88.

Shaugh Prior Church, Devonshire.
Font cover with traces of illumination. 15th cent. Recently recovered to the church, and restored.

Shawbury Church, Shropshire.
N. aisle; monument of Richard Corbet and lady. Circ. 1563. Painted effigies and armorial shields. *Revd. E. Williams,* i. 236.

Shelfhanger Church, Norfolk.
Screen; mouldings and cornice. *Dawson Turner,* xx. 166, 167.

Shiere Church, Surrey.
Colouring found on various parts of the walls.

Shiffnal Church, Shropshire.
N. of chancel; coloured effigy of Thomas Forster. Circ. 1520. *Revd. E. Williams,* i. 322.

Shillington Church, Bedfordshire. (Add.)
E. bay of nave roof; richly coloured. *Repainted.*
N. chancel aisle, on roof; pattern of chevrons.
Chancel roof, ridge beam running E. and W., original colouring.
Walls of S. aisle; various figures. *Destroyed.*
On E. column, N. side of nave; remains of decoration.
Traces of painting visible on N. clerestory wall, and elsewhere.
Crypt beneath E. end of chancel, on the ceiling, masonry pattern. 13th cent.

Shouldham Thorp Church, Norfolk.
St. George and the Dragon. *Dawson Turner,* xxi. 37.

SHREWSBURY, SHROPSHIRE, ST. CHAD'S OLD CHURCH.
(Additional.)

Alabaster slab to Golbard Burton and lady, 1524, with emblazoned shields. Removed to Atcham. *Revd. E. Williams*, i. 54.

SHREWSBURY, SHROPSHIRE, THE FRIAR'S HOUSE.

On wall of a bedroom; two armorial shields. Probably circ. 1550. *D. Parkes, Drawings of Remains of Antiquity, &c. British Museum Library*, No. 21,011.

SMALLBURGH CHURCH, NORFOLK. (Add.)

On screen, add., St. Edward the Confessor, a bishop and ecclesiastic. *Dawson Turner*, xxi. 61.

SMARDEN CHURCH, KENT.

On walls of chancel; the instruments of the Passion, four times repeated, encircled by sentences from the Creed.

Within Easter sepulchre, N. side of Chancel; "carved embattled stones, with colouring upon them."

On reredos, E. wall of nave, N. of chancel arch; a pietà, the entombment, and various figures. *Archæol. Cantiana*, xiv. 20–22, and 30.

Carved stones from chancel screen, retaining their colouring.

Lower part of wooden screen; painted decoration.

N.E. corner of nave; remains of distemper painting.

In window jambs on each side of nave; two niches with rich colouring.

Haselwood, Antiq. of Smarden, pp. 44, 45, 50, 53.

SPARHAM CHURCH, NORFOLK. (Add.)

Rood screen; on S. side, two illustrations of the Dance of Death, on N. The Salutation, and SS. Walstan and Thomas of Canterbury. *Dawson Turner*, xxi. 119–25.

SPARSHOLT CHURCH, HAMPSHIRE.

Niche; coloured and gilt canopy, and at the back, painting of St. Stephen.

STANBRIDGE CHURCH, BEDFORDSHIRE.

Above the chancel arch; pattern of lilies.

S. aisle, E. end of S. wall; decorative designs.

STANFORD LE HOPE CHURCH, ESSEX. (Additional.)
In a chantry chapel, 13th cent. painting in three compartments; in lower, a male figure on his back with
head upon a stone ; in next, a draped figure ascending
an incline ; in upper, a single draped figure with palm
branches overhanging, as if to depict Paradise. "The
whole somewhat resembles Jacob's vision in treatment."
St. Albans Diocesan Calendar, 1880, p. 217.

STARSTON CHURCH, NORFOLK. (Add.)
The Crucifixion painted on a shield.
Norfolk Archæol., vii. 302.

STAUNTON, LONG, CHURCH, SHROPSHIRE.
"Traces of mural painting of which nothing could be
made."
Hereford Diocesan Calendar, 1872, p. 120.

STOKE DRY CHURCH, RUTLANDSHIRE. (Add.)
On S. wall of S. chantry chapel; decorative border,
the Martyrdom of St. Edmund, and the Virgin and Child,
late 13th cent.
Partly painted over these; lower portion of a St.
Christopher.
On splay of S. window; the torture of a female saint,
? St. Agatha.
On N. wall ; an ecclesiastic and other figures.
On panels of Digby monument against the N. wall ;
remains of colouring, time of Henry VIII.
S. of chancel ; monument of Kenelm Digby and lady,
colour and gilding on the effigies, armorial shields, &c.,
circ. 1590.
Rood screen ; painting and gilding on the canopy.
15th cent.

STOTFOLD CHURCH, BEDFORDSHIRE. (Add.)
Panelling round the altar space, probably portions of
a screen; traces of red colouring, visible through the
varnish. 15th cent.

STOW LONGA CHURCH, HUNTINGDONSHIRE.
In the chancel; colouring on 13th cent. stonework,
built into the wall.
Traces of colour on the rood screen, and in various
parts of the church.
At E. end of N. wall of nave; a painting can be
detected under the whitewash.

SUTTON BONNINGTON, NOTTINGHAMSHIRE, ST. MICHAEL'S CHURCH.

" The nave roof, which was of perpendicular character
" and retained the ancient colouring, was unfortunately
" removed twenty years ago." *Lincoln Diocesan Calendar,*
1879, pt. ii., p. 76.

SWAFFHAM PRIOR, CAMBRIDGESHIRE, ST. MARY'S CHURCH.

N. side of chancel, on splay of an Early English lancet
window; remains of a figure.   15th cent.

E. face of tower, N. side of tower arch; figure of an
ecclesiastic.

Under pointed arch on N. side of tower; floral decoration.

Beneath the other paintings; remains of a masonry
pattern.   Circ. 1300.

SWAINSTHORPE CHURCH, NORFOLK.

S. wall of nave; The Expulsion from Paradise.

S. wall; the Agnus Dei, and a female figure.

Roof; crowned " M "s and " IHC " and other decorations.

Dawson Turner, viii., new series, 227, 228, 230.

SWINESHEAD CHURCH, HUNTINGDONSHIRE.

On rood screen, temp. Henry VII. or VIII., traces of
rich painting and gilding.

E. wall of N. aisle; traces of painted figures beneath
the whitewash, apparently demons recoiling from the
Blessed Virgin, whose image occupied a niche in the
wall.   15th cent.

Many parts of the building appear to have been decorated with red colouring.

TAVERHAM CHURCH, NORFOLK.   (Add.)

N. aisle; consecration cross.   *Dawson Turner,* ix.,
new series, 10.

TAVISTOCK ABBEY, DEVONSHIRE.

Various richly gilt and coloured mouldings dug up at
different times.   *Builder,* 1882, vol. xliii., pt. ii., p. 315.

TAVY, PETER, CHURCH, DEVONSHIRE.   (Add.)

Additional figures on panels of screen; SS. Matthew,
John the Evangelist, Thomas, James the Less, and
Philip.

TERRINGTON ST. CLEMENT'S CHURCH, NORFOLK.
Gilding on bosses of roof. *Dawson Turner*, xxiii. 157.

TEVERSHAM CHURCH, CAMBRIDGESHIRE.
Back of sedilia; powdering of the monogram "IHC," and floral decoration. 15th cent.
Traces of colour on the walls and screen.
Builder, 1882, vol. xliii., p. 731. *The Academy*, 1882, p. 420.

THORPE ABBOTS' CHURCH, NORFOLK.
Screen; Saints formerly painted on the panels. *Dawson Turner*, ix., new series, 36.

TIBENHAM CHURCH, NORFOLK.
On lower part of screen; diaper of "IHC," &c., on the panels. *Dawson Turner*, ix., new series, 53.

TIDWORTH, NORTH, CHURCH, WILTSHIRE.
N. wall of nave; St. Christopher.
E. wall of nave, N. side of chancel arch; SS. Lawrence and a bishop, (?) St. Martin. *All destroyed.*
Remains of colour on a bracket, N. side of nave; on a niche, E. wall of nave, on S. of chancel arch; and on a piscina, in S. wall of nave. All late 15th cent.

TILSWORTH CHURCH, BEDFORDSHIRE
On E. pillar, S. side of nave; remains of red colouring on a sculptured rose, &c.
E. wall of nave, on S. side of chancel arch; above two recesses, are painted a row of battlements. 15th cent.

TODDINGTON CHURCH, BEDFORDSHIRE. (Add.)
On S. wall of S. aisle; the Coronation of the Virgin.
Over S. door; St. Michael weighing souls, with the Virgin interceding, and a king being persecuted by a demon, perhaps parts of a Doom; above, a series of medallions enclosing swans and leopards' heads; and above again, (?) the Seven Acts of Mercy. 14th cent.
E. beam of nave roof; decorative painting. 15th cent.

TONG CHURCH, SHROPSHIRE. (Add.)
Armorial shields on the monuments of Sir Henry Vernon, circ. 1494, and Richard Vernon, circ. 1507. *Revd. E. Williams*, ii. 125, 128.

TOWCESTER CHURCH, NORTHAMPTONSHIRE.

Archdeacon Sponne, died 1448, is represented on his monument, habited as a canon or member of some collegiate or conventual foundation, and his vestments were originally painted in their proper colours. They are now all black. *Hartshorne, Recumbent Effigies of Northants*, p. 65.

TRUSHAM CHURCH, DEVONSHIRE. (Add.)

"16th cent. monument for members of the Staplehurst family, represented in painting on panel at the back." *Murray's Handbook for Devonshire*.

UPAVON CHURCH, WILTSHIRE.

On walled-up pillar, S. side of nave; (?) St. Christopher. *Destroyed.*
Various traces of colouring.

UPTON CHURCH, BUCKINGHAMSHIRE. (Add.)

The Adoration of the Magi.
Dedication crosses; "those in the chancel were highly foliated and enriched with colour and gilding." *Destroyed.*
Records of Buckinghamshire, i. 205.

WAKERING, GREAT, CHURCH, ESSEX.

"There are traces of mural paintings in the nave." *Kelly's Post Office Directory for Essex*.

WALKERN CHURCH, HERTFORDSHIRE.

Rood screen; found to have been formerly highly decorated.
On S. wall of S. aisle; an ornamental border to a picture, or early text. Early 16th cent.

WATTON CHURCH, HERTFORDSHIRE.

N. chancel aisle; on incised alabaster slab to John Butteler and his two wives, painted armorial shield. Late 15th cent.

WAVERTON, CHURCH, CHESHIRE.

On N. and S. walls of nave; large painted figures discovered, "too much decayed by whitewash for preservation." *Ormerod's History of Cheshire*, 2nd ed., ii. 790.

WEEKLEY CHURCH, NORTHAMPTONSHIRE.

Traces of colour on the effigy of Sir Edward Montagu, Chief Justice of the Common Pleas, who died Feb. 10, 1556–7.

WELLINGTON CHURCH, SHROPSHIRE.
Monument of William Chorlton and lady, circ. 1524; angels holding blazoned shields. Removed to the Abbey Church, Shrewsbury. *Revd. E. Williams*, i. 3.

WELLS CHURCH, NORFOLK. (Additional.)
Painting of an archangel, partly concealed by texts. *Dawson Turner*, xxiv. 179.

WEOBLEY CHURCH, HEREFORDSHIRE.
Figures of knight and lady, "guilt," on S. of chancel, probably of John Marbury, Esq., and Agnes his wife. *Dingley's History from Marble*, pp. 94, ccxliv.

WESTMINSTER ABBEY, MIDDLESEX. (Add.)
Diaper work in the triforium coloured red and gilded. Reredos of high altar originally richly painted and gilt.
G. G. Scott, An Essay on the Hist. of English Church Architecture, pp. 143, 169.

WESTWELL CHURCH, OXFORDSHIRE.
Painted decorations. 12th or early 13th cent.

WESTWOOD CHURCH, WILTSHIRE. (Add.)
On N. wall of N. aisle; a figure holding a lantern and staff, supposed to have been the hermit in a picture of St. Christopher.

WICKHAM, WEST, CHURCH, KENT.
Two foliated capitals found in the wall, entirely covered with red ochre. *Weale's Quarterly Papers*, vol. iv.

WICKHAMPTON CHURCH, NORFOLK. (Add.)
On N. wall of nave; the Seven Acts of Mercy and the Resurrection. *Dawson Turner*, ix., new series, 184–92.

WIDECOMBE IN THE MOOR CHURCH, DEVONSHIRE. (Add.)
Additional figures on screen; Our Lord, SS. Peter, James Major, and Bartholomew; also SS. Andrew, Mary Magdalene, Sidwella, Edmund, (?) Edward the Confessor, and two bishops.
Bosses of roof carved, one to represent St. Catherine, and painted.
R. Dymond, Things New and Old concerning the Parish of Widecombe in the Moor, p. 12. *Letter signed "Devoniensis," in the "Exeter News."*

WIDFORD CHURCH, HERTFORDSHIRE. (Additional.)
Back of piscina, S. of nave; traces of two figures.

WIGHTON CHURCH, NORFOLK. (Add.)
On N. of chancel; the incredulity of St. Thomas.
Dawson Turner, ix., new series, 200.

WILMSLOW CHURCH, CHESHIRE. (Add.)
"Beneath the whitewash the remains of several mural
paintings were discovered." *Ormerod's History of
Cheshire*, 2nd ed., iii. 597.

WIMBORNE MINSTER, DORSETSHIRE. (Add.)
Remains of alabaster reredos, retaining its original
colouring; found in the Lady Chapel, S. choir aisle.

WISTANSTOW CHURCH, SHROPSHIRE.
Walls covered with painting, illuminated· texts, &c.
Hereford Diocesan Calendar, 1872, p. 120.

WITCHINGHAM, GREAT, CHURCH, NORFOLK. (Add.)
On bowl of font; sculptured representations of the
Seven Sacraments of the Romish Church, and the Assumption of the Virgin. *British Archæol. Assoc. Journ.*, xiv.
52.

WOODBRIDGE CHURCH, SUFFOLK. (Add.)
On bowl of font; the Seven Sacraments of the Romish
Church, and the Crucifixion.

WOODLAND CHURCH, DEVONSHIRE.
Traces of illumination on fragments of screen and
pulpit.

WOODLEIGH CHURCH, DEVONSHIRE.
Over chancel arch; decorative painting.
On N. wall, opposite S. door; St. Christopher. Lower
portion of rood screen; panel paintings of Saints.

WORSTEAD CHURCH, NORFOLK. (Add.)
Mural painting of St. Michael and Satan.
The walls were covered with paintings, which were
destroyed in 1838.
Dawson Turner, xxvi. 55, and ix., new series, 241, 242.

WROXETER CHURCH, SHROPSHIRE. (Add.)
Monument of Sir Richard Newport and lady, circ.
1570; coloured shields. *Revd. E. Williams*, ii. 12.

WYE CHURCH, KENT.
On nave walls; various figures. *Whitewashed over.*

YANWATH HALL, CUMBERLAND.

Walls of ladies' chamber; several figures, portions of a large subject. *R. S. Ferguson, A Handbook to the Principal Places . . . . . . in the Vicinity of Carlisle,* p. 120.

YARMOUTH, GREAT, CHURCH, NORFOLK. (Additional.)

N. wall of N. aisle; David and Goliath.

N. and S. aisle roofs; richly coloured bosses.

S.E. corner of N. transept; diaper.

Colouring on screen work.

In W. arch of first floor of tower towards the belfry; panelling with the monogram "IHC." *Dawson Turner,* xxvii. 142, 153, 158-62, iv., new series, 72, and x., new series, 30–43.

YATESBURY CHURCH, WILTSHIRE.

On N. wall of nave, bordering the arches; bold and effective patterns of ivy leaves in scarlet paint.

On E. wall; faint traces.

ALPHABETICAL INDEX

PRINCIPAL OBJECTS, SUBJECTS, SAINTS, &c.

* Mural and other paintings in distemper.
† Paintings on panels of screens and other woodwork.
‡ Painted sculpture.
§ Paintings of later date.

⁎ On the bosses of the roof of Norwich Cathedral are
numerous representations in sculpture of events from the time
of the Creation to the reign of King Solomon, and from the birth
of Christ to the Final Judgment. *See Goulburn, "The Ancient
Sculptures in the Roof of Norwich Cathedral,"* as, owing to their
number, the several subjects *have not been specified* in "The
List."

AARON.
    Edmundthorpe.†
    Roystone.*

ABDIAS (OBADIAH). *See* PRO-
PHETS, THE.

ABEDNEGO.
    Warblington.*

ABIMELECH.
    Westminster Hall.*

ABNER.
    Westminster Hall.*

ABRAHAM.
    Salisbury Cath.*
    Wissett.*
    Woolborough.†

ACCA, ST.
    Hexham.†

ACTÆON.
    Cowdray.*

ADAM AND EVE.
    Bradninch.†.
    Brooke (Norfolk).*
    Colton.*
    Easby Ch.*
    Easton, Little.*
    Elford.*
    Exeter Cath.†
    Kempston.†
    Newport, I. of Wight.*
    Poringland.†
    Shenley Mansell.*
    Swainsthorpe.*

ADORATION OF THE MAGI, THE.
    See CHRIST (2).

ADORATION OF THE SHEPHERDS,
THE. *See* CHRIST (4).

AGATHA, ST.
Binham Abbey.†
Castor.*
Eton.* (?)
Heavitree.†
Hempstead.† (?)
Holne.†
Manaton.†
Norwich, St. John's Mad-
dermarket.†
Preston in Holderness.‡
Stoke Dry.* (?)
Tor Bryan.†
Ufford.†
Ugborough.†
Upton (Norfolk).†
Wiggenhall, St. Mary
Magdalene.†
Winchester Cath.*

AGES OF MAN, THE.
Hardham.* (?)
Stow, West.* §

AGNES, ST.
Babingley.†
Binham Abbey.†
Cawston.† *
Denton.†
Elmham, North.†
Eton.* (?)
Eye.†
Farnborough.*
Hempstead.† (?)
Kenton.†
Norwich, St. James. †
Plymtree.†
Preston in Holderness.‡ (?)
Repps.†
Tuddenham, North.†
Ufford.†
Ugborough.†
Westhall.†

AGNUS DEI. See CHRIST (32),
also ST. JOHN THE BAPTIST.

AHAZIAH.
Westminster Hall.*

AIDAN, ST.
Carlisle Cath.*
Woolborough.†

ALABASTER SLAB.
Claverley.
Dale Abbey.
Shrewsbury, St. Chad's.
Watton (Herts).

ALCMUND, ST.
Hexham.†

ALTAR SCREEN. See REREDOS.

ALTAR STONE.
Weston in Gordano.

ALTO-RELIEVO. See BAS-RELIEF.

ALWIN, BISHOP.
Ely Cath.*

AMATOR, ST.
Cambridge, Trinity Ch.‡
(?)

AMBROSE, ST., DOCTOR OR
FATHER OF THE WESTERN
CHURCH.
Acre, Castle, Ch.†
Ashton.†
Berry Pomeroy.†
Burnham Norton.†
Cawston.†
Elmham, North.†
Foxley.†
Fritton (Norfolk).†
Gooderstone.†
Gressenhall.†
Heigham, Potter.†
Holne.†
Houghton le Dale.†
Kenn.†
Lanreath.†
Lessingham.†
Ludham.†
Manaton.†
Morston.†
Portlemouth.†
Romsey.†
Roxton.†
Ruston, East.†
Sall.†
Suffield.†
Tunstead.†
Upton (Norfolk).†
Woolborough.†
Worstead.†
Wrotham, Great.†

AMOS. *See also* PROPHETS, THE.
  Crawley, North.†
  Southwold Ch.†
  Stapleton.*

ANASTASIA, ST.
  Hennock.†

ANDREW, ST. *See also* APOSTLES, THE.
  Bovey Tracey.‡
  Brisley.*
  Edingthorpe.†
  Hexham.†
  Horsham, St. Faith's.†
  Kenn.†
  Mainhead.†
  Marholme.*
  Newington.*
  Norwich Cath.*
  Pulham, St. Mary the Virgin.†
  Repps.†
  Salthouse.†
  Somerleyton.†
  Stalham.†
  Swafield.†
  Tavy, Peter.†
  Trusham.†
  Walpole, St. Peter.†
  Whissendine.†
  Widecombe in the Moor.†
  Winchester Cath.*

ANGELS AND ARCHANGELS. *See also* HIERARCHY, THE HEAVENLY; MICHAEL, ST.; *and* ANNUNCIATION, THE.
  Amport.‡
  Ardeley.*
  Arundel.*
  Asgarby.*
  Attleborough.*
  Barfreston.*
  Barnet, East.†
  Bennington.‡
  Berkeley Ch.* (?)
  Blundeston.†
  Blythburgh.‡
  Bolton Abbey.*
  Bradfield Combust.*

ANGELS AND ARCHANGELS— *cont.*
  Bradford Abbas.†
  Bradninch.†
  Bradwell.†
  Bramfield.*
  Buckland Monachorum.‡
  Bunbury.*
  Canterbury Cath.*,†
  Carbrooke.†
  Cassington.*
  Chiltington, West.*
  Cobham, Henhurst.*
  Copford.*
  Dodford.*
  Eaton.*
  Eggington.*
  Elgin.*
  Exeter Cath.†
  Exeter, St. Mary Major.*
  Farleigh Hungerford.* §
  Flaunden.*
  Gloddaeth.*
  Gooderstone.†
  Gorleston Ch.*
  Hadleigh (Essex).*
  Hethersett.†
  Hillesden.‡
  Hitcham.†
  Holne.†
  Houghton Conquest.*
  Impington.*
  Irstead.*
  Keevil.†
  Kelston.*
  Kempley.*
  Knapton.‡
  Knowle.†
  Landbeach.‡
  Leek.*
  Leicester, St. Margaret's.‡
  Llandanwg. †
  London, St. Andrew Undershaft.† §
  Ludlow.* †
  Maidstone.*
  Marston Moretaine.‡
  Milston.*
  Muchelney Ch.†
  Mylor.*
  Newton Bromswold.*

ANGELS AND ARCHANGELS—
cont.

Newton Solney.‡
Norwich, St. Gregory.†
Norwich, St. John's, Mad-
. dermarket.†
Oakley.†
Oxburgh.‡
Oxford, All Souls Coll.†
Oxford Cath.*
Pinchbeck.‡
Pinvin.*
Pirford.*
Pluscardine.*
Plymtree.†
Portlemouth.†
Pulham, St. Mary Mag-
dalene.†
Randworth.†
Raunds.*
Romsey.†
St. Albans Cath.*
St. Davids.*
Sall.†
Southwold Ch.†
Stanford Dingley.*
Stauton.†
Stanton St. John's.†
Stifford.*
Stoke-sub-Hamdon.*
Stow Bardolph.*
Stradbroke.†
Tewkesbury.*
Totham, Great.*
Ugborough.†
Upton (Bucks).*
Wakefield.*
Walsham, North.†
Walsham le Willows.*
Wells (Norfolk).*
Wells, St. Cuthbert's.†
Westhall.†
Weston Baggard.*
Winchester Cath.* †
Winchester, Magdalen
Hosp.*
Winterbourne Dauntsey.*
Worcester Cath.*
Workrop.‡
Yaxley (Suffolk).†

N.B.—Figures of Angels
are also generally found in
representations of "The
Doom," "Our Lord in
Glory," and "The As-
sumption of the Virgin."

ANNE, ST.
Babingley.†
Boston, Rochford Tower.*
Gorleston Ch.*
Haddon Hall.*
Harpley.†
Harting.*
Hereford Cath.*
Higham, Cold.*
Horsham, St. Faith's.†
Houghton le Dale.†
Latton.*
Slaptou.*
Somerleyton.†
Whittlesford.‡
Wiggenhall, St. Mary the
Virgin.†
Winchester, St. Cross.*

ANNUNCIATION, THE. *See*
MARY THE VIRGIN, ST. (2.)

ANTHONY, ST.
Ashton.†
Blythburgh.‡
Boston, Rochford Tower.*
Carlisle Cath.†
Eversden.*
Gressenhall.†
Irthlingborough.*
Kempley.*
Kenton.†
Preston in Holderness.‡
Rauceby.* (?)
Romsey.†
Smallburgh.†
Strensham.†
Tawstock.* (?)
Westhall.†

ANTHONY, ST., OF PADUA.
Ipswich, St Margaret's.* (?)

ANTIOCHUS.
Westminster Hall.*

APOSTLES, THE. *See also*
under individual names.

APOSTLES, THE—*cont.*

N.B.—In most instances St. Paul is included, SS. Matthew or Matthias being omitted.

Acre, Castle, Ch.†
Ashburton.‡
Aylsham.†
Beeston Regis.†
Beighton.†
Belaugh.†
Berkhampstead, Great, Ch.*
Blofield.†
Bovey Tracey.†
Bozeat.†
Brailes.†
Buckland in the Moor.†
Burford (Salop).†
Canterbury Cath.†
Carlisle Cath.†
Cawston.†
Checkendon.*
Chiltington, West.*
Chudleigh.†
Combe Martin.†
Copford.*
Cowdray.*
Cury.‡
Elsing Ch.†
Exeter Cath.*
Farleigh Hungerford.* §
Gisleham.†
Gooderstone.†
Gunwalloe.†
Gyffin.†
Hardham.*
Hereford Cath.*
Hexham.†
Holne.†
Hunstanton.†
Irstead.†
Kempley.*
Kenninghall.†
Kenton.†
Kimbolton.†
Launcells.†
Lessingham.†
Llanwyddyn.*
London, St. Andrew Undershaft.* §

APOSTLES, THE—*cont.*

London, St. Helen's.† §
London, The Savoy Chapel.†
Lynn, South.†
Magor.†
Manaton.† ‡
Marsham.†
Martock.*
Mattishall.†
Middleton.†
Middleton Cheney.†
Milton Abbas.†
Neatishead.†
Necton.†
Norwich, St. Helen's.‡
Pennant Melangell.†
Pickering.*
Pluscardine.*
Poringland.†
Quainton.†
Randworth.†
Reculver.‡
Redenhall.†
Ringland.†
Rotherham.*
Salisbury Cath.*
Salisbury, St. Edmund's.*
Sotterley.†
Southwold Ch.†
Strensham.†
Tewkesbury.*
Thetford, St. Peter's.†
Thirsk.*
Tor Bryan.†
Trunch.†
Tunstead.†
Upwell.†
Walsham, North.†
Wellow (Hants).*
Weston Longville.†
Westwick.†
Woolborough.†
Worstead.†

The Apostles are also generally introduced in pictures of The Ascension, the Death of the Virgin, and sometimes in representations of the Day of Judgment.

Q

APPOLLONIA, ST.
  Ashton.†
  Babingley.†
  Barton Turf.†
  Bunbury.†
  Eton.*
  Holne.†
  Horsham, St. Faith's.†
  Kenton.†
  Lessingham.†
  Ludham.†
  Norwich, St. John's Maddermarket.†
  Tor Bryan.†
  Ugborough.†
  Westhall.†
  Widecombe in the Moor.†
  Woolborough.†

AQUILA AND PRISCILLA.
  Mells.* (?)

ARCHANGELS. See ANGELS AND HIERARCHY, THE HEAVENLY; also ST. MICHAEL, and ANNUNCIATION, THE.

ARCHBISHOPS not specially identified.
  Amport.‡ (?)
  Barfreston.*
  Bristol, St. John's.*
  Chester, St. Mary on the Hill.*
  Easby.*
  Kempley.*
  Minster (Kent).*
  Peterborough.†
  Winchester, Magdalene Hosp.*
  York Minster.†

ARMADA. DESTRUCTION OF THE SPANISH.
  Bratoft.* §

ARMORIAL SHIELDS, HERALDIC BEARINGS, &c.
  Aberdeen.†
  Abergavenny.‡
  Acre, Castle, Priory.*
  Albrighton.‡
  Anstey.*
  Ashbourn.‡
  Aslacton.*

ARMORIAL SHIELDS, HERALDIC BEARINGS, &c.—cont.
  Buckwell.‡
  Barford, Great.‡
  Barking, Eastbury Ho.* §
  Belaugh.†
  Boston, Rochford Tower.*
  Bradford Abbas.†
  Brington, Great.‡
  Bristol, St. Stephen's.‡
  Broughton (Oxon).*
  Broxbourne.‡
  Burford (Salop).‡
  Bury St. Edmunds, St. Mary's.* ‡
  Canterbury Cath.* † ‡
  Cardington.‡
  Cartmel.‡
  Chalgrave.‡
  Chichester Cath.*
  Chichester, Bishop's Palace.†
  Cirencester.*
  Claverley.* ‡
  Clifton.‡
  Clocaenog.*
  Cobham, Henhurst.*
  Colkirk.†
  Cople.‡
  Cove, North.‡
  Dartmouth, St. Petrox.†
  Dartmouth, St. Saviour's.†
  Deeping, Market.*
  Denham.†
  Dodford.*
  Doncaster, St. George's.†
  Dorney.†
  Durham Cath.†
  Eastwick.‡
  Elford.† ‡
  Epworth.†
  Exeter Cath.* §
  Exeter, Residentiary House.†
  Farleigh Hungerford.* §
  Feering.*
  Frampton.†
  Fundenhall.†
  Furneaux Pelham.†
  Glastonbury, St. John's.†
  Hagbourne.*

Harewood.‡
Hazelbury Bryan.*
Hengrave.*
Higham, Cold.*
Hilgay.†
Hillesden.*
Holne.†
Horsham, St. Faith's.* †
Houghton Regis.‡
Hunmanby.*
Hunsdon.*
Ickburgh.†
Impington.*
Isfield.*
Keevil.†
Kingston.‡
Kington.‡
Kirton in Lindsey.*
Knapton.‡
Knebworth.‡
Landbeach.†
Langford.*
Langford, Steeple.‡
Leighton.‡
Levens Hall.‡
Llanfihangel   Yng
    Nghwnfa.†
London, Carpenters' Hall.*
London,   St.   James'
    Palace.*
London,   The   Savoy
    Chapel.†
Ludlow.*
Lurgashall.*
Lytes Cary.* §
Marholme.‡
Marston Moretaine.*
Melford, Long.†
Mendham.*
Mimms, North.‡
Moreton Corbet.‡
Narburgh.‡
Navenby.‡
Naworth.*
Newark.*
Norwich Cath.*
Norwich, St. Helen's.‡
Norwich, St. James.*
Norwich, St. Swithin's.†

Norwich, The Bishop's
    Palace.‡
Nottingham, St. Peter's.†
Orwell.†
Oulton.†
Oxford Cath.‡
Penmynydd.‡
Pennant Melangell.*
Peterborough.*
Pinchbeck.‡
Puttenham.†
Rainham (Kent).†
Randworth.†
Richmond.†
Rochester Cath.*
St. Albans Cath.* †
St. Albans, St. Michael's.*
St. David's.* †
Salisbury Cath.‡
Scropton.‡
Shawbury.‡
Shrewsbury, St. Chad's.‡
Shrewsbury, Friars' Ho.*
Sotterley.*
Spratton.‡
Stackpole Elidur.*
Stanford.‡
Stoke Dry.‡
Sudbury, All Saints.*
Tilney, All Saints.*†
Tong.‡
Totnes, Guildhall.*
Wainfleet.‡
Warblington.*
Watton (Herts).‡
Wellington (Salop).‡
Wells Cath.*
Westhall.†
Westminster Abbey.*†‡
Westminster, Canon's Ho.*
Wheathampstead.‡
Willington.*
Winchester Cath.†
Winchester,   Magdalen
    Hosp.*
Wingfield.†
Wolverhampton.‡
Wroxeter.‡

ARTHUR, PRINCE.
Plymtree.†

ASCENSION, THE. *See* CHRIST (29).

ASSUMPTION, THE, OF THE VIRGIN. *See* MARY, THE VIRGIN, ST. (10).

ATHELSTAN, BISHOP OF ELM-HAM.
Ely Cath.*

ATHELSTAN, BISHOP OF HERE-FORD.
Hereford Cath.*

ATHELSTAN, KING.
Baston.†
Milton Abbas.†

AUDRIE, ST. *See* ETHELDREDA, ST.

AUGUSTINE, ST., BISHOP AND DOCTOR OR FATHER OF THE WESTERN CHURCH.
Acre, Castle, Ch.†
Ashton.†
Berry Pomeroy.†
Burnham Norton.†
Canterbury Cath.†
Carlisle Cath.†
Cawston.†
Elmham, North.†
Foxley.†
Fritton (Norfolk).†
Gateley.† (?)
Gooderstone.†
Gressenhall.†
Heigham, Potter.†
Holne.†
Houghton le Dale.†
Kenn.†
Lanreath.†
Lessingham.†
Ludham.†
Manaton.†
Morston.†
Portlemouth.†
Romsey.†
Roxton.†
Ruston, East.†
Sall.†

AUGUSTINE, ST.—*cont.*
Suffield.†
Tunstead.†
Upton (Norfolk).†
Woolborough.†
Worstead.†
Wrotham, Great.†

BALDREDUS.
Chester Cath.‡

BAPTISTERY. *See* FONT COVER.

BARBARA, ST.
Ashton.†
Babingley.†
Barton Turf.†
Berry Pomeroy.†
Blyth.†
Cassington.*
Denton.†
Elmham, North.†
Eton.*
Eye.†
Filby.†
Holne.†
Jersey, St. Clement's.*
Kenton.†
Lanreath.†
Lustleigh.†
Manaton.†
Norwich, St. Gregory.†
Norwich, St. Peter, Man-croft.‡
Randworth.†
Teignton, King's.†
Thornham.†
Tor Bryan.†
Trimmingham.†
Walpole, St. Peter's.†
Walsham.*
Walsham, North†.
Warwick.‡
Wiggenhall, St. Mary the Virgin.†
Woolborough.†
Yaxley (Suffolk).†

BAPTISM OF CHRIST. *See* CHRIST (9).

BARNABAS, ST.
Woodbridge.†

BARTHOLOMEW, St. *See also*
  APOSTLES, THE.
    Attleborough.†
    Blythburgh.‡
    Brisley.*
    Chalgrove.*
    Clifton.†
    Edingthorpe.†
    Lostwithiel.‡
    Maresfield.*
    Repps.†
    Sall.†
    Wellow (Somerset).*
    Widecombe in the Moor.†

BARUCH.
  Bedfield.†
  Southwold Ch.†
  Stapleton.*

BAS-RELIEF AND ALTO-RELIEVO.
  Bolsover.
  Burnsall.
  Carlton in Lindrick.
  Durham, St. Giles.
  Freckenham.
  Lostwithiel.
  Mabe.
  Melford, Long.
  Nottingham, St. Mary's.
  Pool, South.
  Sandford.
  Stewkley.
  Stoke Charity.
  Thursby.
  Upton (Bucks).
  Wingfield.

BEAM OF ROOF. *See* ROOF.

BEAM, FONT COVER.
  Sall.
  Sheringham.
  Trunch.

BEAM, ROOD.
  Brabourne.
  Martham.
  Postling.
  Ufford.

BEDA (? BRIGIDA), St.
  Westhall.†

BELSHAZZAR'S FEAST.
  Sotby.* (?)

BENCH ENDS. *See* STALLS.

BENEDICT, St.
  Burlingham, St. Andrew.†
  Elmham, North.†
  Horsham, St. Faith's.†
  Milton Abbas.†
  Plumstead, Great.†
  Smallburgh.†

BENEFACTORS, &c., PORTRAITS
  OF. *See* PORTRAITS.

BENORA, REX.
  Chester Cath.‡

BERTWULPH, REX.
  Chester Cath.‡

BETRAYAL, THE. *See* CHRIST,
  (20).

BISHOPS, not specially identified. Does not include monumental effigies.
    Adderbury.*
    Alrewas.*
    Barfreston.*
    Bunbury.*
    Canterbury Cath.*
    Cassington.*
    Chichester Cath.†
    Clocaenog.*
    Colton.*
    Crostwight.*
    Denton.†
    Easton (Suffolk).*.
    Exeter Cath.*†
    Garboldisham.†
    Halifax.*
    Hedingham, Castle.*
    Hennock.†
    Hereford Cath.*
    Hornton.*
    Ipswich, St. Nicholas.‡
    Kelshall.†
    Kempley.*
    Latton.*
    Lichborough.*
    Lingfield.*
    Mabe.‡
    Manaton.†
    Marsham.†
    Merstham.*

BISHOPS, not specially identified —*cont.*

Norwich, St. Michael at Plea.†
Nottingham, St. Mary's.‡
Peterborough.†
Plymtree.†
Preston (Sussex).*
Rushall.*
Salisbury, St. Thomas.*
Smallburgh.†
Soham.*
Stanford Dingley.*
Sutton Bingham.*
Upchurch.*
Upwell.†
Whaddon.*
Whittlesford.‡
Widecombe in the Moor.†
Widford.*
Wilmington.‡
Winchester Cath.†
Winchester, St. Cross.*
Woolborough.†
York Minster.†

Figures of Bishops are generally introduced in representations of the Day of Judgment, *which see.*

BISHOP'S THRONE. *See* THRONE, BISHOP'S.

BLAISE, ST.
Ashton.†
Crawley, North.†
Eye.†
Hempstead.†
Kingston on Thames.*
Manaton.†
Norwich, St. James.†
Norwich, St. John de Sepulchre.†
Strensham.†
Wilburton.*
Woodbridge.†

BLIDA, ST.
Babingley.† (?)
Norwich, St. James.†

BRACKET.
Alkham.
Ashwell (Herts).
Cley.
Coventry, St. Michael's.
Gaddesden, Great.
Hayes.
Hillesdon.
Necton.
Tanworth.
Tidworth, North.

BRASS.
Aspenden.
Cambridge, King's College.
Cople.
Eastwick.
Ketteringham.
Knebworth.
Marholme.
Wing (Bucks).

BRIDGET or BRIGIDA, ST.
Babingley.† (?)
Bradninch.†
Cullompton.*
Horsham, St. Faith's.†
Plymtree.†
Portlemouth.† (?)
Ufford.†
Westhall.† (?)

BRITHNOTH, DUKE.
Ely Cath.*

BRUNO, ST.
Portlemouth.†

BURGHREDUS, REX.
Chester Cath.‡

CANDLESTICK.
Canterbury Cath.*
Exeter, All Hallows Ch.‡
Kempley.*

CANTELUPE, BISHOP.
Hereford Cath.*

CAPTIVITY OF THE JEWS, THE.
Westminster Hall.*

CASSANDRA.
Amberley Castle.†

CATHERINE OF ALEXANDRIA, ST.

Alfriston.*
Amport.‡
Ashby.*
Babingley.†
Bardwell.*
Barton Bendish, St. Mary's.* (?)
Bengeo.* (?)
Beverley, St. Mary's.*
Binham Abbey.†
Bunbury.†
Burlingham, St. Andrew.†
Burton Latimer.*
Castor.*
Catfield.*
Chalfont, St. Giles.*
Cirencester.*
Cleeve, Old.*
Cullompton.*
Eton.*
Eye.†
Filby.†
Gorleston Ch.* (?)
Heavitree.†
Holne.†
Kenn.†
Kenton.†
Kirdford.*
Lanreath.†
Lastingham.*
Latchingdon.†
Leicester, St. Martin's.*
Lessingham.†
Limpenhoe.*
Maidstone.*
Manaton.†
Marholme.*
Merstham.* (?)
Norwich Cath.*
Norwich Castle.‡
Norwich, St. Helen's.‡
Pickering.*
Plymtree.†
Preston (Sussex).*
Raunds.*
Sporle.*
Stonham, Earl.*
Teignton, King's.†
Tempsford.*
Tuddenham, North.†

CATHERINE OF ALEXANDRIA, ST.—cont.

Walpole, St. Peter.†
Walsham, North.†
Warwick.‡
Wellington (Somerset).*
Wenham, Little.*
Westhall.†
Widecombe in the Moor.†
Wiggenhall, St. Mary the Virgin.†
Winchester Cath.*
Winchester; St. Cross.*
Yaxley (Suffolk).†

CATHERINE OF SIENA, ST.

Horsham, St. Faith's.†
Portlemouth.† (?)

CEADDA, ST.

Hereford Cath.*

CEADWALLA.

Chichester Cath.†

CECILIA, ST.

Babingley.†
Burlingham, St. Andrew.†
Denton.†
Elmham, North.†
Filby.†
Holne.†
Kenton.†
Somerleyton.†
Tor Bryan.†
Trimmingham.†
Ufford.†
Yaxley (Suffolk).†

CEILING. See ROOF.

CEOLREDUS, REX.

Chester Cath.‡

CHAIR, BISHOP'S.

Hereford Cath.‡

CHANCEL SCREEN. See SCREEN.

CHERUBIM. See ANGELS, also HIERARCHY, HEAVENLY.

CHEST.

Burgate.
Cratfield.
Durham Cath.

CHEST—*cont.*
Empingham.
Fersfield.
Glastonbury, St. John the Baptist.
Newport (Essex).
Rainham (Kent).
Stonham Aspall.
Swaffham Bulbeck.
Wells (Bubwith Hospital).
Winchester Cath.
Yarmouth, Great.

CHIMNEY-PIECE.
Acre, Castle, Priory.
Bradenstoke.
Waltham Abbey.

CHRIST.
(1.) THE NATIVITY.
Canterbury Cath.*
Chalgrove.*
Chiltington, West.*
Coggeshall, Great.*
Easby Ch.*
Easton (Suffolk).*
Ely Cath.‡
Exeter Cath.†
Faversham.*
Friskney.*
Guernsey, St. Apolline.*
Hardham.*
Headington.*
Islip.*
Latton.*
Loddon.†
Newington.*
Norwich, St. Helen's.‡
Notgrove.*
Preston (Sussex).*
St. German's.†
Sarratt.*
Shulbrede.*§
Stonham, Earl.*
Wakering, Little.*
Winchester Cath.*
Winterbourne Dauntsey.*
Wiston (Suffolk).*

(2.) THE ADORATION OR OFFERINGS OF THE MAGI.
Barfreston.*
Brook.*

CHRIST—*cont.*
Buckland in the Moor.†
Burnsall.‡
Catfield.*
Chalgrove.*
Chiltington, West.*
Easby Ch.*
Faversham.*
Friskney.*
Gloucester, St. Mary de Crypt.*
Islip.*
Jersey, St. Brelade's.*
Kirdford.*
Lichfield.*
Loddon.†
Melford, Long.‡
Newnham Regis.*
Notgrove.* (?)
Pinvin.*
Plymtree.†
Podymore Milton.*
Portslade.*
Preston (Sussex).*
Preston in Holderness.‡
Ripon.*
Rowner.* (?)
St. Albans Cath.*
Salisbury, St. Thomas.*
Salisbury, House in New St.*
Stonham, Earl.*
Timworth.*
Upton (Bucks).*
Westmeston.*
Westminster Abbey.‡
Westminster, St. Stephen's.*
Wickham, East.*
Winchester Cath.*
Winterbourne Dauntsey.*
Wiston (Suffolk).*
Worcester, Guesten Hall.*

(3.) THE ANNUNCIATION TO THE SHEPHERDS.
Chester, St. Peter's.*
Chiltington, West.*
Combe Martin.†
Faversham.*
Orleton.* (?)
Sarratt.*
Stonham, Earl.*

CHRIST—*cont.*

(4.) THE ADORATION OF THE
    SHEPHERDS.
  Catfield.*
  Friskney.*
  Timworth.*
  Westminster,   St. Ste-
    phen's.*
  Wiston (Suffolk).*

(5.) THE PRESENTATION IN
    THE TEMPLE, or CIR-
    CUMCISION.
  Chalgrove.*
  Cowley (Oxon).*
  Faversham.*
  Gyffiliog.* (?)
  Loddon.†
  Westminster,   St. Ste-
    phen's.*

(6.) THE   FLIGHT   INTO
    EGYPT.
  Guernsey, St. Apolline.*
  Haddon Hall.*
  Hardham.*
  Headington.*
  Overton, Cold.*
  Plumpton.*
  St. Clement's.*
  Winterbourne Dauntsey.*

(7.) AMONGST THE DOCTORS.
  Ashridge.*
  Brook.*

(8.) ASSISTING JOSEPH AS A
    CARPENTER.
  London, Carpenters' Hall.*

(9.) THE BAPTISM.
  Ashridge.*
  Crostwight.*
  Exeter Cath.†
  Terrington,   St. Cle-
    ment's.† §

(10.) THE TEMPTATION IN
    THE WILDERNESS.
  Ashridge.*
  Pensax.*
  Terrington,   St. Cle-
    ment's.† §
  Winterbourne Earl's.*

CHRIST—*cont.*

(11.) WITH THE APOSTLES.
  Acre, Castle, Ch.†
  Brailes.†
  Carlisle Cath.†
  Hereford Cath.*
  Hexham.†
  Llanwyddyn.*
  Middleton Cheney.†
  Necton.‡
  Pluscardine.*
  Salisbury, St. Edmund's.*
  Strensham.†
  Tewkesbury.*
  Wellow (Hants).*
  Widecombe in the Moor.†

(12.) PREACHING.
  Catfield.*
  London, Carpenters' Hall.*
  Winchester, St. Cross.*

(13.) WITH THE WOMAN OF
    SAMARIA.
  Broadclist.†
  Catfield.*
  Talland.*

(14.) PERFORMING MIRACLES.
  Ashridge.*
  Brook.*
  Eriswell.*
  Hornchurch.*
  Sherborne Almshouses.†
  Talland.*
  Tew, Great.*
  Warblington.*
  Westminster Abbey.‡
  Winchester Cath.*
  Winchfield.*

(15.) THE TRANSFIGURATION.
  Ashton.†
  Chester Cath.*
  Puckington.*
  Reading, St Lawrence.*
  Westhall.†

(16.) DINING AT THE HOUSE
    OF SIMON THE LEPER.
  Guernsey, Ste. Marie du
    Chastel.*
  Notgrove.*
  Winterbourne Dauntsey.*

CHRIST—*cont.*

(17.) THE TRIUMPHAL EN-
TRY INTO JERUSALEM.
Ashridge.*
Brook.*
Chiltington, West.*
Headington.*
Jersey, St. Helier's.*
St. Clement's.* (?)
Somerton, West.*
Winchester Cath.*

(18.) THE LAST SUPPER.
Ashridge.*
Barton Segrave.*
Brook.*
Canterbury, Eastbridge
Hosp.*
Chiltington, West.*
Cury.‡
Dover, St. Martin's.*
Friskney.*
Hampton Court.†
Horsham.*
Llanwyddyn.*
Moreton, Maids.*
Preston (Sussex).*
Slaugham.*
Stanton Harcourt.*
Winterbourne Dauntsey.*

(19.) WASHING THE DISCI-
PLES' FEET.
Llanwyddyn.*
Stanton Harcourt.*

(20.) THE BETRAYAL, AND
SCENES FROM THE PAS-
SION.
Ashridge.*
Bacton.*
Bampton (Devon).†
Battle Ch.*
Baunton.*
Beddington.*
Bloxham.*
Blunham.‡
Bristol, St. John's.*
Brook.*
Chalgrove.*
Chiltington, West.*
Cove, North.*
Crostwight.*

CHRIST—*cont.*

(20.) THE BETRAYAL AND
SCENES FROM THE PAS-
SION—*cont.*
Dickleburgh.*
Durham Cath.*
Easton, Little.*
Hampton Court.†
Jersey, St. Brelade's.*
Llanwyddyn.*
London, The Savoy
Chapel.†
Madley.*
Mitcheldean.†
Norwich Cath.‡
Norwich, St. Michael at
Plea.†
Norwich, SS. Simon and
Jude.†
Podymore Milton.*
St. Michael's Mount.†
Somerton, West.*
Stanton Harcourt.*
Thetford, St. Cuthbert's.*
Thursby.‡
Upwell.†
Warblington.*
Westmeston.*
Winterbourne Dauntsey.*
Worstead.†
Wrexham.*
York Minster.*

(21.) THE CRUCIFIXION.
Alfold Ch.*
Ashridge.*
Ashton, Long.*
Attleborough.*
Bedfont.*
Bedwin, Great.*
Bere Regis.* (?)
Bradninch.†
Breamore.*
Brinsop.*
Buckland (Gloucestersh.)*
Chaddesden.*
Chalfont, St. Giles.*
Chester, St. Mary on the
Hill.*
Chesterfield.*
Chiltington, West.*
Cleeve, Old.*

347

CHRIST—*cont.*

(21.) THE CRUCIFIXION — *cont.*

Coggeshall, Great.*
Copford.*
Cranborne.*
Crostwight.*
Dereham, East.‡
Doddington (Northants).*
Dorchester.*
Durham Cath.*
Duston.*
Ely Cath.‡
Ely, Prior Crauden's Chapel.*
Faversham.*
Flaunden.*
Fowlis Easter.†
Godshill.*
Goosey.*
Halesowen.*
Hampton Court.†
Hereford, Little.*
Hexham.†
Hoxne.*
Ilketshall, St. Margaret's.*
Kenn.†
Kimble Parva.* (?)
Kirdford.*
Kirton in Lindsey.*
Knockmoy.*
Landkey.*
Lichfield.*
Llanwyddyn.*
Ludham.†
Meon, East.*
Moreton, Maid's.*
Newport (Essex).†
Newton Bromswold.*
Norwich Cath.‡
Norwich, St. John's, Timberhill.*
Norwich, St. Michael at Plea.†
Norwich, Huby's Yard.†
Notgrove.*
Paignton.‡
Pinvin.*
Ringmore.*
Rising, Castle.*
Rushton.‡

CHRIST—*cont.*

(21.) THE CRUCIFIXION — *cont.*

St. Albans Cath.*
St. Clement's.*
St. David's.*
St. German's.†
Sandwich, St. Peter's.*
Starston.*
Talland.*
Tamworth.*
Tong.* (?)
Turvey.*
Ulcomb.*
Walsingham, New.‡
Wellington (Somerset).*
Westmeston.*
Westminster Abbey.*
Whissendine.*
Whittlesford.‡
Winchester Cath.*
Winchester, St. John's.*
Winchester, St. Cross.*
Winsham.†
Winterbourne Dauntsey.*
Wisborough Green.*
Woodbridge.‡
Worthy, Headbourn.‡
See also TRINITY, THE.

(22.) THE DESCENT FROM THE CROSS.

Ashridge.*
Beachamwell.‡
Blunham.‡
Bury St. Edmunds, St. Mary's.*
Castor.*
Chalgrove.*
Cowley (Oxon).*
Crostwight.*
Easby Ch.*
Exeter Cath.†
Ilketshall, St. Margaret's.*
Mitcheldean.†
Newnham Regis.*
Pinvin.*
Smarden.*
Stanton Harcourt.*
Westmeston.*
Winchester Cath.*
Worcester Cath.‡

348

CHRIST—*cont.*
  (23.) "PIETA."
    Ashton.†
    Breadsall.‡
    Brook.* (?)
    Broughton (Bucks).*
    Cherry Hinton.†
    Norwich, St. Michael at Plea.†
    Slapton.*
    Smarden.*
    Winchester, St. Cross.*

  (24.) THE ENTOMBMENT, AND CHRIST IN THE SEPULCHRE.
    Ashridge.*
    Binstead.* (?)
    Brook.*
    Castor.*
    Chalgrove.*
    Easby Ch.*
    Huntingfield.*
    Melford, Long.*
    Mitcheldean.†
    Pinvin.*
    Southwold.†
    Stanton Harcourt.*
    Winchester Cath.*

  (25.) THE DESCENT INTO LIMBUS, OR HELL.
    Ashridge.*
    Chaldon.*
    Chalgrove.*
    Hawkedon.*
    Lanivet.*
    Leigh, South.* (?)
    Mitcheldean.†
    Pinvin.*
    Stanton Harcourt.*
    Winchester Cath.*
    Winterbourne Dauntsey.*

  (26.) THE RESURRECTION.
    Abbotsbury.*
    Amport.‡
    Ashton.†
    Bunbury.*
    Catfield.*
    Chester, St. Mary on the Hill.*
    Chiltington, West.*

CHRIST—*cont.*
  (26.) THE RESURRECTION—*cont.*
    Colton.*
    Dickleburgh.*
    Easby Ch.*
    Exeter Cath.* †
    Friskney.*
    Gloucester, St. Mary de Crypt.*
    Gorleston Ch.‡
    Halesowen.*
    Hampton Court.†
    Hardham.*
    Horbling.‡
    Hoxne.*
    Islip.*
    Kelham.*
    Melford, Long.*
    Milton Abbas.*
    Norwich Cath.‡
    Norwich, St. Helen's.‡
    Norwich, St. Michael at Plea.†
    Pinvin.*
    Pool, South.‡
    Preston in Holderness.‡
    Quat.†
    Romsey.†
    Rothwell.* (?)
    Sarratt.*
    Somerton, West.*
    Staveley.* (?)
    Upwell.†
    Wickhampton.*
    Winterbourne Dauntsey.*

  (27.) WITH ST. MARY MAGDALENE, "NOLI ME TANGERE."
    Bray.*
    Drayton (Norfolk).*
    Exeter Cath.*
    Preston (Sussex).*
    Sotby.*
    Winchester Cath.*
    Yaxley (Hunts).*

  (28.) THE INCREDULITY OF ST. THOMAS.
    Preston (Sussex).*
    St. Albans Cath.*
    Wighton.*

CHRIST—*cont.*

(29.) THE ASCENSION.
Ashridge.*
Berwick, St. James.*
Bowden, Little.*
Brisley.*
Chalgrove.*
Colchester.*
Cove, North.*
Exeter Cath.*
Loddon.†
Milton Abbas.*
Mitcheldean.†
Norwich Cath.‡
Norwich, St. Helen's.‡
Pinvin.*
Preston in Holderness.‡
Rowner.* (?)
Sarratt.*

(30.) CHRIST IN GLORY OR
MAJESTY.
Binstead.*
Bloxham.*
Bolton Abbey.*
Brinsop.* (?)
Brixworth.*
Brook.*
Canterbury Cath.*
Canterbury, Eastbridge
Hosp.*
Chaldon.*
Checkendon.*
Chiltington, West.*
Copford.*
Cowley (Oxon).*
Dormington.*
Drayton (Norfolk).*
Durham, St. Giles.‡
Eggington.*
Guildford, St. Mary's.*
Hardham.*
Hereford Cath.* (?)
Houghton Conquest.*
Kempley.*
Llangwm Ucha.*
Madley.*
Malmesbury.‡
Romsey.†
Rotherham.*
St. Albans Cath.*
Salisbury Cath.*

CHRIST—*cont.*

(30.) CHRIST IN GLORY OR
MAJESTY—*cont.*
Swincombe.*
Waltham, Great.*
Wellow (Somerset).*
Wells, St. Cuthbert's.*
Westminster Abbey.*
Winchester Cath.*†
Winchester, St. John's.*
Winterbourne Dauntsey.*
Wisborough Green.*
Withyam.*

(31.) CHRIST IN JUDGMENT.
Birmingham.†
Huntingfield.*
Kelston.*
Oakley.†
Ripon.*
Westminster Abbey.*
Widford.*
See also DOOM, THE.

(32.) AS THE " AGNUS DEI."
Bovey Tracey.*
Cassington.*
Dereham, East.†
Peterborough Cath.†
Plumpton.*
St. Albans Cath.†
Swainsthorpe.*
Westmeston.*
Also generally intro-
duced as the emblem of
St. John the Baptist.

(33.) SURROUNDED BY IM-
PLEMENTS OF THE PAS-
SION.
Chiltington, West.* (?)
Michaelchurch Eskley.*
Stedham.*

(34.) THE INFANT SAVIOUR
IN THE ARMS OF THE
VIRGIN. *See* ST. MARY
THE VIRGIN (5).

(35.) ON THE SHOULDER OF
ST. CHRISTOPHER. *See*
CHRISTOPHER, ST.

(36.) IN REPRESENTATIONS
OF THE TRINITY. *See*
TRINITY, THE.

CHRIST—*cont.*

(37.) OTHER EXAMPLES;
DETAILS NOT SPECIFIED.
Alton.*
Axbridge.†
Bozeat.†
Bridgham.*
Brook.*
Brooke (Rutland).*
Cartmel Fell.‡
Coggeshall, Little.*
Donington.‡
Fulbourne, All Saints.†
Harnham, West.*
London, St. Andrew Un-
dershaft.* §
Meavy.‡
Swaton.*
Warmington.†

CHRISTIAN, REPRESENTATIVE.
Chiltington, West.* (?)
Hessett.*
Lanivet.*

CHRISTINA, ST.
Elmham, North.†
Eye.†
Portlemouth.† (?)

CHRISTOPHER, ST.
He is always represented
as a man of gigantic sta-
ture, fording a stream, with
the infant Saviour seated
on his shoulder, and with
a hermit standing on the
bank and holding a lan-
tern.
Alburgh.*
Aldburgh.*
Ampney Crucis.*
Ardeley.*
Arminghall.*
Aston-le-Walls.*
Babingley.*
Bardwell.*
Barkston.*
Bartlow.*
Baunton.*
Belton.*
Bersted, South.*

CHRISTOPHER, ST.—*cont.*

Bibury.*
Billingford (Norfolk).*
Binham Abbey.†
Bloxham.*
Blundeston.*
Bolton-on-Swale.*
Bradfield Combust.*
Bradninch.†
Bramley.*
Brisley.*
Brooke (Norfolk).*
Bunbury.*
Burford (Oxon).*
Burgh Castle.*
Burgh, St. Peter.*
Burnham Overy.*
Cambridge, St. John's
Coll.*
Canewdon.*
Canterbury Cath.*
Castor.*
Chellesworth.*
Cherry Hinton.*
Chesham.*
Chesham Bois.*
Chickerell, West.*
Chiltington, West.*
Cirencester.*
Colton.* (?)
Conisborough.*
Crostwick.*
Crostwight.*
Croydon.*
Cullompton.*
Devizes, St. Mary's.*
Ditteridge.*
Drayton (Norfolk).*
Durrington.*
Elmham, South.*
Enford.*
Eversden.*
Exeter, St. Mary Major.*
Fairford.*
Fakenham.*
Feering.*
Freethorpe.*
Fring.*
Fritton (Norfolk).*
Fritton (Suffolk).*
Gawsworth.*

CHRISTOPHER, ST.—*cont.*

Gorleston Ch.*
Grantchester.*
Gravenhurst, Lower.*
Haddiscoe.*
Hardwick (Cambs).*
Hardwick (Norfolk).*
Hargrave.*
Hawkedon.*
Hayes.*
Headington.*
Heigham, Potter.*
Hengrave.*
Henstridge.*
Herringfleet.*
Hessett.*
Hockering.*
Homington.*
Horley (Oxon).*
Horsham, St. Faith's.†
Houghton Conquest.*
Idmiston.*
Ilketshall, St. Margaret.*
Impington.*
Ingatestone.*
Ipswich, St. Margaret's.*
Irthlingborough.* (?)
Ketton.*
Kimpton.* (?)
Knockmoy.* (?)
Latton.*
Layer Marney.*
Limpenhoe.*
Loughborough.*
Loxton.*
Ludgvan.*
Lympstone.*
Margaret Marsh.*
Marston, Long.*
Melcombe Horsey.*
Mells.*
Meon, East.*
Milton.*
Morborne.*
Mylor.*
Newdigate.*
Northolt.*
Norwich, St. Etheldred's.*
Norwich, St. Giles.*
Norwich Castle.‡
Nottingham, St. Mary's.*

CHRISTOPHER, ST.—*cont.*

Ongar, Chipping.*
Overton Longueville.*
Pickering.*
Portisham.*
Poyntington.*
Preston (Suffolk).*
Randworth.*
Raunds.*
Ravenston.*
Ridge.*
Ridlington.*
Ringmore*
Rogate.* (?)
Roxton.†
Rushmere.*
St. Albans Cath.*
St. Clement's.*
Salisbury Cath.*
Sedgford.*
Seething.*
Shorwell.*
Shotteswell.*
Slapton.*
Somerford Keynes.*
Spalding.*
Sproughton.*
Stanton, St. Quintin.*
Stedham.*
Stoke Dry.*
Stokesby.*
Stoneleigh.*
Stow Bardolph.*
Stowlangtoft.*
Talaton.*
Tawton, Bishop's.*
Tewkesbury.*
Tichborne.*
Tidworth, North.*
Toddington.*
Troston.*
Ufford.*
Upavon.* (?)
Wacton Magna.*
Walpole, St. Peter.*
Wangford.*
Warlingham.*
Watford.*
Wedmore.*
Wellington (Somerset).*
Wells (Norfolk).*

CHRISTOPHER, ST—cont.
Westfield (Norfolk).*
Weston, Edith.*
Westwood.*
Whimple.*
Wickham, Child's.*
Wickhampton.*
Wilburton.*
Wilsford and Lake.*
Wimbotsham.*
Winchester Cath.*
Winchester, St. John's.*
Winchester, St. Lawrence.*
Winfrith Newburgh.*
Winterbourne Dauntsey.*
Winterbourne Earls.*
Witton.*
Woodford Halse.*
Woodleigh.*

CITHA, ST. *See* SITHA, ST.

CLARA OR CLARE, ST.
Babingley.†
Cullompton.*
Plymtree.†
Trimmingham.†

CLEMENT, ST.
Beeston, St. Mary's.†
Denton.†
Elmham, North.†
Houghton-le-Dale.†
Leigh, South.*
Lingfield.*
Trimmingham.†
Westhall.†

CLOCK AND CLOCKFACE.
Raunds.
Wells Cath.

COLWULPHUS, REX.
Chester Cath.‡

CONSECRATION CROSSES. *See*
CROSSES, CONSECRATION.
CONSTANTINE.
Kempley.* (?)

CORBEL.
Barnack.
Ely Cath.
Exeter Cath.

CORBEL—cont.
Knapton.
London, Temple Ch.
Navenby.
Stifford.
Westhall.
Yarmouth, Great.

CORNELIUS, ST.
Portlemouth.†

CORNICE AND STRINGCOURSE.
Bristol Cath.
Cambridge, Gt. St. Mary's.
Pershore.
Potterne.
Winchester Cath.

CORONATION OF THE VIRGIN,
THE. *See* MARY THE VIR-
GIN, ST. (11).

COSMO AND DAMIAN, SS.
Manaton.† (St. Cosmo
only.)
Pickering.* (?)
Woolborough.† (St. Da-
mian only.)

CREATION, THE.
Easby Ch.*
Exeter Cath.†

CRIEDA, REX.
Chester Cath.‡

CROSS, ADORATION OF THE.
Attleborough.*
Bramfield.*
Bramford.*
Tewkesbury.*

CROSS, LEGEND OF THE FIND-
ING OF THE.
Stratford on Avon, Chapel
of the Guild of the Holy
Cross.*

CROSSES, CONSECRATION OR
DEDICATION.
Aldwincle, St. Peter's.*
Amberley.*
Arminghall.*
Arundel.*
Barfreston.*

CROSSES, CONSECRATION OR DEDICATION—*cont.*

Barningham Winter.*
Bircham.*
Blofield.*
Blythburgh.‡
Bramley.*
Braxted, Little.*
Brisley.*
Brook.*
Bures.*
Bury St. Edmunds, St. Mary's.*
Byfleet.*
Caerleon.*
Cambridge, Pembroke Coll.*
Canfield, Great.*
Capel.*
Chaldon.*
Cheltenham.*
Chesham.*
Chichester, St. Olave's.*
Chichester, Bishop's Palace.*
Clapton in Gordano.*
Climping.*
Cockerington, South.*
Coggeshall, Great.*
Crostwight.*
Ditteridge.*
Downham Market.*
Drayton (Norfolk).*
Duntisbourne Rous.*
Eaton.*
Exton (Hants).*
Farnborough.*
Flaunden.*
Heckfield.*
Kempley.*
Maidstone.*
Malvern, Great.*
Manningford Bruce.*
Norwich, St. John de Sepulchre.*
Norwich, St. Peter per Mountergate.*
Norwich, St. Saviour's.*
Pevensey.*
Pirton.*
Poling.*

Q 3254.

CROSSES, CONSECRATION OR DEDICATION—*cont.*

Potterne.*
Randworth.*
Repps, North.*
St. Bartholomew's.*
Salisbury Cath.‡
Sherborne, Monk's.*
Shurdington.‡
Sleaford.*
Slindon.*
Slingsby.*
Southfleet.*
Stifford.*
Stone.*‡
Stow Bardolph.*
Sudbury, St. Gregory.*
Swincombe.*
Taverham.*
Thrigby.*
Treyford.*
Uggeshall.*
Upton (Bucks).* ¶
Westminster Abbey.*
Wickhampton.*
Winchester, St. John's.*
Winchester, Magdalene Hosp.*
Winchester, St. Cross.*
Wiston (Suffolk).*
Wolston (Gloucester).*
Worlingworth.*

CRUCIFIXION, THE. *See* CHRIST (21).

CUTHBERT, ST.
Carlisle Cath.*†.
Hexham.†
Pittington.*
Woodbridge.†

CYRIAC, ST.
Hardwick (Cambs).*

DAMIAN, ST. *See* COSMO AND DAMIAN, SS.

DANCE OF DEATH.
Hexham.†
Newark.†
Salisbury Cath.*
Sparham.†
Yoxford.† (?)

DANIEL. *See also* PROPHETS, THE.
    Crawley, North.†
    Poringland.†

DAVID, KING.
    Abbey Dore.*
    Catfield.* (?)
    Chalgrove.*
    Crawley, North.†
    Dereham, West, Abbey.*
    Hoxne.*
    Marston Mortaine.†
    Newport (Isle of Wight).*
    Poringland.†
    Salisbury Cath.*
    Southwold.†
    Stapleton.*
    Thornham.†
    Yarmouth, Great.*
      See also JESSE, STEM OF.
      In series of the Prophets, David is generally included.

DAVID, ST.
    Hereford Cath.*

DAY OF JUDGMENT. *See* DOOM, THE.

DEATH. *See* TIME AND DEATH.

DEATH, DANCE OF. *See* DANCE OF DEATH.

DEDICATION CROSSES. *See* CROSSES, CONSECRATION.

DELUGE, THE.
    Exeter Cath.†
    Shenley Mansell.*

DENIS, or DIONYSIUS, ST.
    Dersingham.†
    Grafton Regis.†
    Hempstead.†
    Teignton, King's.†
    Warminster.* (?)

DESCENT FROM THE CROSS. *See* CHRIST (22).

DIANA.
    Cowdray.*

DIONYSIUS, ST. *See* DENIS, ST.

DOCTORS OF THE CHURCH. *See* AMBROSE, AUGUSTINE, GREGORY, and JEROME, SS.

DOMINATIONES. *See* HIERARCHY, HEAVENLY.

DOMINIC, ST.
    Barling.‡

DOOM, THE. *See also* CHRIST IN JUDGMENT.
    Alfriston.*
    Ampney Crucis.*
    Ardeley.* (?)
    Ashby.*
    Ashby, Mears.*
    Axbridge.*
    Bacton.*
    Bardwell.*
    Barton Segrave.*
    Barton Turf.*
    Beaminster.*
    Beckley.*
    Bedfont.*
    Berkeley Ch.*
    Bloxham.*
    Bonchurch.* (?)
    Bottesford.*
    Bromsgrove.*
    Broughton (Bucks).*
    Cassington.*
    Caythorpe.*
    Chaddesley Corbet.*
    Chalgrove.*
    Chellesworth.*
    Chesterton.*
    Chishill, Great.*
    Cliffe-at-Hoo.*
    Clifton Reynes.*
    Combe.*
    Cove, North.*
    Coventry, Trinity Ch.*
    Cropredy.*
    Dalham.*
    Denham.*
    Devizes, St. Mary's.* (?)
    Ditchingham.*
    Enfield.†
    Eversden.*
    Exeter, St. Mary Major.* (?)
    Eye.*

DOOM, THE—*cont.*
   Fairford.*
   Garboldisham.*
   Gawsworth.*
   Gloucester Cath.†
   Ham, West.*
   Hardham.* (?)
   Harling, East.*
   Hastings.*
   Headington.*
   Hereford, St. Peter's.*
   Heytesbury.* (?)
   Huntingdon.*
   Ibsley.* (?)
   Irthlingborough.*
   Jersey, St. Brelades.*
   Kempley.*
   Kimbolton.* (?)
   Lathbury.*
   Lavendon.*
   Leigh, North.*
   Leigh, South.*
   Llandanwg.*
   Lutterworth.*
   Manningford Bruce.*
   Marston Mortaine.*
   Martham.* (?)
   Meon, East.*
   Mitcheldean.†
   Newington.*
   Newport (Essex).*
   Northwood.*
   Norwich Cath.‡
   Patcham.*
   Pickering.*
   Pickhill.*
   Pinvin.*
   Pirton.*
   Plumpton.*
   Portslade.*
   Quat.*
   Rougham.*
   St. Albans, St. Michael's.*†
   Salisbury, St. Thomas.*
   Shorwell.*
   Sloley.*
   Slymbridge.*
   Snetterton.†
   Somerton, West.*
   Stanford Dingley.*

DOOM, THE—*cont.*
   Stanningfield.*
   Stedham.*
   Stoke by Nayland.*
   Stoke sub Hamdon.*
   Stonham, Earl's.*
   Stow Bardolph.*
   Stratford on Avon, Chapel of the Guild of the Holy Cross.*
   Tew, Great.*
   Toddington.* (?)
   Totham, Great.*
   Westmeston.* (?)
   Winchester, St. John's.*
   Winchfield.*
   Winwick.*
   Wiston (Suffolk).*
   Withyam.*
   Wrexham.*
   Wymondham.*
   Yaxley (Hunts).*
   Yaxley (Suffolk).*

DOOR.
   Cotton.
   Worlingworth.

DOROTHY, ST.
   Ashton.†
   Babingley.†
   Blofield.†
   Chesterton.*
   Denton.†
   Elmham, North.†
   Eton.*
   Eye.†
   Kenton.†
   Manaton.†
   Plymtree.†
   Roxton.†
   Tor Bryan.†
   Tuddenham, North.†
   Walpole, St. Peter's.†
   Westhall.†
   Wiggenhall, St. Mary the Virgin.†
   Woolborough.†
   Yaxley (Suffolk).†

DUNSTAN, ST.
   Broughton (Bucks).*
   Heavitree.†

DUNSTAN, ST.—*cont.*
  Highworth.*
  Holne.†
  Ilsington.‡
  Latton.*
  Plumstead, Great.†
  Stifford.*
  Watford.*

EASTER SEPULCHRE.
  Glastonbury Abbey.
  Gloucester, St. Mary de Crypt.
  Huntingfield.
  Pool, South.
  Preston in Holderness.
  Smarden.
  Stanton Harcourt.
  Withybrook.

EATA, ST.
  Hexham.†

EDBURGA, ST.
  Pinvin.*

EDITH, ST.
  Tamworth.* (?)

EDMUND, ST.
  Adisham.*
  Bardwell.*
  Barton Turf.†
  Blyth.†
  Brinsop.* (?)
  Burlingham, St. Andrew.†
  Catfield.†
  Charlwood.* (?)
  Cliffe at Hoo.*
  Crawley, North.†
  Denton.†
  Easton (Suffolk).* (?)
  Ely Cath.*
  Guilden Morden.†
  Hempstead.†
  Kelshall.†
  Kenton.†
  Kersey.†
  Knapton.‡
  Litcham.†
  Ludham.†
  Norwich, St. Helen's.‡
  Pickering.* (?)
  Preston (Suffolk).*

EDMUND, ST.—*cont.*
  Rackheath.†
  Slapton.*
  Somerleyton.†
  Stalham.† (?)
  Stanford Dingley.*
  Stoke Dry.*
  Stow Bardolph.*
  Strensham.†
  Trimmingham.†
  Troston.*
  Tuddenham, North.† (?)
  Whaddon.*
  Widecombe-in-the-Moor.†
  Wimborne.* (?).

EDNOD, BISHOP.
  Ely Cath. *

EDWARD, ST., KING AND MARTYR.
  Burlingham, St. Andrew.†
  Crostwight.* (?)
  Denton.†
  Litcham.†
  Peterborough.†
  Stokesby.* (?)
  Strensham.†
  Trimmingham.†
  Wimborne.*

EDWARD, ST., KING AND CONFESSOR.
  Attleborough.†
  Barton Turf.†
  Boxford.*
  Burlingham, St. Andrew.†
  Crawley, North.†
  Denton.†
  Exeter Cath.*
  Eye.†
  Faversham.*
  Hempstead.†
  Hereford Cath.*
  Kelshall.†
  Ludham.†
  Norwich Cath.*
  Norwich, St. Helen's.‡
  Norwich, St. Swithin's.†
  Peterborough.†
  Plymtree.†
  Repps.†

EDWARD, ST., KING AND CON-
FESSOR—*cont.*
Romford.*
St. Albans Cath.*
Smallburgh.†
Somerleyton.†
Stalham.†
Westminster Abbey.*
Westminster Hall.*
Widecombe-in-the-Moor.†
Woodbridge.†
Woolborough.†

EDWARD I., KING.
Yarmouth, Great.‡

EDWARD II., KING.
Byfleet.* (?)

EDWARD III., KING, AND
FAMILY.
Westminster, St. Ste-
phen's.*

EDWARD, PRINCE, SON OF
HENRY VI.
Windsor.†

EDWARD IV., KING.
Windsor.†

EDWARD V., KING.
Windsor.†

EDYVE, QUEEN.
Canterbury Cath.†

EFFIGIES, MONUMENTAL. *See*
MONUMENTS.

EGFERTUS, REX.
Chester Cath.‡

EGIDIUS, ST. *See* GILES, ST.

EILFRID, ST.
Hexham.†

ELFGAR, BISHOP.
Ely Cath.*

ELIAS or ELIJAH.
Ashton.†
Chester Cath.*
Olney.†
Puckington.*
Reading, St. Lawrence.*
Southwold.†
Westhall.†
Westminster Hall.*

ELIGIUS, or LOYE, ST.
Freckenham.‡
Heigham, Potter.†
Hempstead.†
Ipswich, St. Matthew.† (?)
Woolborough.†

ELISHA.
Westminster Hall.*

ELIZABETH, ST.
Aconbury.*
Amberley Ch.*
Bradninch.†
Bures, Mount.* (?)
Canterbury Cath.*
Chiltington, West.*
Colton.*
Ely Cath.‡
Faversham.*
Gately.†
Hexham.†
Houghton le Dale.†
Norwich, St. Michael at
Plea.†
Outwell.*
Pinvin.*
Plymtree.†
Salisbury Cath.*
Salisbury, St. Thomas.*
Sparham.†
Timworth.*
Wickham, East.*
Winchester Cath.‡
N.B.—Chiefly portrayed
in representations of the
Salutation or Visitation.

ELIZABETH OF HUNGARY, ST.,
QUEEN.
Fulbourn, All Saints.†
Gately.†
Lanreath.†

ELIZABETH, QUEEN.
Gaddesden, Little.†
Llanaber.* (?)

EMBLEMS OF TRADES, &c.
Broughton (Bucks).*
Chiltington, West.*
Gumfreston.*
Hessett.*

EMBLEMS OF TRADES, &c.—
cont.
Lanivet.*
St. Just in Penwith.*
Stedham.*

EMBLEMS OF THE EVANGE-
LISTS. *See* EVANGELISTIC
EMBLEMS.

ENGLAND, SERIES OF KINGS
OF.
Baston.†
Beverley, St. Mary's.†
Chichester Cath.†
Naworth.†

ENTOMBMENT, THE. *See*
CHRIST (24).

ERASMUS, ST.
Ampney Crucis.*
Buckenham Ferry.‡
Cambridge, Trinity Ch.‡
Cirencester.*
Hempstead.†
Norwich, St. Michael at
Plea.†
Roxton.† (?)
St. Albans Cath.‡
Tawstock.* (?)
Whitwell.*

ERKENWOLD, ST.
Guilden Morden.†

ERMINILDA, ST.
Chester Cath.‡

ETHELBERT, ST.
Burnham Norton.†
Chester Cath.‡
Hereford Cath.*‡

ETHELDREDA, or AUDRIE, ST.
Amport.‡ (?)
Babingley.† (?)
Burlingham, St. Andrew.†
Chester Cath.‡
Eton.*
Gately.†
Gorleston Ch.* (?)
Ham, East.*
Hessett.*
Horsham, St. Faith's.†

ETHELDREDA, or AUDRIE, ST.
—*cont.*
Lanivet.* (?)
Norwich, St. John de Se-
pulchre.†
Norwich, St. Peter Man-
croft.‡
Oxburgh.†
Plymtree.† (?)
Randworth.† (?)
Sudbury.†
Tuddenham, North.†
Upton (Norfolk).†
Westhall.†

ETHELREDUS, REX.
Chester Cath.‡

EUGENIA, ST.
Farnborough.*

EULALIA, ST.
Charlwood.* (?)

EUPHEMIA, ST.
Blyth.†

EUSTACE, ST.
Canterbury Cath.*

EVANGELISTIC EMBLEMS.
Bloxham.†
Canterbury Cath.†
Canterbury, Eastbridge
Hosp.*
Cartmel.†
Durham, St. Giles.‡
Edinburgh.‡
Gloucester, St. Mary de
Crypt.* or ‡.
Gyffin.†
Ludham.‡
Randworth.†
St. Albans Cath.†
St. David's.*
Sherborne Almshouses.†
Terrington, St. Cle-
ment's.†§
Wellingborough.†
Whaddon.*
Whissendine.*
Wiggenhall, St. Mary Mag-
dalene.†

EVANGELISTS, THE. *See* MAT-
. THEW, MARK, LUKE, JOHN,
SS.

EVE. *See* ADAM AND EVE.

EZEKIEL. *See also* PROPHETS,
THE.
    Crawley, North.†
    Southwold.†

FAITH, or FIDES, ST.
    Fring.*
    Horsham, St. Faith's.†
    Marsham.†
    Ufford.†
    Westminster Abbey.*

FATHERS OF THE CHURCH.
  See AMBROSE, AUGUSTINE,
  GREGORY, and JEROME, SS.

FELIX, ST.
    Randworth.† (?)

FIDES, ST. *See* FAITH, ST.

FLORENCE, ST.
    Ufford.†

FONT.
    Acle.
    Acre, Castle, Ch.
    Aslacton.
    Blythburgh.
    Bovey Tracey.
    Bridgham.
    Brooke (Norfolk).
    Broome.
    Bury St. Edmund's, St.
      Mary's.
    Chevening.
    Cockington.
    Cothelstone.
    Cove, North.
    Covehithe.
    Coventry, Trinity Ch.
    Cringleford.
    Dereham, East.
    Dunster.
    Gorleston Ch.
    Gresham.
    Hagbourne.
    Hornton.

FONT—*cont.*
    Kimble, Great.
    Leasingham.
    Lenton.
    Loddon.
    Ludham.
    Martham.
    Merton (Norfolk).
    Northolt.
    Sheringham.
    Sproxton.
    Stalham.
    Sudbury, All Saints' Ch.
    Swanton Morley.
    Tey, Marks.
    Waddington.
    Walsingham, New.
    Wells Cath.
    Westhall.
    Wickham Market.
    Witchingham, Great.
    Wolston.
    Woodbridge.

FONT COVER.
    Acre, Castle, Ch.
    Acre, South.
    Burton Latimer.
    Elsing Ch.
    Ely Cath.
    Foulsham.
    Frieston.
    Horham.
    London, St. Bartholo-
      mew's.
    Merton (Norfolk).
    Norwich, St. Peter Man-
      croft.
    Plymstock.
    Randworth.
    Sall.
    Shaugh Prior.
    Sporle.
    Sudbury, St. Gregory's.
    Terrington, St. Clement's.§
    Trunch.
    Ufford.
    Worlingworth.

FONT COVER BEAM. *See* BEAM,
  FONT COVER.

FORTITUDO.   *See* VIRTUES,
    THE.

FORTUNE, WHEEL OF.
    Catfield.*
    Kempley.*
    Leominster.*
    Padbury.*
    Rochester Cath.*

FOX, BISHOP.
    Plymtree.†

FRANCIS OF ASSISIUM, ST.
    Bradninch.†
    Hempstead.†
    Repps.†
    Romsey.†
    Slapton.*
    Stalham.†
    Stratford-on-Avon, Chapel
        of the Guild of the Holy
        Cross.* (?)
    Winchester, St. John's.*

FRIDBERT, ST.
    Hexham.†

GABRIEL, ST.   *See* MARY THE
    VIRGIN, ST. (2.)

GALLERY, MINSTRELS'.
    Exeter Cath.
    Keevil.

GALLERY, RINGERS'.
    Aylsham.
    Sall.

GENEVIEVE, ST.
    Babingley.†
    Horsham, St. Faith's.†
    Teignton, King's.†

GEORGE, ST.
    Ashton.†
    Astbury.*
    Bedwin, Great.*
    Beeston, St. Mary's.‡
    Berkhampstead, Great.*
    Bovey Tracey.‡
    Bradfield Combust.*
    Bradninch.†
    Bramfield.*
    Braughing.*

GEORGE, ST.—*cont.*
    Broughton (Bucks).*
    Cheddar.* (?)
    Chellesworth.*
    Croydon.*
    Darent.*
    Dartford.*
    Devizes, St. Mary's.*
    Drayton (Norfolk).*
    Evenley.*
    Eversden.*
    Farleigh Hungerford.*§
    Filby.†
    Finchley.*
    Fordington.‡
    Fritton (Norfolk).*
    Gawsworth.*
    Gidleigh.†
    Hadleigh (Essex).*
    Hardham.*
    Hargrave.*
    Hempstead.†
    Hereford Cath.*
    Hornchurch.*
    Hornton.
    Horsham, St. Faith's.†
    Houghton Conquest.*
    Kenton.†
    Kimble Parva.*
    Lavant, Mid.*
    Manaton.†
    Norwich,   St. George
        Tombland.†
    Norwich, St. Gregory's.*
    Norwich, St. John's, Mad-
        dermarket.*
    Norwich, St. John de Se-
        pulchre.†
    Oakwood.*
    Pickering.*
    Pickhill.*
    Pitton.*
    Preston (Suffolk).*
    Randworth.†
    Raunds.
    St. Just-in-Penwith.*
    Salisbury, St. Thomas.*
    Shouldham Thorp.*
    Slapton.*
    Smallburgh.†
    Somerleyton.†

GEORGE, ST.—*cont.*
Sproughton.*
Stedham.*
Stonham, Earl's.*
Stotfold.*
Stratford-on-Avon, Chapel
of the Guild of the Holy
Cross.*
Troston.*
Trusham.†
Westfield (Sussex).* (?)
Whimple.*
Wilsford and Lake.*
Winchester Cath.†
Winfield, North.*
Witton.*
Woolborough.†
Worstead.*

N.B.—Most of the wall
paintings represent St.
George on horseback,
piercing the Dragon with
his spear, the Princess with
a lamb kneeling behind
him, and the King and
Queen viewing the en-
counter from a distant
tower. In the panel paintings St. George is gene-
rally on foot and trampling
on the Dragon.

GERON, or JERON, ST.
Suffield.† (?)
Tuddenham, North.† (?)

GERTRUDE, ST.
Babingley.†
Hennock.†
Woolborough.† (?)

GILES or EGIDIUS, ST.
Bradninch.†
Elmham, North.†
Hempstead.†
Lessingham.†
Plumstead, Great.†
Smallburgh.†

GOBNET, ST.
Ballyvourney.‡

GODIVA.
Hereford Cath.*

GOLIATH.
Hoxne.*
Yarmouth, Great.*

GREGORY, ST., POPE, AND
DOCTOR OR FATHER OF THE
CHURCH.
Acre, Castle, Ch.†
Ashton.†
Berry Pomeroy.†
Burnham Norton.†
Canterbury Cath.†
Cawston.†
Elmham, North.†
Foxley.†
Fritton (Norfolk).†
Gooderstone.†
Gressenhall.†
Heigham, Potter.†
Holne.†
Houghton-le-Dale.†
Kenn.†
Lanreath.†
Lessingham.†
Litcham.†
Ludham.†
Manaton.†
Morston.†
Norwich, St. John de Se-
pulchre.†
Portlemouth.†
Repps.†
Romsey.†
Roxton.†
Ruston, East.†
Sall.†
Suffield.†
Tuddenham, North.†
Tunstead.†
Upton (Norfolk).†
Woolborough.†
Worstead.†

GREGORY'S, ST., MASS, OR THE
LITERAL TRANSUBSTANTIA-
TION OF THE WAFER.
Beverstone.*
Slapton.*
Stoke Charity.‡

GUDULE, ST.
Berry Pomeroy.†
Walpole, St. Peter's.†

GUILDS, INSIGNIA OF.
    Brecon, St. John's.†
    Cawston.*
    Dereham, East.†
    Horstead.†
    Norwich, St. Giles's Hosp.†
    Redenhall.†

HABAKKUK. *See also* PROPHETS,
THE.
    Norwich, St. Peter Man-
       croft.†

HAGGAI. *See also* PROPHETS,
THE.
    Poringland.†

HEAVENLY HIERARCHY. *See*
HIERARCHY, HEAVENLY.

HELEN, ST.
    Babingley.†
    Broughton (Bucks).*
    Cawston.†
    Chalgrove.*
    Eaton.*
    Eye.†
    Harting.*
    Hempstead.†
    Holne.†
    Ilsington.‡
    Kenton.†
    Manaton.†
    Norwich, St. James.†
    Norwich, St. Peter Man-
       croft.‡
    Repps.†
    Roxton.†
    Teignton, King's.†
    Tilbrook.†
    Tor Bryan.†
    Trusham.†
    Upton (Norfolk).†
    Walpole, St. Peter's.†
    Woolborough.†

HELL AND THE VICES.
    Leigh, South.*
    Melbourne (Derby).*
    Westminster Hall.*

HENRY III., KING.
    Westminster Abbey.*

HENRY IV., KING.
    St. David's.* (?)

HENRY VI., KING.
    Alnwick.‡
    Alton.*
    Barton Turf.†
    Binham Abbey.†
    Chester, St. Mary-on-the
       Hill.* (?)
    Eye.†
    Gately.†
    Ilketshall, St. Margaret's.*
    Litcham.†
    Ludham.†
    St. Albans, St. Michael's.†
    Warfield.*
    Wesenham.†
    Witton.*

HENRY VII., KING.
    Plymtree.†
    Windsor.†

HENRY VIII., KING.
    Chichester Cath.†

HEROD'S FEAST AND HERODIAS'
DAUGHTER.
    Chalfont, St. Giles.*
    Pickering.*
    Ugborough.†

HEXAGONAL STAND.
    Burlingham, St. Andrew's.

HEZEKIAH, KING.
    Westminster Hall.*

HIERARCHY, HEAVENLY.
    Barton Turf.†
    Irstead.*
    Madron.‡
    Southwold.†
    Tavistock.†
    Warwick.‡

HIERONYMUS, ST. *See* JEROME,
ST.

HILDEGARDE, ST.
    Norwich, St. Peter Man-
       croft.‡

HOLOFIUS, ST. *See* OLAVE, ST.

HOSEA. ' See also PROPHETS, THE.
    Crawley, North.†
    Norwich, St. Peter Mancroft.†
    Southwold.†

HUBERT, ST.
    Idsworth.* (?)
    Ingham.* (?)
    Lenham.*
    Litcham.†

ICONUELA.
    Amport.

INCREDULITY OF ST. THOMAS.
    See CHRIST (28).

INNOCENTS, MASSACRE OF THE.
    Chalgrove.*
    Headington.*
    Jersey, Holy Trinity.*
    Llanwyddyn.*
    Winterbourne Dauntsey.*

IRENÆUS, ST.
    Woolborough.†

ISAAC.
    Salisbury Cath.*
    Woolborough.† (?)

ISAIAH. See also PROPHETS, THE.
    Attleborough.*
    Crawley, North.†
    Norwich, St. Peter Mancroft.†
    Poringland.†
    Southwold.†
    Winchester, St. John's.*

ISRAEL, CHILDREN OF, CROSSING THE RED SEA.
    Exeter Cath.†

ISRAEL, CHILDREN OF, GATHERING THE MANNA.
    Friskney.*

JACOB.
    Orleton.* (?)
    Salisbury Cath.*
    Stanford le Hope.* (?)
    Woolborough.† (?)

JAMES, ST., MAJOR. See also APOSTLES, THE.
    Belton.*
    Bovey Tracey.‡
    Clifton (Beds).†
    [Denton.†]
    Edingthorpe.†
    Exeter Cath.*
    Houghton le Dale.†
    Ilsington.‡
    Kempley.*
    Kenn.†
    Latchingdon.†
    Mamhead.†
    Norwich, St. John de Sepulchre.†
    Norwich, St. Peter Mancroft.†
    Plymtree.†
    Pulham, St. Mary the Virgin.†
    Randworth.†
    Salisbury, St. Thomas.*
    Salthouse.†
    Swafield.†
    Swanscombe.*
    Trimmingham.†
    Trusham.†
    Walpole, St. Peter's.†
    Westhall.†
    Widecombe-in-the-Moor.†
    Winchester Cath.†
    Wisborough Green.*

JAMES, ST., MINOR. See also APOSTLES, THE.
    Berry Pomeroy.†
    Elmham, North.†
    Houghton le Dale.†
    Ipswich, St. Nicholas.‡ (?)
    Norwich, St. Peter Mancroft.†
    Pulham, St. Mary the Virgin.†
    Randworth.†
    Sall.†
    Salthouse.†
    Swafield.†
    Tavy, Peter.†

JANE OF VALOIS, ST. See JOAN OF VALOIS, ST.

JEHOIACHIN.
Westminster Hall.*

JEREMIAH. *See also* PROPHETS, THE.
Attleborough.*
Crawley, North.†
Poringland.†
Southwold.†

JEROME, ST., CARDINAL, AND DOCTOR OR FATHER OF THE CHURCH.
Acre, Castle, Ch.†
Ashton.†
Berry Pomeroy.†
Burnham Norton. †
Cawston.†
Elmham, North.†
Foxley.†
Fritton (Norfolk).†
Gooderstone.†
Gressenhall.†
Heigham, Potter.†
Holne.†
Houghton le Dale.†
Kenn.†
Lanreath.†
Latchingdon.†
Lessingham.†
Ludham.†
Manaton.†
Morston.†
Portlemouth.†
Romsey.†
Roxton.†
Ruston, East.†
Sall.†
Suffield.†
Tuddenham, North.†
Tunstead.†
Upton (Norfolk).†
Woodbridge.†
Woolborough.†
Worstead.†

JERON, ST. *See* GERON, ST.

JESSE, STEM OF.
Abingdon.†
Buckland (Herts).*
Chalgrove.*
Colchester.†

JESSE, STEM OF—*cont.*
Etton.*
Godshill.*
Llantwit Major.‡
Naworth.†
Wells, St. Cuthbert's.‡

JESUS CHRIST. *See* CHRIST.

JEWS, CAPTIVITY OF THE.
Westminster Hall.*

JEZEBEL.
Pirford.* (?)

JOAB.
Westminster Hall.*

JOACIM, ST.
Harpley.†

JOAN OF VALOIS, or JOANNA, ST.
Barnham Broom.†
Eaton.*
Norwich, St. James.†
Upton (Norfolk).†

JOB.
Salisbury Cath.*

JOEL. *See also* PROPHETS, THE.
Bedfield.†
Crawley, North.†
Norwich, St. Peter Mancroft.†

JOHN THE BAPTIST, ST.
Amport.‡
Ashton.†
Attleborough.†
Aylsham.†
Barkway.‡
Bedwin, Great.*
Belaugh.†
Beverley, St. Mary's.†
Bideford.‡
Blakenham, Little.*
Burlingham, St. Andrew.†
Canterbury Cath.*
Catfield.*
Chalfont, St. Giles.*
Chalgrove.*
Chester, St. John's.*

JOHN THE BAPTIST, ST.—*cont.*
Easton (Hants).‡
Eaton.*
Elsing Ch.*
Friskney.*
Godalming.*
Hastings.*
Hereford Cath.‡
Higham, Cold.*
Holne.†
Horsham, St. Faith's.†
Houghton le Dale.†
Idsworth.*
Manaton.†
Norwich, St. Gregory's.†
Norwich, St. John's, Timberhill.*
Norwich, St. Stephen's.‡
Overton, Cold.*
Oxburgh.†
Plymtree.†
Randworth.†
Repps.†
Salisbury Cath.*
Strensham.†
Terrington, St. Clement's.†§
Ugborough.†
Wiggenhall, St. Mary the Virgin.†
Wilton.†
Winchester Cath.†
Windsor.*
Wiston (Suffolk).*
Witton.*
Woolborough.†
Worstead.†
York, St. Mary's Abbey.‡

JOHN THE EVANGELIST, ST.
See also APOSTLES, THE.
Adisham.†.
Ashton.†
Attleborough.†
Bedfont.*
Beverley, St. Mary's.†
Bloxham.†
Bovey Tracey.‡
Canterbury Cath.*
Catfield.*
Chalgrove.*
Chester Cath.*

JOHN THE EVANGELIST, ST.—*cont.*
Chester, St. Mary on the Hill.*
Cleeve, Old.*
Clifton.†
Durham Cath.*
Eaton.*
Edingthorpe.†
Elmham, North.†
Exeter Cath.*
Eye.†
Faversham.*
Flaunden.*
Foulsham.†
Gidleigh.†
Heigham, Potter.†
Hennock.†
Hexham.†
Horsham, St. Faith's.†
Houghton le Dale.†
Kenn.†
Kirton in Lindsey.*
Llandanwg.†
Ludham.†.
Mamhead.†
Morston.†
Newnham Regis.*
Newport (Essex)†.
Norwich, St. Peter Mancroft.†
Norwich, SS. Simon and Jude.†
Paignton.‡
Pinvin.*
Pluscardine.*
Plymtree.†
Pulham, St. Mary the Virgin.†
Randworth.†
Repps.†
Ruston, East.†
St. Albans Cath.*
St. Davids.*
Salisbury Cath.*
Somerleyton.†
Suffield.†
Swafield.†
Tamworth.*
Tavy, Peter.†
Trunch.†

JOHN THE EVANGELIST, ST.—
cont.
Walpole St. Peter's.*†
Wellington (Somerset).*
Westminster Abbey.*
Whissendine.*
Widecombe in the Moor.†
Wilton.†
Winchester Cath.†
Winchester, St. John's.* (?)
Winchester, St. Cross.*
Woolborough.† §
Worthy, Headbourn.‡

JOHN OF BEVERLEY, ST.
Beverley, St. Mary's.†
Hempstead.† (?)
Hexham.†

JOHN OF BURLINGTON, ST.
Hempstead.† (?)

JONAH. See also PROPHETS,
THE.
Southwold.†

JOSEPH. See also PATRIARCHS,
THE.
Tawton, Bishop's.*

JOSEPH, ST.
Hornton.*
Laycock Abbey.* (?)
London, Carpenters' Hall.*
Tavy, Peter.†
Winterbourne Dauntsey.*
Worstead.†
Also often introduced in
representations of the Na-
tivity, Adoration of the
Magi and Shepherds, Flight
into Egypt, &c.

JOSES.
Houghton le Dale.†
Randworth.†

JOSHUA.
Roystone.*

JOSIAH.
London, Carpenters' Hall.*

JUDAS ISCARIOT. See CHRIST
(11), (18), (19), (20).

JUDAS MACCABEUS.
Westminster Hall.*

JUDE, ST. See also APOSTLES,
THE.
Berry Pomeroy.†
Clifton.†
Denton.†
Elmham, North.†
Exeter Cath.*
Fritton (Norfolk).†
Hennock.†
Houghton le Dale.†
Ilsington.‡ (?)
Norwich, St. James.†
Pulham, St. Mary the Vir-
gin.†
Randworth.†
Swafield.†
Widecombe-in-the-Moor.†

JUDGMENT, DAY OF. See DOOM,
THE.

JULIAN, HOSPITATOR, ST.
Suffield.†

JULIANA, ST.
Bunbury.†
Dersingham.†
Elmham, North.†
Eton.*
Hempstead.†

JUSTINE, ST.
Norwich, St. Peter Man-
croft.‡ (?)

JUSTITIA. See VIRTUES, THE.

KENEBURGA, ST.
Chester Cath.‡ (?)

KENELM, ST.
Chester Cath.‡
Halesowen.*
St. Kenelm's.*
Woodbridge.†

KENREDUS, REX.
Chester Cath.‡

KINGS OF ENGLAND, SERIES OF.
See ENGLAND, SERIES OF
KINGS OF.

KINGS, THE THREE. *See*
CHRIST (2).

KNIGHTS TILTING, &c.
Barrow (Salop).*
Bletsoe.*
Burgate.†
Upchurch.*
Westminster Hall.*

KYNEBURGA, ST. *See* KENE-
BURGA, ST.

LADDER OF SALVATION OF THE
HUMAN SOUL.
Chaldon.*

LANGTON, BISHOP.
Winchester Cath.*

LAW, FIGURE SYMBOLICAL OF
THE JEWISH.
Newport (I. of Wight).*(?)

LAWRENCE, ST.
Catfield.*
Chalgrove.*
Chishill, Great.*
Harpley.†
Harting.*
Hempstead.†
Hennock.†
Holne.†
Ilsington.‡
Kenn.†
Kenton.†
Ludham.†
Milcomb.*
Randworth.†
Rotherfield.*
Ruislip.*
Smallburgh.†
Somerleyton.†
Strensham.†
Tidworth, North.*
Tor Bryan.†
Worstend.†

LAZARUS.
Hornchurch.*
Roxton.†
Thornham.†
Westminster Abbey.‡
Winchester Cath.*

LAZARUS AND DIVES.
Ulcomb.*
Winchfield.*

LECTERN OR LETTERN.
Bigbury.
Eton.
Leighton Buzzard.
Littlebury.
Ottery St. Mary.
Peakirk.
Randworth.

LEODEGAR, ST.
Wilburton.*
Woodbridge.†

LEOFRIC, BISHOP.
Exeter Cath.*

LEONARD, ST.
Bengeo.* (?)
Gressenhall.†
Hempstead.†
Milton.‡
Norwich, St. John's Mad-
dermarket.†
Portlemouth.† (?)
Westhall.†
Woolborough.†

LIMBUS, THE DESCENT INTO.
See CHRIST (25).

LITANY DESK.
Hexham.

LONGINUS, ST.
Suffield.† (?)

LORD, OUR. *See* CHRIST.

LOUIS, ST.
Foxley.†
Gateley.†
Gidleigh.†
Suffield.† (?)

LOY, ST. *See* ELIGIUS, ST.

LUCIA, or LUCY, ST.
Eye.†
Havant.* (?)
Plymtree.†
Stoke by Nayland.*

LUKE, ST., EVANGELIST.
  Adisham.†
  Ashton.†
  Bovey Tracey.‡
  Bramfield.†
  Foulsham.†
  Gidleigh.†
  Heigham, Potter.†
  Holne.†
  Kenn.†
  Llandanwg.†
  Manaton.†
  Morston.†
  Newnham Regis.*
  Norwich, SS. Simon and
    Jude.†
  Paignton.‡
  Pluscardine.*
  Ruston, East.†
  Salisbury Cath.*
  Suffield.†
  Tor Bryan.†
  Winchester Cath.†
  Woolborough.† §

MACCABEUS, JUDAS.   See
  JUDAS MACCABEUS.

MACHUTUS, ST.
  Portlemouth.† (?)

MAGI, THE. See CHRIST, (2).

MAJESTY, CHRIST IN.   See
  CHRIST (30).

MALACHI. See also PROPHETS,
  THE.
  Crawley, North.†
  Poringland.†

MARGARET, ST.
  Babingley.†
  Binstead.*
  Bovey Tracey.‡
  Brington, Great.†
  Cassington.*
  Charlwood.*
  Cleeve, Old.*
  Dormington.* (?)
  Eton.*
  Filby.†
  Garboldisham.†
  Gressenhall.†
  Hennock.†

MARGARET, ST.—cont.
  Holne.†
  Jersey, St. Clement's.* (?)
  Lessingham.†
  Lindfield.*
  Lingfield.*
  Maidstone.* (?)
  Manaton.†
  Mentmore.*
  Norwich Cath.*
  Norwich, St. Michael at
    Plea.†
  Norwich, St. Peter Man-
    croft.‡
  Plymtree.†
  Preston (Sussex).*
  Randworth.†
  Repps.†
  Tilbrook.†
  Ugborough.†
  Walsham.*
  Walsham, North.†
  Warwick.‡
  Wellow (Somerset).*
  Wenham, Little.*
  Westhall.†
  Westminster, St. Mar-
    garet's.‡
  Whissendine.*
  Wiggenhall, St. Mary the
    Virgin.†
  Worstead.†

MARK, ST., EVANGELIST.
  Adisham.†
  Ashton.†
  Bloxham.†
  Bovey Tracey.‡
  Bramfield.†
  Foulsham.†
  Gidleigh.†
  Heigham, Potter.†
  Holne.†
  Kenn.†
  Llandanwg.†
  Morston.†
  Newnham Regis.*
  Norwich, SS. Simon and
    Jude.†
  Paignton.‡
  Pluscardine.*
  Ruston, East.†

MARK, ST., EVANGELIST—*cont.*
    Salisbury Cath.*
    Suffield.†
    Tor Bryan.†
    Winchester Cath.†
    Woolborough.†§

MARTHA, ST.
    Eton.* (?)
    Jersey, St. Clement's.* (?)

MARTIN, ST.
    Birmingham.*
    Crawley, North.†
    Grendon.*
    Milton Abbas.†
    Norwich, St. James.†
    Plumstead, Great.†
    Ruislip.* (?)
    Tidworth, North.*

MARY THE VIRGIN, ST.
  (1.) BEING TAUGHT BY ST. ANNE.
    Babingley.†
    Boston, Rochford Tower.*
    Gorleston Ch.*
    Haddon Hall.*
    Harpley.†
    Hereford Cath.*
    Higham, Cold.*
    Houghton-le-Dale.†
    Latton.*
    Mentmore.*
    Slapton.*
    Somerleyton.†
    Whittlesford.‡
    Winchester, St. Cross.*

  (2.) THE ANNUNCIATION.
    Ashton.†
    Barfreston.*
    Beverley, St. Mary's.†
    Boston, Rochford Tower.*
    Bradninch.†
    Brook.*
    Buckland in the Moor.†
    Bunbury.†
    Canterbury Cath.*
    Cassington.*
    Chalgrove.*
    Chiltington, West.*
    Clifton.†

Q 3254.

MARY THE VIRGIN, ST.—*cont.*
  (2.) THE ANNUNCIATION— *cont.*
    Easby Ch.*
    Ewelme.*
    Faversham.*
    Hastingleigh.*
    Hennock.†
    Hexham.†
    Histon.*
    Horsham.*
    Jersey, Grouville Ch.*
    Jersey, St. Brelade's.*
    Kimpton.* (?)
    Leicester, St. Margaret's.*
    Loddon.†
    Maidstone.*
    Milton Abbas.†
    Norwich, St. Helen's.‡
    Norwich, St. Michael at Plea.†
    Notgrove.*
    Oakwood.*
    Pinvin.*
    Plymtree.†
    Reading, St. Lawrence.*
    St. Alban's Cath.*
    Salisbury, St. Thomas.*
    Salisbury, House in New St.*
    Slapton.*
    Stow Bardolph.*
    Timworth.*
    Tor Bryan.†
    Ugborough.†
    Westminster, St. Margaret's.*
    Winchester Cath.*‡
    Winterbourne Dauntsey.*
    Wiston (Suffolk).*
    Woolborough.†

  (3.) THE SALUTATION or VISITATION.
    Aconbury.*
    Amberley Ch.*
    Ashton.†
    Brinsop.*
    Bures, Mount.* (?)
    Canterbury Cath.*
    Chiltington, West.*

A A

MARY THE VIRGIN, ST.—*cont.*

(3.) THE SALUTATION OR VISITATION—*cont.*

Colton.*
Faversham.*
Gately.†
Hexham.†
Norwich, St. Michael at Plea.†
Outwell.*
Pinvin.*
Plymtree.†
Salisbury Cath.*
Salisbury, St. Thomas.*
Sparham.†
Timworth.*
Wickham, East.*
Winchester Cath.‡

(4.) THE NATIVITY. *See* CHRIST (1).

(5.) WITH INFANT CHRIST. *See also* CHRIST (2), (4), (5), (6).

Amberley Ch.*
Anwick.‡
Ashton.†
Attleborough.†
Barkway.‡
Beckley.*
Bleadon.‡
Blunham.‡
Bosham.*
Braughing.*
Broughton-in-Airedale.‡
Buckland (Herts).*
Canfield, Great.*
Chichester, Bishop's Palace Chap.*
Cowley (Oxon).*
Eaton, Castle.*
Edstaston.*
Elmham, South.*
Haddon Hall.*
Hadleigh (Essex).*
Harpley.†
Hereford Cath.*
Hexham.†
Hornton.*
Horsham, St. Faith.†
Houghton-le-Dale.†

MARY THE VIRGIN, ST.—*cont.*

(5.) WITH INFANT CHRIST —*cont.*

Isleham.*
Latton.*
Loddon.‡
Manaton.†
Melford, Long.*
Mentmore.*
Merstham.*
Milton, Great.*
Norwich Castle.‡ (?)
Pakefield.*
Pinvin.*
Poyntington.*
Randworth.†
Rochester Cath.* ‡
Shimpling.*
Somerton, West.*
Stewkley.‡
Stoke Charity.*
Stoke Dry.*
Stone.*
Tilbrook.†
Walpole, St. Peter's.†
Wells Cath.‡
Wenham, Little.*
Wiggenhall, St. Mary the Virgin.†
Winchester Cath.†
Winchester, St. John's.*

(6.) AT THE CROSS OF CHRIST.

Bedfont.*
Chester, St. Mary-on-the-Hill.*
Cleeve, Old.*
Durham Cath.*
Faversham.*
Flaunden.*
Hexham.†
Kirton-in-Lindsey.*
Ludham.†
Paignton.‡
Pinvin.*
St. Albans Cath.*
St. David's.*
Tamworth.*
Trunch.†
Walpole, St. Peter's.*

MARY THE VIRGIN, ST.—*cont.*

(6.) AT THE CROSS OF
CHRIST—*cont.*
Wellington (Somerset).*
Whissendine.*
Winchester, St. Cross.*·
Worthy, Headbourn.‡

(7.) "MATER DOLOROSA"
or "PIETA." *See*
CHRIST (23).

(8.) THE FIVE JOYS.
Broughton (Oxon).*

(9.) THE DEATH OF.
Burgh, St. Peter.*
Chalgrove.*
Chilton Cantelo.*
Wimborne.*

(10.) THE ASSUMPTION.
Brisley.*
Chalgrove.*
Chilton Cantelo.*
Devizes, St. Mary's.*
Eton.*
Ewelme.*
Exeter Cath.*
Friskney.*.
Jersey, St. Brelade's.*
Ruislip.*
St. David's.*
Sandford.‡
Witchingham, Great.‡

(11.) THE CORONATION.
Buckland Monachorum.‡
Chalgrove.*
Chichester, St. Olave's.*
Chilton Cantelo.* .
Fetcham.*
Gyffiliog.* (?)
Holne.†
Llandaff.†
Norwich, St. Helen's.‡
Notgrove.*
Pickering.*
Portlemouth.†
St. Albans Cath.* †
Sutton Bingham.*
Toddington.*
Westminster Abbey.†
Winchester Cath.* †

MARY THE VIRGIN, ST.—*cont.*

(12.) MIRACLES.
Chalgrove.*
Eton.*
Winchester Cath.*

(13.) OTHER REPRESENTA-
TIONS.
Arundel.‡
Babingley.†
Barling.‡
Barton (Suffolk).†
Bedwin, Great.‡
Bozeat.†
Broughton (Northents).*
Burnham Norton.†
Combe Martin.†
Dersingham.†
Eddlesborough.*
Ely Cath.‡
Gately.†
Horton.*
Kempley.*
Kenn.†
Kenton.†
Knowle.*
Lathbury.*
Leigh, South.*
Mendlesham.*
Necton.‡
Newport (Essex).†
Pluscardine.*
Sittingbourne.* (?)
Sproughton.*
Swanscombe.*
Walsham, North.†
Warton.†
Wellow (Somerset).*
Weston Baggard.*
Worksop.‡
Wotton.*

St. Mary the Virgin is
also generally included in
pictures of the Doom,
often also in representa-
tions of St. Michael weighing souls; in both cases
interceding on behalf of
mankind.

MARY CLEOPAS, ST.
Bunbury.*
Chiltington, West.*

MARY CLEOPAS, ST.—*cont.*
   Easby Ch.*
   Exeter Cath.*
   Faversham.*
   Gloucester, St. Mary de
      Crypt.*
   Houghton le Dale.†
   Lastingham.* (?)
   Randworth.†
   Stedham.*
   Winterbourne Dauntsey.*

MARY MAGDALENE, ST.
   Babingley.†
   Barnham Broom.†
   Berry Pomeroy.†
   Bramfield.†
   Bray.*
   Bunbury.*
   Catfield.*
   Chalgrove.*
   Cherry Hinton.†
   Chiltington, West.*
   Copford.*
   Denton.†
   Drayton (Norfolk).*
   Easby Ch.*
   Exeter Cath.*
   Farnborough.*
   Faversham.*
   Garboldisham.†
   Glatton.*
   Gloucester, St. Mary de
      Crypt.*
   Guernsey, St. Marie du
      Chastel.*
   Holne.†
   Jersey, St. Clement's.*
   Kenn.†
   Kenton.†
   Lastingham.* (?)
   Lessingham.†
   Ludham.†
   Maidstone.* (?)
   Manaton.†
   Norwich, St. Peter Man-
      croft.‡
   Notgrove.*
   Oxburgh.†
   Preston (Sussex).*
   Repps.†
   Somerleyton.†

MARY MAGDELENE, ST.—*cont.*
   Sotby.*
   Stedham.*
   Tavy, Peter.†
   Thornham.†
   Tilbrook.†
   Walpole, St. Peter's.†
   Walsham.*
   Walsham, North.†
   Warwick.‡
   Wenham, Little.*
   Widecombe-in-the-Moor.†
   Wiggenhall, St. Mary the
      Virgin.†
   Winchester Cath.†
   Winchester, St. John's.*(?)
   Winterbourne Dauntsey.*
   Yaxley (Hunts).* ᵇ
   Yaxley (Suffolk).†

MARY SALOME, ST.   *See*
   SALOME, ST.

MARY OF EGYPT, ST.
   Walsham, North.†

MATER DOLOROSA.   *See*
   CHRIST (23).

MATTATHIAS.
   Westminster Hall.*

MATTHEW, ST.   *See also*
   APOSTLES, THE.
   Adisham.†
   Ashton.†
   Bloxham.†
   Bovey Tracey.‡
   Bramfield.†
   Edingthorpe.† (?)
   Foulsham.†
   Gidleigh.†
   Kenn.†
   Llandanwg.†
   Morston.†
   Newnham Regis.*
   Norwich, SS. Simon and
      Jude.†
   Paignton.‡ (?)
   Pluscardine.*
   Rauceby.* (?)
   Ruscombe.* (?)
   Ruston, East.†
   Salisbury Cath.†

MATTHEW, ST.—*cont.*

Salthouse.†
Suffield.†
Tavy, Peter.†
Widecombe-in-the Moor.†
Winchester Cath.†
Woolborough.†§

MATTHIAS, ST. *See also* APOS-
TLES, THE.

Berry Pomeroy.†
Blythburgh.‡
Elmham, North.†
Hennock.†
Norwich, St. Stephen's.‡
Salthouse.†

MELANGELL or MONACELLA,
ST.

Pennant Melangell.†

MERCY, SEVEN ACTS OF.

Arundel.*
Catfield.*
Chesterton.* (?)
Coltishall.*
Cropredy.*
Dalham.*
Hardwick (Cambs).*
Heigham, Potter.*
Ingatestone.*
Irthlingborough.* (?)
Kimpton.*
Milton Abbas.*
Netherbury.*
Quat.*
Ringshall.* (?)
Ruabon.* (?)
Toddington.*
Wickhampton.*
Winchester, St. John's.*

MERWALDUS.

Chester Cath.‡

MESHACH.

Warblington.*

MICAH. *See also* PROPHETS,
THE.

Crawley, North.†
Norwich, St. Peter Man-
croft.†

MICHAEL, ST., ARCHANGEL.

St. Michael is sometimes
represented as contending
with Satan, and sometimes
as weighing souls. The
examples of the former are
distinguished by the affix
(A.), those of the latter by
a (B.)

(A.) and Satan. (B.) weighing souls.

Ashton.†
Beckley.* (B.)
Beeston St. Mary's.‡
Bisley.* (A.)
Blackford.‡
Boston, Rochford Tower.*
Bovey Tracey.* (B.)
Bradninch.† (A.)
Bramfield.*
Bucklaud (Gloucester).*
Chaldon.* (B.)
Chesham.* (B.)
Chiltington, West.* (B.) (?)
Copford.* (A.)
Crostwight.* (A.)
Cullompton.* (B.)
Ditteridge.* (B.)
Elstow.* (A.)
Filby.† (B.)
Guildford, St. Mary's.* (B.)
Hadleigh (Essex).* (?)
Horley (Oxon.)* (B.)
Horsham, St. Faith's.†
Ilsington.‡
Ipswich, St. Nicholas.* (?)
Islip.* (B.)
Jersey, St. Clement's.*(A.)
Kempley.* (B.)
Lathbury.* (B.)
Leigh, South.* (B.)
Lenham.* (B.)
Lindfield.* (B.)
Lingfield.* (B.)
Melcombe Horsey.* (B.)
Netherbury.* (B.)
Norwich Castle.‡ (A.)
Norwich, St. Peter, per
Mountergate.† (A.)
Pickering.* (A.) (?)
Plymtree.† (A.)

374

MICHAEL, ST., ARCHANGEL—
cont.
Portisham.* (B.)
Preston (Sussex).* (B.)
Randworth.† (A.)
Ruislip.* (B.)
Slapton.* (B)
Somerleyton.†
Stotfold.* (B.)
Sturminster Marshall.*
Tawton, Bishop's.* (B.)
Ulcomb.* (A.)
Waltham, Great.* (B.)
Wellington (Somerset).*
(B.)
Westhall.†
Wickham, East.* (A.)
Wilsford and Lake.* (A.)
Winterbourne, Earl's.* (A.)
Withyam.* (A.)
Worstead.* (A.)
The subject of St.
Michael weighing souls is
also included in most of
the large representations
of the Doom.

MIDDLETON, BISHOP.
Yarmouth, Great.‡

MILFRID, KING.
Hereford Cath.*

MILBURGA, ST.
Chester Cath.‡

MILDRIDA, ST.
Chester Cath.‡

MINSTRELS' GALLERY. *See*
GALLERY, MINSTRELS'.

MISERERE SEATS.
Belaugh.
Higham Ferrers.
Landbeach.
Norwich, St. Swithin's.
Randworth.

MODWENNA, ST.
Stratford-on-Avon, Chapel
of the Guild of the Holy
Cross.*

MONACELLA, ST. *See* MELAN-
GELL., ST.

MONICA, ST.
Carlisle Cath.†
Houghton-le-Dale.† (?)

MONTHS AND SEASONS.
Easby Ch.*
Salisbury Cath.*
Woodford (Essex).*§

MONUMENTS, MONUMENTAL
EFFIGIES, &c., arranged
under counties alphabetically.

BEDFORDSHIRE.
Barford, Great.
Cardington.
Chalgrave.
Clifton.
Houghton Regis.
Sandy.
Turvey.
Willington.

BERKSHIRE.
Englefield.
Fyfield.
Poughley Priory.
Wantage.

BUCKINGHAMSHIRE.
Ashendon.
Aylesbury.
Chenies.
Clifton Reynes.
Hillesden.
Wing.

CAMBRIDGESHIRE.
Borough Green.
Ely Cath.
Hildersham.
Rampton.

CHESHIRE.
Barthomley.
Bunbury.
Malpas.

CORNWALL.
Callington.
St. Teath.
Sheviocke.

375

MONUMENTS, &c.—*cont.*

CUMBERLAND.
Carlisle Cath.
Crosthwaite.
Millom.

DERBYSHIRE.
Ashbourn.
Bakewell.
Newton Solney.
Norbury.
Norton.
Scropton.
Staveley.
Youlgrave.

DEVONSHIRE.
Ashburton.
Axminster.
Brent, South.
Crediton.
Downe, West.
Exeter Cath.
Haccombe.
Horwood.
Kerswell, Abbots.
Landkey.
Pool, South.
Shebbear.
Stoke Fleming.
Tawstock.
Totnes.
Trusham.

DORSETSHIRE.
Cranborne.
Mappowder.
Marnhull.
Piddletown.
Whitchurch Canonicorum.
Wimborne.

DURHAM.
Brancepeth.
Durham Cath.
Durham, St. Giles.
Staindrop.

ESSEX.
Latton.

MONUMENTS, &c.—*cont.*

GLOUCESTERSHIRE.
Berkeley Ch.
Bristol Cath.
Bristol, St. Mark's Chapel.
Bristol, St. Stephen's.
Cleeve, Bishop's.
Leckhampton.
Tewkesbury.

HAMPSHIRE AND ISLE OF WIGHT.
Christchurch.
Newport.
Silchester.
Southampton.
Stoke Charity.
Winchester Cath.

HEREFORDSHIRE.
Hereford Cath.
Kington.
Ross.
Weobley.
Weston Baggard.

HERTFORDSHIRE.
Albury.
Bennington.
Berkhampstead, Great.
Bovingdon.
Broxbourne.
Hunsdon.
Mimms, North.
Munden, Little.
Standon.
Stevenage.
Wheathampstead.

KENT.
Ash.
Canterbury Cath.
Canterbury, St. Martin's.
Minster.
Reculver.
Rochester Cath.
Sandwich, St. Peter's.
Southfleet.

LANCASHIRE.
Cartmel.

LEICESTERSHIRE.
Bottesford.
Tilton-on-the-Hill.

LINCOLNSHIRE.
Dowsby.
Grimsby, Great.
Hainton.
Horbling.
Spilsby.
Wainfleet.

MIDDLESEX.
London, St. Bartholomew's.
London, St. Martin Outwich.
London, Temple Ch.
London, the Tower, St. Peter's Chapel.
Stoke Newington.
Westminster Abbey.

MONMOUTHSHIRE.
Abergavenny.
Chepstow.
Monmouth.

NORFOLK.
Ashwellthorpe.
Banham.
Fersfield.
Ingham.
Narburgh.
Norwich Cath.
Norwich, St. Mary in Coslany.
Reepham.
Swaffham.
Yarmouth, Great.

NORTHAMPTONSHIRE.
Brington, Great.
Charwelton.
Dene.
Dodford.
Edgcott.
Fawsley.
Heyford, Nether.
Higham Ferrers.
Marholme.
Orlingbury.
Spratton.
Stanford.

NORTHAMPTONSHIRE—cont.
Towcester.
Weekley.
Woodford.

NORTHUMBERLAND.
Chillingham.

NOTTINGHAMSHIRE.
Gonalston.
Newark.

OXFORDSHIRE.
Broughton.
Dorchester.
Drayton.
Ewelme.
Hampton Poyle.
Oxford Cath.
Oxford, St. Aldate's.
Stanton Harcourt.

RUTLANDSHIRE.
Ashwell.
Exton.
Stoke Dry.

SHROPSHIRE.
Albrighton.
Burford.
Claverley.
Leighton.
Ludlow.
Moreton Corbet.
Shawbury.
Shiffnal.
Tong.
Wellington.
Wroxeter.

SOMERSETSHIRE.
Ashton, Long.
Backwell.
Bathampton.
Cadbury, North.
Cheddar.
Chew Magna.
Curry Rivell.
Dunster.

MONUMENTS, &c.—*cont.*

SOMERSETSHIRE—*cont.*
Farleigh Hungerford.
Glastonbury, St. John's.
Henstridge.
Kingston.
Muchelney Abbey.
Porlock.
Trent.
Wells Cath.
Weston-in-Gordano.
Wraxall.
Yatton.

STAFFORDSHIRE.
Elford.
Tamworth.
Weston.
Wolverhampton.

SUFFOLK.
Bures.
Bury St. Edmunds, St. Mary's.
Dennington.
Erwarton.
Framlingham.
Gorleston Ch.
Hengrave.
Melford, Long.
Stonham Aspall.
Wingfield.

SURREY.
Capel.
Guildford, St. Nicholas.
Merstham.
Southwark.

SUSSEX.
Arundel.
Battle.
Boxgrove.
Broadwater.
Chichester Cath.
Horsted Keynes.
Hurstmonceux.
Hurstpierpoint.
Ifield.

MONUMENTS, &c.—*cont.*

SUSSEX—*cont.*
Isfield.
Lewes Priory.
Robertsbridge.
Winchelsea.
Wiston.

WARWICKSHIRE.
Astley.
Aston.
Birmingham.
Eatington, Lower.
Guy's Cliff.
Hillmorton.
Polesworth.
Stratford-upon-Avon.

WILTSHIRE.
Bedwin, Gt.
Boyton.
Bradford-on-Avon.
Corsham.
Edington.
Langford, Steeple.
Laycock Ch.
Ludgershall.
Monkton Farleigh.
Salisbury Cath.

WORCESTERSHIRE.
Astley.
Bromsgrove.
Holt.
Icomb.
Worcester Cath.

YORKSHIRE.
Bainton.
Bedale.
Beverley, St. Mary's.
Burton Agnes.
Easby Abbey.
Harewood.
Hull.
Leeds.
Methley.
Wath.
York Minster.

378

MONUMENTS, &c.—cont.

WALES.

Beaumaris.
Llanarmon-in-Yale.
Llandawke.
Swansea.

SCOTLAND.

Douglas.
Dunfermline.

IRELAND.

Knockmoy.

MORTON, CARDINAL.
Plymtree.†

MOSES.
Ashton.†
Aylsham.†
Bratton Clovelly.*
Chester Castle.*
Chester Cath.*
Edmonthorpe.†
Friskney.*
Gloucester, St. Mary de
Crypt.*
Guist.†
Norwich, St. Peter Man-
croft.†
Peterborough.†
Poringland.†
Rochester Cath.‡
Roystone.*
Salisbury Cath.*
Southwold.†
Westhall.†
Woolborough.†

NAHUM. See also PROPHETS,
THE.
Norwich, St. Peter Man-
croft.†
Southwold.†

NATHAN.
Catfield.* (?)

NATIVITY, THE. See CHRIST
(1).

NICHE.
Ardeley.
Axbridge.

NICHE—cont.
Aylesbury.
Barton Bendish, St. An-
drew.
Bentley, Great.
Bleadon.
Bolton Abbey.
Bottisham.
Brigstock.
Bristol, St. Peter's.
Burford (Oxon).
Cadbury, North.
Cambridge, Trinity Ch.
Campton.
Canterbury, St. Alphage.
Charlton Horethorne.
Charlwood.
Cheddar.
Chiltington, West.
Combe Martin.
Creech, St. Michael's.
Deddington.
Deeping, Market.
Ditton, Fen.
Eddlesborough.
Edingthorpe.
Ely Cath.
Exeter, St. Mary Major.
Faversham.
Folkingham.
Garvestone.
Gloucester Cath.
Hadleigh (Essex).
Harrow.
Harty.
Heveningham.
Hinxworth.
Horkesley, Little.
Horningsey.
Ipswich, St. Nicholas.
Laycock Ch.
Leicester, St. Margaret's.
Lichfield.
Llantwit Major.
Martock.
Mayfield.
Melbourne (Cambs).
Mendlesham.
Milton.
Mold.
Munden, Great.

NICHE—*cont.*

Newark.
Northallerton.
Notgrove.
Ottery St Mary.
Oxford, St. Mary's.
Pakefield.
Pulham.
Reigate.
Ribbesford.
Rissington, Great.
Roche Abbey.
St. Albans Cath.
Salisbury, St. Edmund's.
Salisbury, St. Thomas.
Sandwich, St. Clement's.
Sedgbrook.
Smarden.
Sparsholt.
Stacpole Elidur.
Stoke-sub-Hamdon.
Tidworth, North.
Tong.
Wakefield Bridge Chapel.
Warwick.
Weston in Gordano.
Whissendine.
Whittlesford.
Winchester Cath.
Winchester, St. John's.
Winchester,   Magdalen
    Hosp.
Witney.
Worthing.

NICHOLAS, ST.
Charlwood.*
Colton.*
Eccles.*
Headington.* (?)
Holne.†
Ingham.†
Inworth.*
Ipswich, St. Matthew's.*(?)
Kirdford.*
Manaton.†
Milton Abbas.†
Norwich Cath.* (?)
Patcham.* (?)
Pirford.* (?)
Rushall.* (?)

NICHOLAS, ST.—*cont.*
Slapton.* (?)
Somerleyton.†
Tamworth.*
Winchester, St. Cross.*

NINIAN, ST.
Turriff.*

NOAH.
London, Carpenters' Hall.*
Shenley Mansell.*

"NOLI ME TANGERE."   *See*
    CHRIST (27).

ODILO, ST.
Plymtree.†

OFFA, REX.
Chester Cath.‡

OLAVE or HOLOFIUS, ST.
    Barton Turf.†
    Manaton.†

ORGAN.
· Faversham.

OSEE.   *See* HOSEA.

OSMUND, BISHOP.
Ely Cath.*

OSTHRID, QUEEN.
Melbourne (Derby).*

OSWALD, ST.
Hornchurch.* (?)
Horsham, St. Faith's.†
Norwich, St. James.†
Woodbridge.†

OSYTH, ST.
Newport (I. of Wight).* (?)

PANCRAS, ST.
Holne.†
Woolborough.†

PANELLING.
Acre, Castle, Ch.
Acre, Castle, Priory.
Addington, Great.
Baston.
Dartmouth, St. Petrox.
Dartmouth, St. Saviour's.
Dorney.
Icomb Manor House.
Kelvedon.

PANELLING—*cont.*
Naworth.
Norwich, St. Miles.
Pengersick.
Sco-Ruston.
Selby Abbey.
Yarmouth, Great.

PANEL PAINTINGS, exclusive of Rood Screens and Roofs.
Adisham.
Amberley Castle.
Astley (Warwick).
Axbridge.
Aylesbury.
Bansfield.
Barton.
Blakenham, Little.
Bradninch.
Brancepeth.
Brington, Great.
Burford (Salop).
Canterbury Cath.
Cartmel Fell.
Cheltenham.
Cove, South.
Creake, North.
Elford.
Friskney.
Fulbourn, All Saints.
Gloucester Cath.
Herringfleet.
Hexham.
Landbeach.
Latchingdon.
Llandaff.
Llandanwg.
Loddon.
London, The Savoy Chapel.
Lynn, King's.
Milton Abbas.
Mitcheldean.
Morley (Norfolk).
Newark.
Norwich, St. George Tombland.
Norwich, St. Michael at Plea.
Norwich, St. Peter Mancroft.
Norwich, St. Swithin's.
Norwich, Huby's Yard.

PANEL PAINTINGS—*cont.*
Quat.
Romsey.
St. Albans, St. Michael's.
St. Donat's.
St. Germans.
Somerton, West.
Southwold.
Strata Florida.
Sudbury.
Warton.
Wesenham.
Wilton.
Winsham.

PARCLOSE. *See* SCREEN.

PASSION, INSTRUMENTS OR IMPLEMENTS OF THE.
Attleborough.†
Brancepeth.†
Cassington.*
Denford.†
Gloddaeth.*
Goosey.*
Gorleston Ch.*
Hitcham.†
Houghton Conquest.*
Ickburgh.†
Knapton.‡
London, The Savoy Chapel.†
Michaelchurch Eskley.*
Norwich, St. Clement's.*
Oakley.†
Raunds.*
St. Albans Cath.†
Salisbury, St. Thomas.*
Smarden.*
Southwold.†
Stanton.†
Stow Bardolph.*
Tywardreth.†
Ugborough.†
Wellingborough.†
Winchester Cath.†
Wrexham.*
Yaxley (Suffolk).*

In representations of "The Doom," Angels holding the Instruments of the Passion are often introduced.

PASSION, SCENES FROM THE.
See CHRIST (20).

PATRIARCHS, THE.
Burton Latimer.*
Castor.*
Doncaster, St. George's.†
Eyam.*
Hargrave.*

PATRON ·SAINT RESCUING A
SOUL.
Crostwight.*
Eaton.*

.PAUL, ST.
Axbridge.†
Aylsham.†
Beckley.*
Belaugh.†
Bovey Tracey.‡
Bramfield.*
Cawston.†
Chalgrove.*
Checkendon.*
Clifton.†
Denton.†
Edingthorpe.†
Elmham, North.†
Eye.†
Faversham.*
Filby.†
Hawkedon.*
Headington.*
Hennock.†
Hexham.†
Hoxne.*
Hunstanton.†
Idsworth.*
Kempley.* (?)
Lessingham.†
Mambead.†
Manaton.† ‡
Marsham.†
Milton Abbas.†
Newington.*
Newport (Essex).†
Norwich Cath.*
Norwich, St. Helen's.‡
Oxford Cath.*
Peterborough.†
Plymtree.†
Randworth.†

PAUL, ST.—cont.
Redenhall.†
Ruscombe.*
Sotterley.†
Southwold.†
Stoke Ash.*
Strensham.†
Tavy, Peter.†
Thornham.†
Trunch.†
Trusham.†
Tunstead.†
Walpole, St. Peter's.†
Walsham, North.†
Westmeston.*
Westwick (Norfolk).†
Winchester, Magdalen
Hosp.*
Wingfield.†
Woodbridge.†
Woolborough.†
Worstead.†
In the series of Apostles,
St. Paul generally occurs
in place of St. Matthew or
St. Matthias.

PENDA, REX.
Chester Cath.‡

PENTECOST, DAY OF.
Exeter Cath.†

PETER, ST. See also APOSTLES,
THE.
Amport.‡
Bacton.*
Beachamwell.‡
Bedale.‡
Beckley.*
Billingford (Suffolk).* (?)
Bisham.* ·
Blundeston.†
Bovey Tracey.‡
Bristol, St. John's.*
Chalgrove.*
Chester Cath.*
Clifton.†
Edingthorpe.†
Filby.†
Flawford.‡
Headington.*
Hennock.†

PETER, ST.—cont.
Hexham.†
Idsworth.*
Impington.*
Kempley.*
Llanbadarn Fawr.*
London. The Savoy
Chapel.†
Lynn, King's.†
Mamhead.†
Newport (Essex).†
Norwich Cath.*
Oxford Cath.*
Peterborough.†
Ruscombe.*
Swafield.†
Tavy, Peter.†
Trusham.†
Walpole, St. Peter's.†
Westmeston.*
Westminster Abbey.‡
Widecombe-in-the-Moor.†
Winchester Cath.†
Winchester, Magdalen
Hosp.*
Wingfield.†
St. Peter standing at the
Gate of Heaven is fre-
quently introduced in pic-
tures of "The Doom."

PETRONILLA, ST.
Elmham, North.†
Litcham.†
Plymtree.†
Trimmingham.†

PEW.
Cartmel Fell.
Llanfihangel Yng-Nghwnfa.

PHILIP, ST. See also APOSTLES,
THE.
Elmham, North.†
Hennock.†
Tavy, Peter.†
Widecombe-in-the-Moor.†

PHILIP THE DEACON, ST.
Maresfield.*

PHILIPPA, QUEEN.
Westminster, St. Stephen's
Chapel.*

PHŒNIX.
Canterbury Cath.*

PIETA. See CHRIST (23).

PILGRIMS.
Wisborough Green.*
Yaxley (Hunts).*
See also SS. JAMES MA-
JOR, ROCHE, and EDWARD
THE CONFESSOR.

PISCINA.
Anstey.
Ashburton.
Bury St. Edmunds, St.
Mary's.
Cadbury, South.
Deddington.
Dunham, Little.
Frome.
Furness.
Horningsey.
Ickenham.
Ipswich, St. Nicholas.
Isleham.
Lichfield.
Mildenhall.
Rissington, Great.
Sodgbrook.
Sproughton.
Tidworth, North.
Widford.
Winchester Cath.

PLATFORM, PORCH.
Weston in Gordano.

POPE, not specially identified.
Nottingham, St. Mary's.‡

PORTRAITS OF BENEFACTORS,&c.
Aylsham.†
Bangor is y Coed.*
Barfreston.* (?)
Bedale.‡
Bloxham.†
Burford (Salop).†
Burnham Norton.†
Cheltenham.†
Chichester Cath.†
Cirencester.*
Cranborne.*
Durham Cath.*
Edgfield.†

383

PORTRAITS OF BENEFACTORS,
&c.—cont.
Ely Cath.*
Exeter Cath.*
Fritton (Norfolk).†
Gaddesden, Little.†
Gloucester, St. Mary de
Crypt.*
Hereford Cath.*
Houghton le Dale.†
Houston.*
Ipswich, St. Matthew.†
Loddon.†
Lynn, King's.†
Maidstone.*
Melford, Long.*
Morley (Norfolk).†
Plymtree.†
Raunds.*
Ridge.* (?)
Romsey.†
St. Douats.†
Salisbury Cath.*
Silchester.*
Slapton.* (?)
Tamworth.*
Tawstock.*
Tewkesbury.*
Wainfleet.‡
Westbury on Trym.*
Westminster Abbey.*
Westminster, St. Ste-
phen's Chapel.*
Whittington.*
Winchester Cath.* †
Windsor.†
Yarmouth, Great.‡

POWERS, POTESTATES. See
HIERARCHY, HEAVENLY.

PRESENTATION IN THE TEMPLE.
See CHRIST (5).

PRINCIPALITIES. See HIER-
ARCHY, HEAVENLY.

PRISCILLA. See AQUILA AND
PRISCILLA.

PRODIGAL SON, THE.
Brooke (Norfolk).*

PROPHETS, THE. See also
under individual names.
Barking (Suffolk).†
Bovey Tracey.†
Bratton Clovelly.*
Chudleigh.†
Clifton.† (?)
Exeter Cath.*
Harpley.†
Kenton.†
Marston Moretaine.†
Poringland.†
Risborough, Monks.†
Salisbury Cath.*
Thornham.†
Winchester Cath.*

PRUDENTIA. See VIRTUES, THE.

PUDSEY, BISHOP.
Durham Cath.* (?)

PUELLA RIDIBOWNE, ST.
Gately.†

PULPIT.
Acre, Castle.
Allington, East.
Bedford.
Bigbury.
Bovey Tracey.
Bridford.
Brigstock.
Burford (Oxon).
Burlingham, St. Edmund.
Burnham Norton.
Cheddar.
Chivelston.
Cockington.
Coventry, St. Michael's.
Creake, South.
Dartmouth, St. Saviour's.
Dersingham.
Harberton.
Holne.
Horsham, St. Faith's.
Ipplepen.
Kenton.
Kilworth, North.
Launceston.
Locking.
Middleton Cheney.
Mitcheldean.

PULPIT—*cont.*
Molton, North.
Paignton.
Potterne.
St. Catherine.
Snettisham.
Southwold.
Stourton Candel.
Sutton, Long.
Tamerton.
Tor Bryan.
Totnes.
Walsingham, New.
Warmington.
Woodland.

PURGATORY.
Bloxham.*
Chaldon.*
Cirencester.*
Fetcham.*
Guildford, St. Mary's.*

QUINTIN, ST.
Woodbridge.†

RELIQUARY.
Blythburgh.
Caldey Island.
Kewstoke.
Salisbury Museum.
Shipley.
Woodford.

REPRESENTATIVE   CHRISTIAN.
See CHRISTIAN, REPRESENTA-
TIVE.

REREDOS, ALTAR SCREEN, &c.
Abergavenny.
Adderbury.
Axbridge.
Bampton (Oxon).
Beauchief Abbey.
Beverley Minster.
Blunham.
Bristol Cath.
Canterbury Cath.
Chaddesden.
Cobham.
Cury.
Devizes, St. John's.
Drayton (Berks).

REREDOS, ALTAR SCREEN, &c.
—*cont.*
Exeter Cath.
Flaunden.
Gloucester Cath.
Guildford, St. Mary's.
Haseley, Great.
Leeds (Kent).
Ludlow.
Marston Moretaine.
Micheldever.
Milton Abbas.
Norwich Cath.
Norwich, SS. Simon and
Jude.
Norwich, St. Stephen's.
Norwich, Huby's Yard.
Ottery St. Mary.
Overbury.
Oxford, All Souls.
Preston in Holderness.
Reigate.
Rushden (Northants).
St. Albans Cath.
Salisbury Cath.
Sandy.
Sherborne Almshouse.
Shrewsbury, St. Chad's.
Smarden.
Southwold.
Stevenage.
Toft.
Wellington (Somerset).
Wells, St. Cuthbert.
Wells, St. John's Priory.
Westminster Abbey.
Whissendine.
Whittlesford.
Wimborne.
Winchester Cath.
Winchester Coll. Chapel.
Winchester, St. Cross.
Wivelsfield.
Worstead.
Yarmouth, Great.
York Minster.

RESURRECTION,   THE.   *See*
CHRIST (26).

RESURRECTION, THE GENERAL.
See DOOM, THE.

385

RICHARD OF CHICHESTER, ST.
  Maidstone.*
  Norwich Cath.*
RICHARD I., KING.
  Durham Cath.* (?)
RICHARD III., KING.
  Baston.†
ROBERT, ST.
  Erpingham.†
  Somerleyton.* (?)
ROCHE, ST.
  Grendon.*
  Holne.†
  Kettering.*
  Launceston.*
  Pinvin.*
  Plymtree.†
  Romsey.†
  St. Thomas by Launceston.*
  Stalham.†
  Tuddenham, North.†
  Woolborough.†
ROMUALD, ST.
  Plymtree.†
ROOD, THE.
  Cartmel Fell.
  Ludham.
  Somerton, West.
  Worthy, Headbourn.
ROOD BEAM. *See* BEAM, ROOD.
ROOD SCREEN. *See* SCREEN.
ROOFS AND CEILINGS, wholly or partially painted, arranged under Counties alphabetically.
  BEDFORDSHIRE.
  Arlesey.
  Bedford.
  Biggleswade.
  Cople.
  Elstow.
  Gravenhurst, Over.
  Harlington.
  Husborne Crawley.
  Keysoe.
  Marston Moretaine.
  Shillington.
  Toddington.
  Wilshampstead.
  Q 3254.

ROOFS AND CEILINGS—*cont.*
  BERKSHIRE.
  Abingdon.
  Windsor.

  BUCKINGHAMSHIRE.
  Bradwell.
  Chesham Bois.
  Crawley, North.
  Denham.
  Hanslope.
  Moreton, Maid's.
  Newton Longueville.
  Risborough, Monk's.
  Stewkley.
  Stoke Hammond.
  Wing.
  Wycombe, High.

  CAMBRIDGESHIRE.
  Barrington.
  Cambridge, Jesus College.
  Cambridge, King's College.
  Cambridge, Queen's College.
  Comberton.
  Ely Cath.
  Foxton.
  Fulbourn, St. Vigor's.
  Haddenham.
  Ickleton.
  Impington.
  Landbeach.
  Meldreth.
  Newton.
  Orwell.
  Willingham.

  CHESHIRE.
  Chester Cath.
  Gawsworth.

  CORNWALL.
  Advent.
  Grade.
  Helland.
  St. Clement's.
  St. Enodoc.
  St. Levan's.
  Saltash.

B B

ROOFS AND CEILINGS—*cont.*

CUMBERLAND.

Carlisle Cath.
Carlisle Deanery.
Naworth.

DERBYSHIRE.

Dovebridge.
Steetly.

DEVONSHIRE.

Ashburton.
Bovey Tracey.
Bratton Clovelly.
Buckland Monachorum.
Cullompton.
Exeter Cath.
Exeter, Bishop's Palace.
Exeter, Residentiary House.
Hartland Ch.
Hatherleigh.
Hennock.
Holcombe Burnell.
Ilfracombe.
Ilsington.
Lympstone.
Martinhoe.
Meavy.
Payhembury.
Swimbridge.
Tiverton.
Trentishoe.
Widecombe-in-the-Moor.

DORSETSHIRE.

Bradford Abbas.
Frampton.
Pulham.
Sherborne Abbey.
Sturminster Newton.
Thornford.
Wimborne.
Yetminster.

DURHAM.

Brancepeth.
Durham, St. Oswald's.

ESSEX.

Blackmore.
Colchester.

ROOFS AND CEILINGS—*cont.*

ESSEX—*cont.*

Margaretting.
Ongar, High.
Saffron Walden.
Shenfield.
Writtle.

GLOUCESTERSHIRE.

Ampney Crucis.
Awre.
Berkeley Castle.
Bledington.
Bristol, St. Mark's Chapel.
Buckland.
Gloucester, St. Mary de Crypt.
Kempley.
Tewkesbury.

HAMPSHIRE.

Christchurch.
Winchester Cath.
Winchester, St. Cross.

HEREFORDSHIRE.

Almeley.
Hereford Cath.

HERTFORDSHIRE.

Aldenham.
Ardeley.
Barnet, East.
Braughing.
Furneaux Pelham.
Hitchin.
Kelshall.
Puttenham.
Rushden.
St. Albans Cath.
St. Albans, St. Michael's.
Ware.

HUNTINGDONSHIRE.

Hemingford Abbas.
Huntingdon.
Kimbolton.
Newton, Water.
St. Neots.

ROOFS AND CEILINGS—*cont.*

KENT.

Biddenden.
Canterbury Cath.
Harbledown.
Horton, Monk's.
Ightham Mote.
Malling, East.
Rainham.
Staplehurst.

LANCASHIRE.

Leyland.
Manchester.
Stydd.

LEICESTERSHIRE.

Ashby Folville.
Barrow-on-Soar.
Burrow-on-the-Hill.
Laund.
Leicester, St. Martin's.
Leicester, St. Mary's.
Leicester, Old Blue Boar
Inn.
Twyford.

LINCOLNSHIRE.

Addlethorpe.
Billinghay.
Boston.
Broughton, Brant.
Friskney.
Lincoln Cath.
Pinchbeck.
Stamford, All Saints.
Stamford, St. George's.
Stamford, St. John's.
Stamford, St. Mary's.
Welbourne.
Winthorpe.

MIDDLESEX.

Hampton Court.
Ickenham.
London, Crosby Hall.
London, St. Andrew Under-
shaft.§
London, St. Bartholomew's.
London, St. Helen's the
Great.§
London, The Temple.

Q 3254.

ROOFS AND CEILINGS—*cont.*

MONMOUTHSHIRE.

Magor.

NORFOLK.

Acre, Castle, Ch.
Acre, Castle, Priory.
Aylmerton.
Aylsham.
Bradfield.
Brockdish.
Carbrooke.
Caston.
Creake, North.
Creake, South.
Cressingham, Great.
Cromer. (?)
Diss.
Eaton.
Edingthorpe.
Garboldisham.
Hemblington.
Hemesby.
Hilgay.
Honing.
Horstead.
Knapton.
Mattishall.
Northwold.
Norwich Cath.
Norwich, St. Clement's.
Norwich, St. Helen's.
Norwich, St. John's Mad-
dermarket.
Norwich, St. Stephen's.
Norwich, St. Giles's Hosp.
Norwich, Bishop's Palace.
Ormesby, St. Margaret.
Outwell.
Oxburgh.
Postwick.
Pulham, St. M. Magdalene.
Randworth.
Redenhall.
Sall.
Sandringham.
Sculthorpe.
Swainsthorpe.
Terrington, St. Clement's.
Tunstead.
Upwell.

C C

ROOFS AND CEILINGS—*cont.*

NORFOLK—*cont.*

Walsingham, New.
Walsoken.
Wimbotsham.
Wymondham.

NORTHAMPTONSHIRE.

Brington, Great.
Cransley.
Haddon, West.
Higham Ferrers.
Middleton Cheney.
Peterborough.
Pytchley.
Rothersthorpe.
Walgrave.
Wellingborough.

NOTTINGHAMSHIRE.

Blyth.
Nottingham, St. Peter's.
Sutton Bonnington.
Wysall.

OXFORDSHIRE.

Alvescott.
Aston, Steeple.
Checkendon.
Haseley, Great.
Hornton.
Mapledurham.
Merton.
Minster Lovel.
Oxford, All Souls College.
Oxford, St. Mary Magdalene College.
Rycote.
Wigginton.

RUTLANDSHIRE.

Empingham.
Luffenham, North.
Lyddington, Bede Ho.

SHROPSHIRE.

Ludlow.
Worfield.

SOMERSETSHIRE.

Bath.
Bruton.

ROOFS AND CEILINGS—*cont.*

SOMERSETSHIRE—*cont.*

Camel, West.
Cheddar.
Cleeve, Old.
Curry, North.
Ditcheat.
Doulting.
Evercreech.
Frome.
Huish Episcopi.
Langport.
Limington.
Muchelney Abbey.
Pilton.
Sutton, Long.
Taunton.
Wellow.
Wells Cath.
Wells, St. Cuthbert's.
Weston in Gordano.

STAFFORDSHIRE.

Arcley, Upper.
Elford.
Lichfield.

SUFFOLK.

Bacton.
Bardwell.
Blythburgh.
Boxted.
Bury St. Edmund's, St. Mary's.
Cratfield.
Darsham.
Eye.
Flempton.
Gorleston, St. Nicholas.
Hadleigh.
Hopton.
Ipswich, St. Margaret's.
Ixworth.
Melford, Long, Ch.
Melford, Long, Chapel of St. James.
Mendlesham.
Oulton.
Palgrave.
Southwold.
Stoke by Clare.

ROOFS AND CEILINGS—*cont.*

SUFFOLK—*cont.*

Stonham Aspall.
Stradbroke.
Sudbury, All Saints.
Sudbury, St. Peter's.
Ufford.
Walsham-le-Willows.
Wangford.
Westley.
Wilby.
Wingfield.
Yaxley.

SURREY.

Alfold House.
Guildford, St. Mary's.
Pirford.

SUSSEX.

Battle Abbey.
Boxgrove.
Chichester Cath.
Chichester, Bishop's Palace.
Cuckfield.
Hastings.
Horsham.
Maresfield.
Shipley.

WARWICKSHIRE.

Astley.
Birmingham.
Brailes.
Compton Wynyate.
Coventry, St. Michael's.
Coventry, Trinity Ch.
Henley in Arden.
Knowle.
Warwick.

WILTSHIRE.

Bradenstoke.
Bromham.
Chippenham.
Combe, Castle.
Devizes, St. John's.
Devizes, St. Mary's.
Edington.
Keevil.
Laycock Abbey.

ROOFS AND CEILINGS—*cont.*

WILTSHIRE—*cont.*

Laycock Ch.
Orcheston, St. Mary.
Salisbury Cath.
Salisbury, St. Thomas.
Westwood.
Wootton Bassett.

WORCESTERSHIRE.

Broadway.
Bromsgrove.
Droitwich.
Flyford Grafton.
Malvern, Great.
Tredington.
Worcester Deanery.

YORKSHIRE.

Bempton.
Beverley Minster.
Beverley, St. Mary's.
Bolton Abbey.
Fishlake.
Hemingborough.
Jervaulx Abbey.
Methley.
Richmond.
Rotherham.
Wakefield Ch.
Watton.
York Minster.
York, St. Martin's.

WALES.

Guilsfield.
Gyffin.
Laugharne.
Llaneilian.
Llanelian.
Michaelchurch on Arrow.
St. David's.

SCOTLAND.

Aberdeen.
Borthwick.
Craigmillar.
Edinburgh.

IRELAND.

Cashel.
Youghal.

RYPPLEY, ABBOT.
Chester Cath.*

SACRAMENTS, THE SEVEN.
Brooke (Norfolk).‡
Catfield.*
Dereham, East.‡
[Eton.*]
Fetcham.*
Gorleston Ch.‡
Lathbury.*
Lavant, Mid.*
Loddon.‡
Pickering.*
Preston in Holderness.‡
Walsingham, New.‡
Westhall.‡
Witchingham, Great.‡
Woodbridge.‡

SALOME, ST. MARY.
Chiltington, West.*
Easby Ch.*
Exeter Cath.*
Faversham.*
Gloucester, St. Mary de Crypt.*
Houghton le Dale.†
Lastingham.*
Randworth.†
Stedham.*
Winterbourne Dauntsey.*

SALUTATION, THE. *See* MARY THE VIRGIN, ST. (3).

SALVATION, LADDER OF. *See* LADDER OF SALVATION.

SAMARIA, WOMAN OF. *See* CHRIST (13).

SAMPSON, ST.
Milton Abbas.†

SAMSON.
Bradninch.†
Stapleton.*

SATIVOLA, ST. *See* SIDWELL, ST.

SAUL.
Dereham, West, Abbey.*

SAVIOUR, OUR. *See* CHRIST.

SCHOLASTICA, ST.
Kenn.†
Romsey.†

SCHORN, SIR JOHN. *See* SHORNE.

SCREENS, ROOD, CHANCEL, AISLE, AND PARCLOSE, arranged under counties alphabetically.

BEDFORDSHIRE.
Barford, Little.
Clifton.
Cople.
Eaton Bray.
Eaton Socon.
Elstow.
Felmersham.
Gravenhurst, Lower.
Kempston.
Luton.
Marston Moretaine.
Oakley.
Odell.
Pertenhall.
Shelton.
Shillington.
Stevington.
Stotfold.
Tilbrook.

BERKSHIRE.
Chilton.
Drayton.
Hanney.
Ruscombe.

BUCKINGHAMSHIRE.
Ashendon.
Astwood.
Aylesbury.
Crawley, North.
Ellesborough.
Marston, North.
Nettleden.
Olney.
Quainton.
Risborough, Monk's.
Wingrave.

SCREENS, &c.—*cont.*

CAMBRIDGESHIRE.
Bourn.
Caldecote.
Cambridge, King's College.
Cambridge, St. Andrew-the-Less.
Cherry Hinton.
Chippenham.
Comberton.
Coton.
Ditton, Wood.
Foxton.
Guilden Morden.
Horningsey.
Kennet.
Oakington.
Soham.
Teversham.
Trumpington.
Whittlesea.
Willingham.

CHESHIRE.
Bunbury.
Siddington.

CORNWALL.
Blisland.
Davidstow.
Gunwalloe.
Lanreath.
Launcells.
Madron.
Mawnan.
Mylor.
Poundstock.
St. Budoc.
St. Buryan.
St. Columb Major.
St. Michael's Mount.
St. Minver Church.
St. Minver, St. Enodoc's Chapel.
St. Winnow.
Sancreed.
Talland.
Tywardreth.

CUMBERLAND.
Carlisle Cath.
Greystoke.

SCREENS, &c.—*cont.*

DERBYSHIRE.
Ashover.

DEVONSHIRE.
Alphington.
Alvington, West.
Ashton.
Atherington.
Bampton.
Beer Ferrers.
Berry Pomeroy.
Bideford.
Bovey Tracey.
Bradninch.
Bratton Clovelly.
Brent, South.
Bridestow.
Bridford.
Buckland-in-the-Moor.
Burlescombe.
Chawleigh.
Chivelston.
Chudleigh.
Chulmleigh.
Churston Ferrars.
Clayhanger.
Clyst St. Lawrence.
Coleridge.
Combe Martin.
Cullompton.
Dartington.
Dartmouth, St. Saviour's.
Dittisham.
Exeter Cath.
Exeter, Coll. of Priests Vicars.
Feniton.
Gidleigh.
Harberton.
Hartland.
Heavitree.
Hempston, Little.
Hennock.
Holcombe Rogus.
Holne.
Honiton.
Ilsington.
Ipplepen.
Kenn.
Kentisbeare.

SCREENS, &c.—*cont.*

DEVONSHIRE—*cont.*

Kenton.
Lapford.
Lustleigh.
Mamhead.
Manaton.
Ogwell, West.
Payhembury.
Pinhoe.
Plymstock.
Plymtree.
Rewe.
Seaton.
Staverton.
Stoke Gabriel.
Stoke in Teignhead.
Talaton.
Tavistock.
Tavy, Peter.
Teignton, King's.
Throwley.
Tiverton.
Tor Bryan.
Totnes.
Trusham.
Uffculme.
Ugborough.
Widecombe-in-the-Moor.
Woodland.
Woodleigh.
Woolborough.

DORSETSHIRE.

Hawkchurch.
Milton Abbas.
Stockland.
Worth Matravers.

DURHAM.

Brancepeth.
Finchale.

ESSEX.

Latchingdon.
Orsett.
Shenfield.
Stanford le Hope.
Upminster.
Weathersfield.
Yeldham, Great.

SCREENS, &c.—*cont.*

GLOUCESTERSHIRE.

Ashchurch.
Berkeley.
Cirencester.

HAMPSHIRE.

Christchurch.
Micheldever.
Romsey.
Winchester, St. Cross.

HEREFORDSHIRE.

Dilwyn.
Hope Mansel.
Kenderchurch.

HERTFORDSHIRE.

Aldenham.
Flamstead.
Kelshall.
St. Albans Cath.
Walden, King's.
Walkern.

HUNTINGDONSHIRE.

Bluntisham.
Easton.
Kimbolton.
Stow Longa.
Swineshead.

KENT.

Birchington.
Canterbury Cath.
Chiselhurst.
Maidstone.
Ruckinge.
St. Lawrence.
Smarden.
Swanscombe.

LANCASHIRE.

Cartmel Fell.
Claughton.
Sefton.

LEICESTERSHIRE.

Ashby Folville.
Edmundthorpe.

SCREENS, &c.—*cont.*

LINCOLNSHIRE.

Addlethorpe.
Alford.
Bytham, Castle.
Corringham.
Croft.
Croyland.
Epworth.
Fulbeck.
Ropsley.
Somerby.
Somercotes, South.
Stamford, St. George's.
Stamford, St. John's.
Winthorpe.

MONMOUTHSHIRE.

Llangwm Isaf.
Llangwm Ucha.

NORFOLK.

Acle.
Acre, Castle.
Acre, South.
Ashmanhaugh.
Attleborough.
Aylsham.
Babingley.
Banham.
Barnham Broom.
Beeston, St. Mary's.
Beeston Regis.
Belaugh.
Billingford.
Binham Abbey.
Blofield.
Breckles.
Bridgham.
Brisley.
Brockdish.
Buckenham, New.
Burlingham, St. Andrew.
Burlingham, St. Edmund.
Burnham Norton.
Buxton.
Carbrooke.
Carlton Rode.
Catfield.
Cawston.
Colkirk.

SCREENS, &c.—*cont.*

NORFOLK—*cont.*

Creake, South.
Cressingham, Great.
Cromer. (?)
Crostwight.
Denton.
Deopham.
Dersingham.
Dickleburgh.
Edgfield.
Edingthorpe.
Emneth.
Erpingham.
Fakenham.
Filby.
Fincham.
Foulden.
Foxley.
Freethorpe.
Fritton.
Garboldisham.
Gately.
Gillingham.
Gooderstone.
Gressenhall.
Grimstone.
Happisburgh.
Hardwick.
Harling, East.
Harpley.
Heigham, Potter.
Hempstead.
Hethersett.
Hickling.
Horsham, St. Faith's.
Houghton-le-Dale.
Hunstanton.
Ickburgh.
Ingham.
Irstead.
Kenninghall.
Lessingham.
Litcham.
Loddon.
Longham.
Ludham.
Lynn, King's.
Lynn, South.
Marsham.
Martham.

NORFOLK—cont.

Massingham, Great.
Mattishall.
Mautby.
Merton.
Middleton.
Moulton.
Neatishead.
,Northwold.
Norwich, St. Gregory's.
Norwich, St. James.
Norwich, St. John's Maddermarket.
Norwich, St. John de Sepulchre.
Norwich, St. Michael at Plea.
Norwich, St. Paul's.
Norwich, St. Peter per Mountergate.
Norwich, SS. Simon and Jude.
Norwich, St. Swithin's.
Outwell.
Oxburgh.
Paston.
Plumstead, Great.
Poringland.
Pulham, St. Mary Magdalene.
Pulham, St. Mary the Virgin.
Rackheath.
Rainham, South.
Randworth.
Redenhall.
Repps.
Ringland.
Rudham.
Rushall.
Ruston, East.
Salhouse.
Sall.
Salthouse.
Saxthorpe.
Scarning.
Shelfhanger.
Shingham.
Smallburgh.
Sparham.

NORFOLK—cont

Stalham.
Stanfield.
Strumpshaw.
Suffield.
Swaffham.
Swafield.
Taverham.
Thetford, St. Cuthbert's.
Thetford, St. Peter's.
Thornham.
Thorpe Abbots.
Tibenham.
Tilney, All Saints.
Toft Monks.
Tofts, West.
Tottington.
Trimmingham.
Trunch.
Tunstead.
Upton.
Upwell.
Walcot.
Walpole, St. Peter's.
Walsham, North.
Walsham, South.
Walsingham, New.
Walsoken.
Weeting.
Wellingham.
Wells.
Wendling.
Wesenham.
Weston Longueville.
Westwick.
Wickmere.
Wiggenhall, St. Mary Magdalene.
Wiggenhall, St. Mary the Virgin.
Wighton.
Worstead.
Wrotham, Great.
Yarmouth, Great.
Yelverton.

NORTHAMPTONSHIRE.

Ashby, St. Leger's.
Badby.
Barton, Earl's.

SCREENS, &c.—*cont.*

NORTHAMPTONSHIRE—*cont.*

Bozeat.
Bugbrooke.
Burton Latimer.
Denford.
Floore.
Grafton Regis.
Hannington.
Harringworth.
Marston, St. Lawrence.
Middleton Cheney.
Newnham.
Ravensthorpe.
Stanford.
Sutton, King's.
Warmington.

NORTHUMBERLAND.

Hexham.

NOTTINGHAMSHIRE.

Blyth.
Collingham, North.
Newark.
Strelley.

OXFORDSHIRE.

Bloxham.
Charlton-on-Otmoor.
Handborough.
Hornton.
Milcomb.
Rollwright, Great.
Shutford.
Stanton, St. John's.
Swalcliffe.
Westcott Barton.

RUTLANDSHIRE.

Egleton.
Lyddington Ch.
Stoke Dry.

SHROPSHIRE.

Ludlow.

SOMERSETSHIRE.

Ashton, Long.
Banwell.
Brympton D'Evercy.
Lydeard, Bishop's.
Minehead.

SCREENS, &c.—*cont.*

SOMERSETSHIRE—*cont.*

Norton Fitzwarren.
Pilton.
Sutton, Long.
Wellow.

SUFFOLK.

Athelington.
Badley.
Barking.
Barningham.
Barrow.
Bedfield.
Billingford.
Blundeston.
Blythburgh.
Bramfield.
Brandon.
Brockley.
Cowling.
Dennington.
Eye.
Gisleham.
Grundisburgh.
Hawkedon.
Hessett.
Hitcham.
Ipswich, St. Matthew's.
Ixworth.
Kersey.
Laxfield.
Mellis.
Mickfield.
Newbourne.
Pakefield.
Parham.
Ringsfield.
Risby.
Sibton.
Sotterley.
Southwold.
Stanton.
Stonham, Earl.
Stowlangtoft.
Sudbury, St. Peter's.
Thurlow.
Troston.
Ufford.
Walberswick.
Walsham-le-Willows.

SCREENS, &c.—cont.

SUFFOLK—cont.

Walton.
Wattisfield.
Wenham, Great.
Westhall.
Wingfield.
Withersfield.
Woodbridge.
Woolpit.
Yaxley.
Yoxford.

SUSSEX.

Horsham.
Rye.

WARWICKSHIRE.

Henley in Arden.

WILTSHIRE.

Amesbury.
Avebury.
Berwick Bassett.
Bremhill.
Chalfield, Gt., Manor Ho.
Clyffe Pypard.
Compton Bassett.
Hullavington.
Kingston Deverill.
Lyneham.
Salisbury Cath.

WORCESTERSHIRE.

Besford.
Bredon.
Hampton Lovett.
Leigh.
Pershore.
Sedgberrow.
Strensham.

YORKSHIRE.

Aysgarth.
Campsall.
Flamborough.
Hornby.
Hubberholme.
Leake.
Skipton.

SCREENS, &c.—cont.

WALES.

Brecon, St. John's.
Llangurig.
Llanrhaidr-in-Kinmerch.
Merthyr Cynog.
Newport.
Newtown.
Pennant Melangell.
St. David's.

SCOTLAND.

Fowlis Easter.

SCREEN, ALTAR. See REREDOS.

SEASONS, THE. See MONTHS AND SEASONS.

SEBASTIAN, ST.

Binham Abbey.†
Bradninch.†
Cashel.* (?)
Charlwood.* (?)
Easton (Suffolk).* (?)
Holne.†
Irthlingborough.*
Knockmoy.*
Pickering.*
Plymtree.†
Preston (Sussex).*
Romsey.†
Roxton.†
Stalham.†
Tuddenham, North.†
Ugborough.†
Wear Gifford.*
Widecombe-in-the-Moor.†

SEBERT, KING.

Westminster Abbey.*

SEDILIA.

Bengeo.
Chatham.
Coggeshall, Little.
Crediton.
Dorchester.
Dunham, Little.
Easby Church.
Exeter Cath.
Furness Abbey.

SEDILIA—*cont.*
   Gloucester, St. Mary de Crypt.
   Hornchurch.
   Lynn, King's.
   Moreton, Maid's.
   Norwich, St. Peter Hungate.
   Oxburgh.
   Paignton.
   Puckington.
   Reading, St. Mary's.
   Rochester Cath.
   St. Albans Cath.
   Salwarpe.
   Stow Bardolph.
   Teversham.
   Tewkesbury.
   Westminster Abbey.
   Winchelsea.
   Yarmouth, Great.

SEPULCHRE, EASTER. *See* EASTER SEPULCHRE.

SERAPHIM. *See* HIERARCHY, HEAVENLY, AND, ANGELS.

SEVEN ACTS OF MERCY. *See* MERCY, SEVEN ACTS OF.

SEVEN DEADLY SINS. *See* SINS, SEVEN DEADLY.

SEVEN SACRAMENTS. *See* SACRAMENTS, SEVEN.

SHADRACH.
   Warblington.*

SHEPHERDS, THE ANNUNCIATION TO AND ADORATION OF THE. *See* CHRIST (3), (4).

SHIELDS, ARMORIAL, &c. *See* ARMORIAL SHIELDS.

SHORNE, SHORN, or SCHORN, SIR JOHN.
   Cawston.†
   Gately.†
   Sudbury.†
   Suffield.†
   Woolborough.†

SHRINE.
   Cerne Abbas.
   Chester Cath.
   Guisborough.
   Lincoln Cath.
   Oxford Cath.
   St. Albans Cath.
   Westminster Abbey.

SIDWELL or SATIVOLA, ST.
   Ashton.†
   Eton.*
   Holne.†
   Kenn.†
   Plymtree.†
   Widecombe-in-the-Moor.†
   Woolborough.†

SILKSTEDE, PRIOR.
   Winchester Cath.*

SIMEON, ST.
   Gloucester, St. Mary de Crypt.* (?)
   Winchester, St. Cross.*

SIMON, ST. *See also* APOSTLES, THE.
   Fritton (Norfolk).†
   Houghton-le-Dale.† ([1])
   Kenn.†
   Norwich, St. James.†
   Norwich, St. Peter Mancroft.†
   Norwich, St. Stephen's.‡
   Pulham, St. Mary the Virgin.†
   Randworth.† ([1])
   Salthouse.†
   Somerleyton.†
   Swafield.†
   Trusham.†

([1]) In these two instances St. Simeon is intended, but he has been confounded with St. Simon.

SINOPE.
   Amberley Castle.†

SINS, TREE OR WHEEL OF THE SEVEN DEADLY.
   Arundel.*
   Bardwell.*

SINS, TREE OR WHEEL OF THE
SEVEN DEADLY—*cont.*
  Bristol, St. John's.*
  Brooke (Norfolk).*
  Brunstead.*
  Catfield.*
  Cropredy.*
  Crostwight.*
  Dalham.*
  Hessett.*
  Ingatestone.*
  Milcomb.*
  Milton Abbas.*
  Netherbury.*
  Raunds.*
  Stokesby.*
  Wisborough Green.*

SIRA, ST.
  Eton.* (?)

SITHA, CITHA, or ZITA, ST.
  Barton Turf.†
  Denton.†
  Elmham, North.†
  Norwich, St. James.†
  St. Albans Cath.*
  Somerleyton.†
  Westhall.†
  Whittlesford.‡

SOLOMON AND THE QUEEN OF
SHEBA.
  Gloucester, St. Mary de
  Crypt.*

SOPHONIAS. *See* ZEPHENIAH.

STALLS AND BENCH ENDS.
  Astley (Warwick).
  Axbridge.
  Blythburgh.
  Brington, Great.
  Cannings, Bishop's.
  Carlisle Cath.
  Chichester Cath.
  Fordington.
  Hemingborough.
  Hereford Cath.
  Lincoln Cath.
  Mulbarton.
  Rochester Cath.
  Shelford, Little.
  Walpole, St. Peter.
  Windsor.

STEM OF JESSE. *See* JESSE
STEM OF.

STEPHEN, ST.
  Ashton.†
  Berry Pomeroy.†
  Blyth.†
  Hempstead.†
  Hennock.†
  Herringfleet.†
  Horsham, St. Faith's.†
  Kenn.†
  Kenton.†
  Ludham.†
  Manaton.‡
  Randworth.†
  Ruscombe.*
  Sparsholt.*
  Strensham.†
  Wellow (Somerset).*
  Windsor.*
  Woolborough.†

STRINGCOURSE. *See* CORNICE.

SUPPER, THE LAST. *See*
CHRIST (18).

SWITHIN, ST.
  Winchester, St. Cross.*

SYBILS, THE.
  Bradninch.†
  Ugborough.† (?)

SYLVESTER, ST.
  Houghton-le-Dale.†

TEMPERANTIA. *See* VIRTUES,
THE.

TEMPLE, DESTRUCTION OF KING
SOLOMON'S.
  Exeter Cath.†

TEMPLE, THE BUILDING OF
THE SECOND.
  Exeter Cath.†

TEMPTATION, REPRESENTATION
OF.
  Strata Florida.†

TEMPTATION OF ADAM AND EVE,
THE. *See* ADAM.

TEMPTATION IN THE WILDER-
NESS, THE. *See* CHRIST (10).

TESTER.
    Goosey.

THECLA, ST.
    Cleeve, Old.*

THEOBALD, ST.
    Hempstead.†

THEODOSIA, ST.
    ETON.* (?)

THOMAS, ST. *See also* APOS-
TLES, THE.
    Berry Pomeroy.†
    Clifton.†
    Drayton (Norfolk).*
    Elmham, North.†
    Ilsington.‡
    Kenn.†
    Norwich, St. Peter Man-
      croft.†
    Plymtree.†
    Preston (Sussex).*
    Repps.†
    St. Albans Cath.*
    Sall.†
    Swafield.†
    Tavy, Peter.†
    Walpole, St. Peter.†
    Wellow (Somerset).*
    Widecombe-in-the-Moor.†
    Wighton.*

THOMAS OF CANTERBURY or
À BECKET, ST.
    Attleborough.† (?)
    Beauchief.‡
    Binham Abbey.†
    Bramley.*
    Brentwood.* (?)
    Burgh, St. Peter.* (?)
    Burlingham, St. Andrew.†
    Burlingham, St. Edmund.*
    Canterbury Cath.†
    Canterbury, Eastbridge
      Hosp.*
    Easton (Norfolk).*
    Eaton.*
    Faversham.*
    Hadleigh (Essex).*
    Hauxton.*
    Hereford Cath.*
    Hingham.*

THOMAS OF CANTERBURY or
À BECKETT, ST.—*cont.*
    Holne.†
    Horsham, St. Faith's.†
    Maidstone.*
    Mentmore.*
    Merstham.*
    Oxburgh.†
    Pickering.*
    Preston (Sussex).*
    Randworth.†
    St. Albans Cath.*
    Somerleyton.†
    Sparham.†
    Stalham.†
    Stoke Charity.*
    Stoke D'Abernon.*
    Stoneleigh.* (?)
    Stow.*
    Stratford-on-Avon, Chapel
      of the Guild of the Holy
      Cross.*
    Strensham.*
    Upchurch.*,
    Whaddon.*
    Winchester, St. John's.*
    Winchester, Magdalen
      Hosp.* (?)
    Winchester, St. Cross.*
    Woolborough.†
    Wootton Bassett.*
    Worsted.†
    Yarmouth, Great.* (?)

THOMAS OF HEREFORD, ST.
    See CANTELUPE, BISHOP.

THRONE, BISHOP'S.
    Durham Cath.
    Exeter Cath.
    Wells Cath.

THRONES. *See* HIERARCHY,
HEAVENLY.

TIME AND DEATH.
    Abbey Dore.*
    Alveley.*
    Caddington.*
    Checkley.*
    Loughborough.*
    Norton, Chipping.* §

TIME AND DEATH—*cont.*
Nuneaton.*
Stoneleigh.*
Worlaby.*

TOBIT.
Westminster, St. Stephen's.*

TRADES, &c., EMBLEMS OF.
See EMBLEMS OF TRADES.

TRANSFIGURATION, THE. *See* CHRIST (15).

TRANSUBSTANTIATION OF THE WAFER, THE LITERAL. *See* GREGORY'S, ST., MASS.

TRINITY, THE BLESSED.
Aldenham.*
Ashridge.*
Ashton Keynes.* (?)
Attleborough.†
Bere Regis.* (?)
Broughton, Brant.‡
Canterbury Cath.†
Carlton in Lindrick.‡
Cowley (Oxon).*
Gorleston Church.*
Gyffiliog.* (?)
Hull.‡
Latton.*
Muchelney Abbey.‡
Norwich Castle.‡
Pinvin.*
St. Albans Cath.*
Tewkesbury.*
Upton (Bucks).‡
Upwell.†
Winterbourne Earls.*

TRINITY BANNER, THE.
Gorleston Church.*
Ickburgh.†
Norwich, St. Swithin's.†
St. Albans Cath.†

TRIUMPHAL ENTRY INTO JERUSALEM, THE. *See* CHRIST (17).

TROIS ROIS MORTS ET LES TROIS ROIS VIFS, LES.
Ampney Crucis.*
Bardwell.*

TROIS ROIS MORTS ET LES TROIS ROIS VIFS, LES—*cont.*
Barnstaple.*
Battle.*
Belton.*
Bovey Tracey.*
Charlwood.*
Ditchingham.*
Edworth.*
Evenley.* (?)
Feteham.*
Gorleston Church.*
Guernsey, Ste. Marie du Chastel.*
Jersey, St. Clement's.*
Knockmoy.*
Limpenhoe.*
Lutterworth.*
Raunds.*
Seething.*
Slapton.*
Stokesby.*
Tettenhall.*
Whaddon.*
Wickhampton.*
Wymondham.*

TYMPANUM, NORMAN.
Bridge.
Ditteridge.
Fordington.
Leckhampstead.
Malmesbury.
Wiston (Suffolk).

ULPH, ST.
Eton.* (?)

URSULA, ST.
Babingley.†
Barnham Broom.†
Blyth.†
Eye.†
Lanivet.* (?)
Litcham.†
Norwich, St. John de Sepulchre.†
Norwich, St. Peter Mancroft.‡
Repps.†
Stedham.*
Stoke by Nayland.*

URSULA, ST.—*cont.*
 Stratford-on-Avon, Chapel of the Guild of the Holy Cross.*
 Woolborough.†
 Yaxley (Suffolk).†

VERONICA, ST.
 Babingley.†
 Creake, North.†
 Kenn.†
 London, The Savoy Chapel.†
 Tor Bryan.†
 Woolborough.†

VINCENT, ST.
 Culford.* (?)
 Wesmcston.*

VIRGIN, THE. *See* MARY THE VIRGIN, ST.

VIRTUES, THE. JUSTITIA, PRUDENTIA, FORTITUDO, TEMPERANTIA.
 Creake, North.†
 Westminster Hall.*
 Wye Coll.* §
 York Minster.†

VISITATION, THE. *See* MARY THE VIRGIN, ST. (3).

WAINFLEET, BISHOP.
 Wainfleet.‡

WALBURGE, ST.
 Winchester, St. John's.*(?)

WALSTAN, ST.
 Barnham Broom.†
 Burlingham, St. Andrew.†
 Denton.†
 Ludham.†
 Norwich, St. James.†
 Sparham.†

WANDRAGESILAS, ST.
 Horsham, St. Faith's.†

WERBURGH, ST.
 Chester, St. Werburga's.*

WHEEL OF FORTUNE. *See* FORTUNE, WHEEL OF.

WIGLAFF REX.
 Chester Cath.‡

WILFRID, ST.
 Chichester Cath.†
 Hexham.†

WILGEFORTIS, ST.
 Walsham, North.† (?)
 Worstead.†

WILLEBROD, ST.
 Oxburgh.†

WILLIAM OF NORWICH, ST.
 Ashby.*
 Eye.†
 Litcham.†
 Loddon.†
 Norwich, St. John's, Maddermarket.†
 Somerleyton.†
 Worstead.†

WILLIAM OF YORK, ST.
 Garboldisham.†
 St. Albans Cath.*

WINIFRED, ST.
 Babingley.†
 Hereford Cath.*
 Holywell.*
 Mells.* (?)
 Wells, St. Cuthbert's.* (?)

WITHBURGHA, ST.
 Barnham Broom.†
 Burlingham, St. Andrew.†
 Chester Cath.‡ (?)
 Oxburgh.†
 Randworth.† (?)

WOLPHERUS, REX.
 Chester Cath.‡ (?)

WOLSEY, CARDINAL.
 Bloxham.†

WOLSTAN, BISHOP.
 Ely Cath.*

WULSTAN, ST.
 Ashby.*
 Norwich Cath.*
 Woolborough.† (?)

402

WULWIVE.
Hereford Cath.*

ZACHARIAS.
Axbridge.†
Canterbury Cath.*
Exeter Cath.†
Salisbury Cath.*
Stifford.*

ZECHARIAH. *See also* PRO-
PHETS, THE.
Poringland.†

ZENO, ST.
Somerleyton.†

ZEPHENIAH (SOPHONIAS). *See
also* PROPHETS, THE.
Crawley, North.†

ZITA, ST. *See* SITHA, ST.

ZODIAC, SIGNS OF THE.
Copford.*
Kempley.*
Westmeston.*

LONDON: Printed by EYRE and SPOTTISWOODE,
Printers to the Queen's most Excellent Majesty.
For Her Majesty's Stationery Office.
[13681.—1000.—10/83.]

Printed in June 2019
by Rotomail Italia S.p.A., Vignate (MI) - Italy